THE NEW ENGLISH BIBLE

COMPANION TO THE
NEW TESTAMENT

BY
A. E. HARVEY

WILLIAM A. BLACK
3 CLEVELAND STREET
LOGANSPORT, IN 46947
PHONE 753-3850

The Gospels

OXFORD UNIVERSITY PRESS
CAMBRIDGE UNIVERSITY PRESS
1972

©

THE DELEGATES OF THE OXFORD UNIVERSITY PRESS
THE SYNDICS OF THE CAMBRIDGE UNIVERSITY PRESS
1970

INTERNATIONAL STANDARD BOOK NUMBERS
OXFORD UNIVERSITY PRESS: 0 19 826168 3
CAMBRIDGE UNIVERSITY PRESS: 0 521 09689 8

FIRST PUBLISHED 1970 AS PART OF
COMPANION TO THE NEW TESTAMENT

Printed in Great Britain
at the University Printing House, Cambridge
(Brooke Crutchley, University Printer)

CONTENTS

PREFACE

This book is a reprint of the first half of *The New English Bible: Companion to the New Testament*, published in 1970. A few minor corrections have been made, but in other respects the text is unchanged.

A. E. H.

WILLIAM A. BLACK
3 CLEVELAND STREET
LOGANSPORT, IN 46947
PHONE 753-3850

THE NEW TESTAMENT

The word TESTAMENT is a technical term with a long history. Strictly speaking, the English word, like the Latin word from which it is derived, means a legal document, a "will"; and the same was true of the Greek word, *diathēkē*, of which TESTAMENT is a translation. But it is obvious that what has been known since the early centuries of the church as the New Testament is not a legal document, and has little in common with a will. That it bears this name is the result of a particular turn in the fortunes of the Greek word.

When, in the third century B.C., a group of Jewish scholars translated the Hebrew scriptures into Greek for the use of the Greek-speaking Jews in Alexandria, they found themselves confronted by a number of words in the original which had no equivalent in the Greek language. One of these was the Hebrew word *berith*, of which the usual English translation is "covenant". This word was an exceedingly important one in the history and religion of the Jewish people: it expressed one of their most fundamental convictions about the relationship between God and man. God, they believed, had shown in the distant past his readiness to protect and care for his own people. He had miraculously rescued them from bondage in Egypt and settled them in a land of their own. He had undertaken to continue this relationship with them, so long as they, for their part, observed in their lives and in their worship those principles which he had revealed to them at the beginning of their history, and which were known to them as the Law of Moses. All this was often described in the Jewish scriptures as the "covenant" into which God had entered with his people. Indeed, the Jews' conception of this covenant embraced their deepest convictions about the faithfulness, the justice and the mercy of God. In rendering this important word by the Greek word *diathēkē*, the translators virtually gave a new meaning to a familiar legal term. Thereafter, any Greek-speaking person who was familiar with the Hebrew scriptures knew that *diathēkē*, though it normally meant "will" or "testament", was also a technical term for that "covenant" which the Jews believed God had made with his own people.

The documentary evidence, so to speak, for this covenant consisted in a collection of sacred books which had been formed gradually over the centuries and which, by the time of Christ, had already been complete for about two hundred years. This collection was not homogeneous. It consisted of books originally written at different times for different purposes. The Jews distinguished three broad divisions: first, the Law (the five books attributed to Moses); then the Prophets (which included most of the historical books); and finally the remaining books, which they called simply the Writings. The first of these divisions, since it included the code of religious and civil laws

5

under which they lived, they regarded as the most important. Consequently, when they wished to refer to the whole collection, they sometimes called it "the Law". Otherwise, they called it "the Holy Writings", "the scriptures". These scriptures were regarded by the Jews with the greatest veneration. Elaborate precautions were taken to prevent the smallest alterations to the text, and the leather scrolls on which they were written were reverently preserved in the temple and the synagogues. It was not just that they were more important or more authoritative than other books. They were in a class by themselves. They were believed to have been inspired by God, and they formed the basis of all worship, all education and all justice in every Jewish community.

The first Christians, being Jews, inherited the same reverence towards the scriptures. When they referred to them, it was sufficient to call them simply "Scripture" or "the scriptures". No other writings had any importance for them. It would not have occurred to them to think that the scriptures had in any way lost their unique authority merely because a new way of understanding them had been made possible by Christ. On the contrary, they continued to take it for granted that the scriptures contained the authentic record of God's dealings with men, and (following the example of Jesus himself) they soon began to find in them numerous prophecies and oracles which seemed to have come alive for the first time in the light of their new faith in Christ. Christianity, they realized, was the crowning chapter of an old story. In Christ, God had done something absolutely new for men, yet it was something which complemented rather than superseded the historic faith of Israel. The matter was neatly expressed by Paul in one of his letters. God's previous relationship with men should be called, no longer "the covenant", but "the old covenant"; for now God had made a new covenant through Christ (2 Corinthians 3). The documents of the old covenant were the scriptures. Paul, indeed, on one occasion called the scriptures themselves 'the old covenant' (2 Corinthians 3.14), in order to help Christians (who now had a new covenant) to place them in the right perspective. But the terminology seems to have stuck. By the end of the second century A.D. the church had grown used to calling the original Jewish scriptures the "old covenant" (the Old Testament), in contrast to which the formative writings of the Christian faith inevitably began to be known as the "new covenant" (the New Testament).

For Paul, of course, no authoritative Christian writings existed. Indeed, he made much of the contrast between the old covenant which was expressed in written documents, and the new covenant which was expressed 'not in a written document, but in a spiritual bond' (2 Corinthians 3.6). The first generation of Christians drew their faith, not from a book, but from a living experience. They may even have shared something of the Jews' distrust for the idea of any religious writing apart from the Old Testament. Nevertheless,

6

circumstances made them into writers. Paul himself travelled constantly, and kept in touch with the widely scattered churches which he had founded by writing them letters in which he strengthened their faith and discussed important points of doctrine. These letters are the earliest Christian writings in existence, and they were followed by others from other Christian leaders, who may or may not always have been in Paul's position of needing to communicate with a distant church, but who adopted the form of an apostolic letter in order to consolidate the faith of their fellow-Christians. At the same time, the need began to be felt to preserve in written form the sayings of Jesus and the events of his life. To meet this need several Christians, probably in different parts of the church, composed the books which we now call the gospels. These relate the story of Christianity from its very beginning; but they appear to have been composed later than Paul's letters, towards the end of the first century A.D. One of them was completed by a second volume (Acts of the Apostles) which carried the story on into the history of the early church.

Thus the first Christian writings were the result of particular circumstances and particular needs encountered during the early decades of the church's existence. Christians did not need to rely on a new "holy book"; their faith was sustained by the spirit active among them, and their teaching was based, partly on the Old Testament, and partly on facts and traditions which were remembered by their elders and which could be traced back to Jesus or to his immediate followers. But in the course of the second century A.D., as living contact with this first age of Christianity began to die out, it became necessary to assemble whatever writings still survived from that period in order to provide a solid and authentic basis for Christian teaching, and also in order to have some standard of Christian truth to appeal to against the attacks and innovations of heretical thinkers. The task was complicated by the fact that there were already books in circulation which purported to have been written by one of the original apostles, but which were in fact the work of later imitators. The church had to decide which of these writings were authentic. In theory, it had a simple criterion: only those which had been written by an apostle could be accepted. In practice, the matter was not so easy, since some of the books were originally anonymous, and some that were attributed to an apostle were plainly imitations. But in general it appears that only those were regarded as "apostolic" which were written during the first seventy years or so of the church's existence, and which seemed always to have held a firm place in the esteem of Christians. In essentials, the selection was settled by the end of the second century A.D., though the inclusion or exclusion of a few books continued to be debated for much longer. On the evidence available, it can be said that the church did its work well. Almost all the writings in the New Testament belong unmistakably to the first century A.D. and have a note of authenticity which is absent from other surviving documents which the church might have been tempted to include.

As soon as the selection was established, it inevitably changed its character. By the end of the second century A.D. the New Testament came to be regarded, like the Old, as Scripture. Its various writings, regardless of the original differences between them, were all treated as equally authoritative documents of the Christian faith. Christianity became, like Judaism, a religion of a book. The methods which had long been used to find the Word of God in any verse of the Old Testament began to be used on the New. The New Testament, along with the Old, began to be called "the Bible", which means simply "the Books". This Bible, like the Old Testament before it (which it still included), became in its turn a book different from all other books, to be interpreted in a special way and possessing in its every part a unique degree of authority and truth.

It was only in comparatively recent times that it began to be realized that this approach does violence to the original diversity and vitality of the individual writings which make up the Old and New Testaments. To regard them as deriving all their authority from the fact that they bear the common name of Scripture is to do them an injustice. This Companion is written in the conviction that the New Testament gains in life and cogency when it is taken for what it originally was, that is, a collection of writings each of which was produced under particular circumstances. Sometimes these circumstances are lost beyond recall; but often it is possible to reconstruct them with reasonable certainty, and so to recapture something of the urgency and authority which these writings possessed for their first Christian readers.

All the books of the New Testament have come down to us in Greek. It is possible that some of them, or small parts of them, originally existed in Aramaic, the language spoken by Jesus himself, and were translated within a few years into Greek; but as we have it, the New Testament is written in the language which was understood by the majority of people in the eastern half of the Roman empire in the first centuries of our era. To understand it we need to know something of the culture of what is loosely called the Hellenistic world, that is, that part of civilization which, since the time of Alexander the Great, had come progressively under the influence of Greek ideas and Greek institutions, even though its political centre had passed to Rome. But Christianity was born in the one part of the Roman empire where there had been determined resistance to the influence of Greek civilization. The great majority of the Jews in the world spoke Greek, but their culture remained essentially Jewish. In Palestine itself they spoke for the most part Aramaic, a language which had spread over much of the Middle East since the days of the Persian empire, and their lives were still regulated by the pattern laid down in their scriptures. Even in the Dispersion they kept themselves at a certain distance from the ideals and institutions of Greek culture, and were allowed to dissociate themselves completely from Greek religion. The society of which we read in the New Testament is therefore not that of the Hellenistic world in general, but of that particular part of it which jealously retained its national religion and culture and way of life.

It happens that not many documents have survived which are evidence for this particular section of the population of the Roman empire. Very few non-Jewish writers had any interest in it; and the Jews in Palestine, for reasons already given, were far from being prolific writers. The recent discovery of the Dead Sea Scrolls has done something to dispel the darkness. They reveal in considerable detail the life and beliefs of a particular religious movement that was flourishing in Palestine in the time of Jesus. Our only other contemporary record is that of Flavius Josephus, a Jewish aristocrat who was involved in the fighting in the Jewish War of A.D. 66–70, and who subsequently wrote both a history of that war and a complete history of the Jewish people, in the hopes of gaining sympathy at Rome for the Jewish cause. Another Greek-speaking Jewish writer, Philo of Alexandria, was meanwhile devoting his life to interpreting the Jewish scriptures in terms that would be familiar to people educated in Greek philosophy. By temperament and circumstances Philo was remote from the concerns of the Jews in Palestine. Yet his writings were intended for readers of similar background to those addressed by early Christian writers, and they can occasionally be usefully compared with passages in the New Testament.

Apart from this, there is very little indeed. A few Jewish writings of a visionary and symbolic character (known as "apocalyptic"), which were subsequently suppressed by the Jewish authorities, were preserved in translation by the Christian church. Otherwise, the characteristic Jewish distrust of any authoritarian writings apart from the scriptures continued right into the second century A.D., and it was only in about the middle of that century that the Jewish rabbis began to write down and codify the traditions which had been handed down to them. These rabbinic writings became voluminous in the centuries that followed, and often contain genuine recollections of customs, events and doctrines of first-century Palestinian Judaism. But their evidence is always fragmentary and often misleading. The picture they present is frequently idealized beyond recognition.

In this respect the New Testament stands very much by itself. Much of it is first-hand evidence for conditions and events of which we should otherwise be totally ignorant. Where we can check it against independent sources of information, it is usually faithful to the facts. Where we cannot, we have to judge it on its merits. On the whole, the historical evidence it provides is consistent and plausible, and for reconstructing the circumstances in which any part of it was written the most important information is usually to be found within the New Testament itself. Yet it is still necessary (and this is one of the objects of this Companion) to supplement this information so far as possible from the little we know about the history, religion and culture of the Jewish people in Palestine and in the Dispersion during the first century A.D.

Not that the Christians were ever merely Jews, or Christianity simply a form of Judaism. The Christian religion and the Christian church represented something new and unique in the ancient world. Yet Jesus was a Jew, and so were all his first followers and all the founders of the first churches. Christianity stood closer to Judaism than to any other religion or philosophy of life, and its history and its beliefs were written in predominantly Jewish terms. The clearest instance of this is the constant use of the Old Testament which is made by nearly every New Testament writer. Sometimes whole passages are quoted, sometimes just a word or a sentence, sometimes there are subtle allusions, and sometimes a writer seems deliberately to imitate the style of the Old Testament without actually quoting it. There is nothing surprising in this. The only form of literature with which most of these writers were familiar was either Scripture itself, or else some kind of commentary upon it; and it was natural that they should see their own work in the same light, however new the message was that they had to convey. To us their use of Scripture, and the interpretation they placed on particular passages, often seems recondite and artificial. It presupposes a long tradition of Jewish scholarly interpretation which was based on principles very different from those which would be acceptable today. But this does not alter the fact that the Old Testament was the most important single element in the background shared by all the New Testament writers.

The NEB, unlike most editions of the New Testament, seldom gives the reader any indication when a passage of Scripture is being quoted. But even if it did, it would not always be easy to turn up the relevant passage of the Old Testament and identify it with the quotation in the New. Most English translations of the Old Testament are based on a Hebrew text which did not become fully standardized until the early centuries of our era. In the time of Christ it is unlikely that every synagogue and religious group in Palestine used an identical text of the scriptures. Moreover, although in Palestine they were read in Hebrew, the reading was usually followed by a translation into Aramaic; and throughout the Dispersion the Jews read and listened to the scriptures in a Greek translation. The most famous of these Greek translations, the Septuagint (so called because of the legend that it was compiled by a team of 70 translators), was made in Egypt in the third century B.C. and had a wide circulation. It still exists, and by comparing it with the quotations which occur in the New Testament we can tell that this was the translation most frequently used by Christian writers. But they did not always use exactly the translation which we now possess. Sometimes their Greek version seems to have been different from that of the Septuagint, sometimes they seem to have quoted a version based on an Aramaic translation, and occasionally they may have made their own translation from the Hebrew. If all these translations had been strictly accurate by modern standards, this would not much matter. But in fact they show striking variations from each other. Sometimes the translators misunderstood the original, sometimes they rephrased it to make it (as they thought) more comprehensible or more edifying to their readers. In addition to this, the Septuagint included more books than were subsequently admitted into the Hebrew text which has survived. These books, having been "hidden away" by the Jewish scholars of Palestine on the grounds that they were not sufficiently important or authoritative to be included, have since the Reformation been printed separately in Protestant Bibles under the title Apocrypha (literally, "hidden books").

For all these reasons, quotations of the Old Testament in the New are not always easy to recognize and identify, and their function in the argument is often difficult to follow. In this matter as in others, this Companion represents an attempt to enter the minds of these writers, and so to bring out the tremendous importance which the Old Testament held for them as a prime source of inspiration and truth. Even the title, THE NEW TESTAMENT, can hardly be understood apart from that other term, "The Old Testament", from which it was originally derived.

THE GOSPEL

To the modern reader, the word GOSPEL denotes the kind of book which has come down to us under the names of Matthew, Mark, Luke and John. But in the early church it was some time before the word took on this meaning. It is clear from the letters of Paul that "the Gospel" existed before any of the "gospels" came to be written down. *Euangelion*, "gospel", was a technical name given by the first generation of Christians to the message they had to impart. Literally, it meant "the good news".

When this message was first preached, it appears to have consisted of a fairly brief summary of those facts about Jesus of Nazareth which had caused his followers to believe that the Messiah, or Christ, of Jewish expectation had now come. For the purpose of convincing their Jewish hearers, the first preachers needed to concentrate primarily upon the fact of Jesus' resurrection, and on the consequences of that fact for faith and conduct. But as time passed, and as the membership of the church began to embrace more and more people of different backgrounds, it became necessary to give flesh to the bare bones of this simple proclamation. New questions were being asked. For example, Christians found themselves caught in a tense controversy with the Jews. What had been Jesus' own attitude to this people? They suffered occasional persecution from the officials of the Roman empire. How far had Jesus himself provoked the hostility of the Roman occupying power in Palestine? They were confronted with problems about life and discipline within the Christian community. Had Jesus left any instructions that were relevant? These and many other questions inevitably arose in the course of the early decades of the church's existence. To answer them, it was necessary to recall the life and teaching of Jesus. His sayings, and the main events of his life, were doubtless reverently preserved in the memories of his followers. We do not know how soon they began to be written down and gathered into collections of sayings or consecutive narratives. But between about A.D. 65 and 100, four books were written in Greek which gathered together much of what was still remembered about the life and work of Jesus. In point of literary form these books were unlike anything that had been written before. They were not biographies, since they omitted a great deal which the reader of a biography would expect to be told; but equally they were not religious treatises. What they contained was the original "Gospel" proclaimed by the church, though cast in extended narrative form. It seemed simplest to refer to them simply by the title of the message they embodied (THE GOSPEL) and to distinguish between them by adding "according to" Matthew, Mark, Luke or John.

These four names do not tell us very much. They were almost certainly intended to stand for four men who appear in the New Testament under the names of 'Matthew', 'John Mark', 'Luke the doctor', and 'John'. But it is only a tradition of the church, going back to the second century A.D., which attributes the gospels to these men; the books themselves are anonymous, and the environment they reflect is not, for the most part, that which one would have expected if they had been written by men who were among the earliest members of the church. Nevertheless, there must have been some reason for preserving these names; two of them (Mark and Luke) are not even the names of apostles. It may well be that at some stage the traditions contained in the gospels passed through the hands of the men whose names they bear.

More significant is the relationship between the four, and in particular between the first three. The gospels according to Matthew, Mark and Luke all tell what is essentially the same story, and sometimes they tell it in almost identical language, while at other times they diverge widely from each other. Usually they agree, sometimes they disagree; and each of the three preserves some material which is absent from both the others. Mark is the shortest of the three, and contains very little which does not appear in Matthew or Luke or both. On the other hand, Matthew and Luke have a number of passages in common which do not appear in Mark. In short, the relationship between the three is close, but very complicated. Evidently they originated in different places, for use in different churches: no church would have needed a second or third one so similar to the first, and it can only have been when they began to be circulated more widely that they were bound up together in the same book. On the other hand, they cannot all have been written quite independently of each other. The occurrence of almost identical passages in two different gospels is explicable only if one writer had the work of the other before him.

There is no completely convincing explanation of all these facts. The most popular hypothesis in modern times has been that Mark was composed first, and was used by both Matthew and Luke; that Matthew and Luke also used another document, now lost, consisting chiefly of sayings of Jesus (hence the appearance of passages common to both of them but absent from Mark); and that each of them had access to traditions not available to either of the others, which they worked as best they could into the narrative framework provided by Mark. To account for all the facts this explanation needs considerable refinement, and it cannot be said to have been proved correct. Nevertheless, as a working hypothesis it has probably aided the study of the first three gospels more than any of the other possible combinations, and it is adopted in this Companion, not because it can be taken for granted as true, but because it is impossible to make sense of the evidence without some explanation of this kind. Moreover, it would have been a waste of space and of the reader's time to provide a full commentary on the same passage each time it appears in different gospels. It was therefore a matter of convenience, as well as a deliberate exploitation of the most widely held hypothesis, to make the commentary on Mark more detailed than any of the others. Any passage which occurs in Mark and in one or more of the other gospels is fully discussed in its context in Mark. The commentary on a parallel passage in another gospel is confined to pointing out significant differences. Further, where a passage occurs in both Matthew and Luke, the discussion will normally be found under Matthew—though this is merely for the reader's convenience: it is not intended to suggest that Luke had read the gospel according to Matthew (although this, theoretically, is also possible).

However, more important consequences follow from adopting this hypothesis than the arrangement of a commentary. If Matthew and Luke used Mark, Mark must have been written first. It seems unlikely, for various reasons, that any of the gospels were written as early as the lifetime of Paul, or later than the end of the first century A.D. To allow time for Mark to have been circulated and then rewritten by Matthew and Luke, it seems sensible to place Mark near the beginning of that period—say between 65 and 70—and the other two a decade or two later. John's gospel seems to reflect external conditions and a stage in the development of Christianity which are somewhat later than those reflected in the other three. It is therefore usually dated between A.D. 90 and 100. But there is virtually nothing by which to check these dates—even the catastrophic event of the fall of Jerusalem in A.D. 70 is not certainly alluded to in any of the New Testament writings.

There is another consequence of accepting this hypothesis which bears more directly on the interpretation of the gospels themselves. When a passage occurs in Mark and in one or two other gospels, it is necessary to account for the changes, sometimes very slight, sometimes quite substantial, which have been made in Matthew or Luke. By studying these changes, one can often see a certain pattern beginning to emerge: it is as if each gospel writer had a particular approach of his own to the material he was recording, an approach which he expressed by subtle editorial changes or careful re-arrangement of the episodes. The case is clearest when we come to John, whose gospel, at first sight, tells a story very different from the others, and in a distinctive style of its own. It is possible that John, like Matthew and Luke, used Mark, but used it much more freely than they did. But he clearly also had other sources of information, and may indeed preserve traditions which are older than Mark's gospel. In any event, it can hardly be doubted that he was consciously recasting his material in a form which he felt expressed better the genius of Jesus' teaching and the significance of Jesus' life and work. Sometimes his narrative is incompatible with that in the other gospels, and we have to make a choice between the two. It is usual to regard Mark's gospel (assuming it is the earliest) as providing the most reliable historical information. But we do not possess the material which Mark himself may have been editing and adapting to his own purpose. It is possible that he, like John, imposed a certain pattern on his sources in order to bring out the significance of the events he was recording. There is no good reason to think that one gospel more than another was ever intended merely to present a bare chronicle of Jesus' life, death and resurrection.

Detailed analysis of the gospels has shown that much of the material out of which they were composed originally consisted of small independent units, sometimes amounting only to a single saying, sometimes running to the length of a complete episode. It was the writers of the gospels who put these units together in the form of a coherent narrative. The NEB sub-headings are intended to indicate the broad shape which the story assumed at their hands; and to this extent a commentary which tries to elucidate the particular style and concerns of each writer is in line with the translators' purpose. But it does not follow from this approach that it is impossible to get behind the gospels and discover the original sayings and actions of Jesus. On the contrary, the individual contribution of each of the gospel writers is very slight and subtle; to present the message in their own way, each had to be content with comparatively small touches. It is as if the material they had to work on, having been reverently preserved by their fellow-Christians, set a strict limit to their editorial freedom. At any point the reader must be prepared to detect their hand; but it seems never to have been a free hand. There is an essential element in the works which have come down to us under the names of Matthew, Mark, Luke and John which the writers could never have created themselves.

Even this does not necessarily take us back to Jesus himself. By the time the gospel writers set to work, the traditions they possessed about Jesus had already been collected and preserved by the church and put to use in preaching, teaching, and defending the faith. They had also at some stage been translated into Greek, with all that that implies of subtle accommodation to a different culture. The gospels as we have them often betray the marks of this process. The circumstances and needs of the early church are discernible in the form in which Jesus' sayings and the events of his life have been preserved. Yet once again there is an essential element in the traditions so preserved which the church could not have created itself. It is this element which makes it possible to say with confidence that the gospels, despite the mysterious and complicated history of their compilation, still preserve an authentic recollection of the life and teaching of Jesus of Nazareth.

THE GOSPEL ACCORDING TO MATTHEW

The coming of Christ

This innocent-looking heading has been placed by the translators at the beginning of each of the gospels; but neither of the terms which it contains is as simple as it looks. In the first place when, and in what sense, did Christ "come"? The New Testament writers themselves were by no means agreed on the point at which the gospel story began. Mark, for example, followed what we may believe to have been the oldest pattern of Christian preaching: he began with Jesus' baptism, and recorded nothing before this except the activity of John the Baptist, Jesus' immediate precursor. Matthew felt it important to record the circumstances of Jesus' birth and parentage, and Luke went back still further to the birth of John the Baptist. John's "beginning" is on another time-scale altogether: Christ had existed with God the Father since the birth of time, and his "coming" was really a "becoming", the appearance of a pre-existent divine being at a certain moment and place in history. These differences of approach and emphasis are characteristic of each gospel; and the similarity of the headings in the NEB should not obscure the fact that for each of these writers the word *coming* might have borne a different meaning.

Secondly, *Christ*. The Greek word *Christos* stands for the Hebrew word *Messiah*, "the Anointed One". This was an old title, originally used of the first kings of Israel. But in the time of Jesus it was reserved for a divinely appointed figure whom (it was widely believed) God would soon send into the world to inaugurate a new and blessed age for the benefit of his elect. Was Jesus this Messiah, this Christ? His work and teaching were such that the question was bound to be constantly raised. In public, he never gave an altogether unambiguous answer to it, and during his lifetime his name remained simply the not uncommon Hebrew name *Yeshua*, represented in Greek as Jesus. It was only after the resurrection that his disciples became completely convinced that he was the Christ. They then began to refer to him as Jesus "the Christ", and soon simply as Jesus Christ.

Many different beliefs were held by Jesus' contemporaries about the exact nature and function of this Messiah; but it was common ground to most of them that he would be a descendant of King David. Jesus apparently fulfilled this qualification: he had a family tree which could be traced back to David; and this is one reason why Matthew begins his gospel with a

1. 1 table of the descent of Jesus Christ. But it may not be the only reason. Jewish writers were fond of establishing the genealogies of their heroes, and of showing them to be descendants of great figures of the past, and Matthew in fact takes the genealogy back, not just to David, but further still, to Abraham. Abraham, for any Jewish thinker, was the decisive figure in the story of God's concern for mankind; and Matthew's genealogy serves to knit Jesus firmly into this story. Moreover, the series of three groups of

17 fourteen generations (which is somewhat artificially imposed upon the list of names) is probably intended to suggest that divine providence had been at work in bringing Jesus into the world at this exact moment of history.

The list itself is demonstrably inaccurate in certain details, but is not

2–12 necessarily entirely untrustworthy. From Abraham to Zerubbabel the genealogy runs through the well-known leaders of the Jewish people. Where it can be checked against similar lists in the Old Testament (such as in the first chapters of 1 Chronicles), it shows certain discrepancies and errors; but it is certain that no single and authoritative genealogy of the leading families in Jewish history existed in Matthew's time, and it need cause no surprise that Matthew's list differs slightly from others, particularly since it had

12–16 to be adjusted a little to fit into a fourteenfold pattern. After Zerubbabel, the line branches off from the main stem in order to reach the immediate ancestors of Jesus, and from this point we have no means of checking it. It is quite different from Luke's table; but this does not necessarily prove either of the tables to be a fiction. The evangelists may have had access to family papers such as many Jewish families possessed, recording one or more family trees (perhaps through different parents or grandparents) and proving that Joseph was among the descendants of David.

But Joseph was not Jesus' father. This difficulty, which was felt suffi-

16 ciently acutely in antiquity to cause some variants in Matthew's text (see the footnote in NEB), arose out of the fact that Matthew had two apparently incompatible things to say about Jesus: first that he was (as the Messiah was expected to be) a descendant of David, and secondly that he was born in a unique way, without a human father. But Jewish law and custom offered a solution to this difficulty. If a Jew formally named and adopted a child, that child became his son. This is the theme of the following paragraph.

18 This is the story of the birth of the Messiah. The birth was miraculous: it was God, and no human father, who caused Mary to conceive. In the Old Testament, the creative power of God was called his "spirit"; and it may still have come naturally to a Jewish writer such as Matthew to use the same language: she was with child by the Holy Spirit. But Matthew does not linger over the miracle itself; he goes straight on to its human consequences. Mary was **betrothed to Joseph,** which meant under Jewish law that she was fully committed to marrying him: the contract had already been signed, and it only remained for the marriage ceremony to take place and for the bride to take up residence in her husband's house. Her pregnancy, if suddenly discovered at this stage by the bridegroom, was therefore a potential source of scandal. **Being a man of principle,** Joseph could 19 not possibly condone it: he must either bring his fiancée publicly before a court in order to prove her guilty, or else repudiate the marriage contract (which he was entitled to do at any time) and leave the question of Mary's shame to be resolved by her family. But a further divine intervention, related this time in the form of a dream and an angel, made him take responsibility himself. If the world believed that he had had intercourse with his betrothed before their marriage, it would not greatly matter: this was not regarded as a serious sin in Jewish society; and by adopting and naming the child, he took him formally into his own family and ensured that Jesus, like himself, could be rightfully called a '**son of David**'. 20

However, Matthew is not only concerned to settle these practical details. He compresses into this short paragraph some important clues to the wider significance of Jesus' birth. The name itself, Jesus, meant **Saviour,** and 21 described something of Jesus' destiny; and the manner of Jesus' birth had a striking parallel in Old Testament prophecy. One of Matthew's particular contributions to the gospel story was to demonstrate that not merely the suffering, death, and resurrection of Jesus but also many other episodes were foretold or prefigured in Scripture. In doing this his methods were not always such as modern scholarship would countenance, though they would have aroused no scruples among Jewish scholars of his time. Here, for example, the original Hebrew of Isaiah 7.14 has, not '**the virgin**', but 'a young 23 woman', and it is unlikely that Isaiah, in this prophecy of future abundance and divine favour, meant to predict anything so miraculous as a virgin birth. But in the Greek translation of the Old Testament, which Matthew used, the word could (though it did not necessarily) mean 'virgin', and so to Matthew's mind the text provided a startlingly exact prophecy of the event he had just recorded.

Jesus was born at Bethlehem in Judaea during the reign of Herod. 2. 1 Herod the Great died, after a long reign, in about 4 B.C. Matthew's narrative implies that Jesus was born not less than two years before this (verse 16), but also not much more (verse 19)—say, 7–6 B.C. This is somewhat earlier than the traditional date (between 1 B.C. and A.D. 1), but the idea of dating world history by the birth of Christ was only invented five hundred years later, and the date which was then chosen was the result of a mistaken calculation. Matthew's date is not improbable in itself; the only difficulty is to reconcile it with the chronology in Luke (see below on Luke 2.1).

In any country where astrology was taken seriously (as it was in most countries in the ancient world, and particularly in those which lay immediately to the east of Palestine) a new star, or a notable conjunction of stars, would quickly attract attention, presaging an important new turn in human affairs. Conversely, it was believed that it was the very regularity of the stars which guaranteed the orderly course of history, and it followed that any really significant event must necessarily be accompanied by some striking phenomenon in the heavens. The birth of Jesus was such an event, and if the following story reads more like legend than history, it is easy to see how such a legend could have originated, particularly since similar legends were told in Jewish folklore about the birth of Moses, and it is arguable that Jesus was regarded by Matthew as, in some sense, a second Moses. On the other hand, the story is by no means incredible. The visitors from the east are called in the Greek *Magi*. The word came originally from Persia, where it denoted influential religious leaders; but in ordinary Greek usage it meant sorcerers or magicians. What does it mean here? These men were certainly not "three kings of Orient"—that is a later legend [a]; and they may not have been quite as dignified as "wise men". But one kind of knowledge they did possess—astrology; and it is certainly correct (though it may not be the 2 whole truth) to call them, with the NEB, **astrologers**. Their observation of the star had satisfied them that some change was impending in the west, that is to say, in Palestine; and they felt sure enough of their interpretation to put to Herod a specific question, '**Where is the child who is born to be king of the Jews?**'. Herod, who doubtless intended to make his own arrangements about the succession to the throne, preferred to regard the star as a sign of that other "king" whom the Jews were awaiting, the Messiah. Many passages of the Old Testament pointed forward to this figure, and it was to be expected that the religious leaders of the Jews, and particularly 4 the **lawyers** (who were the professional expositors of the Old Testament, the law of the Jewish people) would be able to answer the astrologers' question. Their answer could by no means be taken for granted: many opinions were abroad about the place and circumstances in which the 5, 6 Messiah would appear. But there was a **prophecy in Micah 5.2** [b] which was understood by some as an oracle about the birthplace of the Messiah. In Matthew's story the function of the prophecy is to direct the astrologers to the village five miles south of Jerusalem where they would find what the star had led them to expect; but in the wider context of the gospel its apparent fulfilment serves to strengthen Jesus' claim to be both Messiah and "son of David" (for Bethlehem had been David's home).

[a] Based on an application of the prophecy in Isaiah 60.3.
[b] Matthew quotes this in a version a little different from that in either the Hebrew or the Greek of the Septuagint, and combines with it a few words from 2 Samuel 5.2: this may have been one of a collection of texts which the early Christians used to prove that Jesus had fulfilled Old Testament prophecy.

The purpose of the astrologers in seeking the child was to **pay him** 2 **homage**. When they found him, they **offered him gifts: gold, frank-** 11 **incense, and myrrh**—traditional products of the wealth and luxury of the east (compare Isaiah 60.6 for gold and frankincense, Song of Solomon 3.6 for frankincense and myrrh); their gifts showed that they recognized him as the "king" of whom the star was a sign, and theirs was the first testimony to him who was to be crucified as "king of the Jews". Herod's interest, however, was more practical: to eliminate one who might grow up to be, if not a pretender to the throne, at least a cause of dissension in Judaea. It would be in keeping with what we know of the character of Herod that **he** 16 **fell into a passion, and gave orders for the massacre** of all suspect children. His reign, especially in its closing years, was marked by many atrocities. But Matthew may not mean that he killed all the children in Bethlehem of two years or less. The phrase, **corresponding with the time he had ascertained from the astrologers** (which refers back to verse 7 above), suggests that he limited the slaughter to the babies born at the exact season of the star's appearing in the previous two years—possibly quite a small number. Matthew's concern, in any case, was not so much to portray the savagery of Herod as to discern the significance of the episode. He saw it, first, as a direct fulfilment of a prophecy of Jeremiah (31.15), '**A voice** 18 **was heard in Rama ... it was Rachel weeping for her children**'. In Jeremiah, Rachel, the wife of Jacob and mother of two of the "tribes" of Israel, is imagined as weeping over her descendants who are being deported by the Assyrian conquerors past the northern frontier-town of Rama. Matthew evidently imagines her lamenting near Bethlehem, perhaps because there was an old tradition (Genesis 35.19), which is still preserved by a monument today, that Rachel's tomb was close to Bethlehem. Secondly, Herod's massacre was the motive for the flight of Jesus' parents into Egypt, and this too placed Jesus in the line of a great national tradition: God had "called his son"—the people of Israel—"out of Egypt" (Hosea 11.1). 15 Jesus, who was "God's son" *par excellence*, lived through a similar exile and a similar return.

He settled in a town called Nazareth. Matthew's explanation of the 23 move from Bethlehem to Galilee is not very cogent: Galilee was ruled by Herod Antipas, another of Herod's sons, and the danger might have been as great there as in Bethlehem. In practice, however, Nazareth was probably much safer. It was a small and rather isolated town in the hills of Galilee, with none of the Davidic traditions of Bethlehem. Indeed, no one would have expected a native of Nazareth to make any mark in history (John 1.46, 'Can anything good come from Nazareth?'). Jesus, at any rate, became known as 'a Nazarene' and indeed Christians were for many years called "Nazarenes" in Palestine. One of Matthew's purposes in the whole of this chapter has been to show how this Nazarene was nevertheless born in

Bethlehem, as a true descendant of David should be. Even in the name "Nazarene", however, Matthew finds some significance. But here we are at a loss. The Old Testament does not contain the words 'He shall be called a Nazarene'. The nearest phrase occurs in the narrative of the birth of Samson: Samson was to be a "Nazarite" (Judges 13.5), which means an ascetic under vows to God. But Matthew may have had in mind a more subtle allusion to the Hebrew word *netser*, "branch", which occurs in various biblical texts that were held in his time to be prophecies of the Messiah. *a*

3. 1 **About that time.** Literally, "in those days", a phrase which is perhaps deliberately imprecise. Many years have passed in the little gap between chapter 2 and chapter 3. Jesus has grown up. Judaea is now under direct Roman rule, the reign of Archelaus, Herod's successor, having quickly come to an ignominious end (A.D. 6); while the northern and eastern parts of the country, Galilee and Peraea, are still under the more or less independent rule of another of Herod's sons, Herod Antipas. It is in connection with Herod Antipas that **John the Baptist** makes a brief appearance in the pages of another writer nearly contemporary with the author of this gospel, the Jewish historian Josephus. Josephus' interest in him is more political than religious, but his account agrees in the basic facts. John's movement appeared to Herod Antipas as a threat to peace, and in due course Herod imprisoned him.

When Mark introduces John the Baptist he concentrates entirely (apart from a few words devoted to the nature of his baptism) on his rôle as the herald and forerunner of Jesus. Matthew, though he quotes the same
3. 1 prophecy from Isaiah (40.3), presents him at the outset **as a preacher,** making his proclamation in the manner of an Old Testament prophet. John, in any case, resembled a prophet, both by his clothes (compare the description of Elijah in 2 Kings 1.8), and also by his appearance in **the Judaean wilderness.** Large tracts of Palestine, one of them reaching right up to the neighbourhood of Jerusalem, were bare and uncultivable, as against the densely inhabited farmlands of Galilee or the vineyards of other parts of Judaea. Traditionally, a prophet was a man who pondered his message in an austere environment, away from the amenities of sophisticated life. John conformed to this tradition; and his message was correspondingly
2 simple and direct. '**Repent**': the word meant not so much personal remorse as a corporate re-orientation, away from the subtleties of contemporary political and religious life, towards a single-minded attention to the commands of God. '**For the kingdom of Heaven**': this is the same concept as "the kingdom of God", only in somewhat more pious Jewish dress (the Jews liked to avoid using God's name, and preferred to speak of "heaven",

---

[*a*] Especially Isaiah 11.1. **Nazarene** is actually the form used by Mark, and sometimes by Luke. Elsewhere, including this passage, the actual form of the word is "Nazoraean".

"angels" and the like). It means God's rule, that longed-for state of affairs when men will willingly and spontaneously do the will of God. 'Is upon you': literally, the Greek means "has drawn near". How near? From the Greek word alone, it is impossible to tell. But it is clear from what follows that John is giving urgent warning of coming judgement. All Jews expected this some time in the future. John proclaims that it is very near indeed: his word (like that of Jesus, whose preaching, in this gospel, begins in exactly the same way) is meant to drive the point home: it is no longer in the uncertain future, it is 'upon you'.

Among the crowd were **Pharisees and Sadducees.** (It does not strictly 7 follow from the Greek that they came **for baptism.** They may simply have been there to watch.) These people represented a higher level of society than (presumably) the rest of the throng, and in Matthew's account (unlike Luke's) they are singled out for attack by John the Baptist just as, later in this gospel, they are consistently criticized by Jesus. The ground on which they are attacked here is that they claimed a certain immunity from the coming judgement: "**We have Abraham for our father**".ᵃ John—with 9 words also used by Jesus (7.19)—sweeps aside this suggestion of divine favouritism, and returns to the arresting element in his proclamation. The **one who comes** is certainly (as in Mark) a person greater than himself, 11 and his baptism will be not just a ritual washing with water but a personal experience of the power of **the Holy Spirit:** he is also an Elijah-figure (the language recalls Malachi 4, Ecclesiasticus 48), a man of fire, bringing 12 immediate judgement.

We know, and Matthew's first readers knew, who it was for whom John was preparing a way. It was Jesus. But we should not necessarily read this knowledge back into the narrative. For in many respects Jesus does not fit the portrait given here. Jesus himself still expected and proclaimed the coming judgement, he did not immediately precipitate it; and as for an Elijah-figure, Jesus regarded John, not himself, as Elijah (11.14). Matthew, in any case, does not state here that John recognized Jesus as the Man of Fire. All that John recognized was some exceptional quality in Jesus which 14 seemed to make it inappropriate to baptize him "confessing his sins". It looks, indeed, as if this was a difficulty felt by Matthew's readers. They knew that Jesus had been baptized by John, and they knew that John's baptism was 'for the forgiveness of sins' (Mark 1.4). But Jesus did not commit sin; why therefore was he baptized? This passage may have been moulded to suggest an answer: **to conform ... with all that God requires.** 15 The translation is rather free (the literal sense is "to complete all righteousness"), but gives at least a possible meaning: just as Jesus came to "complete" the Law, by endorsing its inner meaning and laying a new form of it on his followers (5.17), so he submitted to John's baptism and, by his action,

[a] This classic argument of the Jew is criticized by Paul in Romans 2.

validated the rite for all future generations of Christians. The account of
Jesus' baptism follows Mark closely (Mark 1.9–11). The same combination
17 of scriptural texts **was heard** (though possibly only by Jesus—the Greek
has simply, "a voice from heaven saying"); but even this did not conclusively identify Jesus as the one whom John was expecting. Indeed, John
was still in doubt some time later (11.2–3).

4. 1 **Jesus was then led away.** Mark, at this point, simply records a period of
contest with the devil in the wilderness. Matthew and Luke evidently knew
a fuller version of the story, and one which puts it in a somewhat different
light. In Mark, one has to imagine a sustained struggle between Jesus and
the devil, Jesus being meanwhile aided and fed by angels. Here, Jesus first
undergoes a prolonged fast (he is only afterwards waited on by the angels,
3 verse 11) and is then approached by the devil in the character of **the tempter,**
3–4 and exposed to three "temptations", or tests. The first of these tests was
a natural consequence of his hunger, and could have taken place on the spot.
5 The other two are also vividly set in Palestinian scenery—the **parapet of**
the temple is usually thought to be the south-east corner of the immense
terrace constructed by Herod the Great around the temple in Jerusalem,
from which there was a sheer drop of some 150 feet into the Kedron valley
below; and many hill-tops in the Judaean desert offer immense views over
the Jordan valley and the mountains beyond which could well be described as
8 a microcosm of **the kingdoms of the world in their glory.** But the actual
tests could not have been carried out in one region of the Judaean desert;
they must have taken place in Jesus' mind. In which case it must be asked,
in what sense is it likely that the story represents a historical episode in the
life of Jesus? One feature in the story bears on this question. All of Jesus'
4 replies are quotations from the Book of Deuteronomy: Deuteronomy 8.3,
7, 10 6.16 (in answer to the devil's quotation of Psalm 91.11–12) and 6.13.
Furthermore, these verses in Deuteronomy are set in the context of
the period of "testing" which the people of Israel underwent in the wilderness. It is clear that the biblical narrative has influenced the form, and
perhaps the content, of the story recounted by Matthew and Luke: Jesus
was re-enacting, in his own person, the formative experience of the desert
generation. But this, of course, is not to say that Jesus did not experience
something of this kind. The disciples could well have been aware that
Jesus treasured these verses of Deuteronomy and had come to realize their
significance during his period of retreat in the wilderness. The remaining
details would not have been hard to fill in.
12 **When he heard that John had been arrested.** Like Mark, Matthew
regards the moment of John's arrest—which he can assume his readers
know all about, and which he only describes later on—as the point in time
at which Jesus appeared in Galilee. But he is a little more specific than Mark

about the details. **Jesus withdrew**—not, presumably, to avoid the same fate as John; for Galilee, just as much as Peraea (where John was probably arrested) belonged to the territory of Herod Antipas. Rather, his "withdrawal" was a natural retirement after the rigorous testing of the desert. Matthew also knew (or at least inferred) that since so many of the events he was about to record were enacted on the shores of the Sea of Galilee, Jesus must have moved from Nazareth (which is some 30 miles from it) and

13 **settled at Capernaum**, the most important Jewish town on the lake (see the map on p. 25); and this enabled him to invoke another prophecy. The

15-16 passage he quotes from Isaiah (9.1–2), with its old tribal names for the region, was written when Galilee was under foreign control (and was therefore **heathen**), and prophesied its restoration to the people of Israel. Matthew sees in Jesus' appearance by the **Way of the Sea** a different and more significant fulfilment of the prophecy.

17   On Jesus' **message** (which in Matthew is identical with that of John the Baptist), see below on Mark 1.15.

18 **Jesus was walking by the Sea of Galilee**. Matthew follows Mark in placing this episode right at the beginning of Jesus' work. It was necessarily located **by the Sea of Galilee**—which is what the Jews called it, though in reality it was a lake, the Lake of Tiberias. The main fishing waters are still at the north end of the lake, where hot springs enter it near the site of Capernaum. Jesus' activity is thus to be thought of as confined, at this stage, to a relatively small area around Capernaum. But Matthew then widens the scene. Jesus' preaching and healing—of which he is about to give examples

23 —extended over **the whole of Galilee**. It was concentrated, for the purpose of teaching, on towns like Capernaum and Chorazin, where there would be a large synagogue, and where the Sabbath congregations would offer him a good opening for his work (see below on Mark 1.21); but we are also to

25 picture him as a healer, moving about over a wide area, and attracting **great crowds**, not only from Galilee and the rest of Jewish Palestine (**Jerusalem**, **Judaea** and **Transjordan**), but also from the more cosmopolitan world of the **Ten Towns** (the Decapolis, a league of wealthy Greco-Roman cities to the south-east of Galilee).

The Sermon on the Mount

This is the title by which the next three chapters of Matthew's gospel have been known since at least the time of Augustine. The NEB adopts the old

5. 1 title, but in verse 1 it replaces "mount" with a more colloquial word, **when he saw the crowds he went up the hill**. This rendering makes one want to

ask, what hill? But the original Greek is probably less precise, and means "up into the hill-country", [a] that is, away from the populous coast of the lake into the more lonely foothills to the west and north, and Jesus' purpose in thus going "up the hill" was usually simply to get away from the crowds in order to pray (Matthew 14.23) or to talk privately with his disciples (Mark 3.13). Accordingly, the opening of his discourse here is specifically addressed to his disciples (who are mentioned here for the first time, and may be assumed to be a group which has grown out of such episodes as Simon's and Andrew's decision to "follow" Jesus, 4.18–20), and the traditional picture of Jesus standing on a high place addressing the multitudes is unwarranted by these opening verses. However, at the end of the discourse (7.28) we find that 'the people (literally, "the crowds") were astounded at his teaching'. If we are to accept these chapters at their face value as the record of a historical occasion, we shall have to assume that the crowds caught up with Jesus while he was talking, and that what began as the giving of teaching to a group of disciples ended, by force of circumstances, as a "sermon" addressed to a large congregation.

This is a possible explanation; but the apparent change in the audience between the beginning and the end is not the only indication that these chapters are not quite what they seem. Some of the sayings they contain must have been originally intended for the disciples, some for the crowds; some of them are found in other gospels in quite different contexts, and some, by the time Matthew wrote them down, seem to have been slightly altered by the early church into a form which it found more relevant to its own situation. Moreover, the discourse as a whole hardly constitutes a "sermon" in the modern sense. There is a logical development of the argument in certain sections, but there is no clear theme, and it is hard to imagine the discourse being delivered on a single occasion and listened to by a single audience. In short, it seems to fit the facts better if we regard these chapters as a collection made by Matthew (or the source he was using) of Jesus' ethical teaching, arranged under certain headings, and provided with an introduction and a conclusion which (since these occur also in the "sermon" in Luke's gospel, 6.20–49) may well reproduce a pattern which Jesus was accustomed to use in his teaching. Such a collection would obviously have been useful for teaching purposes in the early church, and this may be one of the reasons why Matthew incorporated it in his gospel. Another reason may be that Matthew saw Jesus as, in some respects, a new Moses: Jesus' teaching on the mount corresponded to, and was indeed the necessary fulfilment of, Moses' proclamation of the Law on Sinai.

These possibilities must be borne in mind throughout the next three chapters. But they do not necessarily affect our estimate of the "sermon". For however it came into existence, it remains the most comprehensive

[a] The same words are translated 'up to the hills' in Matthew 15.29.

discourse of Jesus of which we have any record. It was regarded by the author of the gospel as a fair summary of what Jesus taught (this follows from the prominent position he assigned to it near the beginning of his narrative), and even if we can at times detect evidence of subsequent editing and retouching by Matthew or by the tradition which he preserves, and although we may suspect that on some points Jesus may originally have expressed himself differently or have had specific situations in mind which are no longer remembered, yet we shall never in fact replace this discourse by something different, nor are we likely to find a better picture of Jesus' ethical teaching than that which Matthew gives us. These are the words through which we must still hear the voice of Jesus; this is the *Sermon on the Mount* which, down the centuries, has left its mark on the church and on the world.

Jesus' teaching begins with a series of "beatitudes". What kind of people are "blest"—that is to say, what are the conditions which a person must fulfil if he is to enter upon the rewards which are promised by religion?

3   **'How blest are those who know their need of God'.** Here the NEB rendering is a bold paraphrase. Literally, the Greek means, "Blest are the poor in spirit", a phrase which sounds unnatural in Greek, and can only be understood in the light of a characteristic Old Testament conception of poverty. In the corresponding passage of Luke's gospel (6.20) Jesus is reported as saying, 'How blest are you who are in need', where there can be little doubt that 'in need' means literally poor. In many ancient cultures, including the Jewish, this would have sounded like nonsense: riches, not poverty, showed that a man was blest. But there was one strain of Jewish piety (represented particularly by some of the psalms) which saw the matter differently. In this tradition, "the poor" had become a religious as well as a social term. As opposed to the rich, the influential, the extortionate and the oppressive, "the poor" were those who, by keeping intact their own righteousness and piety, could be sure that, however much they appeared to be the victims of society, they would ultimately be rewarded and vindicated by God. This tenacious faith of "the poor man" was decisively endorsed by Jesus: the compromises and injustices into which men are inevitably led by wealth and position are incompatible with the integrity demanded by God. Consequently, "Blest are the poor". But of course they are not blest merely because they are poor. There was a spirit of poverty which went with physical poverty, and it was this spirit which was important. The corresponding Hebrew phrase, "poor in spirit", actually occurs in the Dead Sea Scrolls, and was doubtless current in Palestine in the time of Jesus. Matthew was probably trying to put this into Greek when he wrote the words, "poor in spirit". Poor meant literally poor: but it also implied an attitude of simplicity, integrity, and dependence upon God—an attitude which is spelled out in

more detail in the beatitudes which follow. It is this attitude which the NEB has tried to define by the paraphrase, those who know their need of God. [a]

'How blest are the sorrowful; they shall find consolation'. The 4 NEB translation makes this sound a little philosophical, as if it expresses the truth that there is a way of bearing sorrow which enables one to "find" consolation. But the Greek is more direct: "they shall be consoled". It was one of the great truths of the Gospel that it gave men true "consolation" (see also 2 Corinthians 1). And the condition of obtaining that blessing was, again, not the complacency and satisfaction of those who are insulated by their possessions from the general suffering of mankind but —sorrow.

'How blest are those of a gentle spirit'. Almost identical words occur 5 in Psalm 37.11. This "gentleness" (which is the mark, in the Old Testament, of one who accepts his humble status without bitterness) is one of the characteristic notes of "the poor"; and the confidence that it would be rewarded had already found expression in one tradition of Jewish piety.

'How blest are those who hunger and thirst to see right prevail'. 6 Luke, again, preserves a more radical version: 'How blest are you who now go hungry'. The social context is still the same. Those who are poor and oppressed are blest, even though they may in fact go hungry; but the reason why they are blest is not merely that they go hungry—they do not swerve from what is right; and here too Matthew may have added the single word "righteousness" (of which the NEB has brought out the meaning by a paraphrase, to see right prevail) in order to fill in another of the "spiritual" characteristics of the traditional "poor man" of Jewish piety.

After this first group of four beatitudes, three of which are more decisive and radical than anything which is to be found in the Old Testament or in contemporary Jewish piety, the series continues with three more which seem 7-9 rather to recommend certain virtues than to propound a new scale of values. These, which can be paralleled in Jewish literature, are lacking in Luke's more radical version; and they give the opening of the Sermon a distinctly more ethical character than do the abrupt statements in the first beatitudes. Only the last—'How blest are those who have suffered persecution 10 for the cause of right'—returns to the decisive tone of the opening. There had been many in Jewish history who had "suffered persecution for the cause of right". Religious men trusted and prayed that, despite their

[a] In the First Edition of NEB the first beatitude is rendered, "How blest are those who know that they are poor". This is more open to criticism. Any Greek philosopher might have agreed that a man who "knows that he is poor" has made important progress in self-knowledge, and is consequently more "blest" than one who takes a complacent view of his worldly possessions. But for the purpose of achieving this self-knowledge it did not much matter whether one were rich or poor; the important thing was to cultivate a philosophic detachment from whatever wealth one happened to possess. It is unlikely that Jesus was recommending merely this philosophical detachment. His teaching is always concerned as much with people's actual circumstances as with their frame of mind.

apparent humiliation, these martyrs had been accepted and would one day be vindicated by God. Jesus, again, gave his authoritative endorsement to this faith.

Such people, then, are blest. But what does this blessedness consist of? Jewish religion conceived of it as a future state of felicity in a new order which would soon be brought into being by God; and most of Jesus' beatitudes similarly have a future tense: the blessedness cannot be expected in this world, but Jesus promises it, with the full weight of his authority, for the life in heaven. But what of the first and last in the series of beatitudes, 3, 10 which end, 'the kingdom of Heaven is theirs'? Should these also be understood as future, or is there a sense in which the kingdom is already present? This is a question which runs right through the gospel. It is raised by Jesus' very first words, 'The kingdom of Heaven is upon you' (see above on 3.2). For the present, it is important to bear in mind that Jesus saw himself (or at least was seen by the earliest Christians) as fulfilling the prophecy, "The Spirit of the Lord is upon me because the Lord has appointed me to bring good tidings to the poor . . . to comfort all who mourn". (Isaiah 61.1–2). The coming of Jesus inaugurated a new situation, in which many of the world's accepted values would be reversed.

11 'How blest you are'. The language suddenly becomes personal: no longer the broad sweep of a religious teacher pronouncing general truths, but the direct address of a master to his disciples. It seems early yet to think of those who had so recently begun to follow Jesus suffering **insults and persecution and every kind of calumny**. It was the church, after Jesus' death and resurrection, which first began to experience these things, and will have gratefully remembered (if indeed it did not adapt to its own situation) Jesus' warning and Jesus' promise. Similarly, the metaphors which follow clearly apply, not to any casual listeners, but to those who have committed themselves to discipleship.

13 '**You are salt to the world**'. We now use salt mainly for flavouring, and so the metaphor suggests to us a small but necessary element in that total mixture which is human civilization (and this, in fact, is precisely what many would say the Christian contribution to history has been). But in antiquity salt was equally important for preserving food; and the metaphor may be similar to that used by a Christian writer of the second century, "Christians are the soul of the world"—for they are responsible for its continuance in life. But how does salt become **tasteless**? Chemically, it can never lose its saltness. But in the various kinds of use to which it was put in Palestine it could become progressively less and less pure, until finally it was useless—and then nothing could be done to "restore its saltness".

14 '**Light for all the world. A town that stands on a hill**'. The two metaphors probably belong together. Isaiah had declared it to be the destiny

of Israel to be "a light to the nations" (49.6); and the symbol of this destiny was the city of Jerusalem set on a hill, to which the peoples of the world would come to worship the one true God. Jesus' disciples were to become the new Israel, and could be described in the same imagery. (For a note on the meal-tub, see below on Mark 4.21.) 15

'Do not suppose that I have come to abolish the Law and the 17 prophets'. Jesus' ethical teaching was by no means entirely new but, like the teaching of his contemporaries, took as its point of departure the systematic code of behaviour contained in the books of the Old Testament attributed to Moses (which the Jews in fact observed not merely as a moral code but as a legal code, and referred to as the Law), and also the great moral insights contained in the writings of the prophets. Sometimes his teaching was so radical that it seemed a direct contradiction of the Law of Moses—and some of the first Christians were quick to draw the conclusion that Christianity completely superseded the moral and legal code of the Jews. But Matthew was anxious to show that even where Jesus' teaching seemed most at variance with normal Jewish practice, it was still a direct development of the original Law: I did not come to abolish, but to complete. [a] Consequently Jesus' followers, whatever their enemies might say (and we can probably overhear this debate at several places in Matthew's gospel), were as committed to "keeping the Law" as the Jews themselves. To demonstrate this, Matthew arranged the first section of his collection of Jesus' teaching in the form of a new interpretation of the Law of Moses— and indeed Jesus himself is likely to have given his teaching in this form; it was one of the regular patterns followed by Jewish moral teachers in his day. The Pharisees, and those doctors of the law who shared their 20 convictions, devoutly believed that the Law of Moses, though originally formulated many centuries before, was still valid in their own day as a comprehensive guide to conduct; and in order to bring it up to date (so to speak) they evolved certain rules of interpretation by which its provisions could be shown to apply to present-day circumstances. Jesus' quarrel with these men (and again this is a debate which we can often overhear as the gospel progresses) was that their interpretation had become so subtle and casuistical that it often frustrated the original intention of the Law. But in offering his own interpretation, he had no idea of taking the Law less seriously than they did. He too regarded it as unalterable down to the smallest letter or stroke of a letter, and as of eternal validity: and as regards 18 the keeping of its detailed provisions, his followers must show themselves better men even than the Pharisees and the doctors of the law. 20 This, at least, seems to have been Matthew's view of the relation between

[a] The word translated complete can also mean "fulfil", or even (perhaps) "establish". Its exact meaning here must depend upon the way in which the whole passage is understood.

Jesus' teaching and the Law of Moses. But the question was not an easy one, nor was it always answered in the same way by different New Testament writers.

21 **'You have learned that our forefathers were told'**. The phrase is repeated, with slight variations, six times in this chapter. In each case, it refers to a well-known provision of the Law of Moses, and prepares for a new interpretation; and it is likely that this form of argument was one that was frequently used in Jesus' time in learned debates about the application of specific laws. **'Do not commit murder'** is the sixth of the Ten Commandments. But the rest of the sentence, **'anyone who commits murder must be brought to judgement'** is not in fact to be found in the Old Testament (though it is of course implied in it), but is the kind of addition which the doctors of the law made to the original text in order to show its practical application. When Jesus pronounced that anger and abuse were as serious as murder in the eyes of God, many of his contemporaries would have agreed with him—in theory; for the Old Testament said as much itself. But in practice there was a difference: a man who had committed murder could be brought before a court, a man who had merely expressed anger could not—and this difference inevitably made the one seem much less serious than the other. If human justice were perfectly to mirror the judgement of God (as the Jewish law was claimed to do) this difference

22 should not exist: **anyone who nurses anger against his brother** should be as accountable in a human court as a murderer is; for in the divine court both will be sentenced to **the fires of hell.**

23-6 Before the series is continued, two practical examples are given, which in a general way illustrate the same point. Both examples are vividly drawn

23-4 from daily life.[a] In the temple at Jerusalem one of the commonest sights will have been that of individual Jews bringing beasts or birds to be sacrificed at the great altar in the central court. Some of these sacrifices were laid upon them by the Law on certain occasions (Luke 2.24), some were offered voluntarily as thank-offerings or as offerings to atone for some transgression. From the point of view of the temple cult, a personal grievance would have seemed a small matter compared with the due completion of the sacrifice; but from Jesus' statement that any offence against one's brother is as serious as murder, it followed that personal reconciliation must be of infinitely more importance than any ritual act.

25 **'If someone sues you'**. This again seems drawn from life. It follows

26 from the end of the saying (**'you will not be let out till you have paid the last farthing'**) that Jesus was thinking of someone who was really in

[a] The details of private sacrifice, so far as we can discover them, do not fit in too well with Jesus' words: the animal was normally killed by the layman not far from the altar, and the blood then poured on the altar by the priest. But the idea of individual sacrifices was so familiar from the Old Testament that perhaps Jesus did not need to be precise about the details.

debt, and who was ultimately sued by his creditor. In the east, it would be natural (though of course sometimes risky) to play for time by pretending that the debt did not exist, and even to allow the matter to come to court. But this natural litigiousness was an offence against Jesus' moral standard. It was only right (as well as prudent) to come to some agreement about repayment on your way to court. 25

'You have learned that they were told, "Do not commit adultery"'. 27 Jesus' interpretation of the Law is resumed, this time with the Seventh Commandment, interpreted in the light of the Tenth ("You shall not covet your neighbour's wife"). Some of Jesus' contemporaries took much the same view, though none of them, so far as we know, stated the principle in quite such an uncompromising way. The metaphor of the right eye and the 29 right hand, being embedded in the same context, seems to refer to sexual 30 behaviour—and so it has often been taken in Christian history; but in Mark the saying occurs in a more general context, and it may originally have had nothing to do with adultery. 'They were told, "A man who divorces his 31 wife must give her a note of dismissal"'. This same text (Deuteronomy 24.1) is interpreted by Jesus in a later discussion with the Pharisees. It is significant that here an exception is allowed: for any cause other than 32 unchastity (see below on 19.3–9, Mark 10.1–12).

'Again, you have learned that they were told, "Do not break your 33 oath", and, "Oaths sworn to the Lord must be kept"'. These quotations do not occur as they stand in the Old Testament, but they doubtless represent a standard way of summarizing the laws on swearing. Oaths were a serious matter; in principle, they had to be taken on the name of God (Deuteronomy 6.13 and elsewhere). Not surprisingly, many teachers, from the Old Testament onwards, discouraged swearing as much as possible (though it remained necessary on certain occasions, such as in law-courts). But some saw another way of avoiding the extreme seriousness of oaths, that of swearing by lesser things, such as heaven or earth. Jesus exposes the casuistry of this. Swearing is swearing, and nothing will make it less serious. Better to avoid it altogether.

"Eye for eye, tooth for tooth". This basic principle of elementary 38 justice was written into the Old Testament (e.g. Leviticus 24.19), and was still theoretically in force, though more civilized ways of applying the principle had been evolved. In a primitive society, it brought the instinct of revenge under control by limiting the compensation which could be demanded for an injury; but later the Jews, with their reverence for the letter of the law, were apparently somewhat embarrassed by it, and it was only by ingeniously stretching their interpretation of the words that they were able to use it as a rough criterion for assessing damages in court. Jesus doubtless had this debate in mind; but instead of contributing to it himself, he allowed the principle to stand in all its severity, and simply told his followers not to invoke it. Humiliation should be willingly suffered, service should be willingly offered; there should be no threats of recourse to the law.

43   "Love your neighbour, hate your enemy." Only the first phrase stands in the Old Testament: "Love your neighbour" (Leviticus 19.18). But, as we know from Luke's gospel (10.29) as well as from Jewish writings, people asked, Who is my neighbour? And the answer given was usually, Any fellow-Jew, with the addition (in some more liberal quarters) of certain particularly deserving Gentiles. The rest of the world (since it consisted, by definition, of Gentiles and idolaters, God's "enemies") could be treated with something considerably less than love (which is all that a Semitic language like Hebrew or Aramaic, which tends to call things either black or white, need mean by "hating"). "Hate your enemy" was therefore the kind of implication which many of Jesus' contemporaries may have seen in the command to love your neighbour. [a] And it was in opposition to this that Jesus offered his own interpretation.

44   No: you must **love your enemies**—and this becomes, either in Jesus' mouth or in the tradition of the early church, no longer a matter of Jews' attitude to non-Jews, but of the individual's attitude towards his personal enemies, a Christian's attitude towards his persecutors. The injunction in Leviticus, which was taken by most Jews as a guide to the proper attitude of their nation, was translated by Jesus into the universal realm of personal
46 ethics. Yet the teaching is still expressed in typically Jewish idioms: **tax-gatherers**, being somewhat ostracized from Jewish society, tended to "love
47 each other" out of a natural sense of solidarity; and **the heathen**, whatever their other faults (in Jewish eyes), certainly extended hospitality and courtesy to each other. But the followers of Jesus must thrust aside all such social barriers, and fulfil the command, Love your neighbour, in the total and uncompromising sense in which it was intended by God. The Jews were accustomed to being told to imitate God; but since they believed that God extended to their own race a favour and compassion which he withheld from the Gentiles, it seemed to follow that they should show a similar partiality themselves. But in reality a truer picture of God is given by the
45, 48 proverb, He makes his sun rise on good and bad alike. God's goodness knows no bounds, he makes no distinctions. In the same way, there must be no limit to the goodness of his followers. [b]

[a] We now know of one Jewish sect—the community which produced the Dead Sea Scrolls—which enshrined this implication in a maxim and may, for all we know, have taken it quite literally.
[b] Literally, "you must be perfect, as your heavenly Father is perfect". In Greek thought, perfection consisted in an advance towards higher levels of knowledge and understanding. To the Jews, it meant a wholehearted and uncompromising conformity to the ethical standards and practical provisions of the Law. The Greek meaning occurs in Paul: but here only the Jewish meaning is appropriate. The translation "goodness" must therefore be understood, not in a philosophical sense of general moral goodness, but in the completely

'Be careful not to make a show of your religion before men.' Just as 6. 1
Jesus did not attack the Law of Moses as such, but only the way in which
it was being interpreted in his time, so he did not reject the religious practices of his contemporaries, but only criticized the attitude with which these
were often performed, particularly by those who most insisted upon them,
the Pharisees (to whom Jesus—or subsequently the church—seems to have
given what became almost a nickname: the hypocrites). "Acts of charity" 2
were very highly regarded by the Jews, and with this Jesus agreed. But it
had become the custom to announce any substantial gift at the meeting
of the congregation either in synagogue, or at an open-air service in the
streets. By contrast, 'your good deed must be secret'. Again, the Jews 4
regularly prayed (standing up) at certain times of day: either in synagogue, 5
or else wherever they happened to be. This too gave opportunities for
ostentation, particularly if one chose out street-corners for the purpose.
Again, there was a tendency to admire anyone who knew and could recite
especially long prayers (and here there is a sideways glance at heathen 7
worship as well as the synagogue); by contrast, Jesus prescribed a very
short and condensed prayer for his followers. Finally, fasting was a recog- 16–18
nized practice, and was becoming more widely observed in Jewish circles
at the time this gospel was written. Christians were also to fast, but their
fasting must be secret.

'This is how you should pray.' Into this series of contrasts between 9
Jewish and Christian religious practices is slipped the Lord's Prayer. It is
possible that this prayer was originally taught by Jesus in deliberate opposition to traditional Jewish forms of prayer (though Luke offers a quite
different reason, 11.1); and certainly, although many of its clauses belonged
equally to Jewish spirituality, its brevity presents a striking contrast to the
more elaborate prayers which every Jew was supposed to recite daily. It is
given twice in the New Testament, once here in Matthew, and once in Luke
(11.2–4). In each case the basic elements of the prayer are the same, but
Luke's version is considerably shorter. Jesus may, of course, have taught the
prayer in both forms; but it is not difficult to think of reasons why, in the
different churches for which Luke and Matthew wrote, two different
versions of the same prayer should have existed. If, for instance, Luke's
version is original, Matthew's version could be an early expansion of it
under the influence of other Jewish prayers; while if Matthew's is original,
Luke's could be an abbreviation of it for the benefit of a church less accustomed to Jewish forms of prayer. In any case, it is the longer form which
since very early times has become standard in the church. The NEB offers

practical sense of a total and extraordinary conformity to the Law as interpreted by Jesus.
This kind of goodness must be learnt from the goodness (the perfection) of God himself.
God is not called "perfect" anywhere in Jewish literature. But there was a tendency to
regard him as the model for any human virtue. The prototype for such a comparison is
Leviticus 19.2, "Be holy, as I am holy".

a new translation, and attempts to convey some of the extreme brevity and directness of the original Greek. The more polished and rhythmical phrases of the King James version will probably always come more naturally to most people in their prayers; but the importance of grasping the precise meaning of each petition justifies this new rendering of familiar words.

9 **"Our Father in heaven."** Prayers written exclusively for private use are a comparatively modern invention. Jesus' prayer, like all formal Jewish prayers, was primarily intended to be used in corporate worship by a congregation. This gives content to the word **our**. In most religions of the world God is at one time or another addressed as Father, but not always with the same meaning. For the Greeks, God was "father" in the sense of creator: he was therefore everyone's father. From this we inherit such ideas as the universal fatherhood of God and brotherhood of man. The Jews, on the other hand, thought of God as Father in a much more particular way: God was "father" to Israel, in that he had a special relationship with his people, and guided and protected them "like a father". To the Jew, therefore, he was "our" father in a highly exclusive sense. What then could Jesus have meant by '**Our Father**'? There is no evidence in the gospels that he endorsed the Greek view of God's universal fatherhood; and he certainly did not accept the exclusive attitude of the Jews that only they were the true "sons" of God. Jesus' own attitude lies somewhere between. He himself was the Son of God, and God was in a unique way his Father. Moreover, those who followed him became, along with him, God's "sons", and were entitled to address God with that singularly intimate Aramaic word which passed at once into the praying of the earliest Christians, *Abba*, "Father". *a* "Our Father" therefore takes on its meaning from those who use it. It is the distinctive prayer of the community whose members, through Jesus Christ, have become "sons of God".

"Thy name be hallowed." The translators have kept the archaic word, which is probably known to most people only through its occurrence in the Lord's Prayer. To "hallow" is to separate from all that profanes. There is a part of creation where God's name is already perfectly hallowed—**in heaven**; the prayer is that this hallowing should be extended to earth, that the whole of creation should become consonant, instead of discordant, with the divine nature. Two implications of this are drawn out in the next two
10 clauses. **"Thy kingdom come."** Much of Jesus' teaching in the gospel concerns this "kingdom". God is king—that is axiomatic. But his reign is not yet universally acknowledged. Jesus often draws attention to those

[a] See also Romans 8.15. Luke's version of the prayer, which begins with the single word "Father", probably reflects an original which began with this distinctive word *Abba*. Such apparently easy familiarity with God would have seemed shocking to the Jewish mind, and it may have been as a concession to Jewish feelings that Matthew's version had the solemn phrase (which can be paralleled from contemporary writings), **Our Father in heaven.**

moments in the present—often quite unexpected ones—when an individual's response to an ordinary human situation makes this reign actual; but he also constantly looks ahead to the time when God, by his own act, will make his kingdom universal. The prayer presumably envisages both kinds of "coming". **"Thy will be done."** The meaning of this, again, follows from the "hallowing" of God's name. It does not express (as it might in some religions) a resigned acquiescence in an inscrutable providence, but a longing for God's purposes to be accomplished **on earth as in heaven.**

"Give us today our daily bread." This is unlikely to be a metaphor: 11 most Jewish prayers included a petition for bread, and no formal Jewish meal would ever be eaten without thanksgiving to God who provides food for the use of men. But the clause says, not just bread, but **daily bread.** The adjective is strange. This particular Greek word occurs nowhere else in literature, and we can only guess at its meaning here. Still less can we recover the Aramaic word which Jesus originally used. It is true that a "religious" interpretation is possible. Bread came to have a special significance for Jesus: the bread which he broke became a means of communion; and it is possible that, apart from the satisfaction of hunger, this petition with its mysterious adjective contains a reference to the supernatural nourishment given by Jesus to those who worship him. [a] But even if this meaning is present, it can hardly be the whole meaning. Bread is still bread, and the adjective must define the amount that is asked for. This is a remarkable limitation. Men usually pray for a steady supply of bread to last through the year. But a Christian, it seems, is to ask only for what is necessary today (or, at most, tomorrow). [b] We need bread today, because the present weighs upon us, life is to be lived and we have work to do. But tomorrow—next week, next year—is in the hands of God.

"Forgive us the wrong we have done." Literally, "our debts"—a 12 rendering which has prevailed in some English versions of the Lord's Prayer, as it has in the traditional Latin version (*debita nostra*). But "debt" was a strongly religious concept in Hebrew culture: God had laid obligations on his people, and, in so far as they had failed to fulfil them, they felt themselves in debt to God. So our "debts" amount, in fact, to the **wrong we have done** (and in Jesus' own language of Aramaic the same word was used for both). To be released from this debt was the ultimate, if barely attainable, object of Jewish religion, and a constant burden of Jewish prayers. Jesus taught that this release was an immediate possibility —on condition that one had already extended a free pardon in one's own

[a] For this reason, "super-substantial" has been one of the translations current in the Roman Catholic church since the time of Jerome (about A.D. 400).
[b] The alternative translation in the footnote has been suggested since the second century. It would permit the Christian to ask for bread "for the morrow"—but still not for the whole year!

circle. So the clause is added (and the perfect tense is a correct translation of the Greek), "as we have forgiven those who have wronged us".

13   "And do not bring us to the test." Test here replaces the familiar word "temptation", and is probably a more faithful rendering. Temptation is a psychological concept, suggesting a struggle within the individual between good and bad impulses. But this kind of psychological analysis was not characteristic of Hebrew thinking. The nearest corresponding Hebrew concept was that of "testing". In the Old Testament, many of the afflictions suffered by the people of Israel, and many personal catastrophes which befell pious individuals, were understood as a "test" imposed by God. How one would ultimately be judged by God would depend on how one survived this "test"; and the more urgently that judgement was expected (and Christians soon began to expect it in their own lifetime), the more reason there was to dread any decisive moment which might bring out the true worth of the individual and so determine God's final verdict.

"The evil one." The Greek word can mean either "evil" or "the evil one", and translators have to make their choice. Perhaps in the long run it makes little difference whether a personal devil is seen behind the phenomena of evil. In Jesus' time it was natural to think in this way; today it may seem less so. But the reality of evil, with which the follower of Jesus is in perpetual conflict, is acknowledged either way.

Traditionally, the prayer ends with an ascription of glory to God, "For thine is the kingdom and the power and the glory, for ever. Amen". These words are absent in most early manuscripts, and were almost certainly added, under the influence of Jewish prayers, when the prayer began to be used in public worship. The original prayer taught by Jesus contains no liturgical elaborations; indeed the most striking thing about it is the directness and simplicity of its petitions.

14   Just one of these petitions is singled out for comment: 'For if you forgive others the wrongs they have done'—and here a Greek word is used which does literally mean "wrongs". There is a very similar saying (in a quite different context) in Mark 11.25.

So far, the teaching of the sermon seems to have been in conscious opposition to the most prominent religious party among Jesus' contemporaries. It now becomes more general, and continues a tradition that goes back to Old Testament writings such as Proverbs or Ecclesiasticus: the tradition of Hebrew "wisdom", which consisted of an intensely practical attitude to life combined with firm religious values. Accordingly the object of attack is no 19   longer the Jewish 'hypocrites', but 'the heathen'. 'Do not store up for yourselves treasure on earth'—this advice was already centuries old, and was usually taken as an encouragement to generous almsgiving. In Jesus' mouth it has a strongly Palestinian flavour: the "treasure" is not the gold of a rich man locked away in a strongroom, but the cherished possessions of country people, like clothes and carpets, [a] stored in a corner of a mud-brick house, so that thieves could easily **break in** [b] through the walls. '**The lamp of the body is the eye.**' It was quite natural in Greek to call the eye a "light", and the sentence may have been a proverb already. But the elaboration of this in the following metaphors is more puzzling. There may be an allusion to an idiom known in both Hebrew and Greek, according to which the bad eye is a term for meanness, and therefore the "sound eye" for generosity. But the saying can also be taken as a small parable: just as the body moves in darkness if the eyes are bad, so a person lives in spiritual darkness unless his whole personality is trained upon the source of all true light. '**No servant can be the slave of two masters.**' It was a commonplace that a slave who had to take his orders from two different members of a household, say from both father and son, was in a luckless position. With his usual radical approach to worldly possessions, Jesus declares that any attempt to combine the service of God with a concern about money is equally impossible. 22

24

'**Therefore I bid you put away anxious thoughts.**' The word **anxious** occurs four times, and is the key-word of the paragraph. The imagery belongs again to the Palestinian countryside. '**Look at the birds of the air**' —and Jesus makes his point with a certain humour, conjuring up the absurd picture of birds carrying bags of seed and reaping-hooks. '**Consider how the lilies grow in the fields.**' For a few brief weeks in the spring, the fields are a mass of colour, to be compared with the proverbial splendour of Solomon. **Lilies** is the traditional translation, but we do not know exactly which wildflower Jesus was thinking of. [c] However the image is clear enough. A few days of hot sun, and the flowers and bushes (**the grass in the fields** has a falsely European sound) turn brown and dry, and the peasant can gather them to burn in his baking-oven or under his cooking-pot. [d] God has no less concern for mankind than for birds and flowers. Moreover God has given men a more serious concern—to work for his **kingdom and his justice.** '**Each day has troubles enough of its own**'— which is not the sigh of a man who has become resigned to misfortune, but a programme of action. There is plenty of work to be done today, combating and overcoming the evil around us. We are not to take on in addition a useless burden of anxiety about the evil which will have to be faced tomorrow. 25

26

28

30

33, 34

('**Is there a man of you who . . . can add a foot to his height?**' As it 27

[a] If **rust** is a correct translation, presumably one must add things like metal implements. But the meaning of the word is uncertain. It may denote other destructive insects.
[b] The Greek word means literally "dig through".
[c] Many suggestions have been made. A plausible one is the Anthemis, or Easter daisy.
[d] If Palestinian peasants had "stoves", they certainly did not use brushwood as fuel for them. The Greek word probably means "oven".

stands, this seems to be making rather a different point. But the Greek word translated **height** can also mean age, and **a foot** may be metaphorical (see footnote in NEB). Compare Psalm 39.5, "Thou hast made my days a few handbreadths". If so, anxiety about prolonging one's life would fall naturally into series with anxiety about food and clothing.)

7. 1, 2 **'Pass no judgement, and you will not be judged . . . whatever measure you deal out to others will be dealt back to you.'** One of the most powerful generators of proverbs is the old belief that there is a law of retribution in human affairs, and that what you do to others will be returned upon your own head. But Jesus' sayings, even if they have the same proverbial sound, go a good deal deeper. Here, it is not stated whom you may be judged by: but every Jew would have known what was meant. The unexpressed subject is God, the judgement is the verdict God will one day pass on every man, and you are not to anticipate it (as an individual, or a community, or a church) by initiating proceedings yourself. The same goes for the measure that **will be dealt back to you**—not by your fellow-men, but by God. As for the hypocrisy of criticizing others before you look carefully at yourself, the world's literature is full of proverbs about it. Jesus' example is
3 characteristic of him, in that it is almost grotesquely exaggerated—a **great plank** and a **speck of sawdust**.
6 **'Do not give dogs what is holy.'** Proverbial again, and with a perfectly general sound. But perhaps there was originally a sharper edge to it. "Dogs" and "pigs" were words of abuse which the Jews were accustomed to use of Gentiles. Jesus himself used this language (Mark 7.27), but here he presumably meant, not Gentiles in general, but unbelievers.
7 **'Ask, and you will receive.'** The efficacy of prayer was taken for granted, but (since prayers often appear to go unanswered) it was felt that a prayer must fulfil all sorts of conditions (sincerity, humility, etc.) in order to qualify for an answer. Jesus' teaching, by contrast, appears to be quite unconditional, and proceeds from the premise (which also underlies the Lord's Prayer) that God, being Jesus' own father, is therefore also Father of all who follow Jesus. And if God is the Christian's Father, then he will treat his children as a human father does—but tempering his discipline with infinitely more patience and generosity.
12 **'Always treat others as you would like them to treat you'**—the Golden Rule. A somewhat similar moral rule-of-thumb was current among the Jews in Jesus' time, and was indeed thought to sum up the **Law and the prophets**. But it took the negative form, "Do not do to others what you would not wish them to do to you". This is significantly different from Jesus' rule, not just because avoiding evil is a colourless concept compared with doing good, but because there is a totally different presupposition. Beneath the negative form there is an implied threat: Do not do to others

40

what you would not wish them to do to you, otherwise they will retaliate. But there is no such threat in Jesus' rule. Always treat others as you would like them to treat you, otherwise—what? Otherwise they may not do for you all you wish they would? But no one ever expected they would! There is no "otherwise". Jesus' teaching is not prudential at all, but an absolute principle: this is how you are to treat others—regardless!

'**Enter by the narrow gate.**' Moralists in antiquity often represented the 13 choice between good and bad as a decision between "two ways", the narrow, difficult path of virtue, and the easy road of licentiousness. Jesus stands in the same tradition, but he seems to use the metaphor somewhat differently. He combines the image of a road with that of a gate—one should perhaps imagine oneself in a walled city, with its principal gate leading on to a main road, while a small side gate leads to a mountain path; moreover, he does not seem to be drawing just the usual moral—not many are virtuous, but make sure you are yourself. By **the gate that leads to life** he means the path of Christian discipleship; and it has been true ever since the beginning of Christianity that, relatively speaking, **those who find it are few.**

'**Beware of false prophets.**' We know nothing of such people in the time 15 of Jesus; but we do know that during the first century or so of the church's existence "false prophets" constituted a practical problem. Christian "prophecy" was highly esteemed, and itinerant "prophets" were warmly received when they visited local churches. But this hospitality could easily be abused. It was not difficult to play the part of a prophet, and the churches soon had to devise some means of "testing" the inspiration of their visitors. The tests they used are described in various early Christian writings (there is an example in 1 John 4.1); and here it looks as if a general principle of moral judgement—**you will recognize them by their fruits**—which was 20 spoken by Jesus in various contexts (Matthew 12.33, Luke 6.43) came to be applied to the specific problem of **false prophets** in the church. Much the same goes for the following paragraph. Jesus was hardly addressed as "**Lord, Lord**" in his lifetime; but in the church it was an article of faith 21 that Jesus was "Lord", and Christians were by definition those who acknowledged "the Lord Jesus". But was it enough simply to make this confession of faith? Was it enough even to speak inspired words and perform 22 miraculous cures and exorcisms "in his name"? Were such people necessarily Christians, and would they be accepted by Christ at the final judgement? By no means. **When that day comes,** it will be by a man's adherence to the kind of teaching given in the Sermon, more than by his professions of faith or his psychic powers, that he will be judged worthy of entering the kingdom of Heaven.

The Sermon ends, like other discourses of Jesus, with a brief parable. 24-7 Two houses may look outwardly the same; but one, foolishly built on the sandy bed of a *wady*, is suddenly inundated by a deep raging torrent which, after a few days of Palestinian rain, will rush down the valley, sweeping all before it. Outwardly, two men's lives may look much the same. But when the moment of testing comes, all the pretensions of one of them will collapse into ruin.

Teaching and healing

Matthew, Mark and Luke all give a picture of Jesus' activity in Galilee in which the two principal elements are *Teaching and healing*. Matthew, by placing the Sermon on the Mount so early in his narrative, gives special prominence to the teaching. He now devotes a few paragraphs to examples 8.2 of the healing, and begins with the cure of a **leper**. This episode, in Mark (1.40–5), is told in greater detail and with an eye to its social and religious implications; but Matthew omits everything except the bare narrative. The only emphasis he appears to lay on the story is not (as in Mark) on the behaviour of the leper who has been cured, but on Jesus' anxiety to conform 4 with the Law: **make the offering laid down by Moses for your cleansing.**

5 **When he had entered Capernaum.** The next episode is evidently recorded for the sake of the conversation between Jesus and a military officer. Much of the point of the conversation lies in the fact that the man who **came up to ask** Jesus for **his help** was a **centurion** (the Roman title for a junior officer in charge of about a hundred men). This does not reveal his nationality: whether he was in the service of Rome or of one of the vassal kings (Herod Antipas or Philip), he could have been recruited from any part of the eastern empire. But one thing about him is almost certain: he was not a Jew (for Jews did not normally serve in any army in Palestine). The episode is therefore one of the very few in the gospel which illustrate Jesus' attitude towards the Gentiles. The conversation is almost identical in both Matthew and Luke, though the two evangelists seem quite independent of each other when it comes to narrating the episode in which this conversation took place.

6 **'A boy of mine'.** The translators have successfully caught the ambiguity of the Greek phrase: it could mean one of the centurion's children, or one of his servants. Matthew probably intended it to mean his son, in which case the urgency of his request needs no explanation (Luke took a different view, 7.2). Jesus' immediate response to this request by a foreigner was apparently 7 favourable:[a] **'I will come and cure him'.** But the soldier, sensing the

[a] A different punctuation would turn Jesus' reply into a question, as in the footnote in NEB; since early Greek manuscripts had no punctuation, this could equally be correct. In which case Jesus' response will have been initially, not favourable, but unfavourable: "Am I to come and cure him?", i.e. "Do you expect me, a Jew, to defile myself by entering a Gentile's house?"

impropriety of having a Jew of Jesus' renown entering his house (or else out
of pure diffidence) requested Jesus merely to say the word, and made a 8
comparison (which is the other main point of the story) between the
authority of himself as an officer and the authority of Jesus. Just as he, being
under orders[a] himself, had soldiers under him, and in his own small way 9
could get his will done by his subordinates, so, he believed, Jesus had
supreme authority over those powers of evil which caused such things as
the paralysis of his son. Jesus surely did not need to go and encounter the
particular demon concerned; he had only to say the word, and the whole
regiment of the devil would obey him. To credit Jesus with such authority
over the entire realm of evil spirits (unlike ordinary exorcists, who could
only take them on one by one) was a sign of remarkable faith; and Jesus was
led to comment on the contrast between such implicit faith and the much
more reserved and sceptical attitude which he had encountered[b] in Israel. 10

'Many, I tell you, will come from east and west.' This saying occurs in 11
a different context in Luke (13.28–9), and was doubtless remembered for its
own sake, apart from any particular occasion. It is added here as a general
comment on the episode which has just taken place. The Jews looked forward
to a future age of glory, often pictured as a heavenly feast, presided over by
the great patriarchs of the past. In the language of those prophets who
wrote when the Jewish nation was exiled far away from Jerusalem (e.g.
Isaiah 49.12), there would at the same time be a great coming together of
people from east and west—but these, of course, would be Jews, people
born to the kingdom. Jesus here turns this conventional imagery on its 12
head: it is Gentiles who will flock in to enjoy the promised kingdom, while
the Jews who so confidently look forward to it will be driven out into the
dark, the place of wailing and grinding of teeth.

Two brief paragraphs follow which appear to be borrowed from Mark's
gospel (1.32–4), with slight abbreviation. In Mark, the events are included
in his account of a complete day's activity, and since that day was a Sabbath,
the words when evening fell are significant: only after the Sabbath ended 16
at sunset was it permissible to travel any distance or to perform more than
the most necessary tasks for the sick. Matthew, by his rearrangement, has
robbed this of its significance. Characteristically, he sets Jesus' activity in
relation to a prophecy of Isaiah (53.4). This comes from a chapter which 17
the church rapidly came to see as one of the key Old Testament passages
bearing on the person of Jesus; but Matthew quotes the text in an unusual

[a] This phrase is strange: one would expect, not "under orders", but "in a position to
give orders", and it is possible that our present text is at fault on these words. But perhaps
it comes to the same in the end. An officer, if he is to have authority over his men, must
be under a higher authority himself.
[b] Or rather: was to encounter. This may be a saying which Jesus in fact uttered much
later on. But the story had come to be associated with the beginning of Jesus' activity
in Galilee.

version which appropriately makes it apply, not to salvation from sin (its usual sense), but to healing from disease.

Two sayings on discipleship follow, which seem on the face of it to make the demands of Jesus almost impossibly exacting: not only must the disciple do without the security of a home, but he must even be prepared to neglect what was for the Jews (as for most people) one of the most sacred of all family duties, that of providing an honourable burial for one's father. It is true that Jesus often seems to have called men to a break with their previous lives so radical that these demands can be seen as a consistent part of his teaching on discipleship. On the other hand, each of Jesus' replies has something of the ring of a proverb, and may originally have been spoken in a
20 somewhat different context. Thus, 'the Son of Man has nowhere to lay his head' sounds oddly inappropriate immediately after the welcome given to Jesus in Peter's house (verses 14–15 above), and since no teaching has yet been given about the Son of Man it is hard to see how, at this stage, anyone could have understood what Jesus meant. But later on, when Jesus had finally turned his back on his own country and was on his way to meet humiliation, suffering and death in Jerusalem, the saying could well have been one of those in which he tried to convey to his disciples the darker side
22 of his destiny as Son of Man. Again, 'leave the dead to bury their dead' is understandable enough as an invitation to leave the ranks of those whose minds are closed to new possibilities of life and to become, through the gospel, really "alive"; and it may only be Matthew (or the tradition he was reproducing) who, by taking the phrase literally and introducing a circumstantial little story to illustrate it, has made Jesus appear so ruthlessly insensitive to the most precious family ties of his would-be disciples.
23 **Jesus then got into the boat, and his disciples followed.** The word **followed** is a little odd in this sentence: "his disciples went with him" would be more natural. But "following" was the disciples' *métier*, and was the vocation of the church which came after them; and this may be the first of the subtle alterations and adjustments to the story as we know it from Mark (4.35–41) by which Matthew appears to have adapted it to the needs of a Christian community that was struggling against persecution like a small boat caught in a storm, apt to imagine that its Protector was asleep. This record of Jesus' magisterial words to the raging elements may have been intended to reassure the church that its destiny was, after all, in safe hands.
28 **When he reached the other side, in the country of the Gadarenes.** It is likely that a small strip of the southern shore of the lake belonged to the important Greco-Roman city of Gadara (which lay about seven miles away), and to this extent Matthew's correction of Mark's 'Gerasenes' somewhat eases the geographical difficulty of the story (for Gerasa lay much further away); at the same time, the name of the city, as well as the presence

of a herd of pigs, still gives the impression of a predominantly non-Jewish environment. The story clearly reproduces that given by Mark (5.1–10), but is told more briefly, and in a much less sensational form. The man possessed by a whole legion of unclean spirits becomes (unexpectedly) **two men possessed by devils** of considerable violence; and the enormous herd of two thousand pigs becomes simply **a large herd**. Moreover the emphasis 30 here is quite different. In Mark's version the interest is focused upon the state of the man before and after the exorcism, and upon the crowd's reaction to the cure. But here the two sufferers are barely mentioned more than once. The scene is played out entirely between Jesus and the devils, who (as always) recognize him as the Son of God, and expect from him an unwelcome anticipation of that punishment which (according to popular Jewish mythology) the devil and all his company were to receive at the end of time. They beg to be allowed to make a spectacular demonstration of their power before yielding (a common feature of exorcism stories), and this duly takes place in the destruction of the herd of pigs. The consequence is very different from that in Mark's version: instead of a vociferous witness being left behind in gentile territory to spread the word of Jesus' greatness, there was a unanimous reaction of hostility: **all the town . . . begged him to** 34 **leave the district**. According to Matthew, Jesus' work at this stage aroused no response among the Gentiles.

And now some men brought him a paralysed man. The story is told 9. 2 more fully by Mark (2.1–12) and Luke (5.17–26), and the men's exploit in lowering the stretcher through the roof (which is not mentioned by Matthew) seems a necessary presupposition of the story if the words **seeing their faith** are to make good sense. Jesus' first words to the paralytic perhaps bring out the true sequence of events more clearly than in the parallel versions. '**Take heart, my son; your sins are forgiven**'. Since, it was believed, God must forgive a man his sins before he could recover from an illness, this was sufficient reason for saying '**take heart**': if the paralytic's sins were really forgiven, he could now expect to recover. But the unspoken accusation of blasphemy incited Jesus (as in the other accounts) to make a demonstration of his authority to pronounce forgiveness of sins by miraculously performing an instant cure. **The people**, in Matthew, were not merely stunned by the miracle, but appreciated, perhaps, that it was a decisive answer to the charge of blasphemy. Jesus' act proved that God had indeed granted him **such authority**. 8

As he passed on from there. In Mark (2.13–14) and Luke (5.27–28) the 9 name of the customs official is Levi; here it is **Matthew**. There can be no doubt that this is the same incident as in the other two gospels; all the main features of this and the following paragraphs (down to verse 17) are the same. The only important difference is the name of the disciple. One reason for the change is probably that Levi does not occur in any of the lists of the Twelve, and the writer of this gospel (or indeed a later hand, if it was desired to bring the reputed author of the gospel into the narrative) wished to attach this story to one of the names which certainly appeared in the list, and which subsequently appears (10.3) as 'Matthew the tax-gatherer'.

13 The narrative continues exactly as in Mark (2.15–17), save that Jesus' reply to his critics includes a quotation from Hosea (6.6), "**I require mercy, not sacrifice**". Possibly Matthew was dissatisfied with Jesus' brusque and proverbial reply to the Pharisees, and deliberately introduced the quotation from Hosea, which was a classic formulation of the superiority of spontaneous acts of compassion and generosity over the fulfilment of the temple ritual, and which Jesus (at least according to Matthew), also used on another occasion (12.7 below). In this way Jesus could be portrayed as meeting the Pharisees on their own ground. '**Go and learn what that text means**' was, incidentally, a characteristic phrase in Jewish scholarly arguments.

In verses 14–17 Matthew runs very close to Mark (2.18–22), but adds a characteristic touch at the end. The drift of these sayings in Mark, and still more in Luke, is that Jesus' new message is incompatible with the old observances. But for Matthew this must have seemed too bald a statement. Christianity was a new interpretation, but it by no means superseded the
17 Jewish Law: so he adds, '**then both are preserved**'.

A short section follows devoted to miracle stories, which are told very briefly, but in such a way as to bring out the fact that the miracles were performed in
18 response to a gesture of faith. In Mark's version (5.21–43) the **president of the synagogue** (who is actually called simply "a ruler" in Matthew's text, but the translators have filled in his title from the parallel accounts in Mark and Luke) came to Jesus when his daughter, though critically ill, was still alive: he asked only for a healing miracle, and it was Jesus who took the initiative once it was known that the child was dead. But here the child is already dead, and the man's faith in Jesus is demonstrated in that he believes from the outset that Jesus can perform the miracle, exceptional even in Jesus' activity, of restoring the dead to life. Similarly, the story of the woman with haemorrhages is much shortened, but is told in such a way as to bring out the woman's faith and Jesus' approval of that faith. Nevertheless, even within this brief scope, Matthew adds two touches of what we would now call local colour which are not found in Mark. Jesus' garment had
20 an **edge**, which in the Greek is a technical word for the tassels which Jews were bidden to wear on each corner of their cloak (Numbers 15.38); and the
23 house of bereavement had already attracted **flute-players**, whose profession it was to attend mourners.

The gospels contain a number of stories of Jesus curing the blind. There is one in both Matthew (20.29–34) and Luke (18.35–43) which follows the story as told in Mark 10.46–52. But here, Matthew has an additional version, told more briefly than the others but preserving two typical features: first, that the blind recognize Jesus as **Son of David** (which, all the evangelists 27 agree, was correct in a sense, but was not normally discerned by those with whom Jesus came into contact: there may be something symbolic in the fact that it is only the blind who "see" this); and secondly, Matthew on each occasion unexpectedly introduces not one but two blind men, just as, in 8.28, he equally unexpectedly introduces two madmen. In this very brief account Matthew is careful, once again, to emphasize the men's faith: '**As you have** 29 **believed, so let it be**'. The injunction is added, which is more characteristic of Mark's gospel than of Matthew's, '**See that no one hears about this**'. 30 Matthew perhaps understood the matter like this: the fame of Jesus' miracles was bound to have spread whatever happened; but the particular intuition which the blind men had about Jesus' true identity (**Son of David**) ought not, at this stage, to be revealed.

The last in the series of miracles, the exorcism of a devil from a dumb 32–3 man, is told only in barest outline. Since Jesus is dealing here, not with the patient, but with a devil which has assumed control over the patient, there can be no question of the individual's faith. Instead, the interest of the story is shifted to the reaction of the onlookers.

The kernel of the following section is to be found in Mark (6.7–13). Jesus, at some stage in his work in Galilee, commissioned his disciples to go out independently of him as missionaries and healers, and the instructions and advice which he gave them are recorded in each of the first three gospels. But it was perhaps inevitable that the early church, when it meditated on these sayings, was more interested in their application to its own circumstances and problems than in the actual historical situation in which Jesus originally pronounced them. There was consequently a tendency, both to collect together scattered sayings of Jesus which seemed to have a bearing on church life, and to hand them down in language that was appropriate to the time. This tendency, which is present even in Mark's much briefer collection, has clearly influenced this section of Matthew. In the first place, the setting of the discourse has become artificial. In Mark (6.7, 30) and Luke (9. 2, 10), the disciples are sent out on a mission, and when they return they give some account of their exploits. In Matthew, too, they are "sent out" (10.5); but it is never said that they actually go, and there is no reference to their return: Matthew has characteristically allowed the importance he attaches to Jesus' discourse to crowd out the details of the circumstances which inspired it. In the second place, the conditions prevailing in the church when Matthew wrote are clearly discernible in the form in which some of the sayings are recorded (especially 10.17–20, 40–2). And in the third place, Matthew has added to the original collection a number of sayings about the future which lies ahead of the Christian community, sayings which occur in a quite different context in other gospels and which have little relevance to the situation of twelve disciples supposedly about to depart on a missionary tour. In short, Matthew has edited his material in such a way that it has become, not so much the report of words which Jesus may have spoken on a particular occasion in his life, as a manual of Jesus' sayings relevant to the work and witness of the church.

Before proceeding to the task of the disciples, Matthew introduces two similes to characterize, first the people among whom they would work, and secondly the urgency of the mission on which they would be sent. The

36 people were **like sheep without a shepherd**—a well-remembered comparison recorded in another place in Mark (6.34), but serving here to fix in the mind one of the commonest designations of Christian ministers: they

37 were to be "shepherds". The disciples, moreover, were to be like **labourers** when **the crop is heavy**; and the church must pray that God would liberally increase the number of men called to this urgent task—or so Matthew understood the saying. But just as the 'fishers of men' metaphor (Mark 1.17) probably had a different meaning before it became a commonplace in the church, so with the harvesting metaphor. The harvest was one of the commonest biblical images for the Last Judgement; and the Greek phrase,

38 "Lord of the harvest", though it could perhaps mean simply the **owner** of a farm (as it is translated here), would naturally lead the mind to the divine Judge himself. The labourers, at this ultimate harvest, were traditionally to be the angels (as they are, for instance, in the Revelation); but the followers of Jesus were to have their place on the tribunal at this judgement, and might also have their share in the harvesting. '**Beg the owner to send labourers to harvest his crop**', on Jesus' lips, was doubtless a command to pray for the immediate beginning of the Judgement, hastened by the efforts of his followers.

10. 1 **Then he called his twelve disciples.** We have not been told that he had twelve; but the existence of the Twelve was so taken for granted in the church that it was hardly necessary to introduce them: they were simply **his twelve disciples**. Just as there were twelve legendary tribes of Israel, so there were to be twelve leaders of the new People of God. Matthew's list is much the same as Mark's (3.16–19). But only a few of the names are known personalities. The important thing was that the group existed, and

2 consisted of **apostles** (which means men "sent out" on a particular mission) whom the church subsequently recognized as its immediate founders. It

5 followed that the **instructions** given to them were given, through them, to the church.

'**Do not take the road to gentile lands**'. By the time Matthew's gospel was written, Gentiles outnumbered Jews in the church, and the Christian message had penetrated deep into non-Jewish lands. This command of Jesus, recorded only by Matthew, is therefore extremely puzzling. It is true that Jesus himself did not extend his work into **gentile lands,** but quite apart from the specific command which, after his resurrection, he gave to 'make all nations my disciples' (Matthew 28.19) there are numerous hints in his teaching that he thought of his message and his mission as something far wider than a religious movement within Judaism. Why then is he here reported as limiting the scope of the mission to **the house of Israel** (by which Matthew, like other Jewish writers, means the Jewish population of Palestine)? Only two solutions seem possible, and neither is entirely satisfactory. Either the command was (or was subsequently understood to have been) a temporary limitation, which was removed after the resurrection; or else perhaps the church Matthew knew was one engaged in a difficult mission to the Jewish people, tempted to abandon the task and join the more successful mission to the Gentiles, but needing to be recalled to its first duty by the recollection of some stern words that Jesus had once uttered: **'Go rather to the lost sheep of the house of Israel'.**   6

'As you go proclaim the message'. The task of the missionaries was 7 to continue the preaching and healing work of Jesus. Sufficient examples of this work are given in the course of the gospel, and little space is devoted to it here. Instead, the discourse is concerned with the way these missionaries are to live. **You received without cost; give without charge.** Some of 8 the powers which the disciples were to exercise—such as healing and exorcizing—were possessed by others in the ancient world, who accepted payment and hoped to make a living by their exceptional gifts. But Christian missionaries were to use their powers as freely as they had received them. Their bearing, it seems, must be one of complete poverty—**no pack for the** 10 **road,** either for provisions or for accepting alms (see on Mark 6.8); not even shoes and stick (which are allowed in Mark, but forbidden in Matthew), either as a sign of more extreme asceticism, or else because coat, stick and begging-pouch (**pack**) was the uniform of the many wandering philosophers who accepted a beggar's reward in return for their wisdom. How then were they to live? **The worker earns his keep.** However Jesus originally meant this proverb, the early church soon made a clear principle out of it. As in other religious societies, the travelling preacher was to be given hospitality in believers' houses, bringing with him only the customary greeting of peace (though this was not a mere formality: it could be revoked if necessary!). 12 The readiness to hear and receive was a test of ultimate salvation: if a house or a town failed to pass it, the traveller, by "shaking the dust off his feet", 14 would demonstrate that it would have no part in the kingdom—just as a Jew, entering Palestine, would shake off the dust of gentile countries which could not share the sacred destiny of the Holy Land. Its punishment, said Jesus, would be worse even than that of the proverbially sinful cities, Sodom and Gomorrah. Doubtless Jesus was thinking of the serious condemnation brought upon themselves by those who gave no hearing to the first preaching of the gospel; but possibly the church, when it remembered these words, was thinking of the experience of its own members in inhospitable Jewish towns.

However this may be, the sayings which follow plainly reveal a perspective different from that of twelve men sent out on a brief preaching tour. Matthew, in fact, has drawn into this discourse a number of sayings which Mark and Luke place considerably later in the narrative. In those gospels, the sayings are prophecies of the sufferings which Christians will have to endure, and describe some of the traditional tribulations (such as strife within families) which will presage the approaching end. In Matthew, they refer equally clearly to the period, not of Jesus' lifetime (when there is no evidence and little probability that the disciples suffered persecution) but of the church; and they are grouped here for convenience, even though they hardly fit the

16 context. Apart from the opening warning ('**be wary as serpents, innocent as doves**'), which sounds like an old proverb, the next few verses all occur

23 in Mark 13. But Matthew adds a startling new saying at verse 23: '**before you have gone through all the towns of Israel the Son of Man will have come**'. The "coming" of the Son of Man is a phrase which usually seems to stand for the moment when world history will come to an end, the Last Judgement begin, and the righteous be finally vindicated; and the saying looks at first sight like a prophecy of Jesus which was soon proved false. Yet Matthew, half a century later, deliberately included this saying in his "manual for the church". Was he writing for a community of Christians engaged in the difficult task of preaching in Jewish cities, and encouraging them to persevere, despite discouragement and persecution, on the grounds that there were still plenty of towns for them to work through before the end? Or did he understand the figure of the Son of Man in a more sophisticated way, as he in whom the righteous were represented and, in a sense, already vindicated? If so, in so far as Christianity had already been widely accepted, it could be said that the Son of Man had "come". As in other passages, we must beware of imagining that Jesus, when he used the language in which his contemporaries speculated about the future, was indulging in predictions as naïve as theirs. [a]

24 '**A pupil does not rank above his teacher.**' There is a similar proverb in the sermon in Luke (6.40). Here it is applied to persecution of the dis-

25 ciples, who can have nothing worse to endure than their master did. (On

26 Beelzebub, see below on Mark 3.22.) '**There is nothing covered up that**

[a] This verse was the basis of Albert Schweitzer's famous view that Jesus expected the end to take place before the disciples returned from their journey. This view is not widely accepted today, mainly because it appears that the discourse as a whole is an artificial composition by Matthew, and that the sayings it contains were not necessarily spoken on the historical occasion of the disciples' departure for their mission. See below on Jesus' similar prophecy in Mark 9.1.

will not be uncovered'—another proverb, usually somewhat pessimistic: acts which one is ashamed of and hopes to leave concealed, will be known, if not in one's lifetime, certainly at the Judgement. But perhaps there is a larger thought here (as probably also in Mark 4.22): the gospel, in its beginnings, was essentially a mystery, something **covered up** and **hidden**, known only to a few. But Christians need not be discouraged: one day there would be "revelation", a full manifestation to the whole world, and in the strength of this promise they should meanwhile **shout from the house-tops.** 27 The worst that could happen to them would be physical death; while to fail in their mission would expose them to the judgement of God, who alone **is able to destroy both soul and body in hell.** God's concern for them 28 was as certain as for the sparrows that are sold as poor men's food in the market—so long as they were faithful. But **whoever disowns** Jesus **before** 33 **men** loses the right to call God his Father: Jesus will no longer admit him as a brother, and therefore God will no longer be his Father.

'**You must not think that I have come to bring peace to the earth**'— 34 and yet, 'how blest are the peacemakers' (5.9)! The solution of the paradox probably lies, again, in the fact that this saying originally belonged in the context of Jesus' predictions about the time immediately before the end. One of the terrors of that time (it was traditionally believed) would be inter-necine fighting and the reversal of family loyalties (see below on Mark 13.12). Jesus, by precipitating this climactic period of history, would be bringing not peace **but a sword**—and the early church, seeing families divided by the new faith (for Jewish communities were evidently as intolerant of conversions to Christianity in the first century as they were subsequently), saw here a clear sign of the approaching end.

In view of this, loyalty to Jesus must take precedence over all other loyalties—Luke expresses this even more strongly (14.26)—and the sayings 37–9 which follow take on their full meaning in the light of the subsequent experience of the church (see below on Mark 8.34–6). In verses 40–2 one can even overhear something of the church's structure and nomenclature. Travelling "prophets" were frequent visitors to each local church and (so 41 long as they were genuine) it was the Christian's duty to give them hos-pitality. A **good man** seems, for a time at least, to have been a name used by Christians for Christians; and **one of these little ones** was a familiar way 42 of referring to the poor and the gentle, the "little flock" out of which the church was characteristically composed (see below on Mark 9.42). In short, the theme of this short paragraph is the same as that which is worked out on a grand scale in the parable at the end of chapter 25: 'anything you did for one of my brothers here, however humble, you did for me'.

John, who was in prison. The circumstances of John the Baptist's 11. 2 imprisonment are related below, 14.3–12. We learn here for the first time that he had a following of **disciples**: he evidently had a great deal of teaching to give on moral questions (we can glean scraps of this from the various New Testament references to him), but his main importance, at least in Christian eyes, lay in his rôle as precursor. His message was centred upon one who was to come after him, whom he thought of as a Man of Fire, bringing universal judgement; or as the Elijah who (according to Jewish mythology) was to return in supernatural form shortly before the end of the world; or perhaps even as the Messiah who was to inaugurate a New Age. Now Matthew's account of the first meeting between John and Jesus makes it appear that John recognized in Jesus at least some marks of the Person whom he had been announcing. But since then, Jesus' activity, though clearly something out of the ordinary, scarcely measured up to the sensational programme outlined by John. To this extent his question is under-

3 standable: '**Are you the one who is to come?**'

Jesus' answer (as so often when he was questioned about his true nature) was somewhat ambiguous. There were prophecies in the Old Testament (see especially Isaiah 35. 5–6; 61.1) which foretold a time when physical infirmities would be cured and social evils righted; and the usual interpretation of these passages was that this golden age would begin with the coming of the Messiah. Jesus' miracles had already fulfilled the spirit of these prophecies. This meant, at the very least, that a new age was dawning. But how far Jesus himself corresponded to the popular image of the inaugurator of that new age was another matter: John must draw his own conclusions. In particular, Jesus was certainly not the man of unlimited power whom the populace expected. His activity raised questions rather than compelled allegiance. Men had to make up their minds for or against him, and might find him

6 challenging too many of their presuppositions. Hence—'**happy is the man who does not find me a stumbling-block**'.

7 **Jesus began to speak to the people about John.** There were many different versions current of the programme which popular Jewish speculation envisaged for the end of history and the dawning of the promised new age. They tended to revolve around some supernatural Person, be it an Elijah *redivivus* or a Messiah. But they did not normally make room for two such figures: and therefore, given the fact that Jesus was such a person, it was something of a problem (doubtless for subsequent generations of Christians as much as for the contemporaries of these events) to fit in John the Baptist as well. Jesus sharpened this question for his hearers. When they went out **to the wilderness**, what had they expected to find? Not, obviously, something as ordinary as a **reed-bed swept by the wind** (which may or may not be metaphorical: either an actual reed-bed—or reed, as the Greek can also mean—or a man as feeble as a reed); nor yet something as crudely supernatural as a splendidly dressed figure in the depths of the desert. A desert preacher was likely to be one thing only: **a prophet**. But

this prophet was unique, in that he was a herald—the prophecy which fitted him (Malachi 3.1) is given here exactly as at the opening of Mark's 10 gospel. The new state of affairs which he heralded was being even now brought about by Jesus; and if you could accept that, then you could accept that John was after all the great herald of popular expectation, **the destined** 14 **Elijah**, the last figure in the old era of the Law and the prophets. But to recognize this, you had to be able to recognize what was unique in Jesus, and this insight was not given to everyone, just as not everyone could grasp Jesus' parables. And so here (as several times in connection with parables): **'If you have ears, then hear'.** 15

Two very difficult sayings are worked into this section. (i) John was of quite exceptional importance and greatness; **'yet the least in the kingdom** 11 **of Heaven is greater than he.'** Why? Perhaps because all human priorities in the kingdom are turned upside down, so that, by definition, the least become the greatest, the first last. Or else perhaps because John the Baptist only announced the kingdom and came too soon actually to belong to it. It is true that Jesus nowhere else suggests that you have to belong to a particular time or place to enter it. But there are a number of his sayings which do imply that the appearance of Jesus had opened an entirely new chapter in world history, and that the least of his disciples enjoyed a privilege which had been denied to the greatest of the figures of the past (see below, 13.17). (ii) **'Ever since the coming of John the Baptist the kingdom of Heaven** 12 **has been subjected to violence and violent men are seizing it.'** The Greek is capable of more than one meaning (see the footnote in NEB), and the sentence itself appears to be a riddle to which we no longer have the key. The arrival of John the Baptist was a turning-point, so much is clear; but why this should have given their chance to men of violence (who might be over-enthusiastic adherents of Jesus, like zealots, or else ruthless opponents) remains mysterious.

'How can I describe this generation?' The little parable that follows 16 presupposes two groups of children playing a game of marriages and funerals. One group makes the appropriate music, the other goes through the appropriate actions. Both John and Jesus, in their different ways, had sounded a call to repentance; but their hearers, like sulky children, had answered, "You are not playing it right". **'Yet God's wisdom is proved right by its** 19 **results.'** The Greek has simply "wisdom"; but it would seem a trite proverb if it meant merely "it pays to be clever", and quite irrelevant to what has preceded. "Wisdom", in the sense of philosophy, was not much prized among the Hebrews. For them, "wisdom" usually meant God's wisdom— the divine plan which underlies the universe and which is reflected in the righteous deeds of men. John and Jesus were conspicuous agents of that divine plan. Their conduct might seem wrong to some, but **the results** of their work would prove them to be right. (Luke 7.35 has a slightly different version of this saying, which in any case is obscure, and may not have been understood even by the time the gospels were written.)

20 **Then he spoke of the towns in which most of his miracles had been**
21 **performed.** Chorazin lies a few miles inland from Capernaum. It was a smaller and less pretentious town (to judge from the surviving remains), and this is the only indication in the gospels that Jesus worked there. A miracle at **Bethsaida** is recorded in Mark 8.22–6. Jesus here gives high importance to his miracles: the sight of them should have moved people to repentance. According to the gospels, the impression they create is normally favourable, in that people come for more and praise God for what they have seen; but we also hear of frank opposition and scepticism on the part of certain individuals, and in fact (in view of this saying of Jesus) the reaction of most people may have been a good deal less positive than the gospel
21–4 writers suggest. Jesus uses the tones of an Old Testament prophet: Amos (1.9–10), Isaiah (23), Ezekiel (26–28) and Zechariah (9.2–4) had all made of **Tyre and Sidon** a classic example of cities which deserved the imminent wrath of God; Isaiah (14.13–15) had said of Babylon that, even if it thought
23 of itself as **exalted to the skies**, it would soon be **brought down to the depths**; and **Sodom**, since the book of Genesis, was the sinful city *par excellence*. But even these cities were excusable compared with the impenitent witnesses of Jesus' miracles.

25 **At that time Jesus spoke these words.** Verses 25–30 have a solemn ring. Whether or not the sayings they contain originally belonged together, they are cast in a form which was quite frequently used by great teachers in antiquity. The last chapter of Ecclesiasticus (a book that was written about two centuries before the time of Christ) is composed on much the same pattern (thanksgiving for benefits received, verses 1–12; claim to special knowledge, 13–22; invitation to others, 23–30) and contains many phrases which are startlingly similar to the words of Jesus. Similarly, the Stoic philosopher Epictetus, not many years after Jesus' death, appealed to others to follow his manner of life in a sentence of exactly the same structure as
28 '**Come to me … and I will give you relief.**' Therefore if Jesus, at some stage, made a general appeal to the public to come to him for instruction, this was a natural way for him to do it (or for an early editor of his sayings to picture him doing it); and the understandable modern reaction, that such an encomium would have come better from a follower of Jesus than from Jesus himself, probably fails to take account of the literary conventions of the time.

25 '**I thank thee, Father**'. Since the nineteenth century this saying has been called "a meteor from the Johannine sky". Certainly Jesus' intimacy with God, as that of a son with his father, is a leading theme of the fourth gospel, and these words of Jesus, which come as something of a surprise here,

would hardly be noticed in John. Nevertheless the ideas they express belong to Matthew's gospel as much as to any other. The contrast between the misguided learning of the Pharisees and the truer insight of the least of Jesus' followers underlies many episodes in the gospel, and the claim that Jesus was to God as son to father, and that his followers, through their solidarity with him, come to share his sonship and thereby to address God as Father, runs through much of the Sermon on the Mount, and is a presupposition of the Lord's Prayer. Terms such as "knowing", "hiding" and "revealing" suggest at first sight the kind of religion in which the mystical "knowledge" of God is the main object, to be obtained by initiation into successive degrees of intellectual illumination. Almost from the beginning, there were tendencies to assimilate Christianity to this kind of mysticism (see also Colossians, 2. 18); and these verses have often been regarded as evidence for similar influences. But the terminology also has its home in Jewish thought. To the Jew, God was not "known" to the man who searched unaided for religious truth: God "chose" to reveal himself to his people, whom he "knew", in the sense that he had chosen and identified them. In return, his people "knew" God, in the sense that they gave him their allegiance, and were the recipients of his self-revelation. The same deliberate self-revelation was still in progress: but the vehicle of this revelation was now Jesus, and its recipients no longer the historical people of the Jews but those who were "chosen" by Jesus to share in the privilege of Sonship, and to enter into the son's intimate "knowledge" of the Father.

'Come to me, all whose work is hard, whose load is heavy.' Any 28 religious leader lays a "yoke" on his followers, just as any king lays a yoke on his subjects. Men's allegiance can only be expressed in acts of submission and obedience. Moreover, to encourage that allegiance, any ruler or teacher will certainly promise "relief" to those who are under the yoke, and the extent to which that relief seems worth having will depend, in part, on the severity of the previous régime. Now it was a common figure of speech that the Law of Moses by which the Jews were obliged to live, despite the many blessings and privileges which it conferred, was nevertheless a "yoke" which had to be borne with discipline and patience; and one of Jesus' complaints against the Pharisees was that with all their efforts to make the Law fully applicable to present-day conditions they had only succeeded in making the yoke more oppressive. At least a part of what Jesus meant by his "yoke" must be understood in this context: even though he expected from his followers an obedience to the Law as great as that of the most exacting of his contemporaries, yet by returning to the spirit of the Law instead of the letter, by giving assurance that prayers were heard and answered, and by promising blessings both now and in the future to those whom society had traditionally victimized, he was able to say 'My yoke is good to bear, my load is light'. But at the same time, the 30 saying has a generality and a nobility which transcend this particular con-

29 trast. '**I am gentle and humble-hearted**'. These words do not merely describe Jesus' moral character; they define the kind of king which Jesus was—one 'who comes to you in gentleness' (21.5), one who 'humbled himself' (Philippians 2.8). His kingship was so new, his rule such a reversal of the usual structures of authority, that his yoke had nothing to do with oppression. Paul, indeed, was to call it freedom.

Controversy

The first main topic of *Controversy* in Matthew, as in Mark and Luke, is the observance of the Sabbath. The principal exponents of correct Sabbath observance were the Pharisees, and Jesus' criticism of some of the restrictions which beset what was intended to be a day of goodwill and rejoicing, and his own and his disciples' comparative freedom with regard to these restrictions, naturally became a serious issue between himself and the Pharisees. Matthew, in the next two episodes, follows much the same tradition as Mark (2.23–3.6) and Luke (6.1–11), but in each case introduces a somewhat more technical argument which shows Jesus meeting the Pharisees on their own ground. In the first, after referring his opponents (as in Mark) to the difficult but

12. 3-4 indecisive case of David, Jesus adds (using a technical formula of scholarly

5 discussion, **have you not read in the Law**) a logically more powerful argument. It was agreed that the necessities of the temple service made it necessary for the priests to break a Sabbath regulation—for instance, they still had to reap a sheaf for the ritual on the second day of Passover, even

6 if this happened to be a Sabbath. *A fortiori*, if **there is something greater than the temple here** it will provide exemption for other kinds of "reap-

7 ing". An appeal to the general principle expressed in Hosea 6.6, that mercy (which includes charitableness) is superior to ritual observances, rounds off the argument. The validity of this reasoning depends of course ultimately on the authority which Jesus claims for himself. So here (as in Mark and

8 Luke): '**For the Son of Man is sovereign over the Sabbath**'.

9-14 In the second episode the challenge to Jesus is answered, in Mark and Luke, by a simple counter-challenge: 'Is it permitted to do good or to do evil on the Sabbath?' Here, Jesus' reply takes the form of another argument *a fortiori*. It was admitted that it was permissible to rescue a sheep on the

12 Sabbath. How much more then **to do good** to a man!

15-21 The following paragraph appears to offer an explanation of certain rather puzzling statements which are found in Mark. Mark records that, while Jesus was performing cures, the unclean spirits by which some of the sufferers were possessed shouted out who he was, and Jesus 'insisted that they should not make him known' (3.11–12). Matthew uses exactly the same language (**he gave strict injunctions** renders the same Greek word as 16 'he insisted' in Mark) but omits all reference to the spirits. What in Mark takes the form of a dialogue with supernatural powers appears in Matthew as a simple command given to the crowds. Nevertheless, the question still remains as puzzling in Matthew's version as it does in Mark's: why did Jesus insist on this secrecy? Matthew seems to hint, by his introductory words (**Jesus was aware of it and withdrew**) that Jesus' motive was 15 simply prudence: he wished, for the time being, to avoid further controversy with the Pharisees. But he also has a more profound explanation to offer. One of the Old Testament passages which seemed to Matthew (and doubtless to the early church) both to foretell Jesus' coming and to explain his destiny was the opening of Isaiah 42—the prophecy of a "servant" who would establish justice in the world. An allusion to this prophecy seems to underlie the words heard at Jesus' baptism (3.17 above); here Matthew 18–21 quotes it in full. His version does not exactly follow either the Hebrew text or the Greek version of the Septuagint, but is a curious combination of the two, suggesting that the verses had already been much pondered in the church and had been slightly modified in the process. But the point which was important for Matthew here was the silence and modesty of this servant: **He will not strive, he will not shout, nor will his voice be heard in the** 19 **streets**. It was in conformity with this prototype, Matthew suggests, that Jesus maintained his mysterious secrecy.

The following episode is told by Matthew and Luke in a form somewhat different from that which it has in Mark (3.22–30). It begins with a brief account of an exorcism, which aroused in the bystanders a reaction of considerable expectancy: **the word went round: 'Can this be the Son of** 23 **David?'** It was widely believed among the Jews that God would at any moment bring into being the New Age by means of a divinely appointed Person (a Messiah), who would be the true successor of King David, and who was therefore often called (not because of his genealogy, but because of his destiny) **the Son of David**. This Person, it was said, existed already, but his identity would remain unknown until the time for his appearing should come. When that moment came, he would manifest himself with signs and wonders. Jesus' miracles naturally gave rise to the question, **'Can this be the Son of David?'**

The Pharisees were ready with an alternative explanation: **'It is only by** 24 **Beelzebub prince of devils that this man drives the devils out'**. Jesus shows this to be sophistry. His argument is here very close to that in Mark's account (3.22–6) but has an additional point of some interest. It shows that 27 there were exorcists about whom the Pharisees approved of; therefore the argument used against Jesus would apply equally to them. No, the Pharisees

were wrong, and the people (in a sense) were right. Jesus' exorcisms were a
28 sign of the new age: 'the kingdom of God has already come upon you.'
29   The comparison with the strong man's house is almost exactly as in
30 Mark (3.27); the saying in verse 30 is a proverb, expressing the challenge
presented by Jesus' teaching (Jesus appears to say the opposite in Mark 9.40,
but the inconsistency is probably only apparent: see below on that passage).
The saying about the slander against the Spirit is as difficult here as it is in
Mark (3.28–30), even though Matthew, like Luke, has the additional words,
32 'any man who speaks a word against the Son of Man will be forgiven.'
It is possible that the experience of the early church has influenced this
formulation. It was one thing, out of ignorance or perversity, to misunderstand the church's teaching about the nature of Jesus Christ (i.e. "to speak
against the Son of Man"). But if, confronted by the manifest activity of the
Spirit in the church, men still reviled and persecuted, then there seemed no
further hope for them either in this age or in the age to come (as
Matthew puts it, borrowing a standard Jewish idiom).
33   'Either make the tree good and its fruit good.' This is essentially the
same saying as in the Sermon on the Mount (7.16–20). There it was applied
to the problem of discriminating between true and false prophets; here it is
part of an attack on the hypocrisy of the Pharisees, whom Jesus (in Matthew)
34 treats with great asperity ('vipers' brood'). Their words cannot be (as they
claim) "good" when their actions are evil—and the theme of "words"
seems to explain the addition of another completely general saying. That a
36 thoughtless word will have consequences on the day of Judgement
is a conclusion reached by any thinker who takes God's judgement seriously;
but Jesus' contemporaries would not normally have expressed the matter so
uncompromisingly.
38   'Master, we should like you to show us a sign'. This request occurs
in Mark (8.11), and is there refused without any reason being given. Here
39 the refusal is expanded by a reference to Jonah. The book of Jonah was one
of the most popular of the Old Testament. It contained a message both of
hope and of warning. All the other Old Testament prophets had met
resistance, unbelief, even outright rejection; but Jonah had preached and
(much to his discomfiture!) the whole city of Nineveh had attended to him
and repented. This was the hopeful side of the message: repentance was
always possible, and God would reward the penitent as he had rewarded
Nineveh. But Nineveh was a gentile city! This was the note of warning:
was there anything in Jewish history to compare with Nineveh's repentance?
41 And the warning is taken up by Jesus here: 'when this generation is on
trial, the men of Nineveh will appear against it'—a moral that could
42 also be drawn from that other great Old Testament story of the visit of the
Queen of Sheba to Solomon (1 Kings 10). But Matthew (unlike Luke) has
worked in another motif from the legend of Jonah. The decisive "sign"

which Jesus ultimately did give to "that generation" was the resurrection, and the church (whether or not there was originally a saying of Jesus on these lines) very soon came to see Jonah's legendary sojourn in the sea- 40 monster's belly as a prefiguration of Jesus' brief period of physical death.

When an unclean spirit comes out of a man. Given the naïvely realistic 43 language of an age which believed implicitly in spirit-possession, this was, and remains, a valid description of what we would now call a psychological danger, that of removing an obsession without putting anything positive in its place. So Luke (11.24–6) understands it; but Matthew records it as a parable, and it is hard to be sure what it was supposed to illustrate. Perhaps the idea was that "that generation", after an imperfect repentance provoked by Jesus' teaching, would soon be exposed to the dangers of still worse religious and political leaders than they had before.

The scene which closes the section is given almost exactly as in Mark 46–50 (3.31–5).

Matthew now devotes a further chapter to the teaching of Jesus; but this time it is teaching of a new kind. So far, it has taken the form of rules and precepts for the conduct of life. But it was well known that Jesus also spoke 13. 3 **to them in parables,** and Matthew (who follows very closely the account given in the corresponding chapter of Mark) now presents a collection of these parables, and at the same time casts Jesus in a new rôle: that of an inspired teacher of divine mysteries.

The collection begins with a parable of sowing, told almost exactly as in Mark. Just as, however good the harvest, there will always be some wastage, so, despite the apparent success of Jesus' work, there would always be some who opposed it and so excluded themselves from the kingdom. But if this was how the parable was intended by Jesus to be understood (see below on Mark 4.1–10), it was not for this reason that Matthew set it down here. Matthew, in common with Mark, possessed another and much more recondite interpretation; and this led him to see Jesus' parables, not as illustrations intended to make his meaning clearer (which was the most common sense of the Greek word), but as cryptic sayings fully intelligible only to the initiated (which was one of the meanings of the Hebrew word corresponding to "parable"). There was good precedent for an inspired thinker clothing his teaching in mysterious imagery. From time to time visionaries appeared among the Jews who believed that they had been vouchsafed glimpses of the destiny which God had in store for the world, and it was to be expected that they would express the content of their visions in cryptic form; for they were, in effect, divulging "mysteries" or secrets, the full manifestation of which was reserved for the future. Meanwhile, it was only to themselves, and to the privileged few who had the knowledge and understanding to grasp the meaning of their cryptic discourses, that these things were revealed. An example of this kind of writing is the Revelation of John; another is the long series of Jewish "apocalypses" which begins with the Book of Daniel and runs on at least to the end of the first century A.D. Jesus himself was remembered to have conformed to this tradition when he gave some teaching on the "last things" (see below on Matthew 24 and Mark 13); and in Matthew the parables are regarded as part of the same kind of teaching. In the centre of the picture stand the disciples, a privileged group to

11 whom it has been granted **to know the secrets of the kingdom of**

17 **Heaven.** Even the **prophets and saints** of the Old Testament, for all their remarkable insight and vision, did not reach that point of initiation into the purposes of God which the disciples have already reached—and they will go further still: Matthew applies to them a saying of Jesus which

12 stands isolated in Mark (4.25), '**the man who has will be given more**'. The disciples, unlike the people of Israel of old, have been given "eyes to see and ears to hear" (Deuteronomy 29.4), and this makes of them a uniquely privileged class, in sharp contrast to the bemused crowds who are straining to catch the import of Jesus' teaching from the shores of the lake. But what then of these crowds? Why is their fate so different from that of

10 the privileged few? This is the sense of the disciples' question, '**Why do you speak to them in parables?**' (which, in Mark, appears as a question about the nature of the parables themselves). And the answer is that here, once

14-15 again, is a fulfilment of prophecy. Matthew quotes (at far greater length than Mark or Luke) from Isaiah 6.9-10, and his quotation follows word for word the Septuagint version of the Greek Bible, which gives a somewhat different sense from the Hebrew. Jesus is not likely to have used a Greek version, but it does not follow from this that he did not on occasion make use of the same passage in Hebrew (see below on Mark 4.11-13)—only that Matthew has been at work editing his material. The word in the passage which has

14 caught Matthew's imagination is **understand**. It is not opposition, or indifference, or perversity, which has kept the crowds from salvation, but a lack of **understanding**; and Matthew has subtly altered the interpretation of the parable (an interpretation which, for various reasons, is unlikely to go back to Jesus himself: see below on Mark 4.14-20) in order to make the

23 point that the reward belongs to the man who hears the word **and understands it.**

24-30 The second parable also describes the ordinary cultivation of the fields but, unlike the first, contains something of a story. The farming described is again perfectly normal. It was to be expected in any cornfield that there

25 would be weeds, and one of the most troublesome was that species of **darnel** which, in its early stages, is almost indistinguishable from the young blade

26 of corn. Nothing could be done about it, therefore, until the corn **sprouted and began to fill out**: by then (in fact, somewhat before then) it would be easy enough to distinguish the darnel. There were then two possible courses

of action, both of which were quite common practice, but each of which had disadvantages. Either the darnel could be pulled out when the corn was still green—but it had strong roots, and there was a danger of pulling up the corn at the same time; or else it could be left **till harvest**—but then it had 30 either to be carefully separated out in the reaping (which was done, not by the farmer's own labourers alone, but by a force of specially hired men), or else sieved out in the threshing; for the seeds of darnel are poisonous. In the parable, the farmer is made to choose the second course; and if the parable originally existed (like the parable of sowing) in the form of a straight-forward description of familiar farming methods, with the emphasis on the words, **let them both grow together**, then we can guess at the point Jesus was making. Do not judge before the time, do not try to weed out your ranks and form a sect of "holy men". There will be time enough for this at the Last Judgement (for which "harvest" was a familiar symbol).

But, in the present form of the parable, a familiar scene is turned into an anecdote by the addition of a curious feature. The presence of weeds in the field would not normally surprise anyone; it was the commonest of the farmer's difficulties. But here a different explanation is given: "**This is an enemy's** 28 **doing**". This is not necessarily improbable in itself. Stories are told of village feuds being carried on in this way. On the other hand it does not add anything to the point of the parable, which appears to lie in the wheat and the darnel both "growing together" till harvest. The detail of the enemy becomes significant only if the parable is in reality something quite different, that is, a cryptic discourse in which each term stands for something else. As has just been said, the "harvest" is a conventional image of the Last Judgement. The description of the harvesting in verse 30 is difficult to visualize in terms of wheat and darnel, but is apt enough if the real material being harvested is a cross-section of good and bad human beings; and in this case, the enemy is a necessary character, since it is the devil who prompts the evil deeds committed by men.

In this form (which may or may not be the form in which Jesus originally spoke it) the parable fits appropriately into its context in Matthew's gospel. The story, like the previous one, is deliberately mysterious, and only the privileged few have the key to its meaning. Moreover, since its theme is the Last Judgement, it falls naturally into place in the teaching of one who had a special vision of the future to impart to his chosen disciples. As in the case of the previous parable, Matthew has an esoteric interpretation to offer. The 36–43 interpretation, again, has a number of features more characteristic of Matthew's editing than of Jesus' own idiom, and uses terms which are conventional elements in Jewish descriptions of the Last Judgement. There are thus serious reasons for doubting whether it can go back to Jesus himself.

No clue is given for interpreting the next two parables. If they were 31–3 intended to receive the same kind of esoteric interpretation, then each element in them would presumably have to be a cryptogram for something else; and given one correspondence (the kingdom of Heaven is like a mustard-seed, or like yeast) one would have to ask what, for instance, the man who sowed, or the woman who baked, stand for. But it is unlikely that Jesus meant them to be taken in this sense. The phrase, '**the kingdom of Heaven is like . . .**', does not necessarily (or at least did not, in the language that Jesus spoke) mean that the kingdom corresponded to just one person or thing in the parable, but that it was illustrated by the parable as a whole (thus the same Greek phrase is translated in 13.24 'The kingdom of Heaven is like this', and in 13.45 as 'Here is another picture of the kingdom of Heaven'). The point of comparison in each case seems to be simply the contrast: the tiny seed and the huge full-grown plant, or the small amount of yeast with which a baker can leaven a whole day's baking.

34 **In all this teaching to the crowds Jesus spoke in parables; in fact he never spoke to them without a parable.** The word **never** has been inserted by the translators and needs qualifying. Matthew, of course, does not mean that Jesus never spoke to the crowds at all without a parable—after the Sermon on the Mount this would be nonsense. But in his rôle as a revealer of the secrets of providence, his speech to the crowds (Matthew wishes us to understand) was always cryptic, and only his disciples were given the key to his meaning. Matthew again finds a scriptural model for this.

35 The passage he quotes is Psalm 78.2, with a slight modification of the second line: **things kept secret since the world was made** is a phrase which describes the kind of revelation being given by Jesus better than the literal text in either the Greek version or the Hebrew. Although it is from a psalm, it could legitimately be regarded as a **prophecy**: Jesus himself found things in the psalms which were prophetic in the sense that they were still awaiting fulfilment. But why some manuscripts of Matthew's gospel give **Isaiah** it is impossible to say. It is conceivable that Matthew took the text from an anthology of quotations in which it stood next to a passage of Isaiah; otherwise it must be simply a mistake.

44–6 The next pair of parables obviously belong together, and presumably make the same point: the total personal commitment demanded by the kingdom of Heaven. To buy a field, the man in the first parable had to sell everything he had: he was therefore a poor man, doubtless working in the field as a hired labourer. Having found the treasure, he was not necessarily obliged to report it, but he could not expect to be allowed to acquire it
45 unmolested until he became the owner of the field. The **merchant** of the second parable would have been a far more prosperous person. He is to be imagined passing through Galilee on his way from the pearl-fishing seas of the east. On his last journey he was able to acquire an exceptional pearl, for which he willingly surrendered his entire stock, knowing that it would make his fortune when he brought it to the dealers in the big cities.

47 The last parable is drawn from one of the commonest scenes on the lake

(here called the **sea**, which was the way the local inhabitants referred to the   47
Lake of Tiberias). The point about the drag-net is that it catches **fish of
every kind**, which are only sorted out afterwards—and this presumably (as
in the case of the wheat and the darnel) was the original point of the parable.
Do not try to sort out the good from the bad in this life by forming a little
sect of specially pious men and despising all who will not join you: all the
sorting necessary will be done by God at the Last Judgement. The interpretation added by Matthew does not conflict with this, but it shifts the
emphasis from the present to the future, and treats the parable primarily
as a cryptic description of the Last Judgement. This is consonant with
Matthew's picture of Jesus in his rôle of an expounder of the secrets of the
future to a privileged few, but may, once again, represent a later understanding of the parables themselves.

Mark's parable chapter ends with a summary of the way in which Jesus
addressed the crowds (4.33-4). Matthew slightly alters this by focusing
attention on the disciples, who alone have the privilege of "understanding".
The ordinary Jewish **teacher** of the law, in the course of his training, built up   52
an immense store of **the old**—that is, of knowledge of the scriptures themselves and of the traditional interpretations of them that were handed down and
elaborated by generations of scholars. But the training of Jesus' disciples, as
sketched in this chapter, gave them something altogether new to offer as well.

Matthew's account of Jesus' visit to Nazareth follows Mark closely (6.1-6),
and only two slight changes have significance: Jesus is called, not the carpenter,
but **the carpenter's son**—perhaps Christians hesitated to acknowledge that   55
Jesus had actually been a tradesman; and Mark's 'he could work no miracle
there' is altered to **he did not work many miracles there**. Matthew was   58
not prepared to concede that Jesus was less than omnipotent.

Prince Herod. Mark calls him 'king', which is doubtless what he was   **14.** 1
popularly called; but Matthew, more precisely, gives him his official title of
tetrarch, or **Prince.** The tetrarchy of Herod Antipas included the whole of
Galilee, and this was the ruler with whom Jesus had to reckon until he
travelled up to Jerusalem. Herod's attitude to religious movements of the
kind started by John the Baptist and Jesus was clearly an important factor in
the story. It is for this reason that Matthew, who has already alluded to
John's arrest in 4.12, now introduces the full story (the context in Mark is
more contrived). Herod is made to see in Jesus a visitation of his guilty conscience about John the Baptist, and this gives the cue for the story of John's   3-12
execution, told exactly as in Mark (6.14-29), with the omission of a few details.

The news of this execution also sets in motion the sequence of events which   13-27
follows (the context in Mark is again slightly different). The narrative
closely follows that in Mark (6.45-56), leaving out a few details, and showing

21 only a slight tendency to enhance the miracles (**to say nothing of women**
24 **and children . . . some furlongs from the shore**) and to present the
28-33 disciples in a better light. Peter's venture upon the water, however, is told
only by Matthew. It is a vivid illustration of a theme Matthew is fond of:
the importance of faith in a disciple. It is also a perfect illustration of the
impulsiveness of Peter's character and his failures at moments of crisis—
traits which had serious consequences during the trial of Jesus.

The next episode justifies the title under which this section stands,
15. 1 *Controversy*. A critical question from some **Pharisees and lawyers from
Jerusalem** provokes Jesus into a violent counter-attack, which the Pharisees
12 have no difficulty in recognizing as a deliberate challenge to their principles. When Mark comes to this incident (7.1), he elucidates it for non-
Jewish readers by adding an explanation of the Jewish customs alluded to.
Matthew omits these notes. Presumably his readers would have known
2 at once that the Pharisees' comment, '**They do not wash their hands
before meals**', touched a question, not of hygiene, but of ritual purity.
Precisely what the **ancient tradition** was which Jesus was attacking, and
what the target was of Jesus' counter-attack on the Corban-oath (the
technical word is omitted by Matthew, but the argument is the same as in
Mark), are questions of some difficulty (see below on Mark 7.1–13); but the
6, 9 underlying tendency of Pharisaic tradition to overlay **God's law** with **the
commandments of men** is neatly summed up in the quotation from
8-9 Isaiah 29.13 (which Matthew, like Mark, quotes according to the Greek
version), and is here, as elsewhere, made the object of Jesus' criticism. No
12 wonder the Pharisees took **great offence**! But Jesus, in the presence of his
disciples, went further still. The religious leaders of the Jews prided themselves on being 'guides to the blind' (Romans 2.19). Jesus casts this back
14 in their teeth by calling them **blind guides** themselves, and denies that they
have any part in the ordained process of God's self-revelation.
10-11 Woven into this controversy is a saying which appears in Mark (7.15) in a
completely general form: 'nothing that goes into a man from outside can
defile him; no, it is the things that come out of him that defile a man'. This
saying certainly sounded a little mysterious, and needed interpretation; and
the interpretation added by Mark in fact made it apply to the question (much
discussed in the early church, but of less apparent topical interest in the
Jewish environment of Galilee) of ritually permissible foods. Matthew, by
adding the words **into his mouth**, robs the original saying of its generality,
and makes it into one which could have no application except to food. As a
15-20 result, it hardly needs interpretation. But Matthew, who is obviously using
Mark as his model, none the less gives the same detailed explanation for the
16 benefit of the **dull** disciples, and then, with a slight twist at the end, brings
20 it round to the point from which the section started: the washing of hands.

Jesus and his disciples

It is true that the interest of the narrative soon begins to shift from Jesus and the crowds to the more intimate episodes concerning only *Jesus and his disciples*; but there is first a section in which the disciples play little part, and 21-8 which is of some interest in view of the subsequent history of the church. The question to which the passage offers an answer is, What was Jesus' attitude to Gentiles? There can be little doubt that Matthew knew of Mark's version of this story, but he may well have felt that it left the question somewhat in the air. According to Mark (7.24–30), Jesus seemed both to endorse the usual Jewish attitude of exclusiveness towards all non-Jews, and at the same time to make an unexplained exception for the benefit of a woman who was 'a Phoenician of Syria by nationality'. Matthew endeavours to bring more logic into the story by adding a few details which may be in part his own invention, in part drawn from another source of the same story. The woman came **from those parts**—that is (in all probability) from some 22 village at the north end of the Jordan valley, where the administration was carried out from the coastal cities of Tyre (and perhaps even Sidon), but the population was still mainly Jewish. She is here called a **Canaanite**, which is a piece of antiquarianism on the part of Matthew: Canaanite is the Old Testament word for those inhabitants of Palestine, such as the Phoenicians, whom the people of Israel found already in occupation. But it serves to underline the apparent exclusiveness and scriptural correctness of Jesus' reply, **I was sent to the lost sheep of the house of Israel, and to them** 24 **alone.** More clearly than the lively, and perhaps slightly humorous, dialogue which follows, this first reply leaves no doubt of Jesus' attitude towards Gentiles: his mission was not to them. But Matthew also makes clear the reason (which Mark does not) why an exception was made for the Canaanite woman: she had faith. As in the case of the Roman centurion (8.5–10), so here: non-Jews, if they have faith enough, can qualify for the privileges up to now possessed by the Jews alone. Whether or not this was originally Jesus' attitude, it certainly soon became that of the early church. It governs the thought, for instance, of the first few chapters of Paul's letter to the Romans.

Matthew continues to follow closely the order of events in Mark's gospel, but gives them a more logical sequence. What in Mark is a single miracle 29-31 (the healing of a deaf and dumb man, 7.31–7) becomes in Matthew a whole series of miracles. The effect is the same: the prophecy of Isaiah 35.5 is seen to be fulfilled (the three words **dumb, lame** and **blind** all occur in that 30 passage), and the people, doubtless recognizing the significance of these events, give **praise to the God of Israel.** But the episode in Matthew's 31 version, with the crowds flocking to Jesus where he was seated somewhere

29, 32–9 **in the hills,** also sets the scene neatly for the feeding-miracle which follows. The same considerations apply to this narrative as to the version in Mark (8.1–10); Matthew has made only slight alterations, perhaps partly to increase

32 the impression of Jesus' mastery of the situation ('**I do not want to send them away unfed**' for Mark's 'If I send them away', the enlargement of

38, 39 the crowd by the addition of **women and children**). The **neighbourhood of Magadan** is Matthew's alteration of Mark's 'Dalmanutha'. But from our point of view this is no improvement: Magadan is also completely unknown.

16. 1–4 Matthew has already given a full report of the question of the "sign" (12.38–9), doubtless drawn from a source other than Mark; but here, for all that, he continues to follow Mark's order and relates it again, closely following the version in Mark (8.11–12), but avoiding Mark's reference to Jesus' emotion and adding an allusion to **the sign of Jonah** which was mentioned in the earlier conversation.

5–12 Matthew's treatment of the next episode is highly significant. He normally presents the disciples as a privileged group of men, constantly in the company of their Teacher and, in contrast to the multitudes, in a unique position to grasp the meaning of Jesus' teaching. This picture is rudely shattered if we turn to the parallel passage in Mark (8.14–21); for there this episode is the occasion for the severest criticism ever made by Jesus of the disciples' obtuseness and lack of understanding. It is therefore not surprising to find that Matthew gives the incident a different turn. The elements are the same:

6 the saying on **the leaven of the Pharisees and Sadducees,** and the crossing of the lake without a provision of bread. But Matthew's combination of them is different. Instead of concentrating on the disciples' total incomprehension of the feeding miracles, Matthew shifts the emphasis on to Jesus' admittedly somewhat enigmatic saying about leaven. It was this which the disciples had failed to understand. Matthew even suggests that

12 they were trying to take it literally, as a warning against the **baker's leaven.** But of course the saying, like the parables, had a deeper meaning and, by excluding (with a reference to his feeding miracles) the naïve literal meaning, Jesus led them to understand that it was a warning **against the teaching of the Pharisees and Sadducees.** Once more, the disciples are shown to be in possession of an esoteric interpretation of a saying of Jesus. Whether this was the interpretation intended by Jesus is perhaps doubtful. In Mark, the relevant phrase is 'the leaven of the Pharisees and the leaven of Herod', and can hardly mean anything but the common desire of both the religious and political authorities to do away with Jesus. In Matthew, Herod is replaced by the Sadducees. This party certainly had its own **teaching,** to which Jesus was openly opposed. But it was an aristocratic party, more political than religious, and would hardly have been interested in trying to influence men at the social level of Jesus' disciples. It is difficult to see why they should have had to be **on their guard** against the Sadducees' teaching.

The territory of Caesarea Philippi, to the extreme north of Galilee, is 13 the scene (as in Mark) of an important moment in the unfolding of the true nature of Jesus. But this moment, in Matthew's treatment, becomes also a means of drawing attention to one of the disciples, who has so far usually been mentioned only along with the others, but now begins to become prominent in the story (not always to his credit) and who was subsequently a leading figure (if not *the* leading figure) in the early church: Simon Peter.

Who do men say that the Son of Man is? This is a strangely oblique 13 way of speaking,[a] but there can be no doubt that Jesus' question is really about himself: the sequel makes this plain—and in any case the question is clearly not just a theoretical one about that mythological figure who appeared in Jewish speculation as the "Son of Man". The stage reached in the popular estimate of Jesus was that of moderately tense expectancy: he seemed to be bringing the promised kingdom appreciably nearer, and therefore he might well be one of those Old Testament figures who, it was popularly believed, would return to earth as a herald of the impending new age. Indeed, John the Baptist himself had appeared to fulfil so faithfully the traditional rôle of an Old Testament prophet, and had at the same time proclaimed such an urgent message, that Jesus might even be a reincarnation of him. But Simon Peter had advanced to a further stage in understanding who Jesus was: **'You are the Messiah, the Son of the living God'.** That 16 Jesus was in fact these things was of course taken for granted by the church when Matthew was writing; and by relating that Peter offered and Jesus accepted these titles, Matthew incidentally allowed his readers to feel that the language they were accustomed to use of their Lord had been endorsed by Jesus himself. But the significance of the narrative is mainly the light it throws on Peter. Matthew has inserted a saying of Jesus which occurs in 17–19 no other gospel. So far, he has represented the disciples as a group of men who are given the unique privilege of private and esoteric teaching, while the crowds who listen to Jesus are left in doubt and bewilderment about his real meaning. One of them, however, has now shown that he has advanced further still, to the point where he can receive a direct revelation from God. His recognition of the true nature of Jesus is something not to be learnt **from mortal man**: it is the very highest type of knowledge imparted by 17 God alone to those who are **favoured indeed**—and it is doubtless implied by Matthew that all those Christians who come to acknowledge the same truth for themselves are similarly **favoured** (the word is the same as that which is translated 'blest' at the beginning of the Sermon on the Mount).

But if Peter is up to this point the prototype of all Christians who confess Jesus to be Christ and Son of God, the next part of the saying sets him apart in a position by himself. **'You are Peter, the Rock.'** Matthew has already 18

[a] A way which puzzled some copyists, hence the alternative reading in the footnote.

said more than once that Simon was 'called Peter', and Mark states that it was Jesus who gave him the name. Unlike, for instance, the name given to two other disciples ('Boanerges'), Simon's name stuck to him, and he is known throughout the gospels indifferently as Simon or Peter (or its Aramaic equivalent, Kephas). Jesus' intention in so naming Simon is here explained for the one and only time in the New Testament: Peter (in Greek *Petros*, in Aramaic *kephas*) means "stone" or "rock"; and in true Hebrew fashion the full significance of the name is worked out, giving its bearer an apparently unique rôle to play in the subsequent history of the church.

Since it is clear from the New Testament that Peter was in fact not, or at any rate not for long, the universally acknowledged leader of the church; and since, on the other hand, it has been of primary concern to one whole section of Christendom for many centuries past to assert the absolute supremacy of Peter and of his successors over the church at large, the authenticity and meaning of this saying have become a subject of longstanding controversy. Further, the word **church** is very rare in the gospels (it occurs only here and at 18.17, where it is translated 'congregation'), and even though the concept of a community of followers may be implied in Jesus' teaching as a whole, it remains surprising to find him using the actual word **church**, and it is tempting to think that it was only after the church had come into existence that such a saying could have assumed its present form. On the other hand the building metaphor, as applied to the church, seems to have been used from very early times by Christians: it is taken for granted, for instance, by Paul. The metaphor is not unparalleled in Jewish writings; but it remains a striking one, and it is only reasonable to assume that it goes back to Jesus himself. Moreover, if Jesus gave Simon a name which means "stone" or "rock", it need not surprise us if at some moment he put the two ideas together and ascribed to this disciple an important function in the "building" which was to come. To this extent, the saying may well go back to Jesus, even if the subsequent evolution of a Christian "church" has modified the form in which we now possess it.

18 **'The powers of death shall never conquer it.'** [a] Again, it is easier to understand the birth of this saying after the resurrection than before it; for it was the resurrection which assured Christians that they no longer had anything to fear from the powers of death. Yet if Jesus did in fact make predictions about the community which was soon to arise, these predictions

19 could well have included some form of this saying. The expression, **the keys of the kingdom of Heaven**, appears to be explained in the sentence which

[a] Literally, "The gates of hell will not prevail over it". This suggests a more concrete image: when men die, the gates of "hell" (understood in the ordinary Greek sense, not as a place of torment, but as the shadowy dwelling-place of all the dead) close irrevocably behind them. But for Christians, death is not irrevocable. The church (in a sense) can pass back and forth through the gates. This is the sense of the alternative rendering in the NEB footnote.

follows. The Greek means literally, "what you bind . . . and what you loose", and the NEB rendering, **what you forbid . . . and what you allow**, represents a possible interpretation of the words. A qualified lawyer had the authority to decide, in disputed matters, precisely what was "allowed" by the Law and precisely what was "forbidden" by it. Similarly, it could perhaps be said of Peter (and, if of him, possibly of other leaders of the church) that he would have the authority to decide what was, and what was not, permissible for Christians. This authority would doubtless imply the decision when to excommunicate a member of the church (which is another possible meaning of "bind" and "loose"); and it is not altogether easy to reconcile this responsibility of Peter's (or of any single church leader) with the more democratic procedure described in chapter 18 below. The precise interpretation of these words depends, once again, on whether it is thought credible that Jesus should have made detailed predictions about the organization of the church, and on whether it is admitted that the subsequent practice of the church may have influenced the form in which the sayings have been handed down.

The remainder of the section reproduces the corresponding passage in 24–8 Mark (8.34–8) with only a few alterations. The final saying, on the coming of the kingdom, has been modified significantly. One of the rôles of the Son of Man (suggested by the Son of Man passage in Daniel 7) was to assist at the final Judgement, when each man would receive 'the due reward for 27 what he has done.' So far, the saying merely endorses what was probably a current Jewish belief. But the sequel, 'there are some of those standing 28 here who will not taste death before they have seen the Son of Man coming in his kingdom', is more startling. It appears to predict (erroneously) the coming of the end of the world in the lifetime of Jesus' own generation. Matthew, unlike Mark, made the saying turn on the figure of the Son of Man, and in so doing was perhaps trying to reconcile it with the experience of the church; for there was a sense in which Christians had already seen **the Son of Man coming in his kingdom**—compare Stephen's vision in Acts 7.55–6. Nevertheless, the saying remains a puzzling one: see below on Mark 9.1.

He was transfigured. Matthew's account of the Transfiguration follows 17. 1 closely that in Mark (9.2–8), and the details, as in Mark, frequently suggest a symbolical interpretation, even if (again as in Mark) they do not necessarily demand it. The small changes made by Matthew nevertheless indicate a slightly different understanding of the scene. Moses comes before Elijah, so that the two figures are clearer symbols of the Law and the prophets; and certain small touches, such as the radiance of Jesus' face, the brightness of the cloud, and the prostration of the disciples after (instead of before) the heavenly voice, bring the experience of Moses on Mount Sinai more vividly to mind (Exodus 34.29–35). These details perhaps show Matthew at work, deliberately presenting Jesus as the new Moses, the definitive lawgiver. The scene is followed, as in Mark, by the disciples' question about Elijah,

10 'Why then do our teachers say that Elijah must come first?' The teachers are the "doctors of the law", whose traditional interpretation of the prophecy in Malachi 4.5 (that Elijah was to come "before the day of the Lord") had given to this Elijah-figure an ever greater rôle, so that he was

11 now popularly believed to be one who would set everything right. Matthew, compared with Mark, somewhat simplifies Jesus' reply. Elijah's rôle was compatible (contrary to popular belief) both with remaining unrecognized and with suffering execution. Similarly, the Son of Man (again contrary to

12 popular belief) was to suffer. That such could be the destiny of Elijah (who was now at last recognized by the disciples in the figure of John the Baptist) should help them to understand how such too could eventually be the destiny of the Son of Man.

14–18 The exorcism which follows is related more briefly in Matthew than in Mark (9.14–29), and there is here no dialogue on the subject of faith. Nevertheless, Matthew makes faith the point of the story. To the question, why did Jesus' disciples (and presumably also the early Christians) not always succeed in their exorcisms, the answer, in Mark, is: they do not pray

20 enough! The saying of Jesus given here suggests a different answer: they have not sufficient faith!

A further prediction of the fate in store for the Son of Man is recorded here in Matthew as it is in Mark and Luke, but with a characteristic difference. In the other gospels the disciples failed to understand; but here they under-

23 stood so well that they were filled with grief.

24 'Does your master not pay temple-tax?' It was an almost universal custom among the Jews, not only in Palestine but all over the Roman empire, to pay an annual tax of a "half-shekel" or (in Greek money) a "double drachma" for the upkeep of the temple in Jerusalem. The amount of this tax was relatively small: it was just twice the labourer's wage for a day's work (20.2), and the obligation to pay it was taken for granted by rich and poor alike. But in fact it is doubtful whether any legal sanctions attached to it, and it was the view of the Sadducees, for example, that since the only description of the tax in the Law of Moses (Exodus 30.11–16) made no mention of it as a recurrent tax, the institution must be a product of a later "tradition", and was therefore not binding. The question of the collectors did not therefore necessarily amount to asking whether Jesus was a law-abiding person in this respect, but implied that Jesus, as a new religious teacher, might possibly have a view of his own on the matter.

25 Jesus answered with a simple analogy. 'From whom do earthly monarchs collect tax or toll?' The monarchs of whom the Jews had

experience were those lesser kings whom the Romans allowed to administer parts of Palestine under the general jurisdiction of the Roman empire. The **tax** which these princes exacted was a capitation tax levied on all subject peoples; the "tolls" were customs dues. Roman citizens were exempt from both these; but all others—**aliens** from the Roman point of view—were subject to them. Jesus' answer implied that, just as Roman citizens were exempt from taxes, so Jews should have a similar immunity with regard to taxes for their own institutions. This might give the impression that Jesus was opposed to the institution of the temple as such; but this is not borne out by his attitude at other times, and is indeed contradicted by his approval of free-will offerings to the temple treasury (Mark 12.41–4). What he objected to was probably the notion of a formal obligation to pay the tax, instead of spontaneous offerings. '**But as we do not want to cause offence** 27 . . .' This was clearly not the moment to make an issue out of it, and Jesus complied with the collectors' demand.

The story of how he did so is reminiscent of many folk tales, and is often thought to be an example of the kind of legend which very soon attached itself to the person of Jesus: similar stories came to be told of other famous Jewish rabbis, by way of emphasizing their exceptional holiness. Alternatively, some saying of Jesus—a parable or a simile—may in the course of telling have been changed into a story about Jesus himself. The **silver coin** in the fish's mouth was a *stater*, which corresponded to four drachmas, or two persons' temple-tax. Matthew alone records this story; it may have been preserved (and possibly modified) in a Jewish-Christian church because of its bearing on what may have been a delicate question for Palestinian Jews converted to Christianity: should they or should they not continue to pay the temple-tax? They may have found their answer in the words, '**we do not want to cause offence**'.

At that time the disciples came to Jesus and asked. Matthew calls 18. 1 Jesus' long answer a 'discourse' (19.1), and the chapter constitutes one of the five substantial discourses with which this gospel is punctuated. It is addressed specifically to **the disciples**; but the topics it deals with are unmistakably those which were later to arise in the life of the church.

'**Who is the greatest in the kingdom of Heaven?**' The question looks innocent enough; but the context in Mark (9.33–4) reveals why it was originally asked—the disciples had been discussing 'who was the greatest' among them. We can probably detect in Matthew's handling of this his desire to present the disciples in a more favourable light: he simply omitted the disreputable argument which was the original cue for the question. Whether or not the church was interested in the order of precedence which may have obtained among Jesus' first disciples, it was intensely interested in the order of precedence which should be observed among its own members, and in the problems of organizing its community life; and it doubtless found all the sayings of Jesus which are collected here relevant to these questions.

2   **He called a child, set him in front of them, and said.** In the narrative in Mark (9.36), Jesus answers the disciples' question with the same gesture: he makes them concentrate their attention on a mere child, and declares himself present even in such an insignificant member of the community.

5   Matthew repeats this: '**Whoever receives one such child in my name**

3   **receives me**', but he adds to it other children-sayings. '**Unless you turn round and become like children**'. **Turn** is a synonym (with more of an Old Testament than a New Testament feeling: compare Mark 4.12, where it occurs in a quotation from Isaiah) of the more common "repent". In what respect must they become like children? What Jesus' original meaning may have been is a deep question; but in the immediate context given to the saying by Matthew—that of order and priority in the church—the

4   point is probably quite simple. As the text goes on to say, '**Let a man humble himself till he is like this child**', not so as to become child-like (for children are not necessarily humble), but so as willingly to occupy a child's humble place in the community.

In the corresponding passage of Mark, sayings about children lead on to sayings about 'little ones' (9.42), but there are signs that this is a superficial connection: 'little ones' was a name given to the weaker members of the Christian fellowship. The case is even clearer here. The notion of a small child "having faith in Jesus" is a modern one; in antiquity, children were deemed simply to go along with their parents. A man became a Christian 'with his household', and nobody asked questions about the quality of his children's "faith". Therefore, when Matthew presents us with the phrase,

6   **one of these little ones who have faith in me**, we must beware of

7   assuming that the discourse is still about children. In the church, **causes of stumbling** were bound to appear, in the form of persecutions, heresies and betrayals—the ever-active devil would see to that. But deliberately to add to these causes by making life still more difficult for the "weaker brethren" would be a very serious matter—and one which had a natural place in this discourse about the life of the church.

8   '**If your hand or your foot is your undoing**'. Almost the same saying occurs in the Sermon on the Mount (5.29–30) in the context of personal renunciation. Why does Matthew repeat it here? Possibly because he found it in the corresponding passage in Mark (9.42–7); or perhaps he saw a new meaning for it in this context. The church is the "body" of Christ. Offensive members must be thrown out rather than the whole community be corrupted.

10   By contrast, the **little ones** must never be despised, for **they have their guardian angels in heaven.** The function of angels in Jewish literature was twofold. First, they constituted the court of God in heaven, offering him unceasing praise and worship; secondly, they acted as the messengers

and agents through which God intervened in the affairs of men (there are a number of examples of this in the early chapters of Matthew and Luke). Popular belief also ascribed a third function to them, that of **guardian angels** of individuals and nations (this is clear from Acts 12.15, and became officially recognized in Jewish writings in the following centuries). But these guardian angels were not excused their duties in heaven: they still had their place in the heavenly court. As to the order of precedence of these angels: it was usually thought that only a very few actually had the privilege of standing in God's presence and (to use a court metaphor) of "looking continually on his face". If the guardian angels of **these little ones** had this dignity, what must be the worth in God's sight of the individuals whom they guarded!

'**Suppose a man has a hundred sheep**'—an easy supposition: this was a 12 reasonable-sized flock for a single-handed shepherd; and if one strayed, he would not necessarily abandon it just to stay close to the rest of the flock. But the parable is given a quite different application from the more famous one it has in Luke's gospel. There, all the emphasis is on the joy of the shepherd that the "lost" sheep is found; here, it is on the duty of the shepherd not to let a "straying" sheep get lost. The lesson for the leaders of the church is obvious.

'**If your brother commits a sin**'. These sentences are not (like what has 15 gone before) mere exhortation, they lay down a strict procedure to be followed. From the language it is possible almost to date the words to a particular phase in the growth of Christianity. There was already a **con-** 17 **gregation** [a]—that is to say, there is no pretence that the words were applicable to the disciples in Jesus' lifetime. But this congregation was still completely Jewish: it shared, with an exclusiveness that was hardly characteristic of Jesus, the attitude that all whose nationality or occupation disqualified them from membership of the Jewish people were incapable of salvation. Hence, it treated its own recalcitrants as the Jewish community treated a **pagan or a tax-gatherer**. Nevertheless, the actual procedure it followed was by no means characteristically Jewish. It is true that the Dead Sea sect had a very similar procedure (and the similarity between these verses and a passage in the Scrolls shows, at the very least, that at this stage the Palestinian church was in touch with ideas that had shaped other communities); but the patience which Christians were to show towards a sinner (expressed in its most radical form in Jesus' reply to Peter about forgiving **seventy** 22 **times seven** times) is very different from the normal procedure of the synagogue, where excommunication normally followed the commission of certain sins automatically. Nevertheless, moments would come when the leaders of the church would have to apply the ultimate sanction of exclusion.

[a] This word can also be translated "church". Apart from 16.18 above, this is the only occurrence of the word in the gospels.

When this happened, there was a saying of Christ (see above on 16.19) which
18 authorized them to act: 'Whatever you forbid on earth shall be forbidden in heaven, and whatever you allow on earth shall be allowed
in heaven'.

19 'If two of you agree on earth'. This "agreement" was the united
prayer of the church, for the church was the place where two or three
individuals were gathered together "in Christ's name"; and just as a later
Rabbi could say, "When two sit occupied with the words of the Law, the
divine glory is in the midst of them", so the fact of being united in the
worship of Christ guaranteed his presence among them.

23 'The kingdom of Heaven, therefore, should be thought of in this
way'. The parable is clearly intended to be an illustration of the teaching
which has just been given about forgiveness, and makes its point, as so
often, by a touch of exaggeration. The scene is the court of a king: Jesus may
have been thinking of one of the sons of Herod the Great who ruled as
vassals of Rome, or else of a more distant and perhaps legendary oriental
monarch. Among the men who served this king were officials entrusted with
the taxation of his realm, or perhaps local governors set over certain areas
24 of the kingdom. There appeared before him a man whose debt ran
into millions. Here is the first touch of exaggeration. Ten thousand talents
(the sum named in the Greek) would have been more than the total tribute
paid by Galilee to Rome in 15 years—an immense sum, but it would be just
conceivable for a local governor to fall into arrears to this extent; if he did,
he would presumably enrich himself enormously by so doing, and the king
could hope to recoup much of the revenue by confiscating the man's
27 property. However, out of pity the king remitted the debt—that is (in
practical terms) he wrote off the revenue or at least postponed the date
when payment would be due. [a] By contrast, another official owed the first
28 a few pounds, and the first had every right to bring him to court and, if
convicted, have him jailed; but the affair, as being between court officials,
31 was noticed by the other servants (or courtiers [b]), with the consequences
described. At the end of the story there is another touch, if not of exaggera-
34 tion, at least of the exotic: the Jews did not practise torture, and did not
normally suffer it at the hands of the Romans; but they had all heard
vaguely of the methods used by oriental despots, and torturing was in any
case the obvious way of forcing a debtor to reveal what assets and credits he
really had. Jesus' parable describes a situation which is by no means impossible but which, by being slightly larger than life, makes the point all the
more cogently.

[a] Literally, the Greek means "remitted the loan", which may be meant to imply that the
king turned the servant's debt into a loan repayable at some future date.
[b] In an eastern court no distinction would be made between a king's "servants" and his
officials. Both could easily be slaves.

He left Galilee. The geography, both here and in Mark (10.1), is some- **19.** 1
what obscure. One of the pilgrims' routes from Galilee to Jerusalem crossed
the Jordan south of the lake, followed the east side of the valley through
"Transjordan" (i.e. Peraea, which like Galilee was part of the territory
of Herod Antipas) and then recrossed the Jordan to Jericho. If Jesus
took this route, it would effectively have taken him **across Jordan;**
and since Peraea was predominantly Jewish, the presence, for instance, of
some Pharisees need cause no surprise. The difficulty is that Matthew 3

1 appears to call this part of the country **the region of Judaea.** Strictly speaking, Judaea (the area administered by a Roman procurator) lay on the west side of the Jordan; but the word was sometimes used as a name for Jewish Palestine generally.

The Pharisees' question reflects a controversy which certainly existed in the time of Jesus. The relevant passage in the Law of Moses runs (Deuteronomy 24.1): "When a man has married a wife, but she does not win his favour because he finds something shameful in her, and he writes her a note of divorce . . ." Divorce, in this passage, is taken for granted; and the grounds on which it is permitted are defined as "something shameful" in the wife. But what does this phrase mean? The most rigorous school of thought considered that it referred only to adultery; but those more favourable to divorce interpreted it in the most general way possible, to cover quite trivial misdemeanours by the wife. We know that in the time of Jesus this wider interpretation was the usually accepted one: the historian Josephus, for example, tells us that he divorced his own wife because he was "displeased with her conduct"; but at the same time there were some who disapproved of such permissiveness and endeavoured to tighten up the application of the law. Jesus was evidently being challenged to enter this debate when he was asked (according to Matthew, who was doubtless

3 familiar with the controversy), '**Is it lawful for a man to divorce his wife on any and every ground?**'

Jesus' answer was characteristic. Instead of concentrating on a text which

4-5 referred only to the practical and legal question of divorce, he drew attention to another part of Scripture which was generally agreed to provide positive teaching about the nature of marriage.[a] From these texts it could be deduced

6 that man and wife **are no longer two individuals: they are one flesh.** The will of God, as revealed in the narrative of the creation of Adam and Eve, clearly presupposed a union of man and wife so profound that ideally it excluded any possibility of divorce.

According to their own principles of interpreting Scripture, the Pharisees' objection to this was a fair one. If the Law of Moses allowed for divorce, how could anyone say that divorce was contrary to the will of God? Jesus' answer reveals, by comparison, a somewhat radical approach to Scripture. Even though the Law was unquestionably the revealed will of God for men, Jesus frankly pronounced it to have been conditioned by the circumstances

8 in which it was given. '**It was because your minds were closed that Moses gave you permission to divorce your wives.**' The permission was a secondary development; the real will of God in the matter must be deduced from the account of the creation.

However, this did not necessarily mean that Jesus was recommending a

[a] For the force of these two passages of Genesis in the argument (1.27; 2.24) see below on Mark 10.1–12.

new law on divorce. It was an agreed principle among legal experts that no rules of conduct were legally binding that could not be deduced from explicit commandments in Scripture. Principles deduced from statements of fact— such as that **the two shall become one flesh** (Genesis 2.24)—could never 5 be more than morally binding. And in fact Jesus' answer reads more like a moral judgement than a legal one. '**If a man divorces his wife . . . he** 9 **commits adultery.**' Adultery was regarded by the Jews as a very serious sin. Jesus' words show that he regarded divorce as just as serious. Ideally, it should never occur.

Yet his answer also reveals his attitude to the practical debate about the permissible grounds for divorce. It contains the exception, **for any cause other than unchastity.** By this, Jesus showed that he sided with those of his contemporaries who interpreted the law on divorce as strictly as possible. In allowing this exception, he implicitly acknowledged that the relevant clause of the Law of Moses, with its recognition of the principle of divorce, was still in force; but by appealing to the narrative of creation he demon- strated that divorce itself was something deserving the very strongest moral condemnation. It is characteristic of Matthew's gospel that Jesus should be represented as taking part in a technical dispute of this kind. Mark's gospel, by contrast, records only Jesus' general moral condemnation of divorce as such—which is indeed the more striking part of his teaching on the subject (Mark 10.1–12).

The meaning of the following short paragraph depends on how much of it goes back to a historical conversation between Jesus and his disciples, and how much is an addition by the church in the interests of making Jesus' ethical teaching more practicable. That the sequence of thought is due to Matthew is suggested at once by a comparison with the corresponding passage in Mark (10.10–12). There, Jesus' pronouncement on marriage is followed by a private conversation with the disciples about the practical implications of it. Matthew follows the same pattern, but gives it a quite different content: the disciples' question is a more pointed one, and Jesus' answer to it leads into a fresh saying altogether. It appears, therefore, to be Matthew who has taken advantage of the change of scene recorded in Mark in order to add an important piece of ethical teaching, ostensibly for the benefit of the disciples, but in reality of greater relevance to the life of the church.

Seen in this light the disciples' comment, though banal, is quite natural. Jesus' teaching on marriage seemed to the church to set an impossibly high standard: might it not be better **not to marry** at all? The answer given 10 was a saying of Jesus about the renunciation of marriage which seemed, by implication, to accept the point of view of the disciples, and to concede that his teaching could not be literally carried out by more than a few. Marriage without divorce, he seemed to be saying, is indeed an impossible

11 ideal. The only safe way is to renounce marriage—but of course **that is something which not everyone can accept.** Thereby, the church might well feel authorized to countenance divorce among its own members: Jesus' absolute teaching about marriage was never intended to be taken literally except by those few who could be sure of not transgressing it—by renouncing marriage altogether.

This, in view of palpable assimilation in certain parts of Matthew's gospel to conditions prevailing subsequently in the church, is a possible reading of the passage. However, if we assume that the dialogue is historical, and transpose it back into the context of first-century Palestine, we get a very different result. Among the Jews, one matter on which there could be absolutely no question was that a man had an unqualified obligation to marry and beget children. "Be fruitful and multiply" (Genesis 1.28) was regarded as a command binding on every Jew; and only certain extremist sects, which regarded ritual pollution caused by intercourse with women as a still more serious matter than the command to bring up children, ever thought of recommending a celibate life. Against this background, the disciples'
10 objection takes on a very different sense. '**If that is the position with husband and wife, it is better not to marry**'. But (in view of God's clear command) it cannot ever be better not to marry; therefore that cannot "be the position": marriage without the possibility of divorce is absurd. Read in this way, the disciples' objection is a real one: it seeks, by a *reductio ad absurdum*, to show that Jesus' teaching cannot hold; the divorce permitted by Moses must belong to the nature of things. Jesus' reply [a] then goes some way to meet the point: to most people it will seem like this, but there will be some (and here doubtless the disciples are in mind and those followers of Christ who are their successors) who, by God's appointment, can accept it. It is God's will that some, at least, should be able to fulfil the nature of marriage as God originally intended it to be.

The discussion (at least as Matthew presents it) runs on into a saying
12 about those who are **incapable of marriage.** The original character of the saying is a little obscured by the NEB rendering. A more literal translation would run:

> "For some are eunuchs because they are born so,
> And some are eunuchs because they were made so by men,
> And some have made eunuchs of themselves for the sake of the kingdom of Heaven."

The saying, in fact, is concerned, not with those who are **incapable of marriage** (for it was by no means unknown for a sexually impotent man to

[a] In the Greek, the words 'That is something which not everyone can accept', can refer equally to (i) the saying in verse 9, (ii) the disciples' remark in verse 10, (iii) the implication of their remark that celibacy is desirable, or even (iv) the saying in verse 12. The translators settled, without complete conviction, for the third of these possibilities.

marry) but with those who are incapable of consummating a marriage. Jewish society recognized two classes of impotent men, those who were **born so**, and those who became so by accident or the action of enemies. But "eunuchs", in the sense of men who had been deliberately and willingly castrated, represented something utterly foreign to their culture, a repellent phenomenon which they took to be explicitly forbidden in the Law (Deuteronomy 23.1). In a Jewish setting, the first two lines of Jesus' saying would have seemed to exhaust the possibilities; and one would have expected the third line of the epigram to be a statement about men other than eunuchs, or else an expression of utter condemnation of those who have "made eunuchs of themselves". Hence the extreme originality of Jesus' saying. The meaning is of course metaphorical: the last class of "eunuchs" are those who have voluntarily and decisively **renounced marriage**. But by setting this class in series with those who were genuinely eunuchs, [a] Jesus was expressing in a forcible and almost paradoxical way his opposition to the contemporary Jewish view that procreation was an absolute duty laid on every male who was capable of it. This too (like riches further on in the chapter) was something which it might be proper to renounce **for the sake of the kingdom of Heaven**.

From this point to the end of the chapter Matthew follows Mark closely (10.13-31), and it is only necessary here to draw attention to certain small changes he has introduced.

They brought children for him to lay his hands on them with **prayer.** Mark writes simply 'for him to touch': Matthew makes it clear from the start that what they wanted was a blessing such as a parent or respected teacher would often be asked for. He omits one of the sayings recorded by Mark, but retains the essential one for the sake of which the incident was doubtless remembered: '**the kingdom of Heaven belongs to** **such as these**'. [13] [14]

And now a man came up. Matthew appears to have inferred from the enthusiasm of his approach (as described by Mark) that he was a **young** **man**; but he has eliminated some of Mark's more striking details. In particular, instead of the pointed exchange, 'Good Master . . .' 'Why do you call me good?', he makes the conversation open with the very ordinary question, '**What good must I do to gain eternal life?**' (which makes Jesus' answer, 'One alone is good', appear a little irrelevant). Good works, particularly almsgiving, were generally regarded as a qualification for a reward in heaven, and the young man may have desired some direction on what kind of munificence he should aspire to. Jesus directed him instead to **keep the commandments**, mentioning some of the Ten Commandments, [16] [20] [16] [17] [17]

[a] It is just possible that Jesus was criticized by his enemies for not marrying, and that the saying was originally his answer to insulting insinuations that he was a "eunuch". If so, Matthew, or his source, has given it an entirely different context, that of private instruction to the disciples.

and adding the very general commandment from Leviticus (19.18) to
19 **love your neighbour as yourself,** which he himself regarded as a summary
of the Law. But he attached no value, apparently, to any extra works of piety
which his questioner may have had in mind. The only alternative he gave
21 him was **to go the whole way,** a new ethic altogether demanding a decisive
break with the past.

28   The reply to Peter on the question of rewards gives a specially privileged
place to the disciples in a way characteristic of Matthew. The imagery of
the saying about **thrones** stems from the book of Daniel (7.9–14): "As I
looked, thrones were placed . . . the court sat in judgement . . . and behold,
with the clouds of heaven there came one like a son of man". The significance
of Jesus' title, 'Son of Man', in Matthew's gospel is concentrated in the rôle
which this figure was to play in the final Judgement, and those of Jesus'
followers who were admitted to know the 'secrets of the kingdom' (13.11)
would also play their part in the same drama. **The twelve tribes of Israel**
was an archaic title that could be used for the contemporary Jewish nation.
A possible meaning of the saying (which has a totally different context in
Luke 22.28) is that the nation as a whole would be "judged" by those few
individuals who had accepted Jesus as Lord. But **the twelve tribes of
Israel** was also a way of describing the New Israel constituted by the
Christian church (see also Revelation 7.4–8); and the saying could equally
well mean that the disciples were to "judge" the church, in the sense
(which followed the Old Testament concept of "judging") of assuring its
29 members of their rightful reward. This second sense leads more naturally
into the following saying, which is again concerned with rewards in heaven.
Matthew is still apparently following Mark (10.29–31); but he smooths out
the apparent materialism of Mark's version by omitting the words, 'in this
age'.

20. 1 **'The kingdom of Heaven is like this.'** The setting of the parable is
vintage-time in Palestine, the only time in the year when unskilled labourers
would be needed in a vineyard. Normally the **landowner** would hire all
the men he needed first thing in the morning; but the story required that he
should have miscalculated and taken the rather unusual step of engaging
6 further labourers right up to **an hour before sunset.** At the end of the day,
he was bound by law (Leviticus 19.13) to pay the stipulated wage to those
who had done a day's work; but, with regard to the rest, he could either wait
till they came again the next day and made up the full time (this was the
4 usual procedure) or else, if the work were finished, pay **a fair wage** for the
number of hours worked. On this occasion he instructed his steward to
8 settle the men's wages, **beginning with those who came last**—that is to
say, the eleventh-hour men were not to be allowed to go home and return
in the morning, but were to be paid off at once. The surprise came in the
9 fact that they **were paid the full day's wage.**

Matthew has shown how he understood the parable by enclosing it in the motto, 'the first will be last and the last first' (19.30 and 20.16), a motto which was highly relevant to the subject in hand, namely the correct ordering of the Christian community. But it is clear that this is not really the point of the parable: the fact that the last to be employed were paid first is an unimportant one in the story; the emphasis is on their being given, not first treatment, but equal treatment with the others. What was the original point of the parable? We may guess that the question which caused Jesus to tell it was not that of priorities in the church of the future, but of his own converse with 'tax collectors and sinners'. According to strict justice, those who had devoted their whole lives to observing the law in all its detailed provisions (especially the Pharisees) deserved a reward far greater than the men and women who, after lives of irresponsibility or even immorality, had responded at the eleventh hour to the preaching of Jesus. The logic of the parable was intended to force Jesus' hearers to see the question of ultimate rewards from the point of view of a God who is not only just but generous.

Challenge to Jerusalem

Jesus was journeying towards Jerusalem. During his activity in Galilee, 17 Jesus' activity could be characterized by the heading *Teaching and healing*, which gave rise, not so much to overt opposition, as to *Controversy*. This was followed by an itinerant period, when the bulk of what Matthew records was in the nature of private instruction to Jesus' immediate followers (*Jesus and his disciples*). But on his arrival at Jerusalem, Jesus' actions were such as to make an official reaction inevitable, and the heading consequently changes to *Challenge to Jerusalem*, even though there are still a few sections to come which consist of teaching addressed to the disciples.

Matthew here follows Mark closely (10.32–52), but makes a few changes of detail. As so often, he appears to have been unwilling to present the disciples in an unfavourable light, and the blame for ambitious sentiments is laid, not on James and John themselves, but on their mother. (The 20 difficult saying in Mark about 'a baptism' is also omitted.) The miracle-story is a doublet of the one already told earlier (9.27–31). The blind man of 29–34 Mark has for some reason again become **two blind men**, and the theme of 29 faith, which was kept in the previous version (9.29), is omitted here.

When they reached Bethphage at the Mount of Olives. Matthew has 21. 1 the most exact geography here of any of the gospels. The road from Jericho, just before it reached the crest of the Mount of Olives, had a turning off to the left leading to the small village of Bethphage and after that to Bethany.

It was the natural place for Jesus to pause while obtaining a mount for his entry into Jerusalem. All the gospel accounts see this episode as a symbolic act and interpret it with reference to Old Testament prophecies of the coming Messiah, in particular Zechariah 9.9 (see below on Mark 11.1–10).
4 Matthew characteristically makes this correspondence quite explicit—**this was to fulfil the prophecy**—and quotes the verse from Zechariah in full, prefacing it with a phrase from Isaiah (62.11), '**Tell the daughter of Zion**'.
2 However, he also adds a curious detail: there were two beasts, **a donkey tethered with her foal beside her**. It is true that the prophecy of Zechariah
5 has a double description of the animal—**riding on an ass, riding on the foal of a beast of burden**—but this was simply a common idiom of Hebrew poetry, which often, in the two halves of a single line, likes to say the same thing in slightly different words. So far as we know, no Jewish interpreter ever thought of reading Zechariah's words as if they meant two animals; but Matthew appears to have done so—unless, of course, he knew of a tradition that Jesus entered Jerusalem with two mounts, and then offered a literal interpretation of Zechariah to explain it. But he offers no
7 explanation of how Jesus actually used the two animals: **they laid their cloaks on them and Jesus mounted** is a translation which smooths out the awkwardness. The Greek has "Jesus mounted *them*".
9   '**Hosanna to the Son of David!**' The relevant words of Psalm 118.25–6 are as follows:

> "Save us, we beseech thee (*Hosanna*), O Lord ...
> Blessed be he who enters in the name of the Lord."

The psalm was used at a number of annual festivals, and in the course of its liturgical use the Hebrew word *Hosanna* seems to have lost its literal meaning, "save us now", and to have become a general cry of acclamation or shout of praise. The Septuagint version of the Old Testament translates the word into Greek; but both Matthew and Mark are content to leave it as it stands, without offering any explanation of its meaning. The reason must be that this was one of the Hebrew words (*Amen* is another) which the Greek-speaking church had taken over into its worship, so that it would have been already familiar to Matthew's readers.

Matthew makes one significant change to the text of the psalm. He adds: **to the Son of David.** It is an important theme of the gospel that Jesus' Messiahship was confirmed by his physical ancestry, which could be traced back to David. Indeed, **Son of David** is Matthew's distinctive title for the Messiah. The crowds, therefore, if they shouted out this title, must have recognized that Jesus was the Messiah, and this would explain Matthew's comment that **the whole city went wild with excitement.** Jesus' entry, 10 according to Matthew, was not directly into the temple area, but by way of a detour through the city. But, curiously, the recognition that here at last was the awaited Messiah was not sustained. Once in the city, the crowd seems to have dropped the portentous title **Son of David,** and given to inquirers the much less sensational reply, '**This is the prophet Jesus, from Nazareth** 11 **in Galilee**'.

It seems likely, therefore, that Matthew has allowed the subsequent faith of the church, which thought of Jesus as riding triumphantly into Jerusalem as the awaited Christ, the Son of David, to colour his description of the scene. At any rate, the status of Messiah is hinted at much less obviously in what follows. (On the details of Jesus' action **in the temple precincts,** 12 see below on Mark 11.15–17.) The healing of **blind men and cripples** 14 could be interpreted, by those who wished, as the breaking in of the Messiah's kingdom, but equally it could be regarded as of no decisive significance. This was the view of **the chief priests and doctors of the** 15 **law.** Matthew contrasts them, not with the crowds (whose attitude had now become uncertain), but with **the boys in the temple** who continued the cry started on the Mount of Olives, '**Hosanna to the Son of David!**' Matthew has said elsewhere (19.14) that it is children who are closest to the kingdom; and the fact that these boys intuitively recognized Jesus as the Messiah is explained in the words of a psalm (8.2): "**Thou hast made children and** 16 **babes at the breast sound aloud thy praise**". In the Hebrew, the last word of this text is, not "praise", but "strength". Matthew's quotation is according to the Greek version, and fits the situation perfectly. But the Hebrew or Aramaic text known to Jesus would have been less appropriate: and our impression is thereby strengthened that Matthew has written up this section fairly freely, to bring out the ambiguity of Jesus' reception in Jerusalem.

23   Matthew somewhat abbreviates the story of the fig-tree, but follows Mark
      closely in verses 23–7 (see below on Mark 11.20–33). He then inserts a
28   parable not found elsewhere. **A man had two sons.** The story itself is
      perfectly clear; and its immediate application by Jesus is plausible enough:
31   **'tax-gatherers and prostitutes are entering the kingdom of God
      ahead of you.'** These were the two classes of people whose way of life most
30   flagrantly (in the view of strict Jews) expressed a clear "I will not" to the
      commands of God, but for whom Jesus consistently kept open the pos-
      sibility of "changing their mind"; whereas the Pharisees, for all their
      profession of obedience, remained obstinately inactive in the things that
      really mattered. Thus far, the point is clear enough; but Matthew has
      added (at least so it would appear from the fact that Luke (7.29–30) records
      a similar saying in a quite different context) a second saying about John the
      Baptist, which is a little difficult to relate to the preceding parable, and is
32   perhaps better understood separately. **John came to show you the right
      way to live.** This is a rather free translation, and takes the sense differently
      from most English versions. Linguistically, it may be correct; but John the
      Baptist's message, apart from a few ethical rules given in Luke's gospel
      (3.10–14), is usually presented as more concerned with preparation for a
      coming event than with instructions about the right way to live. An alter-
      native rendering would be, "When John came on his mission to you, he
      lived in strict observance of the Law; but even so you did not believe him".
      In this case there would of course be an implied contrast between John,
      whose austerity made it almost impossible to criticize him for breaking any
      ritual regulation, and Jesus, whose way of life showed notorious freedom
      with regard to the detailed provisions of the Law.

33   **'Listen to another parable.'** The problems this parable raises are dis-
      cussed in detail below on Mark 12.1–12. Except for a slight change in the
      number of servants, the details of the story are exactly as in Mark. But if,
      in Mark, the story shows signs of having had an interpretation imposed upon
      it by the early church, in Matthew this is very much clearer. The passage of
      Isaiah (5.1) on which the opening words are based, continues (verse 3): "And
      now, O inhabitants of Jerusalem and men of Judah, judge, I pray you,
      between me and my vineyard." Hence, perhaps, the extra dramatization in
40   Matthew, when Jesus puts the question to his hearers, **'How do you think
      he will deal with those tenants?'** The reply, at any rate, shows a clear
      tendency to interpret the parable. The main crime of the tenants is of course
      their maltreatment of the owner's servants and their murder of the son; but
      Matthew makes it sound as if their real guilt was that they did not let the
41   owner **have his share of the crop.** This, applied to the Jewish people, was
      a constant theme of Jesus' preaching (at least in Matthew's gospel): they had
      failed to bring forth fruit (or "a crop"—the word is the same in the Greek)
      comparable with the blessings God had bestowed upon them. Consequently

(and Matthew draws out a consequence which was in fact only slowly realized by the church), 'the kingdom of God will be taken away from 43 you, and given to a nation that yields the proper fruit'—that is, the Gentiles! The parable thus becomes, in Matthew, an attack on the Jewish people as a whole; and it is perhaps by a slight oversight that he reproduces from Mark the statement that the chief priests and Pharisees saw that he 45 was referring to them.

'The kingdom of Heaven is like this'. A parable occurs in Luke's gospel 22. 2 so similar to this one that both must go back to the same original. But in Matthew the story is considerably less lifelike, and sometimes appears even far-fetched, whereas in Luke it seems to spring (like most of Jesus' parables) straight from Palestinian daily life. It is tempting to see here an instance of what was originally a straightforward story with a single point having been transformed, in the course of telling, into an elaborate piece of allegory. The setting is a royal wedding-feast. Invitations had been sent out to the notables among the city-dwellers, and when the day came the king, following the courteous custom of the time, sent his servants to inform the guests that 3 all was ready and to conduct them to the palace. But—they would not come! No reason is given for their rude and disloyal behaviour; and at this point the story becomes frankly implausible. Why should the king, after receiving the first affront, have demeaned himself still further by sending a second set of servants with a renewed invitation? And why should the invited guests have then attacked them brutally, and killed them? As a 6 story, the sequence of events is fantastic; but as an allegory, it has a logic of its own. A wedding-feast was a familiar image for the kingdom of glory promised to the elect people of God. "Servants"—the prophets—had been repeatedly sent to invite the guests to prepare themselves, but had been ignored, or maltreated, or killed. As a result, Jerusalem (as the prophets themselves had foretold) had been taken and destroyed—once by the Assyrians centuries before, and now, shortly before Matthew's gospel was written, by the Romans. The story so far is clearly an allegory of these things. But what of the wedding-feast? Was God's purpose now frustrated, and his promise void? Regardless of factual verisimilitude, the story continues as if only an hour had passed. "The guests I invited did not 8 deserve the honour", but there are others to whom it can be offered instead. "Go out to the main thoroughfares". The Greek means 9 literally the places where the narrow city streets debouch into public squares and open country places, that is, the places where people congregate. It was a fact, both of Jesus' own practice and of the missionary experience of the church, that the gospel, after its rejection by the Jewish leaders, was offered to a much wider public, good and bad alike. 10

'When the king came in to see the company at table.' The story goes 11

on, but the sequel is again quite implausible. How could those who had just been "collected" from the streets have been expected to provide themselves with wedding clothes? There is no evidence for the solution sometimes proposed that a festal garment was issued to each guest on arrival; and even if this had been the case, the refusal of one guest, to put it on would be incomprehensible. To make sense of it, we have to assume that another, and originally separate, piece of allegory has been added by Matthew, and somewhat inexpertly welded into a single story. The kingdom of Heaven is like a royal wedding-feast: and woe to him who comes not properly prepared (with repentance? with righteous deeds?). The penalty will be exclusion; and on the last day the consequence will be hell, in all its traditional horror.
14 The essential thing is to be among the few who are chosen.

15 **Then the Pharisees went away and agreed on a plan.** The four questions and answers which follow are very much the same as in Mark (12.13–37), but Matthew builds up a slightly more dramatic setting for them by presenting them as a series of attacks by different sections of Jesus' opponents, while the people stand by in amazement. The scene culminates in a devastating
46 counter-attack by Jesus, after which **no one dared ask him another question.** Within the conversations themselves, it is only in the third that
34-40 Matthew's hand can be seen at work. In Mark, Jesus' interlocutor is a 'lawyer', who appears to ask the question about the greatest commandment in perfectly good faith, and is then warmly commended by Jesus on his own attitude to the Law. But in Matthew the question has a different tone. The speaker is one of the Pharisees (which is often Matthew's way of saying, an
35 enemy of Jesus) who **tested him with this question.** The question, we know, was one which was earnestly discussed in Pharisaic circles; but in what sense was it a "test" for Jesus? Did his enemies want to see whether Jesus had the technical skill and knowledge to take part in their debates? Or did they hope to lead him down the path (a dangerous one, as they saw it) of calling some laws more important than others—a position which would imply a lack of respect for some provisions of the Law? In Mark's version, the question, in the course of the conversation, becomes a fundamental one of moral principles. But Matthew, who was more familiar than Mark with the rules of Palestinian scholarship, reports Jesus' reply in a form that would
40 have been regarded as technically correct. '**Everything in the Law and the prophets hangs on these two commandments**' implies that Jesus understood the question as an academic one and answered it in the same terms. The words could not be construed as emphasizing some parts of the Law at the expense of others; they merely stated that all the rest of the Law (and indeed the regulative utterances of the prophets) could be deduced from these two commandments. In saying this, Jesus was making precisely the kind of judgement his opponents made themselves; and the scene contri-

butes to Matthew's careful portrait of Jesus as a perfectly correct (even though sometimes startlingly original) interpreter of the Law.

Jesus then addressed the people and his disciples. The discourse which 23. 1 follows consists of a sustained attack on **the doctors of the law and the** 2 **Pharisees.** In the time of Jesus, these two groups were by no means identical. The **doctors of the law** (the "scribes" of older versions) were a professional class, who underwent a formal and exacting training in the interpretation of the Law of Moses, and were then qualified to undertake the education of others, to sit as justices in the law-courts, and to give their ruling on questions of law and conduct. For these services they received no payment, and most of them followed another profession at the same time; but since the Law of Moses was determinative in Jewish society for both religious and civil matters, their learning gave them considerable authority, and they were beginning to displace the old landed aristocracy of the Jewish nation as the most influential class in society. The Pharisees, on the other hand, had no official status as such. The origin of their name is obscure, but their emergence as a distinctive party can be dated to the time of the Maccabean revolution (second century B.C.), when, under the name of "Hasideans", they were "volunteers in the cause of the Law" (1 Maccabees 2.42), and became the most devoted and intransigent defenders of the traditional Jewish way of life against Hellenistic influences. Their successors, the Pharisees of Jesus' day, were thus not so much a professional class as a school of thought. Their original concern to preserve the ancestral Law uncontaminated by foreign influences had developed into a distinctive approach to the Law itself. They found in Scripture not only a code of law sufficient for the civil and religious ordering of the community, but a detailed and comprehensive system of commandments which (given their own subtle methods of interpretation) could be shown to govern every aspect of an individual's life. To demonstrate this, these men formed themselves into fellowships whose members were committed to carrying out every detail of the law according to its distinctive Pharisaic interpretation, and to keeping themselves ritually "pure" by shunning the society of all non-Pharisees. These fellowships did not consist only of scholars; indeed the majority of their members were laymen. But they formed an increasingly important and exclusive element in Jewish society, and both in their lives and in their teaching the Pharisees treated Scripture with a seriousness and a determined obedience which far exceeded that of society as a whole.

The natural way for Pharisaism to extend its influence was through the administration of justice and through education; and in fact in the time of Jesus many of the doctors of the law belonged to the Pharisees' fellowships. Nevertheless the two groups remained distinct: the doctors of the law were qualified professionals, the Pharisees were exponents of an unofficial idea;

and not all the lawyers were Pharisees. Consequently, though both had failings which came under sharp criticism from Jesus, these failings were not necessarily the same in each case. The lawyers, though required to be professionally competent in the Law, were not thereby committed to make their lives morally superior to other people's, and as a class they may often have deserved the charge of oppressing others while keeping on the right side of the law themselves. The Pharisees, on the other hand, aimed at a very high standard of moral conduct, and strove to bring their lives into conformity with a detailed and comprehensive interpretation of the Law. Their distinctive failing was that of allowing an elaborate system of outward legal observances to obscure the original humanitarian basis of the Law and to lead them into an exclusiveness which ignored the real needs of their fellowmen. It was for this reason that Jesus so often called them 'hypocrites'.

Why then in this chapter of Matthew (as often in Luke, though not in Mark or John) are the two classes grouped together as the object of Jesus' attacks? Some of the charges brought against them fit the lawyers, some the Pharisees, but not all fit both. Moreover, Luke's gospel (especially 11.37–52) makes a distinction between those of Jesus' criticisms which were aimed at the lawyers and those which were aimed at the Pharisees. The reason may be simply some confusion in the tradition. But it must also be remembered that by the time Matthew's gospel came to be written, towards the end of the first century, conditions in Palestine were no longer what they had been in the days of Jesus. Jerusalem had fallen; and in the dispersed and disorganized Jewish population authority and influence had passed to a "school" of learned men which had recently been founded at Jamnia, on the coastal plain west of Jerusalem. These men were Pharisees; and from then on there ceased to be any real distinction between them and the lawyers; for, in their efforts to consolidate and codify the traditions and observances of the old Jewish nation, the Pharisees gained complete control over the administration of justice and education. The Judaism with which Christianity was confronted when Matthew wrote his gospel was therefore becoming increasingly Pharisaic; and we can probably overhear, in these attacks of Jesus which Matthew records against **the doctors of the law and the Pharisees**, something of the polemic which was being carried on by Christians against the leaders of neighbouring synagogues.

2   **'The doctors of the law and the Pharisees sit in the chair of Moses'.** This may not be pure metaphor. An imposing stone seat has been found in the ruins of several ancient synagogues, placed in the centre of the rear wall facing the congregation. This may have been called **the chair of Moses**. But in any case the name describes the function of him who sits there. Moses both promulgated the law and acted as judge. His successors were those who interpreted the law and gave judgement on transgressions of it. Christians, as much in Jewish as in Gentile communities, were to be law-abiding: **'do**

what they tell you'. But these professional judges were not to be regarded as models of behaviour: their knowledge of the intricacies of the law enabled them to discover exemptions and saving clauses which greatly eased the burden of keeping it personally, and so it could be said of them that 'they say one thing and do another.' The law, to the ordinary layman, was a burden, and could be made oppressive by judges who elaborated its application but had the skill to circumvent it themselves. 3

'Whatever they do is done for show.' This refers to a custom that was widespread among pious Jews. The two passages referred to in the NEB footnote (Deuteronomy 6.8–9 and Exodus 13.9) were commonly interpreted as instructions to wear short texts from the Law bound on to forehead or wrist, and many Jews in fact carried such texts on their persons in little leather boxes. These boxes looked, of course, very similar to the amulets or charms carried by those who believed in magic, and when, in Matthew, they are called **phylacteries** (which means "charms"), this looks like a deliberately derogatory description of them. There appears, in any case, to have been a practice of carrying especially **broad** and ostentatious ones, and of wearing especially **large tassels** on one's robes (for all Jews, following Deuteronomy 22.12, wore distinctive tassels at the corners of their outer garment): and these affectations, along with a desire for **places of honour** and for public respect (which is singled out also in Mark's gospel, 12.38–9), were characteristic of a profession that was becoming increasingly conscious of its influence, and offering increasingly attractive rewards to the vain and the ambitious. 5 6

'You must not be called "rabbi"'. "Rabbi" became a technical title for an ordained doctor of the law in the period after the fall of Jersualem (A.D. 70) when authority in religious matters was concentrated in the school of Jamnia. In the time of Jesus it was simply a term of respect, given spontaneously to distinguished teachers. While the disciples had Jesus, their "master", with them, it is unlikely that anyone would have thought of addressing them as "rabbi"; but later, when the leaders of the Christian community began to exercise authority in a way somewhat similar to the leaders of the local synagogues, there may have been a tendency to follow the Jews in introducing the technical title, "rabbi". But the Christian community, if it were to remain faithful to Jesus' teaching, must be in important respects distinct from the Jewish community, and must eschew such titles. (A slightly different point seems to underlie the saying, '**Do not call any man on earth "father"**'. This time it is not an injunction to the disciples to avoid such titles themselves, but a warning to dissociate themselves from a particular Jewish doctrine. When the Jewish people talked about their "fathers", they meant the patriarchs (and, in more recent times, distinguished rabbis). They held that the virtues of these men laid up a kind of treasury of merit for the nation in the eyes of God. This saying seems to 8 9 be an attack on the whole conception; compare the treatment of the characteristic Jewish claim, 'We have Abraham for our father', 3.9; John 8.33.)

10 'Nor must you be called "teacher"'. The Greek word here is an unusual one: perhaps it was a title being tried out in the church when Matthew wrote, perhaps it was simply the Greek equivalent of "rabbi". But it came under the same condemnation: Christians (for this saying can hardly have been spoken in its present form by Jesus, who never referred to himself without explanation as "the Messiah") have one Teacher, the Messiah. Only one principle could properly obtain in the church, one which Jesus

11 laid down on several different occasions (20.26; Mark 9.35); 'the greatest among you must be your servant'. And this in turn depended on a principle of God's dealings with men which had already found expression

12 in the Old Testament (Proverbs 29.23; Job 22.29 etc.): 'whoever exalts himself will be humbled'.

13 'Alas, alas for you'. Seven of these "woes" follow, still aimed indiscriminately at the lawyers and Pharisees, and perhaps again influenced by the strained relations existing in Matthew's time between the church and the new leaders of Judaism. 'You shut the door of the kingdom of Heaven in men's faces'. Jesus himself proclaimed the coming of the kingdom, and his opponents could hardly keep people away from it; but later, when the Christian community was thought of as an (at least partial) realization of God's kingdom on earth, it was a cause of deep concern to Christians that the Jews not only refused to join, but stopped others from joining. Moreover, some sections of Judaism believed in vigorous proselytizing, and this often happened in direct competition with the Christian mission. We can probably detect the language of very strained relations when

15 one side calls the other 'fit for hell'.

16 'Blind guides'. Jesus called his opponents this more than once (15.14; Luke 6.39), and the phrase became part of the language of Christian polemic against the Jews (Romans 2.19). The point of attack here is similar to that in the Sermon on the Mount (5.33–7): no casuistry can mitigate the seriousness of oaths and vows, which are all, even if they do not seem so, sworn by the name of God—and perhaps we should supply the same conclusion as Jesus draws in the Sermon, 'you are not to swear at all'.

23 'You pay tithes of mint and dill and cummin'. This was a typical Pharisaic elaboration of the law (Deuteronomy 14.22–3) that all Israelites must pay tithes of their grain, wine and oil: the Pharisees extended this even to herbs, and although none of them would have admitted to overlooking the weightier demands of the Law, the burden of Jesus' attack on them was that this excessive attention to detail caused them to lose sight of the great general principles upon which the whole law was based. This and the following accusation must both have originally been directed specifically against the Pharisees (as indeed they are in Luke 11.39–42).

'**You clean the outside of cup and dish**'. The ritual cleansing of 25 vessels used in the worship of the temple was being extended by the Pharisees to apply even to the cups and dishes of daily household use, and in the following centuries they developed an astonishingly complicated system of rules applying to almost any household utensil. Jesus saw in this tendency (for there is no reason to doubt that this saying at least goes right back to Jesus) material for a trenchant simile: all this attention to the outside of crockery vessels was like their attention to the externals of religion. But what were they like **inside**? If they would begin there, the externals would look after themselves. The same thought continues in the next simile. '**You are** 27 **like tombs covered with whitewash**'. Jewish tombs were mostly hewn out of rock, and if they were whitewashed it was not for display but (as Luke rightly sees, 11.44) to mark the spot. Jesus was probably thinking of the conspicuous pagan tombs, built of white marble or perhaps of whitewashed stone, which were to be seen near the Greco-Roman cities of Palestine. All this exterior show made no difference to the fact that the contents of the tomb were, to the Jewish way of thinking, repugnant and ritually unclean.

Nevertheless, the Jews did raise up monuments to the memory of the great figures of their history. '**You build up the tombs of the prophets**'. 29 We know nothing of any "prophets' tombs" in the neighbourhood of Jerusalem. The so-called "Tomb of Zechariah" which still stands in the Kedron valley is Hellenistic, and was not associated with the prophet before the Christian era. But we do know that legends were growing up in this period about the lives, deaths and burial places of the Old Testament prophets; and at Hebron there were certainly famous monuments which were (and still are) reputed to be the tombs of Abraham, Isaac and Jacob, the **saints** of the remote past. But this did not alter the fact that the ancestors of Jesus' contemporaries (and this last "woe" seems to apply to the Jewish nation as a whole, rather than to the lawyers and Pharisees in particular) had taken part in the **murder of the prophets**. Only one such murder is men- 30 tioned in the Old Testament, that of a certain Zechariah (2 Chronicles 24.20–2); but Jewish legend had added five more of the great prophets to the list of national martyrs. Jesus, who was in some sense a "prophet", doubtless saw his own impending death as part of the same tradition, and these words challenge his opponents to play their appointed part in the grim drama. '**I** 34 **send you therefore prophets, sages, and teachers**'. An old theme of Scripture is adapted to the destiny of the Christian church. Just as God "sent prophets among them" (the same passage from 2 Chronicles), so Jesus is made to say '**I send**' the men who were to become the leaders of Christian communities, among whom there would be **prophets** (see above on 10.41), **sages and teachers**. Their fate would follow a pattern which filled the Old Testament from cover to cover: the death of Abel was the first murder in the book of Genesis (4.8), that of Zechariah *a* the last in 2 Chronicles, which was at that time the last of the books in the canon of Hebrew scriptures.

37 'O Jerusalem, Jerusalem'. Jerusalem was not in fact, or even in legend, the place where many of the prophets met their death; yet it was the symbolic centre of a religion which again and again had rejected the prophetic voice. Jesus, to end this discourse of condemnation, once again assumes the rôle of a prophet destined to suffer a similar fate, upbraiding the city which should have accepted his message, using the classic metaphor of the protective wings of a bird (Deuteronomy 32.11; Isaiah 31.5 etc.), and prophesy-

38 ing, as if he saw it before his eyes, the day when the great temple *b* in the midst of it would be made meaningless by the departure of God from its sanctuary and by the destruction of its magnificent buildings. It was not for Jesus to reverse this terrible destiny by compelling the inhabitants to repent. On the contrary, their very recognition of him would be delayed until such a time (perhaps at his final vindication in glory) as there rose spontaneously to

39 their lips that traditional phrase of acclamation (Psalm 118.26), "**Blessings on him who comes in the name of the Lord**".

Prophecies and warnings

24. 1 **Jesus was leaving the temple.** The setting for the discourse of *Prophecies and warnings* is as vivid and realistic as in Mark (13.1–3). The immense scale of Herod the Great's architectural achievement on the temple mount

2 evoked both the disciples' admiration and Jesus' prophecy that **not one stone will be left upon another**; and Jesus' long answer to the disciples' astonished question about this prophecy was appropriately delivered on the Mount of Olives, which commanded a magnificent view of the whole temple area. The elements of this answer are the same as in Mark's version, and Matthew has made only a few rearrangements and additions. The catastrophes and tribulations which were normal in history were to be intensified, the faithful would be put to a severe test; but these things would be no mere accidents, they would be signs that the end was about to come. The disciples' question (in Matthew) invited such an answer. They did not wish to know merely when the temple would be destroyed: they realized that such a staggering reversal of Jerusalem's present splendour must be a presage of still

[a] In 2 Chronicles 24.20 Zechariah is called "son of Jehoiada". It is only in the Book of Zechariah that the prophet (who may or may not be the same person) is called **son of Berachiah**. The confusion here may have existed in many minds in Jesus' time; it may be a mistake of Matthew's; or the words **son of Berachiah** may even be the addition of a well-meaning but misguided copyist not long after Matthew wrote.

[b] The Greek may mean, either the **temple**, or else, more generally, the place where God makes his dwelling with his people. See the footnote in NEB.

more significant events; and the only two events which they could envisage as being on the required scale were the **coming** of Jesus in glory and **the end** 3 **of the age**. They realized (with that deeper insight which Matthew, unlike the other evangelists, ascribes to the disciples) that all these things must be related; and they asked Jesus for further precision.

The reply includes conventional elements: the danger of being **misled,** 5 the intensification of warfare, **famines,** and **earthquakes.** The persecution 7 of the faithful also belonged to the picture of the bitter period before the end (which Matthew, like Mark, calls by the technical name, **the birth-pangs** 8 **of the new age**); but Matthew has already recorded sayings about this in an earlier discourse (chapter 10) and includes only brief allusions to it here; whereas more space is given to the implications of a period in which, inevitably, **lawlessness spreads.** 12

And then the end will come. The reader is disconcerted to find that it 14 does not, but that other calamities are still to be recorded which clearly belong to the time before the end. But it is a feature of the kind of literature to which this chapter belongs (of which we possess numerous Jewish examples, such as 2 Esdras in the Apocrypha, and also one Christian example, the Revelation) that the drama is not made to unfold in an orderly progression, but the description keeps turning back on itself to fill in details belonging to an earlier phase. So here: the next events predicted (whatever the precise meaning of the cryptogram from **the prophet Daniel**—see 15 below on Mark 13.14) are not those of the end at all, but of an incursion of military strength into Palestine on a scale that makes immediate flight the only sensible course; and, since mainly Jews will be affected, Matthew adds that it will be as well if it does not happen on the **Sabbath,** when all journey- 20 ing is forbidden, and fugitives will have a crisis of conscience to contend with as well as their other troubles.

The danger from impostors is made precise. The fanatics who proclaimed themselves divinely inspired leaders and attempted to lead a nationalist rising did in fact often begin by gathering a following **in the wilderness;** 26 alternatively they might form a conspiracy in an **inner room**. But the coming of the Son of Man (as the next verses make clear) will be totally different: it will be as quickly and clearly recognized by all as a corpse is spotted by 28 vultures (if this is the sense of the proverb inserted at verse 28). The language used of it is like that of the Old Testament prophets when they looked forward to the "day of the Lord": disorder among the heavenly bodies 29 (Isaiah 13.10; 34.4), **lamentation** among the peoples, a **sign** (which is 30 probably an ensign, Isaiah 11.12), a **trumpet blast** (Isaiah 27.13, Joel 2.1), 31 and the gathering of the **chosen from the four winds** (Zechariah 2.6; Deuteronomy 30.4). All these conventional features are gathered round Daniel's description of the coming of the **Son of Man** (Daniel 7.13, 14).

With the simile of the fig-tree the discourse moves (as in Mark) from 32

description to exhortation: this must be your posture in the face of all these developments, neither scepticism because of the apparent delay of the end,
36 nor agitated preoccupation with the exact day and hour (which **only the**
42 **Father** knows). The watchword (as in Mark) is '**keep awake**'.

Matthew goes on to illustrate this lesson of wakefulness with a series of parables and similes, which emphasize (at least in Matthew's presentation of them, if not in their original form) the suddenness with which the end must be expected, and the error of not taking seriously the teaching which has just
37 been given. '**As things were in Noah's days**'. The narrative in Genesis concentrates entirely upon Noah and his family. Apart from the brief statement (6.11–13) that "the earth was corrupt" and that God had "determined to make an end of all flesh", nothing is said about the behaviour of all those who were doomed to destruction. But as the Jews meditated upon this story they began to be impressed by the attitude of Noah. Even though there were no signs in advance of the coming deluge, he put such trust in the word of God that he unhesitatingly set about the immense and apparently absurd task of building a great ship on dry land. He became, in fact, one of the classic examples, along with Abraham, of those who unhesitatingly put their whole faith in God (Hebrews 11.7). If Jesus mentioned him in his teaching, one would have expected him to have drawn the same moral: When I preach to you, be like Noah, who believed the message of God, and not like those
39 others who, since they neither heard nor believed—**they knew nothing**— were consigned to destruction. But here, all the emphasis is not on Noah but
37 on the men and women of **Noah's days**, who showed by their manner of living that they had no idea of the calamity which threatened them. How different must be the lives of Christians (this seems to be the moral) who are aware of what is impending! There will be no time for last-minute repent-
41 ance. Suddenly, in the midst of daily occupations, **one will be taken** (to join the company of the elect) **the other left** (to face the Judgement).

45 The parable of **the trusty servant** may have had a somewhat different point when Jesus first told it from the simple lesson of vigilance which it is used to illustrate here. The background to it is one of the many estates in Palestine which were owned by foreign magnates and managed in their absence by stewards or agents. The **household staff**, which included all who worked on the estate, will normally have consisted of slaves, and the landlord's agent will also probably have been a slave (this was quite usual, and the Greek word translated **servant** also means "slave") since his reward was to be, not higher wages, but a position of still greater respon-
48 sibility in his master's establishment. Similarly, if he turned out to be a **bad servant** he could be punished, not just with dismissal, but with death—but at this point the details become blurred. "Cutting in pieces" was not unknown as a punishment, but seems unnecessarily brutal here (it is possible that Jesus used an Aramaic idiom "divide out to him" (his punishment)

which was subsequently misunderstood as "divide him"); and by the end of the parable the landlord seems to have become the divine Judge, and the slave's punishment the punishment which will be meted out to all **hypocrites** 51 on the Last Day. Clearly the parable, at some stage in its progress from the lips of Jesus to the written page of the gospel, has been adapted to yield teaching about the proper behaviour of Christians in view of the impending return of their Lord: all the emphasis is now on the suddenness of the master's home-coming. But the natural structure of the story, with its balanced contrast between a trust deserved and a trust betrayed, points in a different direction. Who, among Jesus' contemporaries, had been set over God's household? The Jewish leaders, the lawyers and Pharisees. Now the hour of reckoning had come, and they had been found unworthy of their trust!

'**When that day comes, the kingdom of Heaven will be like this**'. 25. 1 Another parable follows, which Matthew evidently saw as a further illustration of the same theme of watchfulness and preparedness for the last day. It ends with the same message—**keep awake then**—and the detail that the 13, 5 **bridegroom was late in coming** suggests the context in which the parable may have been used in the church. The Last Day, and the coming of Jesus, was being delayed longer than expected: those who relaxed their vigilance would be like the girls who failed to reckon with the possibility of delay, and were not ready for the moment when it came. But it can be seen at once that this interpretation of the parable is somewhat forced. If five of the girls had fallen asleep, and the other five had remained awake and ready, the moral—**keep awake then**—would have been exactly right. But in the story **they all dozed off to sleep**, and there is no suggestion that there was 5 anything wrong about doing so. The error of the five foolish girls was not that they fell asleep, but that they did not allow for the possibility of delay. Was the original point of the parable therefore to warn Jesus' followers that they must be prepared for a longer period of waiting than they thought?

We are unfortunately not in a position to fill in the background of the story with any certainty. Marriage customs vary from place to place, and from one period to another, and we possess no independent description of marriage festivities in Palestine in the first half of the first century A.D.: in particular, we hear nowhere else about a procession at night, or about attendants with lamps. On the other hand, one of the high-points of marriage festivities all over the ancient world was the moment when the bridegroom was escorted, either to the house of the bride, or (with his bride) to his own house. This was a moment for singing and dancing; and when the procession got indoors the guests would sit down to the wedding feast. In broad outline the story of the ten girls fits well enough into this pattern. The story is about **ten girls who took their lamps and went out to meet the bride-** 1 groom. [a] The lamps one usually thinks of are the small domestic oil lamps used all over the ancient world, which consist simply of a shallow container of oil and a wick fitted into a hole in one end. But it is difficult to imagine how such lamps could have been used on this occasion. For one thing, they would instantly blow out when taken out of doors; for another, they were quite inappropriate for carrying about; and thirdly, they would normally have lasted all night without being refilled. Some kind of hurricane lamps are another possibility; but the Greek word used here never (so far as we know) meant this, and anyway, being made of horn, they would have given out a very subdued and unfestive light. Far the most likely kind of lights for the girls to have used (and this is what the Greek word normally means) were torches—the only lights which could be carried by anyone running or dancing, and which were certainly the normal thing for any procession at night. But torches usually consisted of long cones of wood coated with pitch; if this was what the girls were carrying, they cannot possibly have needed oil as well. The only convincing solution which has yet been found to this mystery is a custom which has been observed in comparatively modern times in Palestine. This consists of wrapping the head of the torch with some material impregnated in olive oil. The torch will then burn for a short time, say a quarter of an hour, but will need soaking in oil again if it is to be made to blaze up suddenly or to last for a longer time. If this is what the girls were to carry, the fault of the foolish ones was not that they did not allow for the delay, but that they came at the beginning without an essential part of their equipment; and having slept during the time they might have put this right, they had no chance to make good their negligence when the critical moment came. The bridegroom went in to **the wedding** (probably the wedding feast) with the girls who had lighted his way; but he was not going to admit some more girls whom he had never seen until the moment they came to the door.

If this is the true explanation—and it cannot claim, in the present state of our knowledge, to be much more than a conjecture—then it gives a very different point to the parable. The moral which Matthew himself draws—

13 keep awake then—has already been shown not to fit the parable; and the suggestion that the original emphasis was on the unexpected delay of the bridegroom now fares no better: the fault of the foolish girls was not that they had brought too little oil, but that they had forgotten to bring any oil at all. The parable in fact falls into place beside that of the man without a wedding garment. The new life promised to believers (often described in the image of a feast) is freely offered to all—but on condition that they prepare themselves (presumably with repentance, or perhaps with good deeds). Those who take this condition lightly must expect to be turned away.

[a] The first four verses must be in the nature of an introduction, setting the scene for the story itself, which begins at verse 5, "As the bridegroom was late in coming". Otherwise, we would be left with the very improbable circumstance that the girls fell asleep out of doors.

'It is like a man going abroad'. Precisely what is like this is not said: as 14 with many parables of Jesus, the original application was not preserved, though Matthew (as we shall see) found reason to include this one in the general context of teaching about the Last Things. The parable reflects commercial conditions in Palestine. Jews were not permitted to practise usury among themselves; therefore the **man going abroad** could not simply invest his capital in someone else's business. He had to find agents whom he could trust to initiate and carry on commercial enterprises on his behalf. It was natural that he should choose **his servants** for this. These would not have been slaves (who had not sufficient rights at law to carry on a business), but salaried men whom he had been employing as agents or administrators while he lived in Palestine. Among these servants, some would have proved themselves more capable than others, and it was natural to divide up the capital, not into equal parts, but to each **according to his** 15 **capacity**: he would not risk losing a large sum by giving it as working capital to an inexperienced or incompetent agent. The sums involved were substantial, and reckoned by *talents* (the NEB has translated this **bags of gold**, which well describes the way in which such large sums of money were in fact transferred from one owner to another). A *talent* was equivalent to 6,000 standard silver coins (*denarii*), which, by the scale of values adopted in the NEB, would have been worth about £600. In the story, therefore, the capital sums involved were (very roughly) £3,000, £1,200 and £600. If the servants went bankrupt, they probably had to compensate their master out of their own pockets for up to half the capital sum. If they made a profit (and high rates of profit and interest were normal in antiquity), most of this, as well as the original capital, would be due to be repaid to their master; for the servants were still his agents, they had not been set up in business on their own. It followed that although they had to take a part of the risk for losses they could not expect to enrich themselves by their profits. Their principal reward would be the prospect of promotion in their master's employment.

So much for the setting; now for the characters. Two of them are vividly drawn, the master and the third servant. This servant, compared with the two others, was given only a small capital to work with: clearly he was not regarded as very competent. But a small capital is more difficult to trade with than a large one; he could not expect a large profit, and there was always the risk of loss. So he buried the money—this was regarded as the safest way of minding a deposit. And when he had to settle accounts with his master, he stood up to him firmly. "**I knew you to be a hard man**", that is, one who 24 expected the maximum return on his money (and so would leave little or nothing of any profit to his servants), and who made as small an outlay as possible (by way of "sowing" or "scattering" his money for the benefit of his agents or his debtors) and pressed for the highest possible rate of return.

The servant feared the risk of losing the capital more than that of forfeiting his own exiguous share of any possible profit. We see him, not only as a timid and incompetent businessman, but as a servant with a sense of grievance towards his master.

The description of the master is equally vivid. Far from denying the servant's description of him, he proceeds to substantiate it. **"You ought to have put my money on deposit"**. In modern terms this makes good sense: a deposit account at a bank is a safe and painless way of securing a small increase of capital. But in antiquity one did not normally deposit money for interest, but only for safety. It is possible that a more literal translation gives a better sense: "you should have given my coins to the money-changers". Gold and silver coins were minted outside Palestine, and money-changers charged a small commission for exchanging them for the local bronze coinage. The suggestion seems to be that the servant with a substantial capital of such coins could at least have gone into nominal partnership with a money-changer and secured some interest that way. At any rate the master, true to character, could not accept the servant's point that, with a small capital, it is better to be safe than sorry.

'Take the bag of gold from him, and give it to the one with the ten bags'. This was no punishment: he was due to pay back the capital in any case; and it was only logical for the master to add it to the capital of the servant who had shown himself the most efficient businessman. But, as we read the parable in Matthew, this comparatively trivial detail becomes the most important point in the story. For it appears to be a perfect illustration of a saying of Jesus that is recorded also (though without any particular context) in Mark's gospel: **'the man who has will always be given more . . . and the man who has not will forfeit even what he has'**. Precisely what Jesus originally meant by this saying (which was probably a proverb drawn from the market—see below on Mark 4.25) we do not know. But Matthew seems to have seen in it a commentary on the rewarding of a man's spiritual resources at the Last Judgement; for he goes on to consign the **useless servant** to hell (for which **the place of wailing and grinding of teeth** is his favourite expression), and we are left in little doubt that, as he tells the story, the return of the master has turned into a symbol of Christ's final Coming, and that the reward of the "good" servants has been deliberately spiritualized, so that they are not merely given a position of greater responsibility on earth, but are invited to share their **master's delight**— that is (as the striking Greek phrase suggests), to enter into the joy of the heavenly kingdom. In Matthew's hands, if not before, the parable has become an allegory of the Last Judgement.

Was this the original meaning? It seems hardly likely that Jesus would have given the main figure in the parable the character of a hard and unscrupulous businessman if he had intended him to stand for the divine Judge himself! The parable is probably best understood alongside that of the 'trusty servant' (24.45–51). The theme, again, is trust. Even an extortionate capitalist could justly blame an agent who did nothing at all with the capital entrusted to him. And what had Jesus' opponents done with the immense capital of their ancestral religion which had been entrusted to them?

The discourse ends with a grand tableau of the Last Judgement, built up out of a number of separate images. **When the Son of Man comes in his** 31 **glory** is the language of Daniel's prophecy (7.13–15) describing the solemn moment of divine judgement, when **all the nations** would become subject 32 to the righteous Son of Man and the elect whom he represented. **As a shepherd separates the sheep from the goats** is a simile of judgement as old as Ezekiel (34.17): the Palestinian shepherd would pasture his flocks of sheep and goats together, but at some stage he would **separate** the one from the other; the white sheep were a natural symbol for the pure apparel of the righteous, the black goats for the dark deeds of the wicked. And finally, a **king** on his throne was one of the commonest of images for the God of 34 justice who would one day bring all men to account for the "acts of kindness" [a] which they had done or failed to do. All these elements, including even the dialogue between the king and those who appear before him, are conventional enough. But the way these elements are combined and exploited is unique and arresting. That Jesus was himself the Son of Man who would "come in glory" has already been intimated several times in the gospel, and it followed from the title itself, and from the destiny traditionally connected with it, that he would play an important part in the Last Judgement. But here the thought is taken a step further—he becomes the Judge himself, the King who gives sentence—though still in some way subordinate to God the Father ("**You have my Father's blessing**"). This represents a greater 34 concentration of attributes in the person of the Son than appears anywhere else in the gospels, and if these are to be taken literally, rather than as a poetic accumulation of images, they confront the interpreter with difficult problems about the true nature and status of Christ. But the real originality of the passage, as well as its beauty and symmetry, lies in the dialogue. That men would be richly rewarded for their acts of kindness was taken for granted by Jesus' contemporaries; and that these acts (rather than the fact of belonging to the Jewish race, or the fact of having faithfully observed the Law) would serve as the principal basis of distinction between the blest and the damned was a point of view that many would have been prepared to accept. But the reason given here must have seemed revolutionary: it was not just that acts of this kind are specially meritorious, but that in doing them to certain people one is doing them to Jesus himself. Who are these people in whom lurks the Son of Man? It is tempting to answer, All who are in need.

[a] See below on Mark 14.3–9. The only act listed here which does not occur in similar Jewish lists is visiting prisoners.

4-2

40 But this is not what is said here. "Anything you did for one of my brothers here, however humble, you did for me". "Brothers", in this gospel (and indeed throughout the New Testament) is almost a technical name for Christians; moreover, Jesus called his "brothers", not mankind in general, but those who, with him, have God as their father. In short, the reward

46 of **eternal life** is promised here to those who show kindness to Christians, for it is in the Christian community that Jesus lives on, bringing men face to face with the ultimate issues of life and death, reward and condemnation, just as he did when he preached and worked on earth.

The final conflict

From this point on Matthew follows the account in Mark very closely, and it will be sufficient to notice a few details which he has changed or added.

26. 2 **'You know that in two days' time it will be Passover'**: This is exactly the same chronology as in Mark, but here, in Jesus' own mouth, the dating takes on deeper meaning: Jesus knows in advance that this particular Passover will be unique as being the exact moment when the **Son of Man is to be handed over for crucifixion**—and the stage is set for this "handing

3 over" at a meeting, which only Matthew mentions, **in the palace of the High Priest, Caiaphas** (whom we know to have held this office from A.D. 18 to 36). Already there is conflict: Jesus is prophesying his crucifixion during the Passover, while his enemies are endeavouring to avoid exactly

5 this. **'It must not be during the festival,'** they said.

6 **Jesus was at Bethany.** Compared with Mark's account (14.3–9), Matthew's is less startling. Instead of breaking the neck of the bottle and emptying the

7 entire contents over Jesus' head, the woman merely **began to pour it,** and the value of the ointment is not the very large figure of thirty pounds (which

9 Mark gives) but merely **a good sum.** Any reader who still found in Mark's version of the story, despite its symbolic meaning, an unnecessarily wasteful gesture, would been considerably less shocked when reading Matthew, where almsgiving and this particular act of charity are kept more in proportion with each other.

14 **Then one of the Twelve.** Matthew alone gives the details of the bargain made between Judas and the chief priests. How did he know the exact figure? Possibly some Christian was able to find it out afterwards, and passed on the information; but possibly Matthew inferred it from a passage of the Old Testament which he regarded as a prophecy of the events he was recording. Zechariah 11.12 runs, "they weighed out as my wages thirty

pieces of silver". In Zechariah's time these silver pieces were doubtless shekels; in the time of Jesus the equivalent was the tetradrachm, which was the largest silver coin in currency, and which had been minted all over the Greek-speaking world since the time of Alexander the Great. The sum of money would therefore amount to 120 Roman *denarii*, or (according to the scale adopted by the NEB) twelve English pounds. There is slight doubt whether the verb in the Greek means that the chief priests paid Judas at once ("weighing out" the coins in case any should be under weight) or 16 merely promised to pay (as Mark has it). But the rendering adopted in the main text comes closer to the meaning in Zechariah and is not improbable in itself.

On the first day of Unleavened Bread. Strictly speaking this is 17 inaccurate: it was the afternoon (as Mark makes clear) preceding the evening which, by Jewish reckoning, began the new day of 15th Nisan, the first day of Unleavened Bread. But a non-Palestinian reader, counting the days as we do from midnight to midnight, would not have been misled. The miraculous details in Mark's account of the finding of a room are omitted by Matthew, who evidently assumed that the matter was prearranged. This was Jesus' 'appointed time', the Passover which would be the signal for his 18 crucifixion.

Matthew's additions to Mark's account of the supper (14.17–25) are very 20-9 small. The traitor is explicitly identified as Judas—though perhaps not so clearly and unambiguously that anyone but Jesus and Judas himself would have realized what was going to happen. It is not said when Judas left the company to carry out his plot; but this point (i.e. after verse 25) is the most likely one; and if the traitor was then out of the room, the slightly greater emphasis in this account (compared with Mark's) on the privileged circle of the disciples (**'Drink from it, all of you'** . . . **'when I drink it new with** 27, 29 **you'**) is understandable. There is one further addition of significance: the blood is shed **for the forgiveness of sins.** To the image of the old **covenant,** 28 sealed by the blood of a sacrifice, is added that of the "new covenant", foreseen by Jeremiah (31.31–4), which would be brought into effect by God's forgiveness of his people's sins.

Jesus then came with his disciples to a place called Gethsemane. 36 This episode is told almost exactly as in Mark (14.32–42): Matthew has merely modified some of Mark's more forcible expressions and clarified a few obscurities—adding, however, a fresh one. Jesus' reply to Judas, **'Friend,** 50 **do what you are here to do'** is a puzzling piece of Greek. Jesus certainly returned Judas' greeting, but in just what tone of voice we cannot tell (see the footnote in NEB). Matthew makes one significant addition to the narrative. The scuffle which led to the High Priest's servant losing an ear is only mentioned in passing by Mark, but in Matthew it leads to two sayings

52 of Jesus. The first, 'All who take the sword die by the sword', sounds like a proverb—possibly, like another proverb used by Jesus, originating in a reaction against the violent tactics of fanatical rebels against the Roman régime (see below on Mark 9.40): Jesus made a point of dissociating himself from any movement of that kind. The second raises the conflict to a different level. As Luke puts it, this moment was 'the hour when darkness reigns', which is not just a metaphor, but a clear indication of the way the crisis presented itself to the gospel writers (and doubtless to Jesus). The contest was not merely between Jesus and the secular powers. Behind this was raging a supernatural battle against Satan and all the evil powers. We now know from the Dead Sea Scrolls how this battle was imagined in the time of Jesus: huge detachments of angels arrayed in military order were lined up against each other in readiness for the final conflict. The discipline and organization of the Roman occupying army were projected by these writers into the scene 53 of heavenly warfare; hence Jesus' somewhat surprising expression, 'twelve legions of angels'.

57 **Jesus was led off under arrest to the house of Caiaphas the High Priest.** Matthew, unlike Luke and John, follows exactly the same order of events as Mark: immediately after Jesus' arrest there was a formal session of the Sanhedrin, not in its usual meeting place, but in the house of Caiaphas, 59 who was probably president of the court. The court consisted of other **chief** 57 **priests, the lawyers** (who were mainly Pharisees) and **elders** (who were probably influential and aristocratic laymen). There was nothing unusual in members of the court themselves presenting evidence against the accused. But for any charge to be substantiated, it was necessary for two witnesses independently to give consistent evidence, and this seems to have been the 61 court's first difficulty. **Finally two men alleged.** It seems that valid evidence was obtained on only one point, a saying of Jesus which in fact John's gospel records in another context (2.14). Matthew's version of the saying is a little milder than Mark's: not, 'I will pull down the temple', but '**I can pull down the temple**'—a form which will have troubled subsequent Christians less, since it did not raise the question (as Mark's perhaps more original version does) of when and how this promise was fulfilled. Nevertheless, the allegation was serious. "Prophesying against the temple" had once nearly cost Jeremiah his life (Jeremiah 26) and was the kind of thing which, if uttered in the precincts of the temple, could doubtless be regarded as blasphemy. Here, *prima facie*, was damning evidence; and when Jesus refused to speak a word in his own defence, a case seemed to have been made out. The critical point which proceedings had reached is marked by 62 the fact that **the High Priest rose**; but before passing judgement he had one further question to put which would explain and confirm the evidence so far given. It was generally expected that when the Messiah came one of

the marks of his reign would be a period of new holiness and new splendour in the temple in Jerusalem. Could it be that Jesus' saying was not just blasphemous arrogance, but was a sign that he believed himself to be the Messiah? If so, this would by no means lessen his guilt, since it must have seemed obvious to the court that their silent prisoner could not possibly be the glorious deliverer expected by the whole Jewish people; but it would make Jesus' saying about the temple intelligible and give the judges a more substantial case to pronounce on. Jesus was therefore put on oath to answer the question, '**Are you the Messiah, the Son of God?**' (where **Son of** 63 **God** would be understood, not in the deep sense propounded by the early church, but simply as a successor to the long line of Old Testament figures who, by virtue of their divine commission, were called Sons of God).

Jesus' reply to the specific question seems, as usual, to have been ambiguous: to have accepted without qualification the title of Messiah would perhaps have been to accept too many of the secular and superficial ideas which his contemporaries attached to it. But, by means of allusions to two Old Testament passages (Daniel 7.13; Psalm 110.1) which described a personage honoured and glorified by God, Jesus affirmed that at least one of the implications of the title was true of himself. '**From now on**'—not in 64 some theoretical future, but by an immediate reversal of fortune—Jesus would be seen to be vindicated and given a unique status **at the right hand of God**. Matthew doubtless saw this claim as having been fulfilled by the resurrection and ascension of Jesus: the church did in fact come to know and experience its Lord as glorified and vindicated. But to the judges such a claim seemed merely to aggravate the original blasphemy. '**He is guilty,**' 66 **they answered**; '**he should die.**'

But, under the Roman administration, the Jewish court had apparently lost the power to carry out the death penalty, and further measures were necessary to secure Jesus' execution. Meanwhile, in a scene of brutality, Jesus' claim to be Messiah was put to the test. The Messiah would have the gift of prophecy—for instance, he would know who people were without being told. It was a fair test: '**Now, Messiah, if you are a prophet, tell** 68 **us who hit you**'. But Jesus offered no such spectacular confirmation of the possibility that he was the Messiah.

Meanwhile Peter was sitting outside. Here Matthew has rearranged 69 Mark's narrative very little, omitting only the curious feature of two separate cock-crows. The story of Peter's denial occurs in all the gospels: see below on Mark 15. 66–72.

When morning came. Does Matthew mean to record a second formal 27. 1 session of the Sanhedrin? A meeting in the morning would certainly harmonize better with the accounts in Luke and John, but after the proceedings which Matthew had just described, taking place during the night and ending with a verdict and a sentence, a further session seems superfluous. All that remained to be done was **to plan the death of Jesus**—in the sense that, since the court was not competent to carry out its own sentence, it was necessary to have Jesus sentenced also by the Roman governor. Deciding on their tactics need not have taken the judges very long, nor required another formal session; in any case it was necessary for them to hand Jesus over to

2 **Pilate, the Roman Governor,** as early as possible, so as to catch him when he would be available.

At this point Matthew inserts an episode which is recorded in none of the other gospels (though it is mentioned in Acts 1.18–19): the death of Judas.

3 It comes in a little awkwardly, for **the chief priests and elders** are at this moment at Caiaphas' house, whereas Judas' gesture of returning the money

5 presupposes that he is **in the temple**—that is to say, at least in one of those courtyards of the temple where there were arrangements for receiving money (see below on Mark 12.41–4). Matthew, in fact, is adding an excursus on the working-out of Judas' destiny, without too much concern for its connection with the main narrative (a modern writer would probably use a footnote for the purpose). It is clear that the interest of the early Christians was not merely biographical. There were other reasons for the tradition being preserved. One was that the Christian community in Jerusalem came to associate a particular spot with Judas' sinister death. They named it, in Aramaic,

8 Akeldama (Acts 1.19), which meant **'Blood Acre'**; but to everyone else it

7 was known as **the Potter's Field.** The site of it is fairly certain. The "Potter's Gate" of Jerusalem lay at the extreme south-east corner of the city, at the mouth of the ill-famed valley of Gehinnom. Nearby were tombs cut into the rock: the whole area, with its smoking industries, its sinister historical associations, and the ritual uncleanness which belonged to any cemetery, was a fit place to bear the memory of the death of the traitor. Precisely what the connection was between Judas and this place was perhaps (by the time the gospel was written) no longer remembered, and it was necessary to work back from the name the Christians themselves had given it. A quite different explanation is given in Acts (1.18–19); here, an inference is drawn which at least shows Matthew's expert knowledge. The area belonged to the temple authorities and was used **as a burial-place for foreigners** (for whom, of course, the associations of the place were less sinister—in later centuries it became an honoured burial-place for Christian pilgrims). How did they acquire it? What better explanation than that they used Judas' money which, being blood-money, could not be put into **the**

6 **temple fund?** These details are quite correct. Deuteronomy 23.18 runs: "You shall not bring the hire of a harlot or the wages of a sodomite into the house of the Lord your God". *A fortiori*, blood-money could not be put into **the temple fund** (literally *Corban*, another technical term).

But there was also a more fundamental reason for this interest in the circumstances of Judas' death. His treachery did not present itself to the first Christians as something demanding a psychological explanation: it was intended and destined by God. But things which had long been prepared in the purposes of God might be expected to be alluded to in prophecy. Sure enough, Zechariah 11.12–13 runs as follows:

> "They weighed out my wages, thirty pieces of silver. The Lord said to me, Throw it back into the treasury. I took the thirty pieces of silver— that noble sum at which I was valued and rejected by them—and threw them into the house of the Lord, into the treasury."

This text was always somewhat obscure and widely different versions of it exist. Moreover, it had a curious variant. Only certain versions gave "throw it into the treasury"; the original Hebrew appears to mean, "cast it to the potter". It looks as if Matthew knew both these interpretations and he was also able to exploit the fact that, when translated into Greek, the word meaning "I took" was identical with the word meaning "they took". Consequently, it only needed a little skilful manipulation of the original (which scholars in his time took very much for granted) to yield an impressive prophecy of the events of Judas' suicide. Only one problem remains: why does Matthew say **Jeremiah** instead of Zechariah? It is true that there were two well-known 9 passages of Jeremiah in which the prophet "went to the house of the potter" (18.3) and "bought a field" (29.9); but even if these lay at the back of Matthew's mind, it was Zechariah, not Jeremiah, that he was quoting. The most likely answer is that this was simply a mistake. It is in any case likely that early Christian writers, when quoting from the Old Testament, used, not a complete copy, but a collection of short prophecies which the church had found particularly relevant to the proclamation and defence of the Christian faith; and it is quite possible that these short passages were not always correctly arranged under their respective authors (for another example, see below on Mark 1.2–3).

Jesus was now brought before the Governor. After this digression, 11 Matthew returns to the hearing before Pilate, and his account closely follows that of Mark, though it presupposes on the part of his readers less familiarity with the original circumstances than Mark's does. Mark's readers were evidently expected to have heard of Barabbas; but here he is introduced with the slightly more precise name, **Jesus Bar-Abbas,** [a] and the scene is 16 given a new element of drama by the confrontation of two criminals called Jesus—**Jesus Bar-Abbas, or Jesus called Messiah.** Matthew has two new 17 details to add to the narrative. One is the intervention of Pilate's wife. 19

[a] That Barabbas had the first name **Jesus** is the evidence of a number of early manuscripts, and also of the third-century writer Origen. It would be more understandable that the piety of later generations suppressed a second Jesus than that their fantasy invented one, and the NEB translators have therefore adopted this reading. Bar-Abbas (if that is the correct division of the syllables) is not an uncommon name. It means "father's son".

Roman provincial governors had recently begun to take their wives with them when on foreign service. Her dream is very much the kind of portent which ancient historians often recorded before a battle or a crisis. The

24 other detail is Pilate's gesture of washing his hands **in full view of the people.** The gesture would be intelligible in any culture, but it was also a classical biblical way of expressing innocence (Deuteronomy 21.6; Psalm 73.13). By recording it, Matthew emphatically attaches the blame for what followed to the Jewish people as a whole.

27 **Pilate's soldiers then took Jesus into the Governor's headquarters.** Matthew is still following Mark very closely—and the fact that he uses the

32 same rather uncommon word (said to be of Persian origin) for **pressed him into service** is one of the detailed pieces of evidence which show that he must have had a copy of Mark's gospel in front of him. [a] He leaves out the names of Simon of Cyrene's sons (which Mark gives as Alexander and Rufus), since these men, who must have been known to the Christians who first read Mark's gospel, were presumably of no interest to Matthew's readers. At the same time he adds or alters certain details. When the soldiers

28 mocked Jesus, they **dressed him in a scarlet mantle**—not the royal purple of Mark's version, but the Roman Emperor's colour: there may be a touch of historical precision here, for it would have been difficult for the soldiers to procure purple, but they could perhaps have borrowed the scarlet mantle of one of the official attendants of Pilate (who was the Emperor's

34 representative). It is not clear why Matthew substitutes **wine mixed with gall** for Mark's 'drugged wine': possibly a recollection of Psalm 69.21 (which, in the Greek version, contains the words "for my food they gave me gall") influenced him. In any case, the point is the same. The drink was a narcotic, such as was normally provided by the Jews for prisoners who were about to be executed. To the description of the mockery to which Jesus was

39-40 subjected, Matthew adds a further touch, drawn again from the repertory of Old Testament poetry describing innocent suffering. The closest parallel is Psalm 22.8 (the psalm which provides the most impressive precedent for and commentary on the details of Jesus' crucifixion):

> " 'He committed his cause to the Lord; let him deliver him,
> let him rescue him, for he holds him dear.' "

But there is another passage which must also have been in Matthew's mind. The first chapters of the Wisdom of Solomon are concerned precisely with the problem of the righteous sufferer, and in chapter 2 the mockery of the

[a] For many centuries it was believed that the dependence is the other way round, and that Mark is simply an abridged edition of Matthew; hence the comparative neglect of Mark's gospel until recent times. But it is now generally thought that the differences between the two gospels are easier to explain on the hypothesis that Mark's gospel was written first. See the introductory note to THE GOSPEL, p. 14.

unrighteous is described. The following phrases (from verses 13–18) will show how closely Matthew's account conforms to what had already become a classical model in Jewish literature: "He styles himself 'the son of the Lord' . . . he boasts that God is his father . . . let us test the truth of his words . . . for if the just man is God's son, God will stretch out a hand to him and save him."

Matthew diverges significantly from Mark's account only when it comes to the moment of Jesus' death. At this point (15.38) Mark mentions one event which he must have regarded as supernatural: the tearing of the curtain of the temple. In this Mark is probably making use of an ancient and somewhat oriental convention: the reference to miraculous events accompanying a person's death is an element of commentary on the significance of the moment rather than of meticulous historical reporting. Matthew takes this somewhat further, and thereby starts a trend which produces a mass of increasingly improbable miracles in the accounts of the later apocryphal gospels. The symbolism may have in fact begun with the **curtain of the** 51 **temple** itself. This huge piece of tapestry was a famous sight. It was hung in front of the doors of the main temple building, and could be seen even by non-Jews when they looked through the gateway of the Court of the Israelites towards the temple entrance. Embroidered upon it was the firmament of heaven. The most obvious symbolism in the tearing of this curtain **from top to bottom** was the end of the importance of the temple in religious life and the removal of the barrier which had hitherto excluded non-Jews from the worship of the true God. But a further meaning may have been suggested by the picture woven upon it. Not the curtain only, but the heavens themselves, were rent asunder (one of the traditional signs of the Day of the Lord); and this was answered on earth by an **earthquake.** To this extent Matthew's 52 miracle-commentary on the moment of Jesus' death is of a piece. That **the graves opened** is more strange; but resurrection was also an element of the Day of the Lord, even though, as Matthew admits, the time for such a miracle was really **after his resurrection.** 53

'**Truly this man was a son of God**'. This is a total reversal of the 54 mockery of a few minutes earlier. At the very moment of Jesus' death, God had acted to vindicate his righteous servant, and even the foreigners standing by—**the centurion and his men**—were moved to recognize something divine in Jesus. In Mark it is Jesus' bearing at his death which impresses the centurion; here it is the accompanying portents which overwhelm the whole group of soldiers. Their confession was valid: it was as "Son of God" that the church soon began to worship Jesus. But if we are to ask what the phrase could have meant in the mouths of the soldiers, the answer, in Matthew, is quite clear: Jesus was one of those so-called "sons of God" who would work miracles and whose death would appropriately be marked by an earthquake.

55 **A number of women were also present.** Matthew mentions the same
56 names as Mark, except that he seems to identify Mark's Salome with **the
mother of the sons of Zebedee.** But only two of them remain to witness
the burial, and only two return on Sunday morning to the tomb, Mary of
Magdala and the other Mary (28.1). Joseph of Arimathaea, too, has undergone
a significant change at Matthew's hands. In Mark, he is presented as a devout
and influential Jew, whose main motive in undertaking the burial of Jesus
was probably that of saving the city and its surrounding country from the
defilement of an unburied corpse. But in Matthew his motive is quite
57 different: he is a man who **had himself become a disciple of Jesus** (which
might have been difficult if, as Mark says, he was a member of the Sanhedrin: Matthew omits this detail), and his action is that much more devoted
60 in that he lays Jesus **in his own unused tomb.** What in Mark was a hasty
burial perfunctorily performed by a stranger has become in Matthew a work
of charity undertaken by an influential disciple.

62   **Next day, the morning after that Friday.** Matthew alone reports this
episode, which accounts for the presence (in his account) of soldiers at the
tomb, and so makes the events of Sunday morning still more miraculous.
It is a little surprising to find the Jewish authorities taking action of this kind
on the Sabbath, and in any case one would have thought that they should
have taken the precaution as soon as Jesus was buried. However, Pilate
65 provided **a guard** (Matthew uses the Latin word *custodia*, suggesting a
contingent from the Roman army, not from the Jewish temple police), and
the Jews, as an additional precaution, placed some kind of seal on the stone
so that any unauthorized opening could be detected.

28. 1 **The Sabbath was over.** The scene is recognizably the same as that in
Mark, but is told with less detail and a greater emphasis on the supernatural.
2 **The earthquake,** the description of **the angel of the Lord,** and the
paralysed fear of the guards, are all features that belong less to a factual
narrative of the discovery that the tomb was empty than to an imaginative
description of a supernatural experience. Such importance as the empty tomb
itself may have had is still further played down when the vision of the angel
is immediately followed by an encounter with the risen Jesus. This brings
the women's experience into line with that of the church as a whole. It was
not the empty tomb, but the appearances of Jesus himself, which gave them
9 confidence to proclaim the resurrection. The women were the first to
worship him in his risen state. **Clasped his feet, falling prostrate before
him,** are signs of the deepest reverence.

11-15   Matthew has his own explanation to offer (different from Mark's) of why
the discovery that Jesus' tomb was empty was not immediately seized upon
and proclaimed by the church: a counter-story was deliberately put about
by the Jews; and since the Christian version of the matter rested only on the

testimony of two women (whose evidence would not have been admitted in a Jewish court), this could presumably never have had much force in disputes (such as we can frequently overhear in Matthew's gospel) between the Christian church and its Jewish opponents. Matthew simply reports the two versions of the facts and leaves the reader to decide between them.

The eleven disciples made their way to Galilee. Matthew, like Mark, 16 has faithfully recorded (26.32) the somewhat puzzling statement of Jesus that after the resurrection he would 'go on before' his disciples to Galilee. The promise has just been repeated by the angel at the tomb (28.7) and by the risen Jesus himself (28.10); and Matthew ends his gospel by recounting its fulfilment. The mention of **the eleven disciples** sounds deliberately precise. The 'twelve' were last mentioned at the Passover supper (26.20). Since then Judas had defected and killed himself; but although Peter had denied Jesus, and the rest had deserted him, these eleven were still evidently (at least to Matthew's way of thinking, if not in historical fact) the only appropriate group to receive the final revelation of Jesus' authority and commission. Matthew reports that they **made their way to Galilee.** This contradicts Luke's account, according to which all Jesus' last appearances took place in or near Jerusalem. But it is possible that Matthew was more interested in the symbolic significance of the setting than in the geographical spot where the vision was actually seen. In his gospel, Matthew has said nothing of a **mountain where Jesus had told them to meet him:** this phrase does 16 not help us to locate the scene. On the other hand, the greatest moments of Jesus' self-revelation, whether of his true nature (the Transfiguration) or of his moral demands (the Sermon on the Mount), were conceived of as taking place on a mountain, and just as the definitive revelation of God in the Old Testament took place on Mount Sinai, so Matthew may well have taken it for granted that the scene he was about to relate must have taken place on a mountain, and therefore that Jesus must previously have arranged this meeting-place with his disciples.

They fell prostrate before him. The appearance of Jesus is not de- 17 scribed, and has to be inferred from the disciples' reaction. On meeting the earthly Jesus, their greeting would have been respectful, certainly—that of disciples to master; but they would hardly have prostrated themselves, for this was regarded as a subservient action only appropriate to the great monarchs of the east. The only reason for prostration would have been some vision of the supernatural—and this is clearly what is intended here, though not a word is used to describe what the disciples saw. **Some were doubtful.** Possibly the vision was ambiguous: the figure was certainly Jesus, but there was not such a radiance in his person that all those who saw him were led to recognize that they were in the presence of a divine being. Nevertheless, their doubt at this stage seems surprising—particularly since Matthew is usually careful to present the disciples so far as he can as models of Christian discipleship. This may perhaps be Matthew's momentary admission of the fact, which is clearly stated in Luke and John, that some of the disciples took time to be convinced of the reality of the resurrection.

18 'Full authority in heaven and on earth has been committed to me.' This is the fulfilment of the destiny of the Son of Man—"Sovereignty and glory and kingly power were given to him, so that all people and nations of every language should serve him" (Daniel 7.14). The words provide the answer to the question, What was Jesus' status after the resurrection? He was the one to whom supreme power had been given under God. The church had various ways of expressing this, one drawn from Psalm 110—"You shall sit at my right hand, until I make your enemies the footstool under your feet"—and others besides. But most appropriate to the triumphant end of the story of the suffering Son of Man were these words from Daniel; and the following sentences offer a commentary on the **authority** which was now exercised by the risen Jesus. It was effective, not when men were blindly

19 subservient, but when they became Jesus' **disciples**, by accepting baptism and by observing his teaching. However much Jesus may have limited the range of his disciples' mission during his life on earth, their task was now world-wide. Indeed, by the time Matthew's gospel was written, Christianity had spread so far round the civilization of the Mediterranean that it seemed already to have reached **all nations**. For the language of these sentences is the language of the early church: baptizing and instructing were the main activities of Christian ministers, and it is of a piece with the emphasis which, throughout his gospel, Matthew lays upon Jesus' ethical teaching that Jesus

20 should say, '**teach them to observe all that I have commanded you**'. Doubtless the conviction of the first generations of Christians that this was their task and mission, and that the risen Christ was perceptibly "with them", went back to an assurance of Jesus, given in the course of an experience such as Matthew here describes. But plain reporting cannot do justice to such experiences; an author has to add what personal touches he can to draw out their meaning. And we can hardly be wrong in detecting, in the last words of the gospel, an allusion to one of the very first things which Matthew reports about Jesus (1.23): 'He shall be called Emmanuel—a name which means "God is with us."'

THE GOSPEL ACCORDING
TO MARK

The coming of Christ

Here begins the Gospel. When a messenger brought news of a victory in 1. 1
war or of some stroke of personal good fortune, the correct Greek word for
his tidings was *euangelion*, "good news". In the Roman empire, happy
events of this kind were ascribed to the apparently superhuman power of the
reigning Emperor. It was the Emperor's genius which gave men victory,
peace and prosperity. The Emperor was the saviour of mankind, and the
news of a new Emperor's birth or accession was therefore the most important
euangelion of all. The essence of the Christian message was that a new
Saviour had now appeared among men and had ascended his throne in
heaven. It was no stretch of language to call this message a *euangelion*, and
the word soon became a technical term in the Christian vocabulary. The
equivalent, in English, has always been the Anglo-Saxon word **Gospel**.

The content of this Gospel concerned **Jesus Christ the Son of God.**
At least a generation before Mark wrote (as is evident from Paul's letters)
the title **Son of God** had become attached to Jesus. Nevertheless in the
gospels it is used only sparingly, and its occurrence here in the very first
verse of Mark's gospel is significant: evidently one of the main purposes of
Mark's work was to demonstrate that Jesus was in fact the Son of God.
To feel the force of this claim, it is important to know what the title would
have suggested to Mark's first readers. Among Greek-speaking people, the
phrase **Son of God** denoted nothing very much out of the ordinary. The
many miracle-workers and men of exceptional psychic or ascetic powers
who moved about the ancient world were often so described; and the
citizens of the Roman empire had become accustomed to the Emperor being
called "son of a god". But (as is clear from the temptation stories in Matthew
and Luke) Jesus vigorously rejected any connotations of this sort. If he
was the Son of God, this did not mean that he was just one among the
many "sons of God" of the ancient world; for he was unique. The meaning
of the title for the earliest Christians (and perhaps for Jesus himself) must
therefore be looked for, not in the secular language of Greece and Rome,
but in Jewish religion; and here it is clear that the title was much more
specific. It meant one who was specially singled out by God for an important
rôle in the unfolding of the destiny of his people. In the past, certain kings
and prophets had had such a vocation. But in recent times no comparable
person had appeared, and hopes were concentrated instead on a single,

almost legendary figure, the Messiah (in Greek, the Christ) who was to appear at the end of the present age. Tentatively before the resurrection, and confidently after it, the disciples recognized that Jesus was indeed this Christ (albeit a very different Christ from that of Jewish expectation). Similarly they were led to the point, by the life, death and resurrection of Jesus, of seeing in him **the Son of God**—though, once again, the title when applied to Jesus meant a great deal more than it ever had in the Old Testament: Jesus was not merely the chosen instrument of God, he was uniquely related to God with the intimacy which a son has with his father. That any man should claim such intimacy with God was a source of scandal to the religious men of Palestine, and was one of their reasons for securing Jesus' execution. But the disciples had intimations during Jesus' life on earth that this intimacy was a fact; and they saw the resurrection as decisive proof of it. Thereafter they could talk confidently of **Jesus Christ the Son of God.** It is one of the themes of Mark's gospel that this sonship was already apparent, to those few who could discern it, during Jesus' life on earth.

The writers of the gospels each chose a different point at which their story could be said to "begin". Mark starts later than any of them with the appearance of John the Baptist—which is in fact where early Christian sermons seem often to have begun (Acts 10.37). Here John is introduced with an Old Testament prophecy; but only the second part of the quotation

2–3 (**A voice crying aloud** etc.) can be found in **the prophet Isaiah** (40.3); the first part appears to be a combination of Malachi 3.1 and Exodus 23.20. It is possible that Christians had come to see references to John the Baptist in all these texts from Scripture, and that after they had been quoted together a few times they were thought of as a single passage of prophecy and attributed as a whole to **the prophet Isaiah**. In any case the prophecy serves here to stress that element in the mission of John which was of supreme importance for Christians: John was the immediate forerunner of Jesus.

4　**And so it was.** The prophecy simply announced a "herald". Mark now fills out the picture of the historical figure, John, who fulfilled the prophecy. He appeared **in the wilderness.** This, for anyone who knew Palestine, was a sufficient indication: although a large part of the country was desert, it was the arid and wild mountainous area which begins dramatically just below the Mount of Olives and stretches down to the Jordan valley over 3,000 feet below which was the "wilderness" any local inhabitant would think of at once. John's appearance there doubtless helped to emphasize the austere and challenging message which he had come to proclaim (see above on Matthew 3.1–6). It was also close to the Jordan, where John carried out his characteristic work of **baptism.** This baptism was something quite new. The Jews practised many forms of ritual washing as part of the ceremonies needed to remove the impurities of sin, and we now know (from the Dead Sea Scrolls) that in one Jewish sect at least such washing was the principal rite by which it was felt that men could be made morally "clean". But nothing in such practices prepares us for the baptism of John. Admittedly John's baptism was also in token of repentance, for the forgiveness of sins. But it was clearly not intended to be understood merely as a new supplement to existing institutions. It was proclaimed as something quite decisive, an act which everyone should submit to, regardless of their religious upbringing; it was a necessary preparation for a new state of affairs which was shortly to come into being. Some of the implications of this radically simple message are worked out in the narratives of the other gospels. Here it seems to have been sufficient to indicate the barest elements of the scene: a new rite of moral cleansing, readily undergone by a great multitude of people, performed by an austere preacher in the wilderness of the Jordan valley, far from the usual holy places and institutions of the Jewish religion. The essence of it was that the people, however scrupulously they had been abiding by the moral and ceremonial laws of their religion, came confessing their sins. John's baptism, like the teaching of Jesus, 5 marked a new stage in the progress of religion from a system of observances to an attitude of uncompromising moral sincerity.

The quotation from Malachi (3.1), "Here is my herald whom I send on ahead of you", has already prepared the reader to think of John as Elijah; for Elijah was not merely a great figure of the past: it was prophesied that he would one day return (Malachi 3.23). The description of John's clothes reinforces this impression: in 2 Kings 1.8 Elijah is described as "a man wearing a garment of hair cloth and a leather belt". Moreover the returning Elijah was to herald the day of the Lord; John heralded not only one who was mightier than himself, but one whose baptism would be of a different 7 order altogether.

The readers of the gospel knew who this was, and Mark spends no time on the questions which worry the other evangelists, such as whether John recognized Jesus, or whether it was appropriate for Jesus to be baptized. He relates the important facts in a single sentence and proceeds at once to 9 interpret the significance of Jesus' baptism. The dove appears to be a visible 10–11 symbol of what was essentially an invisible event: Jesus' endowment with the Holy Spirit. The voice from heaven, given in words drawn from Ps. 2.7 or Isaiah 42.1 (or both), serves to justify the title given to Jesus in the first sentence of the gospel: Son of God. 1

Matthew and Luke each give a full account of the "temptation" of Jesus. According to them, it consisted of certain choices suggested to Jesus by Satan. Mark's account is so brief that we cannot be sure whether he intended the same interpretation. The details are more or less traditional. Forty days was a biblical round number, the time Moses spent on Mount 13 Sinai (Exodus 24.28), the time Elijah spent on his pilgrimage to Horeb (1 Kings 19.8); and the angels waited on him (provided him with food) exactly as they did on Elijah (1 Kings 19). All the meaning of the passage is concentrated in the words **tempted by Satan**. If we do not supply the details from the other accounts we need not think of this as a succession of specific "temptations" so much as a trial of strength between the Son of God and the powers of evil—a contest which remains present in the background of many other episodes as the gospel progresses.

In Galilee: success and opposition

14 **After John had been arrested, Jesus came into Galilee.** Mark's readers evidently were expected to be familiar with the story of John's arrest (which Mark in fact tells later on, 6.17–29): it is mentioned here simply in order to mark the moment at which Jesus' work in Galilee could properly be said to have begun—that is, not immediately after the baptism and temptation, but after a certain interval. What Jesus was doing in that interval (whether, for instance, he remained in company with John the Baptist) is not explained by Mark, who is less concerned to fill the gaps in his biography than to divide the narrative into clearly marked sections. For him (contrast, for example, John's gospel) the activity of Jesus has two main phases: first in Galilee, where Jesus has both *Success and opposition*—though the emphasis is on the success rather than on the opposition; and secondly in Jerusalem, where *The final conflict* leads to his death. This simple arrangement of the material concerning Jesus is logical and plausible, and is followed with only slight modification by Matthew and Luke. But the fact that John's gospel follows a different pattern, weaving together Jesus' activity in Galilee and Jerusalem, suggests that Mark's arrangement may be schematic rather than historical; and there are hints even in Mark's narrative that Jesus made more journeys to Jerusalem (as a pious Jew living in Galilee would normally do) than the single one which he records. However this may be, Mark clearly intends Jesus' appearance in his home country to mark the beginning of the first period, that of preaching, healing and controversy in Galilee. He devotes the next few chapters to giving some typical examples of these activities.

14 **Proclaiming the Gospel of God.** The modern reader is curious to know what Jesus' message was like, and will probably find Mark's summary of it somewhat disappointing. In this respect Matthew, who places the Sermon on the Mount right at the beginning of his account of Jesus' work, may seem much more satisfactory. The reason why Mark was content with such a brief summary is probably that when he used the phrase **the Gospel of God** he could be sure that his first readers would be thoroughly familiar with what was meant by it. The Gospel was the preaching which they

themselves had heard and responded to when they became Christians; and Mark gives here, not the content which Jesus must have given to this Gospel when he first preached it, so much as the tone in which he preached, and in which indeed the message was still preached in the church.

'The time has come.' Every Jew would have known what this meant. 15 History as recorded in the Old Testament was all preparation for a consummation that still lay in the future; Jesus was proclaiming that the time of preparation was at last over. 'The kingdom of God is upon you.' Again, the meaning of the phrase the kingdom of God was one which Mark's readers would have come to grasp for themselves. It could not be easily defined; it would only gradually be demonstrated in the teaching and destiny of Jesus and in the new experience of the church. The point here is that it was upon you: unlike his predecessors, Jesus did not merely teach about the kingdom, he proclaimed its imminent arrival. 'Repent, and believe the Gospel.' It will have made no difference that Jesus' hearers already professed a religion in which repentance played an important part. It will have been no good answering, "But we repented yesterday". For Jesus' appearance was the irruption of something new, and the urgency of his preaching demanded (as the next two paragraphs will show) a single-minded and immediate response, a turning away from old habits, and a total commitment to a new standard and a new master. Christian preaching doubtless had this urgent and demanding tone in Mark's time and continued to have it for a long time. Mark is showing here that it had the same tone when first formulated by Jesus.

Jesus was walking. Mark has now set the scene: Jesus is in Galilee 16 proclaiming the Gospel by his deeds, as we shall see, as much as by his words. The next events hardly fall into a biographical sequence: they are presented as typical examples of Jesus' activities, somewhat loosely strung together. The first such event is Jesus' summons to two pairs of brothers to accompany him. How much they knew of Jesus beforehand, and how much they were prepared for this sudden call, are details which Mark does not trouble to record. The only important point for him (as doubtless it was the important point also for the young church, when it reflected upon the experience of conversion) was the immediacy of the disciples' response. They were fishermen: not peasants (for Zebedee employed hired men) but 20 partners in a family fishing business. Jesus said he would make them fishers 17 of men. The metaphor is obvious enough in the context of the life of the church, where "fishing for men" meant drawing them in from the pagan world outside into the security of the "net" of the church. But when Jesus used the phrase, he probably meant something different. The fishing net in the teaching of Jesus (as in the Old Testament) is usually a symbol of the Last Judgement: when that judgement comes, men and women will be caught up into it inescapably. Simon and Andrew, James and John, are to share in Jesus' work of confronting men with a judgement which is already beginning and which (like a fishing net) they cannot evade.

21 **They came to Capernaum.** Jesus, Mark has informed us, came from Nazareth: but the centre of his teaching was to be Capernaum, some 30 miles away from Nazareth and some 1,500 feet lower in altitude—a different world altogether from that of his native highland village. Capernaum was the largest town on the lake, it had a brisk commercial life (it was situated on the important trade route from Damascus to the Mediterranean) and was an important centre of the fishing industry. Its synagogue would certainly have been (as the existing ruins show it to have been in the following century) one of the largest in the country, and here Jesus went **on the Sabbath** for the normal service of prayer, readings from the Old Testament, and exposition. It was normal for the president of the synagogue to invite a qualified layman to give the teaching, and it was natural that Jesus, who was exceptionally well versed in Scripture, should receive such an invitation. Indeed we find him often (like the apostles after him) seizing just such an opportunity to proclaim his message. Mark does not say what the teaching was: but we may assume that (as in Luke 4) it took the usual form of exposition of Scripture. But it was nevertheless something very different from the

22 ordinary run of Sabbath sermons. **Unlike the doctors of the law, he taught with a note of authority.** It is possible that the Galilean congregation would have been equally impressed by the **authority** of, say, a learned scholar from Jerusalem, compared with the less highly qualified local **doctors of the law** (the "scribes" of older versions) to whom they were accustomed: but Mark, who has already stated that Jesus was the Son of God, doubtless has a more significant kind of authority in mind, something which would invest Jesus' words with a greater weight than would proceed from the mere scholarship of an expert. He proceeds to illustrate this, not by an example of Jesus' teaching, but by what we would call a "miraculous cure". By calling it this, we misdescribe it. Mark sees it as another encounter between Jesus and the forces of evil, and the onlookers are made to have the same interest. They are impressed by the fact, not that the sufferer is cured,

27 but that **even the unclean spirits submit.** Popular belief in Palestine— as indeed in many parts of the ancient world—was inclined to find demons and spirits (as agents of the devil) operative in many spheres of life. A fairly obvious case of their activity was felt to be any kind of mental or physical illness, such as epilepsy or some forms of schizophrenia, in which the

23 sufferer behaved as if controlled from outside, i.e. **possessed.** Furthermore, if (as was usually the case) this condition compelled the victim to commit acts which made him ritually "unclean", then the agent possessing him was called an **unclean spirit.** The proper technique for dealing with this condition was exorcism, and the power to perform exorcisms was by no means uncommon (Matthew 12.27; Acts 19.13). The normal procedure was

to make the spirit confess who or what it was and then to invoke the name of a mightier power in order to drive it out. Clearly (at least in Mark's understanding) Jesus had no need to invoke any authority apart from his own: the spirit instantly recognized him and submitted (with the usual final manifestation of its power—in this case **convulsions**). The episode falls naturally 26 into place. After the trial of strength with the devil himself (1.12–13) Jesus shows his mastery of the devil's agents. The people, impressed both by the authority of his teaching and the effectiveness of his exorcism, rapidly spread abroad the news.

The case of **Simon's mother-in-law** is told quite simply and is one of 29–31 the passages in Mark which seems most likely to go back to the personal testimony of the apostles.

That evening after sunset. Mark is very precise about the timing. The 32 Sabbath ended at sunset, and only then would it have been lawful to bring (if that meant carrying) **all who were ill** out of their own houses to the house where Jesus was: they came in fact at the first possible moment after Jesus' appearance in the synagogue that morning. Jesus **drove out many** 34 **devils**, presumably in much the same way as in the story recorded a few verses earlier. The devils had to submit because they knew who he was. But Jesus was evidently anxious to keep his true nature dark—a motive which is characteristic of Mark's presentation of Jesus.

Very early next morning. The phrase in the original is rough and vivid: 35 "very early, it was still night". Mark does not say what Jesus' motive was— whether simply to gain time for prayer, or to escape from the pressure of the crowds in Capernaum. The episode marks the transition from Jesus' initial appearance in Capernaum to his wider activity **all through** 39 **Galilee.**

Once he was approached. Mark has been giving a sequence of events 40 that fill out the picture of Jesus' first twenty-four hours in Capernaum, culminating in his departure to undertake a wider field of work. From now on it is clear that the episodes are less carefully linked together and are more in the nature of a selection of Jesus' activities, which perhaps came into Mark's possession without any clear order or sequence. The healing of the **leper** is a typical instance of these activities. It is not at all certain that the biblical disease of leprosy was the same as the terrible paralysis, anaesthesia and rotting of limbs which bears that name today. Descriptions of it in the Bible (see especially Leviticus 13–14) suggest a variety of skin diseases which were certainly severe and difficult to cure, but which cannot have been regarded as totally incurable, as modern leprosy would have been: for there are elaborate directions both in the Old Testament (Leviticus 14) and in later Jewish literature about the formalities of ritual cleansing which must be performed by the patient when he recovered. The real terror of the disease was seen, not in the physical suffering which it involved, but in the ritual "uncleanness" which was imposed upon the sufferer. Strictly speaking (though it is possible that the severity of these rules was partially relaxed in the time of Jesus) a leper was allowed no physical contact with the persons or the houses and possessions of other Jews, and this social ostracism was inspired not so much by the fear of contagion as by the ritual "contamination" which was believed to be involved in any such contact. There is

41 therefore significance in the detail that Jesus **touched him**, and the **warm indignation** [a] which accompanied the act may have been a feeling aroused by the inhumanity of the social regulations which added so much suffering to the physical condition of lepers. Jesus seems to have been careless of the implications for himself of having touched him—indeed, it is just possible

45 that this was the reason why Jesus **could no longer show himself in any town**: as a result of contact with the leper, he would have been ritually unclean. Nevertheless, he instructed him to conform to the regulations governing recovery. Anyone whose leprosy healed had to go and show

44 himself **to the priest** who would examine him; if the priest confirmed that the recovery was complete, he would allow him to be readmitted to the community after making the prescribed offering (all these regulations can be found in Leviticus 14 and were still in force). Only the completion of this ritual would **certify the cure** and allow him to resume normal social

43 contacts. The vehemence with which Jesus **dismissed him** and told him, '**Be sure you say nothing to anybody**', was perhaps due simply to the desire to avoid making a stir; Jesus was anxious not to become known at this stage for an activity which could be regarded as a threat to the authority of the priests. But the subject of the cure, even if he subsequently travelled to Jerusalem to fulfil his ritual obligations, clearly did not wait before mingling freely with others and spreading the news of the miracle.

2. 1 **The news went round that he was at home.** The scene of the next episode is once again Capernaum, where Jesus seems to have made his home with the family of Simon (1.29). It should not be imagined that such a house would have been large enough for Jesus to preach to a great number of people inside (though Luke (5.18–19), who was more familiar with the larger houses of the west, evidently pictured the whole scene as taking place indoors). Rather he will have stood in front of the door and addressed the

2 crowd in the street or open space outside—though even [b] that space **was not big enough to hold them**. Because of the press of people, the four men carrying the paralysed man could not force their way through; so they must have found a way up to the roof of the house, perhaps at the side or at the back. Small houses in Palestine normally had flat roofs: one would have

[a] This is not certainly the correct reading: the majority of manuscripts give "sorry for him"; but **in warm indignation**, being more difficult, was thought by the translators more likely to be original.
[b] The word "even" is in the Greek, but has been omitted by the translators.

thought it would have been easier for them to have let down the stretcher from the edge of it, directly in front of Jesus. But presumably the closely packed throng of people made even this impossible; so they broke through the roof (which would have been of dried mud and wattle, and of no great thickness) and lowered the stretcher on to the only spot where there would have been any room, inside the house, behind Jesus. Their faith was that Jesus must ultimately turn back into the house and would then be forced to attend to the sufferer.

When Jesus saw their faith, he said to the paralysed man, 'My son, 5 **your sins are forgiven'.** It was widely believed among the Jews that illness came to men as a direct punishment for sin. This theory was obviously inadequate to explain the whole problem of suffering (and Jesus certainly did not accept the theory unreservedly); nevertheless no one denied that there was a close connection between sin and sickness, and to be forgiven by God was regarded as an essential precondition of recovery. Now, since people did certainly recover, it followed that God must often forgive them their sins, either of his free mercy or in view of their repentance and their meritorious acts. But God could not be forced to forgive them: he retained his sovereign freedom to give or to withhold forgiveness, and no man (unless perhaps he was a prophet to whom God had given intimations of the future) could presume to know whether God would forgive or had forgiven until unmistakable signs of physical recovery could be seen. Jesus' unequivocal statement, **your sins are forgiven,** therefore embodied a striking claim. He was not just speaking with the voice of a prophet (who might have claimed to know that the man was about to recover, and who could have said, in virtue of this knowledge, that it must be the case that the Lord had forgiven him). Jesus declared outright that the man was forgiven, and so implicitly claimed the authority (which of course Mark's readers knew that he possessed) to dispense God's forgiveness himself. **The lawyers with their** 6 professional knowledge of Scripture were naturally quick to recognize the implication as blasphemous. **'Who but God alone can forgive sins?'** 7

Jesus' claim was certainly blasphemous—unless it was true. Could it be proved true? How (since a man's forgiveness was entirely a concern between him and God) could it ever be known whether he had been forgiven? If it was a simple blasphemy, it was a singularly "easy" one to utter, since there could be no evidence to show that it was false. If on the other hand the claim was true, it was a stupendous one. It was no "easier" to make such a declaration than to effect immediately the physical improvement which, if the forgiveness was authentic, could be expected to follow in any case in due course. Jesus therefore authenticated his claim by what we now call a miracle: by giving the man an immediate recovery from his paralysis, he demonstrated that his declaration "your sins are forgiven" had been effective. Mark does not say whether the lawyers were convinced. This is just the beginning of a long series of events which built up the tension between Jesus and the religious authorities. Instead, he brings the story to a close by describing the impression made on the crowd, who were less interested in the theological point at issue than in the unprecedented evidence of a supernatural power at work among them.

10   This is the first use of the title **Son of Man** in the gospel. It occurs again, perhaps with a somewhat different meaning, later in the chapter, but otherwise its occurrences are all concentrated in the second half of the gospel. The title appears never to have established itself in the early church as a formal title of Jesus, but the evidence of the gospels is unanimous that Jesus frequently used it himself. Why did Jesus refer to himself in this cryptic way, and how did he intend the title to be understood? In his own language (Aramaic), the equivalent must have been *bar nasha*, "son of a man"; and just as the frequent biblical phrase, "sons of men", often means nothing more than "men", so this idiom may have been used in certain circumstances to mean simply "a man" or "a certain man". It is therefore possible that there are some instances in the gospels where Jesus originally used the expression, not of anyone in particular, but of men in general. But these instances are the exception; normally it is quite clear that when Jesus talked about the Son of Man he was referring to a particular individual. There are reasons for thinking that in Aramaic the idiom was sometimes understood as a deliberately enigmatic and oblique way of referring to oneself. If so, Jesus' use of it may have been of a piece with his characteristic manner of speaking: instead of making explicit claims for himself, he challenged his hearers to make up their own minds whether or not he was a person about whom such claims could be made. Nevertheless, his use of the expression had far-reaching implications. It suggested, for instance, not just "a man", but "the Man", that is to say, a particular man who had been singled out by God to perform an important and perhaps representative rôle in the destiny of his people or of mankind at large. There was much speculation in the ancient world about the appearance or return of the perfect Man, who would restore mankind to its pristine glory and inaugurate a new age. But the only form in which such speculation is likely to have impinged on the society in which Jesus moved was that which stemmed from some verses in the book of Daniel. "I was still watching in visions of the night, and I saw one like a son of man coming with the clouds of heaven; he approached the Ancient in Years and was presented to him. Sovereignty and glory and kingly power were given to him . . ." (7.13–14). This "son of man" in Daniel is again a little mysterious—the book was deliberately written in cryptic imagery—but certain things can be said about him with reasonable certainty. The context in Daniel shows that he appeared before God (the "Ancient of Years") at the moment when the divine judgement of the world was about to begin. He was in some sense a representative figure: he stood for the righteous men

who (at the time the book of Daniel was written) were being brutally oppressed by a foreign power; and Daniel's vision was that in God's judgement their destiny would be reversed: they would be vindicated, and there would be given to them that ascendancy among the peoples of the world which was being denied them at the present time. We know that this Son of Man figure fired the imagination of the Jews and enjoyed some popularity in later writings. Unfortunately we cannot say for certain how far the idea had been embellished in Jesus' day or what the popular image of the Son of Man would have been. But certain elements in it must have been constant. In particular, the Son of Man was always a personage who was (or would be) vindicated at God's final judgement, and he always had some connection—whether as representative or as leader—with those who suffered on account of their faith. When therefore Jesus used the expression—which he did most frequently (at least according to Mark) in connection with his own impending sufferings—he must have been understood by at least some of his hearers to be tacitly claiming that, whatever his present humiliations, he was destined to be vindicated by God; and also that he had a unique degree of solidarity, if not with all mankind, at least with those whom God regarded as righteous. Now Jesus healed the paralysed man to convince those who accused him of blasphemy that **the Son of Man has the right . . . to forgive sins.** These 10 lawyers will have known that the Son of Man was a person to whom there would ultimately be given **authority** (this was an implication of the word "sovereignty" in Daniel). The conclusion forced upon them by Jesus' words and actions will have been twofold: first, that Jesus was in some sense the person prefigured in the prophet's vision of the Son of Man; and secondly, that the authority given to this person included **the right** (which is the same word as **authority** in the Greek) **on earth to forgive sins,** and therefore to heal the sick.

As he went along. The exact locality of the call of Levi is left vague by 14 Mark, except that it was in the neighbourhood of the Lake; but we can fill in the details from the geography of Galilee. Capernaum, which was built on the northern shore of the lake, was a station on the important "road to the sea" which carried trade between the cities of the Decapolis and the Mediterranean ports. It was also close to the frontier between the territories of Herod Antipas and Philip, and was the centre of the fishing industry on the lake. It was the obvious place for a **custom-house;** and since Jesus had already become well known in Capernaum there is no reason to suppose that Levi did not have time to ponder the message of Jesus before he responded to Jesus' summons. Curiously, Levi does not appear in the list of the Twelve in 3.14–19 below (although his brother James does): this is perhaps the reason why in Matthew's gospel the same story is told, not of Levi, but of one who was known to have been one of the Twelve: Matthew.

The social status of Levi can be inferred from the next paragraph. His house ^a was large enough to accommodate a fair number round the table; he was therefore probably a senior customs officer in the service of Herod

15 Antipas. But the profession of **tax-gatherers** (including customs officials) was one of those which was very severely judged by Jewish society. It was assumed that it invariably involved extortion and dishonesty—for how else could these officials make a good living?—and it was usually exercised on behalf of a foreign power. Morally speaking such people were thought to be no better than thieves and criminals. They were therefore shunned by the stricter members of society and were even denied certain civic and religious rights. They tended consequently to make their friends mainly among themselves and with members of similarly "disreputable" professions; and a group of such people would be looked upon as by definition **bad characters**.

At the other extreme of society were the Pharisees, who not merely avoided contact with all such people but constituted a closed society of their own, observing a code of moral obligations and ritual observances more elaborate than that accepted by the majority of Jews. They would naturally have expected a religious teacher such as Jesus to observe the same rule of life as themselves, and this was doubtless an initial cause of tension between Jesus and the Pharisees. But now Jesus was behaving in a way that scandal-

16 ized them still more. It happened that some of them who were also **doctors of the law** (with whom Jesus had already had some controversy) observed him not merely conversing with these disreputable members of society but

15 actually sitting **at table** with them, which according to Jewish custom was the principal way in which a man could express his solidarity with his friends. And not only this: Jesus, like many teachers of his time, had now gathered a number of "disciples" around him (**for there were many who followed him**: Mark has recounted the call of only five disciples, and he hastily makes good his omission here), and he was allowing

16 these also to associate with **bad company**. In reply to their scandalized comments, Jesus quoted a familiar proverb and then boldly applied it to his

17 own rôle in contemporary society. '**I did not come to invite virtuous people, but sinners.**' This saying will have been understood by the church of Mark's time in a general and spiritual sense: it will have been their experience that Christ's invitation had come to them, not as specially "virtuous people", but as "sinners"; and it is possible that their understanding of this saying has influenced the form in which it has come down to us. Nevertheless the application of Jesus' words to the social conditions of his time is still intelligible and is borne out by one of the most characteristic features of his activity: he found himself constantly in opposition to those who were widely regarded as the most **virtuous** people in society, and

[a] In the Greek, as in the translation, verse 15 is ambiguous: it could mean Levi's house or Jesus' house. But Jesus had no house in Capernaum; he apparently stayed in that of Simon's family. Luke at any rate understood the house to be that of Levi (5.29).

sought out those who were shunned as **sinners.** It was these people whom he came **to invite**—that is, these were the people with whom he expressed solidarity by offering them a place at that heavenly banquet which (in traditional Jewish imagery) was the destined reward of the righteous.

Once, when John's disciples and the Pharisees were keeping a fast. 18 Fasting was an obligation laid on all the Jewish people on one day of the year; but stricter religious sects tended to lay upon themselves additional fast days. This was certainly true of the Pharisees (Luke 18.12) and Mark says that it was true of their **disciples** (though strictly speaking they were a closed society and did not have disciples, except in so far as some of them were "doctors of the law" and therefore had students). We are not surprised to hear that it was also true of the religious movement initiated by John the Baptist. Seeing Jesus surrounded by disciples, people naturally expected it to to be true also of his "sect", and when they found that he laid down no such practices for his followers, they asked the reason. Jesus replied with a comparison. It was the task of the **bridegroom's friends** at a wedding banquet 19 to contribute gaiety to the proceedings. Fasting—which meant of course doing without drink as well as food—would be quite out of place and was in fact waived even by the Pharisees on such occasions. **'As long as they have the bridegroom with them, there can be no fasting.'** By this it is clearly meant that Jesus' presence with his disciples was a time of rejoicing: fasting was appropriate to a time of waiting and preparation, but now the awaited moment had come, and the old observances had lost their meaning. Jesus was not merely initiating a variant of the Jewish religion, he was proclaiming something entirely new which the old forms of religion could not contain. Two similes help to make the point: old material will not take the strain of a 21 new patch that pulls on it when it begins to shrink; and new wine (which 22 was poured off from the vats into jars or skins before it had finished fermenting) needed new and supple wineskins, not old and brittle ones which would burst under the pressure.

Thus understood, these verses form a connected and intelligible whole. But the sequence is interrupted by a verse which appears to say something quite different: **'But the time will come when the bridegroom will be** 20 **taken away from them, and on that day they will fast.'** Jesus, we have said, appears to have been answering the question about fasting by showing in three short similes that the new dispensation which he had come to proclaim superseded all older observances. Why then did he prophesy a time when they would be resumed? Furthermore it was the firm belief of the church, expressed in words attributed to Jesus himself (e.g. Matthew 28.20, 'I am with you always, to the end of time'), that the Lord was always, and always would be, present among those who acknowledged him. What moment then can be in mind when Jesus is reported as saying, **'the time will come when the bridegroom will be taken away from them'?** Was

Jesus already hinting at the dark days between the cruciflxion and the resurrection? If so, the hint comes a long time before Jesus (at least in Mark's gospel) makes any clear allusion to his destiny in Jerusalem. Alternatively, is this a saying which was invented or adapted by the early church to justify its observance of days of fasting? The verse remains mysterious.

23   **One Sabbath he was going through the cornfields.** A short sequence of sayings and episodes follows which illustrates Jesus' attitude to the most fundamental and widely observed of all Jewish institutions, the Sabbath. The Sabbath was regarded as one of God's greatest gifts. It was the privilege of the Jew to observe it and to hand down the tradition of its observance from generation to generation. Much of this tradition was of a very positive character: the Sabbath was a day for rest, for rejoicing, for family gatherings, and of course for worship in the synagogue. But it had also its negative side. The simple direction in the Law of Moses, "Thou shalt do no manner of work", had been elaborated into a long series of complicated and often oppressive prohibitions, and it is with these petty restrictions—which were insisted upon most vigorously by the Pharisees—that Jesus is shown frequently taking issue in the gospels. One of the pettiest is illustrated by the first episode. **His disciples, as they went, began to pluck ears of corn.** It was expressly allowed in Jewish law for anyone to satisfy his hunger by taking a handful of fruit or corn from someone else's field (Deuteronomy 23.24–5). Normally this would offend no one. But on the Sabbath, according to the Pharisees' point of view, such an action must be regarded differently: it fell in the same category as reaping, which was "work", and therefore

24   **forbidden.** Jesus, in reply, appealed to a passage of Scripture which the rigorists themselves had some difficulty in explaining. The story about David is told in 1 Samuel 21: David was being pursued by Saul, and coming

26   to the sanctuary (**the House of God**) which then existed at Nob demanded food for himself and his men. (The priest concerned was actually Ahimelek and not his son **Abiathar**; but Abiathar was one of the two most famous priests in the time of David, and the error, whether it be Mark's or Jesus', is trivial.) It happened that the only bread available consisted of the **sacred bread** which was placed each week before the sanctuary, and which could afterwards be eaten only by the priests (Leviticus 24.5–9). Jewish scholars were in some embarrassment to explain how it could have been right for David and his men to eat this bread. Jesus, in recalling the incident, may simply have been trying to silence his critics by pointing to an instance where their own technique of interpretation left them in difficulties; but there may also be an unspoken implication (made explicit in Matthew's account, 12.1–8) that "a greater than David was here" who, even more than David, had the authority to exempt his followers from particular regulations of the law.

27   **He also said to them.** This is one of Mark's ways of binding into the context of his narrative a saying of Jesus which may originally have been

remembered in isolation. The saying adds a further touch to Mark's portrait of Jesus' attitude to the Sabbath. Even the Pharisees were prepared to concede that, if a human life were in danger, it was allowable to ignore a Sabbath restriction in order to save it; and they would have agreed that **the Sabbath was made for the sake of man**, in the sense that it conferred a great blessing on those who observed it. But they would certainly not have agreed with the much more liberal attitude which doubtless underlay Jesus' use of these words. It is possible that verse 28 should be understood in the same way. It was pointed out above that in the Greek the phrase **Son of Man** 28 may sometimes be a mistranslation of an expression which in Jesus' own language of Aramaic meant simply "man". If this is the case here, Jesus will have been saying that, not just when life is in danger, but in countless other cases besides, man is **sovereign even over the Sabbath** and not the Sabbath over man. On the other hand, if Mark has here correctly recorded Jesus' use of the title Son of Man, then Jesus must be once again understood as making a particular claim for himself: by virtue of his unique status he could legislate even on such matters as the observance of the Sabbath.

On another occasion. Mark adds one more dispute between Jesus and 3. 1 the Pharisees over the Sabbath, this time leading up to a clear breach between them. The presence of **a man in the congregation who had a withered arm** constituted a test case; for although it was permissible on the Sabbath to save a life that was in danger, it was generally forbidden to perform services for the sick on the grounds that, apart from the danger of infringing minute regulations about permitted work and movement, too much concern for those who were ill would be incompatible with the sense of joy and well-being which a Jew should feel on the Sabbath. It seems to have been, once again, the sheer inhumanity of such an interpretation of the Sabbath which moved Jesus to **anger and sorrow at their obstinate stupidity** and 5 caused him to make a public issue out of an act of healing. This was sufficient, according to Mark, to set in motion a plot against his life, the Pharisees making common cause with the **partisans of Herod.** These men, who 6 reappear later (12.13), were presumably influential citizens who gave their support to the administration of Herod Antipas and saw in Jesus' movement a threat to the peace of the district.

Jesus went away to the lake-side. The scene changes from an ordinary 7 Sabbath congregation in a synagogue to a huge gathering on the shore of the lake. Mark's list of the districts from which Jesus' hearers had come seems to include all the main areas of Jewish population in Palestine. So far, the movement had been confined to Galilee; but now the whole of the Jewish nation in Palestine came to hear him: from **Judaea and Jerusalem** in the south (omitting of course Samaria, which was regarded as a hostile and alien district) and, still further south, from **Idumaea,** the Edom of the Old 8

Testament; from **Transjordan**, that is, the narrow strip of valley and the highlands immediately to the east of the Jordan (officially called Peraea); and from the **neighbourhood of Tyre and Sidon**, to the north-west of Galilee, where there were substantial communities of Jews. It was, it seems, Jesus' reputation as a healer which brought the crowds. Healing involved exorcism, and therefore contact with spirits who knew (as Mark and his readers knew, but as the crowds did not know) that Jesus was the **Son of God**. But once **11** again Jesus refused to allow his true status to be known to the multitudes who came for healing.

He then went up into the hill-country. Steep and therefore unin- **13** habited country lay not far from the lake, and was an appropriate setting for a moment which demanded quiet and privacy. **He appointed twelve as his 14 companions**, a statement which becomes more significant a moment later in the form **he appointed the Twelve.** Mark's readers knew, not just that **16** Jesus had had a certain number of **companions** entrusted with specific tasks during his work in Galilee, but that he had left behind him a group of men known as the Twelve, who (or at least some of whom) constituted an essential link between Jesus' work on earth and the continuing existence of the church. Some members of this group were well known to Mark and his readers, either because of the part they played in the gospel narrative, or because of their subsequent rôle in the church: this goes for the first four in the list, and of course for Judas Iscariot. But the rest seem to have been little more than names, and the lists given in different parts of the New Testament do not always agree with each other. The important thing was evidently not the name and character of each, but the fact that there were **twelve**, symbolizing perhaps that the new people of God was in important respects the successor of the old Israel with its legendary Twelve Tribes.

To Simon he gave the name Peter. The name means "a stone", as is **16** explained in John's gospel (1.42); and a reason for the name is suggested by a passage in Matthew (16.18). The name **Boanerges** is mysterious. We do **17** not know precisely what these letters are supposed to represent in Aramaic or Hebrew, nor what Jesus intended by renaming the two brothers. Mark tells us that the name meant **Sons of Thunder.** This may be right, but it does not take us much further; nor is there any record of these two disciples ever having been called by this name subsequently. **Thaddaeus** occurs only in Mark's list, **18** replaced in Matthew (10.3) by Lebbaeus, *a* in Luke (6.16) by 'Judas the son of James'. **Simon** (as the NEB makes explicit) *b* was a **member of the Zealot party.** Not much is known of the Zealot party before the beginning **19** of the Jewish War (60–66 A.D.), when its members became champions of revolt against the Roman occupying forces; but there is no reason to doubt

[a] Some manuscripts give Thaddaeus also in Matthew's list.
[b] The Greek has *kananaios* ("Canaanite"), which probably, though not certainly, bears this technical meaning here. Luke calls him 'Simon who was called the Zealot' (6.15).

that this fanatical anti-Roman movement was active during the previous decades, especially in Galilee, and Simon seems to have been a member of it.

Up to this point in Mark's narrative, such opposition as Jesus had encountered (which first comes to the surface in 3.6) had been created by his attitude to Sabbath regulations. The next two episodes illustrate the beginnings of a deeper antagonism. That the activity of Jesus should have collected

21 a large crowd inevitably suggested to some[a] **that he was out of his mind**, and that the crowds had been attracted by mere curiosity. Consequently his family (who are to be imagined a day's journey away in Nazareth) **set out to take charge of him.** Meanwhile Jesus was being confronted with a more

22 menacing accusation. The **doctors of the law**—whom Mark probably assumes to have **come down** to Galilee from Jerusalem specially to investigate the reports about Jesus—admitted the reality of Jesus' exorcisms but gave them a sinister explanation. The power by which Jesus drove out the demons and spirits that caused (it was believed) so much of people's illness, was not a good power, but was a worse power still. '**He drives out devils by the prince of devils.**' The man who professed to cure those who were "possessed by devils" was in a worse case himself—he was **possessed by Beelzebub,**[b] who was, if not the devil in person (as Matthew states, 12.24), at least a prince among devils. Jesus showed this up as sheer sophistry. It was one thing to believe (as Jesus and his contemporaries certainly believed) that there was an objective and personal force of evil abroad which could enter a man and make him act in a way untrue to his nature; and it made sense, on this view of the matter, to talk of devils, spirits, demons and so forth in the plural: these were all different manifestations of the same supernatural power. But it was quite another thing to infer from this terminology that different "devils" could be played off against each other for the benefit of human beings. Evil was ultimately one single power, and to talk of evil being

25 **divided against itself** was a contradiction in terms. It was as silly as saying

24 that "Satan could drive out Satan".

23 Jesus put his answer in the form of two **parables.** To see what a parable is one must look at the parables of Jesus: it was he who made the form immortal. But the word itself did not necessarily mean anything so extended and elaborate as most of Jesus' stories. In Greek it meant any "comparison" or "simile"; and the Hebrew word to which this corresponded had an even wider range of meanings—proverbs, riddles, illustrations and stories. Thus

24-7 Jesus' answer here consists of two quite simple and obvious illustrations.

[a] Perhaps indeed to his own family—the Greek reads as easily in this sense. See the footnote in NEB.

[b] The name occurs nowhere outside the New Testament and its origin and meaning are unknown. An old theory is that it is a form of Baalzebub, "the God of Ekron" (2 Kings 1.2), and in view of this theory many Latin versions and the older English translations, followed by NEB, reproduce the name in the form *Beelzebub*. But all Greek manuscripts have the still more mysterious name *Beelzebul* (or, in some cases, *Beezebul*).

The only deeper meaning which may possibly be present lies in the phrase
the strong man. According to contemporary Jewish mythology, the mon- 27
strous power of evil was due to be "bound" for a period before the end of
the world (see also Revelation 9.1); so that underneath the comparison may
lie a claim of Jesus to be stronger than the devil himself and to be the person
destined to bring evil into subjection.

On any interpretation the saying which follows is hard to understand. The
first part of it fits easily enough into the general pattern of Jesus' teaching.
Some Jewish thinkers had drawn up a whole list of sins which in their view
put the sinner outside the range of divine forgiveness and deprived him of
his share (as they put it) in the life to come. Jesus' teaching stands at the
opposite extreme to such legalism: it is open to anyone to repent and be
forgiven. '**No sin, no slander, is beyond forgiveness for men.**' Why then 28
does he make the severe exception which follows? And what does it mean, to
"slander the Holy Spirit"? Mark indicates the way he understands this
himself: **He said this because they had declared that he was possessed** 30
by an unclean spirit. Confronted, that is to say, by a clear instance of the
defeat of evil powers (which in Mark's theology indicated that the Holy
Spirit was at work), they had rejected this clear evidence of God's activity.
Mark may have wished his readers to infer that, since no clearer case could be
given them of the presence of the Spirit, nothing further could happen which
would lead them to repentance, and therefore there was no chance that they
would adopt the attitude necessary to obtain forgiveness. In the wider context
of a doctrine of God's mercy, this is a hard saying. But Mark's concern is a
more limited one. He has to explain how it happened that men crucified the
Son of God. If they were capable even of "slandering" the clearest manifestations of his divine power, then it was understandable that they would
not stop short of destroying Jesus. Nothing would move them to repentance:
therefore nothing could qualify them for forgiveness.

Then his mother and his brothers arrived. We were told in verse 21 31
that they were setting out from Nazareth to 'take charge' of Jesus. Mark
does not say what happened when they tried to do so; their arrival in
Capernaum simply gives him the cue for recording a saying of Jesus which
was perhaps remembered apart from any particular context (it appears to be
alluded to by Paul in Romans 8.29): '**Whoever does the will of God is my** 35
brother, my sister, my mother.' The word **brothers** is less precise in
Greek than in Hebrew: it could mean half-brothers (i.e. sons of Joseph by
another wife) or even cousins. It does not follow from this passage (even
if it seems likely for other reasons) that Mark knew nothing of the tradition
that Jesus was born of a virgin.

On another occasion. But it was clearly, in Mark's view, an important 4. 1
occasion. Just as Jesus' fame as a healer had drawn such crowds that he had

to have a boat ready to 'save him from being crushed' (3.9), so too his teaching drew a crowd **so large that he had to get into a boat**. Mark evidently intended to set the two scenes in parallel, and just as in the first he gave some notable examples of Jesus' works of healing, so now, for the first time in his gospel, he gives a specimen of Jesus' teaching, introduced by a word which would have had solemn overtones for Jewish listeners, since it stood at the beginning of a formula which they used every day in their

3 prayers ("Listen O Israel, the Lord is our God, the Lord is one"): '**Listen**'.

In fact however this sample of Jesus' teaching can hardly have been typical. Admittedly it consists mainly of "parables", which were one of Jesus' most characteristic figures of speech; but the point of these particular parables is not so much to convey new religious or ethical truths as to illustrate how Jesus' teaching as a whole was to be understood. In this they continue an important theme from the previous chapter. Just as Jesus' works of healing had provoked opposition as well as admiration, with the result that his opponents, having "slandered the Holy Spirit", had now lost all chance of repenting and being forgiven, so his teaching was such as to arouse different reactions among his hearers, some of whom would inevitably be

9 deaf to his message—God would not give them **ears to hear** (a phrase which evokes Deuteronomy 29.4, and recalls the pristine obstinacy of the people of Israel in the face of the spectacular benefits they received at the time of the Exodus). What was the explanation of this? Why was the teaching of the Son of God ignored or rejected by some of those who heard it? In the case of the acts of healing, Mark was able to give two reasons for this opposition: some thought Jesus was mad, others that he was inspired by the devil. Neither of these reasons would account for the mixed reception given to his teaching; and so Mark opens his collection of Jesus' sayings with a discourse which bears upon this very question.

3 '**A sower went out to sow.**' The first of the parables describes what we know to have been usual farming practice in Mediterranean lands in antiquity, and its freshness comes more from Jesus' vivid and poetic observation than from any intrinsic interest in the narrative. After the harvest (around June) the farmer would probably plough his fields at least once, perhaps several times, during the dry summer months, both to prevent the dry earth from becoming hard and to keep it free of weeds. In November or December (the time of the first heavy rains, when there was enough moisture in the ground to allow the seed to germinate) the field would be sown, the sower casting the seed by hand and probably varying the quantity of seed according to the quality of the soil. Very soon after the sowing, the seed would be ploughed in to protect it from the birds. In these circumstances a certain amount of wastage was inevitable. The field would be bounded at least on

4 one side by a path. Some seed would naturally fall on it, but since the farmer would not plough over the path, it would remain on the surface and

be eaten by the birds. Some would fall **on rocky ground**, that is to say, 5
places where the limestone rock which underlies the soil in Galilee came close
to the surface. Probably the farmer would not expect much of a crop from
it: the soil would be too shallow to hold moisture, and the fierce heat of the
sun would quickly scorch the plant as soon as it began to grow. But he would
not for that reason leave such patches completely unsown. Some seed would
fall among **thistles**, which could never be completely eradicated from the 7
soil and which were always a serious nuisance to the farmer. But this amount
of wastage was only what was to be expected. Most of the seeds sown would
grow to fruition, often producing several side-shoots. A return of thirty to
sixty grains from each plant was normal, a return of a hundred was exceptional (though not unheard of)—Jesus was fond of a touch of exaggeration.

The parable then is a description of ordinary farming practice with which
Jesus' hearers will have been perfectly familiar. Nevertheless it dwells on a
number of details which would not normally come to mind. From the
farmer's point of view the wastage would be negligible: it would hardly
occur to him to pay much attention to it, or to censure the sower for allowing
a few seeds to fall on the path. But Jesus, by recounting three different ways
in which the grain might be lost, drew attention to the fact that even when the
harvest was good some wastage was inevitable, some seeds would come to
nothing. Similarly: however successful his own work might appear to be, it
was perfectly natural that there should be some wastage, some indifference,
even some opposition.

If this is the natural interpretation of the parable, it is also one that is
entirely consistent with Jesus' understanding of himself and his work: he
presented an unavoidable challenge, and it was inevitable that some would
react against him. But Mark evidently saw a further meaning in the parable,
and knew of a more subtle interpretation of it. Consequently, before going on
with the scene of Jesus teaching the crowds, he recorded some conversation
which Jesus had in private with **the Twelve and others who were round** 10
him. This change of scene puts the matter in a different perspective. The
emphasis in the parable was on the small but necessary amount of wastage:
a few will always remain unfruitful even though the main harvest develops
normally. But now it is the other way round. The phenomenon being
explained is no longer the small (though potent) opposition to Jesus' teaching,
compared with the crowds who press in to hear it. It is those who accept
who are now a small and privileged minority, and what has to be explained
is the fact that the great majority remain **outside.** 11

At this stage of his work, Jesus had had more *success* than *opposition.*
He was more aware of the crowds who strained to see and hear him
than of the enemies who were already plotting against him. But for the early
church things were very different. The Christians were a small movement
set in the midst of a large and (particularly on the Jewish side) hostile world;

and to account for this hostility they were glad to find an explanation in a prophecy of Isaiah (6.9–10). That great prophet had been entrusted with the authentic word of God. Yet the people would not listen. Why? It must have been because God himself had intended it that way and dulled their under-

12 standing—**that they may look and look, but see nothing**—and it was this which was preventing them from turning to God and obtaining his forgiveness. Paul used the same text when confronted by the opposition of fellow-Jews in Rome (according to Acts 28.26–7); and doubtless the prophecy helped many Christians in the early days of the church to understand their own position and the attitude of their neighbours.

Did Jesus quote this text himself? Mark says that he did, and there is no good reason to doubt it: there will have been many occasions later on when it may have helped him to understand and interpret the massive opposition which he encountered. But it is hardly appropriate to the context here, where Jesus has more admirers than opponents; and it looks as though Mark (or the source from which he derived his narrative) introduced it in order to explain a somewhat different sense of the word "parable" from that which is exemplified by the story of the sower. The word parable (or its Hebrew equivalent) could mean a variety of figures of speech, including riddles and enigmatic sayings. The parables of Jesus, though they may have been perfectly clear to those who first heard them, were often inspired by the circumstances and context in which they were delivered, and there may soon have come a time when, since their original setting had been forgotten, the parables themselves could no longer be understood: they then became "parables" in the sense of mysterious, enigmatic utterances. In which case the fact that Jesus taught in "parables" could be held to explain why some (indeed the majority, as it seemed to the first Christians) did not accept his teaching: they did not understand it! It was only to his intimate disciples (so this explanation ran), and through them to the church, that Jesus had given

11 the clue—**the secret of the kingdom of God**. As one example of the kind of esoteric understanding which (on this view) was necessary in order to grasp the meaning of Jesus' teaching, Mark appends a detailed interpretation of the parable of the sowing. He attributes the interpretation to Jesus, and it may well have come down to Mark along with the parable itself. But there are serious reasons for doubting whether Jesus was the author of it. While the parable bears some traces of the idioms of the language (Aramaic) which Jesus spoke, the interpretation contains many expressions which do not occur elsewhere in the gospels but are characteristic of the preaching of the Greek-speaking church. Further, the circumstances which prevent the proper reception of the word (**trouble, persecution, false glamour of wealth**) belong more to the experience of the church than to that of the crowd which first listened to Jesus' teaching in Galilee. Most significant of all: the psychological analysis of different kinds of unbelief, profound though it may be,

does not spring from the parable itself (as the meaning springs from most of Jesus' parables). It has to be read into it. Mark was right: if this was the way in which the parables were intended to be understood, then they would indeed be mysterious to anyone who did not possess the clue. If Jesus taught like this, no wonder that only a few followed him. Mark indeed goes on to suggest that Jesus' parables were all like this. '**You do not understand this parable? How then are you to understand any parable?**' And at the end of the chapter he explicitly makes the same point: the disciples were privately given the key to all the teaching which to everyone else remained simply "parables"—mysterious and perplexing. This is one of Mark's answers to a question which runs through his gospel: why was Jesus not universally recognized as the Son of God? Because he deliberately gave his teaching in a form which few could understand. Mark develops this idea here, at the expense of breaking into the scene of Jesus' public teaching—which is resumed without apology at verse 21. 13, 33-4

He said to them. Clearly the section containing private instruction to the disciples is finished, and the scene is once again the lake-side, with the crowds straining to hear Jesus' teaching, just as on a previous occasion they had pressed upon him to witness his powers of healing. According to Mark, the parables were such as to mystify all except those who belonged to the privileged circle of the disciples and were given the clue to their interpretation. He now gives some examples of precisely this kind of enigmatic parable. All but one of them (that of the seed scattered on the land) reappear in Matthew and Luke, who, by placing them in a certain context, or by making minor alterations, often give some hint as to how they understood them. But Mark neither gives an esoteric explanation of them (as he does for the parable of the sowing) nor offers by his editing any suggestion about their meaning. He evidently intends the sayings to remain mysterious, as an illustration of what he has just said about their effect on their hearers. It may well be that the point of them was already obscure to him. 21

The sayings themselves are characteristically vivid, drawn from life, and often with the ring of proverbs. The **lamp** is the ordinary oil-lamp that has been found by thousands among the ruins of the ancient world, shaped like a small flattened teapot with the wick in the spout. To light a room, it would have to be put on a **lamp-stand**, not underneath one of the pieces of furniture in the room such as **the bed** or the **meal-tub** (there is a little evidence that this part of the equipment of a peasant house might be mounted on legs; otherwise we should have to think of the tub being placed upside down over the lamp in order to extinguish it, which is a rather different idea). Proverbially, anything hidden away (the meaning of the parables? the true nature of Jesus? the infant church in the world?) will be brought into view one day. The two proverbs in verses 24 and 25 seem drawn from the bazaar: the fair and generous merchant does better in the end, but (as in all economies) the 21, 24, 25

poor get poorer, the rich richer (in understanding the parables? in understanding the gospel? in faith?). The seed is sown, the farmer continues his
normal activities, and does nothing to it until the moment comes for
the decision to harvest (judgement will be sudden and unprepared?—
the harvest, at all events, was a biblical symbol of the Last Judgement
29 often used by Jesus, and the words **he plies the sickle, because harvest-**
31 **time has come** are a quotation from Joel 3.13). The **mustard-seed**
was proverbially the smallest seed in the ground, and by comparison the
plant which sprang from it (which grows over six feet tall in Galilee) was
prodigious—though Jesus was once again exaggerating when he used language about it which in Daniel (4.12) and Ezekiel (17.23; 31.6) is applied
to a massive tree (small beginning of the gospel? of the church? of faith in
26, 30 the human heart?). These last two parables are said to illustrate **the kingdom of God**—but what aspect of the kingdom remains mysterious. Mark
has kept faithfully to his programme of showing that Jesus' teaching was
likely to be unintelligible to the mass of his hearers.

Miracles of Christ

So far Jesus' activity had all been situated on the west side (or rather in the
north-west corner) of the Lake of Tiberias. Now Jesus crossed over to the
37 east side, and the **heavy squall** which his boat encountered was of the kind
for which the lake is notorious, and which can take even the most experienced
fisherman by surprise. It is a little curious that the crossing should have been
35 undertaken **in the evening**. Jesus would then have reached the other side
two or three hours later, long after nightfall; but the events which immediately followed his landing clearly took place in daylight. We cannot be
sure that Mark was really concerned about such details; but if he was, then
he must have envisaged the crossing as being combined with an all-night
fishing expedition, during which it would have been natural for Jesus to take
the opportunity to get some sleep. The episode is told quite simply, with
some details which are usually thought to suggest the use of an eye-witness
account (the other boats, the cushion, the disciples' almost reproachful cry
to Jesus, and Jesus' words which, in the Greek, recall the way he spoke
to devils). It is interesting to compare the accounts in Matthew and
Luke, who see a more symbolic meaning in the story (Matthew 8.23–7;
Luke 8.22–5).

5. 1 **So they came to the other side of the lake, into the country of the
Gerasenes.** Gerasa was one of the most important of the group of Greco-
Roman cities which lay for the most part on the eastern side of the Jordan
and which, though subject to Rome, constituted a league known as the

Decapolis (the Ten Towns). Later in the century Gerasa began an 20
ambitious building programme and became one of the most splendid Roman
cities of the east. But even before that, those of Mark's readers who knew
little about Palestine were likely to have heard of it. This may be the reason
why Mark calls the scene of this episode the country of the Gerasenes: 1
with the name, and with the detail of a herd of pigs (which was unthinkable
in Jewish territory), he will have succeeded in conveying an impression of the
very different Greco-Roman world in which Jesus set foot when he crossed
over the lake. But as a matter of geographical detail his description creates
difficulties. The scene is laid by the shore, not too far from a town (verse 14).
Gerasa lay some thirty miles away from the lake, more than a day's walk
across the mountains, and no part of the shore could properly be called "the
country of the Gerasenes". A few Greek manuscripts, following the version
of the story in Matthew, give "Gadarene": Gadara was another city of the
Decapolis, somewhat closer than Gerasa, in the hills within sight of the lake;
but even this city was too far away to fit the details of the story. Either the
name conceals that of an unknown smaller town near the lake, or else Mark,
for the reason suggested, was more anxious to give the area a pagan atmosphere than to be precise about geographical details (of which in any case he
may have been ignorant).

Just as the area was exceptional for Jesus' activity, so too the case of
possession is described as an exceptional one. The unclean spirit gave its 2
victim superhuman strength, and its name, Legion (a Roman military unit 9
of over six thousand men), put it in a class apart from the more common
cases of possession by, say, seven demons. Yet on seeing Jesus it reacted just
as other unclean spirits had: it recognized him by his name (Jesus) and his 7
real nature (son of the Most High God), and acknowledged his superiority.
And it was doubtless to illustrate Jesus' power even over such a demon, and
even in gentile surroundings, that Mark recorded the story. But there are
some further details which make the story unlike any other in the gospels.
The first is Jesus' conversation with the spirit. Usually he simply commands
it to come out. Here he also asks its name (which was standard exorcists'
technique, though it was normally done before, not after, the command to
come out, as a way of getting control of the spirit). The second is the occurrence of the title, Most High God, which was not a Jewish phrase, but
belonged to the common vocabulary of many Hellenistic cults—another
detail which gives a non-Jewish tone to the whole scene. The third
is the destruction of the pigs. It was to be expected in an exorcism that
the devil would make a final demonstration of its power before leaving
its victim. This usually took the form of a paroxysm in the victim himself, though stories were told of other violent manifestations (such as a
statue being overturned near by). In this way the onlookers would be
assured that the spirit had been decisively overcome. A herd of two

thousand pigs can hardly have been a common sight, and their loss would have been a major calamity for their owner. But neither the interest of the narrator nor, it seems, of the crowd which soon collected was attracted by this aspect of the matter. The miracle, in the eyes of all, was the recovery of one who had been possessed by so formidable a spirit. It was
15 because of this that **they were afraid** and begged such a potent exorcist
16 **to leave the district.** Nevertheless, since Jesus would not allow the subject of the cure to go with him, the evidence of the miracle, in the person of a notorious demoniac suddenly restored to health, was soon widely acknowledged in an area far outside the normal range of Jesus' activity.

The two miracles which follow are woven into each other in a way which suggests the hand of an expert narrator (Mark was particularly adept at this).
22 The **president** of a synagogue was in charge of the maintenance and worship of the synagogue, and was necessarily one of the dignitaries of any Jewish community. [a] That he should have appealed to Jesus was therefore a clear sign that Jesus had by now achieved considerable fame as a miracle-worker. But although the present section of Mark's gospel contains a group of miracles which give substance to this reputation, Mark is careful not to tell the stories as mere miracles. It was said of a number of people in antiquity that contact even with their clothes could heal diseases (compare Acts 5.16; 19.12); and this was explained in terms of a magical "power" going out of them. Mark does not reject this explanation, but he makes it clear that the
34 cure was nevertheless much more than magic: 'My daughter, your faith has cured you'. Similarly with the restoring to life of a little girl who had just died. This was of course the supreme miracle for anyone to perform— though Jesus was by no means the only miracle-worker of his time to be credited with it. The story is told with vivid detail, down to the actual words
41 spoken by Jesus in his own language, Aramaic; and in outline it could be regarded as a typical miracle story. But again, Mark preserves a dimension
36 which raises it above mere miracle: 'Do not be afraid; only have faith.' And (though this can hardly be conveyed in a modern English translation) the words used of the girl's recovery are full of deeper meaning. For those (Jews and Christians alike) who believed in a future resurrection, the
39 righteous who had died were in reality **asleep,** waiting for the great moment
41-2 of awakening; and the words translated **get up, got up,** are those which the first Christians always used of the raising of Jesus himself from the dead. The miracle did not merely bring the girl back to life; it was a demonstration of the wonderful fact, known to faith, of resurrection from the dead. Even so, Mark hastens to add, the demonstration could not yet be made fully public,

[a] The Greek means literally "one of the synagogue-presidents". There was only one effective president of each synagogue, but there is some evidence that the title was also an honorary one, so that the text does not necessarily imply (as the NEB translation does) that there was more than one synagogue in the town.

but was deliberately veiled by Jesus: **he gave them strict orders to let no** 43
one hear about it.

This (at least according to Mark) was Jesus' **one visit to his home town** 6. 1
(Nazareth). Jesus followed his regular practice of attending the synagogue
on the Sabbath and making use of an invitation to preach in order to spread
his teaching. As always, he made an impression; but the dominant reaction
of his audience was sceptical. How could one who had grown up among them
and practised a trade, [a] and whose family was still well known to them,
pretend to speak as if he had had all the training and authority of a professional expositor of Scripture? Their incredulity was an obstacle—it prevented
them from accepting his authority and believing in him. The translation,
they fell foul of him, is an English colloquialism suggesting the break-up 4
of a partnership. But the word in the Greek is not colloquial at all; it was a
technical expression, drawn from the Greek Old Testament, for the shatter-
ing of religious faith. The incredulity of Jesus' hearers was an obstacle, a
snare (*skandalon*), which prevented them from accepting his authority and
believing in him. Jesus, presumably detecting the intransigence of their
attitude, replied to them with a familiar proverb. Apparently the strong
feeling against him prevented him from performing the miracles which
usually went with his appearance in synagogue.

On one of his teaching journeys. At some stage in his activity in Galilee 7
(Mark evidently did not know at what stage) Jesus enlarged the scope of his
work by sending out his disciples as missionaries. They had the double task
of calling for repentance and of carrying on Jesus' onslaught against the
powers of evil in the form of the **unclean spirits.** This mission was very
similar to that which was subsequently entrusted to the church, and there
can be little doubt that, at least in some of the gospel accounts, the practice
and experience of early Christian missionaries have influenced the record of
Jesus' instructions to his disciples (see above on Matthew 10). It is hard to
be sure, for instance, whether the detail of anointing the sick **with oil** (which 13
is not mentioned anywhere else in connection with Jesus' activity) is an
authentic element of the disciples' mission or is a reflection of the subsequent practice of the church (James 5.15). In either case it is clearly not
thought of as a medicinal treatment (for which indeed oil was often used, as
in Luke 10.34) but as an instrument or sign of supernatural power over
disease. But even if such details are uncertain, there is no reason to doubt
either that Jesus, on at least one occasion, [b] sent his disciples out on a mission,
or that his charge to them was faithfully remembered. The way they were to

[a] The alternative reading 'son of the carpenter and Mary' is probably an assimilation to
Matthew's version. It was a repugnant idea in some quarters that Jesus should actually
have been a carpenter.
[b] Luke records two: see below on Luke 10.1.

proceed is vividly drawn: apart from what was basically necessary for any-
8–9 one walking across the country—sandals and stick—they were not to take any
of the provisions of food, clothes and money with which a prudent traveller
always equipped himself before a long journey. (There may also be the implication that they were not to go as beggars—the word translated **pack** can
mean the pouch in which a beggar put what was given to him.) The reason for
travelling so light was probably twofold. In the first place, the mission seems
to have taken place in Galilee, which was densely populated: the distance
between one town or village and the next was never so great as to warrant
serious preparations. Secondly (and this is more important), they were to
expect hospitality (as any traveller could who had a good reason for his visit)
and to accept it. They were not to exploit this by moving from house to
house in turn: their work was presumably too urgent, and time too precious.
On the other hand, the kind of reception they had would be a clear sign of
people's readiness to hear them. If it were unfavourable, they were to perform
a gesture which was a characteristic Jewish way of emphasizing the holiness
of Palestine: after being abroad, or in any place regarded as "unclean", Jews
would shake the dust from their feet before they stepped in the holy land,
so as not to contaminate it. The disciples' gesture could be interpreted only
in one way: the place which did not receive them could have no part in the
coming kingdom.

Mark separates the departure of the disciples from their return by a
narrative which bears only indirectly on the theme of the gospel. It is
certainly true that John the Baptist was put to death by Herod Antipas: the
fact is recorded by Josephus. It is also true that, just as John's preaching
was the forerunner of Jesus' preaching, so his death prefigured Jesus' death,
and perhaps for that reason won a place in the gospel story. But the vivid
17–28 details of Mark's account are clearly there for their own sake. The story as
told in Mark is somewhat different from Josephus' account: according to
Josephus, Herod's motive was political. But it is perfectly consistent with
what is known of Herod's character; and although it is told more in the
manner of a *raconteur* than of a serious historian, it may well have a basis in
history.

14, 15 **People were saying . . . others said.** The kind of rumours to which
Jesus' activity gave rise all tended in one direction. There was no special
16 reason to think that a man who had been **raised from the dead** would be
capable of performing miracles; on the other hand, it was a widespread
popular belief that the new age, which the Jews confidently expected in the
near future, and which would be marked by a miraculous triumph of good
over evil, would be ushered in by the return of one of the great Old Testa-
15 ment figures, Moses, Elijah or **one of the old prophets.** In so far, then, as
the activity of Jesus seemed to betoken the arrival of the new age, it was
natural to identify him with one of these; and following the same line of

thought, it might even have seemed possible that John the Baptist himself had been a person in the same tradition who would "come again" at the appointed time, and Mark, by way of introducing the following story, makes Herod think the same.

This same Herod. Herod Antipas had been tetrarch (and doubtless 17 known locally as king) of Galilee and Transjordan (Peraea) since the death 14 of his father, Herod the Great, in 4 B.C. He had recently, while returning from a visit to Rome, fallen in love with Herodias, the wife of his brother. This brother did not possess a kingdom of his own at the time, which may be one of the reasons why Herodias left him and was prepared to marry Herod Antipas. So far as we know, the brother's name, like his father's, was simply Herod: that Mark calls him **Philip** is perhaps no more than a mistake. Herod Antipas then prepared to divorce his first wife (who anticipated him by returning to her father's court at Petra) and duly married Herodias, who brought with her the child of her first marriage, Salome (Josephus gives us her name). The girl would have been around twenty years old. All sorts of unfortunate results followed from this marriage, including, predictably enough, a war with the Nabataean king of Petra, the father of Herod Antipas' first wife. But in the eyes of strict Jews there was a further reason for disapproval in that it was unlawful to marry a brother's wife while the brother was still alive. This is the background to John the Baptist's remonstrances and Herodias' grudge against him. According to Josephus the scene of John's imprisonment and execution was Machaerus, Herod's frontier stronghold east of the Dead Sea. The gospel narrative is not incompatible with this, although Herod's luxurious palace in Tiberias on the Sea of Galilee would certainly have been a more appropriate setting for the story of the fatal banquet.

The apostles now rejoined Jesus. For the first and only time in Mark's 30 gospel the disciples, on their return from their mission, are called **the apostles.** The word, which means literally "one who is sent out", was a technical one used by the Jews for a messenger entrusted with an official mission; but in the early church it had only one significance: it meant the select group of disciples who, having witnessed the Resurrection, were entrusted with the task of founding the church. It is a striking fact that this title is seldom read back into the gospel narrative; but there is perhaps reason for it here in that the disciples had just acquitted themselves of the kind of task which was subsequently to be the particular mission of the apostles.

Jesus' reaction to the crowds who had just frustrated his intention of sailing **to some lonely place** was that they were **like sheep without a** 31, 34 **shepherd.** This biblical expression (Numbers 27.17, Ezekiel 34.5) was more than a picturesque metaphor for an aimless multitude. It evoked the whole history and destiny of Israel. God himself had shepherded his people, keeping them as one flock in the face of all disintegrating pressures and leading them into their own land towards the fulfilment of that ideal of perfection which their religion constantly held before them. But God had also deputed this shepherding to the people's own political and religious leaders, who had again and again failed to discharge their responsibility—the classic description of this failure is in Ezekiel 34. And it was the same in the time of Jesus. The religious leaders—particularly the Pharisees and the doctors of the law—had failed to give the guidance expected of them (this is a recurring motif in Jesus' discourses). And it was because of this failure that Jesus' heart went out to the crowd—**they were like sheep without a shepherd**. But there is more still in this phrase: it was promised in the Old Testament (and the hope was still alive in later Jewish writings) that God would send a leader who would be a true shepherd. Jesus knew himself to be this shepherd; and he deliberately began to fulfil the rôle by showing, first that **he had much to teach them**, and secondly that he was aware of their physical needs.

34

The four gospels between them give no less than six accounts of a feeding miracle of this kind, and clearly the church cherished the memory of it. Just as, in Mark at least, the healing miracles are not presented merely as the feats of a wonder worker, so the miracle of the feeding has a deeper significance. The scene is not a picnic but a formal meal: the men are made to sit in an orderly way as for a banquet; *a* and Jesus proceeds, like a devout Jewish host, to say the blessing and break the bread himself. The crowd is thus brought into table fellowship with him—the most expressive symbol the Jews knew of solidarity between one man and another; and the whole scene could hardly fail to be remembered when in later years the Christian church began to meet together for that eucharistic meal by which they were still miraculously fed and at which their Lord was still somehow present as host.

The traditional site of this miracle is a small and very luxuriant plain in the north-west corner of the lake, which appears not to have been populated in the time of Christ and which lay about an hour's walk west of Capernaum. If this was in fact the place, and if Mark or the tradition he was making use of was sufficiently familiar with the country for us to be able to rely on the details—and both these assumptions are open to question—then the course of the following events is to be imagined as follows. It had been quite possible for the crowds to gather on the shore from the neighbouring towns before the boat reached the spot: the boat had therefore clearly not crossed the lake from one side to the other (which would have been a much quicker way of crossing than walking all the way round), but had simply moved some distance westward along the shore in order to reach a **lonely place**. If it

31

[a] **A hundred rows of fifty each** gives the required total of five thousand: but it is the translators' idea. The traditional translation "by hundreds and by fifties" may equally well be right.

started from Capernaum (which was the centre of Jesus' activities) then the traditional site of the feeding miracle would be about the right distance away. After the miracle Jesus apparently intended to do what the crowds had done, that is to say, to walk round on foot while the boat returned the way it had come.

Thus, **he made his disciples embark and cross to Bethsaida ahead** 45 **of him.** Bethsaida was in fact a few miles further east than Capernaum on the other side of the mouth of the Jordan. However, the disciples found themselves rowing **against a head-wind** so powerful that by the early hours 48 of the morning (Mark uses the Roman reckoning, "the fourth watch of the night") they had not merely made no headway but were actually (we must suppose) drifting in the opposite direction. Seeing this, Jesus turned west to meet them and apparently struck out across the water. [a] **He was going to pass them by,** presumably because he wished to get to the land in time to meet them. But once they had seen him he joined them in the boat. **So they** 53 **finished the crossing and came to land at Gennesaret.** The plain of Gennesaret lay still further to the west, and they were now further from home than when they had set out. The contrary wind had in fact prevented

[a] The plain of the feeding miracle and the plain of Gennesaret are separated by a rocky hill which runs right up to the shore of the lake. Normally Jesus would have had to walk round it or climb over it, so losing sight of the boat. This could explain why he chose to cut across over the water.

them from making the **crossing** at all; but they were now at least in a different place (which is all that the Greek, taken literally, need mean by **finished the crossing**).

In some such way as this the events recorded by Mark can be fitted into the geography of the lake. But geographical precision was not his main concern. What he had to record was a miraculous feat which Jesus was remembered to have performed. As usual he was anxious not to present it simply as a freak or as the ostentatious performance of a wonder-man, and
52 so he concentrated on the reaction of the disciples. **Their minds were closed**: the word in the Greek is a form of that translated "obstinate stupidity" in 3.5 above. It denotes an almost wilful lack of response to a revelation of the true nature of God. Just as the disciples **had not understood the incident of the loaves**, failing to see in it Jesus' assumption of the rôle of the true shepherd, so now, we are to suppose, they failed to see the implications of his power over the elements: their minds still worked at the level of popular ghost-stories, and their only reaction was fear.

Yet for all this deeper purpose, the fact remained that Jesus performed
53-6 many miracles, particularly miracles of healing; and the section ends with a brief summary of this constant activity without any attempt at interpretation.

Growing tension

7. 1 **A group of Pharisees, with some doctors of the law**. Almost from the beginning of the gospel these men have been constantly in the background, representing a sinister and powerful opposition to Jesus. Not only were they allied to the civil authorities in Galilee (the 'Herodians'), but they were in touch with the religious leaders in Jerusalem (some of these lawyers **had come from Jerusalem**, perhaps for the express purpose of reporting on Jesus' activities). So far, conflict with them had been sporadic and inconclusive, and had been focused mainly on specific questions of Sabbath observance. But now the antagonism came further into the open, beginning with some criticism made of Jesus' disciples on a technical question of purity, but developing into a fierce counter-attack by Jesus against the whole principle on which his opponents' religious practices were based.

The dispute began because some of Jesus' disciples were observed to be
2 **eating their food with 'defiled' hands—in other words, without washing them**. It is known that a hundred years later (if not earlier) it was indeed a strict rule among orthodox Pharisaic Jews to wash their hands before eating, in order to avoid the risk of contaminating their food with any ritually "unclean" substance which might be on their hands; and since this
3 rule was not to be found in Scripture they appealed **to an old-**

established tradition. But strangely enough there is no evidence for this having been a general rule in the time of Jesus, and the most that can be said is that at a formal meal it was normal for guests to wash their hands (Luke 11.38), and that some exceedingly strict Jews of Pharisaic tendencies may already have been regarding hand-washing as essential for the ritual purity of the ordinary layman in his daily life, just as it was for the priest in the performance of his temple duties. In support of this they may have appealed to a traditional interpretation of some passage of Scripture. Mark's comment, in any case, which is clearly intended for readers unfamiliar with Jewish customs, is certainly an exaggeration in so far as it attributes this kind of scrupulousness to the Jews in general; and in other respects it offers information which is barely credible for Palestine in the time of Jesus. It may, however, reflect the conduct of Jewish communities in a city such as Rome where the risks of ritual "defilement" through contact with pagan institutions were so much greater.[a] Moreover, the passage from Isaiah 6 (29.13) is quoted according to the Greek version of the Septuagint, which is somewhat different from the original Hebrew text. Jesus himself could not have used this version, but the church did so, and indeed in Colossians 2.22 we find the passage quoted in the same form as in Mark, again in the context of a discussion about ritually permissible food. It may well be that discussion of this kind between Jews and non-Jewish Christians has left its traces upon the gospel; consequently we have to go behind it to reach the nerve of the original controversy as it would have been conducted between Jesus and the Pharisees.

If it is not true that the Jews in general observed this rule about the 3 washing of hands, the offence given by Jesus' disciples must have been similar to their failure to fast: they were not adopting those practices of extra piety which were expected of any serious religious movement within Judaism. Jesus' reply, assuming that he quoted from the Hebrew text of Isaiah, would have ended: "their religion is but a precept of men, learned by rote". He was endorsing, in fact, the prophet's criticism of any religious practice which diverted the pious from their basic moral obligations; and he was applying it directly to his critics with the words, 'You neglect the 8 commandment of God, in order to maintain the tradition of men'. The many detailed observances which the Pharisees regarded as binding were based, not on the Law of Moses itself, but on a traditional interpretation of the law which sought to make all injunctions relevant to the conditions of contemporary life. The sheer complexity of these observances made the mastery of them a matter which seemed at times to crowd out any

[a] The details are also somewhat obscure. We know of no rules about washing after visiting a "market-place" (which was the name for the civic centre of any Greco-Roman city), and the phrase "washing the hands with the fist", which appears in the best manuscripts and ought probably to be kept in the text, has baffled interpreters. A recent suggestion is that it means holding the hands out, not flat, but cupped.

balanced understanding of the spirit in which the divine law had been given; and it is on this point that Jesus' most characteristic attacks against the Pharisees were made. Their attempt to secure perfect obedience to the law by fencing it round with a mass of detailed regulations had resulted in an actual neglect of the original commandments.

9 But Jesus, in Mark's narrative, carried his attack a stage further. The Pharisees not merely distracted attention from **the commandment of God** by the mass of their detailed applications of it, they actually **set aside** commandments by developing traditions which were incompatible with them. This was a serious charge indeed. The particular example chosen by Jesus is surprising at first sight. From all we know of Pharisaic tradition, it is

10 clear that they placed very high value on the commandment **Honour your father and your mother** (Exodus 20.12 and the negative form of it, Exodus 21.17), and were prepared to waive all sorts of other obligations in order to ensure that it would be observed. The case envisaged by Jesus is

11 that of a son who, in a moment of anger, says "**Corban**". Literally, this meant **set apart for God**. But the word had become an element in a very common form of oath. What the son said amounted to the oath: "I swear you shall have no benefit from anything of mine" (literally, "If I give you anything, it will have to be set apart for God and paid into the temple treasury"). Now the Jews, like many people in antiquity, took oaths very seriously: it was laid down in their law that a man must fulfil his oath (Deuteronomy 23.21), and fearful consequences were expected if he failed to do so. Therefore it made no difference if, when the moment had passed, the son repented of his precipitate words. He was now bound by an oath which prevented him from fulfilling his normal duties to his parents. Clearly such a use of oaths had the makings of a serious abuse. It is true that the Pharisees attempted to remedy it by arguing that a large number of popular ways of swearing were not valid oaths at all and therefore constituted no excuse for failing to observe a clear commandment of the law. Nevertheless, we know from the Dead Sea Scrolls as well as from later rabbinical writings that abuses of this kind flourished in the time of Jesus, and it was fair to attack the Pharisees for having countenanced them. It was their own thoroughly casuistical interpretation of the law which had given the word "Corban" the status of an oath, and so had made it possible for a man to evade his clear duty to his parents simply by uttering the word. This was

13 a good example of their **own tradition** having made an important article of **God's word null and void**.

14 **On another occasion he called the people.** This introductory sentence is so general that it gives no hint of Jesus' motive in making the pronounce-

15 ment which follows. On the face of it, the saying, '**Nothing that goes into a man from outside can defile him**', is of a piece with Jesus' prophetic criticisms of the religion of his day: outward observances are valueless

compared with the pure intentions of the heart. But there is no clue to its precise application; and we can understand why it was subsequently thought of as an enigmatic saying (which is one of the meanings of the word **parable**). 17 Following the pattern which he used when explaining the parable of sowing in chapter 4, Mark appends an interpretation that was given privately to the disciples. This interpretation makes the saying apply specifically to regulations about food; but is this the point which Jesus originally had in mind? The topic was not particularly appropriate to Jesus' work among the Jewish population of Galilee. It was clearly stated in the Old Testament (Leviticus 11, Deuteronomy 14) that certain kinds of meat and fish were not to be eaten, and no Jew would ever have thought of doing so. It was only in a mixed community of Jews and non-Jews that the question became urgent. Moreover, the list of evil deeds and vices is more typical of the conventional 21-2 language of Hellenistic ethics than of the teaching of Jesus. The principle given here was certainly accepted in the church by the time this gospel was written; but there is abundant evidence, both in Acts (10.15; 15.29) and in Paul's letters (Galatians 2.11–14; 1 Corinthians 8 and elsewhere) that the traditional Jewish scruples over "unclean" foods continued to cause divisions of opinion among Christians. Jesus' general statement doubtless implied a liberal attitude towards food; but the implication may not have been worked out by the church until the whole question of the application of Jewish ordinances to Christians had been settled. **Thus he declared all** 19 **foods clean** appears to be a comment by Mark himself, reflecting the position on this matter at last reached by the church.

Then he left that place and went away into the territory of Tyre. 24 The predominantly Jewish region of Galilee was bounded on most sides by territories that were mainly gentile. To the west, the plain lying between the mountains of Galilee and the Mediterranean sea belonged to the Roman province of Syria, and its inhabitants were called "Phoenicians of Syria" to 26 distinguish them from the Phoenician settlers who founded Carthage, in Libya. The principal Phoenician cities in Syria were Tyre and Sidon, which were both cosmopolitan Mediterranean ports; but there is some evidence that politically the **territory of Tyre** extended eastwards over the mountains 24 as far as the upper reaches of the Jordan, and therefore included an area where the population was still mainly Jewish. Mark's meaning therefore may be that Jesus travelled to the extreme north of the Jordan valley (where he would have been still among his fellow-countrymen), and not that he took the more drastic step of crossing the mountains into the completely non-Jewish environment of the coastal plain.

Nevertheless the point of the following story was that it put to the test for the first time Jesus' attitude to Gentiles. What would he do when accosted by a gentile woman? Was he prepared to extend his miraculous and compassionate powers to pagans? Jesus' first response, though a little cryptic

and perhaps spoken with sufficient humour not to give offence, was dis-
couraging: everyone knew that the Jews, themselves in a special sense the
27 'children' of God, were not above referring to non-Jews as 'dogs'; and
Jesus seemed to be endorsing the usual Jewish attitude. But the woman,
instead of protesting at this order of priority, accepted that Jesus' mission
was primarily to his own people, but surmised (with a prophetic insight
which may well have seemed significant to Mark and to the many non-Jews
in the church to which he wrote) that its effect could not be limited to the
Jewish race. For this insight she was rewarded by a rare miracle: exorcism
from a distance.

31   Jesus' **return journey from Tyrian territory** is exceedingly puzzling.
Assuming that Mark intended to continue the series of episodes which took
place in the outposts of Jewish territory, it is reasonable that Jesus' destination should have been that part of the Sea of Galilee which lay in **the territory of the Ten Towns** (the Decapolis, a league of Greco-Roman cities to

146

the east and south of Galilee), and it is just intelligible to describe the journey there as having been **through** this territory, even though this territory was the last he came to. Jesus' route would then have kept to a direction roughly south-east. But **Sidon** (and its territory which, like that of Tyre, extended far inland) lay considerably to the north. If Jesus went literally **by way of Sidon**, he must have made an immense detour, and his journey would have taken several weeks. If he went even into the territory of Sidon at its nearest, he must have gone substantially out of his way, and it seems preferable to assume, either that Mark was ignorant of the geography, or else that Sidon is mentioned only because, since early times, it was customary to refer to it in the same breath as Tyre.

The cure of the man **who was deaf and had an impediment in his** 32 **speech** is described in some detail, and Jesus' procedure conforms closely to that of miracle-healers in many parts of the world: the touch, the spittle, and the solemn word of command (for **Ephphatha** probably represents the 34 Hebrew form of the word, and Jesus would have used Hebrew as a sacred language) are all typical details; and the raising of the eyes to heaven and the sigh can also be paralleled from magical techniques (though they may of course also indicate something of Jesus' emotion on this occasion). But Mark characteristically avoids giving the impression of a mere miracle. He adds once again Jesus' curious injunction forbidding them **to tell anyone**; and 36 he records the very strong impression made on the crowds in words which 37 suggest that they saw the miracle as a sign of greater things to come. For had not Isaiah prophesied (35.5) that in the promised new age "the ears of the deaf shall be unstopped and the tongue of the dumb shout aloud"?

There was another occasion. Mark seems to have had no information 8. 1 about the place or the time of this miracle; and it is of no help to us when he records that the place Jesus went to immediately after it was **Dalmanutha**, 10 since nothing whatever is known about this place. [a] Nor has he attempted to read a deeper meaning into the story, as he did for the remarkably similar incident in 6.30–44. He simply presents the miracle as a notable feat of Jesus, motivated this time (unlike the previous one) by the sheer physical necessity of the people who had followed him: they were now too far from civilization to procure themselves food, and could have come to serious harm unless something were done. It is true that the words **after giving thanks to God**, 6 **he broke the bread** recall Jesus' institution of the eucharist; but they do not in themselves provide a satisfactory explanation why Mark, whose gospel contains on the whole a highly economical selection of Jesus' words and deeds, records two such similar episodes, even if there were in fact (as both Mark

[a] This is the reason why some manuscripts offer the variants Magedan (which is the name, equally unknown, given in Matthew's gospel) or Magdala, which can be identified with a town on the west side of the lake.

and Matthew relate) two such feeding miracles in the course of Jesus' work in Galilee.

11 **They asked him for a sign from heaven.** Coming straight after the report of some remarkable miracles, this request may seem puzzling. What more impressive "signs" could be given than the feats which Jesus had been performing? But from the point of view of sophisticated and sceptical onlookers like the Pharisees, the vital question about Jesus could not be so easily settled. However much deeper meaning the miracle-stories may have possessed (and Mark takes care to show that most of them were more than mere miracles), they were never entirely cogent or unambiguous. Jesus' exorcisms, it was suggested, were carried out in collusion with the devil himself; his healings used recognized techniques of magic; his apparent control of the forces of nature could be accounted for in terms of harnessing powers considerably inferior to that of God himself. There were too many miracle-workers about for it to be prudent to give one's allegiance to any particular one of them without very careful "testing". Moreover Jesus' teaching constituted a direct challenge to existing institutions and traditional piety. If the Pharisees were to own his authority, they would be forced to abandon much of what they stood for. If indeed it were true, as Jesus was proclaiming, that 'the kingdom of God is at hand', then a decisive response of penitence and self-preparation could no longer be postponed. Naturally the Pharisees (and doubtless many others) were unwilling to draw such disturbing conclusions from their encounters with Jesus unless they had a clear and unambiguous "sign" that he had full authority to say what he said and do what he did. What would they have regarded as such a sign? Here we can only speculate; but parallels from the Old Testament and from later Jewish sources suggest that a dramatic fulfilment by Jesus of a specific prophecy, or a miraculous confirmation of one of his own predictions, would have confronted them with a challenge which they could no longer evade.

12 **Jesus sighed deeply to himself.** The signs of emotion which, to a notable extent in this gospel, are attributed to Jesus seem to be provoked by impatience with the religious observances and attitudes by which he was surrounded. So here: the religious mentality which will not yield its allegiance without first being given what it will recognize as unassailable evidence makes Jesus impatient. He sees his questioners as representatives of a whole **generation** which, like the "generation" of Israelites in the wilderness, is too obstinate to recognize the source and implications of the wonders done in its midst.

15 **'Be on your guard against the leaven of the Pharisees and the leaven of Herod.'** These words are not elucidated by the story in which they occur, and since they are found in a quite different context in Luke (12.1) it is likely that they were remembered as an isolated and somewhat

enigmatic saying of Jesus which Mark thought it appropriate to work in at this point. Leaven, because of its impressive power of transforming a mass of dough many times greater than itself, was often used metaphorically. Sometimes good things were compared to it (Matthew 13.33), sometimes bad (1 Corinthians 5.6). The only clue to its meaning here is that it must have been something which the Pharisees and Herod had in common; and this (particularly since an alliance of Pharisees and Herodians on the very point is recorded in 3.6 above) can hardly have been anything but a common disposition to suppress Jesus and his movement. Jesus' warning, in fact, was entirely practical.

But the story in which the saying is embedded (and in which it plays virtually no part) has a very different point. It gives Jesus an opportunity to castigate his disciples severely for their still unenlightened response to the great things he is doing in their presence. He repeats the condemnation of them already recorded by Mark after the first of the two feeding miracles (6.52). Their **minds** were **closed**—a biblical phrase suggesting that they 17 were still in that state of obtuseness which, in the face of divine revelation, had characterized the people of Israel throughout its history; indeed Jesus goes so far as to apply to his disciples those fatalistic words of Isaiah (6.9) 18 which (at least according to Mark) he used of the crowds at large when they failed to understand his parables (4.11–12). The distinction between the disciples and the crowds is here at vanishing point: Mark, unlike Matthew, makes no attempt to portray them in a favourable light. Their moment of glory came later, after Easter, and belonged not to the gospel story but to the history of the church. Meanwhile, even after witnessing Jesus' feeding miracles, they remained blind. The sections which follow show Jesus taking steps to penetrate their blindness.

For Jesus could heal the physically blind. It may be in order to point to a deliberate contrast between his power over blindness and the continuing obtuseness of the disciples that Mark inserts here a second healing story remarkably similar to that given at the end of the previous chapter (the two stories have in common the privacy of the cure, the use of touch and spittle, and the injunction to secrecy, and what was said above about the conventional traits of this kind of miracle applies with equal force here). This one takes place at **Bethsaida**, which was on the far side of the Jordan, in the 22 tetrarchy of Herod Antipas' brother Philip. Philip had begun to found a new city on the site, named Julias after Augustus' daughter Julia; but, since very little is heard about this "city", and since no buildings of any pretension have ever been found on the site, it may be that his plans never got very far, and Mark may not be altogether inaccurate in calling it a **village**; in any 23 case, there is no reason to think that its population must have been much less Jewish than that of, say, Capernaum, or that Mark intends us to imagine that the blind man was a Gentile. The unique feature of the cure is that it was gradual. If a parallel was intended between the man's blindness and the disciples' obtuseness, it is possible that it was this detail which led Mark to place the story here: the next three chapters relate the gradual (and in fact only partial) enlightenment of the disciples.

From Bethsaida, a day's walk northward through the territory of Philip
27 would have been more than sufficient to reach the **villages of Caesarea Philippi,** a town which had been refounded by Philip as a Hellenistic city, without presumably much affecting the character of the villages round it. The
28 beginning of the conversation is a little contrived: Jesus presumably did not need to ask the disciples for information about what people were saying; and their answer to Jesus' question has already been given once by Mark in connection with Herod (6.14). But it serves to point up the significance of the disciples' reply. The people at large had certainly come to see in Jesus more than a mere miracle-worker: he appeared to be a sign that God's promises to his people were about to be fulfilled, and they therefore inclined to identify him with one of those prophetic figures of the past who, it was believed, would return to earth as a herald of the new age. But since the world around them still remained very much the same as it was, they did not take the further step of identifying Jesus with that unique person, the Messiah, who would be the central figure in the inauguration of a new age. The new age, it seemed, had not yet come, even though there might be signs of its dawning in the liberating activity of Jesus. Moreover Jesus himself had not openly admitted to the title of Messiah. Now all the Christians for whom Mark's gospel was written knew that Jesus was in fact the Messiah: indeed they had come to call him, as a matter of course, Jesus "Christ". Mark here relates that even before the resurrection the disciples (for whom Peter appears simply as the spokesman, since Jesus' response to what he says seems on each occasion to embrace all the disciples) had come to recognize
29 the same truth: '**You are the Messiah**' (the Christ).
30   This truth however was not yet to be openly revealed. The injunction to silence continues the series of such injunctions which (particularly in Mark's gospel) Jesus often gives after the performance of a miracle. It is debatable whether these injunctions go back to Jesus (in which case they may have been motivated by a desire for privacy, an anxiety to avoid conflict with the government, or a sense that a popular following was a form of temptation to be resisted), or whether they were (at least in part) inserted by Mark in order to explain the comparatively small following which Jesus obtained in Galilee. But here the injunction makes a clear distinction between the disciples and the people in general: the disciples are shown to have advanced, despite their previous failures, to the point of recognizing Jesus as Messiah, whereas this is something which must still be concealed from the crowd.

Their progress however does not go very far. Jesus immediately gives

them some further teaching which finds no response in them whatever. The ₃₁
Son of Man was a phrase which suggested a glorious and vindicated figure;
but he was to come into this state of glory only after he, or the righteous
people whom he represented, had suffered, and even been martyred, for
their faith. It was perhaps natural that popular thought should concentrate
more on the glory to come than on the necessary condition that the righteous
people of God (of whom everyone hoped to be a member) should first undergo severe tribulation; and the effect of Jesus' words here is to correct this bias
and to emphasize the things which have got to happen first, before glory
and vindication can be contemplated. He does this in some detail; and the
details are an unmistakable description of his own rejection, death and resurrection. According to Mark, therefore, Jesus both identifies himself completely with the Son of Man and gives a detailed forecast of his own destiny.
How near we stand to historical truth at this point is a tantalizing question.
On the one hand it was only be to expected that the words in which the
church was accustomed to recite the bare facts of Jesus' life, death and
resurrection should have influenced at least the form in which Jesus'
prophecy was remembered (and there are vestiges of this process in the
Greek text of Mark). On the other hand it is difficult to make sense of Jesus'
mission unless it is granted that he had at least a premonition of the fate in
store for him, and some consciousness of his destiny.

He spoke about it plainly. Much of his teaching was in parables, much ₃₂
of it enigmatic; the disciples had as much difficulty in understanding it as
anyone else unless, as sometimes happened, Jesus gave them a clue to his
meaning. But on this occasion Mark relates that Jesus talked to them
plainly, that is, in a way they could not possibly misunderstand. Their
reaction, for all that, was no more enlightened than usual. Instead of their
usual bewilderment, they registered frank opposition to the idea that Jesus
(and perhaps also themselves, as members of the people whom the Son of
Man would represent) should suffer rejection and execution. This amounted
to a frank substitution of human preferences for obedience to the divine
purpose. It was a manifestation, in the very circle of Jesus' own disciples (for
whom, again, Peter stands as spokesman), of the seductive power of the
devil with which Jesus had already had to wrestle in the "temptation" with
which his work began.

Since the disciples were unresponsive to this message of suffering, Jesus
called the people to him for some more general teaching on the same theme ₃₄
—or so, at least, Mark or his source arranged this group of Jesus' sayings:
the whole difficulty of this passage is to determine how far the later experience of the church has influenced the record of this important moment in
Jesus' self-revelation. That there has been some influence is difficult to deny.
'He must take up his cross', for example, is a phrase which can hardly have
had much meaning before the crucifixion of Jesus. Crucifixion was the

Romans' normal method of executing those of their subjects in Palestine who were convicted of causing sedition; but before Jesus' own passion and crucifixion set the pattern for his followers, the call to "take up one's cross" could hardly have been understood except as an invitation to risk one's life in acts of resistance or rebellion against the Roman occupying power— which is hardly likely to have been Jesus' intention. Again, whatever teaching

34 Jesus may himself have given about the necessity to **leave self behind** (which is the NEB translators' interpretation of the Greek phrase "to deny

36 oneself") and to maintain one's **true self** at all costs (which is an attempt to bring out the double sense of the word "life" in the original phrase, "whoever shall lose his life ... shall save it"), there can be no doubt that these sayings take on far more relevance and significance if they are read in the context of a Christian community which is being persecuted. The same goes

38 for the final sentence. There may have been moments in Jesus' life (such as Peter's denial of him) when this saying would have been relevant; but it reads more easily as a subsequent warning to the church that anyone who is **ashamed** of Jesus and his followers [a]—that is, who has not the courage to confess his allegiance in the face of persecution—cannot expect to be numbered among those who will share the Son of Man's glorious vindication at the end of history.

9. 1 **He also said.** This is one of Mark's usual ways of adding a saying of Jesus which did not originally belong to the context. The saying presents great difficulty because (taken in its plainest sense) it was soon proved false; but equally, since no one would have thought of attributing to Jesus an apparently unfulfilled prediction if he did not make it himself, it is almost certain to be authentic. In the context both of Jesus' own teaching and of contemporary Jewish expectation, **the kingdom of God ... come in power** could only have meant one thing: the moment when God would bring the present course of world history to an end and institute a new order which would be unmistakably his **kingdom.** If this is what Jesus in fact predicted in the lifetime of his hearers, then he was mistaken; and many interpreters have felt bound to accept this clear limitation of Jesus' understanding of the future, particularly since it is clear from the New Testament letters that the early Christians in general expected the end to come within their own generation. On the other hand a number of decisive events, of less finality than the end of the world, but of considerable significance in the working out of the divine purpose, did in fact take place before the passing of Jesus' generation. One was the destruction of Jerusalem by the Romans in A.D. 70 which seemed to many to symbolize God's final judgement passed on the Jewish religion;

[a] Jesus had no "followers" (people whom he could call **mine**) in the sense of a steady community of which a wavering member might be **ashamed**, until after the resurrection. This would be clear evidence that the saying took its present form not on the lips of Jesus but in the church, were it not that it is far from certain that this is the correct manuscript reading. See the footnote in NEB.

another was the vindication of Jesus (the Son of Man) by the resurrection; a third was the manifest power released in the church which caused the gospel to be accepted on a scale beyond all human expectation, and seemed a clear foretaste of the **kingdom of God already come in power**. It is possible that Jesus' prediction originally referred to one or more of these events; in addition to which, the kingdom of God in Jesus' teaching was never a concept confined to the future: his message was that, though the consummation was still to come, vital things were happening and vital decisions were being asked of men even now in the course of his own activity. Since all his teaching about the coming of the kingdom was thus a great deal richer in meaning than the simple prophecies of doom or glory made by some of his contemporaries, it is reasonable to think that the saying here, whatever its original form, was neither so naïve nor so misguided as it now appears.

The episode which follows is traditionally known as the Transfiguration, **transfigured** being derived from the Latin word which corresponds most 2 nearly to the Greek *metemorphōthē*, "changed his form". The account is brief and succinct; but the difficulty is to know whether it is intended simply to report an eyewitness account or whether some of the details derive from a symbolical interpretation of the event. **Elijah ... and Moses with him,** 4 for example, are clearly not just extras on the stage, but are intended by their presence to point to the nature of him with whom they are conversing. But what on this occasion do they stand for? Are they symbols of the Law and the prophets which Jesus was destined to fulfil and supersede? Elijah was commonly thought of as the first of the prophets, and Moses was of course the lawgiver (though it is surprising to find him in second place after Elijah: it is just possible that he was added later to the original story to fill out the symbolism). Or does Elijah appear in his usual rôle of precursor of the Messiah? In which case Moses is presumably there for the same reason: and it may well be that there was a belief in the time of Jesus (as there certainly was at a later date) that Moses, as well as Elijah, would return at the inauguration of the new age. **Shall we make three shelters?** Again, this could be a 5 purely practical suggestion of Peter's, an effort to offer hospitality on the mountain to the disciples' distinguished guests—and Mark himself notes how inappropriate the suggestion was: **he did not know what to say.** But 6 equally the **shelters** (the word means literally "tents") could be an allusion to the fact that in the earliest history of Israel it was in a "tent" that God came to meet his people (Exodus 33.7–11), and the image of a tent continued to serve as a description both of the actual temple in Jerusalem and also of the true sanctuary of God in the heavens (Hebrews 9.1–14). After this, however, the symbolism of the details becomes apparent: the **cloud** was a 7 traditional sign of the presence of God (Exodus 16.10; 19.9, and many other Old Testament passages); and, since the extinction of the prophetic spirit with the death of the last of the Old Testament prophets, the **voice** from heaven was the most frequent of the ways in which God was believed to reveal himself to men. The words spoken by the heavenly voice are identical with those spoken at Jesus' baptism; the significant difference here is that they are addressed to the disciples, who are henceforward (though their behaviour might seem to belie such knowledge) in possession of the key to Jesus' true nature. One more clue to the mystery of Jesus may lie in the final phrase, 'listen to him'. Deuteronomy 18.15 reads (Moses is speaking): "The Lord your God will raise up for you a prophet like me from among you, from your brethren—listen to him." Jesus (it is doubtless implied) is this prophet.

The vision, then, is cast in a Jewish mould: some if not all the details take on their significance from traditions that originate in the Old Testament. All the more striking therefore is the one verse in the section which describes,

3 in language of an almost peasant simplicity (**with a whiteness no bleacher on earth could equal**), the transfiguration of Jesus himself. To this there is no parallel in Jewish literature: to find anything comparable one has to go to Greek myths, where gods often enough assume human form and then suddenly, by their dazzling appearance, betray their real nature. The vision is unparalleled for good reason. Jewish religion, unlike Greek religion, did not conceive of another and more glorious reality lying in some sense "behind" the physical world and occasionally breaking through to the senses of men. The Jews thought of this other world not metaphysically but temporally. It lay, not in the present behind the outward appearance of things, but in the future: it was the content of God's promises to his people and would one day, by an act of God, be fully revealed to them. The substance of Jewish religious visions was therefore 'what must happen hereafter' (Revelation 4.1), and it may be that Jesus' transfiguration should in part be understood in this sense: the "glorification" of Jesus lay in the future, it was the state he would assume after the resurrection, and what the three privileged disciples were being vouchsafed was a glimpse of that which was to come. But clearly the vision was more than this. Jesus was already Son of God and Messiah; therefore he was already (for those who could see it) a figure of glory. In his transfiguration, as in his preaching of the kingdom and in his power over the forces of evil, Jesus brought decisively into the present things which until then all Jewish religious thinkers had reserved for the future.

In Mark, any spectacular action of Jesus is very often followed by an injunction to secrecy. The transfiguration evidently falls into the same category of things not, or not yet, to be revealed. Jesus refers to himself

9 again (as in 8.31) as **the Son of Man**, and places for the first time a limit to the period of secrecy—**until he had risen from the dead.** The NEB offers

10 an entirely original translation of the following phrase: **They seized upon those words.** The sense is excellent, making a smooth transition to the

question about 'rising from the dead'. But it is doubtful whether the Greek can mean this: it is normally translated "They observed his commandment" or (following a different punctuation) "they kept these things to themselves". In any case their question about rising from the dead arose out of the last words of Jesus' injunction. It was not of course a question about the meaning of "resurrection" itself, for this concept was part of everyone's stock of religious knowledge. One of the most widely held beliefs in Palestine was that at the end of the world all men would "rise from the dead" in order to receive judgement and just reward. What presumably puzzled them about Jesus' saying was that it implied that the Son of Man would rise from the dead, not at, but before the general resurrection. If so, his rising would doubtless (according to the accepted scheme) be a signal for the speedy coming of the end; and this accounts (if strict logic is to be applied to this somewhat jerky paragraph) for their second question: if the end was to come so soon, why had not all things yet come to pass which were due to happen first?

'Why do our teachers say that Elijah must come first?' These 11 teachers are the "lawyers" of a few verses further on, those who profession it was to determine, by reference to their own tradition of interpretation, the precise bearing upon any matter of conduct or belief of a given passage of Scripture. The passage in question here was Malachi 4.5–6: "Look, I will send you the prophet Elijah before the great and terrible day of the Lord comes. He will reconcile fathers to sons and sons to fathers..." The original prophecy was straightforward enough: before the day of the Lord a new prophet would appear who would be none other than the first of the prophets, who had in fact never died (but had been taken up to heaven) and who would return to establish peace in the families of Israel before the end came. But from earliest times there was a tendency to elaborate the rôle of this future Elijah. The Septuagint Greek version of the Old Testament (by adding the words, "and a man to his neighbour") had already extended the area of his peacemaking from family life to the life of the nation as a whole, and Ecclesiasticus 47.13 gives him further tasks. By the time of Christ he had become an important figure in the scheme of the Last Things, and his rôle had grown from that of domestic peacemaking to that of restoring all things to their pristine perfection (to set everything right is a colourless and not 12 entirely accurate translation). Whether he was to be a precursor of the Messiah, or himself to fulfil part of the traditional task of the Messiah, was a matter on which opinions were probably divided. But in any case it was inconceivable that the end could take place without the previous appearance of this Elijah-figure; and the words of Jesus, which seemed to bring the end sensationally close at hand, naturally raised the question in the disciples' minds how, in Jesus' scheme of things, Elijah could be fitted in.

Jesus' reply is somewhat obscure. The correctness of a traditional interpretation of a passage of Scripture could be established or refuted by reference to another passage, and this seems to be Jesus' technique here.

12 Prophecies that the Son of Man himself was **to endure great sufferings and to be treated with contempt** are frequently appealed to in the New Testament, but are not easy to find: Isaiah 53 is usually thought to come nearest to what is required, and doubtless the Son of Man passage itself in Daniel 7 implies that the now vindicated and glorious figure had recently (in the persons of the saints) suffered persecution. But such prophecies seemed to conflict with the Elijah traditions, for the Son of Man unquestionably belonged to the final act of the drama, and if Elijah had already **set everything right**, it was hard to see what would be left to cause **great sufferings**

13 for the Son of Man. For the true answer, Jesus appeals to another prophecy which stated that Elijah too was to suffer at the hands of men. No such prophecy occurs in the Old Testament or the surviving Apocrypha; but we must assume that it occurred in some writing now lost which was sufficiently reputable for Jesus to quote it in the same breath as "the scriptures" (it is just possible that this tradition underlies the passage in Revelation 11 which is concerned with two suffering "witnesses"). If this prophecy was to be preferred to the tradition of a glorious and well-nigh omnipotent Elijah, then the disciples could look among their own contemporaries for a man who fulfilled this rôle. If we turn to Matthew (11.14), his account makes explicit what is doubtless implicit in Mark. They need not look far: the person in question was John the Baptist.

15 **As soon as they saw Jesus the whole crowd were overcome with awe.** The last phrase in the sentence is a strong one, a little stronger perhaps in the translation than it is in the Greek, which could mean simply that the crowd was "astonished" to see Jesus arriving at the precise moment when his presence was required. But **overcome with awe** may be correct. When Moses came down from Mount Sinai "the skin of his face shone" (Exodus 34.30), and the people were "afraid to come near him". Since the story of the transfiguration itself is full of Old Testament allusions, this may well be one more: Mark thought of a reflection of glory still visible in Jesus, as in Moses, some hours after the event, and producing awe in those who saw him.

The argument seems to have started with the disciples' failure to perform an exorcism. That they were empowered to exorcize is stated in 6.7; but that they should have occasionally failed is not surprising in itself (for some spirits were stronger than others) and must also have given the story a particular interest for the early church, in which exorcism was still practised but doubtless not always with success. What was the reason for these failures? Surely the disciples, and the Christians after them, either had the power or did not have it? A possible answer lay in words attributed to Jesus and added here by Mark as a piece of private instruction to the disciples:

'There is no means of casting out this sort but prayer'. If they failed, 29
it must be because they did not pray enough![a]

The exorcism, the last recorded by Mark, concerns a severe case of what
we would now call epilepsy or hysteria, but was then ascribed to the activity of
a spirit. The episode contains elements which allow Mark to present it, not
as a mere miracle, but as a characteristic manifestation of the power and true
nature of Jesus. Jesus' reaction to the all too human scene which met him
on his descent from the mountain recalls the impatience and resignation of
an Old Testament prophet: in the face of the signal acts of God performed
before their eyes, the people remained (as so often in their history: the words
clearly evoke Deuteronomy 32.5) **an unbelieving and perverse genera-** 19
tion. The justification for such severe language is immediately provided by
the tentative approach of the boy's father: **'if it is at all possible for you'.** 22
This showed a clear lack of faith in Jesus' power, only partly made good by
his impassioned appeal, **'I have faith . . . help me where faith falls** 24
short' (literally "help my lack of faith"); for it was apparently the approach
of the crowd, rather than the singularly candid confession of the father,
which spurred Jesus to perform the exorcism, and cure the boy, not just of
his present fit, but of his illness altogether: **'come out of him and never** 25
go back'. Nevertheless it was doubtless because of these words about faith,
and because of Jesus' statement which formed part of the dialogue and which
must have been a source of great encouragement to Mark's readers—
'everything is possible to one who has faith'—that Mark included this 23
exorcism story in his gospel. It is possible also (as his use of the technical
Greek words for "rising from the dead" may suggest) that in the very lifelike
details of the boy looking **like a corpse,** and in the judgement of **many** that 26
he was dead, Mark saw a prefigurement of that victory over death which was
to be accomplished in Jesus' resurrection and shared by all who had faith
in him.

He was teaching his disciples. Mark now devotes a section explicitly 31
to Jesus' instruction of his disciples. The main burden of this teaching was
the prediction of the fate in store for the Son of Man, which is here repeated in very much the same terms as before (8.31); and just as on that
occasion the disciples refused to accept it, so now **they did not understand** 32
what he said, and were afraid to ask. For us, who have come to regard
the Son of Man simply as a title for Jesus, the teaching seems to be a 31
straightforward statement of what was going to happen, and we find it hard
to believe that anyone could have failed to understand it. But **Son of Man**
to Jesus' contemporaries meant (so far as we can now establish its meaning)
a figure who was first and foremost vindicated and glorified; he embodied

[a] Many manuscripts add the words "and fasting". This looks like an early Christian
addition giving a further reason for failure: they did not fast enough!

the splendid destiny to which God's righteous and elect people could confidently look forward. The disciples may not have found any difficulty in Jesus' use of the title as such, for they saw in him a person of unique power and authority; but the teaching which Jesus was giving them about the rôle which suffering was to play in the destiny of this figure (and doubtless in the destiny of that community of righteous and elect men whom the Son of Man represented) was apparently too much for their preconceptions.

Nevertheless the teaching—or at least that part of the teaching which concerned what would be demanded of the community, and which gave guidance to that community in times of stress—was remembered; and it is possible that we can detect in the apparently illogical sequence of these paragraphs one of the ways in which it was in fact held in the memory. For these sayings were clearly not originally spoken in the order, or even necessarily in the context, in which we have them. There is little apparent logical connection between them; and several of them occur in Matthew or Luke in quite different (and sometimes more appropriate) surroundings. On the other hand, one saying often contains a word or an idea which occurs again in the next, so that the memory would be assisted in moving from one to the other. Thus, **in my name** in the saying about children (verse 37) is picked up by **in your name ... in my name** in the saying about non-Christian exorcists; **is a cause of stumbling** in verse 42 is picked up by **is your undoing** (which is the same word in the Greek) in verse 43; **fire** in connection with hell leads on to **everyone will be salted with fire**; and this again leads on to two further sayings about **salt** (verse 50). It is even possible that the word **servant** in verse 35 represents a word in Jesus' own language (Aramaic) which also meant **child**, in which case a further link would be established between the saying about greatness (35) and the saying about receiving children (37). In short the easiest explanation of the inconsequential character of this paragraph is that it reproduces a kind of crude mnemonic system used by teachers in the early church.

To understand these sayings it is therefore necessary to take them separately.

35   (i) The saying, 'If anyone wants to be first, he must make himself last of all and servant of all' occurs again at 10.43–4 and in various other places in Matthew and Luke, and the context is always that of Jesus' instruction to the circle of his disciples; but the saying was clearly remembered as one of Jesus' most fundamental pieces of teaching about human relationships.

37   (ii) 'Whoever receives one of these children'. Two presuppositions seem to underlie this saying. First, to maltreat an accredited envoy is to maltreat him who sent him (the idea was as much taken for granted in antiquity as it is now); and secondly, Jesus is in some way present in the poor and needy to whom one gives, or refuses, hospitality, help and service (this is worked out in Matthew 25.31–46). But neither of these presuppositions

explains why the saying is about **children**. It is true that Jesus had an unusual (for his time) interest in children as such (10.13–16). But it is also possible that the original saying was, like verse 42, about 'little ones who have faith', that is, the weaker and more humble of the followers of Jesus, and that at some stage the expression 'little ones' was taken too literally and turned into **children**.

(iii) Part of the ordinary technique of exorcism was to find out the name 38 and so the power of the devil concerned, and then to invoke by name a stronger power with which to cast the devil out. There is nothing surprising in the report that a contemporary exorcist, hearing of Jesus' power over a large number of "unclean spirits", should have been using his name without any sense of obligation to join Jesus' following. The reaction of Jesus' disciples is human and understandable: that of Jesus suggests that he was anxious to avoid forming any kind of militant and exclusive sect. To make the point, he used what was almost certainly a proverb: '**he who is not** 40 **against us is on our side**'. The proverb was presumably a political one, and represented the attitude of a liberal and conciliatory party, as opposed to that of the more fanatical nationalist sects which were continually spring-ing up under the Roman administration in Palestine. The fact that Jesus appears to say the opposite in Matthew 12.30, Luke 11.23, is probably again because the proverb existed in reverse, "He who is not with us is against us". This would have been the watchword of the more fanatical parties; and there were certainly aspects of Jesus' teaching which had a certain exclusive-ness, and which he (or an evangelist) may have found it appropriate to express by this severer version of the same proverb.

(iv) '**I tell you this**'—one of Mark's characteristic ways of adding an 41 isolated saying of Jesus. The saying occurs in Matthew (10.24) in the context of instructions about the reception to be given to Christian missionaries.

(v) '**As for the man who is a cause of stumbling to one of these little** 42 **ones**'. The **little ones** are doubtless the weaker members of the community of followers of Jesus, and a commentary on this saying can be found in Romans 14; indeed it may have been the kind of situation described there which caused this saying to assume its present form.

(vi) The necessity for sacrifice and single-mindedness is described with all 43–8 Jesus' usual vividness and lack of compromise. Cutting off **hand or foot** was certainly intended as a metaphor; and since the language is metaphorical, the saying should not be pressed for teaching about hell and eternal punish-ment. Jesus accepted and used the language of his contemporaries about these things. In the Greek, the word for **hell** in this passage is *Gehenna*, the precipitous valley on the south side of Jerusalem which was of baneful memory in Old Testament history ("Hinnom" in 2 Kings 23.10, Jeremiah 7.31 etc.) and was in the time of Jesus smoking with the refuse of the city. It was in common use as a name for "hell", and other conventional touches

43 are added, like the **unquenchable fire** and the phrase (which is a quotation
48 from Isaiah 66.24) **where the devouring worm never dies and the fire
is not quenched.**

49 (vii) **'For everyone will be salted with fire.'** Salt preserves; and that
which will make Jesus' disciples worthy of eternal life and preserve them in
a state of preparedness for it will be the fire of persecution. (This at least is
one possible meaning of this difficult sentence.)

50 (viii) **'Salt is a good thing.'** It is clear from the form given to this saying
by Matthew in the Sermon on the Mount that it is the followers of Jesus who
are to be like salt. For the rest, see above on Matthew 5.13.

50 (ix) **'Have salt in yourselves.'** This appears to come close to the Greek
idiom in which salt means sharpness of mind and speech—'never insipid' as
the very similar phrase is translated in Colossians 4.6. [a]

10. 1 **On leaving those parts he came into the regions of Judaea and
Transjordan.** The journey was destined to be of the greatest significance.
Jesus was leaving the comparative freedom of the somewhat provincial
territory of Galilee and would soon be facing a direct confrontation with the
religious leaders in Jerusalem. On the way, however, there was no reason
why things should be any different for him, since the populations and
political conditions through which he passed would have been much the
same as they were in Galilee. The shortest route from Galilee to Jerusalem
was due south along the mountain ridge on the west side of the Jordan. But
this meant going through Samaria, and since relations between the Jews and
the Samaritans were exceedingly strained at this period, Jewish travellers
sometimes preferred to cross the Jordan south of the lake and proceed down
the east side of the valley through territory which was also, like Galilee,
under the administration of Herod Antipas and in which the population was
predominantly Jewish. This territory was called Peraea (rendered in the
NEB as **Transjordan**). They would then re-cross the Jordan in order to
reach Jericho, and by so doing enter **Judaea**, having skirted both Samaria
and most of the Decapolis, and having remained for almost the entire
journey on what could reasonably be described as Jewish soil. Mark's description of the route is a little vague, and is often thought to be an indication
that he had no first-hand knowledge of the geography of Palestine; but
whether or not this is so, his words suggest one of the routes which were
normally taken by Jewish travellers and pilgrims to Jerusalem.

2 **The question was put to him: 'Is it lawful for a man to divorce his
wife?'** It is not easy to be sure what prompted this question. There was
considerable discussion in the time of Jesus on the question of what constituted adequate grounds for divorce, for the relevant text of Scripture

[a] "Sharing salt" was also an expression for giving hospitality: hence the possible rendering in the footnote.

(Deuteronomy 24.1–4) was not precise, and the opinions of the professional interpreters (the 'doctors of the law') were divided, some taking a strict view, some a more permissive one. Matthew, who had greater familiarity than Mark with conditions in Palestine, set Jesus' sayings on marriage and divorce in the context of such a discussion (19.3–9). But in Mark the question is more general: not, Under what circumstances is divorce permissible? but, Is it lawful at all? On the face of it, this question could hardly have arisen in a Jewish community, for there was a passage in the Law of Moses (again Deuteronomy 24.1) which expressly sanctioned divorce. The only practical question was the definition of the grounds on which a divorce could be obtained. Nevertheless, there was at least one Jewish sect in Palestine which disapproved of divorce as such; but anyone who held this extreme view had then to explain away the explicit sanction of divorce in Deuteronomy 24.1. If Mark is correct, and the question was put to Jesus in this general form (and not in the more technical form recorded in Matthew), it must have been because it was thought he would take an extreme view on the matter, and

could be challenged to reconcile his view with Scripture. In this sense, the
2 question could have been asked **to test him.**

Jesus' answer, compared with the ordinary run of expert discussion, was
radical. The premise of all such discussions was that the Law of Moses was
the definitive word of God to man. An obscure clause could be explained by
reference to another passage, and apparent inconsistencies could be smoothed
out by subtle interpretation; but every clause was regarded as in principle
absolutely binding. But Jesus was apparently prepared to regard a clause of
the Law as less important than a principle that could be deduced from
5 another part of Scripture. **It was because your minds were closed that
he made this rule for you.** Moses' dispensation was only a concession to
the obstinacy of human nature. The real will of God must be looked for
6 **in the beginning, that is, at the creation.**

To prove his point, Jesus quoted two passages from Genesis (1.27; 2.24).
The relevance of the first is not immediately obvious. It is true that the verse
in question was something of a puzzle to Jewish scholars. It runs: "So God
created man in his own image, in the image of God he created him; male
and female he created them." Why does the text suddenly break into the
plural? Whatever the real reason, there is some evidence that scholars in the
time of Jesus had an ingenious interpretation based on the legend (made
famous by Plato) that man was originally an androgynous being, made up of
a male half and a female half, which then got separated and for ever after
yearned for each other. It was this original double being, it was believed,
which explained the mysterious appearance of the plural "them" in the
Genesis account of the creation of man. Jesus may have known of this
interpretation; in some circles the text was certainly used in order to propound a somewhat mystical view of the true nature of marriage. In any case,
7 the argument becomes clearer with the second quotation. The words, **for
this reason,** are part of the quotation, and immediately follow the account of
the creation of the woman from the rib of the man. The biblical explanation
8 of the fact that man and wife become **one flesh** is rather similar to Plato's
legend: originally, woman was actually a part of man's flesh. By the institu-
9 tion of marriage, God simply **joined together** what originally belonged
together. On the basis of this passage, Jesus could argue that divorce as such
is contrary to the will of God.

10 **The disciples questioned him about this matter.** The disciples may
simply not have understood this somewhat sophisticated piece of reasoning,
or else they were puzzled (as Christians have been puzzled ever since) about
11 its practical implications. But Jesus' reply to them was quite uncompromising. He was not, it seems, offering an interpretation of the law as it stood; for
in theory (though this seldom happened in practice) Jewish law permitted
polygamy, and therefore a prohibition of divorce would hardly have affected
the position of the husband: he was permitted to have more than one wife in

any case. Rather, Jesus was making a judgement on divorce in general. Adultery was one of the acts which Jews regarded with the greatest abhorrence and punished very severely: its prevalence among non-Jews was one of their most constant complaints against gentile society. By calling the remarriage of divorced persons **adultery**, Jesus condemned it in very strong terms indeed. As for the second part of Jesus' reply, it is difficult to see how 12 it could possibly have had this form in Palestine, where a wife had no right to institute divorce proceedings, and where consequently the words **if she divorces her husband** would have made little sense. She might however ask her husband for a divorce, and if he gave it to her the law permitted her to marry another man; [a] this may originally have been the point of Jesus' saying.

They brought children for him to touch. Their purpose (as Matthew 13 explains, 19.13) was to obtain his blessing: it was something very commonly asked of a religious teacher. Why the disciples objected is left to our imagination; but Jesus' reaction, as described by Mark (who hesitated less than any of the evangelists to ascribe expressions of emotion to him), was a strong one: **he was indignant.** What was the quality in children which Jesus prized so 14 highly? We have to clear our minds of all those concepts of children's innocence, freshness of vision and spontaneity of motive which have come to be taken for granted in the west only since the Romantic movement, and have probably never had much currency in the east. The child, in antiquity, was valued not for his childishness but only for the promise in him of adult manhood; and the "blessing" of a parent or a teacher would be in effect a prayer that the promise would be fulfilled: it was a blessing entirely for the future. It is therefore a new and curiously modern tone which we hear in Jesus' voice when he appears to value children as children, in the present and not the future. It is possible, of course, that he was not doing anything of the sort. **Children** in this passage may be simply symbols for the poor and meek and humble of heart, a nickname for Christians (as perhaps in 9.37); or the episode may even (as some maintain) owe its form, if not its origin, to disputes in the early church about the propriety of baptizing infants. But neither of these explanations does full justice to the saying, '**the kingdom of** 14 **God belongs to such as these**', which implies a clear recognition that there is something in children, as children, of real religious importance. The nearest the Bible (or indeed any ancient literature) comes to this is a passage such as Psalm 131.2—"I have calmed and quieted my soul like a child quieted at its mother's breast"—where the total dependence of a small child on its parents is an image of the dependence, trust and humility a man should feel before God. We can only guess how much more than this was intended by Jesus, or would have been understood by his hearers.

[a] A manuscript reading exists (not noted in NEB) which, since it gives "departing from her husband" instead of "divorcing him", is compatible with Jewish law. It is possible that this is what Mark originally wrote and that the text was subsequently changed to correspond with Roman law.

17   **A stranger ran up, and, kneeling before him, asked, 'Good Master
. . .'** This scene, which contains some notably vivid details, has also a striking
beginning. It was not customary for one Jew to kneel to another—the
gesture was associated more with the cringing behaviour expected in the
presence of an oriental monarch—and **'Good Master'** was a form of address
so unusual that Jesus was moved to comment on it. This is hard to convey in
English, for in a phrase like "Good Sir" the word "good" is nothing more
than an expression of courtesy. The same was true to some extent in Greek
society, and a Greek reader would probably have found the phrase, **'Good
Master,'** as innocuous as a modern English reader does. But in Jewish
conversation this polite idiom was unknown. To say of someone that he was
"good" would not even have been understood as a professional compliment:
a Jew would not have said that Jesus was "good" in the sense of being a
good teacher, better than other teachers. To call someone "good" was to
use the word in all seriousness of his moral character and personal conduct.
Furthermore it was to use of a human being an absolute term that was
proper to God alone. Hence Jesus' objection. It has often been felt (as it
appears to have been felt by Matthew, who altered the sense of the remark)
that the objection came oddly from Jesus: surely he, if anyone, merited the
title "good"? But it may be that Jesus was objecting less to the word itself,
which might in fact have been appropriate to him, than to the attitude of his
questioner, who was prepared to use so serious a concept as a term of
courtesy or even flattery.

17   **'What must I do to win eternal life?'** The question was a standard one.
After death, at the general resurrection, men would be judged on their
record, and those whose good deeds and way of life had merited it would
win eternal life while the rest would be consigned to hell. This, at any rate,
was the usual way of looking at the matter in the time of Jesus and in the
circles in which he moved, and the ultimate purpose and goal of religious life
and moral conduct was to "gain a share in the world to come" or to **win
eternal life.** In broad terms the Jews were agreed on the way this could be
achieved. God's will for man was revealed in the Law of Moses, and those
who kept this law would automatically qualify for their promised share in the
life to come. Did the stranger expect from Jesus some kind of practical
precision and elaboration of the Law in answer to his question, or did he hope
for a new ethic altogether, superseding the old? His words alone do not tell
us, though the eagerness of his approach suggests that he expected some-
19 thing quite new. Jesus' reply was almost brusque. **'You know the commandments'.** Jesus simply referred him back, without any refinements of
interpretation, to that basic section of the Ten Commandments which
20 governs conduct towards one's neighbour. **'But, Master', he replied, 'I
have kept all these since I was a boy'.** This reply was not pretentious. A
devout Jew treasured his consciousness of living correctly by the law, and it

was only the immense elaboration introduced into the observance of the law by certain schools of Pharisaic thought which made scrupulous souls such as Paul despair of keeping the law in its entirety. Jesus at any rate did not criticize his reply; on the contrary, **his heart warmed to him.** Perhaps he 21 valued especially the man's dissatisfaction with a moral achievement which would have seemed adequate to most men of his circumstances (for we learn at the end that **he was a man of great wealth**). The obvious advice to give 22 him would have been to recommend a drastic increase in his almsgiving, for this was valued by the Jews as one of the most meritorious acts of all, a sure way of amassing **riches in heaven**; and the rich were regarded as 21 fortunate in having the resources to do this on a large scale. But Jesus pushed this far beyond the limit that would have been thought desirable by most of his contemporaries (some of whom actually discouraged excessive almsgiving, on the grounds that a man had a duty not to impoverish himself). The man must give away everything. Only total "giving to the poor" would answer to his situation. And to the question, What should he do then, as a pauper? Jesus had an answer ready: '**Come, follow me**'.

The story is one of a personal encounter between Jesus and a particular wealthy man. The question must immediately have been raised (as it has been raised ever since), Would the same apply to every rich man? The normal Jewish view (which was shared by all but the most sophisticated thinkers in antiquity) was that a man's riches were a sign of God's blessing, and that he could turn his wealth to a source of still greater blessing by generous acts of charity. The obverse of this, of course, was that the poor were not blest; and in a society like the Jewish, where throughout their history the rich were few and the poor were many, a more refined view had developed, according to which the poor had other virtues and opportunities of service which they could cultivate, and other evidence in their lives of God's blessing upon them, which compensated for their lack of wealth and privilege. Jesus very strongly endorsed this attitude. He went so far as to say, without qualification, 'How blest are you who are in need' (Luke 6.20). But it would not necessarily have occurred to his listeners to draw the conclusion which Jesus drew, 'Alas for you who are rich', for this would have drastically upset their presuppositions. When therefore Jesus generalized the case of this particular rich man by saying, '**How hard it will be for the wealthy to enter the kingdom of** 23 **God**', the reaction of his disciples was one of bewildered astonishment.

'**It is easier for a camel to pass through the eye of a needle.**' The 25 almost grotesque disproportion of the simile is characteristic of Jesus' speech: there is no reason to think (as some have thought) that the original saying in his own language was misunderstood when it came to be translated into Greek. It is possible indeed that the saying was originally even more general and paradoxical than it appears; for the reading of the majority of manuscripts (as given in the NEB text as opposed to the footnote) gives in

24 verse 24 'how hard it is to enter the kingdom of God', without any mention of riches, and it is possible that all these sayings were originally quite general: the possibility of anyone entering the kingdom of God is one created only by God; no human qualifications (let alone riches) make any difference.

28 **At this Peter spoke.** The disciples had responded to the challenge which the rich man had failed to meet. Could they at least be sure of their reward? Jesus' reply should probably be understood as that of a man who was even now leading a small group of impoverished disciples towards an uncertain destiny. A religious leader with political aspirations (and there were several

30 in first-century Palestine) would naturally promise **in this age** material rewards, as well as **in the age to come eternal life**. On the other hand, a teacher whose concern was entirely with religious truth would be likely to content himself with promising his followers spiritual benefits after death. Jesus' rôle was clearly of the second type, and that part of the saying which promises **eternal life** seems the more characteristic of him. But it was also a feature of his teaching that much of what was normally reserved for the promised future life, Jesus brought startlingly into the experience of the present. It is therefore perhaps not surprising that part of Jesus' answer to Peter's question should have dealt with the question of rewards **in this age**. Nevertheless the apparently unashamed materialism of these promises comes as a shock, only slightly mitigated by the addition that there would be **persecutions besides**. Jesus may have been speaking metaphorically; but the saying is none the less puzzling, and it is possible (particularly in view of the conflicting evidence of a number of manuscripts) that some confusion crept in soon after the saying was written down.

31 **'But many who are first will be last and the last first.'** This saying occurs in a different context in each gospel (compare Matthew 20.16, Luke 13.30), and was evidently remembered as an isolated dictum, to be inserted by the evangelists into their narratives wherever it fitted best. Its setting in Luke's gospel seems the most appropriate.

Challenge to Jerusalem

32 **They were on the road, going up to Jerusalem.** They were about to come to Jericho, whence the road begins the long steep climb up to Jerusalem. The summit of the Mount of Olives could already be seen, some four thousand feet above. They were therefore, in the most literal sense, **going up to Jerusalem**. But "going up" meant more than this. It was the expression used of going to Jerusalem as a pilgrim on one of the great festivals (and the road may already have been crowded with pilgrims on their way to join in the

Passover); and the deliberate and public confrontation which Jesus seemed to be seeking with the centre of religious authority in the land may be a sufficient explanation of the awe of his disciples and the fear of those who followed behind. Nevertheless, the awed reaction of his followers, though understandable under the circumstances, remains a little strange. Mark may have deliberately anticipated, at this point, something of the dark drama which was soon to begin. He has certainly done this, in any case, in his report of Jesus' pronouncement to the Twelve. The two previous predictions of the destiny awaiting the Son of Man (8.31; 9.31) were in general terms, and could well have been spoken out of Jesus' awareness of the nature of the part he had soon to play. But this third prediction includes details drawn directly from the history of Jesus' subsequent trial; and unless we wish to credit Jesus with the most literal kind of second sight, we must recognize the hand of the narrator, writing up this saying of Jesus in the light of its ful-filment a few days later.

On the two previous occasions, the disciples had failed to understand how the glorious title, Son of Man, could be compatible with so menacing a future. Here, this failure is not mentioned; but the request of James and John perhaps indicates that understanding had still not dawned. '**Grant us the** 37 **right to sit in state with you**'. They may have imagined that in Jerusalem Jesus would become a real king, and that they would be his chief courtiers; or they may have been looking forward to the supernatural transformation of things in the age to come—the Greek phrase translated **in state** means literally "in glory". In either case, they were making the disciples' usual mistake of looking ahead to the future glory without reckoning on the tribu-lations which must come first, both for the Son of Man and for those whom he represented. Jesus' reply, once again, insisted on this necessary pre-liminary. '**Can you drink the cup that I drink, or be baptized with the** 38 **baptism I am baptized with?**' Cup and baptism were soon to have their own specific place in Christian worship, and this may have influenced the form in which Jesus' saying has come down to us; but it is possible to attach meaning to the saying without reference to the later technical meaning of these words. The **cup** was an obvious symbol for a destiny of suffering (as in 14.36), and was a standard Old Testament expression for the severe judge-ment of God; and to be **baptized** was probably (though there are too few instances in ancient literature for us to be sure) a not uncommon metaphor, meaning to be overwhelmed by a wave of afflictions. Jesus was in effect challenging the two disciples to share in that destiny of suffering which must precede his own ultimate glorification. They accepted the challenge, and so qualified for a share in the Son of Man's glory. But the further privilege of absolute precedence in the court of heaven was not so readily granted. [a]

[a] There are grounds for believing that John died of old age in Ephesus; but another tradition relates that he was martyred at the same time as James (Acts 12.2). This is

43 'Whoever wants to be great must be your servant'. This radical teaching on personal relationships is repeated here (after its appearance already at 9.35) as Jesus' response to signs of ambition among his disciples; but this time it is firmly based upon the example of Jesus himself. The Son 45 of Man, in Daniel 7.14, is indeed exalted to a position where he is to be served "by all peoples". But that lies in the future, when he will be glorified. Meanwhile (and this is the side of the Son of Man's destiny upon which Jesus lays special stress in these chapters) his rôle is the exact opposite: he has come to serve; and since he is a representative figure, it follows that each 44 of those who throw in their lot with his must also be the willing slave of all. The full extent of the service which is to be demanded of Jesus is defined in 45 the words which follow: 'to give up his life as a ransom for many'. At first sight this somewhat technical phrase looks more like the later language of the church than that of Jesus himself. But although there are passages, in Paul for instance, which use similar language (Romans 3.25, Colossians 1.14 and elsewhere), there is no other instance in the New Testament of this precise phrase, and there is nothing in the phrase itself which would necessarily have been strange to Jesus' own way of thinking. The idea of a ransom was a common metaphor in the Old Testament: God's interventions on behalf of his people were often described as acts by which he "ransomed" his people from their enemies; and since, in the time of Jesus, people thought of themselves as under the power, not merely of the occupying Roman forces, but (in a deeper sense) of the forces of the devil and indeed of the only too obvious consequences of their own sins, the metaphor of being rescued from all this by the payment of a ransom was very much alive. But how could the death of one man have such a result? The explanation is often sought in Isaiah chapter 53, where the exiled prophet seems to have had some intimation that the death of a righteous man could atone for "the sin of many" (53.12). But, apart from the word many, the saying of Jesus is barely reminiscent of this passage, and it may not be necessary to look so far for the origin of the idea of a vicarious and atoning death. Not long after the time of the Maccabees, some two centuries previously, the deaths of those who were martyred for their loyalty to the Jewish religion were regarded as an expiation for the misdeeds of their nation (2 Maccabees 7.37–8); and it appears that many Jewish thinkers soon came to take the same view of the vicarious effect of the martyrdom of a righteous man. If Jesus expressed the significance of his own death in such terms as these, there is no reason to think that the idea would have been altogether strange to his hearers.

46 They came to Jericho. The last healing miracle recorded in this gospel

unlikely to be correct; if it were, it would lend support to the view that Jesus' words are a prophecy of the two martyrs' death, a prophecy perhaps attributed to Jesus soon after. The reason why they were denied the two places of honour is sometimes thought to be that it was Peter, and then James "the Lord's brother", and not the sons of Zebedee, who subsequently emerged as the leaders of the church.

is told with much circumstantial detail. The place of it was remembered as the road which led out of Jericho towards Jerusalem; there was a crowd around Jesus, probably of pilgrims who, like him, were "going up to Jerusalem" for the Passover, but who were possibly already curious about Jesus himself and ready, if given the signal, to proclaim him their leader; and a third detail, which is unusual in Mark, is that the subject of the cure is named: **Bartimaeus** (which simply means **son of Timaeus** as Mark explains). Perhaps the fact that after his cure he **followed Jesus on the road** 52 caused his name to be remembered. A further touch of colour suggests that the story goes back to an eyewitness account: when Bartimaeus speaks to Jesus he uses the Aramaic word *Rabbuni*, which is a particularly respectful form of the title "Rabbi". In John 20.16 the Aramaic word is both recorded and translated. Here Mark simply reproduces it, without translating it: his readers, even if they knew little about Palestine, were evidently expected to understand it (the NEB aids the reader, but eliminates the local flavour of the words, by writing **Master**). On the other hand, there are two elements 51 which betray Mark's usual concern to reveal that the cure was more than a mere miracle. **'Son of David'** is a title which has not been used before in 47 this gospel. It does not mean that Bartimaeus knew anything about Jesus' physical ancestry. It was simply one of the names by which it was natural to refer to the person who (it was popularly believed) was destined to restore the fortunes of Israel: the Messiah, or Christ. The following which Jesus had gathered, and the air of expectancy which surrounded his approach to Jerusalem, were doubtless sufficient to suggest to Bartimaeus that **Jesus of Nazareth** was this Messiah. And since a well-known prophecy (Isaiah 61.1), which was usually held to refer to the coming of the Messiah, promised that he would bring "recovery of sight to the blind", Bartimaeus' excitement needs no further explanation. But, from the point of view of the narrator, his cry had a further significance: Jesus *was* the Christ. So far only his disciples had recognized the fact; now a blind man had come to the same decisive realization, and it was in response to this that Jesus opened his eyes: **'your faith has cured you'**. If there is any symbolism in the previous 52 cure of a blind man (8.22–6), the same implication is doubtless intended here: after a series of attempts to open the eyes of the disciples to his true nature and destiny, Jesus demonstrates that even the physically blind can be made to see.

When they reached Bethphage and Bethany, at the Mount of Olives. 11. 1 These two villages did not lie on the direct route from Jericho to Jerusalem, but would have been reached by turning off southwards just before the road began to climb over the crest of the Mount of Olives. It is not clear why Mark mentions both the villages, which lay at least a mile apart; but if Jesus had in fact reached the crossroads from which the road straight on led to Jerusa-

lem, while that to the left went through the small village of Bethphage to the larger village of Bethany, it is not difficult to imagine him sending two
2 disciples 'to the village opposite' to fetch a colt.

The details of the episode are all capable of a thoroughly prosaic interpretation. Jesus could have made prior arrangements about the colt, in which case there is nothing surprising in the way it was provided for him; and the acclamation and the brushwood may have an equally simple explanation. It is often thought likely, for other reasons, that Mark may have been wrong in stating that Jesus entered Jerusalem only once, at Passover-time. At two other annual festivals it was customary for people to gather green branches from the countryside and bring them into Jerusalem; and on one of them
9 Psalm 118 (from which the words 'Hosanna...' are a quotation) was one of the prescribed liturgical songs. It is therefore perfectly possible that the story in the gospels has grown out of an almost accidental involvement with a crowd of pilgrims on the road. This would incidentally explain why the procession had no immediate consequences, and apparently provoked no official counter-measures.

However, even if this was the origin of the story, it was not the way any of the evangelists understood it. Mark's account is the simplest; but even so the details are evidently intended to carry a deeper significance. One point which is crucial to the story, and which tells against a too rationalistic interpretation of it, is that Jesus, having travelled the whole way from Jericho on foot, chose to ride into Jerusalem. Pilgrims were expected to enter the city on foot. Thus Jesus' action was a deliberate gesture, intended to draw attention to himself. Furthermore, the manner in which he acquired his mount is narrated in great detail. It is true that the matter could have been pre-arranged by Jesus, but it is unlikely that Mark would have recorded it so carefully if he had thought of it simply as a detail of organization. For him, and for those who first remembered and recorded the episode, it must almost certainly have appeared as an instance of Jesus' supernatural prescience. There is significance, too, in the animal he rode on. Mark and Luke use a word for it which, in ordinary Greek, would normally mean a horse's colt. But this was also the word which the Septuagint translators of the Old 2 Testament used to represent the Hebrew word meaning "foal of an ass". Two Old Testament texts in particular use this Hebrew expression. One is Genesis 49.11, a rather mysterious oracle about someone who would some day come to rule over Judah and over "all the nations", and would "tether his ass to the vine and his ass's foal to the red vine". This oracle was certainly interpreted as a prophecy of a coming Messiah in the time of Jesus. The other text is Zechariah 9.9: "Your king is coming to you . . . humble and mounted on an ass, on a foal, the young of an ass"; and this again was regarded as a prediction of the Messiah who was to come. Matthew and John, by quoting the text from Zechariah, make it quite clear that they understand Jesus' mount to be "the foal of an ass", and Jesus' ride into Jerusalem to be the fulfilment of a prophecy about the advent of the Messiah. The matter is not so clear in Mark: but certain details point in the same direction. The colt was **tethered**, as in Genesis 49.11; and it was one **which no one has yet ridden**—a fact about it which would hardly have struck the disciples when they went to fetch it; but it was axiomatic that any beast used for a sacred purpose must never have been ridden, and in fact the Septuagint Greek version of Zechariah adds the detail that the foal the king was riding was "new". Thus the details of Mark's account seem to imply that, like Matthew and John, he thought of the **colt**, not as a young horse, but as the symbolic and sacred "ass's foal" on which people expected the Messiah to ride.

Jesus' deliberate and ostentatious ride from the Mount of Olives (a spot which also had a place in Zechariah's prophecies of the ultimate coming of the Lord, Zech. 14.4) was therefore staged in such a way as to alert those who could interpret it to the fact that he was himself the promised Christ. But, just as throughout Mark's gospel it had only been a very few who had recognized Jesus for what he really was, so here there was no open and unmistakable declaration of his true nature; and the response of the crowds, though it had all the enthusiasm to be expected in view of Jesus' reputation, does not give anything away. Their cry 'Hosanna' (which originally meant 9 "save now" but had probably become a very general word of religious acclamation), '**Blessings on him who comes in the name of the Lord**', was a quotation from a psalm (118.25–6) that was particularly associated with

the carrying of green branches at religious festivals, and the evocation of the
10 **coming kingdom of our father David** was a sign, certainly, of a lively
expectation of the Messiah, but did not necessarily single out Jesus as the
Messiah himself. Mark's readers knew who Jesus was and would have found
many hints of his true nature in the narrative; but it is nowhere stated that
the crowds who thronged round Jesus recognized him for what he really was.

11 **He entered Jerusalem and went into the temple.** "Going up to
Jerusalem" reached its goal when the pilgrim descended the west side of the
Mount of Olives, crossed the Kedron valley, and climbed up the other side
to the tremendous terrace on which Herod the Great had built the temple.
The terrace formed part of the city wall, and one gate on this side led straight
into the immense area of colonnaded porches, open courtyards and subsidiary buildings which surrounded the temple itself. To look **at the whole
scene,** Jesus could well have spent some time there; but he soon retired for
the night to Bethany, where (if we may supply details from the other gospels)
he had friends and the assurance of hospitality.

The story of Jesus cursing the fig-tree is odd in so many respects that it is
widely believed to have been misreported by the gospel writers. Why should
12 Jesus have **felt hungry** on the short walk (barely two miles in all) from
Bethany to Jerusalem? How can he have expected to find fruit on the tree
13 **if it was not the season for figs?** And is not his curse on the tree both quite
unreasonable in the circumstances and also out of character? Of all these
oddities, the greatest is the detail that **it was not the season for figs.** If this
phrase were removed, the story, though still puzzling, would at least be
plausible; and it is possible to think of reasons why the phrase may not
belong to the original version. If it was the case (as John's gospel maintains,
and as certain details in Mark's account make us suspect) that Jesus went up
to Jerusalem at other festivals besides this Passover, then the story may have
belonged originally to one of his earlier visits at a different time of year (say
for the autumn feast of Tabernacles, when figs would be ripe). But Mark, or
the source he was using, recounts only one visit to Jerusalem, at Passover-
time, that is to say March–April, too early by some two months for any ripe
figs to be found on the trees. The story could not be inserted anywhere else
in the gospel, since it was set in the neighbourhood of Bethany; and either
Mark, or else some scribe working over the manuscript not long after it was
written, may have added the words, **for it was not the season for figs.** In
the framework of Mark's narrative this was correct: but unfortunately it
made nonsense of the story.

Even if this explanation is accepted, the story is still puzzling. Why did
Jesus curse the tree? Two possibilities are often suggested. One is that the
story was originally a parable told by Jesus to express the point that a
husbandman's patience could not be expected to last for ever, and that the
parable subsequently became confused with an actual event in Jesus' life;

the other is that the action was symbolic, in the tradition of the Old Testament prophets: for all its early promise, the "tree" of Israel had failed to produce any fruit, and the time had come for its destruction. The literal withering of the fig-tree could have been intended as a lesson for the Jewish people of Jesus' time.

Jesus **began driving out those who bought and sold in the temple.** 15 The **temple** comprised not only the sanctuary itself and the central buildings connected with the cult, but also a series of large colonnaded courts, one of which, since it was open to non-Jews, was known as the Court of the Gentiles. The whole precinct was sacred, and subject to ritual regulations which were enforced by Jewish temple police; nevertheless there is no reason to doubt that people came to the outer courts for many purposes. It was here, under Herod's colonnades, that Jesus 'taught day after day in the temple' (14.49), and here that crowds gathered to hear him. But the target of Jesus' action on this first day after his arrival in Jerusalem was apparently quite specific: **those who bought and sold . . . the tables of the money-changers and the seats of the dealers in pigeons.** The curious thing here is that these seem to have been necessary and (granting the whole principle of the temple's existence and function) unobjectionable institutions. Contributions to the temple treasury, whether the annual temple tax or offerings for other purposes, had to be made in the purest and most exact coinage known in Palestine, the silver coins minted in Tyre. These could be obtained from money-changers, who charged a small commission on the exchange; and at least at one time of year (a short period ending about a fortnight before the Passover) these money-changers were officially permitted to have their **tables** (or banks) inside the temple precincts. This is all we know about such trading in the temple; and if this is what Jesus objected to, then it is not easy to interpret his action. If he had wanted to attack the whole temple system, we should have expected some gesture directed at the priests and administrators, not at such a small and comparatively harmless part of the organization as was represented by the money-changers. On the other hand, it is not at all unlikely that, out of this small beginning, a considerable amount of commercial business had developed. The money-changers may have combined their technical function of providing the ritual silver coins with full-scale commercial banking (there are many parallels to this in the ancient world: the comparative security of a shrine made it the natural place for a bank); the necessary dealing in birds and animals for sacrifices, which should have been confined to markets outside the temple area, seems, from Mark's reference to **dealers in pigeons,** to have made its way into the temple courts; and for all we know, trading of other kinds may have followed in its wake. Jesus' protest, in this case, will have been against an abuse which had grown up with the connivance, but presumably without the official sanction, of the temple authorities; and if the practices he was attacking were

technically illegal, this would explain why the temple police did not imme-
16 diately intervene. His action in not allowing anyone **to use the temple court
as a thoroughfare for carrying goods** will have been of exactly the same
kind. There is some evidence that this too was technically prohibited, and
Jesus may have found that the prohibition was not being enforced.

So far Jesus' action (if this is the correct interpretation of it) reads like
that of a reformer anxious to stamp out abuses which the authorities had
complaisantly allowed to creep into the administration of the temple. It
reflects an extreme reverence for the sanctity of the place and for the importance of the ritual which took place there. But the saying with which Jesus
is recorded to have interpreted his action sets it in a different light. It consists
17 of two quotations. The first, **"My house shall be called a house of
prayer for all the nations"** (Isaiah 56.7) is drawn from a well-known Old
Testament prophecy that the worship of the God of Israel would one day
be shared by men of all nationalities, who would therefore have free access to
the temple. In Jesus' time, non-Jews were admitted into the so-called Court
of the Gentiles, but were very strictly prohibited from penetrating any
further; and the natural target of such a saying would have been the
prominent notices which were set up to warn Gentiles from trespassing any
further. The second quotation is from Jeremiah 7.11: the prophet was
attacking the people of Jerusalem for assuming that, because they maintained
the worship of the temple, the violence, injustice and idolatry of the city's
life would be condoned by God. On the contrary, argued Jeremiah, the
presence of such people in the temple showed that they thought of it simply
as some sort of protection against the consequences of their unlawful
behaviour, rather like a **robbers' cave.** The translation of this phrase in the
NEB reads, at first sight, like a poor substitute for the traditional rendering,
"den of thieves"; for if the object of Jesus' attack was the presence of
extortionate traders in the holy place, then the description of their offices as a
"den of thieves" is as apt as one could wish. But the old translation in fact
begs the question. Nothing in the account so far has suggested that the
bankers and dealers were dishonest, and moreover the original phrase, both
in the Hebrew of Jeremiah and in the Greek translation used by Mark, does
not mean anything of the sort. The essence of a "thief" is that he acts
surreptitiously; but the word used here means, not a surreptitious thief, but
a man of violence, an armed robber or brigand. In the time of Jesus the word
became almost a technical word for fanatical rebels against the Roman
régime, who conducted guerrilla warfare, terrorized peaceable citizens, and
very often had their hideouts in the caves which are to be found in the
mountains all over Palestine. The NEB translation is thus a great deal more
accurate than the traditional one—if indeed it goes far enough: "brigands'
cave" would probably come still nearer to the meaning the phrase would
have conveyed to Jesus' contemporaries. Clearly, the quotation cannot have

been intended as a comment on ordinary commercial transactions: it implies that the temple had become a place of violence, or at least a meeting-place of violent men.

It seems necessary, therefore, to assume that Jesus' saying on this occasion has nothing to do with his action in turning out the bankers and traders, but is a separate piece of teaching directed against the exclusive Jewishness of the temple and perhaps also against incidents of violence which had taken place within it (such as Josephus tells us took place quite frequently at this period), or at any rate at the hands of those who frequented it. If so, we must ask what was the intention of this whole sequence of actions and sayings which marked Jesus' first complete day in the temple. On the face of it, they appear as a protest against abuses of the proper function and sanctity of the temple. But a further meaning may lie in the background. On the previous day, Jesus had entered Jerusalem in a manner calculated to suggest that a prophecy in Zechariah about the coming Messiah was even now being fulfilled. The same book ends, "When that time comes, no trader shall again be seen in the house of the Lord of Hosts" (14.21). Moreover, it was a tradi-tional belief, inspired by the visions of the prophet Ezekiel (40–8), that in the days of the Messiah the temple would be renewed. All these thoughts will have been present in the minds of Mark's first readers; and Mark may have wished it to be understood that the same inferences could have been drawn by those who actually witnessed the scene, had they had eyes to see and ears to hear.

Early next morning. The miraculous sequel of the cursing of the fig-tree 20 gives Mark the cue to introduce three sayings about prayer which, since two of them occur in other gospels in a quite different connection (Matthew 22–5 6.14–15; Luke 17.6), were presumably remembered separately. The form of the first saying was proverbial. "Moving mountains" was nearly as common an expression for doing the apparently impossible as it is now. Nevertheless, the Mount of Olives would have been a singularly striking setting for the saying. From it the Dead Sea can be seen nearly four thousand feet below, and a cataclysm which "lifted it from its place" would naturally 23 be thought of as "hurling it into the sea". There may also be in the back-ground (at least of Mark's consciousness) a final echo of Zechariah (14.4): "On that day . . . the Mount of Olives . . . shall be cleft in two by an immense valley running east and west."

'**Believe that you have received it and it will be yours**'. This sounds 24 a little like permission to use the power of prayer for any purpose whatever, along with a hint on how to do it. But Jesus was fond of exaggerations and striking simplifications. The point is surely, as so often in Mark's gospel, and doubtless also in Jesus' original teaching, the critical importance of faith. The same point is made explicit in Matthew (21.22), and is related to other aspects of Christian spirituality by Paul (1 Corinthians 13.2). There is perhaps a commentary on it in 1 John 5.14–15.

25   The third saying, besides being a characteristic element of Jesus' teaching, reads like a commentary on the Lord's Prayer. Mark, unlike Matthew and Luke, does not include the Lord's prayer in his gospel; but this saying, and the phrase, **your Father in heaven**, strongly suggest that he knew it.

27   **They came once more to Jerusalem.** According to Mark's scheme, this was the second full day of Jesus' activity in Jerusalem. It was taken up with controversy between himself and the Jewish authorities, whose supreme council, the Sanhedrin, had its meeting-place and offices in or near the temple precincts. The members of this body are often described in the gospels as **the chief priests, lawyers, and elders,** and it was therefore probably in their official capacity as members of the Sanhedrin that they accosted

28 Jesus **as he was walking in the temple court.** Their question, '**By what authority are you acting like this?**' was one to which it was important for the Sanhedrin to have an answer. Jesus was attracting crowds by his teaching (11.18), and much of his teaching took the form of a new exposition of Scripture. But the exposition of Scripture was the prerogative of professionally qualified "lawyers". Did Jesus have the necessary qualification? Their question may also have concerned Jesus' reforming actions the day before (11.15–17). Had the High Priest (who was the ultimate authority for the conduct of temple affairs) sanctioned this?

Regarded as a matter of official qualifications and sanctions, the question had a straightforward factual answer: Jesus had received no authority. This was doubtless the answer the deputation hoped to extract. But Jesus (or Mark, or the tradition he used) chose to see the question as a far more searching one. He had not merely assumed the privilege of a qualified lawyer or official representative of the temple authorities; he had acted as a prophet, a preacher and a miracle-worker. For such activity it was meaningless to ask for human authorization. It was either inspired by God or it was not, and a witness of these things had to make up his own mind. Taking the question in this sense, Jesus was justified in returning it to his questioners. It was ultimately the same question as was posed by the person of John the Baptist; and the presence of a crowd of people more ready to see the hand of God in the preaching of a John or a Jesus than in the policies of the official religious leaders put Jesus' questioners at a temporary disadvantage.

12. 1   **He went on to speak to them in parables.** The word "parable" was one with a wide range of meanings (see above on 3.23). Sometimes it was an illustration intended to make the speaker's meaning clearer; sometimes it was riddling and enigmatic, leaving its hearers guessing. What was the meaning here? In the chapter devoted to Jesus' parables earlier in the gospel (chapter 4), Mark seems deliberately to have represented them as obscure and enigmatic to all but those who were specially privileged to understand them. But

here Mark allows that the point was more obvious. Jesus' enemies **saw that** 12
the parable was aimed at them.

'A man planted a vineyard'. At first sight the opening of the story is in 1
the characteristic style of Jesus' parables: the stage is set with a careful
description of a familiar scene. The essential features of a Palestinian vineyard are mentioned: **a wall** built all round to protect the precious vines
from the depredations of men and of beasts; **a winepress,** which was
usually constructed over a trough that had been "hewn out" of rock; and a
watch-tower which was essential for guarding the vineyard, particularly at
vintage time. But this straightforward beginning leads into a story which
(unlike most of Jesus' parables) appears to be singularly implausible, and
the beginning itself turns out to be not at all what it seems. Compare the
following verses from Isaiah (5.1–2):

> "My beloved had a vineyard
> high up on a fertile hill-side.
> He trenched it and cleared it of stones
> and planted it with red vines;
> he built a watch-tower in the middle
> and then hewed out a winepress in it."

The details of the watch-tower and the winepress are identical; and in the
Septuagint Greek version of Isaiah (which Mark, but not Jesus, may have
used) the **wall** occurs also. Now in Isaiah the vineyard is an allegory for
the people of Israel. If Jesus began his parable in words so closely reminiscent of this well-known text, his listeners must have been prepared to find
the same kind of allegory in it.

But if the vineyard stood for Israel, then it was to be expected that other
features of the story would be equally symbolic. And along these lines the
interpretation of the story is so obvious that one ceases to ask whether such a
thing could have happened in real life. The owner of the vineyard is God;
his servants are the prophets (the prophets are often called "God's servants"
in the Old Testament), who were consistently maltreated by the people to
whom they were sent; and the only son is Jesus himself. The question,
Whom do the **vine-growers** stand for? is answered by Mark himself. Jesus'
interlocutors were the religious leaders of Jerusalem; and **they saw that the** 12
parable was aimed at them. The only remaining doubtful point is to
determine who were the **others** to whom the vineyard would be given. 9
Reading the story after the event, we have to answer: the Christian church.

On this reading of the parable, it would be beside the point to ask for a
plausible explanation of the apparently absurd expectation of the vine-
growers that they would acquire the property by murdering the heir, or of
the imprudence of the owner in sending his son into such a dangerous
situation. The course of events would have been dictated, not by the con-

ditions of real life, but by the relationship of God with his people which the characters in the story were intended to illustrate. But there are considerable difficulties involved in taking the parable in this way. Could Jesus have foreseen his own condemnation by the Sanhedrin and his subsequent execution so clearly that he worked it into an allegory? Did he ever refer to himself as the "only son" of God, and would he have been understood by a Jewish audience if he had? Moreover, since his parables are usually entirely realistic stories, is it likely that he would have made up one that was quite improbable in order to illustrate what was about to happen? These questions are difficult to answer with any degree of certainty, but, once raised, they suggest two other approaches to the parable. (i) Since the allegorical interpretation fits more easily into the thinking of the early church than that of Jesus (for it was the church which recognized Jesus to be the only Son of God, it was the church which saw in the crucifixion the decisive climax of God's dealings with his people, it was the church which clearly represented those "others" to whom the inheritance would pass—even if these truths were implicit in the teaching of Jesus), then the parable may have been invented altogether after Jesus' death, or at least (if Jesus told some such story) so modified and adapted by the church that we can no longer recover the original story. (ii) Alternatively, even if some of the details have been altered under the pressure of a later interpretation, it may still be possible to reconstruct the circumstances of the story in such a way that it ceases to be implausible and takes its place alongside the precise and vivid scenes of real life with which Jesus usually illustrated his teaching. The following reconstruction can only be tentative, but may help the reader to choose between these possibilities.

Planting a vineyard was a long-term investment. In the long run it could be highly lucrative, but for the first few years expenses were liable to exceed profits. No fruit could be gathered at all for the first three years; but during that time the new vines would need constant and expert tending. The owner, being a man of property with other more urgent interests abroad, would naturally commit the care of the vineyard for these first years to experienced vine-growers. No return could be expected from the vines; but it was normal to plant them sufficiently far apart to allow vegetables to be grown between, and the profits on these might be sufficient to pay the wages of the vine-growers and perhaps a nominal interest to the owner. During these first three years, it was sufficient to send a servant to collect the nominal rent; but if the vine-growers had been unable to make a profit on the vegetables, the servant's arrival could well have led to a dispute and ended in blows. In the parable, this scene is repeated at the end of each of the first three years.[a]

[a] In verse 2, the First Edition of NEB has "the vintage season", which is incompatible with this interpretation. But in the Greek the word means simply the season, as it is translated in the Second Edition.

In the fourth year matters would be different. For the first time there would be a vintage. This, being "first-fruits", was subject to ritual regulations, and the profit could be appropriated freely only in the fifth year. Nevertheless, it was important for the owner, or his accredited representative, to be present—Jews were even excused military service for the purpose (Deuteronomy 20.6). Moreover, the owner in the parable had special reason to take personal action. His tenants, three years in succession, had refused to pay rent; and since he had received no rent, he had nothing but the title deed to prove he was the owner. If (as was possible in Jewish law) the tenants were contemplating claiming ownership of the vineyard on the basis of three years' undisputed possession, he would be in a weak position, since servants (if they were slaves) were not admitted as legal witnesses, and he would have no evidence that he had attempted to collect his rent during the last three years. It was therefore essential that in the fourth year he should come himself or, if his other interests kept him abroad, that he should send a reliable representative. In fact he sent his son.[a]

The tenants could not of course have acquired the vineyard simply by killing the heir of the owner. But they may have argued that if they repudiated the claims of the owner's representative—if necessary by force—they would by now have a fairly strong case in a court of law; and that if the owner no longer had an heir who would benefit from the investment in the vineyard, he might not think it worth his while to return to Palestine to press his claim. They therefore allowed the son's arrival to develop into a fight—they could say it was self-defence—which resulted in the death of the son. With an eye on future developments, they flung the body unburied **out of the vineyard** 8 as evidence of the battle (and possibly also to avoid having to forfeit the vines as being ritually polluted by a corpse). But if they had been counting on the continued absence abroad of the owner, and on the strong points of their case if meanwhile it came into a Jewish court, they were rudely disillusioned. The owner unexpectedly arrived with a strong following and punished their resistance with death.

Such a reconstruction would make the parable plausible as a story. It may seem unduly complicated; but if there had recently been a well-known case of such a thing in Palestine, Jesus' hearers would have had no difficulty in following it. The church, however, might have very soon lost the original point, and seized upon the allegorical meaning implicit in the vineyard, the servants and the son; with the result that when it came to retell the story it concentrated on these details and omitted many others. If the above reconstruction is anywhere near the mark, the parable will fall into place as one of those which illustrate the folly of prevaricating with God: now is the time

[a] See the footnote in NEB. The Greek word means literally **dear son**, but often meant "only son", and was particularly used in the early church of Jesus Christ, God's "only son". This is another detail which may be due to a later interpretation of the original parable.

to recognize the messengers of God and repent! If so, Mark may well be
12 right in saying that the religious leaders saw that the parable was aimed
at them. Not much help is to be gained from the following quotation of
10 Psalm 118.22–3. It follows exactly the existing Greek version of the Old
Testament; if Jesus quoted it, he will have done so in Hebrew. 'Can it be
that you have never read this text?' Of course they had; but they did not
necessarily know how to interpret it. Some said it referred to Abraham,
some to David; in the early church (which had become accustomed to the
idea of the Messiah being rejected) it was unhesitatingly used of Christ (Acts
4.11; I Peter 2.6–8). It has no obvious relevance to the parable; but Jesus,
conscious of the opposition gathering against him, may well have used it of
himself on some such occasion; and the evangelist may have placed it in this
position as a hint that the death of the "son" was by no means the end of
the story.

13 A number of Pharisees and men of Herod's party. These two groups
were mentioned earlier (3.6) as being in league together against Jesus,
doubtless seeing in him a threat alike to the religious and the political *status
quo*. (It is a little surprising to find representatives of Herod's party in
Jerusalem, for Jerusalem lay outside the dominions of any of the Herods
and was ruled directly by a Roman procurator. It is possible therefore that
the story originally belonged to Jesus' activity in Galilee.) They now hoped
to trap him by extracting from him a declaration of disobedience towards
14 political authority. The taxes in question consisted of the annual poll-tax
levied on every citizen of Palestine and paid direct into the treasury of the
Roman Emperor. The question was a subtle one. The tax was imposed
by the Romans, and no Jew who was liable to pay it could refuse to do so
without being prosecuted. At first sight, therefore, the question, 'Are we
or are we not permitted to pay taxes?' sounds academic: they had in
practice no option. But, after addressing Jesus somewhat fulsomely as someone who had a special insight into the way of life that God requires, the
questioners hoped perhaps that he would produce some proof from Scripture
to show that paying tax to a foreign power was contrary to the way of life
which God had laid down for his people the Jews. If he did so, he would
align himself decisively with those extreme nationalists who regarded the
tax as an intolerable symbol of subordination, and it would then be easy to
have him arraigned before the Roman authorities. But the trap was cleverly
laid; for if Jesus produced no learned argument against payment, his reply
would amount to an expression of acquiescence in the tax. And since the
tax was by all accounts exceedingly unpopular, such a reply might discredit
him in front of the crowd.
15 'Fetch me a silver piece'. Coins minted in Palestine—for instance by
the Herods—took account of Jewish sensitivity to portraits and pagan

images, and the small coins in any man's pocket would probably have little on them to remind him that his country was ruled by a foreign and heathen power. But only copper coins were minted in Palestine; the silver coins in circulation were all—apart from the special Phoenician pieces used for the temple treasury—the standard coinage of the empire, bearing on one side the head of the reigning Emperor. One of these silver coins—called a *denarius*, which is the word used here in the Greek[a]—was equivalent to a day's wage, or to half the annual tax which every Jew paid to the temple. The Roman tax must have amounted to at least this sum, and the Roman silver coinage will have been the usual, if not the obligatory, currency in which to pay it. When Jesus therefore asked his questioners to "fetch a silver piece" he was in effect casting the question back at them. If they possessed such a piece, it meant that they used the Emperor's coinage, and if they used his coinage, they implicitly accepted his authority, and if they accepted his authority, then they could have no grounds to refuse to pay his taxes. His reply has a brilliance and a finality which caused **astonishment** 17 at the time, and has inevitably influenced all subsequent discussions about the relationship of church and state; but it must never be forgotten that when he made it his interlocutors were holding in their hands a piece of coinage which already committed them to the same answer. The Romans probably did not think of their coinage as minted for the convenience of their subjects throughout the empire. Its primary purpose was to be a means of paying the army in any part of the world; and in theory it was expected that the coins, after being spent abroad, would be recovered through taxation. In this sense, a silver coin bearing the image of the Roman Emperor was literally **due to Caesar**. By analogy, a human being, made in the image of God, could be said to be **due to God**.

Next Sadducees came to him. The Sadducees represented an important 18 party. Most of the high priests and other important officials belonged to their number; and in matters of scriptural interpretation they were sharply opposed to the teaching of the Pharisees. Jesus, with his expertise in the law and his authority as a teacher, will have appeared to them as likely to share the views of the Pharisees; and so they presented him with a question calculated to cast ridicule on a specifically Pharisaic belief.

Apart from the Sadducees, the great majority of Jews in the time of Jesus believed in the future resurrection of the dead. But this doctrine was a comparatively new one. It had become generally accepted only during the last two centuries, and the Old Testament contained at most some faint intimations of it. To prove it, the Pharisaic interpreters of Scripture had to resort to a rather subtle use of texts, and to appeal more to their own tradition on the subject than to any clear proof from the Old Testament. It was

[a] The old translation, "a penny", which now suggests a bronze coin, has become entirely misleading.

precisely for this reason that the Sadducees differed from them on the question. They denied the validity of the Pharisees' "tradition", and held that, since the Old Testament makes no mention of it, **there is no resurrection.**

But their question shows them taking a stronger position than this: not merely does the Old Testament make no mention of resurrection, it contains provisions which make the idea absurd. The particular provision of the Law
19 of Moses referred to here is in Deuteronomy 25.5–6—the institution of so-called "Levirate marriage". This institution belonged to an early stage of Israel's history, when it was regarded as a desirable way of keeping property in one family and of keeping the family name alive. But it could only flourish in a polygamous society, and although attempts had been made to give it a higher moral significance (the Book of Ruth was probably one such attempt) it is unlikely that it was often put into practice in the time of Jesus. Nevertheless, the commandment stood in the Law, and may still have occasionally been observed, and the Sadducees were perfectly justified in quoting it to make their point, and in weaving a story around it.

23 'At the resurrection, when they come back to life, whose wife will she be?' The absurdity of the conclusion was probably a fair point in view of the crudity with which the belief in resurrection was often held. Writings have come down to us from this period in which the future life is portrayed with the naïvest materialism as a mere continuation, under beatific conditions, of ordinary human existence. Such crude beliefs deserved the Sadducees' ridicule. At the same time there were many thinkers who were ready to formulate the doctrine in a much more sophisticated and spiritual form; against them, the Sadducees' argument would have had no force. Jesus
25 aligned himself with this more developed view: '**When they rise from the dead, men and women do not marry; they are like angels in heaven.**'

Jesus then attacked the Sadducees' own position by quoting a passage from Exodus (3.6). Since it was recognized that the Old Testament provides no clear proof of the resurrection, how was this text going to carry his point? Was he going to give it a new and subtle interpretation, in the manner of the Pharisees? Jesus' commentary on it is so brief that it is not easy to say. But his usual procedure with Old Testament texts was very different from that of the Pharisees. Instead of manipulating the literal sense of the words, he liked to reveal their underlying purpose, and this may be his technique here.
26 The phrase, **the God of Abraham, the God of Isaac, and the God of Jacob,** which occurred in the Jews' daily prayers and was one of their characteristic ways of referring to "the God of Israel", carried a heavy load of meaning. God was the God of these patriarchs in the sense that he had led them, protected them, and above all promised to them that he would be eternally concerned for their descendants. In early centuries this promise was understood as being fulfilled in the prosperity and (at times) glorious history of the people of Israel. But in the time of Jesus, when that history

had become anything but glorious, and when, in any case, religious interest had at last become focused upon the destiny of the individual as much as of the nation, the promise had to be understood differently. Since so many generations of pious Israelites had died without seeing any material evidence of the fulfilment of God's promises, either these promises were false (which was inconceivable) or else they would have to be fulfilled for every righteous Jew in a future life. God had not made his promises to **the dead** but to **the** 27 **living**. By such reasoning, the Old Testament as a whole could be seen to imply the resurrection, even if it did not actually state it. The Sadducees, in short, had failed to understand both the true sense of the **scriptures** and the 25 **power of God** who, despite the apparent finality of human death, was still able to fulfil his promises.

Then one of the lawyers . . . asked him. The question was not neces- 28 sarily asked in order to embarrass Jesus, for it was one which we know to have been a subject of discussion among **lawyers** in the time of Jesus. But the question was probably intended in a rather technical sense. 'Which commandment is first of all?' sounds to us like a question about the most important principle by which to direct one's life. But in the mouth of the questioner it must have meant something different. For a professional expounder of the law, there could be no question of one part of the law, or one principle contained in it, being more important than the rest. A Jew was strictly obliged to keep the whole law—all the 613 commandments of it (as the Rabbis were soon to calculate the number), and the question, **Which commandment is first of all?** could not have been a question about what part of the law one ought particularly to observe (for one had to observe all parts of it equally). It could only have been the more academic question, from what part of the law (if any) could the rest of the law be deduced? Or, in any systematic arrangement of the many individual laws, which law should come at the head of the list? We know that this question was debated (even though some disapproved of the debate, thinking that it might tempt people to concentrate on some laws at the expense of others and so fail to do their duty by the whole law); and the lawyer may well have been genuinely interested to know what Jesus' own position was.

Jesus' reply keeps well within the usual bounds of such a discussion. The first phrase, "Hear, O Israel: The Lord our God is the only Lord" 29 sounds at first inappropriate, since it is not a "commandment" at all, but is in the nature of a statement of faith. But in fact it is the beginning of a text (Deuteronomy 6.4–5) which was a basic part of Jewish devotion. It was recited by everyone twice a day, and there was general agreement that it did in fact sum up the essentials of the Jewish faith and the Jewish life. There- fore it was not inappropriate for Jesus to preface his answer with this intro- duction: it served to put the first great "commandment" in the perspective of the Jew's daily profession of faith. To complete his answer, Jesus somewhat 31 unexpectedly added a second "commandment", taken from Leviticus 19.18, "Love your neighbour as yourself".

Thus far, the conversation had run on lines which would have caused no surprise in scholarly circles. Both the first and the second of these commandments were quite often quoted as being basic to the whole structure of the Law of Moses, and even though we do not happen to know of any other teacher who explicitly paired these two commandments together as Jesus did, it does not follow that, simply by putting them together, Jesus was doing anything startlingly original. Indeed, Matthew in his version (22.40) ends the episode at this point, and uses it precisely in order to reveal Jesus in the rôle of an authoritative Jewish teacher. Luke attaches to it the parable of the Good Samaritan, in order to illustrate Jesus' radical interpretation of the commandment to "love your neighbour". Mark alone allows the conversation with the lawyer to develop in such a way as to throw a new light on the sense in which Jesus understood the "commandments".

32   'Well said, Master.' The lawyer agreed with Jesus; but his commentary on Jesus' answer set it in a totally different light. The keeping of these two
33   commandments was **far more than any burnt offerings or sacrifices.** At a stroke, this phrase turned the question from an academic one into a practical one. Instead of being an attempt to subsume all other laws (including those concerning burnt offerings and sacrifices) under one or two general principles, Jesus' answer became, in the lawyer's commentary (what it was doubtless always intended to be) a clear statement that the spirit and basic motivation of the law was **more important** than the observance of its detailed ritual provisions. We can infer, from other parts of Jesus' teaching, that this was in fact Jesus' view. Mark here allows it to be expressed by a member of that party which was normally opposed to him; and Jesus, to show how closely this formulation came to his own teaching, reversed his
34   usual judgement on the lawyers, and said of this one, '**You are not far from the kingdom of God**'—the highest compliment he ever paid to anyone.

There is a further point to notice about the narrative. The liberal view of the law which is implied in the lawyer's answer was certainly not an orthodox one at the time; but we cannot say for certain that a professional lawyer could not have held it, and we ought probably to leave open the question whether this conversation actually took place as Mark (unlike Matthew and Luke) records it, or whether Mark deliberately constructed it in order to bring out Jesus' understanding of the Jewish law. On the other hand, there are certain details which suggest that at some stage the story has been edited to suit a different *milieu*. When the Jewish faith was being presented to educated Greeks, it tended to be formulated somewhat differently from the way in which it was discussed among Jews in Palestine. It was proclaimed, first and foremost, as the one great monotheistic religion of the world (as compared with the many deities of Greek, Roman and oriental religions); secondly, greater stress was laid on its intellectual content than came naturally to traditional Jewish psychology; and thirdly, there was a tendency to play down the ritual side of it, particularly the sacrificial system of the temple, which struck the Greeks as crude and unnecessary. In Mark's narrative it is noticeable, first, that the lawyer's paraphrase of the Jewish confession of faith reads remarkably like a conscious defence of monotheism; secondly, that an intellectual term, **mind**, is added to **heart, soul** and 30 **strength** (the three terms which stand in the Hebrew text of Deuteronomy); and thirdly, that the conversation ends with a depreciation of **burnt** 33 **offerings or sacrifices.** From this, one conclusion suggests itself. This was the language Mark had often heard being used by Greek-speaking Jews while commending their faith to pagans. If he allowed it to influence his composition of the dialogue between Jesus and a lawyer in the temple at Jerusalem, it was because he realized that the liberal Judaism being preached, say, at Rome or Alexandria was in essence an approximation to the teaching of Jesus: it was **not far from the kingdom of God.** 34

The last of this series of questions is asked by Jesus himself, and in form it is the kind of question that was much discussed at the time: given such and such a doctrine, which we infer from the Old Testament, how is a certain text, which seems at first sight to contradict that doctrine, to be reconciled with it? The doctrine concerned was that **the Messiah is "Son of David".** 35 On this subject, **the teachers of the law** could hardly maintain anything else. It is true that the Old Testament itself does not say in so many words that the coming Messiah would be a physical descendant of David—though some passages come very near it (Isaiah 11.1-9; Jeremiah 33.14-18); but that this would be so had become a very widely held belief, and the gospels themselves, when they show Jesus to be a descendant of David, presuppose that this was regarded as one reason for claiming that he was the Messiah. It is very unlikely, therefore, that Jesus meant to cast doubt on this doctrine. Rather, his question (in the manner of such discussions) drew attention, not to any uncertainty about the doctrine itself, but to a text which had not previously been brought into harmony with it. This text (Psalm 110.1) was subsequently used by the early church as an important prophecy of the ascension and exaltation of Christ (Acts 2.34; 1 Corinthians 15.25 and else-where). Here, Jesus apparently quoted it to bring a new element into the usual understanding of what was meant by a Messiah who was "Son of David". The psalm, which was almost certainly written later, and possibly many centuries later, than David's time, was nevertheless found by Jesus' contemporaries among the collection of the "Psalms of David", and it would have occurred to none of them to question its authorship. Moreover, it occurred in the sacred scriptures, every part of which was **inspired by the** 36 **Holy Spirit,** and must therefore be taken seriously as a word of God. In the first line, **The Lord** clearly meant God, and **my** meant David's; but who was David's "Lord"? There was nothing in the psalm to say; and this was just the kind of ambiguity in the sacred text which later scholars came to regard as full of deeper meaning. "David's Lord" must be a kind of cryptogram for some other important person in the present or future destiny of Israel. Some two centuries after the date of this conversation, there is evidence that this person was thought by Jewish scholars to be the awaited Messiah. The Christian church evidently drew the same conclusion when, soon after the death and resurrection of Jesus, it began using the psalm as a prophecy about the risen Christ. Was "David's Lord" popularly thought to be the Messiah even earlier? This narrative, if it was not composed after the event (as some believe it was) seems to presuppose that he was; and in an age in which expectation of a coming Messiah was a marked feature of many Jews' religion, it would not be at all surprising if the cryptogram was popularly interpreted in this way. But if so, it raised a difficulty: how could the Messiah, whom all agreed must be David's "son", be addressed by his father as if he was a superior being—"Lord"? This was the difficulty which Jesus wanted to emphasize: it would not do to use this somewhat grandiose verse as a prophecy about the Messiah without thinking out its implications. Could someone who was human enough to be called David's "son" also be "lordly" enough to sit at God's right hand? Jesus did not offer an answer to this at once: the answer (so at least the first Christians believed) was given, not in a single word, but by the whole life, death and resurrection of Jesus.

38 **'Beware of the doctors of the law'.** In both Matthew and Luke a substantial section is devoted to an attack on the Pharisees and upon the professional experts in the law. In Mark, even though no secret is made of the opposition between Jesus and these people, only three verses (38–40) are devoted to an explicit attack on their character. Yet perhaps more is implied than is actually said. The real reason to **beware** of them was not, of course, the rather trivial signs of petty ambition and ostentation which are mentioned here, but the hypocrisy of which these things were a symptom and which Jesus attacks elsewhere (7.6–8) as being their really serious fault. This fundamental hypocrisy proceeded from their whole understanding of religion; and it was presumably as particularly striking manifestations of this hypocrisy that Jesus singled out certain instances of arrogant behaviour of which, perhaps, only a few were guilty. Similarly with verse 40: the con-
40 demnation of **men who eat up the property of widows** was as old as the prophets (e.g. Isaiah 10.1–2), and one which religious groups often used as ammunition against each other. The obligation laid on wealthy women to give hospitality to travelling teachers could have given rise to such an abuse, though it is doubtful whether many lawyers were guilty of it, any more than Jesus' own acceptance of hospitality could be regarded as reprehensible. But if there were even a few cases of it they were sufficient to make Jesus' point: saying **long prayers for appearance' sake** made these acts of injustice into

particularly scandalous examples of that same hypocrisy of which the lawyers, as a class, were guilty. [a]

Once he was standing opposite the temple treasury. It is not possible 41 to reconstruct this scene with any certainty. There were a large number of "treasuries" in the temple, and contributions (some obligatory, some voluntary) were made for many different purposes. Clearly the story is about free-will offerings and not about taxes; and it is usually thought that the scene must have taken place in the Women's Court of the temple, where thirteen trumpet-shaped receptacles were set up for receiving various kinds of contributions. But it is superfluous to press the details: how, for instance, Jesus could have seen how much money everyone gave is an unanswerable question. The narrative, in fact, is in the style of a story deliberately told to point a moral, and it is even possible that it was originally told by Jesus as a story and subsequently projected back as an episode in his life—for the story itself has parallels both in Jewish tradition and in the religious literature of other cultures. Its moral is obvious enough, and only one vivid detail requires comment. **Two tiny coins**: the Greek word (*lepton*) was used for the 42 smallest coin in currency in Palestine. It was little more than a quarter of an inch in diameter, and 128 of them went to the silver *denarius*. In Rome it was unknown; the smallest coin there was the *quadrans*, which was twice the size of the widow's coin, and Mark may have had his non-Palestinian readers in mind when he added the explanation, **together worth a farthing** (*quadrans*).

'**Look, Master, what huge stones.**' This is still the visitor's reaction 13. 1 today. The buildings of Herod the Great can be recognized anywhere in Palestine by the immense rectangular blocks of beautifully hewn stone with which their walls are constructed. The temple, with its surrounding buildings and colonnades, was the greatest of his building enterprises, and not the least spectacular part of it was the huge substructure by which the top of the sacred hill had been extended to form a terrace of some 35 acres. The great east wall of this substructure, which rose vertically from the floor of the valley over 100 feet below, is in position today and still excites admiration. On the occasion of Jesus' visit it will have been quite recently completed. The exclamation of Jesus' disciples as they left the temple area and passed through the gate in this gigantic wall is exactly what one would expect. Indeed, the setting for the long discourse which follows is vivid and plausible. From the Mount of Olives, **facing the temple**, one could look 3 down across the steep valley between, and the whole of the temple area, perhaps the most grandiose and impressive architectural achievement of

[a] The alternative rendering in the footnote is perhaps a smoother translation of the Greek, but gives the last saying a much more general application. If it was not aimed at the Pharisees and lawyers, it was a sentiment any pious Jew might have uttered.

antiquity, lay spread out before one's eyes. That it should ever be totally destroyed must have seemed almost unimaginable; yet this is what Jesus had just prophesied. No wonder then that Jesus was questioned privately about it by some of his disciples.

Yet however realistic the setting, Jesus' answer, which is the longest continuous discourse recorded by Mark, shows signs of being an artificial composition. When a master gave "private teaching" to his disciples, it might be merely a matter of clarifying for their benefit difficult or enigmatic points made in public (Mark 4—the parable chapter—provides a good example of this). But another type of private teaching consisted of esoteric truths about the ultimate destiny of the world and of instructions on correctly reading the signs of the times. To impart teaching of this kind, Jewish writers had to hand a well-developed literary form, the so-called "apocalypse" or "revelation". They described the approaching end of the world in terms of a supernatural drama, in which the main events were fairly constant, but to which new details were added according to the particular vision of each writer; and these details could often be interpreted, by those sufficiently instructed to do so, as cryptic references to persons and events of their own time. In the time of Jesus, and particularly also in the second half of the first century A.D. (the period when the gospels were written) a number of these "apocalypses" were composed by visionaries who were inspired to see, in contemporary events, clues to the shape of that final cosmic drama which (they earnestly believed) God was about to initiate. If Jesus gave some teaching of this kind, it need cause no surprise that he utilized some of the elements of traditional apocalypses; and it would be still less surprising if, when that teaching came to be written down, it became further assimilated to the pattern of contemporary apocalyptic writings.

14 There is one clear instance of this process in the present chapter. **Let the reader understand** is an admonition which could not possibly have occurred in a spoken discourse of Jesus; but it is just the kind of hint by which a visionary writer of the period was accustomed to indicate that a phrase or image he had just used was a symbol or a cryptogram for some familiar person, place or event. It shows that at some stage Jesus' teaching on the future has been assimilated to the conventions of a written apocalypse.

Not only the form but also the content of Jesus' discourse has been influenced by these conventions. Speculations about the future tended to assume that the ultimate act of the drama, when God would finally manifest his sovereignty and save his elect, would be preceded by a period of exceptional calamity and tribulation, when the powers of evil would be unleashed to an unheard-of degree, and all but the most faithful and courageous of the saints of God might be tempted to despair. This dark period before the end

8 came to be known in some circles as the **birth-pangs of the new age** (this almost technical expression occurs in Mark's narrative); and moreover it had

a purpose: it would prepare for the impending judgement by putting men to a decisive test. Those whose faith was already wavering would lose heart, and those whose grasp of the truth was insecure would be **misled** (again 6 an almost technical word in this context) by various manifestations of a spirit of deliberate deception. But, severe though the ordeal would be, the righteous could take courage. '**For the sake of his own, whom he has chosen,**' God '**has cut short the time**'—another feature which, if it was not 20 already conventional, was soon to occur regularly in Jewish apocalypses; for the ultimate purpose of these writers was to encourage and sustain their readers. Once these calamitous events had got under way, the final act could not be long delayed, and the righteous could begin to look forward to their promised reward. The important thing was to be able to recognize what stage the drama had reached.

For these reasons, it has become customary to refer to this chapter as a "little apocalypse", with the implication that, since an "apocalypse" is essentially a literary creation, the teaching it contains can hardly have been given by Jesus in anything like its present form. But at the same time it is important to notice the difference between this discourse and a typical "apocalypse". In the Revelation, for example (which is a true Christian apocalypse), the basic pattern is the same—a period of intensified tribulation, followed by the judgement, the new age, and the reward of the righteous; but the treatment is totally different. The tribulations are not the kind of ordinary catastrophes which might be encountered in the course of history: they consist of altogether supernatural upheavals in the processes of nature, accompanied by—or rather caused by—desperate conflicts between cosmic and mythological powers; and the climax to which the book builds up is the establishment of a new order by God, in which his chosen people will at last take their rightful place. In short, the setting is throughout mythological, the powers at work supernatural. The style is that of poetry, not of prose. By contrast, the greater part of Jesus' discourse is set firmly within history. The events predicted are little larger than life, the warnings which accompany the predictions are meant to be serious and practical, and very little space is devoted to the scene which is in fact the *raison d'être* of an "apocalypse"— the final phase of judgement and glory. For the most part, the nearest parallels are to be found, not in the Book of Daniel (the first of the Jewish apocalypses), but in the Old Testament prophets; and the discourse as a whole is more concerned with interpreting the significance of contemporary history (which is the main part of what the Bible means by "prophecy") than with painting a mythological picture of the age to come.

The question the disciples put to Jesus was in any case not a general one about the future of the world, but was quite specific. After Jesus' astounding prophecy of the total destruction of the temple, they asked, '**When will this** 4 **happen?**' In the course of his reply, Jesus gave an equally specific answer:

30 'the present generation will live to see it all.' And he was right. In A.D. 70 (shortly after the date when this gospel is likely to have been written) the Jewish revolt, which had begun four years earlier, was finally crushed. The Romans captured Jerusalem, set fire to the temple, and subsequently levelled it to the ground. That events were already moving in this direction some forty years before must have been clear to a man of Jesus' prophetic insight.

But the essence of prophecy was not merely to discern the course which history was taking, but to set these events in the wider context of God's judgement upon his people, and to prepare men to see in them the signs of a greater providence. The discourse is an essay in reading the signs of the times, and weaves together predictions of actual events or circumstances which Jesus foresaw (or which the next generation of Christians filled in from their experience) with some of the traditional elements which the prophets had incorporated in their descriptions of the impending climactic phase of history. To take each detail as it comes:

6 (i) 'Many will come claiming my name.' Fanatics who claimed to have divine authority to lead the Jewish people in revolt against the Romans had already appeared in Jesus' lifetime and were to appear again before A.D. 70. This was the historical form in which the mythological "spirit of deception" was to appear in the final period before the end. Possibly Jesus' own appearance and death would accentuate the danger: men might claim to be Jesus himself, returned from the dead with power.

7 (ii) 'The noise of battle . . . the news of battles.' An intensification of the political upheavals of which Palestine had always been a victim was a
8 standard feature expected in the last days. Verse 8 is only a slight adaptation of Isaiah 19.2.

9 (iii) 'You will be handed over to the courts.' How far the experience of the early church has coloured these verses we cannot tell. For instance, they would serve as an accurate description of the things which Paul had to endure; but equally it would not have been difficult for Jesus to foresee that his followers had these trials ahead of them. Governors and kings do not necessarily shift the scene outside Palestine: "governor" was a usual word for a senior Roman administrator, and those of Herod's sons who still ruled over parts of Palestine by leave of the Roman empire were commonly known as "kings". On the other hand, a wider perspective than was usual in Jesus'
10 teaching is opened up in the words, 'the Gospel must be proclaimed to all nations.' It soon became a firm conviction of Paul's that this must happen before the end (literally, "first"); but it took the church as a whole some time to accept the proposition that the Gospel was intended, not merely for the Jews and their immediate neighbours, but for the whole Greco-Roman world; and if Jesus made such a clear statement about it, we must assume
30 that the church did not at first take it as a practical commission, but assumed

that he was predicting some supernatural proclamation which would be made immediately before the end.

(iv) 'Brother will betray brother to death'. This prophecy occurs in 12 Micah (7.6). The Jews set particular store by the solidarity of family and of race, and this desecration of family ties was, in their eyes, one of the most horrifying features of the terrible last days.

(v) 'But when you see the "abomination of desolation"'. The 14 phrase is as meaningless in the Greek as it is in English. It was the deliberately cryptographic translation which the Greek version of the Old Testament offered for a subtle piece of Hebrew invective. In 168–167 B.C. Antiochus Epiphanes set up a statue of Zeus in front of the temple in Jerusalem (I Maccabees 1.54). The author of the book of Daniel (9.27 and elsewhere), by a kind of word-play on the Hebrew equivalent to the title "Olympian Zeus", called this "the abominable thing which desolates". Anyone who came across the phrase, either in Greek or in Hebrew, would automatically think of this notorious case of deliberate desecration; and he would be led to look for a similar meaning here by the unexpected parenthesis, let the reader understand. It is probably useless to speculate on precisely what kind of desecration Jesus would have had in mind, if indeed he used this particular cryptogram at all. Possibly he imagined the ensigns of the Roman legions, which were regarded by the Jews as idolatrous, being set up as a sign of victory and conquest in the temple precincts. But by the time Mark wrote one event had taken place which may have suggested how the oracle was likely to be fulfilled. In A.D. 40 the Emperor Gaius (Caligula) attempted to have a statue of himself placed in the temple, thereby nearly causing an insurrection. It may be the memory of this which led Mark to make the idol sound like a live person (at the expense, in the Greek, of correct grammar): usurping a place which is not his.

'Then those who are in Judaea must take to the hills'. The event just mentioned was clearly meant to be regarded as a real possibility. When it happened, the only course would be immediate flight to the caves and inaccessible places in the mountains where no victorious soldiers were likely to follow up fugitives. The haste required is described with conventional but vivid details drawn from life in Palestine. Inside staircases to the roof 15 of one-storied houses were not usual. If a man were on the roof (where many domestic tasks were done), he would have to come down outside before going into his house—and there would not be time for him to go in. Work in the 16 countryside was done without a coat on—and there would not be time for him to go and fetch it. The winter in Palestine sometimes brings rains so heavy that travel is virtually impossible—so pray that it may not come in 18 winter. Those days will bring distress, the kind of distress the Jews had 19 so often endured at the hands of conquering or marauding armies, but this time of an intensity so great that it could only be the fulfilment of well-known prophecies about the great tribulation immediately preceding the end (the language of verse 18 is an almost exact quotation from Daniel 12.1).

21   (vi) "Look, here is the Messiah". Another instance of the manifestation of the spirit of deception, calculated to mislead, similar to (i) above.

24   (vii) 'The sun will be darkened'. At this point one might get the impression that the discourse moves from the realm of reality to that of mythology, from events which can be imagined as taking place in history to cataclysms which mark the end of all history. But the words (which are in any case a tissue of allusions to Isaiah 13.10 and 34.4—the imagery was quite conventional) would not necessarily have suggested, as they do to us, a general disintegration of the universe. The sun, the moon and the stars were thought of as being much the same size as they look; and the main function of them
25   (and of the spirits or powers which were thought to control them, the celestial powers) was to maintain life on earth in an orderly system. The sun and the moon assured the orderly procession of night and day, the stars (by the principles of astrology, which were widely accepted) regulated, not only the seasons, but the destinies of men. Even a minor dislocation (such as an eclipse was thought to be) was regarded as the sign of some extraordinary portent or disaster. *A fortiori*, disorganization in heaven would unleash chaos on earth.

26   (viii) 'Then they will see the Son of Man'. This, at last, is the final moment towards which the whole process has been tending. The language again is conventional: compare Daniel 7.13, Zechariah 2.6, and also Paul's description of the same scene in 1 Thessalonians 4.16 (a passage which perhaps gives the clue to the final phrase: the chosen who are to be gathered
27   from the farthest bounds of heaven may be those of the faithful who have died). The manifestation of the Son of Man will be the climax of the whole drama.

28   'Learn a lesson from the fig-tree.' The discourse, which has mainly consisted of prophecies of what is to happen, now becomes concerned with the proper attitude which men should have in face of the impending future. Two dangers very soon presented themselves in the early church: first, that of assuming that since the end had not come at once it would not come at all, and that vigilance could be relaxed; secondly, that of becoming distracted with all kinds of speculation about exactly "what day or what hour" these things would happen. Jesus, like other Jewish teachers, seems to have had these two dangers in mind. The end would be preceded by signs, just as certainly as summer is preceded by spring. In England we would probably express the simile differently (and Luke may have been adapting it to European conditions when he wrote (21.29) 'look at the fig-tree or any other tree'): for us, spring is the time of the return of green life after the dead colours of winter. But in Palestine the winter, with all its rains, is the one time when the mountains look green: greenness as such is not a sign that

summer is near. But the fig-tree, which is one of Palestine's few deciduous trees, stands strikingly bare in the winter, and only puts on fresh green leaves in the spring. The transition between winter and summer is short: it is completed between March and early May; and the appearance of leaves on the fig-tree is a sure sign that this rapid period of change is beginning.

'**In the same way**'. How exactly is the simile to be applied? What in the 29 previous discourse corresponds to the sign of spring and what corresponds to the summer? '**When you see all this happening, you may know that the end is near**'. As the NEB footnote shows, the Greek is ambiguous: it does not say just what it is which will be near. Further, the phrase '**all this**' is vague, and the next saying, '**the present generation will live to see it all**', 30 only increases the obscurity; for it is clear that there are many things in the previous discourse which the generation contemporary with Jesus did not live to see. We are confronted once again by the same difficulties as are presented by 9.1 (on which see above), and many have inferred that Jesus was in error, or was misunderstood, or even that he never said anything of the kind. In fact, the same considerations apply here as there. Many of the things which Jesus predicted actually happened "in that generation"— civil strife, a famine, persecution of Christians, and a terrible war culminating in the siege and destruction of Jerusalem. Moreover, there was a sense in which Christians did in fact see **the Son of Man coming in the clouds** 26 **with great power and glory**: this was one of their ways of expressing the conviction that Jesus had risen from the dead and was now at the right hand of God (Acts 7.56). But one thing did not happen: the final judgement at the end of history. Jesus may have been in error or have been misunderstood about the temporal relation between this ultimate culmination and the catastrophes and trials which those who heard him would have to endure; but this in any case may not have been the main point which he was making. He was speaking in the tones of ancient prophecy. The course of events which he so clearly foresaw was not meaningless, but predetermined and significant. Men would be able to read from them the lesson that God's purpose was being accomplished, and the universal judgement of mankind brought nearer. What might seem like senseless suffering and catastrophe was an essential precondition of the coming of that state of affairs for which men longed, and was therefore, if rightly interpreted, a cause for encouragement rather than despair. The discourse was an exercise in correctly reading the signs of the times.

'**Heaven and earth will pass away; my words will never pass away.**' 31 If the consummation were delayed, men might cease to believe in it, and find history once again bitter and meaningless. Jesus, in effect, refuses to admit any excuse for this attitude. Whatever time world history may take, its conclusion will always be the same. And against the opposite danger of fussy speculation about the exact timing of **that day or that hour,** he stresses 32 that no human calculation can reveal it. God is free to choose the moment. Surprisingly, even the Son is excluded from the secret. (This is the one occasion in this gospel on which Jesus explicitly claims unique sonship of God. Significantly, he does so in the context, not of his divine power, but of his human limitations.)

33 Between these two attitudes—the one of ceasing to believe, the other of agitated preoccupation—is the true one. 'Be alert, be wakeful.' Another brief simile illustrates it, similar to many others which Jesus uses for the same theme (and perhaps, in the telling, this one has been slightly contaminated by those others: there seems no reason why it should be only the door-keeper who has to keep awake and not the other servants, unless the master of the house is expected at night. But in the east a traveller on a long journey seldom travelled by night; the task of a door-keeper was to be awake to open to him only if he returned late from dinner, or to detect the entry of a thief—and Jesus used these similes too). With that, the discourse, which began as private instruction to three disciples, is now declared to be

37 destined for the whole community of Jesus' followers: 'What I say to you, I say to everyone: Keep awake'.

The final conflict

14. 1 **Now the festival of Passover and Unleavened Bread was only two days off.** This sentence gives, or appears to give, a precise date; and indeed, from this point on, events move rapidly, and in a fairly strict chronological sequence. Passover was a springtime festival, at which the slaughter of lambs before the temple and the eating of them by household groups was understood as a re-enactment of one of the great moments of the Exodus from Egypt (Exodus 12). The Festival of Unleavened Bread, on the other hand, which involved removing all old leaven from the house and eating only unleavened bread for the following week, must have been originally connected with the renewal of life at the beginning of each New Year. Long before the New Testament period, these two festivals had been combined, and the order of events was as follows. The main preparations were made on the 14th day of the month Nisan (which normally fell between March and May, though the Jewish calendar, being lunar and not solar, had constantly to be adjusted). Search was made for leaven and leavened food in all houses, and all that was found was destroyed; and in the afternoon the Passover lambs were slaughtered according to a prescribed ritual at the great altar in front of the temple. After sunset (which, for the Jews, meant the beginning of a new day, so by their reckoning we must now call it 15th Nisan) the people assembled by families or small groups to make a solemn meal of

roasted lamb, one lamb having been brought to the altar by each group that afternoon. At this meal (since the festival of Unleavened Bread was now combined with Passover) all the bread and cakes were unleavened; and the festival continued for a further week, during which all bread was prepared without leaven.

Which of these days is Mark referring to when he speaks of **the festival**? Properly speaking neither Passover nor Unleavened Bread began until after sunset, which by Jewish reckoning was a new day, 15th Nisan; but if Mark was reckoning in the Roman manner (midnight to midnight) and not in the Jewish manner (sunset to sunset), both the preparation in the afternoon and the ritual meal in the evening will have appeared to him as happening on the same "day", the first day of the festival. It is likely, therefore, though by no means certain, that Mark was counting back from that day, which, as we shall see, he believed to be a Thursday. But how far did he count back? **Two days off** suggests to us the previous Tuesday; but when Greeks and Romans counted days, they tended to include the day they started counting from. If today is Tuesday, tomorrow is the second day, and so Wednesday, not Thursday, is **two days off**. For all these reasons, we cannot be sure whether Mark meant to place these events on the Tuesday or the Wednesday of the week of *The final conflict*.

Apart from this uncertainty, the chronology in Mark is clear, and appears to be followed by Matthew and Luke. Jesus celebrated the Passover meal with his disciples in the evening, was tried during the following night and early morning, and was executed the same day, which was a Friday. It follows that the Passover festival, properly speaking, took place after sunset on the Thursday, which was therefore the beginning of 15th Nisan by Jewish reckoning. But against this has to be set the clear evidence of John's gospel that in that year the festival fell one day later, that is to say, that the Thursday evening was only the beginning of the preparation day, 14th Nisan, and that the Jews did not eat the Passover meal until after sunset on the Friday, by which time Jesus had been crucified. This difference between John's gospel and the other accounts prevents us from accepting Mark's time-scheme uncritically; and certain details in Mark's own narrative also fit in a little awkwardly. Not the least significant of these details is the attitude of the chief priests and the doctors of the law. '**It must not be** 2 **during the festival**', they said.[a] But, according to Mark's account, "during the festival" was exactly the moment when the betrayal and arrest took place.

Meanwhile an episode is introduced which has no exact date. **Jesus was** 3 **at Bethany, in the house of Simon the leper.** The story, or one like it, occurs in all the gospels. In Matthew, its position in the narrative and most

[a] It is just possible that the Greek was intended to mean, instead of "not during the festival", "not in the festival crowd". This would considerably ease the difficulty.

of its details are the same; but Luke places a somewhat similar story much earlier in his gospel and gives it a totally different application; and John tells a similar story (though many of the details are different) not two, but six days before the Passover. Evidently the story circulated in more than one form, and it is likely that Mark himself chose to introduce it at this point and placed his own interpretation upon it.

It was customary to anoint face, hands and feet with olive oil, especially before any kind of social occasion, and those who could afford it mixed a little perfume with the oil. Perfume was expensive, and was sold in bottles of alabaster or pottery with long narrow necks, so that it would pour very slowly. But the woman **broke it open**, that is, she broke off the neck, and poured out the entire contents at once. This was extravagant. 300 *denarii*
5 (**thirty pounds** in the NEB) was perhaps the total which a labourer might
4 earn in a year. The reaction of **some of those present** was perfectly understandable.

Jesus' reply is perhaps illuminated by the contemporary Jewish attitude to "good works". Giving alms to the poor was always praiseworthy, and was indeed constantly expected of all who could afford it. But still more praiseworthy were certain exceptional acts of kindness, such as hospitality to strangers. (There is a list of these acts of kindness in a parable in Matthew 25.35–6.) One of these acts was that of giving decent burial to a friend; and it seems that decent burial was held to include anointing the corpse. Compared, then, with an unremarkable act of almsgiving, the woman's gesture
7 was seen by Jesus as a highly praiseworthy act of kindness—'**It is a fine thing she has done for me**'; and whatever the original meaning of her action (Luke gives a different explanation, John offers none) Mark evidently understood it as the fulfilment in advance of an act of kindness which he
8 would soon have no one else to perform for him—'**anointing my body for**
9 **burial. I tell you this:**' the saying which follows has a perfectly obvious meaning. The woman's act was so remarkable that some mention of it was bound to be made wherever the story of Jesus was told. Nevertheless, it is curious that the woman has no name (only in John's version is she called Mary)—it is odd to perpetuate the memory of a good deed but not to record the name of the person who did it; and the phrase, **wherever in all the world the Gospel is proclaimed,** sounds a little strangely in Jesus' mouth (for it is hard to understand why it took the church so long to accept the necessity of a world-wide mission if Jesus had so clearly predicted it, see above on Mark 13.10). Therefore an alternative translation is sometimes suggested: "When the Gospel is proclaimed to all the world (i.e. at the end of the world), then what she has done will be told (at the Last Judgement) so that God may remember her with favour."

After this interlude, the narrative continues from the point reached in
1 verse 2. Jesus' enemies were **trying to devise some cunning plan to seize**

him; one of the twelve disciples listed in 3.13–19 was ready to betray him. It was not in Mark's manner to give reasons for Judas' treachery. Jesus had predicted that he would be betrayed, and here was Judas fulfilling the prediction. Such things happened according to the secret providence of God; there was no need to enquire about human motives as well.

Now on the first day of Unleavened Bread, when the Passover lambs 12 **were being slaughtered.** By Jewish reckoning, these were two different days. The festival of Unleavened Bread began only after sunset (a new day according to the Jewish calendar, so 15th Nisan) whereas the Passover lambs were slaughtered earlier on the same afternoon (14th Nisan). But Mark's expression, though technically inexact, is quite unambiguous: he means the afternoon of 14th Nisan, which (according at least to his information) fell that year on a Thursday, and was the time when each family or group of pilgrims made their preparations for celebrating the festival. These preparations included bringing a lamb to the temple to be slaughtered by the priests in the proper ritual manner. Jesus and his disciples had come to Jerusalem along with the thousands of pilgrims who travelled from all over Palestine to attend the festival; and his disciples took it for granted that he would be observing the festival like everyone else: '**Where would you like us to go and prepare for your Passover supper?**'

The first necessity was to find a room. In earlier times the Passover lamb had been roasted and eaten by all male Israelites over 20 years old in the precincts of the temple; but by now it had become a more domestic festival, and the meal was held in private houses. Nevertheless, although the practice had changed, the theory remained the same: on Passover night, the whole city of Jerusalem was deemed, by a special dispensation, to form part of the temple precincts. This meant that those who lived in Jerusalem could hold the meal in their own homes; but those who came as pilgrims from outside had to find a room in the city where they could do the same. It appears to have been expected of the residents that they should lend the upstairs rooms in their houses for this purpose; and in this way even the many thousands of pilgrims were apparently accommodated. Nevertheless, finding a room was an urgent matter, and the disciples were naturally anxious to press on with it. To the modern reader, it sounds as if Jesus had already made arrangements. It was probably as unusual then as it is now in Palestine to see **a man,** 13 instead of a woman, carrying an earthenware **jar of water,** and the signal could easily have been prearranged. But the episode is remarkably similar to the requisitioning of an ass at the beginning of chapter 11; and it is likely that Mark regarded both that and the finding of the room as instances of Jesus' miraculous foresight.

A large room upstairs, set out in readiness. Since all who possessed 15 a large enough spare room were bound to have it filled on that evening, it is not surprising that this one should have been already **set out in readiness** with the necessary tables and couches (for on special occasions such as this the Jews followed the Greek and Roman custom of reclining on couches, leaning on their left arm). But this would still leave the two disciples with many things to be **prepared for Passover.** A lamb would have to be bought, taken to the temple for slaughter by the priests, skinned and prepared for roasting; besides this, unleavened bread, herbs and wine would have to be obtained.

17   **In the evening he came to the house with the Twelve.** The number of people who shared the same Passover meal followed from the number for whom one lamb would provide sufficient meat. It was normally not less than ten, nor more than twenty. These groups might be family groups: married women and male children over 12 years old were allowed to take part (Luke 2.41–2). But equally, men who had come to Jerusalem as pilgrims could make up "fellowships" for the purpose. The lamb was then slaughtered in the name of each member of the fellowship, and from that moment no further members could be admitted. So long as the meal lasted, the members of such a "fellowship" felt themselves to be intimately bound together by the fact of having shared it; when it was over, they were free to separate. Jesus and his twelve disciples formed an appropriate group to observe the celebration together.

18   **As they sat at supper.** This is good modern English, but conveys a false impression: they were not sitting but reclining, as was the custom on special occasions. **'One of you will betray me—one who is eating with me'.** Since table-fellowship was a particularly strong expression of solidarity between individuals, the betrayal of one who had shared a meal had long been regarded as a particularly base form of treachery: "Even the friend whom I trusted, who ate at my table, exults over my misfortune" (Psalm 41.9, a passage which is clearly alluded to here). On this occasion, the traitor 20 was one who was **dipping into the same bowl** with Jesus. Particularly in the Passover meal, but also at other meals, pieces of bread or vegetable were dipped into a bowl of sweet sauce. Judas must have been lying fairly close to Jesus to use the same bowl; but the point of the saying was probably not to help the disciples to identify the traitor, so much as to emphasize the table-solidarity which the traitor was breaking. As a sin, that was already serious enough; but again, the narrative does not permit us to be sentimental 21 about it. **'The Son of Man is going the way appointed for him in the scriptures'** (an allusion doubtless to the darker side of the destiny of the Son of Man, and of the righteous people whom he represented, that is hinted at in Daniel 7.21). It was God, not Judas, who was guiding events along their predestined course.

22   **During supper.** It may seem surprising that Mark's description of the meal makes no mention of its central feature, the eating of the lamb. But his

concern was not to provide a consecutive account of the details of a Jewish observance, but to record certain acts and words of Jesus which, though they may have been prompted by the original character of the meal, were in themselves something entirely new. The Christian "Lord's Supper", in almost every one of its various manifestations, has from its inception centred round these acts and words, and when Mark came to record them he can hardly have failed to be influenced by the recital of them which took place every time the Supper was celebrated in the Christian community. It is understandable, therefore, that he should have omitted those details of the Jewish rite which had no interest for his Christian readers. Nevertheless, he preserves sufficient indication of the sequence of events during the meal for us to be able to place Jesus' innovations in their original context. **During** 22 **supper he took bread.** It is significant that the breaking of bread took place after the meal had begun. Almost all formal meals among the Jews began with the host saying the blessing and breaking a loaf of bread, which he then divided out among the guests. This was the beginning of the meal: unless it was a luxurious occasion, when hors d'œuvres might first be eaten in another room, nothing would have been eaten until this moment. But there was one exception to this. At the Passover, the supper began with "bitter herbs"—lettuce and the like—which were dipped into a dish of sweet sauce. This was the moment for the Judas episode which has just been narrated. The breaking of bread seems to have had no important rôle in the meal, and certainly did not take its usual place at the beginning. To this extent, it is intelligible that Jesus' action should have been **during supper**, though so far as we know the **blessing** (which took a form such as, "Blessed be thou who bringest forth bread from the earth") and breaking, though usual on any other occasion, normally played no special part in the Passover meal.

'Take this; this is my body.' Another feature of the Passover meal, which certainly goes back to the time of Jesus (though it was much elaborated in later times) was that the host—or the father, if it was a family group—had to explain the significance of the special food that was being eaten. The whole meal was to be seen as a re-enactment of the exodus of the Jews out of Egypt (Exodus 12); and the explanation took the form of a commentary on a passage such as Deuteronomy 26.5–9, where these events are summarized. For instance, the Passover lamb stood for the original sacrifice made in Egypt; its blood for the blood which was painted on the Israelites' doorposts so that the punishment of the Lord should "pass over" them (Exodus 12.27); and the bitter herbs for the days of bitter slavery which God's people had undergone in Egypt. But what did the unleavened bread stand for? This (since it probably did not belong to the original festival) was more difficult, and differing answers were given. It may have been in this context that Jesus pronounced the words, 'this is my body.'

What do the words mean? The question can only be fully answered out of the subsequent reflection and experience of the church. Here it is sufficient to ask how the disciples would originally have understood them. They would have been accustomed, at every formal meal, to the head of the household breaking a loaf of bread with a prayer of thanksgiving to God (a "blessing"), and when each person at the table received and ate a piece of this loaf as it was given to him, he thereby associated himself with the blessing which had been spoken. To this extent, when Jesus **took bread, and having said the blessing he broke it**, the disciples, when they ate the bread he gave them, were doing something entirely familiar: they were expressing their solidarity with Jesus and saying Amen to his blessing. But when Jesus added the words, **'this is my body'**, he went far beyond the meaning of an ordinary family blessing. The only "body" which it would make sense to them to "eat" was the body of an animal which had been offered as a sacrifice—like the lamb which was doubtless (though it is not mentioned here) the main element of the meal which Mark is describing, and which had been ritually slaughtered earlier the same afternoon at the altar before the temple. When Jesus called the bread "his body", his disciples are likely to have grasped that he was likening himself to a sacrificial victim; and when he said, **'take this'**, he was inviting them to share in the benefits which would flow from the sacrifice being offered.

23 **Then he took a cup.** If the meal was following the usual course of a Passover, some time will have elapsed since the breaking of bread: the lamb itself will have been eaten, and the prescribed explanation given of the meaning of the special food that was served. But the Christian community had no interest in these details (though an echo of them survives in Paul's phrase, 'he took the cup after supper', 1 Corinthians 11.25), and Mark goes straight on to the moment, at the end of the meal, when the host took a cup of wine in his hands and **offered thanks to God** in much the same way as he had said the blessing over the bread. Once again, the disciples would have found it natural to associate themselves with Jesus in this by immediately drinking with him, and it is likely (though this cannot be proved from the evidence available) that they would have been used to passing round a common cup on such an occasion. But, once again, Jesus went far beyond this ordinary
24 ceremony by adding the words, **'This is my blood, the blood of the covenant, shed for many.'** This, more clearly than the saying over the bread, was the language of sacrifice. The most important moment in the ritual slaughter of a victim at the altar in Jerusalem was the shedding of its blood. It was by virtue of the blood poured upon the altar that the sacrifice was deemed effective. Certain sacrifices made by the priests were moreover made **for many** (though Jesus probably had in mind a larger section of humanity than would have been envisaged at a normal Jewish sacrifice); and on one occasion the blood of a sacrifice had been sprinkled upon the whole

people of Israel to seal **the covenant** made with them by God (Exodus 24.8). The Old Testament looked forward to a "new covenant" of an inner, spiritual kind (Jeremiah 31.31–4), and the work of Jesus was soon to be understood by Christians as the inauguration of this new covenant. The wine, therefore, which the disciples were to drink[a] was interpreted by Jesus as the blood of himself as a sacrificial victim, whose death would be on behalf of many and would seal a new covenant between God and men.

'**I tell you this: never again shall I drink from the fruit of the vine**'. 25 As it stands here (the meaning is different in Luke), the saying appears to be a simple prophecy by Jesus that he would not live to partake of any further meals at which wine was drunk; and since the narrative implies that he was by now certain of his impending death, it can be taken as one more solemn prediction of what was about to happen. But the saying does not stop there. It continues with a rich sequence of biblical ideas: '**until that day when I drink it new in the kingdom of God**'. The **kingdom of God** was often described as a heavenly banquet, at which the Messiah would preside, and all things would be made **new**; and Jesus seems to have been deliberately relating the meal he had just shared with his disciples to the heavenly reality which, he prophesied, would shortly come to pass. The one was a foretaste of the other, just as the traditional Jewish Passover meal was often interpreted as an anticipation of the coming redemption which God had promised to his people.

After singing the Passover Hymn. The Passover meal ended with the 26 singing of part of the so-called *Hallel*, which consisted of Psalms 113–18. The Greek says simply, "after singing a hymn", but the translators are doubtless right that this special **Passover Hymn** is meant. **They went out to the Mount of Olives.** It was obligatory upon all who kept the festival to remain in Jerusalem until sunrise; but in view of the very large number of pilgrims, a technical dispensation had been introduced under which, for this one night, "Jerusalem" was deemed to embrace a number of outlying areas, including the Mount of Olives, but not including Bethany, where Jesus had been spending the night during the earlier part of the week. We can assume, therefore, that it was long before sunrise when Jesus left the city, crossed the Kedron valley and approached the lower slopes of the Mount of Olives. His prediction, '**you will all fall from your faith**', is 27 supported by a quotation from Zechariah 13.7 (in a form slightly different from that of any version which has come down to us). It is remarkable that in the gospels no attempt is made to conceal or mitigate the failure of the disciples to stand by Jesus; on the other hand, it may have helped them to live it down, so to speak, when they remembered an Old Testament prophecy

[a] Presumably red wine, to make the symbolism obvious. But all wine looks dark red when drunk out of pottery cups, and the "blood of grapes" was a common metaphor for wine in Hebrew poetry.

which made their conduct seem predestined. In any case, all Jesus' predictions seem to presuppose that he knew he was to suffer alone. What may have made the realization all the more poignant is that this denial and desertion took place even before the end of the night, during which he and his disciples should have been particularly closely bound together by their table-fellowship. As on previous occasions in this gospel, Peter is singled out from the disciples, but apparently only to represent them all in their apostasy: 'You will all fall from your faith' applies to them all, 'you . . . will disown me' is the particular way in which Peter will fulfil the prediction. 'Before the cock crows twice'. In the east there is often a remarkably regular cock-crow, the first soon after midnight, another about an hour later, and a third one an hour later still, leaving two or three hours of silence before the chorus at dawn. Certainly, the third of the four "watches" into which the Romans divided the night (and this way of reckoning the parts of the night now prevailed in Palestine, as can be seen from 13.35) was popularly called "cock-crow", as was the bugle-blast with which a Roman military garrison would announce it. Whatever therefore Mark meant precisely by the cock crowing twice, the moment referred to was one which was going to be easy to recognize, well before dawn.

30

28   The section contains one very curious prophecy. 'Nevertheless, after I am raised again I will go on before you into Galilee.' After the flock has been scattered through the striking down of the shepherd, it will once more gather behind its leader as he moves away northward into Galilee. This, at any rate, is the natural meaning of the Greek words, which are repeated below at 16.7; and the difficulty is to see in what way, if any, they were fulfilled. After the resurrection, Jesus appeared to the disciples in Jerusalem, and the fact that there are two traces in the gospels of an appearance in Galilee (Matthew 28.16–20 and John 21) does not really affect the fact that the church began its life, not following its master back to Galilee, but waiting upon his appearances and the manifestations of his power in Jerusalem. On the other hand, the church did soon find itself in movement, being guided by the Holy Spirit from its centre in Jerusalem to all parts of the civilized world. Jesus, in his lifetime, barely went further from the centre of Jewish life than Galilee; but Galilee, compared with Jerusalem, already represented an excursion into a partly non-Jewish world. Moreover, "Galilee" itself was a symbolic name: in its Old Testament form, it meant "land of the heathen" (as in Matthew 4.15). It is just possible that by this prophecy Jesus meant that after the resurrection he would lead his church far beyond the confines of the Jewish world. And this indeed took place.

32   When they reached a place called Gethsemane. The name is likely to mean "oil-press". John's gospel calls it a 'garden' on the far side (from Jerusalem) of the Kedron valley which separates Jerusalem from the Mount

of Olives. All the gospel accounts imply that it was somewhere on the Mount of Olives itself. The traditional site, not far from a cave on the slope of the mount facing Jerusalem, fits these data as well as any, and we should visualize a secluded and perhaps enclosed spot not far from the road that led over the Mount of Olives to Bethany. Jesus' purpose in coming to it was to pray, for which he usually preferred to be alone; but on this occasion he allowed near him the three privileged disciples who had earlier been witnesses of his transfiguration.

From this perfectly natural and quiet beginning, two altogether unexpected sequences of events unfold. First, Jesus' steady resolution and apparent foresight of what was to happen suddenly forsook him. For no reason that the gospels explain, **horror and dismay came over him,** and 34 his prayer, which we may suppose normally took the form of intimate communion with his Father, was on this occasion an anguished mixture of rebellion and resignation. It may be asked, did Jesus really pray like this? Were his actual words heard and remembered (despite the fact that the only witnesses fell asleep), or did a subsequent tradition compose the kind of prayer which Jesus is likely to have prayed, just as ancient historians, from Thucydides on, freely composed the speeches which generals or statesmen were likely to have made on critical occasions? Not all these words of Jesus are (in the modern sense) original: **'My heart is ready to break with** 34 **grief'** is not an exact quotation, but it recalls both the tone of a psalmist whose faith in God is tested to breaking point (Psalm 42.6), and also the exclamation of the prophet Jonah, when the most recent turn of events had made him feel that it would be better that he should die rather than attempt any longer to fulfil his vocation (Jonah 4.9). **'Abba',** an intimate Aramaic 36 word for **'Father',** was the way in which the first Christians believed they should now address their prayers to God (very likely following Jesus' own example). **'Not what I will, but what thou wilt'** is a clear allusion to the Lord's Prayer itself. In short, the materials for composing the prayer lay ready to hand in the spirituality of the Old Testament and of the early church; and if it is thought unlikely that any reliable record of Jesus' words could have been preserved, there is no difficulty in seeing how the first Christians, meditating on Jesus' last hours of solitude in Gethsemane, may have composed and attributed to him a prayer of this nature. Moreover, however surprising it may seem that Jesus underwent such agony, both the Letter to the Hebrews (5.7) and the Gospel according to John (12.27) offer apparently independent testimony to some experience of Jesus comparable with that recorded here; and the episode is so unexpected that it is difficult to see how it could have been invented by the church.

The second unexpected sequence of events concerns the disciples. At the outset Jesus merely bade them, without explanation, to **stay awake.** If we 34 are to understand that Jesus was still deliberately observing the customs of

Passover night, then the injunction is natural: if one of the group which had eaten the supper together fell asleep, the table-fellowship was deemed to have been broken. For the sake of their solidarity with him, Jesus may have warned them to **stay awake**. But there is no hint of this in the narrative. And when Jesus found that they had nevertheless fallen asleep (for it was by

38 now doubtless late in the night), he urged them again to '**stay awake**', and this time gave the reason: '**pray that you may be spared the test**'. What test? The prayer, again, sounds like a reminiscence of the Lord's Prayer: Christians are always to pray, 'Do not bring us to the test' (Matthew 6.13). But clearly a special "test" is in mind here with which the disciples were threatened. Was there a danger that they would be arrested and executed along with Jesus? Or was it precisely the temptation to flee danger and deny Jesus which constituted their "test", and about which they ought to be praying just as Jesus was praying about his own greater test? We are not told; nor do we know in what tone of voice Jesus commented on their

38 failure **to stay awake for one hour**: '**The spirit is willing, but the flesh is weak.**' Was this a proverb, wryly appropriate to the situation? Or an indulgent comment, made by one who suffered no weakness of the flesh himself? Or a general observation on human psychology? We do not know. Once again, it is true that "stay awake" became a very common moral exhortation in the early church, that "do not bring us to the test" was a prayer which Christians uttered every day, and that the power of the spirit and the weakness of the flesh became a familiar contrast in the experience of the first Christian communities. Moreover, '**the spirit is willing, but the flesh is weak**' is the kind of balanced antithesis more characteristic of literary Greek than (so far as we know) of spoken Aramaic, and is hardly likely to have been said by Jesus in exactly this form. In short, there is no difficulty in detecting signs that the subsequent reflection of the church may have influenced or even created the narrative. But equally, if the disciples did not in fact fall asleep, it is difficult to see why anyone in the church should have wanted to cast discredit on them by making up the story; and if the story of their failure to stay awake is true, the rest flows from that. We are left with an account which, though puzzling in its details, is vivid, moving and apparently authentic.

41 '**Still sleeping? Still taking your ease?**' The force of these words depends on the punctuation, and since, when the gospels were first written, punctuation signs were not much used, we can only tell from the context whether here Jesus was giving a command ("Go on sleeping!"), making an exclamation ("Still asleep!") or asking a question ("Still sleeping?"). Most older translations take the words as a command; more recent ones, like the NEB, take them as a comment on the disciples' repeated failure to stay awake. This has the advantage of making better sense with what follows, though there is still considerable obscurity about the Greek word translated

'Enough!'. *a* At any rate, the tone is now abrupt and commanding. Jesus knows that the hour has come.

Suddenly, while he was still speaking. It is difficult, in translation, to 43 reproduce the finer points of an author's style without falling into pedantry. But here there is some significance in the exact word which Mark uses to introduce the next episode. It means, not **suddenly**, but "at once" (as it is translated in verse 45), and is Mark's favourite way of joining one episode to another. The detail is important, because it is at this point that the narratives of all four gospels converge and begin to move forward together along very similar lines; and this convergence is most easily explained if, in the early church, the account of Jesus' arrest, trial and crucifixion was the first part of the gospel narrative to assume a fairly standardized form, leaving each evangelist little freedom to rearrange it. If such a common tradition existed, it apparently began with Jesus' arrest. In Mark's gospel, however, the arrest seems to be so closely linked with what goes before (**suddenly, while he was still speaking**) that it looks at first sight improbable that a new chapter, so to speak, originally began at this point; but the word "at once" (**suddenly**) betrays Mark's editorial hand: it was he who joined up the episodes into a single sequence.

The characters in the scene are clearly identified. **Judas, one of the Twelve:** there seems to be a deliberate emphasis (as in verse 10 above) on the fact that Jesus was betrayed by one of his own disciples; the fact that he was to be "handed over" to his enemies was one which Jesus constantly mentioned when he predicted his own death, and we are left in no doubt that this was the way it turned out. The **crowd armed with swords and cudgels** might sound like an unofficial gang of ruffians were it not that it is explicitly said that they were **sent by the chief priests, lawyers, and elders.** These three classes of people made up the supreme Jewish Council known as the Sanhedrin, which was actually assembling at this moment (verse 53). This Council, though many of its civil powers had been taken over by the Roman administration, exercised legal authority in all religious matters, and maintained some kind of police or body of armed men to ensure that its authority was observed. It was these men, according to Mark, who arrived with Judas to arrest Jesus.

Now the traitor had agreed with them upon a signal. The kiss 44 strikes us as a particularly repellent gesture of betrayal, but this may be a modern reaction. It was customary for a pupil to greet his master with a kiss: when Judas kissed Jesus and called him '**Rabbi**', he was using the ordinary 45 form of greeting, and at the same time identifying, for the benefit of the armed band, the one man in the group who could be addressed in this way. One thing which is clear from his action is that the authorities had no inten-

[a] A further possible rendering might be mentioned, which would give the sense: "Your untimely sleep has its reward: we are caught!"

tion of arresting Jesus' disciples. If they had, they would have needed no signal from Judas: it would have been sufficient to arrest the whole group and identify Jesus afterwards. Therefore we probably should not make too
50 much of the fact that the disciples **all deserted him and ran away.** Physical resistance to the armed party was presumably both out of the question and also contrary to Jesus' wishes; John's gospel states that Jesus actually intended them to escape. Their desertion, in fact, may have been more in accord with Jesus' wishes than the preliminary scuffle. Indeed, Mark seems
47 a little embarrassed by this incident when he says that it was caused by **one of the party.** The Greek word is vague (see the alternative translation in the footnote), as if the perpetrator might have been some casual onlooker. But in fact, apart from Jesus' disciples, there is unlikely to have been anyone there.

48 **Then Jesus spoke.** His words are recorded, with slight variations, in all
49 the gospels, and show that he had no thought of resistance. '**Let the scriptures be fulfilled**' summarizes his attitude. With **the scriptures**, perhaps he had in mind those passages of the Old Testament which seemed to point to a Messiah who must suffer, or perhaps he was thinking of a particular prophecy like that which is given in Luke's version (22.37) "And he was counted among the outlaws" (Isaiah 53.12). Despite his resignation, he
49 allowed himself the irony of saying, '**day after day I was within your reach as I taught in the temple**'—words which present a critical problem, since according to Mark's narrative Jesus had spent at most three days teaching in the temple. This is another small hint that Mark's chronology of these last days may be artificial.

51 Mark alone mentions the **young man with nothing on but a linen cloth.** The Greek says simply "linen", and means that his only outer garment was made of linen—a sign that he was not poor. The detail is so vivid and unexpected that it has often been suggested that Mark put it in because the young man was none other than the writer of the gospel himself. But this is pure speculation.

53 **Then they led Jesus away to the High Priest's house.** There follows a hearing before the **chief priests, elders, and doctors of the law.** These were the people of influence in Jerusalem, and members of these three classes composed the supreme Jewish judicial Council (the Sanhedrin). There can be little doubt that Mark believed that it was before this Council, or a committee of it, that Jesus appeared. But compared with what we know of the usual procedure of the Council, the hearing has some unusual features. The Council's official meeting place was a building inside (or at least close to) the temple precincts, but on this occasion it met in the High Priest's house. Sittings were permitted only during the day, but this one took place in the middle of the night. Capital sentences required confirmation by a further

sitting not less than twenty-four hours after the first, and no capital case could be heard on the eve of a Sabbath or feast day; but on this occasion the judges proceeded immediately to secure the carrying out of the sentence, the following day was a Sabbath, and the night of the hearing was the beginning of the Passover festival. However, it is only fair to say that almost all our information about the procedure of the Sanhedrin is unreliable, in the sense that it was first written down and codified over a century after Jerusalem had been destroyed and the Council, at any rate as a judicial authority with civil powers, had ceased to exist. These later Jewish sources provide us with a picture which may well be idealized and artificial. In the troubled period which preceded the Jewish revolt, it must often have been necessary to improvise and adapt; and the gospel accounts should not be suspected merely because they fail to conform with all the details of a procedure which was worked out theoretically some time later.

However, if the hour and the place are unusual, the hearing itself follows the usual pattern of Jewish legal proceedings. Witnesses were called; but the only way in which a charge could be sustained was by securing two witnesses who, when examined independently (and out of each other's hearing), gave identical evidence. This **the chief priests and the whole Council** failed 55 to do: **many gave false evidence against him, but their statements** 56 **did not tally.** One accusation is mentioned which, if substantiated, would have been very damaging. The temple was the holiest possession of the Jews, the central shrine of the national religion, the place where, above all, God was felt to be present among his people. The threat, "**I will pull down this** 58 **temple**", could presumably have been interpreted as blasphemy—and we read in John's gospel (2.19) that Jesus did in fact say something about building a new temple to replace the old (though we may be sure that he did not mean literally to destroy the existing temple). [a] **But even on this point** 59 **their evidence did not agree.** Apparently, on this point like the others, no two people could be found whose independent evidence was sufficiently consistent to form the basis of a charge.

In the absence of witnesses, the only course left to the Council was to try to get Jesus to incriminate himself. The High Priest's first attempt was simply to put Jesus on the defensive: '**Have you no answer to the charges** 60 **that these witnesses bring against you?**' But, since no charge had been substantiated, Jesus had nothing to gain by replying. **He kept silence.** The first attempt was a failure.

Surprisingly, the second attempt was successful. **Again the High Priest** 61 **questioned him: 'Are you the Messiah, the Son of the Blessed One?'** When Mark called Jesus 'Son of God' (as in the first sentence of his gospel) he intended the full range of meanings which, by the time he wrote, the church had come to associate with the title. But in the mouth of the High

[a] For other versions of this accusation, see Matthew 26.61; Acts 6.14.

Priest the same title (**the Blessed One** stands for God: the Jews preferred to avoid using the divine name) clearly meant the same as **Messiah**, that is, the supernaturally endowed figure whom the Jewish people expected to institute a new age, and who would necessarily stand in the line of those great figures of the Old Testament who were called "Sons of God". Would Jesus admit to being that figure? So far, Jesus had always avoided making any public declaration of his Messiahship. At most he had given hints of it, and his understanding of the title was clearly very different from that of his contemporaries. But asked point blank, he now gave an unequivocal answer,

62 '**I am**',[a] and, by means of two Old Testament allusions, proceeded to draw out one of the implications of his answer. In the course of Daniel's vision (7.13), these words occur: "I saw one like a son of man coming with the clouds of heaven; he approached the Ancient of Years and was presented to him." The scene was the Last Judgement, and the meaning of the vision was that this Son of Man was then to be given a position of the highest honour and authority. Similarly, Psalm 110 was currently interpreted as a prophecy that One was to come who would have supremacy next only to God:[b] "The Lord says . . . sit at my right hand". By means of these two allusions, Jesus accredited himself not merely with a unique mission and with unique power, but with a unique status in all creation.

64 '**You have heard the blasphemy**'. Exactly what constituted blasphemy is not defined in the Old Testament, and we do not know what definitions were in use in the time of Jesus. On the face of it, Jesus' words were not blasphemous in themselves, unless the claim they expressed was obviously false; and it may be that the fact that they were uttered by one who, far from being a person of glory and power, was actually a prisoner of the court, was sufficient for the judges to dismiss Jesus' claim out of hand. At any rate the

63 High Priest **tore his robes** (the action which was required of anyone who heard words of blasphemy) and the rest of the court signified its agreement. Jesus had uttered blasphemy; and blasphemy, according to Jewish law (Leviticus 24.16) was punishable by death.

However, in a province governed by a Roman magistrate, it would have been unusual for a local court to have had the power to impose the death penalty. This power was normally kept firmly in the hands of the Roman governor. John's gospel explicitly informs us that the Sanhedrin refused to carry out the sentence for this reason (18.31), and although there is little independent evidence for Judaea at this period, there is no convincing reason for doubting what John says. The Jews could not execute Jesus themselves, and had to take the further measures which are described in the next chapter. Meanwhile they vented their feelings in a scene of mockery and

[a] The answer is less decisive in Matthew and Luke, and also in some manuscripts of Mark.
[b] "The Power" (see footnote in NEB) was another Jewish periphrasis for God.

insult. The gospels all offer slightly different accounts at this point, and it is difficult to be sure what really happened, but certain ideas seem always to be in the background. The main feature of the scene, in all three accounts, is the sarcastic command, 'Prophesy!' If Jesus was truly the Messiah, then the 65 easiest proof he could give would be to show that he possessed the "spirit" promised to the Messiah, a spirit which would surely manifest itself especially through the gift of prophecy—and the fact that Jesus did not, there and then, give a demonstration of prophecy may have confirmed his judges in their view that he was an impostor. In addition, there seems to have been an element of teasing cruelty in the blindfolding of Jesus. And a third point which doubtless influenced the narrative was a prophecy of Isaiah (50.6),

> "I offered my back to the lash . . .
> I did not hide my face from spitting and insult"

—one of those passages about a "suffering servant" of the Lord which Christians very soon came to see as having been fulfilled in the destiny of Jesus.

Meanwhile Peter was still below in the courtyard. The High Priest's 66 house must be imagined as a substantial building round a courtyard, with the principal rooms (of which one was large enough to hold the whole Council) on the first floor, the ground-floor rooms presumably accommodating servants and guards. Peter, we are told in verse 54, had penetrated right into this courtyard—John's gospel (18.16) provides the explanation that another of the disciples was well known there and was able to get him admitted. He was sitting among the attendants, warming himself at 54 the fire. There it was light enough (either because of the fire, or because of torches) for him to be recognized by one of the High Priest's serving- 66 maids, and after a stammering denial he retreated outside into the porch, 68 that is to say, out of the courtyard, to the street side of the main door of the house where, despite the hour, there were some bystanders who had 69 perhaps been attracted by the news of the unusual sitting of the Council. But the serving-maid noticed him still lingering near the house, and passed on her suspicions to others in the throng. Finally, Peter was identified as a Galilean, perhaps by his accent (as Matthew reports), perhaps by his 70 clothes. This was more incriminating than the maid's personal suspicion, and Peter became vehement: At this he broke out into curses. "May 71 God destroy me if I know the man" is the kind of language the phrase suggests. Then the cock crew a second time. We cannot be sure whether 72 Mark mentioned the first cock-crow: only some manuscripts give it (at the end of verse 68), and if Peter had heard it, why did he not notice it and realize what he was doing? At any rate, the cock crowing a second time brings the scene into harmony with Jesus' prediction (14.30); and Peter

burst into tears (if that is what the very difficult Greek word means: "He rushed out and wept" would be another possible rendering, but in the present state of our knowledge the NEB translation is as likely to be correct as any).

15. 1 **As soon as morning came.** The position at this point was that the Sanhedrin had found Jesus guilty on a capital charge, but not having the power to carry out the sentence they had either to let him off with a flogging or else bring the matter before the Roman governor in the hope that he would arrive at the same verdict and authorize the death penalty. The time for approaching a senior Roman official was the very early morning. The working day of a Roman gentleman began at dawn or even earlier; later in the morning he would have finished his official work and have been unavailable. Consequently the Council **having made their plan** *a*—that is, having decided on an approach to the Roman governor and on the kind of case to put before him—lost no time after their night session but immediately **put Jesus in chains . . . led him away and handed him over to Pilate.** Pilate was the governor of Judaea from A.D. 26 to 36. He had a bad record of tactless and provocative actions aimed at the Jews, but there is nothing in the following narrative to suggest that he acted irregularly. Under Roman law, his task, in a case of this kind, was simply to take note of the charges being brought, make sure that the accused was given opportunity to defend himself, decide what law, if any, the accused's conduct contravened, give his verdict, declare the sentence, and give orders for it to be carried out. Mark does not attempt to give a systematic account of this procedure; but the points which he records all fit into it well enough.

2 **Pilate asked him, 'Are you the king of the Jews?'** From this question we can infer (what Luke, for instance, makes explicit) that the "plan" of the Jewish authorities consisted in bringing Jesus before Pilate on a political charge. A Roman governor, as we can guess from similar hearings in Acts, would not have felt willing or qualified to give a decision on a matter of Jewish law; and the only charge against Jesus which had so far been substantiated was that of blasphemy, the definition of which was entirely a matter for Jewish jurists. To justify their action in bringing Jesus before Pilate, it was necessary to present a different charge. Jesus had admitted to being the Messiah, and this could be represented as a claim to be **the king of the Jews** (which, taken literally, was of course an act of sedition). We must assume that the **many charges** they brought against him before Pilate's tribunal centred round this one accusation.

Now there was certainly a sense in which one who was the Messiah must

[a] The NEB does not indicate the fact that at this point a number of manuscripts offer a reading which would almost certainly mean not, having made their plan but, "having convened a meeting". If this is the correct reading, we must allow for the possibility that Mark knew of two sessions, one before and one after dawn. This becomes important when his account is compared with those of Luke and John.

also be "the king of the Jews". The Messiah was to be the successor of King David, and some kind of kingship was inseparable from his status. Therefore Jesus once again, when asked point blank, did not deny that there was truth 2 in the allegation (though his answer in the Greek is too ambiguous— perhaps intentionally so—for us to be able to say that he actually affirmed it). But it is clear from a later remark of Pilate—'**Why, what harm has he** 14 **done?**'—that this admission was not such as to make Jesus appear as a dangerous revolutionary: Pilate must have understood—and in the account in John's gospel Jesus explains this to him—that Jesus' aspirations to king-ship were not primarily political, and he was presumably not convinced by the allegations of ambition, amounting to sedition, which the prosecutors were able to bring forward. Nevertheless, he did not omit the regular procedure of giving the accused an opportunity to make his defence. **But, to** 5 **Pilate's astonishment, Jesus made no further reply.** This silence of Jesus, both here and in the earlier proceedings before the Council, is much insisted on in all the gospel accounts. It is true that, once again, since the prosecution had apparently failed to make out a case, Jesus had little to gain by trying to defend himself. But there is probably more to it than that. In the first place, his silence was a fulfilment of one of the "suffering servant" passages of Isaiah which the first Christians (and possibly Jesus himself) regarded as an important clue to the meaning of these events:

> "He was afflicted, he submitted to be struck down
>   and did not open his mouth;
> he was led like a sheep to the slaughter
> like a ewe that is dumb before the shearers,
> and he would not open his mouth." (Isaiah 53.7)

In the second place, his refusal to say a word in his own defence was so unusual and so unexpected that it doubtless stuck in the mind of anyone who witnessed it. It is not surprising that it is one of the best-attested facts of Jesus' trial.

The Governor used to release one prisoner. We have no other 6 evidence of this custom in Judaea, but it is not inherently improbable. The custom provided Pilate with the possibility of an easy solution; if the people requested the release of Jesus, he would be relieved of the task of making a decision in the case. But there was another prisoner **in custody** whom 7 apparently the crowd knew well, and indeed Mark introduces him as if both the man and his past were well known to his readers. Barabbas is not a distinctive name—indeed rather the opposite if it represents Bar-Abbas, "Father's son"; and Mark does not trouble to tell us who the other **rebels** were and what **the rising** was they had taken part in (and we know nothing about this from any source outside the gospels). He seems to assume that the whole episode was well known, and it presumably had nothing to do with

8 Jesus' trial that **the crowd appeared**[a] **asking for the usual favour**. This early-morning "office hour" of Pilate was the right time for the crowd to present their request, just as it was for the members of the Sanhedrin to bring to Pilate's notice the case of Jesus of Nazareth. Pilate evidently knew that Jesus was more popular with the people than with the Jewish authorities, and

10 that he had been brought before him **out of malice**. Consequently, the fortuitous arrival of people who might be expected to support Jesus seemed

9 to give him his opportunity: '**Do you wish me to release for you the king of the Jews?**'

However, under the influence of the chief priests, the people kept to their original purpose of asking for the release of Barabbas. It is not clear why Pilate then drew them into Jesus' case. Possibly he hoped that, if they showed themselves sympathetic to Jesus, they would provide him with further reasons for releasing a man who (he was now satisfied) was not a source of political danger; and this would give him the satisfaction of disappointing the Jewish leaders whom (as we know from other sources) he disliked and

13 despised. But **they shouted back, 'Crucify him!'** Again Mark gives no explanation. Up to now the crowd had been on Jesus' side. Why this sudden animosity against him? It may be simply that the presence of the chief priests was sufficient to make them change their mind (though we should not have guessed, otherwise, that the chief priests had so much influence with the populace). Alternatively, Pilate's question was understood—and perhaps intended—as a test of their loyalty. Here was a man who called himself "king of the Jews". On the face of it, this meant that he was an insurrectionary. In the presence of the Roman governor, what would be the reaction of the crowd? To acclaim Jesus as king, and expose themselves to the same charge of attempted insurrection? Or to demand the appropriate punishment under Roman law for a public enemy? These were the alternatives. Understandably they chose the second: '**Crucify him!**' Without more ado (for in such cases the Governor was not bound to any precise legal procedure) Pilate pronounced Jesus guilty and sentenced him to crucifixion, the penalty prescribed for action taken "against the Roman people". As usual, the sentence was to be carried out straight away; and it was normal for the

15 condemned man first to be **flogged**, probably to weaken him so that he would die more quickly on the cross.

16 **Then the soldiers took him inside the courtyard.** When the Roman governor came up to Jerusalem from his capital (the port of Caesarea), he normally brought with him his own **company** of troops; the word used here was the technical Greek name for a Roman cohort, consisting of between two hundred and six hundred men. These he will have lodged in the building

[a] Literally "went up" (according to the most probable reading of the manuscripts). Both the sites which have been suggested for the Praetorium were on high ground: see below on John 19.13.

he used as his **headquarters** (*praetorium*), [a] and it is no surprise to find them here ready to carry out the sentence passed on Jesus. The soldiers themselves are unlikely to have been either Jews (who were not enlisted for military service in Palestine) or Romans (who were reserved for the regular legions of the Roman army), but non-Jewish local men recruited from Palestine and Syria for the auxiliary forces. They will therefore have had some idea of the religious and political pretensions of a man who called himself "king of the Jews", and their mockery of the prisoner was a natural consequence. **They** 17 **dressed him in purple**—this was the distinctive mark of a monarch in the eastern part of the empire; **and plaiting a crown of thorns, placed it on his head**—not a crown in the modern sense, but an insulting travesty of a wreath such as the Emperor's head always bears on Roman coins. So dressed, they greeted Jesus with a parody of a royal acclamation, **'Hail,** 18 **King of the Jews!'**

Then they took him out to crucify him. Crucifixion, though generally 21 regarded as a cruel and barbarous form of execution, was a common enough sight in Palestine under the Roman administration, since it was the usual punishment for those who committed violence and insurrection. **The two** 27 **bandits** (the word was often used for members of armed resistance movements) who were crucified along with Jesus were typical victims of it, and the fact that Jesus received this penalty proclaimed, as clearly as the inscription placed on his cross, that the charge against him was political: he had claimed to be **'The king of the Jews'**. Few details are given in the gospels about 26 how it was carried out, but the traditional representation of the scene is probably roughly correct: the cross might be in the shape of a T or a +, the prisoner was fastened to it either with cords or with nails (John 20.25 proves that Jesus' hands and feet had scars from nails). A peg was driven into the upright of the cross to support the body either between the legs or under the feet. Elsewhere in the empire the victims were stripped naked; but in Judaea the Romans may have respected the Jewish abhorrence of nakedness and allowed a loincloth. All executions, whether Jewish or Roman, took place outside the city walls (**they took him out** could mean 21 out of the praetorium, or out of the city), but since crucifixions were intended to be a warning example, they usually took place not far from a city gate, so that many people would be compelled to see them on their way in or out of the city (John 19.20 confirms that the place was 'near to the city'). The traditional site of Jesus' crucifixion, where in the fourth century Constantine built his great church, is at a spot which, until new city walls were built some ten years later, would have lain just outside one angle of the walls, a few hundred yards from one of the gates, in an area which had once been a quarry but which now held some tombs. A rocky mound jutted up from

[a] On the question where this was, see below on John 19.13.

this area (and still exists inside the present church) which, by its shape,
22 could have suggested the name 'Place of a skull'; of this name, Golgotha
(more correctly *Golgoltha*) is the Aramaic equivalent, and Calvary (*Calvarium*)
the traditional Latin translation. The identification of this spot with the site
of Jesus' crucifixion is by no means certain, but recent archaeological
research has made it seem increasingly probable. In any case, the few details
which are given by the gospels are entirely consistent with what we know
otherwise both about the ancient city of Jerusalem and about the customary
procedure at executions in the Roman empire.

21   A man called Simon, from Cyrene. Mark seldom gives the name of
the subsidiary characters in his story, but here he gives not only his name but
his country of origin. There were substantial Jewish settlements in North
Africa, and Simon may have been a Jew who either owned land in Palestine
(and so could be on his way in from the country) or who had come up
to Jerusalem for the festival. *a* Mark reveals his reason for naming Simon
when he adds that he was the father of Alexander and Rufus. These
names mean nothing to us, but they must have been known to Mark's first
readers. That is to say, the gospel must have been written for use in a
community which counted among its members the children of one of the
witnesses of the crucifixion. If Rufus could be shown to be the same Rufus
as Paul mentions in his letter to the Romans, we could go further and locate
this community at Rome; but the name is fairly common, and Simon's sons
could just as well have belonged to the church in North Africa (which is
another place where Mark's gospel is often thought to have been composed).
They pressed him into service to carry his cross. Criminals on their way
to execution were normally made to carry the cross-beam of their cross
themselves (which is how John's gospel represents Jesus on the way to
Golgotha), but Jesus may already have been too exhausted to carry it the
22 whole way—indeed the Greek word translated they brought him is a
rather physical one, and suggests that Jesus was dragged or helped along
rather than simply led under escort.

Two more details are given which again correspond with normal practice.
23 He was offered drugged wine. This was an anaesthetic, and was normally
given to Jews before execution; indeed, in view of Proverbs 31.6 ("Give
strong drink to him who is perishing, and wine to those in bitter distress"),
it was thought meritorious to do so, if not actually obligatory, and it was
doubtless Jews—and very likely Jewish women—who offered the anaesthetic
24 to Jesus. On the other hand, those who divided his clothes among them
were the soldiers of the execution squad, who had a customary right to them.

[a] It is often argued that travelling was not permitted on the first day of the Feast any more
than on a Sabbath, and that this detail is a sign that Mark's chronology is artificial, and that
(as in John's gospel) the Passover had not yet begun. But "from the country" need not
mean a longer distance than was permitted; and in any case, Simon may not have been a
Jew at all.

That they should have cast lots **to decide what each should have** sounds perfectly natural; but Mark's language shows that he had in mind a precedent. The author of Psalm 22, writing out of a situation very similar to that of Jesus—that of an innocent man brought to the last degree of suffering and humiliation by his enemies—included the same detail in his description of his own abject circumstances (verse 18):

"They share out my garments among them
and cast lots for my clothes."

The hour of the crucifixion was nine in the morning. This trans- 25 lation is correct, but suggests greater precision than perhaps Mark intended. The day was divided into twelve hours between sunrise and sunset (and in a country such as Palestine where the length of the days does not vary more than two or three hours between mid-summer and mid-winter this worked well enough). Ordinary citizens did not use a water-clock or hour-glass to tell which "hour" it was; they looked at the sun, and observed when it was noon (the "sixth hour"), when it was mid-morning (the "third hour"), and when mid-afternoon (the "ninth hour")—and these are the three hours which are in fact most frequently mentioned in the New Testament. The last two were of course approximations: one cannot have more than a rough idea when the sun has got half-way between sunrise and noon, or noon and sunset. Here, Mark says it was "the third hour". If anyone was taking the trouble to find out the correct time by a clock, then this would certainly be equivalent to **nine in the morning.** But there is no reason to think that Mark intended such accuracy. He meant that Jesus was crucified in the middle of the morning, and died in the middle of the afternoon (verse 33). That is to say, Mark spread the main events of Good Friday evenly over the day. John follows a slightly different scheme, and places the crucifixion at midday.

The passers-by hurled abuse at him. Classic descriptions of mockery 29 can be found in the Old Testament. Sometimes it was Jerusalem in ruins which was the object of scorn—"All those who pass by . . . hiss and wag their heads at you" (Lamentations 2.15); sometimes it was a stricken man who had claimed to be pious and good—"All who see me jeer at me, make mouths at me, and wag their heads" (Psalm 22.7); "I have become the victim of their taunts; when they see me, they toss their heads" (Psalm 109.25). Mark uses the conventional vocabulary, but for the content of the taunts he has drawn on earlier scenes from his own narrative—the saying on the temple (14.58), Jesus' "saving" (i.e. healing) of the sick, his assertion that he was the Messiah (14.62). Jesus was subjected in full measure to the insults received by the righteous sufferers of Old Testament poetry.

At midday a darkness fell over the whole land. An eclipse of the sun 33 would have been impossible at full moon, but a dust-storm could have made the day unusually dark—if indeed it was a natural phenomenon that Mark meant to describe; but the notion that the sun is "darkened" at a great king's death was so common in antiquity, and the expectation that the heavenly bodies would leave their regular courses at a moment of universal crisis, occurred so often in Jewish imaginative writing that we cannot be sure whether Mark was intending to give a literal description of the weather, or a

34 symbolic clue to the unique significance of Jesus' death. The cry, '*Eli, Eli, lema sabachthani*', represents a quotation from the first line of Psalm 22. The last two words are in Aramaic—and Mark preserves other sayings of Jesus in his own language. *Eli* is more difficult: it certainly means '**My God**', but it sounds more like the original Hebrew of the psalm than its Aramaic equivalent (which would be *Elāhi*, when the *ā* might have a sound rather like the "a" in "law", and so be transliterated *Eloi*). [a] On the other hand, this Hebrew form of the word for God is likely to have come quite naturally even to Aramaic-speakers who (unlike Jesus) knew no Hebrew; and if Jesus' cry was mistaken for Elijah (*eliyya*), then it is clear that the one sound that was clearly heard by everyone from his lips was *eli*. Elijah was a figure as much of popular folk-lore as of serious religion. Having been "caught up to heaven" instead of undergoing death, it was widely believed that he was still alive and capable of supernatural interventions in human affairs. A common

35 criminal might well have been thought to be **calling Elijah**. But a disciple with sharper ears, or a more inspired imagination, explained the cry in a different way. Jesus was entering into the depths of the desolating experience undergone by many righteous sufferers in the Old Testament. Their predicament was a result of the religious presuppositions of their time. (i) God was just, and therefore bound to reward those who served him in perfect uprightness. (ii) This reward must take some visible form, such as health, prosperity and honour: the absence of these could be interpreted by others only as a sign that God was punishing the sufferer for some misdeed. (iii) The reward must be given in this life; after death it would be too late. If a man was convinced of his own innocence before God, and yet found himself in extreme misfortune; if, in addition, he fell ill and knew himself to be in danger of death—then, on these presuppositions, his predicament became agonizing. Everyone around him was drawing the obvious conclusion that he must have somehow deserved his fate. He knew this to be false, but unless God acted soon, his faith in himself, and even in the God whom he served, would be unable to bear the strain, and his mockers and persecutors would have the last word—and there was not much time left: something must happen very soon! This predicament of the righteous sufferer was in

[a] Most manuscripts of Mark give the first word in the form *eloi*; but the translators evidently thought that, although Jesus is more likely to have quoted the line as a whole in Aramaic than in Hebrew (which would give *lāmā azaphtani*), he must have pronounced the first word *eli* for his cry to be mistaken for *eliyya*. They therefore adopted the reading of a group of manuscripts which gives the same text as in Matthew 27.46, continuing the Hebrew word *Eli* with the remaining words in Aramaic.

fact the classic way in which the problem of evil presented itself to a reflective Jew of the Old Testament period, and it finds one of its most eloquent and agonized expressions in the twenty-second psalm, which describes a whole range of emotions, from near-despair to a triumphant confidence that, despite everything, God would yet bring good out of the present evil. It was the conviction of some witness of the crucifixion that when Jesus uttered the cry '*Eli*' he was experiencing the deepest strain of what we would now call the problem of evil, and confronting it with the spirituality he had inherited from the religious tradition of his own people. He was praying, in his own language, the prayer of the psalmist, '**My God, my God, why hast thou** 34 **forsaken me?**'. *a*

A man ran and soaked a sponge. This seems to have been another effect 36 of Jesus' cry. The **sour wine** was probably the cheap drink which soldiers and labourers carried about with them, and it was presumably a soldier who offered it. We cannot be sure what his motive was. The soldiers employed by the Romans in Palestine, though they were not Jews, were probably recruited locally. There would therefore be nothing surprising in this one sharing the popular belief about Elijah and, seeing that Jesus was about to die, endeavouring to prolong his life with a drink in order to see '**if Elijah will come to take him down**'. Alternatively, he may have simply interpreted Jesus' cry as one of physical agony, and had an impulse of pity. There is no reason to doubt that the episode took place; at the same time, when recording it Mark certainly had in mind a verse from another of the "righteous sufferer" psalms (69.20–1):

> "I looked for consolation and received none,
>   for comfort and did not find any.
> They put poison in my food
> and gave me vinegar when I was thirsty."

Then Jesus gave a loud cry and died. And the curtain of the temple 37, 38 **was torn in two from top to bottom.** The rending of the curtain, like the three hours of darkness, seems to add a touch of the supernatural to what is otherwise a sober and factual account. Admittedly a natural explanation is possible. If the darkness was caused by the *hamsin* wind, which frequently blows in from the desert during April and can bring with it such clouds of dust that there is even a kind of 'darkness over the whole land', then a gust of the same wind (which sometimes reaches gale force) could have split the heavy curtain which was hung over the main eastern porch of the temple. *b* That is to say, it is possible that someone familiar with Palestine

[a] That Jesus should have had this experience evidently seemed inconceivable to some Christians at an early period, who altered the text to the form given in the footnote.

[b] There was in fact another curtain—a double one—hung over the entrance of the Holy of Holies itself. Mark gives no clue which curtain he means.

would have seen nothing extraordinary about these two events. On the other hand, Mark was not writing for Palestinians, and he nowhere mentions the wind, so that no one who did not know the country could possibly have understood how these things were supposed to have happened. Moreover, we know from the Letter to the Hebrews (10.19–20) that the **curtain of the temple** had symbolic value for Christians: that which separated the Jewish sanctuary (that is, the special dwelling-place of God) from the eyes of all non-Jews was now destroyed by the death of Jesus, who had opened up a direct way to the presence of God for Jews and Gentiles alike. This was certainly one of the ways in which the significance of Jesus' death was very soon understood. It is more foreign to the western mentality than to the eastern to confuse fact with symbol, and it seems to us difficult to take two apparently factual statements ("Jesus died" and "the curtain was torn") in two quite different ways, as if one was prose and the other poetry. But when Jewish tradition reported, for instance, that at the death of a certain famous rabbi "the stars became visible in broad daylight", the statement was meant neither to deceive the credulous nor to be dismissed as a scientific impossibility. It was the author's way of describing the significance of the life and death of the rabbi. So with Mark: he gives, in the guise of a bare fact, a hint of the meaning of Jesus' death on the cross.

39 **The centurion who was standing opposite** was the officer in charge of the execution squad. Again, he was certainly not a Jew, but he may still have been a Palestinian. The manner of Jesus' death elicited from him the comment, 'Truly this man was a son of God.' "A son of God" has a very different sound (in English) from the phrase with which Mark describes Jesus in the very first sentence of his gospel, 'The Son of God'. In the mouth of the ordinary Greek-speaking citizen of the empire, "son of God" was a way of describing any man (particularly a ruler) who seemed endowed with supernatural powers or blessed with exceptional marks of the divine favour; and the way in which Jesus met his death may have brought this expression to the mind of the centurion. Nevertheless, although the English translation quite legitimately makes the centurion say "a son of God" and not "the Son of God", the Greek words so translated are exactly the same as those with which Mark prefaces his gospel. [a] The saying thus takes on a stronger meaning. That Jesus was the Son of God had become a central article of faith in the church when Mark's gospel was written; but the fact was recognized immediately after his death—by a Gentile.

40 **A number of women were also present.** Mary of Magdala (Magdala being an identifiable site on the north-west shore of the Lake of Galilee) is known to us from Luke 8.2; nothing is known of the other two women named, but it is interesting that Mark identifies them for his readers by connecting

[a] See the footnote in NEB (Second Edition).

them with two other names which were presumably familiar in the Church where his gospel was read. **James the younger** could be James the son of Alphaeus (5.18)—distinguished perhaps by his age from James the son of Zebedee—but there is no proof. **Salome** appears to be identified by Matthew (27.56) as 'the mother of the sons of Zebedee'.

Preparation-day could equally well be translated Friday, the day before 42 the Sabbath. As soon as darkness fell, it would no longer be permitted to do any kind of work, and in strict Jewish eyes the land would be "defiled" (Deuteronomy 21.23) if the body of a Jew was allowed to remain in the place of execution unburied until the next day. A pious and public-spirited Jew (for whom **a man who looked forward to the kingdom of God** would be 43 a perfectly appropriate description: the phrase itself certainly does not suggest that he was a clandestine Christian,[a] even though Matthew assumes that he was) might understandably be anxious that consciences should not be scandalized by the sight of Jesus' dead body so close to the city. Moreover, the Jews attached great importance to burial: it was esteemed a work of great charity to perform the last duties for a man whose own relatives were not present to do it. **Joseph of Arimathaea** (which was probably, though not certainly, a town about twenty miles north of Jerusalem) therefore **bravely went in to Pilate and asked for the body.** We do not know how far, if at all, the Roman administration was in the habit of accommodating Jewish scruples in such a matter. The usual Roman practice was to leave the dead bodies exposed, and refuse them proper burial. Moreover, victims of crucifixion often took two or three days to die, and indeed **Pilate was surprised** 44 **to hear that Jesus was already dead,** and made certain of the fact before taking any action. However, Joseph's request was granted, and Mark gives a reason why: he was **a respected member of the Council.** A less influential 43 person (say, a relative of Jesus) might have had no success.

So Joseph bought a linen sheet. The Jews did not bury in coffins, but 46 wrapped the corpse firmly and laid it in one of the numerous rock tombs to be found outside any town in Palestine. Usually the tombs were family tombs, a large chamber in the rock having a number of small cavities carved out of it; and the **entrance** would often be sealed by a massive stone (in more pretentious tombs shaped like a mill-stone and rolling into place along a groove in the rock) that was rolled **against the entrance.** Jesus could not be buried in a family tomb: according to Jewish law, the bones of a criminal defiled those of others; and it was presumably too late in the day to convey him right away from the city to one of the common tombs reserved for criminals. So Joseph gave him a rapid burial in a tomb that happened to be empty near by.

That Jesus rose from the dead on "the third day" (that is to say, by the inclusive reckoning generally used in the ancient world, on the Sunday

[a] Luke uses a similar phrase in 2.38, where it cannot possibly mean "Christian".

following the Friday on which he was put to death) was the central point in all the preaching of the early church; and we can tell from the sermons and the summaries of the Christian faith which are recorded in the New Testament (especially 1 Corinthians 15.3–6) that they based this startling assertion on the evidence of those who had actually seen the risen Christ, either on that first Sunday, or on one of the days which followed. This was the evidence on which the first Christians rested their faith: after his crucifixion and his burial, Jesus was seen by a number of reliable witnesses under circumstances which made them say, not that they had seen a ghost, or that Jesus had "come back" from the dead, or even that his death had been an illusion, but that he had now entered upon a new and glorious mode of existence of which they had had visible and tangible evidence, and which, using contemporary religious language, they described in terms of Jesus having "risen from the dead". Now it is true that, to the Jew, "resurrection" meant the calling back to life of a person complete with his mortal body—transformed, no doubt, and adapted to a supernatural existence, but still recognizably his own. It followed that, if Jesus had indeed "risen from the dead", his body must already have undergone this transformation, and that his tomb would be empty. But the absence of Jesus' body from the tomb was apparently never regarded as the main evidence for the resurrection—it was, after all, capable of other explanations: the body might have been removed, or stolen. The whole weight of the Christians' case was placed upon the testimony of those who had actually seen that Jesus was alive, "risen from the dead"; and this short paragraph in Mark's gospel is the earliest reference in Christian literature to the fact that, on Sunday morning, the tomb was found to be empty.

16. 8   Why was this fact not immediately seized upon and proclaimed? The gospel writers seem to have been conscious of this question, and to have suggested different answers. Mark says that the women kept it a secret: **they said nothing to anybody, for they were afraid.** Luke says that, on the contrary, they told the disciples, but were not believed (Luke 24.11). Matthew says that the authorities tried to cover up the fact by spreading the story that the body had been stolen (Matthew 28.11–15). And a further reason can be suggested: the first Christians rested their case on the evidence of witnesses, and in a Jewish court women were not permitted to give evidence. The report brought back from the tomb by the three women would have been of little use to them as a formal proof of Jesus' resurrection.

1   Moreover, Mark's narrative contains some peculiar details. First: it was probably a regular custom to **anoint** a corpse as part of the preparation for burial, and this was doubtless omitted by Joseph of Arimathaea, who had no time to give Jesus more than a hasty burial. But thirty-six hours had passed since Jesus' death. It was too late to do it now. Secondly: the time of their

2   arrival is a little obscure. **Very early on the Sunday morning** ought to

mean before sunrise (**the Sabbath was over** at sunset the previous evening), 1
and just after sunrise appears to be a somewhat clumsy correction. 2
Thirdly: since they knew that the tomb was closed by a heavy stone, their
whole enterprise sounds curiously unrealistic. On the other hand, the scene
which Mark goes on to describe can easily be imagined taking place in a
typical Jewish tomb. Once the **stone . . . had been rolled back** along the 4
vertical face of the rock, an aperture would have been revealed. Through this,
the women **went into the tomb**—a large rock chamber, with small tunnels 5
opening out of it for individual burials. They would not have known which
of these openings was used for Jesus' burial; but the angel (conventionally
described as **a youth . . .**, **wearing a white robe**) pointed it out to them: 6
'**Look, there is the place where they laid him**'. The angel then repeated
Jesus' prediction about Galilee (see above on 14.28), and the scene ends with
the understandable **terror** of the women. 8

For they were afraid. These words, according to a number of important
manuscripts, are the last words of the gospel. It is certain that the following
paragraphs, which occur in some manuscripts, are not by the same author.
Even in English, the phrase, **the sacred and imperishable message of** 8
eternal salvation is recognizably un-Marcan: it belongs to the theological
language of the later church, and is quite unlike the idiom of Mark's sober
narrative; and the longer ending (verses 9–20) is mainly a summary of episodes that are reported in other places, and betrays in its details the hand of a
later editor. [a]

Did Mark intend to end his gospel on this note of fear and uncertainty, or
has the original ending of his book been accidentally lost? On this question
opinion is still divided, and there is no evidence to support a decision. One
point can be made: we know how books normally ended in the ancient world,
and if Mark meant to finish his work with the words, **for they were afraid,**
he was doing something very unusual. But then this would not be the only
respect in which his gospel is a very remarkable book.

[a] Verses 9–11: cf. John 20.14–18; Luke 24.11. Verses 12–13: cf. Luke 24.13–35. Verse 14:
cf. Luke 24.36–43. Verse 15: cf. Matthew 28.16–20. Verse 16 suggests a later conception of
baptism (and the confession of faith which accompanies baptism) as a guarantee of salvation.
Verses 17–18: casting out devils and healing the sick are powers given to the disciples in
the gospels (Mark 6.12–13), speaking in strange tongues is referred to in Acts and the
letters of Paul, handling snakes is reminiscent of Acts 28.3–6, and drinking poison without
coming to harm occurs in a number of second-century legends. Verses 19–20 are a general
summary of the first chapters of Acts.

THE GOSPEL ACCORDING TO LUKE

1. ₁ **The Author to Theophilus.** With this introductory phrase (which does not stand, as such, in the Greek original) the NEB allows one to see at a glance that the first four verses of this gospel are what we should now call a preface. It is the preface to the writings of the author whose name tradition has preserved as Luke, and who may in fact (though we cannot be sure of it) have been the same person as 'Luke the doctor' (Colossians 4.14), the friend and companion of Paul. Then as now, writing a preface was a literary convention. But the books of the New Testament were written for religious, not literary purposes; it is only here, and at the beginning of Acts (which is the second part of Luke's work), that any kind of preface occurs. Immediately, Luke presents himself to us as someone unusual among the New Testament writers: a conscious literary stylist (this opening paragraph is a smooth and polished piece of Greek prose), ready to make use of the conventions of the world of letters.

Greek historians took it for granted that their work should begin with a preface explaining the writer's purpose and methods; and Luke, who certainly felt himself to be writing a chapter of world history, followed the same convention. Moreover, however wide a readership a book was intended for, it was customary to dedicate it to a personal friend or an influential acquaintance. Luke's preface, though it is shorter and less fulsome than most, is entirely in the spirit of his age. But this conformity to convention also makes it impossible for us to draw any precise conclusions from his language. **Theophilus** could be almost anyone—Greek, Roman or Jew, pagan or
₃ Christian, senior civil servant or private gentleman (**your Excellency** suggests a person of some rank, but the Greek word was a very general term
₁ of respect). **Many writers** could be a rhetorical exaggeration of the fact that Mark, and possibly Matthew, had already completed their gospels; or it could be an indication that far more accounts of the gospel story were current in Luke's day than have survived to ours. And Luke's own decision
₃ **to write a connected narrative** of these events could be due to a desire to improve on the work of his predecessors, an anxiety to refute false information that had been coming to the ears of inquirers such as Theophilus, or simply a sense that there was a need for a third "gospel" based, as such
₂ history ought to be, on **the traditions handed down to us by the original eyewitnesses.** The language of the preface does not allow us to decide between these possibilities. But the fact that Luke wrote such a preface at all, and moreover that he extended his work (through his "Acts of the Apostles")

to embrace the story of the spread of Christianity from Jerusalem to Rome, shows that he was aware of tackling a more ambitious task than the other gospel writers, and that, unlike them, he had at his disposal many of the techniques and the literary conventions of the professional Greek historian.

The coming of Christ

In the days of Herod king of Judaea. By contrast with the Hellenistic 5 polish of the preface, and indeed with the historical precision Luke shows elsewhere (see especially 3.1), the narrative begins in a way more reminiscent of the Old Testament than of contemporary history books. Herod the Great reigned for over thirty years, and died in 4 B.C. So Luke's indication of date is extremely vague. On the other hand, "in the days of so-and-so king of Judah" is a standard Old Testament formula for introducing an episode in the history of the Jewish kingdoms, and this is only the first of many touches by which Luke, in these first two chapters, gives an Old Testament atmosphere to his narrative. [a]

There was a priest named Zechariah, of the division of the priesthood called after Abijah. The ritual of the temple in Jerusalem was performed by members of all the families which could trace their ancestry back to Aaron and who formed the priestly class in Jewish society. Twenty-four such families had returned from the exile, each tracing its descent back to one of the grandsons of Aaron (one of whom was **Abijah**), and each of these families (or "divisions of the priesthood") still existed as a distinct clan in some part of Judaea and Galilee, and twice a year took responsibility for a week's duty in the temple. The whole clan took up residence in Jerusalem for its week's duty, and the several families of the clan each took responsibility for one day of the week, casting lots on the morning of the day to determine the duty of each individual. Luke was evidently well acquainted with this system, and was able to show how it came about that Zechariah was officiating in the temple on a particular day. **It was the turn of his division,** 8 that is, it was one of the two weeks in the year when his clan attended the temple; **he was there to take part in divine service,** that is, it was the day appointed for the family to which he belonged; and **it fell to his lot** to be 9 the individual who on that day received the coveted privilege **to enter the sanctuary of the Lord and offer the incense.**

[a] Most of these touches are linguistic, and can hardly be reproduced in translation. Sometimes, indeed, the idioms are more Semitic than Greek, and many believe that Luke's infancy narratives are a translation of a Hebrew or Aramaic original. But phrases thoroughly characteristic of Luke also occur, and it is at least as likely that Luke, who could in any case write in more than one style, is here composing the story in language modelled mainly upon the Greek translation of the Old Testament.

Twice a day, morning and evening, a lamb was sacrificed and burnt at the
10 altar before the temple. The hour of the incense offering came just before
this sacrifice in the morning, and just after it in the evening (we cannot tell
whether morning or evening is meant here): it was the moment when the
chosen priest left his two assistants outside by the altar and entered the
sanctuary. This was the first room in the temple proper, being a kind of
anteroom to the Most Holy Place (which only the High Priest could enter,
and that only on one day of the year). Here stood a small altar for burning
incense; and the mysterious sanctity of the place, combined with the smoke
of the incense and the complete solitude of the priest, made this moment a
particularly likely one for visions and intimations of the divine. Certainly
many stories are told in Jewish literature of similar experiences in the temple;
so much so, that the people who were waiting outside (who were probably
laymen from the district where the clan lived, come to worship with their
own priests) had little doubt what had happened when Zechariah stayed so
long inside and was unable to give them the customary blessing when he
22 emerged from the sanctuary: they realized that he had had a vision.

13 'Your prayer has been heard'. A divine intervention, granting the birth
of a child to a woman who had been barren and was now past the age of
childbearing, was a feature of many Old Testament stories; and these stories
often included the apparition of an angel and a supernatural intimation of the
name which the child was to bear. Almost all the details of Luke's narrative
(and much of the actual language) can be found in one or other of these Old
Testament stories, and a comparison of these shows how deeply Luke was
influenced by such precedents. [a] But this is not to say that his own combination of these conventional elements was simply due to his imagination;
for certain known facts about the subsequent life of John the Baptist, if not
a reliable tradition about the circumstances of his birth, must have suggested
to him that it would be true of John (as it had been true of Samson and
15 certain other Old Testament persons [b]) that he would be sworn never to
touch wine or strong drink; that, like an Old Testament prophet, he
would be filled with the Holy Spirit, and this from his very birth; [c]
and that he would be a figure fulfilling many of the prophecies and
17 expectations which had gathered round the name of Elijah (see above on
Mark 9.11).

19 Again, that the angel was Gabriel (the angel-messenger *par excellence*
since his appearance in the Book of Daniel), that Zechariah asked for a sign
18 ('How can I be sure of this?'), and that he was rewarded (or punished)

[a] Compare especially Genesis 17.15–21; 18.4–15 (the promise of the birth of Isaac to
Abraham and Sarah), Judges 13 (Samson), 1 Samuel 1 (Samuel).
[b] Such as Rechabites (Jeremiah 35) and Nazirites (Numbers 6).
[c] The Greek is a biblical idiom, which can mean from the moment of conception. Luke
may have seen the stirring of the baby in the womb (1.41) as the first proof that John was
filled with the Spirit.

with temporary loss of speech, are all typical elements of this kind of story;[a] but this hardly affects the question whether Luke's story is legend or truth. Experiences of this kind, whether true or fictitious, tend to fall into a certain pattern. Some eye witness may well have remembered the vivid moment when Zechariah **stood there making signs to them, and remained** 22 **dumb,** even if the rest of the story is the writer's attempt to make explicit what was essentially an incommunicable experience.

Failure to bear children was keenly felt by Jewish women as a cause of 'reproach among men', and Elizabeth's thankful reaction is the same as 25 that of Rachel when, after years of barrenness, she gave birth to Joseph: "God has taken away my reproach" (Genesis 30.23). Why did Elizabeth then live **in seclusion** for five months? We know of no custom that would have 24 obliged her to do so; but her seclusion gives added point to the surprise of the meeting which took place between her and Mary **in the sixth month.** 26

Woven into the story of the strange circumstances of John the Baptist's birth is the story of the birth of Jesus. This too comprises a supernatural message and a miraculous birth, but it no longer recalls the stories of Jewish literature and folklore, since it culminates in a happening which was unique and unparalleled,[b] the birth of a child whose mother was a virgin. Matthew and Luke are the only New Testament writers who explicitly mention this. Matthew simply states it in a single sentence, with very little comment. Luke, on the other hand, devotes a whole paragraph to it, and his account is clearly intended to give some explanation of its meaning. He introduces the scene very carefully. Mary was **a girl betrothed to a man named Joseph.** The 27 Greek word translated **girl** has traditionally been translated "virgin", and it is true that it often meant this; but it was also one of the commonest words for "girl", and there is no reason to think that Luke intends to stress Mary's virginity at this stage of the story. Mary is introduced simply as a young fiancée, already legally committed to her future husband, but not yet living with him. Unlike Zechariah, who received his vision when performing a ritual act in a holy place, Mary is no one in particular and has done nothing special, and the words of the angel's greeting seem to recognize this: 'most 28 favoured one'—the phrase shows that God has regarded her with exceptional favour, not that there is necessarily anything in her to have drawn the favour upon herself. How will this divine favour be shown? The angel's answer still holds back the critical point: for the present, he simply promises to Mary a son who will be qualified to bear the titles and attributes of many

[a] Asking for a sign: Genesis 15.8. Dumbness: Daniel 10.15. Paul was similarly struck blind for a while, Acts 9.9. Compare the temporary blindness of Elymas, Acts 13.11.
[b] In Greek mythology there are numerous stories of unions between an immortal God and a mortal woman. But Luke's account shows no traces of influence from such sources. The setting is entirely Jewish, and Jewish traditions knew nothing of such things. Any miraculous birth always involved a human father. So far as Luke and his readers were concerned, Jesus' birth was absolutely unique.

of the great figures of Old Testament history and prophecy, and who will be
32 a worthy successor of **his ancestor** (through Joseph) **David.** (The angel's
words are a tissue of scriptural allusions: compare especially Genesis 16.11,
Isaiah 9.7, Micah 4.7.) Such promises had been made to women in the past.

34 **'How can this be?'** said Mary; **'I am still a virgin.'** Mary's reaction
is puzzling. She is about to be married, and can expect to have a son; and it
is necessary to read a good deal into the text if we are to find there some
reason for Mary thinking it impossible that she should give birth to a child. *a*
However, the difficulty disappears if we ask, not why Mary should have said
these words, but why Luke placed them in her mouth. From the story-teller's
point of view, the question has a clear purpose: it is the cue *b* for the angel's
35 decisive declaration that the child is to have no human father at all. **'The
Holy Spirit will come upon you, and the power of the Most High will
overshadow you'.** Matthew says simply that Mary became 'with child by
the Holy Spirit'. Luke uses some more poetic and suggestive idioms to convey
the proposition that God would himself take the place of a human father,
and that the child would therefore be, in a unique and literal sense, "Son of
God". Mary's apparently naïve question is the key to the whole mystery:
to have this child she will not need, physically, to cease being a virgin.

36 **'Moreover . . .'** In the Old Testament, the recipients of divine promises
commonly ask for a "sign". Mary does not ask; but a sign is given. **'Your
kinswoman*c* Elizabeth has herself conceived a son in her old age.'**
When Mary has seen this, she will have no difficulty in believing that for her,
37 as for Elizabeth, **'God's promises can never fail'** (a phrase from Exodus
13.12).

39 In response, Mary went **straight** (the Greek implies haste and deter-
mination) to visit Elizabeth. **A town in the uplands of Judah** is probably
intentionally vague, Judah being the old tribal name for the mountainous
area around Jerusalem; it implies no more than that Mary took the angel's
message seriously enough to make a three days' journey south from Galilee.
Her purpose was presumably to confirm the angel's words by seeing for
45 herself that Elizabeth was pregnant. This, at least, was **proof of her faith
that the Lord's promise would be fulfilled,** and would have been sufficient
to elicit Elizabeth's blessing. But the coincidence of the baby stirring in
Elizabeth's womb at the moment of Mary's arrival gave the scene a new turn.
41 **Elizabeth was filled with the Holy Spirit**—Luke's way of describing a
sudden gift of prophecy—and declared that her baby had not merely stirred,

[a] It has been suggested that Mary had made a vow of virginity; or that she understood
the angel to mean that she was to conceive immediately. But there is no support for such
explanations in the text.
[b] Luke is fond of introducing such "cues". Compare 13.23; 17.37; 3.10, 14 and elsewhere.
[c] The word is very vague. It could mean belonging to the same nation, or the same tribe
within the nation, or the same family within the tribe. We do not know what the relationship
was.

it had **leapt for joy**. The Greek word used for **joy** here was rich with scrip- 44
tural overtones: it suggested the joy of the people of God in the presence of
their long-awaited Lord, the Messiah.

And Mary said. The narrative is interrupted by a song of praise. There 46
was good precedent for this. In Old Testament narratives, when a barren
woman was granted her prayer for a child, she was often found to break out
in a cry of joy and thanksgiving. The finest example is in 1 Samuel 2: when
Hannah was at last blest with a son, she uttered a song which fills a whole
page of text, and which is so similar in tone to Mary's song that the one can
hardly be regarded as completely independent of the other. Yet Hannah's
great song is anything but personal; it is mostly a hymn on the justice and
the mercies of God, with barely a word that bears upon Hannah's own
situation—so much so, that it is quite possible that the verses originally had
an independent existence, and were only subsequently inserted into the story
of Hannah. Very much the same is true of Mary's song here. The greater part
of it is concerned with themes which occur again and again in the psalms and
in later Hebrew poetry: the fidelity of God to his people, and the ultimate
vindication of the cause of the poor and oppressed against the proud and the
rich. Almost every phrase occurs at one place or another in the Greek translation of the Old Testament, there is not a word in it that is distinctively
Christian, and barely a sentence which is characteristic of Luke. To all in-
tents and purposes, the song is a beautiful example of a Jewish psalm. As
such, there is no reason why it should not have risen spontaneously to the
lips of the joyful mother-to-be. But equally (if one concedes that Luke was
writing up the scene fairly freely), it could have been inserted by the writer
to comply with the convention that the apparently miraculous gift of a child
should be answered by a cry of praise.

But who sang the song? It was Elizabeth, not Mary, who was in the
classic situation of one whose "reproach" of barrenness had been taken
away, and some manuscripts actually give her name in this verse. Moreover,
there is one point at which the song seems to become personal, and to spring
from the events which have just been narrated:

> 'so tenderly has he looked upon his servant,   48
> humble as she is.'

This last phrase could mean literally, "her humiliation". And who has been
"humiliated"? Not Mary, but Elizabeth, who has borne the reproach of
barrenness all her life. In short, were no name given in the text for the singer
of the song (which may indeed originally have been the case, later copyists
adding one name or the other as they thought best), we should probably not
hesitate to ascribe it to Elizabeth, and to regard those few manuscripts which
give her name in verse 46 as having correctly divined the original intention of
the writer.

However, the last of these arguments is double-edged. "Humiliation" is a correct translation in verse 48, but so is "humility", and in so far as the song is a typical utterance of that strain of Jewish piety which fervently believed in the blessedness and ultimate vindication of the poor, the meek and the humble, the speaker could just as well be anyone (or any group of people) who belonged to that class. Mary, just as much as Elizabeth, is to be imagined as an upright and "humble" person to whom God had shown particular favour; therefore the translators (though not without hesitation) decided to abide by the traditional ascription of the song to Mary. The song is throughout in general but fervent terms. If it does not allude specifically to this moment in Mary's life, it is nevertheless a fine expression of what she may have been feeling. Its spirituality, though entirely Jewish in origin, has a universal quality which, since early centuries, has won for it a firm place in the worship of the Christian church.

57 **Now the time came for Elizabeth's child to be born.** Luke is very soon to recount the circumstances surrounding the birth of Jesus: but the way he has chosen to weave together the strands of the two stories makes it necessary for him to balance this by first working in the birth of John. The main interest of this story lay in the apparently inexplicable agreement of the child's parents to call him John. This was a miracle, sufficient for those who wit-
65 nessed it to be **struck with awe.** The impressiveness of the story is marred by the banality of the language in the NEB translation. Luke is here still writing in the idiom of the Greek Old Testament, and thus imparting more solemnity to these events than the English version conveys.

59 **On the eighth day.** This was the normal time for circumcision (Leviticus 12.3), but it is a little surprising to find a Jewish family at this date naming the child (as the Greeks did) when a week or so old instead of at birth. It was by no means invariable to call a child after its father, even in a priestly family; in fact it was more common to call it after its grandfather. But
60 doubtless if the name **John** (which had been fairly popular since the time of the Maccabees) had never been given to a member of this family, the sudden consensus of mother and father must have seemed striking, particularly since the narrator seems to assume that, since his vision in the temple, Zechariah had been not just dumb, but deaf and dumb. (In Greek, a single word meant deaf-and-dumb, and was often used for either affliction.)

67 **And Zechariah his father was filled with the Holy Spirit and uttered this prophecy.** Another song of praise, this time with rather more allusion to the events of the gospel, and therefore justly called a **prophecy**—prophesying was regarded by Luke, as by Jewish writers of the period, as the characteristic manifestation of **the Holy Spirit.** Perhaps it makes little difference whether the words go back to Zechariah's own inspiration, whether they were composed for the purpose by Luke, or whether they

originally had an independent existence as a hymn and were incorporated and perhaps adapted by Luke. This song, like Mary's, is a typical example of Jewish religious poetry, with only small touches added to bring it into line with Christian experience in general and with the story of John the Baptist in particular. Its style, accumulating clause upon clause with little regard for logic or syntax, is reminiscent of some of the psalms in the Bible, and still more of the psalms composed during the century before the birth of Christ and known as the "Psalms of Solomon". Its language, like that of Mary's song, is impregnated with scriptural idioms. Its content departs little from the mainstream of Jewish piety. Thus the first stanza [a] is a typical 68–9 expression of the old Jewish hope that God would "raise up" a deliverer. For Luke's readers, this hope had now been fulfilled by Jesus in a startlingly unexpected form; but the language used here is still perfectly traditional. The second and third stanzas dwell on God's promises that he would guarantee 70–5 to his own people a land of their own in which they would dwell in safety and peace. And the last stanza returns to the theme of the promised Messiah (for whom **the morning sun from heaven** had become an almost technical 78 expression). Only verses 76–7 bear on John the Baptist, who was to be **the** 76 **Lord's forerunner,** and to baptize for **the forgiveness of . . . sins.** 77

As the child grew up. Luke had nothing further to record between 80 John's infancy and his public appearance some thirty years later. But he could infer that John, being a prophet, must during that time have become **strong in spirit** (for prophecy was a gift of the Spirit of God), and also that his appearance in the wilderness was prepared for by a long ascetic apprenticeship **in the wilds.** [b]

In those days a decree was issued by the Emperor Augustus. One of 2. 1 the innovations of Augustus was to replace the existing somewhat haphazard system of taxation in the provinces of the Roman empire by a uniform system based on a census of the population in each province. This policy gradually became effective **throughout the Roman world**; but we happen to know, independently of Luke's gospel, when it was applied to Judaea. Archelaus, one of Herod the Great's sons, ruled over Judaea from his father's death until A.D. 6, when he was banished by Augustus and his kingdom became part of the Roman province of Syria. This was the moment to introduce the new system of taxation, and it fell to **Quirinius,** who became 2 governor of Syria in that year, to carry it out. This imposition of direct taxation was exceedingly unpopular, and actually caused a minor revolt. It

[a] According to the NEB arrangement; but many arrangements are possible. The Greek text has no clear divisions.
[b] There is a certain similarity between the teaching and activity of John and the ideals of the community which produced the Dead Sea Scrolls; but beyond this there is no evidence that he was in any way associated with that community. It is quite possible that during his years in the wilds he came in contact with it; but this remains pure speculation.

was the **first registration of its kind** in Judaea, and it was not liable to be quickly forgotten (Luke in fact refers to it again in Acts 5.37).

If, therefore, Luke intended to provide his narrative at this point with a date (as he does at the beginning of chapter 3), then there can be no doubt that the date in question was A.D. 6–7. But this date causes difficulties. In the next chapter (3.23) Luke says that Jesus was "about 30 years old" in A.D. 28–9. This is probably only approximate; nevertheless, if Jesus was born in A.D. 6–7 he would have been only twenty-two in 28–9, which is rather young for him to be described as "about thirty". Moreover Matthew places Jesus' birth in the lifetime of Herod the Great (that is, before 4 B.C.), and Luke himself states that John the Baptist, who was only six months older than Jesus, was born 'in the days of Herod king of Judaea' (1.5). Luke's date here (A.D. 6–7) seems about ten years too late.

But it is far from certain that Luke is concerned to specify a date at this point. At the beginning of this paragraph he is still using scriptural language:

1 the vague phrase, **in those days,** is typical of the style. His interest in chronology begins only with the very elaborate dating in the next chapter (3.1–2). Here he mentions the census in order to explain how it came about that Jesus of Nazareth, a Galilean, was born at Bethlehem, a village situated in another part of the country altogether. His explanation is at first sight quite plausible. Although a census of this kind was normally based upon people's actual place of residence, not on their ancestral town, at least one other part of the Roman empire is known where subjects had to register according to their place of birth; and this may have been the case in Judaea. And the explanation may have appealed to Luke on other grounds also: it enabled him to establish a direct connection between the birth of Jesus and an act of the supreme ruler of the Mediterranean world—the gospel story is presented, right from the start, as a chapter of world history. But was there in fact such a census at the time when Jesus was born? There are reasons for doubting whether it could have taken place while Herod the Great or his son Archelaus still ruled Judaea; there is no other record of a census before that of A.D. 6–7, and it is not at all easy to fit Quirinius into the picture some ten years before his only recorded governorship of Syria. If Luke is writing serious history at this point, we ought perhaps to be ready to take his word for all this; but if he is merely working a memory of Quirinius' famous census into his narrative in an attempt to explain the circumstances of Jesus' birth, we must be prepared to admit that, from a historical point of view, he has fallen into error.

7 **She wrapped him in his swaddling clothes, and laid him in a manger.** The manger is the pivot of the story. Already in the gospel there have been two interventions by angels, and each of them has ended with the promise of a sign. This third intervention follows exactly the same pattern, and the sign consists in the new-born baby being found **wrapped in his**

swaddling clothes (i.e. in a tight little bundle, as is still the custom of Arab women), in a manger. Why was the baby in such an unusual place? Luke offers a thoroughly practical reason: because there was no room for them 7 to lodge in the house. The words, to lodge, do not occur in the Greek, and may give a misleading impression. In the east, it is unlikely that travellers would have been refused "lodging", either in a private house or in an inn; but it is possible that all the houses were too crowded to offer Mary a room to herself for having her baby, in which case a shed or a cave *a* used for sheltering cattle might have been the best the village could provide—thus giving fulfilment to the angel's "sign". For what really impressed the shepherds was this miraculous confirmation of the angel's words: it had all 20 happened as they had been told. It is only by the way that Luke works in some deeper comment on the event. The angel proclaimed that the baby would be deliverer (saviour), Messiah, and Lord, titles which Jesus hardly 11 bore in his lifetime on earth, but which the church was soon to ascribe to him; and the event (like the fulfilment of each of the previous "signs") was the cue for another song of praise, this time quite brief and sung by the angels. One of the main blessings of the age of the Messiah—so it was believed— would be on earth his peace, to be enjoyed by all those whom God had 14 chosen to benefit from it. To Jewish readers this would have meant the Jews; but Luke was writing for Christians, who now knew that there existed a much wider company of men on whom his favour rests. *b*

Eight days later. Luke shows himself to be thoroughly conversant with 21 everything that was customary under the Law for Jewish parents after 27 the birth of a first male child, and he seems to lay great emphasis (by stating it three times, verses 22, 27 and 39) on the fact that Jesus' parents meticulously fulfilled all the legal requirements. First, after eight days, came circumcision and naming (as with John the Baptist, 1.59). Then, forty days after childbirth (during which she remained at home awaiting her purification) *c* 22 the mother had to offer a sacrifice of a lamb (which, in the case of poorer people, was remitted to a pair of turtle doves or two young pigeons, 24 Leviticus 12.8), after which the priest declared her "clean". A further obligation arose when the child was the mother's first-born and a male; for

[*a*] There is a tradition, dating back to at least the second century, that Jesus was born in a cave. Constantine's great church at Bethlehem was also built over a cave, but this is indecisive: caves very commonly attracted such traditions anyway. A certain cave on the mount of Olives soon became associated with many episodes in the life of Jesus.

[*b*] The traditional rendering, "goodwill towards men", is of a manuscript reading which is less likely to be original (see NEB footnote). "Men of goodwill" is a possible, but unlikely, translation.

[*c*] Their purification is puzzling. Luke's phrase is taken straight from the Old Testament (Leviticus 12.6), where it means, "when the days of (i.e. preliminary to) purifying were completed". The difficulty is in Luke's addition of the word their. It was only to the mother that these requirements applied. On the other hand, Joseph and the baby could be regarded as ritually "unclean" through contact with her, and their presence at the temple sacrifice may have been necessary.

23 it was a very old and strong religious principle in Judaism that 'every first-born male shall be deemed to belong to the Lord' (Exodus 13.2). In primitive times this probably meant that every family had its own priest; but later it was applied literally only to the descendants of Aaron and Levi (the priests and the Levites), and all other families "redeemed" their first-born sons from temple duties by paying a tax of five silver pieces (Numbers 18. 15-16). But Luke mentions no such payment here; instead, the parents of Jesus
22 brought him up to Jerusalem to present him to the Lord. It looks as if Luke is offering a special interpretation of the rule about first-born males:
23 this particular baby was 'to belong to the Lord' in a unique sense. It was therefore inappropriate to "redeem" him from the Lord's service by a payment: he must on the contrary be taken to the temple to be "presented" to
27 the Lord. Thus everything was done as prescribed in the law—but with a highly significant difference.

25 **There was at that time in Jerusalem a man called Simeon.** Two further witnesses are called (so to speak) to give their evidence that the birth of Jesus was of unique significance. The first was a man **upright and devout,** qualified by his blameless life, like Zechariah and his wife (1.6), to play a small part in these critical events. He was also **one who watched and waited for the restoration of Israel,** that is to say, he believed with an exceptional earnestness and eagerness that the glorious destiny which God had promised for his people (the Greek word meaning "consolation" was almost a technical term for this, and so may perhaps be translated **restoration**) was shortly to come to pass, and like many of his contemporaries he
25, 26 expected the herald of this to be **the Lord's Messiah. The Holy Spirit was upon him,** giving him, not just guidance and supernatural knowledge, but above all the gift of prophecy; and when he recognized that the moment had come for which he had been living, he gave his prophetic testimony in the form of the last of the songs with which Luke adorns this part of his gospel. The song begins quite personally: the sight of the baby gives Simeon
29 his **discharge,** and he can now die **in peace.** But to describe what the baby
31 is, language and imagery are borrowed from Isaiah: the promised **deliverance** (Isaiah 40.5) is not only for Israel, but will shine forth far beyond the
32 confines of the Jewish religion as a **light that will be a revelation to the heathen** (Isaiah 42.6). Yet this Messiah by no means conforms to the popular image of a figure of glory and power: the story is to have its darker
35 side. Simeon adds some enigmatic oracles addressed to the parents, which Luke doubtless intends the reader to solve for himself as the gospel unfolds.

36 The second witness is a **prophetess.** The official view in Judaism was that the gift of prophecy had ceased with the last of the Old Testament prophets, and would only be revived in the new age with the coming of the Messiah. But in Jesus the Messiah had come; and so Luke presents the

revival of prophecy as one of the signs accompanying his birth. What this meant was by no means clear to all; but those **who were looking for the** 38 **liberation of Jerusalem** (another almost technical expression for this new age) would have been alive to the significance of Anna's prophetic words **about the child.**

When he was twelve. Nothing is said in any of the other gospels about 42 the years which Jesus spent in Nazareth. But Luke, who has just hinted at the kind of training received by John the Baptist (1.80), provides an anecdote which does the same for Jesus. To anyone familiar with Greek culture, it was axiomatic that these early years would be devoted to education: accordingly Luke reports that Jesus grew **full of wisdom,** and the story of Jesus' 40 precocity can be paralleled from the biographies of many famous figures of antiquity. But Jesus' learning was of an entirely Jewish character. In Hebrew culture "wisdom" consisted of an understanding of the ways of God as revealed in Scripture, and there can be no doubt that the questions being discussed by the twelve-year-old boy and **the teachers** in one of the colon- 46 naded courts of the temple turned upon the interpretation of certain passages of the Old Testament: Jesus had already learned enough in the local synagogue in Nazareth to be able to hold his own with the scholars of the capital. The occasion was a Passover pilgrimage to Jerusalem, which was often made in family groups; but Jesus' answer already betrays a loyalty stronger even than to his family. For him, the temple was not just "God's house", it was 'my **Father's house'.** [a] But addressing God as one's own 49 "Father" made little sense to ordinary people. Even his parents **did not** 50 **understand what he meant.**

There is now a lapse of time; and in the manner of a professional historian Luke carefully fixes the date at which his story comes within the range of world history. The commonly received system of dating throughout the Roman empire was by the year of the reigning Emperor. So here: **in the** 3. 1 **fifteenth year of the Emperor Tiberius,** A.D. 28–9. This sounds, to modern ears, as precise and reliable an indication as one could wish. But in antiquity an accurate chronology was a great deal more difficult to obtain than it is now, and historians often liked to provide some chronological cross-references at the beginning of their work. Luke's list is not exceptional, though it is unusually detailed, and it also serves to fill out the picture of the political conditions of the time. After the death of Herod the Great (4 B.C.) his kingdom had been divided into four, each part being governed by a *tetrarch*, which means "ruler of a fourth part". It was this word *tetrarch* (always translated **prince** in the NEB) which perhaps led Luke to specify, for the sake of completeness, the ruler of each of the four parts. Judaea, after

[a] The old translation, "about my father's business", is much less likely to be the meaning of the Greek phrase, though this is admittedly imprecise.

the unsuccessful reign of its first tetrarch, Archelaus, had come directly under Roman rule in A.D. 6 and was governed by a Roman official called, first, a *praefectus* and subsequently a *procurator*. Pontius Pilate held this office from A.D. 26 to 36, and Luke gives him the general title that was used in Greek for such officials, **governor.** Herod (Antipas, son of Herod the Great) became tetrarch of Galilee and Peraea ('Transjordan') at his father's death, and remained in power until A.D. 39. Philip, another of Herod's sons, ruled his tetrarchy in the north-east until A.D. 33. **Abilene,** the northernmost part of Herod's original kingdom, lay in the Lebanon, and we know little about its history; but there is no serious reason to doubt Luke's statement that its ruler's name was **Lysanias.** Luke then completes the picture with

2 the **high-priesthood.** Only one high priest held office at a time: he normally presided over the supreme Jewish Council (the Sanhedrin) in Jerusalem. The high priest in this year was Caiaphas; but Annas, his father-in-law, had also held the office from A.D. 6 to 15, and he probably still exercised so much influence that Luke may have thought it right to couple his name with that of Caiaphas.

2   **The word of God came to John.** The phrase is an Old Testament one, appropriate to a prophet (compare Jeremiah 1.1). It is one of the touches by

4–6 which Luke fills in the prophetic side of John's ministry. The quotation from Isaiah (40.3) is common to the accounts in all the gospels, though it is given

7–9 at greater length by Luke; and John's first speech (except that it is delivered generally to the crowds and not to the Pharisees and Sadducees) runs closely parallel with the version in Matthew (3.7–10). But after this Luke's narrative takes a different course. From the other gospels the impression might easily be gained that John's preaching consisted entirely of an announcement of the Coming One and an urgent call to repent and be baptized. But it is clear, both from other passages in the gospels and Acts, and from the fact that his movement lasted long after the appearance of Jesus, that he must also have

12 given moral teaching. The people, indeed, addressed him as **Master,** a form of address which was often used when speaking to Jesus, and which implied

11 that John, too, was regarded as a teacher. Luke gives a sample of John's teaching here. Sharing food and clothing with the needy was recognized as a social obligation and as a highly meritorious act throughout the history of Judaism. John's attitude to tax-gatherers and soldiers, however, was more liberal than that of his contemporaries, who regarded these professions as incompatible with a strict observance of the law, and excluded them from the true community of Israel. John by contrast (and here his attitude was closer to that of Jesus) accepted these people, only warning them against the special temptations of their professions. Yet even he showed a certain intolerance

12 towards **tax-gatherers:** if they had done what he said, they would have deprived themselves altogether of their source of livelihood (see below on 18.9–14).

234

The people were on the tiptoe of expectation. Luke gives the Baptist's 15 proclamation of the Coming One in much the same terms as Matthew, but characteristically sets the scene for it a little more carefully and vividly. Any prophetic figure preaching a radical message in the wilderness was liable to arouse expectations about the promised Deliverer, and indeed we know that there were a number of pretenders to this rôle during the century, culminating in the figure of Bar Kochba, who led the last revolt of the Jews against the Romans in A.D. 135. It was against this background that John announced the coming of a greater successor, not so much relaxing the expectation of the people as turning it away from himself to another who was still to come.

The subsequent fate of John is recounted by Mark and Matthew in some detail at a later stage in their gospels (Mark 6, Matthew 11). Luke is content 18–20 merely to summarize it (the story was presumably well known to his readers) and, with perhaps a historian's concern to round off a story and draw a moral, he places his summary here. After this, John does not appear again in his gospel: the stage is left clear for Jesus.

During a general baptism of the people. Jesus was last mentioned 21 growing up in Nazareth. Here it is simply taken for granted that he was among the crowd who came to be baptized, and the vision which accompanied his baptism serves to bring him out of obscurity and indicates that he is from now on the protagonist of the story. Who was this Jesus? Luke's previous chapters have given, so to speak, his divine parentage—but this was only recognized by the faithful. Who was he in the eyes of ordinary people? Luke answers, **the son, as people thought, of Joseph,** and 23 impressively proceeds to trace his ancestry right back to **Adam, son of God.** 38 A similar genealogy in Matthew (though it offers a quite different list of names for Jesus' immediate ancestors) serves to answer the question, How was Jesus a son of David? But Luke's interest seems to be simply that of a historian: this is who Jesus was. (On the genealogy itself, see above on Matthew 1.1–17).

Luke's account of Jesus' temptation is very similar to that of Matthew (4.1–11), except that the episodes are in a different order. There are some slight differences of detail which suggest that Luke was less familiar with Palestine than Matthew and Mark, and found it harder to visualize the setting of Jesus' experience. **Jesus returned from the Jordan.** Did Luke 4. 1 think that the wilderness was in a different part of the country? In fact it began close to the edge of the Jordan valley, and Mark and Matthew are much more convincing when they say that Jesus entered it straight after his baptism. **Next the devil led him up and showed him in a flash all the** 5 **kingdoms of the world.** According to Matthew, Jesus was taken 'to a very high mountain'. In the wilderness of Judaea there are many such mountains which command an immense view over the Jordan valley and would have offered an appropriate setting for Jesus' temptation. But Luke prefers to think of the experience as an inner vision: Jesus saw all the kingdoms of the world in a flash.

In Galilee: success and opposition

Success and opposition describes Jesus' progress through Galilee as aptly in Luke's narrative as it does in Mark's. But Luke, unlike the other evangelists, places a notable case of opposition (recounted more briefly in Mark and Matthew) right at the beginning, perhaps seeing in it a foretaste of Jesus' ultimate destiny at the hands of his fellow-countrymen. He was doubtless familiar with the tradition which made Jesus' activity in Galilee open with a number of "successes", and he makes a brief allusion to these in verse 15. But he does not linger over them; instead he hurries on to the main episode, which serves to lay down the pattern of Jesus' subsequent activity.

16 **So he came to Nazareth, where he had been brought up.** Matthew and Mark call it simply his 'home town', but Luke is careful to maintain consistency with the account he has given of Jesus' infancy. Strictly speaking, Nazareth was not Jesus' 'home town', it was only **where he had been brought up.** No followers were with him, as they are in Matthew's and Mark's narratives; but in those two gospels the episode comes later in the story, whereas here the disciples have not yet been called. He **went to synagogue on the Sabbath day as he regularly did**—and what follows is consistent with what we know from Jewish sources about the order of service in a synagogue on a Sabbath morning. After prayers came a reading from the Law of Moses (the first five books of the Bible). After that, a member of the congregation was invited to stand and read a lection from one of the prophets, and then to sit and expound it. Jesus had already made a reputation by his teaching, and when he visited a town it was natural that he should be asked to give the exposition. Indeed it is likely that he (like the apostles after him) eagerly accepted these opportunities of proclaiming his message, and the exposition which he gave on this occasion was doubtless

15 typical of his teaching **in their synagogues** in many other places. The
18 passage chosen by Jesus (Isaiah 61.1–2, with the addition of a phrase from Isaiah 58.6) was originally a prophecy that, after the exile in Babylon, the Jewish people would once again be free to return to Jerusalem and celebrate
19 the "jubilee year" (Leviticus 25.10), **the year of the Lord's favour.** But in the time of Jesus it was certainly understood as a still unfulfilled prophecy of the new age to which the Jews looked forward. Luke gives the quotation at length (following the Septuagint version of the Greek Bible, which gives a slightly different sense from the Hebrew text which Jesus is likely to have

used), but offers only the barest summary of Jesus' sermon ('Today...in 21 **your very hearing this text has come true**'). Yet the weight of Jesus' words is vividly captured. In referring Isaiah's prophecy to himself he was making a prodigious claim. This claim at first excited admiration; but doubt and disbelief crept in with the remark, '**Is not this Joseph's son?**'—for so, 22 'as people thought' (3.23), he was. Mark, in his account of this scene (6.1–6), goes on to describe the effects of this scepticism: Jesus 'could work no miracle there'. Luke implies the same consequence, even though he does not state it; for the same picture of Jesus unable to perform miracles or to gain acceptance among his own kinsfolk is what gives point to the harsh sayings which follow. Nevertheless, Jesus' words seem to apply, not just to the people of Nazareth, but to the Jewish people as a whole. "**Physician, heal your-** 23 **self!**" There was no obvious reason at this stage why anyone should have cast this well-known proverb in Jesus' teeth, but these were exactly the terms in which the Jews taunted Jesus at the crucifixion (Matthew 27.42)—Luke is again using the scene as a foretaste of the treatment received by Jesus, not just at Nazareth, but (in a wider sense) **in his own country**. Again, Jesus' 24 saying, '**no prophet is recognized in his own country**' is not seen by Luke (as it is by Mark and Matthew) merely as a comment on his treatment at Nazareth. It is a paradigm of the progress of his entire mission (and indeed of the subsequent mission of the church). And the Old Testament examples which follow are relevant, not so much to the matter in hand, as to what was to become the recurring pattern of Jesus' work, seeking out either those whose profession or way of life was thought to disqualify them from member- ship of the holy people of God, or else even those who were not Jews at all. The story of Elijah and the widow of Sarepta is found in 1 Kings 17, that of 25 Naaman in 2 Kings 5. The implication of both these stories was that, in 27 God's saving purpose, it could happen that foreigners might be more favourably placed than Jews; and the result of Jesus quoting them was that **the whole congregation were infuriated.** They evidently intended to put 28 him to death by throwing him down a cliff (and there are many steep places in the neighbourhood of Nazareth, even though the village was not built on a hill, but rather in a hollow among hills). Luke evidently saw something miraculous in Jesus' escape: **he walked straight through them all, and** 30 **went away.**

Coming down to Capernaum, a town in Galilee. The phrase is typical 31 of Luke, who does not expect his readers to be familiar with Palestine, and is careful to explain that what to Greek ears was nothing but a barbarous col- lection of syllables (*Kapharnaoum*) was **a town in Galilee**. Luke may not have been familiar with Galilee himself, but he probably knew that Caper- naum was on the lake, and he is accurate when he says that Jesus must have "come down" to it from the mountain village of Nazareth. From this point to the end of the chapter his narrative closely follows Mark (1.21–34). The

only notable difference is that the fever of Simon's mother-in-law is per-
39 sonified: Jesus **rebuked the fever** as he had rebuked the devil in the
previous incident. By this touch Luke perhaps wishes to make the whole
paragraph into a series of encounters with devils, culminating in the devils'
41 recognition that Jesus was **the Son of God** and **the Messiah**. Jesus' retreat
42 next morning **to a lonely spot** serves, as in Mark, to make the transition
44 from Capernaum to a wider field of work. Luke places this wider field **in the
synagogues of Judaea**. Strictly speaking, Judaea was a long way to the south
of Galilee, and if Luke means this literally he is in conflict with the other
gospels. [a] But, along with other Greek and Latin writers, Luke sometimes
uses "Judaea" to mean Palestine in general, and his intention here is probably only to say that Jesus' preaching extended far over Jewish lands.

By this time, in the other gospels, Jesus had gathered disciples round him.
Luke has not yet mentioned this; but he now tells the story of how he was
joined by Simon, James and John (who were of course so well known to
Luke's readers that they needed no introduction). In Matthew and Mark,
this was a simple summons, followed by an immediate response. But Luke
leads up to it with a story which is clearly intended to offer some explanation
of the disciples' instant decision to follow Jesus—and which also incidentally
gives early prominence to Simon Peter among Jesus' followers. Both Mark
(4.1-2) and Matthew (13.1-3) record that Jesus, when teaching by the
5. 1 **Lake of Gennesaret** (a more precise name for the lake which the Jews
usually called the "Sea of Galilee"), liked to put out a little from the shore
in a boat. Luke takes the story on from there. The details are entirely lifelike.
The best time for fishing in the lake was (and still is) at night; and the co-
operation of two boats to bring in a heavy haul of fish was regular practice.
10 The sequel was Jesus' word (here addressed only to Simon), '**from now on
you will be catching men**'. The story finds a suggestive echo in John 21,
where Jesus (this time after the resurrection) again enables Simon to make
an exceptional haul. Both the stories appear to have been freely written up
by the evangelists to bring out a symbolic meaning, and both may go back
to what was perhaps originally a single event.
12-14 The narrative of the healing of a leper follows Mark (1.40-5) very closely,
only omitting Mark's references to Jesus' anger and sternness (which were
perhaps as puzzling to Luke as they are to us). Jesus, indeed, moves more
gently in this gospel: instead of being forced to leave the town by the numbers of those who were pressing upon him (Mark 1.45), it is merely said that,
16 on his own initiative, **from time to time he would withdraw to lonely
places for prayer**.
17-25 The next scene (the healing of a paralysed man) reproduces the actual
words of Jesus almost verbatim from the account in Mark (2.1-12), but

[a] This apparent conflict caused early copyists to make the alteration in the manuscripts
which is noted in the NEB footnote.

shows considerable freedom in the narrative. In part, Luke appears simply
to have written the scene in a more polished Greek style—'You would 26
never believe the things we have seen today' is, in the original, a fluent
and idiomatic expression compared with Mark's 'Never before have we
seen the like' (2.12); in part also, he makes it easier for the non-Palestinian
reader to visualize: he sets the story inside one of the large tiled houses of
western cities, instead of outside the flat-roofed, baked mud houses of the
east. But in essential points his narrative follows the tradition preserved in
Mark.

In the events and sayings following the call of Levi, Luke has again made 27–39
only minor alterations to the details—he interprets Jesus' "invitation" to
sinners as being, not to a metaphorical banquet (as in Mark), but to repent- 32
ance; and he explains the observance of fasting among John's disciples and
the Pharisees as an aid to the practice of prayer. But whereas in Mark 33
(2.13–22) there is only a loose and general connection between each paragraph, Luke has neatly worked them into the setting of Levi's big reception 29
and, by slight editorial touches to Jesus' sayings, has made them all relevant
to the Pharisees' complaint that his disciples, instead of following the usual
austerities of a strict religious sect, could be seen to eat and drink. The 33
comparison with the wedding feast fits this context just as well as the context 34–5
given to it in Mark, and Luke makes no significant alteration to it (the
presence of verse 35 here is just as puzzling as the corresponding verse in
Mark). But the following parables are given a different slant. The point is no 36
longer, as in Mark, that the sheer novelty of Jesus' message demands an
altogether new medium of expression—this would have no relevance to the
question of the presence of the disciples of Jesus at Levi's reception. The
point is now that any attempt to combine the new with the old (the new
freedom of Jesus' message with the old practices of fasting) is fatal to both.
And Luke adds a further saying, which is in fact an old proverb, and seems 37–9
to fit a little awkwardly here. Once you have tasted the superior quality of
old, matured wine, you cannot go back to cheap, new stuff (or perhaps: you
are prejudiced against anything new). The complaints of the Pharisees were
based on assumptions which were now superseded. To have tried to combine
them with Jesus' new principles would have been to render both meaningless.

The two Sabbath stories run even closer to Mark (2.23–36). In the first, 6. 1–5
Luke characteristically adds a detail which makes the story easier to visualize:
the disciples were plucking the ears of corn, rubbing them in their 1
hands, and eating them; and he also omits, as Matthew does, one of the
general sayings about the Sabbath ('the Sabbath was made for the sake of
man', etc.) recorded by Mark—perhaps, like us, he found it difficult to
understand. In the second story the changes are even more trivial, unless it is 6–11
significant that Luke does not mention Jesus' 'anger' on this occasion: such
an emotion did not fit into Luke's portrait of Jesus as it did into Mark's.

12   **During this time.** Luke now begins to set the stage for a major discourse
17   of Jesus. The discourse itself, though it takes place **on level ground,** is
clearly a version of the same collection of teaching as Matthew presents in
his Sermon on the Mount and, as in Matthew, it presupposes a double
audience: an inner group of disciples, and a large crowd. Luke's narrative,
while still running close to that of Mark (3.7–19) is arranged so as to account
for the presence of these two groups. The sequence begins with Jesus spend-
12   ing **the night in prayer**—Luke insists far more on the importance of prayer
in Jesus' life than any of the other evangelists. Jesus then, out of an existing
group of disciples (the presence of which was presupposed in chapter 5)
13   **chose twelve and named them Apostles.** Even in the less portentous
account in Mark, these twelve are clearly mentioned for the sake of their part
in the subsequent history of the church. Luke makes this even more explicit,
by recording that Jesus actually called them **Apostles** (the title by which
the founders of the early church came to be known), and by subsequently
referring to them by this title four times in his narrative. His list corresponds
to that in Mark and Matthew, except that the Thaddaeus of Mark, or the
16   Lebbaeus of Matthew, is replaced by a mysterious **Judas son of James**—a
name also apparently known to John (14.22).

The inner group of listeners being now identified, Luke brings Jesus down
17   to **level ground** (which he presumably thought more appropriate as a setting
for a sermon than a hill—he seems to have reserved hills for supernatural
experiences) and accounts for the presence of a crowd by the spread of Jesus'
fame far to the south and the north of Galilee. It was not merely that he had
19   been known to perform miraculous cures; there was **power** in him (recognized also by Mark, 5.30) which could be released if a sick person so much as
touched him.

20   **Then turning to his disciples he began to speak.** Luke, like Matthew,
places a long discourse of Jesus early in his narrative, and if we compare
Matthew's Sermon on the Mount, we see at once that here is another version
of the same thing. Both begin with "beatitudes" and end with a parable;
Luke's version, though it is much shorter, contains only a few verses which
are not in Matthew's; and there is even the same indeterminacy of audience:
at the beginning Jesus is speaking 'to his disciples', at the end (7.1) we hear
that he has been 'addressing the people'—exactly as in Matthew. Yet Luke's
"sermon" is not merely an abridged version of Matthew's. It has its own
distinctive tone, and in certain details it presents Jesus' teaching in a somewhat different light.

20   **'How blest are you who are in need'.** The first and most striking
difference between these beatitudes and those in Matthew is that they are
all in the second person: they presuppose an audience of people who were
actually in need, hungry, weeping and reviled. And this goes with a second

difference. In Matthew (5.3), the needy are 'those who know their need of God' (literally, "poor in spirit"), the hungry are those who 'hunger and thirst to see right prevail'. In other words, the blessing is pronounced as a reward for a certain moral and religious disposition. But here, the needy are really needy, the hungry really hungry; and the promise is that their condition will be reversed **on that day**, that is, at the future coming of the king- 23 dom of God. Doubtless many of the religious connotations of poverty and hunger, which are spelled out in Matthew's version (particularly in those beatitudes which Luke omits), are also present here; but the emphasis is on the dramatic reversal of fortune which awaits those who are literally poor and in need.

The same emphasis runs through the "woes" ('**Alas for you**') with which 24–6 Luke balances each of the beatitudes (these do not occur in Matthew's Sermon on the Mount, though rather similar woes appear at another place in his gospel, 23.13–30). '**Alas for you who are rich.**' This is the logical corol- 24 lary of 'how blest are you who are in need', but although there was a strong strain in Jewish piety which was prepared to find a blessing in poverty, it would have come hard to deny that there was also a blessing in riches. Yet this was Jesus' teaching, embodied here in an unambiguous condemnation of whole classes of society which recalls the manner of an Old Testament prophet. One other detail characterizes those who were to be blest: like the 26 prophets (as a Jewish tradition had begun to say—see above on Matthew 23.31) they would be persecuted for their faith; and their persecutors would be the descendants of those who had persecuted the prophets—not the world in general, but the Jews.

'**But to you who hear me I say**'. The rich and prosperous were not in the 27 audience, and little time is spent over denunciations of the world at large: the sermon is for those who will follow Jesus. The next sayings are placed under a single bold heading, '**Love your enemies**'. In the Sermon on the 28 Mount, this radical injunction developed out of Jesus' interpretation of the familiar commandment, Love your neighbour; here it is bluntly stated as a distinctive ethical principle, and illustrated by a series of examples. The examples are familiar from Matthew (5.39–48), but Luke has added touches of his own. '**When a man takes your coat**': evidently a robber who tears off 29 the first garment he can get hold of, not a litigant (as in Matthew) who is prepared to take a shirt as a pledge before he insists on a coat. '**Even sinners** 33 **love those who love them.**' Matthew contrasts the conduct of Christians with that of the outcasts of Jewish society (tax-collectors) or of "the heathen". Luke is more general: **sinners** are simply non-Christians. In Matthew, impartiality is inculcated on the grounds that God dispenses sun and rain impartially to just and unjust. Luke sharpens this, so that loving your **enemies** can be seen to be a way of imitating the God who is **kind to the** 35 **ungrateful.** Similarly, God is to be imitated not (as in Matthew) because

241

he is 'perfect', but—and this is more relevant in the present context—
36 because he is **compassionate**.

37   **'Pass no judgement, and you will not be judged.'** In Matthew's version (7.1–2), the judgement is the Last Judgement, the rewards are other-worldly. The same doubtless goes for these sentences (which, if taken as this-worldly
38 advice, would sound like either opportunism or wishful thinking). The **good measure** of a truly generous corn-merchant is an image of the reward which awaits the generous giver in heaven.

39   **He also offered them a parable.** The word often means "a riddle", and these two sayings, which both have the ring of proverbs, are certainly enigmatic. (Matthew (15.14) applies the first to the Pharisees, and there is
40 an echo of it in a similar context in Romans 2.19. The second, **'A pupil is not superior to his teacher,'** is made into a rule of discipleship in Matthew 10.24; but Luke has a different ending, and the meaning is mysterious.)

41–2   Other parables follow: the speck of sawdust and the plank almost exactly
43–5 as in Matthew, the fruit-metaphor much more generalized so that it becomes a test, not of the authenticity of a prophet (as in Matthew), but of whatever
46 goes on in the heart. Generalized too is the saying about calling Jesus "Lord, Lord"—it is not a question of deciding who is and who is not a Christian (as in Matthew) but of relating the worship of Christ to a sincere intention to perform his exceedingly exacting ethic.

47–9   And so, with the same parable of two houses as in Matthew (though Luke perhaps imagines a house near a European river like the Tiber rather than near a Palestinian *wady*), the sermon comes to an end. It contains much less teaching than Matthew's sermon (though much of what is omitted here appears elsewhere in Luke's gospel), but its tone is both sharper and more general—sharper, because the most radical elements in it are presented without qualification or interpretation; more general, because the debate between Christians and Jews, which is so prominent in Matthew, can hardly be overheard in Luke, and the ethic stands alone as a guide for life under any circumstances whatever. Whether Matthew and Luke themselves were responsible for these two different versions, or whether two different collections of Jesus' moral teaching already existed before these gospels came to be written, is a tantalizing question. But both versions reflect a teacher of outstanding originality, whose influence has disturbed not only those of his first followers who undertook to write down his words, but the many generations of Christians who, in a great variety of ways, have endeavoured to bend their lives to his teaching.

7. 1   **He went to Capernaum.** As in Matthew, so in Luke, the great sermon is immediately followed by a petition addressed to Jesus by a Gentile. In both gospels, the dialogue between Jesus and the centurion is virtually identical; but Luke presents the episode itself somewhat differently. In Matthew, the

sufferer is 'a boy of mine'—which is ambiguous. Matthew apparently takes it to mean the centurion's son; but Luke chooses the other alternative, a servant. However, he then has to explain why the officer was so anxious about this particular servant, and so he adds the explanation: whom he valued highly. In Matthew, again, the point of the episode, with the dialogue it contains, is the comparison between the authority of a military officer over his men and that of Jesus over the world of spirits; but in Luke this point is almost incidental (and indeed fits somewhat awkwardly into the story). All the stress is on the character and behaviour of the centurion; he was "a friend of the Jewish nation", he was so respected by the Jews that some of their elders were willing to press his case, and at the same time he had too much humility to approach Jesus in person. No Gentile could have been better qualified to gain his petition from Jesus; and Luke doubtless saw all these moral excellences comprised in the faith which Jesus promptly rewarded.

Afterwards Jesus went to a town called Nain. The site of this town is known: it lies just off one of the roads leading from the lake to the coast, on the side of a steep hill. As Jesus approached it from the main road he would have had before him the principal gate of the town. Out of this gate was coming a funeral procession. The Jews normally buried within a few hours of death. The body, wrapped in a linen cloth, was carried from the house on a bier (for coffins were not used) to a family grave cut in the rock; and since graves were always outside the walls of a town, the procession had at some stage to pass through the gate. This was the moment at which Jesus intervened, and performed what was regarded as the greatest of all miracles, that of bringing a dead person back to life. Two such miracles are recorded in the gospels apart from this one: Jairus' daughter (Luke 8.40, Mark 5.21, Matthew 9.18) and Lazarus (John 11). Here the story is told quite simply, and there is little to distinguish it from similar stories told about other miracle-workers in antiquity. On the other hand, the reaction of the bystanders was conditioned by their religious beliefs. 'A great prophet has arisen among us'. Elijah and Elisha, the first great prophets, had performed similar miracles (1 Kings 17; 2 Kings 4): Jesus must be another of the same calibre. Moreover, raising from the dead was a sign of the new age that was to come: 'God has shown his care for his people'—the same phrase as is translated 'has turned to his people' in Zechariah's prophetic song (1.68). The miracle was evidence of a new relationship beginning between God and man.

John too was informed of all this by his disciples. This episode, with its sayings about John the Baptist, occurs in Matthew 11, where it reads like a digression. By placing it immediately after the account of two notable miracles, and by inserting the note that there and then Jesus cured many sufferers, Luke knits the same material more neatly into his narrative. In other respects his version is much the same, apart from verses 29–30. This

243

comment, which draws a clear distinction between Jesus' supporters and opponents, occurs only in Luke's gospel (though it is possibly echoed, in a quite different context, in Matthew 21.32). The only difficulty is to know (since Greek manuscripts originally had no inverted commas) whether the comment is that of the narrator or is to be attributed to Jesus himself (see the footnote in NEB).

36 **One of the Pharisees invited him to eat with him**—evidently a formal meal, since the word translated **took his place at table** literally means "lay on a couch", and it was only on more formal occasions that the Jews adopted the Greek and Roman custom of reclining, instead of sitting, at table. Moreover, an ordinary family meal might have been held in private; but any kind of larger dinner-party always attracted visitors other than the invited guests (whether people simply wishing to listen to the conversation or beggars
37 hoping for scraps of food). It was only on such an occasion that **a woman who was living an immoral life in the town** could have gained admission to a Pharisee's house and, finding the guests reclining on couches with their legs stretched out behind them, could have discreetly ministered to Jesus, taking **her place behind him, by his feet.** Jesus' host evidently had certain presuppositions about his guest. He assumed that, like himself, Jesus would be particular about who touched him, in order to remain ritually "clean" (particularly before a meal); and he was interested to see whether Jesus had the prophetic gift of knowing intuitively about the personal lives of those
40 with whom he came in contact. Jesus ignored the first point, but **took him**
41-3 **up** on the second. First, he told a brief and pointed parable, and then he drew attention to the signs of powerful emotion in the woman. Washing a guest's feet or anointing him with oil and perfume were not courtesies normally offered to guests at a banquet; they were part of a specially careful toilet which a guest might make before he left home. Jesus therefore was not criticizing his host on the subject of his hospitality, but pointing out that these attentions from a woman were clear signs of her feelings. He did not need to be a prophet to see that her actions expressed a love and gratitude towards himself which could only be due to the fact that she was indeed a "sinner", but now knew herself to have been forgiven. By contrast, the
47 formal hospitality of the Pharisee expressed no such emotion. '**Where little has been forgiven, little love is shown**'.

To this extent, the point of the dialogue is clear: Jesus wins his point against the Pharisee. But there is evidently far more to the story than this; and as soon as it is examined more carefully, difficulties and uncertainties appear. A somewhat similar story (set in the house of a certain 'Simon the leper', Mark 14.3) occurs in the other gospels shortly before the narrative of the passion. Luke has no such story in that place: has he adapted it to a different purpose here, or were there originally two episodes which both involved a woman with a flask of ointment? Did Jesus originally speak the parable on this occasion, or has Luke added it to his story? Do the final verses belong to the original story, or is it Luke's own explanation that the woman had been forgiven because of her faith in Jesus, perhaps as a result of his preaching earlier in the day? If the paragraph seems less than perfectly coherent, the reason may be that all its parts did not originally belong together. At the same time, the episode is bound together by a very strong association of ideas. Sins, in Jewish teaching, were often described as debts —this links the parable firmly to the dialogue; and the English word love must not mislead us into thinking that the scene is intended to offer an analysis of deep emotions. In Jesus' own language, such words meant, not lasting affection, but the outward expression of loyalty and gratitude; indeed, the same word was used for "love" and "thank". The generous gestures of the woman and the response of the pardoned debtors would have been described by the same word, only imperfectly represented by *agapē* in Greek or love in English.

After this he went journeying. This marks a new stage in the narrative: **8. 1** Jesus left the area around Capernaum, where he could count on the hospitality of friends, and became an itinerant preacher, moving at first from town to town without any clear sense of direction, and then 'setting his face resolutely towards Jerusalem' (9.51). Luke (alone of the evangelists) allows us a glimpse of the way in which Jesus and his disciples were provided for: women who had been cured by him offered **their own resources.** Luke's **3** list of names overlaps with that in other gospels (Matthew 27.55–6; Mark 15.40–1), in so far as they all include **Mary of Magdala. Joanna** reappears **2** below (24.10), **Susanna** is otherwise unknown. It is interesting (and was **3** doubtless of interest to Luke, with his concern for connections with secular history) that Jesus' following extended to the household of **Herod** Antipas, the tetrarch of Galilee.

At this point in the narrative both Mark (chapter 4) and Matthew (chapter 13) introduce a section devoted to Jesus' parable-teaching, and offer some hints on the place of this teaching in Jesus' work as a whole. Luke follows the same tradition, but (perhaps because he has so many other parables to put in later on) he makes much less of it. **He said in a parable:** only the parable **4** of sowing is given, followed by two short sayings; and although Luke retains the difficult quotation from Isaiah 6.9 (**so that they may look but see** **10** **nothing, hear but understand nothing**), he gives it in the briefest possible form, and softens the contrast between the disciples to whom it has been granted **to know the secrets of the kingdom of God** and those who are not so privileged, whom indeed he vaguely calls **the others.** Some, perhaps many, may have reacted with the stubborn obstinacy foretold by Isaiah, but no clear line is drawn. The disciples are not singled out again, nor does Luke suggest that they are given any private instruction. He reserves his full treatment of the Isaiah passage until the very end of his two-volume work (Acts 28.26–7), where he identifies the people from whom God has withheld understanding with that majority of the Jewish race who, though given the first opportunity to hear and accept the gospel message, have persistently rejected it. Meanwhile, the possibility of Jesus' hearers coming to a full understanding of his teaching remains open. Luke accordingly sums up the paragraph with words which represent a slight but significant alteration of the saying which is given in Matthew and Mark (4.24), and which are clearly

18 addressed to the crowds at large: 'Take care, then, how you listen'.

For the details of the parables, see above on Mark 4. Luke has made only slight changes. He appears to have thought that the seed on the footpath

5 would fail to grow because it was **trampled on,** and for that reason would ultimately be eaten by the birds. The interpretation of the parable only differs from the parallel versions in that it introduces still more of the

12 language of the Greek-speaking church, such as **believe and be saved,**

13, 15 **time of testing** and, most striking of all, **a good and honest heart,** which is a cliché of classical Greek ethics.

Some incidents follow which, in Mark, are carefully woven into the narrative but which appear to be assembled together by Luke without much concern for a proper sequence. The parable-teaching which has just finished was clearly given out of doors; but, when Jesus' family arrives (and no reason is given for their visit, as it is in Mark 3.21), he seems suddenly to be indoors,

20 and is told that his mother and brothers **are standing outside.** Similarly,

22 the crossing of the lake is given no context: it simply happens **one day,** though in other respects the paragraph seems to be a straightforward re-writing of the version in Mark (4.35–41), omitting extraneous details and considerably softening the severity with which Jesus reproves his disciples

26–39 for their lack of faith. The following story also runs closely parallel to Mark (5.1–12), and the differences are no more than might be expected from Luke's attention to stylistic detail. He places the episode (according to the testimony

26 of a number of important manuscripts), in the **country of the Gergesenes.** Matthew and Mark give the names of two cities, Gadara and Gerasa, neither of which is close enough to the lake to give any clear indication of the locality. Gergesa (if this is what Luke meant) is totally unknown; all we can say for sure is that Luke correctly understood the place to have been on the east side of the lake, **opposite Galilee**—that is to say, in predominantly gentile territory. The devils however (as in Matthew 8.29) use the language of

31 Jewish mythology: **the Abyss** was the place in which the powers of evil were destined to be imprisoned at the end of time (Revelation 20.1–3).

40–56 In the two interwoven episodes which follow, Luke is faithful to the account in Mark (5.21–43). The few changes he has made are only those which a writer might be expected to introduce in order to make a story his own.

The departure and return of the Twelve are separated, as in Mark 6, by the device of a brief change of scene to the court of Herod. But Luke, though he follows Mark's arrangement, has greatly abbreviated it. The words, '**As for** **9.** 9 **John, I beheaded him myself**', are all that is left of the well-known story of Salome's dance. Herod himself is also presented in a more sophisticated light. He is called (as in Matthew) by his correct title of "tetrarch" (**Prince**) 7 and not (as in Mark) by the popular name of 'king', and he is not made to share the somewhat naïve view (which is more characteristic of Jewish folk-lore than of a Hellenistic ruler) that Jesus might be John the Baptist **raised** **from the dead**. His reaction is more pragmatic: after disposing of John he now finds himself with another religious leader to come to terms with. His desire to see Jesus for himself is referred to again in 23.8.

In other respects the narrative in Mark is clearly the model for Luke's account, and the differences are unimportant. '**Neither stick nor pack**' 3 agrees with Matthew (10.9–10) against Mark (6.9) in forbidding even a stick —perhaps because the main use of the travellers' stick was self-defence, and this was felt inappropriate for the peace-loving disciples of Jesus. The only serious discrepancy in Luke is the mention of **Bethsaida**. This village, 10 which lay on the east side of the mouth of the Jordan, and therefore in the jurisdiction of the tetrarch Philip, had recently been rebuilt as a town of some pretensions. It was hardly a place to choose for withdrawing privately, and the miracle which follows can hardly have been in its vicinity, since it 10–17 presupposes **a lonely place**. By introducing the name, Luke has made the 12 scene extremely hard to visualize. On the other hand, his approach to the geography of Galilee is rather different from that of the other evangelists. He mentions very few place-names, and is usually content to situate the various incidents quite vaguely in the countryside. He is about to omit a series of episodes recorded in Mark, which end with one at Bethsaida (Mark 8.22). His concern may simply have been to bring the general course of Jesus' progress roughly into line with the narratives he was using as his sources, without much attention to the exact setting of any particular episode.

One day when he was praying alone in the presence of his disciples. 18 The translators have made no attempt to soften the contradiction contained in this sentence, and it is Luke who must bear the blame. What appears to have happened is that Luke liked to represent important experiences in the life of Jesus as taking place when Jesus was at prayer: see, for example, the baptism (3.21) and the transfiguration (9.28). But it was also necessary to have the disciples present for the sake of the conversation which follows. Hence, **praying alone in the presence of his disciples**. Luke omits much of the detail of this conversation (compared with Mark (8.27–30), whose narrative he seems now to pick up again, having passed over the contents of several pages, and compared still more with Matthew (16.13–20), who has some altogether original material to insert at this point). He preserves only

20 the two most significant points: Peter's recognition that Jesus is **God's Messiah** (and Luke for once follows Mark in reporting Jesus' injunction
22 to secrecy on the matter), and the prophecy that '**the Son of Man has to undergo great sufferings**'.

23 **And to all he said.** There is again little attention paid to actual circumstances. If Jesus was 'praying alone' there can have been no **all** within earshot to whom Jesus could have addressed his teaching. But the sayings which (following Mark) Luke had now to record were obviously not part of Jesus' private instruction to his disciples, and so the presence of a larger audience had simply to be taken for granted. '**Day after day he must take up his cross**': the expression, "taking up" (or "carrying") one's cross is one which must have been formulated after Jesus' execution (see above on Mark 8.34); and Luke adapts it still more to the purpose of strengthening the resolve of Christian congregations by making it sound like a constant spiritual exercise —**day after day**. In other respects, the sayings stand much as they are in
27 Mark, including the most difficult of them, '**there are some of those standing here who will not taste death before they have seen the kingdom of God.**' Only Mark's final words, 'already come in power', are omitted; and this omission perhaps made the oracle easier for Luke's readers to interpret. The **kingdom of God,** so long as it did not involve a manifestation of power on a cosmic scale, was a reality already sometimes present in the activity of Jesus, and certainly now experienced in the life of the church. To this extent, Jesus' prediction had come true.

One should not properly use the word "transfiguration" as the name of
29 the next episode in Luke. Instead of 'he was transfigured', Luke writes **the appearance of his face changed,** and his account of the scene, while it
32 retains an emphasis on the supernatural **glory** of Jesus and the two figures who appeared with him, nevertheless adds a few touches to make the sequence of events more credible and logical, at the expense of the symbolic meanings present in Mark (9.2–8) and Matthew (17.1–8). Thus: the disciples **had been in a deep sleep**; only on waking did they see the three resplendent figures. Peter's suggestion of making shelters was motivated by the fact that the
33 figures **were moving away,** and he hoped (somewhat inappropriately, Luke admits) to detain them; the disciples' fear was caused, not by the vision (which should not have been particularly frightening) but by their being suddenly enveloped in a cloud. Yet despite these touches of rationalization, the scene in Luke retains its other-worldly quality, and has a clear message
31 to give. Moses and Elijah spoke of Jesus' **departure, the destiny he was to fulfil in Jerusalem.** The Greek word is *exodos*, which certainly meant departure, but was also used as a euphemism for "death", and was furthermore a word which Luke could hardly have chosen to use if he had not intended his readers to be reminded of the Exodus of Israel from Egypt. Moses had had an *exodos*, a "destiny", to fulfil, and had died before it was

completed; and the force of the disciples' vision was not only (as in Matthew) that Jesus was a new Moses, and that (as in Mark) he would shortly be clothed with a glory which was even now momentarily visible in his person, but that meanwhile there was a **destiny he was to fulfil in Jerusalem,** which would involve his "departure" (or death)—that is, an *exodos*. The disciples, according to Luke, needed no injunction to secrecy: they **told** 36 **nobody anything of what they had seen.**

Next day. It is just possible that Luke thought of the vision as having 37 taken place at night (hence the 'deep sleep' of the disciples), in which case he may have deliberately added this note of an interval in time. His account of the exorcism is otherwise a much-abbreviated version of that in Mark (9.14–29), but has a different ending: **they were all struck with awe at the** 43 **majesty of God.** This atmosphere of **general wonder** is built up still more in the next phrase, and provides the setting for the solemn announcement which Jesus makes to his disciples. The announcement is introduced in 44 strikingly biblical language, a point which is lost in this translation. According to Mark (9.32), the disciples 'did not understand what he said and were afraid to ask him'. Mark offers no reason for their incomprehension. But Luke has a simple (if somewhat artificial) explanation. Judging by their subsequent conduct, the disciples had clearly not grasped Jesus' unambiguous prediction. The reason must have been that they were not intended to grasp it: **it had been hidden from them.** 45

To conclude the section, Luke makes a very brief selection from the 46–50 sayings recorded at this point by Mark (9.34–41), without apparently attempting to bring them into a more logical order.

Journeys and encounters

The NEB inserts a new heading at this point; and certainly the next ten chapters form a section sufficiently distinct to deserve its own title. In the narrative of Mark (10.1), Jesus now begins his decisive journey from Galilee to Jerusalem, and in both Mark and Matthew it is possible, at least approximately, to plot this journey on the map. In Luke, Jesus also begins his journey shortly after the episode of the transfiguration; but the journey is so packed with sayings and events that it becomes quite impossible to visualize the progress made by the travellers or to be sure which route from Galilee to Jerusalem they are supposed to have taken. The journey, in fact, which would normally have taken three or four days at most, and which is recorded quite briefly in Mark, becomes a whole series of *Journeys and encounters*, lasting perhaps several weeks.

If Luke were a little more precise about Jesus' route, and offered some indication, as the journey progressed, of the places Jesus had reached, we might conclude that he was better informed about this part of Jesus' activity and was therefore in a position to expand his account of the journey. But in fact he is so vague on these points that a different explanation seems preferable. Practically none of the material in these chapters appears in Mark, and only some of it (in other contexts) in Matthew. We must imagine that Luke had received a substantial amount of information about Jesus' teaching and activities which had no fixed place in any connected narrative, and which he had to work in as best he could. He knew that, at a certain point, Jesus travelled from Galilee to Jerusalem; and it occurred to him to fill out the picture of Jesus as a travelling teacher (a picture which his Greek and Roman readers will have found familiar, since such teachers were a common phenomenon in the Hellenistic world) by inserting into this journey most of the extra material which he possessed. It did not greatly matter exactly what route Jesus took; all that was necessary was to remind his readers from time to time that Jesus was on the road, and to help them to visualize the itinerant life of one who had said that he had **nowhere to lay his head.**

58

There may also be another reason why Luke, though he devotes so much space to the journey, is vague about the route which was actually taken. He may not have known the country; and reliable maps did not exist. He knew that Galilee was a separate region from Judaea, and he was well informed about the political differences between each region. But both regions were essentially Jewish; and he may not have known that they were in fact separated by the alien territory of Samaria, so that to go from one to the other it was necessary to go either through Samaria or round it. He may have visualized Galilee and Judaea (as the Roman geographer Pliny appears to have done) as a continuous stretch of country, with Samaria lying alongside. He knew that Jesus must have entered Samaria at some stage, since one or two episodes clearly belonged there; but whereas in fact a traveller who took the route through Samaria would soon have left Galilee far behind him, Luke may have imagined that Jesus could have crossed the border at any time during his journey and then have crossed back to continue through Galilee to Judaea. If so, he would have felt free to work in the Samaritan episodes at almost any point he liked.

In any case, it was no ordinary journey. For Jesus, it was a necessary
51 prelude to being **taken up to heaven** (Acts 1.2,11), and it fixed his course as being from now on directed inexorably towards Jerusalem. All this Luke expresses in a sentence rich in scriptural overtones; his language leaves no doubt that a new chapter is beginning in the story of Jesus. At the same time, one of these overtones sounds right through the first of these "encounters". One Old Testament figure in particular—Elijah—had been "taken up into heaven" (2 Kings 2.11). Many thought that Jesus must be this same Elijah,
54 now returned to earth; and **the disciples James and John** (appropriately

called 'Sons of Thunder', Mark 3.17) were probably simply echoing this popular view when they expected Jesus to do what Elijah had done to his enemies (2 Kings 1.10) and **burn them up** by calling down fire from heaven. The scene took place in a **Samaritan village.** For several centuries 52 the Samaritans had been something of a race apart from the rest of the Jewish nation. They possessed a different version of the Old Testament (consisting of only the first five books) and regarded Mount Gerizim, near their own capital, as the "chosen place" where God should be worshipped, believing this, and not Jerusalem, to be the true site of the temple. More recently, Samaria had been brought under the same administration as Judaea; but relations between the two races were still strained, and little more than twenty years before Jesus' visit the Samaritans had caused a crisis by deliberately defiling the temple in Jerusalem at the time of the Passover. It was not unknown for them to attack pilgrims on their way through Samaria from Galilee to Jerusalem; and when Jesus tried to make the same journey, the Samaritan villagers were behaving true to form when they **would not** 53 **have him because he was making for Jerusalem.** The disciples' reaction was probably equally typical of Jews; but Jesus (as several stories in this section show) dissociated himself altogether from the traditional animosity between the two races.

Jesus (as Luke will be constantly reminding us) was on the road; and **the** 57 **road** is the cue for three sayings about "following". Two of these occur also 57–60 in Matthew (8.18–22), and what was said of them there may apply equally here: the sayings themselves (including the third, added by Luke) have a 61–2 general and proverbial sound, and it may have been only later that a little anecdote was added to each, thereby making the sayings more particular and more radical.

After this the Lord appointed a further seventy-two. It is clearly 10. 1 stated in each of the first three gospels that Jesus had a distinct group of twelve disciples and that on one occasion he sent them out on an independent mission; and in the early church the existence of this original Twelve was taken for granted. Luke alone mentions **a further seventy-two** and a further mission; but he says practically nothing to explain the function of this second group. The instructions given to them are almost exactly the same as those in his own (9.1–5) or Matthew's (10) version of the charge to the Twelve (the only addition here is that they are to travel so hastily that they must **exchange no greetings on the road**—oriental courtesies con- 4 sume a lot of time!); and after their return they play no further part in the story. What is their significance? Luke was a historian: he knew the importance of the mission to non-Jews in the subsequent history of the church, and he knew that this had been conducted by apostles who were not members of the original Twelve. He may have wished to justify the credentials of this larger circle of apostles by mentioning the **further seventy-two** in the 1 gospel. Alternatively, seventy-two (or seventy: there was constant oscillation between the two) was an important round number in Jewish legend and history. Moses commissioned 72 (or 70) elders (Numbers 11); 70 (or 72) elders had translated the Old Testament into Greek under divine inspiration. Any of these motives may have been in Luke's mind: more we cannot say.

13 **'Alas for you, Chorazin!'** This condemnation of cities of Galilee occurs (more appropriately in a Galilean context) in Matthew 11.20-4; and the
16 final words to the seventy-two (**'whoever listens to you listens to me'**) are evidently another version of the saying at the end of the charge in Matthew (10.40), which appears also, in a slightly different form and in another context, in Mark 9.37.

17 **The seventy-two came back jubilant.** The mission and return of this larger group conforms to the pattern of that of the Twelve (9.1,10), who had also been given 'power and authority to overcome all the devils' (9.1). Invocation of the **name** of Jesus could effect an exorcism, even if the exorcist was not a follower of Jesus (9.49). The reason was Jesus' victory over Satan.
18 **'I watched how Satan fell'.** Jesus' vision of this victory is in terms
19 of Jewish mythology (Isaiah 14.12), his promise to the disciples of **power to tread underfoot snakes and scorpions** (of which Luke later gives an instance in the case of Paul, Acts 28.6) is a fulfilment of Psalm 91.13. The
20 idea of names **enrolled in heaven**—meaning a secure place in the age to come—is a commonplace in the Bible.

21 **At that moment Jesus exulted in the Holy Spirit.** The startling saying
21-2 that follows occurs in Matthew 11.25-7. Here perhaps it is better in place, since the scene concerns only Jesus and his disciples; and if Luke was thinking of the seventy-two as the prototypes of subsequent apostles, then he
23-4 may have found in this saying (and in the next, which in Matthew occurs in the parable-chapter, 13.16-17) a validation of their authority: they were
22 those to whom the Son may choose to reveal the Father.

25 **A lawyer came forward to put this test question to him.** It is the same question as was put to Jesus on another occasion (18.18; Mark 10.17), and the answer is the same as that given to a slightly different (and perhaps more "testing") question in Mark 12.28, Matthew 22.34. This dialogue in Luke may be a record of a different occasion altogether, or it may be a conflation of the others; in either event, it shows Jesus and the professional lawyer in complete agreement—at least so far as general principles were concerned.
29 But on the practical application of these principles—**'And who is my neighbour?'**—Jesus had something quite new to say.
30 **'A man was on his way from Jerusalem down to Jericho.'** The long steep descent through the mountains, winding along the courses of the *wadys*, was a notorious haunt of robbers until quite recent times. The robbery was nothing out of the ordinary; the interest of the story turns entirely upon the

response of the three other travellers. We may feel that the response of the
first two was strangely inhuman; but their conduct was probably due, not
to any lack of human feelings, but to a deliberate choice between conflicting
obligations. On the one hand, there was a clear commandment to help any
"neighbour" (normally interpreted as any fellow-Jew) whose life was in
danger; on the other hand, if the victim were already dead (which, by his
appearance, this one presumably might have been) both a priest and a Levite
would incur ritual defilement by touching or even by approaching the
corpse, and this might prevent them from fulfilling their duties in the temple,
or from collecting the tithes to which they were entitled. It would probably
not have surprised Jesus' contemporaries to hear that in this case caution
overcame charity: they decided to avoid all risk of defilement and **went past** 32
on the other side.

We know what Jesus thought of such an attitude: just as it was absurd to
invoke rules about the keeping of the Sabbath as a pretext for refusing to cure
a sick man, so it was indefensible to regard rules about ritual purity as more
binding than the needs of a human sufferer. But if this were the point which
Jesus intended here, we should expect the third traveller to have been an
ordinary Jewish layman, whose simple understanding of the law would put
to shame the casuistry of the professional religious classes. The element
of surprise in the story consists in the fact that the third traveller was, of all
things, **a Samaritan.** It is true that the Samaritans, according to their own 33
version of the Law of Moses, were also commanded to "love their neighbour as themselves"; and it is true that there was a familiar story in the Old
Testament about the mercifulness of certain Samaritans (2 Chronicles 18).
But at the time when Jesus told this story, Jews and Samaritans hated each
other with great bitterness. The Samaritan had every reason for not regarding
the wounded Jew as his "neighbour". Yet he did for him all—if not more
than all—that one Jew would feel obliged to do for another.

'**Go and do as he did**'. It is tempting to regard these words as permission 37
to use the parable as a moral tale, and to make the Samaritan into an example
of how one should behave when one finds oneself, say, at the scene of a road
accident. But this can hardly be what Jesus intended. The Samaritan's
behaviour was only what, at their best, human beings can be expected to do
for each other. It did not need a parable of Jesus to inculcate such an ideal:
people already knew that this was what one ought to do, and doubtless Jesus'
listeners each hoped that, in a similar situation, he would have done as much
himself. Nevertheless, they would have had more sympathy than we have
with the priest and the Levite, whom they would have realized to be in the
grip of conflicting obligations; and they would have been virtually forced by
their Jewish upbringing to regard the concept of "neighbour" in a very
narrow sense, and to feel no obligation to come to the help of any of the
traditional enemies of the Jewish race, such as the Romans, the Samaritans

or indeed most Gentiles. The example of the Samaritan, who was prepared
36 to regard his worst traditional enemy as his **neighbour,** was designed to
shock them out of this attitude. '**Go and do as he did**' meant, treat anyone,
of any race and background, as your neighbour, with all in the way of help
and charity which the word implies. The parable found its target in the
exclusive nationalism of the Jewish people in the time of Jesus; but there
has never yet been a society or a civilization in which it would have no
relevance.

38 **A woman named Martha made him welcome in her home.** Hospitality was offered to a visiting preacher as a matter of course; but we are
rarely given a glimpse of the domestic strains which it caused. Jesus' hostess
40 was **distracted** by her many tasks (the word meets us often in harassed
private letters of the period), while her sister took up the position of a listener
at the teacher's feet. Jesus' reply speaks for itself: it is an application of the
old adage that it is better to concentrate on one thing than to dissipate one's
energies on many (compare Ecclesiasticus 11.10). But what the moral was for
Jesus' contemporaries or for Luke's readers is a harder question. Simple fare
for visiting teachers? The rights of women in the Christian church? Or
simply the very modern tension between domestic chores and "the things
that matter"? We cannot tell. For Luke's readers, in any case, the whole
39 point probably lay in the one phrase, **listening to his words.** "Listening
42 to Jesus' words" was the "best part" that anyone could possibly choose.

11. 1 **Once, in a certain place, Jesus was at prayer.** In Matthew (6.5–13)
the Lord's Prayer is deliberately contrasted with the lengthy and ostentatious
prayers of Jews and pagans. Luke gives it in a different context. Jesus was a
man of prayer (a point which Luke likes to emphasize), and his disciples
naturally wished to imitate him: '**Lord, teach us to pray.**' Modern instruction on prayer usually concentrates on mental and psychological techniques
for becoming aware of the presence of God. But, whatever experience and
methods the religious men of antiquity may have had, their teaching on
prayer had a slightly different function: it defined the relationship which the
worshipper had to God, the rewards and benefits which his faith justified
him in praying for, and the conditions he must fulfil if his prayer was to be
accepted. It was in this sense that the Pharisees and other religious groups in
Judaism "taught their disciples to pray": they each used distinctive prayers
to formulate their doctrine of the relationship of God and man and of the
destiny which God had promised to his chosen people. We learn from this
passage that John the Baptist had composed such prayers; and we are now
given Jesus' own instruction, which can be regarded, from one point of
view, as a succinct summary of his teaching.

The version in Luke is even briefer [a] than that in Matthew. It is also less

[a] There was a tendency for copyists to fill out Luke's version with clauses from Matthew's.
Later manuscripts therefore offer a text very similar to that in Matthew, and this is why

Jewish, in the sense that the additional clauses in Matthew can all be paralleled from Jewish prayers of the period, and that some of the phrases would
have been easier for a non-Jew to understand in Luke's version than in
Matthew's. Whether this makes Luke's text more likely to represent the
prayer which Jesus originally taught is open to question; but it certainly
lays bare, even more starkly than Matthew's, the radical economy of Jesus'
teaching.

"Father". Even in Greek, this sounds strikingly direct and intimate, and 2
there can be little doubt that it represents the Aramaic word *Abba*. This was
a child's familiar name for its father; it was Jesus' own way of addressing his
heavenly Father; and it became a distinctive mark of the praying of Christians: through Jesus, Christians are admitted to an intimate relationship with
God, such as sons have with their father. The directness of the opening in
Luke, compared with Matthew's more formal address, expresses that new
boldness in prayer which we know to have been characteristic of Christians
from earliest times (see also Romans 8.15). The next change is Luke's **each
day** for Matthew's 'today': the meaning of **daily bread** is still obscure 3
but, in Luke, life seems a little less provisional; we can look forward to
praying for bread **each day** rather than confining ourselves to 'today' and
leaving the future entirely to God. And thirdly, Luke uses the natural Greek
word for **sins** (instead of "debts"), though he brings back the Hebraic 4
concept of debt in the next words: **all who have done us wrong** (literally,
"all our debtors").

'**Ask, and you will receive.**' This apparently unconditional affirmation 9
that a Christian's prayer is always heard is illustrated, as in Matthew (7.7–11),
by the analogy of an earthly father: if God is your father—and that he is so
is a premise of the Lord's prayer and of all Christian praying that begins
Abba, "Father"—how much more will he grant the prayers of his children!
But what prayers? Luke may have been conscious of the obvious question:
surely God does not answer all prayers? In Matthew's version of the saying,
the promise seems quite general: God will give 'good things' to those who
ask him. According to Luke, there is only one prayer that will certainly be
answered, the prayer for **the Holy Spirit**. Luke also gives another small 13
parable. '**Suppose one of you has a friend**'. The scene is a Palestinian 5
one-room house, with the family all in bed; the conflict is between the rules 7
of hospitality that would be normal in village life in the east, and the trouble
caused to a whole family by such an appeal at midnight. The moral seems to
be: a pressing request (even if it looks like **shamelessness**) makes a man 8
give a friend **all he needs**. How much greater the efficacy of even an
apparently shameless prayer, given the overwhelming "friendship" of God!

older translations such as the Authorized Version (which was based on late manuscripts)
offer virtually the same text in Luke as in Matthew (see the footnotes in NEB). But it is
certain that Luke originally had a much briefer prayer than Matthew.

14 **The people were astonished, but some of them said.** The only substantial difference between Luke and Matthew (12.22–30) in this paragraph is that in Luke the objectors are, not the Pharisees, but one section of the crowd: the scene represents, not a deliberate attack by opponents, but a puzzled reaction on the part of some of Jesus' listeners. Luke has also changed
20 one or two details. **'If it is by the finger of God'.** Matthew has, 'by the Spirit of God'. Luke's phase is more biblical: "finger of God" occurs in Exodus 8.19, "hand of God" frequently in the Old Testament; and these are evidently equivalent expressions for "spirit" (compare Ezekiel 8.1 and
21 3). In verse 21 Matthew's 'strong man in his house' has become **'a strong man fully armed . . . on guard over his castle'.** We should probably think of a local prince, such as one of the sons of Herod the Great: many of their palaces were heavily fortified against insurgents or against belligerent
27 neighbours from the east. **'Happy the womb that carried you'.** This brief exchange occurs only in Luke. **Happy** is the word translated 'Blest' at the beginning of the Sermon on the Mount. The woman's blessing is in perfectly conventional language. Jesus caps it with another, which would have again been unremarkable on the lips of any Jewish teacher. But the reader who was
28 aware of the uniqueness of Jesus and of the **word of God** which he preached would have seen that the saying had a special point for the disciples and their successors.

15-19, 24-6   For the remaining details, see the comments on the parallel passages in
29-30, 33-6 Mark and Matthew: Beelzebub, Mark 3.22–7; the unclean spirit, Matthew 12.43–5; the sign of Jonah, Matthew 12.38–42 and Mark 8.11–12; the sayings about a lamp, Mark 4.21 and Matthew 6.22–3.

The two following sections are a striking example of Luke's way of arranging and editing his material. The setting, a meal in a Pharisee's house, is due to Luke (and appears to be quickly forgotten as the chapter progresses). The
38-41 background of the discussion about inner and outer cleansing is drawn from Mark 7.1–9, and the various accusations against the Pharisees and lawyers
53-4 are all found (though in a different order) in Matthew 23. The section ends with a summary account of Jesus' controversies which is, like the opening, apparently due to Luke.
41   In the details, Luke's changes are very slight. **'Let what is in the cup be given in charity'** is an obscure expansion of the simpler phrase in Matthew (23.25). The NEB footnote suggests a possible alternative rendering, which would involve a pun on a Greek word which can mean both "what is inside" and "what is possible" but it may be that the Aramaic original has been
44 misunderstood. **'Alas, alas, you are like unmarked graves over which men may walk without knowing it.'** The Jews took elaborate precautions to avoid the defilement which followed walking over a grave: Luke's version of this saying has an authentic Palestinian ring. So also has his introduction

of a quotation from Scripture (which however we cannot place exactly, though it is close to 2 Chronicles 24.19) with the phrase, 'the Wisdom of God said'. The Jews were fond of referring to God in this kind of oblique way. By contrast, the 'key of knowledge' is an expression more at home in the world of Greek religious speculation than of Jewish controversy. On the whole, Luke shows himself to be expert on political and social conditions in Palestine, and his recognition that only some of Jesus' accusations were applicable equally to the Pharisees and the lawyers corresponds to the facts better than Matthew's more simplified picture. 49 52

Meanwhile, when a crowd of many thousands had gathered. Luke slightly changes the setting, but continues to offer a selection of sayings (occurring in different contexts in other gospels), some of which are addressed to the disciples, some to the crowd. The scene with which the previous chapter closed—the Pharisees submitting Jesus to intensive cross-questioning —is the cue for the first saying about the leaven of the Pharisees. In Mark (8.15) the phrase is unexplained, but seems to refer to political activity. In Matthew (16.5–12) the 'leaven' is the teaching of the Pharisees and Sadducees. Here, it becomes the hypocrisy of the Pharisees: what lies behind their profession of piety will be revealed at the Judgement—and Luke sets in this context (of the darker things of the soul being one day brought to light) a saying which in Matthew (10.26–7) has a quite different application. 12. 1 2, 3

'To you who are my friends I say'. Friends is a new word, but clearly refers to an inner ring of already loyal followers rather than to the crowd outside, and introduces a series of sayings intended to give encouragement under persecution. Down to verse 9, the sequence is the same as in Matthew 10.26–33. The only significant difference is that the saying in verses 8–9 introduces the figure of the Son of Man: here he is not a figure of glory and triumph (as in Mark 8.38) so much as an "advocate" at the heavenly assize that will be held by God with his angels. Verse 10 (on slandering the Holy Spirit) is an abbreviated version of Matthew 12.31–2 (Mark 3.28–30). Verses 11–12 correspond to Matthew 10.19–20 (Mark 13.11). 4 4–12 8

'Master, tell my brother to divide the family property with me'. In Palestine, disputes about inheritance were complicated by the fact that wills had to be made in accordance with detailed provisions in the Law of Moses which defined the rights of eldest sons and of other members of the family. At the same time there was a strong instinct to keep the family property so far as possible intact, and not to divide it among a number of inheritors. The lawyers who dealt with such disputes needed, in this as in other matters, to be experts in the interpretation of Scripture. Jesus had proved himself an expert, and it was perhaps natural for a man in the crowd to assume that he could be appealed to as a qualified judge. Jesus was reluctant; and the exchange led (at least in Luke's editing) to a general discourse about 13

15 **greed of every kind.** The parable which illustrates it is unusually philo-
16-21 sophical for Jesus. Instead of pressing upon its hearers the demands of a
new situation (like most of the parables), it appears to be simply an illustration of the age-old truth that man proposes and God disposes. Its vividness
comes more from the style of telling (the debate of the man with himself, the
dramatic divine summons) and from the unexpected use of some of the catch-
19 words of popular philosophical debate ("**eat, drink, and enjoy yourself**",
20 "**You fool**") than from the intrinsic interest of the story. The moral—that
true riches are of another kind—is also an old one. There is a rather similar
expression of it in Ecclesiasticus 11.14–19.
22 '**I bid you put away anxious thoughts.**' These warnings against
anxiety occur, in much the same words, in the Sermon on the Mount
(Matthew 6.25–34). Luke, who is particularly interested in the degree of
actual renunciation and poverty required in the followers of Jesus, focuses
the same teaching upon every kind of preoccupation with worldly posses-
33-4 sions and, in the saying about thieves and moths, makes a little more of the
contrast (again a cliché of popular philosophy) between material wealth and
33 **never-failing treasure** than is present in the more poetically balanced
32 version in Matthew (6.19–21). Jesus' followers are a **little flock**, the new
elect people of God. They correspond to that faithful remnant of Israel whom
Isaiah sought to strengthen in terms very similar to these words of Jesus
33 (41.8–20; 43.1–7). '**Sell your possessions and give in charity**'. Luke is
clear about the distinctive way of life demanded of this small group of followers, and he is to show how it was put into practice at the very beginning
of the history of the church (Acts 2.44–6).
35 '**Be ready for action**'. A Christian must be constantly alert: this theme
occurs in all the gospels, and is illustrated here by several variations on the
theme of a servant who is not taken by surprise when his master unexpectedly
returns. In Matthew and Mark these illustrations occur when Jesus is explicitly teaching about the imminent but still unpredictable hour of general
judgement which is to come upon the whole world; and in Matthew (25.1–13)
the parable of the 'ten girls' (whatever its original significance may have
been) is offered as an illustration of the same theme. Echoes of that parable
may perhaps be heard here also. But in this chapter of Luke very little is said
about the future. It looks as if Luke has deliberately shifted the emphasis of
this teaching from the prediction of future woes and rewards to the inculca-
tion of the right attitude in the present. Whether the culmination of all things
was far or near (and perhaps it was beginning to seem farther than nearer by
the time Luke wrote), the same vigilance and alertness were still demanded
of Jesus' followers. Of course it remained true that, when the great Day
finally came, there would be a stupendous reversal of accepted values: the
poor, not the rich, would be blest, the last would be first, the least would be
greatest. In such an age, one could even imagine the master and the servants

changing places at supper. But again, this was not only a matter of the future. In the Christian church, the paradox had already been experienced in the present. Their Master had come to serve (Mark 10.45) and actually **wait on** **them** (John 13). At this point the master–servant illustration leaves the world of ordinary experience and points unmistakably to him whom the church came to recognize as its Servant-Lord. 37

Peter said. Luke makes the next paragraph (which is almost identical with 41, 42–6 Matthew 24.45–51) depend on a question of Peter's. The question is not directly answered; but the illustration (as in Matthew) points to the Last Judgement. The vigilance shown now will be one of the criteria by which it will then be known whether any individual belongs to **us** or to **everyone**, whether **he will find his place** among the faithful or **among the faithless.**

'**The servant who knew his master's wishes**'. Another servant illustra- 47 tion, this time preserved only by Luke. Its point seems to be different from the others, but we are given no clue how to interpret it. The situation it fits best is the debate which was soon to begin between Jews and Christians. The Jews, since they possessed the Law of Moses, claimed that they knew their **master's wishes**. This, they believed, assured them of salvation. Most of them shaped their lives in such a way as to **carry them out** (or so they thought). Even those who **made no attempt** to do so could still perhaps be saved through their solidarity with a race which was committed, as a whole, to observing the revealed will of God. On the other hand the Gentiles (they argued) did not know the **master's wishes**; they did not possess the Law of Moses. The verdict on them would surely be infinitely more severe. But suppose Jesus' merciless analysis of their way of life was right; suppose that the Jews did not in fact succeed in keeping the Law. They might find it was the Gentiles, not themselves, who were judged **less severely.** 48

'**I have come to set fire to the earth**'. Fire: a symbol of the Last 49 Judgement and an attribute of the Elijah-figure whom John the Baptist had predicted and who was to precipitate the final phase of history. The saying is one of those which show Jesus in this rôle of inaugurating a new and critical epoch, and it suggests (as does the baptism saying in Mark 10.38) that he knew that he too would be near-submerged by it—for **baptism**, in this 50 saying, is probably correctly understood by the translators as an **ordeal,** rather than as an anticipation of the sacrament of the church. **For from now** 52 **on**: this note of time is Luke's most significant addition to Matthew's version of the saying (10.34–6). **Division** within families was an outrage to Jewish 51 morals, but it was one of the features of that period of intensified evil which (it was believed) would immediately precede the end. Jesus had said (so at least Luke presents the matter) that such division would occur **from now on**; and when the church found that the new faith was in fact tearing families apart, it knew how to interpret these tragedies: they were signs of the critical

54 age which had begun, as surely as, in Palestine, clouds **in the west** mean
55 rain, and a **wind . . . from the south** brings parching heat.
58   '**When you are going with your opponent to court**'. The saying, in the Sermon on the Mount (Matthew 5.25–6), is a simple everyday illustration of the kind of conduct demanded by Jesus. Luke may simply have added it here for want of a better place; or he may have seen a rather different point in it. The **opponent** could be understood as the Christian's persecutor: in view of the urgency of the times, it was better not to get involved with him at all!

13. 1 **At that very time:** Luke was a conscious historian, and this is another instance of his concern to tie his story in with contemporary events. Unfortunately the allusions are lost on us: the historian Josephus does not mention these events, and we have to reconstruct them as best we can from the little Luke says about them. If Galileans were sacrificing in Jerusalem the occasion must have been a Passover, when thousands of pilgrims came in and slaughtered their lambs in the temple. We know that this was often an occasion for civil disorders, and it is quite possible that Pilate had to use
4 force to restore order even in the temple area. It is less surprising that the disaster at Siloam is not mentioned by Josephus. The south-east corner of the city walls of Jerusalem stood on high ground looking over the Pool of Siloam. Some repairs to one of the towers were doubtless the occasion for this accident, which may have been very much in the news in the last year of Jesus' life, but would have been completely forgotten a few years later had not Jesus commented upon it. The contemporary Jewish explanation of why such calamities befall individuals was very simple (though it was often made more plausible by some subtle refinements): they must have sinned, and this was their punishment. Jesus did not altogether reject this solution; there were certainly occasions on which he seems to have regarded illness as a consequence of sin. But here he offers a more prophetic explanation: these catastrophes are warnings, they are typical of the fate which awaits you all
5 —'**unless you repent.**'
6   **He told them this parable**—and its theme is the same: repentance. Fruit and vegetables were grown in vineyards alongside the vines, but clearly a tree had to yield fruit if it were to justify the amount of good it took out of the soil. Manuring a fig-tree would be a somewhat exceptional measure. So too the activity of Jesus was exceptional, and gave his hearers an exceptional opportunity to repent.
10   **One Sabbath he was teaching in a synagogue**—a typical instance of a Sabbath controversy provoked by a miracle of healing. Luke has already recorded one such episode (6.6–11), and this one (which has no exact parallel in the other gospels) follows the same pattern, but with slightly different
11 details. The sufferer was **bent double.** In modern terms, we would say her

condition was one of physical deformity; but it was apparently quite natural to think of this, no less than an obviously mental disorder like epilepsy, as a case of being **possessed by a spirit**. The miracle, then, was an exorcism; and there is considerable play, throughout the paragraph, on the words "binding" and "freeing" (though this can hardly be reproduced in an English translation). We can detect, below the surface, a whole mythology of evil: Satan "binds" his victims, but when he himself is "bound" by one who is stronger (see above on Mark 3.27), his victims are "freed". However, the real interest of the story lies in the dialogue between Jesus and **the presi- 14 dent of the synagogue**. Granted their own premises, it is a little difficult to see why Jesus' opponents should have been **covered with confusion**. In 17 the following centuries, careful regulations were made which permitted Jews to do what was necessary for their animals without infringing the Sabbath rest; and doubtless some such regulations were already in force. If so, they could well have answered that they did not neglect the needs of their animals, but they still kept the Sabbath, and a permanently crippled woman could just as well have been healed another day. In his attack on them, Jesus seems to have argued *ad hominem*. The woman is called a **daughter of Abraham** 16 —an appeal to the solidarity of the Jewish race—and a rather artificial parallel is drawn between loosing an animal from a manger and loosing a person from Satan. But if the argument seems thin, the point was gained in any case by the miraculous cure: only blinkered legalists could regard such an action as wrong, even on the Sabbath.

The two brief parables of mustard-seed and yeast occur (without any 18–20 interpretation) in the parable-chapters of Matthew and Mark (Matthew 13.31–3; Mark 4.30–2).

He continued his journey. So much has happened since Luke told us that 22 Jesus had begun his journey from Galilee to Jerusalem that we need to be reminded of it; for the journey is in reality little more than the literary framework for a collection of otherwise disconnected sayings and episodes. In this section, as so often, Luke gets the dialogue moving with a question from one of Jesus' listeners. The reply, and the sayings which follow it, are all familiar from Matthew's gospel, but appear in a strangely different combination. The 'narrow gate' of Matthew 7.13 has become a **narrow door**, and the difficulty 24 is not to find it (Matthew 7.14) but, having found it, **to enter**—for there is a danger of being too late, and the door may be shut (as it is in the parable in Matthew 25.10). Those who are too late are greeted only with a fierce dismissal—**"Out of my sight, all of you, you and your wicked ways!"** (a 27 quotation from Psalm 6.8)—regardless of their apparent right to enter. Here again Luke offers a different application from that in Matthew (7.22–3), where those excluded are spurious Christian prophets. Here they are Jesus' own society and nation, the Jews—and this leads to the strongly anti-Jewish

29 picture of Gentiles having precedence over Jews in the coming **feast in the kingdom of God,** almost exactly as in Matthew (8.11–12), and complete with a phrase which is otherwise entirely confined to Matthew's gospel,
28 **wailing and grinding of teeth.**
31 **At that time a number of Pharisees came to him.** Mark says (3.6) that the Pharisees were in league with the partisans of Herod. Were they now plotting an ambush together, or had the Pharisees suddenly become anxious to save Jesus' life? We do not know—though it is interesting that in Acts Luke represents the Pharisees as initially sympathetic to Christianity. In any case Jesus' reply was doubtless remembered for its own sake, and not for the light it threw on his relations with Herod and the Pharisees. It also shows that Luke imagined Jesus' journey to be still through the territory of Herod
32 Antipas, that is to say, through Galilee or Transjordan. **He replied, 'Go and tell that fox'.** To the Greeks, as to us, the fox was a by-word for cunning; but in Hebrew writings it more often stood simply for a puny creature, and Jesus may have been saying, "Go and tell your little king". His reply, nevertheless, was very much to the point. Herod wished to put an end to Jesus' activity of **casting out devils and working cures.** But he did not need to trouble himself. **On the third day**—three days was a natural way of describing any short space of time (e.g. Jonah 1.17)—it would all be brought to an end by the will of a power far greater than Herod's, and Jesus would have reached his **goal.** The Greek word here is as ambiguous as the English, and leads on to a saying about the geographical "goal" of Jesus'
33 journey, Jerusalem. **'It is unthinkable for a prophet to meet his death anywhere but in Jerusalem.'** This seems to put it very strongly: it was only a fairly recent tradition which asserted that most of the prophets had in fact been killed in Jerusalem. [a] But for Luke, with a historian's bird's-eye view of religious developments in Palestine, any other destiny for Jesus may well have seemed **unthinkable.** And there follows, with great appropriate-
34-5 ness, a lament over Jerusalem in virtually the same words as in Matthew 23.37-9.

14. 1 **One Sabbath he went to have a meal.** The main meal on a Sabbath took place after the morning service in the synagogue, and guests were often invited. Perhaps Jesus had been preaching, and was invited to the meal afterwards; in any case, his presence on such an occasion **in the house of a leading Pharisee** (that is to say, probably a leading member of the community who also happened to be a Pharisee) was perfectly natural—and Luke makes it the occasion for a number of sayings to do with feasts and banquets. But first, there was a healing miracle to record. Jesus' question,
3 **'Is it permitted to cure people on the Sabbath or not?'** probably had a perfectly clear-cut answer in the teaching of the lawyers and the Pharisees:

[a] See above on Matthew 23.29.

it was permitted when it was a question of saving life, but otherwise not. The man with dropsy was not in immediate danger, therefore it was not permitted to treat him. But possibly the sheer inhumanity of this principle when there was a prospect of an immediate miraculous cure reduced them to silence, and **they said nothing.** If the Law permitted them (as it did) to save even **4** an animal's life on the Sabbath, how could they be so casuistical as to regard it as wrong to heal a man?

Elsewhere, Jesus explicitly criticizes the lawyers and Pharisees for their tendency to seek **the places of honour** (for at any formal meal the seating **7** at table was strictly by seniority). Here, he contrasts this fashion with a rule of his own—which is what, in this instance, the word **parable** seems to mean. *a* The rule itself (**'Do not sit down in the place of honour'**) was an **8** old one (Proverbs 25.6–7) and was not strange to Jesus' contemporaries; and even the motive Jesus gave for it was not unmixed modesty but a desire that the **fellow-guests will see the respect in which you are held.** However, **10** a saying is added (perhaps by Luke, for it occurs also in other contexts, Luke 18.14, Matthew 23.12) which makes the rule into a **parable** in another sense: it is an illustration of that great reversal of values which will be a feature of the kingdom of God. **'Whoever humbles himself will be 11 exalted'.**

Then he said to his host. Another rule, this time based on Jesus' **12** distinctive principle (6.33) that one must do good without expecting any return. Jewish culture was very conscious of the curse of poverty, and when any large party was given it was not done to exclude paupers and beggars who might be fed on what was left over. Moreover, many devout Jews made a point of keeping open house to the poor. Jesus' rule only goes further than this in that the poor were to be invited, not in addition to the usual guests, but instead of them.

One of the company, after hearing all this. Practical questions **15** about hospitality led the mind naturally to the **feast in the kingdom of God.** This was an image which, ever since Old Testament times, the Jews loved to use for the promised reward which awaited the just and devout of their nation. **'Happy the man who shall sit at the feast'** was a typical "beatitude": a Jewish teacher might well use it to encourage his students to greater virtue. But Jesus' beatitudes struck a different note: 'how blest are those in need' (6.20); and the story that follows illustrates the contrast. The story itself runs more smoothly in Luke than in Matthew (22.1–14), whether because of Luke's more careful editing or because he had access to a purer version of it. It faithfully reflects Palestinian customs; but at the same time it has one or two touches which point to a subsequent adaptation of the story to the needs of the church. It was a normal courtesy to send a servant to inform the invited guests when the dinner was ready; but if it was a **big 16**

[a] On the wide range of meanings of this word, see above on Mark 3.23.

dinner party, one servant could hardly have managed the task alone. Matthew, more plausibly, makes the host send 'his servants', but Luke's single servant may be intended to help the reader to think of Jesus, sent by God with the final summons to the kingdom. The first two excuses (which are here made more explicit than in Matthew) are entirely plausible: the last hour of daylight, after the day's work was finished, was the natural time to complete a purchase of land or livestock, and since large dinner parties normally lasted well into the night, the guest would normally lose nothing by giving his apologies to the servant and arriving somewhat later. For this

21 seems to be the point of the story. Instead of keeping these guests' places for them (as would have been usual) the indignant host sent his servant **out quickly** to bring in all the beggars who could be found, so that those whom he had invited (who were men of considerable substance if they could afford five yoke of oxen) would suffer the indignity of arriving at the house and

15 being turned away because there was no room for them. '**Happy the man who shall sit at the feast in the kingdom of God!**' Yes, but (Jesus replies) this happiness may be enjoyed by those whom you least expect. It is the poor who are **happy** (or "blest", the same word in the Greek). The

24 others, by putting it off, have missed their chance: '**I tell you that not one of those who were invited shall taste my banquet**'. However, two further details suggest how this story was used in the early church. First, the

20 third excuse: "**I have just got married and for that reason I cannot come**". There is no hint of this in Matthew's version, and it fits awkwardly into the story; for unlike the others, who could have come late, a newly married man could not have come at all, and it is difficult to see how he could have accepted the invitation in the first place. On the other hand, some Christians soon came to see marriage, as well as possessions, as an obstacle to following the call of Jesus (the servant), and this, as well as artistic symmetry (for most good stories contain groups of three) may have helped this extra detail to come into the story. Secondly, the servant is commanded to go,

21 not only into **the streets and alleys** (as in Matthew) but also **on to the**

23 **highways and along the hedgerows**. This is perfectly plausible; beggars were to be found outside cities on the roads, especially in the shelter of a wall that enclosed some estate or vineyard (there were no **hedgerows** in Palestine: the Greek word here means a wall or a fence). But it is also a perfectly intelligible symbol for those who were "outside" the Jewish nation—the Gentiles. The subsequent history of the church was to demonstrate that it was these people, not the Jews, who got in first.

26 '**If anyone comes to me and does not hate his father and mother**'. Matthew (10.37) has 'who cares more for father or mother', and this is clearly the meaning; Luke's more violent version may nevertheless be closer to Jesus' own language (see above on Matthew 5.43). Moreover, the saying in Matthew is addressed to those who are already disciples. Luke, by bringing

in **great crowds**, has given this and the following sayings a rather different 25
meaning: this is what you must be prepared for if you are contemplating
following me. '**None of you can be a disciple of mine without parting** 33
with all his possessions'. This extreme implication of Jesus' teaching
about poverty and detachment occurs only in Luke; and it is a question in
which Luke seems to be particularly interested, both when recording Jesus'
sayings and when relating the church's attempt to put the principle into
practice (Acts 2.44; 5.1–12). It comes in here as the corollary of two little
illustrations which seem to have the moral: Count the cost first! But, though 28–32
the paragraph hangs together well enough, the examples of the man building
a tower and the king planning a campaign do not quite do what is expected
of them; for their natural meaning is that one should not begin at all unless
one is sure one can finish. This seems an unlikely thing for Jesus to have
said about Christian discipleship in general. But if the sayings were originally 34
intended, not for the crowds (as here), but for the small group of disciples
who were steeling themselves to face whatever lay ahead of Jesus, then they
would make good sense if they were spoken by way of encouragement at a
moment when the disciples were faltering: you cannot give up now, you
should have counted the cost before you began following me!

'**This fellow**', they said, '**welcomes sinners and eats with them**'. 15. 2
Several other episodes have illustrated the offence Jesus gave by consorting
with **sinners**—that is, with those whose profession or way of life excluded
them from the privileged position which all law-abiding Jews claimed to
possess in the economy of God. It was clearly expected of him, as the leader
of a new religious movement, to be as careful about the company he kept as
the highly exclusive fellowships of the Pharisees. The defence Jesus made
on this occasion involved a small but very important difference between
himself and his opponents. It could not be said of the Pharisees, or indeed of
Jewish religious thinkers generally, that they did not value repentance. On
the contrary, they took it for granted that a truly penitent man was accepted
by God, and they made no objection to welcoming a "sinner" into their
company if he had shown genuine signs of repentance. But it was essential
that the sinner should take the initiative: he must first repent, and only then
could he be "welcomed", either by God or by his fellow-men. There was no
question of having anything to do with him until he showed signs of renouncing his old ways. Jesus' offence consisted in not waiting for these signs.

On this occasion, Jesus justified his initiative with a group of parables (the
first of which occurs also in Matthew 18.12–14, but with a quite different
point). Luke, compared with Matthew, dwells a little more on the moment
of finding: the shepherd lifts the sheep **on to his shoulders** (the only way 5
of carrying an injured or exhausted animal), the woman (and also, less
appropriately, the shepherd) invites friends and neighbours in to celebrate

8 the find—she is evidently very poor, for the value of the **ten silver pieces** (Luke gives them the name of the equivalent Greek coins, *drachmas*) only amounts to a pound by NEB values. All the emphasis is on the joy which follows finding what was lost; and if it is true that the sinner is also someone who is "lost", it is legitimate to read off from these simple illustrations

7 something of the **joy in heaven over one sinner who repents.** It follows that repentance is not (as the Pharisees would probably have put it) just a way of making amends for past misdeeds and rejoining the ranks of the just. It belongs to a different order of things altogether.

11-32   The third parable (for which "The Prodigal Son" is perhaps not the best title, since all the emphasis is on the behaviour of the father) illustrates the same point, but takes it a great deal further. The opening reflects actual conditions in Palestine. A father could either bequeath his property in his will (in which case it was laid down by law how he must divide it between his heirs), or else make a gift of it before he died, in which case he was free to dispose of it as he wished, but was entitled to the produce or the interest until his death. The younger son's request was quite normal: the main part of the property would in any case go to his elder brother, and he could expect

13 to do better by turning **his share into cash**[a] and setting himself up in business among the Jews of the Dispersion in some foreign city, than by trying to live on a small-holding in the over-populated farmland of Palestine.

14 However, his taste for **reckless living**, combined with **a severe famine** (which would have sent up the price of food) soon brought him to total poverty. He hired himself out to a gentile employer (and minding pigs would have been a job particularly repugnant to a Jew), but even so his wages were not sufficient to buy himself food (at least in famine conditions), and he

16 would have been content even with the pauper's diet of carob-tree pods— had he been able to get them, but they were jealously guarded for the pigs. In despair, he decided to return home.

    So far, the story is a typical rake's progress. But the reaction of the father

20 is new and arresting. **He ran to meet him**—which was very much beneath the dignity of the head of a family—and instead of listening to his son's

22 request or testing his penitence, he invested him in the **robe** reserved for an honoured guest, and showed, with the gift of **ring** and **shoes**, how far he was

17 from treating the prodigal as one of his **paid servants.** The welcome, the presents, the feast were all tokens of his joy at finding one who was lost. The story, thus far, is a humanly convincing example of that same joy which is the point of the preceding two parables. But, if it is legitimate to read off from it a general lesson about the nature of God's forgiveness (and it is irresistible to do so, since it yields such riches in the process), one point in particular seems relevant to Jesus' controversy with his opponents. They laid

[a] This is probably, but not certainly, what the Greek phrase means. Older versions have "gathered all he had together", which is also possible.

down all kinds of conditions (genuineness, lastingness, a will to make repara-
tion, etc.) which a sinner's repentance had to fulfil if it were to be accepted.
But in the parable, it was sufficient for the son simply to return to his father.
Similarly, it was not necessary for the "sinners" with whom Jesus consorted
to prove their penitence: it was sufficient that they sought his company.

This already provided part of the answer to those who were criticizing
Jesus for consorting with sinners. But the parable goes on. From the point
of view of strict fairness, the elder son had a genuine grievance: while he
had **slaved** for years to work his father's estate, and had gone on working it 29
for his father's benefit even after it had become legally his own, his brother,
by squandering his inheritance, had deprived his father of the interest due
to him. Surely, therefore, the rewards given to the younger brother were
inappropriate and unfair. Once again, the father acted with striking generosity.
Instead of waiting until his elder son approached him (as fitted his dignity),
he **came out and pleaded with him.** "**Everything I have is yours**". 29, 31
This was technically true: the original gift of the entire property to the elder
son was a sign of much greater esteem than the killing of the fatted calf for
the younger. But the main force of the appeal depended, not on technicali-
ties, but on humanity: "**How could we help celebrating this happy** 32
day?" Jesus' strongest argument against his critics likewise depended, not
on technical definitions of repentance, but on those ultimate principles of
humanity which are a sure guide to the nature of God's dealings with men.

'**There was a rich man who had a steward**'. The situation must have 16. 1
been a common one in Palestine, where there were many large estates, owned
by absentee landlords, and administered by a **steward**. But the story itself
is puzzling. On the face of it, the steward's action was dishonest and unscrupulous, and we are astonished to read at the end that **the master** 8
applauded the dishonest steward. It is true that this last sentence is
ambiguous. The Greek words for **the master** could also mean "the Lord".
The sentence might therefore be, not a continuation of the story, but a
comment on it by Luke: "Jesus applauded the dishonest steward". But this
does not make the matter any easier. Why should Jesus, any more than the
rich man in the parable, have **applauded** a blatant case of dishonesty?

However, the situation presupposed in the parable may not be quite what
it seems at first sight. The steward had been accused of **squandering the** 1
property. What does this mean? Simply helping himself to more than his
due from the revenues would hardly have constituted **squandering**—the
word is that used of the younger son of the previous parable who 'squan-
dered' his whole fortune in reckless living. More likely, the steward had been
trying to enrich himself by lending out at a high rate of interest large sums
from his master's fortune, to the detriment of the proper management of the
estate. In Jewish circles, this was strictly illegal (for usury was forbidden);
but there were many ways round this prohibition, and a steward who behaved

8 in this way, though he would certainly be morally **dishonest,** might nevertheless succeed in keeping on the right side of the law. It is true that there is
1 not a word in this parable to say that this was the kind of **squandering**
involved;[a] but if we suppose that it was, then the negotiations with the
debtors become more plausible. The amount they owed was very large—too
large, surely to represent arrears of rent payable by tenants to a landlord;
and the steward is hardly to be imagined as having paid large sums on account
to merchants who had then failed to honour their contracts (for this was not
the usual way of doing business and could anyway hardly be described as
squandering). On the other hand, if the debtors were borrowers, the
situation immediately becomes intelligible. Repayment in kind was regular
practice (and incidentally provided many loopholes for avoiding the technical
prohibition of usury). The difference between a thousand and eight hundred
bushels of wheat represents interest at twenty-five per cent (a normal rate),
and the difference between a thousand and five hundred gallons of olive oil
represents interest at one hundred per cent, which sounds very high, but is
not without parallel in antiquity, since oil was a much riskier commodity
than wheat. This interest the steward had hoped to receive as personal
profit; the rest represented what had to be repaid to his master. But in view
of his imminent dismissal, he decided to forgo the profit, and by voluntarily
liquidating the original contracts and replacing them with bare statements
of the amount of the original loan, he earned the gratitude of the debtors and
the approbation of society at large—for easing or remitting the repayment
of a loan was regarded by the Jews as a singularly meritorious act.

8   **The master applauded the dishonest steward for acting so astutely.**
If this explanation of the parable is on the right lines, the comment becomes
intelligible. The master had not been cheated as a result of the steward's hasty
transactions. On the contrary, the steward, seeing where his true interests
lay, had abandoned his own chances of immediate profit, and the master had
quickly recovered his capital. The steward offered a commendable example
of radical action in the face of a crisis. This may well have been the point
Jesus wished to make, here as elsewhere. Judgement was imminent: no time
must be lost in remitting debts, forgiving offences, and preparing oneself
for the kingdom of God.

    Nevertheless, in the form in which it has come down to us, the parable is
exceedingly obscure. A great many details have to be read into it in order
to make it yield an acceptable sense. What did Luke think was the moral?

    He appears to offer no less than three, but two of these are unfortunately
8 as obscure as the story itself. (i) '**The worldly are more astute than the
other-worldly in dealing with their own kind**'. The steward was certainly **astute** (this is strongly emphasized in the parable); but if this saying

[a] Though the word used for "squandering" is the same as that translated 'scattered' in
Matthew 25.24, and there it does seem to carry the meaning, "lending out for interest".

is to be seen as anything more than a cheap comment on unpractical pietists, it is necessary to find something admirable in his astuteness. If in fact it consisted of the praiseworthy act of freely remitting debts then, even if his motives were astute and self-regarding, his conduct could be held up as an example to Christians who, with their infinitely more altruistic ideals, could hardly afford to be less generous than a **dishonest steward**. But does **the other-worldly** mean Christians? Literally, the phrase means "the sons of light", which is as unusual an expression for religious people as **the worldly** (literally, "the sons of this age") is usual for the irreligious. It appears to be a phrase which some religious sects (if we may judge from the Dead Sea Scrolls) liked to use of their own members. It is quite likely that at some stage the Christian community began to use similar language about itself. (ii) **'Use your worldly wealth to win friends for yourselves'**. This again 9 clearly refers back to the parable. The steward had "made friends" by his prompt action (verse 4). Christians are to do the same, though in a more lasting sense, in that instead of procuring for themselves hospitable homes on earth they are to obtain **an eternal home** in heaven. But how is **worldly wealth** to be used for this purpose? If the steward of the parable was dishonest all along the line, it is hard to draw any moral; but if he genuinely remitted debts to his own disadvantage, then again he can serve as an example to Christians, who are to secure their ultimate reward by renouncing every kind of monetary gain. (The phrase translated **worldly wealth** is a curious one, and means literally "unrighteous mammon". This may correspond to a Hebrew expression meaning any kind of financial profit which, strictly speaking, was forbidden under the Law.) (iii) **'The man who can be** 10 **trusted in little things can be trusted also in great'**. This group of 10–12 sayings simply commends trustworthiness, and would be a more appropriate comment on the parable of the pounds (19.11–27) than on this one; but perhaps it also serves here as a warning against taking the dishonest steward as an example of the wrong kind of "astuteness".

There is no obvious connection between the sayings which follow, and all 13–18 except one of them have parallels in different parts of Matthew or Mark: verse 13 = Matthew 6.24, verse 16 = Matthew 11.12–13, verse 17 = Matthew 5.18, verse 18 = Mark 10.11–12 (and, with a significant variation, Matthew 5.32). Verses 14–15 however are found only in Luke. **The Pharisees, who** 14 **loved money**. It is unlikely that the Pharisees as a class were wealthy; indeed we know of several learned Pharisees who were very poor. But there were certainly some who were not above turning their reputation for sound learning to financial advantage, and even the strictest of them found means of accommodating their interpretation of the law to the necessity of commercial transactions. Much as they praised the virtue of alms-giving, they regarded it as positively undesirable to impoverish oneself by too much generosity, and their attitude to money was a great deal less radical than that of Jesus. Jesus' criticism of them here is a variation of his usual attack on their "hypocrisy". Their outward show of strict observance is a cloak, not just for a lack of humanity, but for a preoccupation with worldly gain. The social position they achieve by these means puts them in the category of those who must expect a reversal of fortune: as it is expressed in Mary's song at the beginning of the gospel (1.51), 'the arrogant of heart and mind God

15 has put to rout'. Or, still more drastically, 'What sets itself up to be admired by men is detestable in the sight of God'.

19 'There was once a rich man'—unnamed, like most of the characters in the parables (though in the course of time he has acquired a name, Dives, which is simply the Latin for "rich man"). Surprisingly, the poor man has

20 a name: Lazarus (the Greek form of a common Jewish name, Eleazar). The contrast is carefully drawn: purple and fine linen and daily feasting were marks of the greatest luxury, while the beggar was a cripple (he lay) who had no one even to keep the dogs from trying to slake their thirst by licking his sores (as they would in a dry summer, when water was far too precious

21 to give to dogs). It is true that it was unusual not to allow beggars the scraps from the table, but nothing is said by way of moral judgement on either the rich man or Lazarus. All we are told is that one was very rich, the other very poor. In the next scene the contrast is equally vivid, though the setting is drawn from contemporary Jewish folklore and popular religion. Whatever might be said in theory about a general resurrection and a universal Last Judgement, ordinary people in Palestine certainly believed (as ordinary people have always believed in many parts of the world) that immediately after death some go to heaven and some go to hell. Clearly Jesus was not using the parable as an opportunity to give new teaching about the after-life.

22 On the contrary, the angels escorting Lazarus, the presence of Abraham
24 in heaven, the fire in hell, and the glimpse given to the damned of the better lot they might have had, were all standard features of popular Jewish belief. Again there is no moralizing. It is a simple contrast; one is very happy, the other very unhappy, not because of their virtues and vices, but because of a necessary reversal of fortunes. Thus far, the parable is a pictorial statement of that great change in values proclaimed in Jesus' beatitudes: 'How blest are you who now go hungry; your hunger shall be satisfied' (Luke 6.21); 'how blest are the sorrowful; they shall find consolation' (Matthew 5.4).

'Blest are you who are in need', 'Alas for you who are rich' (Luke 6.20, 24). The message is stark and clear (especially in Luke's gospel). But can nothing be done, cannot the rich still be saved? Certainly not after death: it will be

26 too late then, there is a great chasm fixed. But suppose a messenger were sent to the rich who are still alive, to warn them? The parable goes on to deny even this possibility—and here it seems to point to the very heart of Jesus' understanding of himself and the people among whom he worked.

29 'They have Moses and the prophets'. The Jews were uniquely privileged

in having, in the Old Testament, an authoritative guide to the conduct required of them by God. But even to this they could be indifferent—they "hear and hear but understand nothing" in the words of Isaiah quoted by Jesus on another occasion (Mark 4.12)—so much so that they could still tolerate extremes of riches and poverty in their own society. No further prompting by God would help these "children of Abraham" (like the rich man of the parable) to live worthily of their inheritance, not even if someone should rise from the dead—and the parable ends with tantalizing allusions 31 to another Lazarus who did "rise from the dead" (John 11—did Luke know of this?), and to Jesus himself, whose own resurrection at first aroused incredulity and even mockery (Acts 17.32).

'Causes of stumbling are bound to arise'. The phrase is barely English, 17. 1 and in the original it is barely Greek. The reason is that causes of stumbling is an expression so loaded with meaning from the Old Testament that it almost serves as shorthand for a number of distinctive Jewish beliefs. The underlying metaphor is of a snare into which one falls or an obstacle over which one stumbles. To us, the metaphor suggests the kind of things which cause accidents. But the Hebrews seldom thought of things happening by accident: either someone had deliberately laid a snare, or else it was intended by God that a person should be tripped. And so the metaphor was used of all sorts of catastrophes or dangers which God laid in the path of his people or of an individual in order to test or to punish them (Isaiah 8.14; Jeremiah 6.21; Ezekiel 3.20). Jesus' followers would not be immune from such trials: there would be persecutions from outside and heresy and schism from within. Such things were bound to arise. But this would be no excuse for any member of the community willingly precipitating further trials by thoughtless or malicious behaviour.

By the little ones who must not be made to stumble, Jesus may originally 2 have meant small children: he was exceptionally interested in them for a religious teacher of his time. Children must always have been following him about, as they still do any unusual person in the east; and Jesus took notice of them instead of ignoring them. But the church was more interested in its own "little ones", the weaker brethren who might stumble over the radical implications of Jesus' teaching; and this is probably how Luke (like Matthew, 18.6) understood the phrase here.

'If your brother wrongs you'. Compare Matthew 18.15, 21–2, where the 3 same rule is given as part of the order of the church. Seven times in a day is 4 equivalent to Matthew's 'seventy times seven'—an unlimited number of times.

The apostles (seldom so called in the gospels, see above on 6.13) said 5 to the Lord—a typically Lucan introduction to a saying also recorded in Mark (11.23) and Matthew (17.20). Luke replaces 'mountain' by mulberry- 6 tree, we do not know why.

7   'Suppose one of you has a servant'. The application of this little parable is built into it from the start. It was a common idiom of religious speech to call oneself "God's servant", and what was true of the relationship of master and servant could be seen to be true, in important respects, of that between God and man. If the relationship described in the parable sounds austere, it must be remembered that the word **servant** meant literally a slave. The master here is of modest means, having only one slave both to work on his farm and to look after the house. He is under no obligation to put his slave's comfort before his own. Equally, the slave is in no position

10   to take credit[a] for completing his usual routine. '**So with you: when you have carried out all your orders**'. Men's **orders** from God were the detailed commands and prohibitions of the Law of Moses. There were many of Jesus' contemporaries who believed they "deserved credit" for their meticulous observance of them, and failed to realize that the demands of God upon man are far more fundamental than can be expressed in any set of **orders**.

11   **He was travelling through the borderlands of Samaria and Galilee.** On the map this makes little sense (and the translation **through the borderlands** is itself a simplification of a puzzling Greek phrase). By now—since Jesus' "journey" has lasted through eight chapters—he should have left Galilee far behind. But Luke may have had a rather different picture of the geography and imagined that much of Jesus' journey lay close to the Samaritan frontier (see above, p. 250). If so, he would have seen nothing inappropriate in placing a story involving a Samaritan at this stage in the journey.

12   **Ten men with leprosy.** On the disease and its social consequences, see above on Mark 1.40–5. The lepers were necessarily on the edge of the village, and **stood some way off** to avoid contact. Jesus' reply to their appeal

14   took the unexpected form of a command to '**go and show yourselves to the priests**'. The command occurs in Mark's story (1.44) of the cleansing of a single leper, and we can see the point of it from Jesus' point of view: he did not wish to come into conflict with the priests by trespassing on their prerogatives. But, in Luke's story, what sort of answer was it to the lepers' appeal? They must have known that, in their present state, they had no hope of being certified **clean** by a priest—otherwise they would have gone for examination long ago. Jesus' answer could only mean that, if they went now, they would be well enough by the time they arrived at the temple to be certified clean—which is just what happened. We can assume that nine of them were Jews, and had to go to Jerusalem for the purpose; but the tenth, being a Samaritan, must have gone to the ruins of the Samaritan temple on

15   Mount Gerizim in Samaria. Precisely when he **turned back** (whether before or after he had seen a priest) is not stated; nor is it clear exactly what the

[a] The translation, **deserve no credit**, is probably correct, though the usual meaning of the word is that given by older translations, "unprofitable".

others ought to have done. But these details probably did not trouble the narrator, who saw in the story a clear illustration of two points he had already made elsewhere: first, even a Samaritan can be an example to a Jew; secondly, a man's faith is more important than the race he belongs to. 19

The Pharisees asked him, 'When will the kingdom of God come?' 20 Given the earnest expectation for a new order of things which (at least in Palestine) ran right through the Jewish religion, and given the fact that this new order was expected to come, not by gradual evolution, but by a sudden act of God, the question was an obvious one to put to Jesus, and was asked by friends and enemies alike. When asked by the Pharisees, the question may have been intended to elicit a reply which (if it were at all naïve or literal) would bring Jesus into ridicule; but Jesus avoided the trap. **'You cannot tell by observation'**—the word suggests particularly astrological observation, calculations from the conjunctions of stars with historical events—and Jesus showed that he agreed with all those learned and responsible Jews who tried to discourage this kind of fanciful speculation about the future. **'There will be no saying, "Look, here it is!"'**, as if it were 21 likely to be something doubtful and ambiguous, needing careful inspection to check its authenticity. Jesus then went on to add a positive answer of his own to the question—but exactly what that answer was is obscured from us by the imprecise Greek in which it is recorded. **'The kingdom of God is among you'** (or within you, or within your grasp—see the footnote in NEB). Several meanings are possible—and it may be that the preposition in Jesus' own language was equally ambiguous, since Jewish scholars themselves debated what was meant by saying that God was "among them": did it mean, God saw that they were clothed and fed, or that God knew their innermost thoughts? Older translations of Jesus' saying have mainly preferred "within you". But this suggests an inner spiritual experience, which is something very different from what the Jews—and, it appears, Jesus—meant by the kingdom of God. Jesus seems to have talked of the kingdom both as a future consummation and as an already perceptible reality. Something of his new and rich understanding of the old Jewish phrase probably lurks in this difficult saying.

He said to the disciples. Luke changes the setting, even though the 22 subject is still the same: the culmination of history in the Last Judgement and the inauguration of a new age. Jesus projected himself into this drama in the rôle of the Son of Man; and Christians, therefore, looked forward to it as **one of the days of the Son of Man.** Perhaps, when Luke wrote, there was already a disappointed longing for this "day", and this saying seemed to offer an antidote; certainly there was for a long time a temptation to abandon ordinary occupations and **go running off in** 23 **pursuit** of anything which seemed to promise the advent of the new era.

There were sayings of Jesus to discourage this (compare Matthew 24.26–7); there were also sayings about the darker side of the destiny of the Son of Man which should have corrected a one-sided preoccupation with his ultimate glory (see above on Mark 8.31).

26 'As things were in Noah's days'. The rest of the chapter inculcates the
27–37 attitude of vigilance and readiness for immediate action which must be maintained in the face of what is to come. The sayings are almost all found (somewhat differently arranged) in Matthew 24. Luke adds to the example of Noah that of Lot (the two were often paired together—see 2 Peter 2.5–6 for
32 another example), and gives us the proverb, 'Remember Lot's wife'. The two biblical stories not only warn against neglecting the signs of the times. It is also fatal (doubtless in the Christian life in general, as well as at the last critical moment) to look back!

18. 1 He spoke to them in a parable. One of the characters in this little story is
6 called the unjust judge, and this has given its name to the parable. But it is important to see in what sense he was unjust. The setting was a small town.
3 A widow—which was a byword for someone reduced to poverty through no fault of her own—had been the victim of some fraud or sharp practice, and in order to recover her money she had to go to law. In such cases, this did not involve a formal sitting of a court; it was sufficient for the parties to agree upon a qualified lawyer to arbitrate between them. The little town, in any case, may have possessed only one such lawyer; if so, the widow's only hope of redress lay in persuading this lawyer to attend to her case. Now it was a fundamental principle of Jewish justice that a judge received no payment. There was therefore only a moral obligation for the lawyer to attend to all the cases brought before him. This particular lawyer was not
2 sensitive to his moral obligations—he cared nothing for God or man; possibly he waited until litigants brought him a present before he concerned himself with their affairs. But the widow, by again and again thrusting her papers in front of him, finally got her way.
6 The unjust judge, therefore, was not necessarily guilty of perverting justice; indeed it might be less misleading to call him "the unrighteous judge", [a] since it was his unreadiness to do his duty and hear cases brought before him which was reprehensible. The justice of the widow's claim is taken for granted; the point is the difficulty she had in getting it attended to. The application of the parable follows easily. Christians needed to have no doubts about the rightness of their cause; but, in the face of calumny and persecution, they longed for vindication. This was expected to take the form of a reversal of present values, a bringing to light of the things known

[a] This is an equally faithful translation of the original, which probably represents a Hebrew idiom, "judge belonging to the world of unrighteousness, the world of inadequate observance of the Law".

only to faith, and the visible establishment of the Christian community as the chosen people of God—in short, the end of the present order, the judgement, and the new age. Those things were taking longer to come than perhaps the earliest generation of Christians expected (a disappointment which may underlie the difficult phrase, **while he listens patiently to them**; an 7 alternative rendering is given in the NEB footnote—"while he delays to help them"—which would make this clearer). But they must **keep on praying** 1 for them. If even a neglectful human judge yielded at last to constant entreaties, how much more certainly would God **vindicate his chosen!** 6 But that moment of vindication would always involve judgement. Anyone who had lost faith (perhaps because of the delay) would have reason to fear it. '**When the Son of Man comes, will he find faith on earth?**' 8

And here is another parable that he told. The scene this time is set 9 in the main inner quadrangle of the temple at Jerusalem at the hour of the morning or evening sacrifice. At these two times in the day every Jew was bidden to pray, either in the synagogue or else wherever he happened to be; but if he was near by, he **went up to the temple** for the purpose, and 10 joined the crowd of those who were present at the sacrifice. The Pharisee's prayer probably sounded a great deal less objectionable then than it does to us now. He was not necessarily priding himself on his virtues; rather, he was thanking God for the privilege of leading a life which, both in public and in private, laid him open to no charge of rapacity, failure to observe the law, or adultery. For example: far from ever failing to observe the annual fast-day of the Jews, he followed the pious practice of the stricter groups and fasted **twice a week.** Far from ever failing to pay the necessary tithes on his agri- 12 cultural produce, he paid tithes on everything in his possession. In short, his way of life was that of a Pharisee, it was an example of one of the most sustained efforts any Jewish group had ever made to observe the law in every detail—and he thanked God for it: thanksgiving, it was said, was the most precious of all forms of prayer. The tax-gatherer, by contrast, was committed to a way of life which made any such prayer impossible for him. He lived by raising slightly more taxes from his fellow-citizens than he was bound to pay to the government, and the fundamental dishonesty inherent in his profession branded him, in the eyes of Jewish society, as one who was for ever "outside the law". It was beyond his power to make the kind of amends (say, giving away most of his profits) which would alone be regarded by his fellow-citizens as a sign of true repentance and allow him to be re-admitted to the society of the just. His prayer was despairing and simple—but not new: it echoed the opening of Psalm 51; and later in that psalm come the words, "A broken and humbled heart, O God, thou wilt not despise". Jesus' parable is a vivid illustration of that wonderful document of Hebrew spirituality. Luke says, **it was aimed at those who were sure of their own goodness and looked** 9 **down on everyone else.** Certainly, the Pharisees believed (and not only they) that their way of life assured them of salvation to a greater extent than that of any of their contemporaries; and this was one of the instances of human pretension which was destined to be exposed by that great reversal of values which Jesus proclaimed. In the words of a saying that occurs in a

14 number of different contexts, 'everyone who exalts himself will be humbled'.

15 **They even brought babies for him to touch.** At this point Luke returns to the order of events in Mark, and reproduces Mark's narrative

15–30 (10.13–31) with only a small amount of rewriting. The children who are brought to Jesus for his blessing become **babies** in Luke; and the 'rich man' of Mark's narrative (who is inferred by Matthew to be 'young') becomes a

18 **man of the ruling class,** which is logical enough: riches secure social position.

Challenge to Jerusalem

31 **'We are now going up to Jerusalem'.** After the long section of *Journeys and encounters* which, though Jerusalem was given at the outset as the ultimate destination, gave little feeling of actual progress southward, the narrative now begins to move again. As in Mark (10.33–4), the disciples are once more taken into Jesus' confidence about the impending destiny of the Son of Man. The rejection and humiliation of this figure, who was traditionally thought of as vindicated and glorified, was something the disciples found it hard to accept, and Mark makes no secret of their bewilderment. But Luke presents the matter more from the point of view of a church historian. The early church must have momentarily felt the same difficulty in reconciling the glorified Christ of their faith with the humiliated Jesus of their memory. How did they overcome it? They went back to the Old Testament and found evidence there (doubtless in such passages as Isaiah 53) that this was what had to happen: **all that was written by the prophets** had **come true for the Son of Man.** But the disciples did not yet realize this: the true interpretation of these prophecies was only revealed to them later (24.27). Meanwhile, their failure to grasp Jesus' prediction—a failure demonstrated by their subsequent conduct—could only be explained (as Luke also suggests,

34 9.45) as part of God's purpose: **its meaning was concealed from them.** Luke has omitted from Mark's account (10.46–52) the name of the beggar (Bartimaeus) and the word of Aramaic with which he addressed Jesus (*Rabbuni*), but in other respects he has followed Mark closely, except for adding a conclusion which he seems to have felt appropriate to a number of

43 Jesus' miracles, **And all the people gave praise.**

19. 1 **Entering Jericho.** The Jordan valley between the Lake of Tiberias and the Dead Sea consists of a long narrow plain which is for the most part

parched and treeless. But at Jericho, which lies toward the southern end of this plain close to the mountains of Judaea, there is a spring which irrigates the fields and orchards and makes the town a veritable oasis in the desert. In the time of Jesus it was a prosperous city, rich in date-palms and balsam trees, and the home of a well-to-do Jewish community. It was also the principal eastern frontier town of Judaea; Herod the Great had built a winter palace there, and it had a large traffic of merchants and travellers. **There was** 2 **a man there named Zacchaeus.** This is the Greek form of a common Jewish name, Zakkai. The man was a Jew, a wealthy **superintendent of taxes.** This does not mean a civil servant in the employment of the government; for the government did not collect its own taxes, but offered the job to any firm of tax-collectors which could offer to return the highest revenue from a given area. These firms made their money, partly by exacting a slightly higher rate of taxation than they returned to the government, partly by investing the revenues in business interests before paying over the total assessment. Zacchaeus is to be imagined as the head of one of these companies. In this profession he had enriched himself; but he had also incurred social disapproval, since the principles upon which tax-collectors made their living could be regarded as extortionate and usurious, and as therefore incompatible with Jewish law. In the eyes of strict Jews, at least, such a man was a **sinner,** and excluded from the society of those who maintained 8 a careful observance of the law. Hence the **general murmur of disapproval** 7 when Jesus deliberately sought lodging with him. But on this occasion Jesus' action was spectacularly vindicated. It was always possible for a tax-collector to repent and rejoin the society of the righteous, so long as he made restitution to all from whom he had exacted more than was due. It was recognized that it was probably impossible for him to identify and repay more than a small number of those whose taxes he had collected, and it was considered adequate if he made up the rest by making a proportionate contribution to the public good. The result of Jesus' visit was that Zacchaeus resolved to do all this—and more. He **stood there**—the word suggests that he was making 8 a public declaration—and promised to give away half his possessions (which was more than would have been considered adequate), and to anyone who could prove he had been **cheated** in the tax collection to pay back the difference, not merely plus twenty per cent (as the Jewish Law required, Leviticus 6.1), but plus 400 per cent. After this, no one could call Zacchaeus **a sinner** again; he and his family would recover their full rights in the 7 Jewish community—'**Salvation has come to this house today**'. But this 9 had happened because Jesus, instead of shunning him as his pious contemporaries did, had deliberately sought his company.

They thought the reign of God might dawn at any moment. This 11 is Luke's introduction to a parable which, in its main features, is familiar from Matthew's gospel (25.14–30), where it is told as an allegory of the Last

Judgement. Whatever people thought of Jesus, there was inevitably a temptation to see in one who gave such notable signs of miraculous power the harbinger of that new age—**the reign of God**—which the majority of Jews earnestly awaited; and Jesus' arrival at the Holy City must have seemed to many a likely moment for the promised new age to begin. Such crude expectations were politically dangerous to Jesus in his lifetime; but they lived on after his death and resurrection, and we know (from the letters of Paul, for example) that Christian leaders had strenuously to discourage those who tried to contract out of all the normal responsibilities of daily life because **they thought the reign of God might dawn at any moment.** The question, at any rate, was still very much alive in Luke's day, and by subtly emphasizing certain details in the parable (the **long journey abroad** of the king, the necessity to be **trustworthy in a very small matter**), Luke made the parable teach a lesson of patience and responsible social conduct. But Luke's version also has some original features which suggest that the parable had already had a complicated history before it came into his hands. It now contains a by-plot; the capitalist who starts his servants in business is also **a man of noble birth** who has hopes of being **appointed king.** This supplies the destination of his **journey.** All "kings" in Palestine held their kingdoms by appointment of the Roman Emperor; and in fact one of Herod the Great's sons, Archelaus, acquired his right to rule over Judaea by making the journey to Rome in circumstances exactly similar to those described here, so much so that Jesus' story may well be an allusion to this actual event (4 B.C.). But what has this political episode to do with the story of the three servants? On the face of it, very little; indeed the two fit together so badly that it seems likely that (as in Matthew 22.1–10) what were originally two separate stories have somehow been combined into one. Nevertheless, the political setting of the by-plot has influenced the telling of the main story; for the capitalist is now also a king, and is able to reward his servants, not just with more capital and more responsibility, but with governorships over cities. And this introduces a new point into the story: these glittering rewards seem out of all proportion to the very modest commercial successes of the servants, all the more so since the sizeable capital sums mentioned by Matthew ('talents') appear in Luke as the almost unworkably small assets of a few pounds. [a] This makes the detail of giving the third servant's capital to the first servant seem slightly grotesque—he had by now become a provincial governor! Hence, perhaps, the protest, **"he has ten already".** But it considerably heightens the point which Luke saw in the parable: your attention now to small and humble things will gain you a reward out of all proportion in the kingdom of God. One further detail sharpens the point. In Matthew,

[a] The NEB translators seem to have abandoned their own principles here. The Greek *mina* (which is the sum in the text) was worth 100 *denarii*, and the NEB normally makes ten denarii equivalent to a modern pound. The servants had the equivalent of roughly ten pounds sterling to trade with.

the third servant buried his money in the ground, which was regarded as the most prudent way of keeping it safe. But here, he put it away **in a handker-** 20 **chief**, which was improvident and dangerous. At Luke's hands he has become a typical example of one who is definitely not **trustworthy in a very** 17 **small matter**.

The **ascent to Jerusalem** from Jericho was a walk of some twenty miles up 28 a road which climbed nearly four thousand feet from the plain to the crest of the Mount of Olives. Luke follows Mark in mentioning **Bethphage and** 29 **Bethany** (which lay just off the road to the south), but prefers an alternative (and possibly more exact) name for the Mount of Olives, **the hill called** "olive plantation" (which in Latin is *olivetum*, hence **Olivet**).

The details of the narrative of finding the colt follow Mark closely 29-35 (11.1-10). As in Mark, the episode is doubtless meant to be understood as a miraculous confirmation of Jesus' authority, not as a piece of prior organization. But Luke gives Jesus' ride a slightly different interpretation. The branches and greenery, with their Jewish festival associations, disappear; instead, the disciples throw their cloaks on the ground in front of Jesus, which is the gesture of acclaiming a king. The Zechariah prophecy, "Here is your king, who comes to you in gentleness, riding on an ass", which is implicit in Mark's account and is expressly quoted in Matthew, is no more than distantly suggested here; but the word **king** is deliberately introduced 38 into the cry of the disciples (who take the place of the crowds in the other versions). Their cry, as in the other accounts, uses the words of Psalm 118.25-6. But Luke has made it sound somewhat less Jewish, omitting the Hebrew word Hosanna, and adding words reminiscent of the angels' song at Jesus' birth. Jesus' entry thus becomes, no longer an uncertain recognition by the crowds of the nearness of the Messiah, but a proclamation by Jesus' own disciples that he is a divinely commissioned king. And Jesus accepts the proclamation. Using a familiar proverb, he tells those who question his right to the title, 'If my disciples keep silence the stones will shout 40 aloud'.

As soon as the procession had come over the saddle of the Mount of Olives the whole city of Jerusalem would have appeared before their eyes, spread out on the opposite side of the valley, with the immense and magnificent buildings of the temple in the foreground and Herod's citadel commanding the city from its highest point behind. According to popular etymology, the name Jerusalem meant "vision of peace". In the manner of a prophet, 41-4 Jesus based his lament over the city upon the name itself and, foreseeing the inevitable course which events were taking and which his own intervention would do nothing to deflect, he prophesied, not peace, but siege and destruction. By the time Luke wrote, these things had in fact taken place (A.D. 70); but the details of Jesus' prophecy have not necessarily been rewritten in the light of subsequent history. They can all be found in the Old Testament (see especially Isaiah 37.33; Psalm 137.9; and the description of Nebuchadrez-zar's siege of Jerusalem in Jeremiah 52); they were already conventional terms for describing a besieged and conquered city. There is no reason to doubt that Jesus foresaw such a fate coming upon Jerusalem as clearly as Isaiah had before him. It must indeed have been clear to any man of vision that the increasing turbulence of Jewish nationalist groups under the Roman administration could only lead to disaster. Nothing short of a change of 44 heart could avert it. The moment—God's moment—for such a change of heart had arrived in the person of Jesus. But the opportunity had been, and would be, rejected.

45 **Then he went into the temple and began driving out the traders.** The episode, told in full by Mark (11.15–19) and Matthew (21.12–13), is no more than briefly summarized by Luke, and is also detached from Mark's strict chronological scheme; for whereas, in Mark, it is placed in the last week in Jesus' life, in Luke it forms only the beginning of a substantial 47 period of activity in Jerusalem: **Day by day he taught in the temple.**

20. 1 **One day.** The question about Jesus' authority, which in Mark (11.20–5) follows close upon his violent action in the temple, is recorded by Luke as having been put to him in the course of his daily teaching, and so becomes a 2 question specifically about his authority as a teacher. '**Acting like this**' must mean, "setting yourself up as a qualified expounder of Scripture". The only authority his questioners were prepared to recognize was that which they conferred themselves; but Jesus was in effect questioning all their pre-suppositions when he returned their challenge with reference to John the Baptist: John had received no **authority** from them to baptize; was his activity therefore invalid?

9–16 The parable of the vineyard is told very much as in Mark (12.1–12), and Luke's only changes (such as the reduction of the number of servants to one each time) are signs of literary artistry rather than of any different under-standing of the story. But there can be little doubt that in the son of the story he saw Jesus himself. The slight alteration (made also by Matthew) that 15 the son was **flung out of the vineyard** before being killed is perhaps deliberately intended to suggest Jesus' crucifixion outside Jerusalem; and the two texts which follow the parable, though they have no very clear application to the story, have much to say about the destiny of the Son of 17 God. "**The stone which the builders rejected has become the main corner-stone**" (Psalm 118.22) was originally an image for the miraculous restoration by God of the fortunes of any righteous man who had seemed to his enemies ruined and God-forsaken, and it was an image which the early church eagerly added to the complex series of building metaphors with which it strove to express the idea of the Christian community as God's new temple. But here it expresses a straightforward claim that Jesus, though now to be rejected and killed, will subsequently be vindicated and glorified. The continuation (found only in Luke), 'Any man who falls on that stone will 18 be dashed to pieces' is not a logical sequel, but another stone-saying which Luke felt it appropriate to insert at this point. It is not an exact quotation: the idea, and some of the wording, is drawn from Daniel 2.34—where a great stone smashes an idolatrous statue—with possibly also a hint of Isaiah 8.14 (the "rock of stumbling"). Later Jewish scholars interpreted the Daniel passage as a prophecy about the Messiah, and this interpretation may have been current in Jesus' time. But in any case, in its context here it clearly expresses the reverse side of the Son's coming glorification: all who do not accept him now will then experience, not the thrill of his glory, but the severity of his judgement.

The following sections follow Mark (12.13–44) very closely. Luke, like 19-21. 4 Matthew, has simply added a few narrator's touches in order to keep the action moving. In particular, he connects the question about paying taxes with one of the accusations actually made against Jesus later on (23.2). One point of detail is corrected. Jesus' answer to the Sadducees in Mark 12.25 ('When they rise from the dead, men and women do not marry; they are like angels in heaven') could conceivably have been misunderstood as a promise of heaven to everyone, good and bad, without distinction. Luke removes the ambiguity: Jesus was talking only of **those who have been judged worthy** 35 **of a place in the other world.**

Some people were talking about the temple. The new temple, begun 5 by Herod the Great in 20 B.C., was still not entirely completed; but it was already one of the most spectacular pieces of architecture in the ancient world. Like the great pagan temples which could be seen everywhere in the Roman Empire, the temple building itself had a façade of brilliant white marble, and its appearance was enriched by **votive offerings,** among which was a great golden vine set up over the door by Herod the Great himself. It is these features, which would have been of a kind familiar to any Greek reader, rather than the exceptional size of the masonry (which only those who had seen it could appreciate) that Luke (unlike Mark) singles out for mention.

The same concern to give, for his Greek readers, a less alien character to a discourse which in Mark (chapter 13) is expressed in a thoroughly Jewish idiom, accounts for some of the detailed alterations which Luke has made in this chapter. But there are also some more significant changes. It is possible that Luke was combining the material in Mark with some other source; but at the same time certain deliberate touches which he gave to the discourse show that he had an editorial policy of his own. He wrote his gospel a decade or two later than Mark, and the church, though still firmly believing in the impending end of the world, had nevertheless had to revise its idea of the course which history was going to follow. In Mark, the disciples' question ('When will this happen?') was elicited by Jesus' startling prophecy that the massive temple buildings were to be totally destroyed; and Jesus answered that all this would take place within their own generation, but that it must be understood in a wider context of world history: it would be no isolated catastrophe, but only one of the events in that turbulent period which must necessarily precede the end. These prophecies were spoken, and perhaps also written down by Mark, before Jerusalem was in fact taken and the temple desecrated and destroyed by the Roman army in A.D. 70. Naïve Christians, up to that time, may well have thought that the end of the world would follow immediately. But as the years passed, and history continued as before, a more sophisticated interpretation was placed on Jesus' words. A part of what he had prophesied—in particular the fall of Jerusalem and the persecution of Christians—had already been fulfilled; but the climax presaged by these events—the Last Judgement and the glorious coming of the Son of Man—still lay in the future. To be precise (and this appears to be

9 Luke's own formulation of the matter): '**These things are bound to happen first; but the end does not follow immediately**'.

This concern to present a slightly more sophisticated and less esoterically Jewish version of Jesus' discourse appears in a number of small details. The setting itself is different in Luke. In Mark, the discourse is a piece of private instruction given to four disciples as they sit on the Mount of Olives overlooking the temple; but here, it is a part of Jesus' general teaching given in

7 the temple itself. The audience are all those who call him '**Master**', and the words are clearly destined, in Luke's account, for the encouragement of subsequent generations of Christians. Those Christians have experience, not

8 of political agitators in Palestine who claimed to be the Messiah (**saying, "I am he"**), but of over-enthusiastic preachers in the church who unsettle their congregations by proclaiming "**The Day is upon us**" (a phrase which

12 occurs only in Luke). **Before all this happens**—that is to say, in the continuing experience of the church—those same Christians are to suffer persecution; and in their frequent appearances in law-courts (**synagogues** both in Palestine and elsewhere were constituted as judicial bodies) they are

14 **not to prepare their defence beforehand** (Luke uses the technical
16 language of a Greek court). '**Some of you will be put to death**': doubtless this had already happened when Luke wrote; but there was a saying of

18 Jesus, '**not a hair of your head shall be lost**'. How was this saying to be reconciled with the fact that Christians had already been martyred? Perhaps along the lines, suggested more clearly by the NEB translation than by the Greek text, that Jesus was talking, not of physical safety and physical death,

19 but of **true life** and true death.

20   '**But when you see Jerusalem encircled by armies.**' The historical

event around which Jesus' prophecies turned was the siege and destruction of Jerusalem. In Mark and Matthew it is referred to, in the conventionally cryptic language of apocalyptic writing, as the 'abomination of desolation'. Luke drops the convention, and makes Jesus refer explicitly to the siege. If Mark was written before the event, and Luke after it, this might seem a sufficient explanation of the difference between them. But Luke's procedure is by no means just to write an account of the siege as it happened and to put this into Jesus' mouth as a prophecy. He does not mention any of the things which (as we know from the contemporary historian Josephus) were particularly notable in the siege of Jerusalem; his language is entirely that which the Old Testament prophets used in their premonition of a similar event, and which, therefore, Jesus may well have used himself when prophesying the fate of Jerusalem. Moreover, the catastrophe is not merely prophesied, it is also interpreted, and interpreted in a fully Old Testament manner: it will be 'the time of retribution, when all that stands written is to be 22 fulfilled' (Deuteronomy 32.35; Hosea 9.7; Jeremiah 5.29); and its consequences will fulfil other oracles, Zechariah 12.3 (where the Septuagint Greek 24 version is much closer to the text of Luke than to its Hebrew original) and Isaiah 63.18. Only the last words are mysterious: until their day has run its course. The foreigners, it would seem, cannot be destined to trample on Jerusalem indefinitely. Jerusalem (even if only metaphorically) has still a part to play in the salvation of mankind—a hint, perhaps, of that view of history which is worked out by Paul in Romans 9–11.

'Portents will appear.' All the calamities described so far, however severe, 25 were the kind of thing which could happen in the ordinary course of history. Even the fall of Jerusalem must not be regarded as so unexampled that it was necessarily a sign of the imminence of the end (Luke, as a historian, and indeed many of his non-Palestinian readers, were doubtless able to keep a sense of proportion about it). Nothing, in short, which the church had experienced so far was to be interpreted as an immediate presage of the last things. These would be heralded by events of another order, by a serious break in the continuity and orderliness of the physical world. The portents to be looked for would be in the sky: if the heavenly bodies lost their regularity—and still more if the celestial powers which controlled those bodies 26 were shaken—then chaos must be expected on earth (for most people took a certain amount of astrology for granted: it was the regular movement of sun, moon and stars which guaranteed the regular succession of cause and effect on earth). The roar and surge of the sea, too, means more than an 25 ordinary storm. It was believed that only God's firm hand held the sea back from engulfing dry land; if this were relaxed, a great tidal wave would make men not know which way to turn. It would be signs such as these, and not the familiar vicissitudes of history, which must be read as heralding the coming of the Son of Man. But that coming would also put an end to the

28 tribulations of the church; therefore it would be the moment to **hold your heads high.**

The tone of this is comparatively optimistic: as soon as things get really severe, Christians may take courage because their **liberation is near.** But 31 it is still necessary to utter warnings. Although **the kingdom of God** (so Luke fills out the cryptic blank left by Mark and Matthew—see above on Mark 13.29) will follow the portents as surely as summer follows the budding 29 of the fig-tree **(or any other tree,** as Luke adds for the benefit of his European readers, see above on Mark 13.28), nevertheless in the meantime the apparent delay of these things must not lead either to scepticism or to 32 moral laxity. Jesus had authoritatively predicted that **the present generation** would **live to see it all,** and when it came it would not just be a cataclysm in Palestine (as the purely Jewish language in which Christians 35 tended to describe it might make others think) but **the whole world over.** 34 **Dissipation and drunkenness and worldly cares**—which Luke perhaps saw already taking hold of some Christian communities—would only dull the mind in the face of this prospect: in this state, men would fail to read the signs and would be caught **suddenly like a trap.** They must pray for strength, so that, whether or not they died before the end, they would at all 36 events win the right to **stand in the presence of the Son of Man.** Luke has written this final exhortation in such a way that it could serve as the end of a sermon to the church at any time, whether or not the "portents" had begun to appear. In a subtle way, he has adapted material that was originally all conditioned by expectation of an immediate end to the needs of a church which was beginning to accept the indefinite continuation of the present.

37 **His days were given to teaching in the temple.** Luke has not yet fallen in with the careful time-scheme propounded by Mark, but allows an indefinite number of days to elapse before *The final conflict.* To **spend the night on the hill called Olivet** does not necessarily imply camping out. The village of Bethany, where (according to Mark) Jesus lodged during these days, lay on the far slopes of the Mount of Olives.

The final conflict

22. 1 **Now the festival of Unleavened Bread, known as Passover, was approaching.** Luke's narrative of the Supper follows the outlines of Mark's version, but also diverges from it at a number of points. Either he was rewriting the passage somewhat freely, or else he was drawing on a different tradition. In either event, the resultant picture is a new one. The introduction seems aimed, as so often in Luke, at giving a slightly more consequential account of events. There is no attempt to offer a date (as in Mark): the

festival was simply **approaching**, and this gave urgency to the schemes of
the authorities to do away with Jesus. It is not quite clear from the other
gospel accounts how Judas' treachery in fact helped them; but Luke makes
this explicit: Judas' task was **to betray him . . . without collecting a** 6
crowd, at a time when Jerusalem was packed with pilgrims. He effectively
did so by leading the authorities to a spot where he knew that Jesus would go
for solitude during the night. He acted, Luke says, under the impulsion of
Satan. Whereas we might now be tempted to speculate on Judas' motives, 3
the first-century approach was less psychological: the events of *The final
conflict* were set in motion by supernatural powers, who used human beings
as the instruments of their purpose. *a*

The preparations for the Passover supper, on the afternoon **on which the** 7
Passover victim had to be slaughtered, are told almost exactly as in
Mark; and it follows that Luke, like Mark and Matthew, thought of this
supper as a celebration of the Passover meal, with its special dishes of bitter
herbs, roasted lamb and unleavened bread, and its recital of the miraculous
deliverance of Israel out of captivity. This meal was always a formal one. The
people in each group which shared it were bound together by table-fellow
ship, which they signified by partaking of the bread and the wine which
their host had blessed. Like Mark and Matthew again, Luke does not trouble
to mention all the normal details of this meal, but singles out certain words
and actions of Jesus which made this celebration exceptional; and it is
precisely in the words and actions which he reports that Luke shows how
differently he understands the occasion.

'**How I have longed to eat this Passover with you before my death!**' 15
The Greek, like the English, is ambiguous (see the footnote in NEB): did
Jesus eat with them or did he not? The phrase in the following verse, '**never** 16
again shall I eat it', sounds less ambiguous, and seems on the face of it to
settle the matter: Jesus shared this Passover with his disciples, but would
do so **never again**—a prophecy which occurs in similar terms in Matthew
and Mark. But the words **never again** occur only in certain manuscripts
(see the footnote); indeed the majority of the most authoritative manuscripts
omit the word in question, and give simply "I shall not". In itself, this
does not settle the matter. The text in the NEB may still be the right one.
But we must keep open the possibility that Jesus' saying was not a prophecy
at all but a vow of abstinence. He had longed to share this Passover with his
friends, but when it came to the point he may have refused to partake of it.
If so, his abstinence would certainly have been surprising. Not only do
Matthew and Mark give no hint of it *b* (the most they suggest is that after the
cup of blessing Jesus refused any further wine: the final "cup" of the formal

[*a*] Nevertheless, the story recorded in Matthew (26.14–16) may be intended to supply a
human explanation: Judas betrayed Jesus for money.
[*b*] Unless Jesus' refusal to accept wine just before the crucifixion was connected with
such a vow of abstinence (Mark 15.23).

meal was waived, not only for himself, but probably also for his disciples), but it would have been odd in itself on such a solemn occasion. [a] Could Luke really have meant this? In view of the ambiguities already mentioned, it is hard to be sure; but there is one further point which bears on it. Both Matthew and Mark lay some emphasis on the fact that Judas' act of betrayal was an instance of that basest form of treachery which consists in betraying someone with whom one has become intimate through the solidarity of table-fellowship: Jesus was betrayed by one who had 'eaten with him' (Mark 14.18; Matthew 26.23). But if Luke believed that Jesus himself ate nothing at this meal, he would have needed to make some change at this point; and sure enough we find that Judas is not identified as one who "ate

21 with" Jesus, but as one whose "hand was with his on the table"; there is no mention of eating together.

However this may be, the point serves to focus attention on one respect in which Luke's account is different from any other. Few words are spoken in

16, 18 explanation of the cup and the bread; but twice over Jesus uses the present meal to point forward to a greater reality, that of the **kingdom of God**, in

16 which the Old Passover ritual will find **its fulfilment**. The coming "Messianic Age"—that is to say, the paradise which (it was confidently expected) God would one day create for his elect by the agency of his Messiah—was often described in the imagery of a banquet; and the principal interpretation placed, in Luke's account, on the disciples' Passover supper is that it was the last that would be celebrated in the old manner. Soon—indeed very soon, if Jesus' sayings are intended to be taken as an indication of his intention to fast until this came about—it would be superseded by an experience which would reveal the coming of the kingdom of God. The purpose of this present meal was to foreshadow something greater in the near future.

19 Little else is added by way of interpretation except the words, '**This is my body**', which follow the blessing and breaking of the bread. The saying points in the direction of the longer versions in Mark and Matthew, where Jesus calls the bread his body because he sees himself as a victim about to be sacrificed, and his disciples can appropriate the benefits of this sacrifice by partaking of the victim's flesh. But Luke gives us no explicitly sacrificial imagery. The saying stands in complete isolation, and could just as well be interpreted as John interprets it in his gospel: Jesus gives men, in his body, the bread of eternal life.

It can now be seen how differently Luke presents the Passover supper. It is not merely that he reverses the order of the cup and the bread—the breaking of the bread had no fixed place in the Passover ritual, and his account can be fitted into its Passover context as well as the others. More

[a] It was for some centuries the practice of a part of the church to fast during the Jewish Passover as a religious act performed on behalf of the Jews. It has been suggested that this provides an explanation of Jesus' fast: he fasted on behalf of his own people.

striking is the fact that, instead of offering an interpretation of Jesus' words over the bread and the wine, Luke appears to concentrate on the significance of the whole meal as a foretaste of the greater realities of the coming kingdom of God. Only at the very end, with the words 'This is my body', does he come near the sacrificial imagery that occurs in Mark and Matthew. This is, in fact, the only vestige in his narrative of that understanding of the bread and wine which was adumbrated by Mark and Matthew, was slightly elaborated by Paul, and then became normative in the church at large.

Or so, at least, the matter stands as the main text runs in the NEB. But this is by no means the only, or even the best-attested, text. The majority of manuscripts give a longer text which brings the narrative much closer to that in Matthew and Mark, and also reproduces some details from Paul's account in 1 Corinthians 11.24–5. If this text is adopted, many of the peculiarities of Luke's account disappear: the usual order is restored of the cup following the bread, and an interpretation is given of Jesus' sayings over the bread and wine which corresponds closely with that in the other accounts. Even so, certain oddities remain, in particular the extra cup of wine shared by the disciples before the breaking of bread; and the critic is left with the very difficult task of explaining how the shorter version ever came into existence. Many believe that it is easier to explain the longer text as a subsequent amplification of an original shorter one than to explain why an original longer one should ever have been abbreviated; and it is for this reason that the NEB translators decided to relegate the longer version to a footnote.

Then a jealous dispute broke out. It is natural, in the light of sub- 24 sequent Christian devotion, to think of the breaking of bread and the sharing of a cup as the most important, if not the only important, features of this meal. But this was not Luke's view. Luke saw the Passover supper as the occasion for a farewell speech by Jesus to his disciples. Such farewell speeches were one of the conventional devices used by ancient historians; Luke himself provides another example in Paul's farewell to the elders of Ephesus (Acts 20.18–35), and the gospel of John considerably extends the convention in reporting a long discourse of Jesus to his disciples on the night before his death. For the content of the speech, Luke draws partly on sayings which are recorded in other gospels in different contexts. In particular, the question, **Who among them should rank highest,** was raised, according to Mark (10.41) and Matthew (20.24), as a result of the indiscreet request of the two sons of Zebedee on the way up to Jerusalem. The answer given by Jesus here is very similar to the one recorded in those accounts. A new detail is the word "Benefactors". Some of the Hellenistic kings of the east 25 liked to adopt this title (*Euergetēs*): by their wealth (however acquired) and by the peace they procured for their kingdoms (however precarious) they were pleased to characterize their rule (however tyrannical) as a benefaction to their subjects. The use of the word here is perhaps ironical; at any rate

26 the highest among Jesus' disciples must have no such pretensions. As in the versions in Mark (10.42–5) and Matthew (20.25–8), the image invoked
27 for this reversal of ordinary precedence is that of the one who sits at table or the servant who waits on him; but Jesus' final word, 'Yet here am I among you like a servant', though it rings true in a general sense, seems a little inappropriate in its setting here, where Jesus is to be imagined reclining at the head of the table. Did Luke know anything of the tradition in John's gospel that, before the meal began, Jesus washed his disciples' feet?
28   'You are the men who have stood firmly by me in my times of trial'. This surprising description stands in the place of the simple phrase, 'you my followers', in Matthew's version of the same saying (19.28). It is difficult to see to what moments in Jesus' life it can refer. The disciples were not present when he was "tempted" (the same word, in the Greek, as "tried") in the wilderness; and there are few occasions in the main part of Luke's narrative on which it could be said that the disciples distinguished themselves by their constancy in moments of trial. Moreover, in the "trials" that were about to begin, they first fell asleep when they might have supported Jesus in his suffering, and then forsook him altogether. The description, therefore, seems hardly appropriate—unless it is a reminiscence of some times of trial which happen not to be recorded in the gospels. On the other hand, after the resurrection, when the church was subjected to severe "trials", and Christians were notably "standing firm", the phrase will have sounded particularly apt; and since, in Luke's gospel, the disciples often stand as representative figures for Christians in general, we may suspect here a certain amount of reading back into the lifetime of Jesus the subsequent experience of the
29 church. 'And now I vest in you the kingship'. This translation is not quite accurate, and fails to evoke the associations present in the Greek word. In Matthew and Mark, Jesus calls the wine shared by the disciples at the Passover 'my blood of the covenant'. Luke says nothing of this, but it may be significant that he makes up for it by introducing the word "covenant" here. Jesus is not, at this moment, "vesting" his disciples with a kingship that will begin at once, but (to take the Greek word literally) "covenanting" or "bequeathing" to them a status which they will enjoy, not immediately, but after his death and resurrection. The symbol of this is one which has been
30 used a few verses before—the coming heavenly banquet; and, in slightly uneasy juxtaposition, [a] a further image is added belonging not to the festivities of the new age but to the Judgement which will inaugurate it. Exactly as in Matthew's version of the saying (19.28), the disciples are promised a
30 part to play at the coming Judgement: they will 'sit on thrones as judges'.
31   'Simon, Simon, take heed.' All the gospels record Jesus' prediction of Peter's threefold denial. Matthew and Mark place it a little later, on the

[a] Though feasting in full view of one's humiliated enemies was traditionally one of the rewards to which the righteous looked forward: Psalm 23.5.

walk out of the city to Gethsemane; Luke and John set it in the context of Jesus' farewell discourse. Luke, moreover, introduces it with some words which seem, like the rest of the speech, to look further forward into the future. Peter would indeed (by the time this gospel was written) have gone to prison and death; and there would certainly be times when it was the 33 responsibility of any church leader, in times of stress, to lend strength to 32 his brothers ("brother" became almost a technical term for "fellow-Christian"). Jesus could have foreseen these things. But in any case there was a severe test to be undergone in the near future. We have seen that, instead of speculating about Judas' motives in betraying Jesus, the tradition ascribed the cause of his action to Satan (22.3). In the same way, there is no psychological reflection in the gospels about the disciples' behaviour in forsaking Jesus at his arrest. This too happened through the intervention of Satan. But this time Satan was not permitted to destroy his instruments; he was merely given leave to put them to the test (as he was given leave to torment Job; 31 see Job 1.12; 2.6). The metaphor used is a strange one (though well in the manner of Jesus). Wheat is either sifted in a coarse sieve to separate it from the chaff and other rubbish (in which case the wheat falls through), or else, after threshing, in a fine sieve to separate it from smaller seeds and impurities (in which case the wheat remains in the sieve). Either way, it is tested and separated out. What the disciples were about to undergo was an equally rigorous test; but because of Jesus' prayer, and with the aid, apparently, of Peter's timely recovery (when you have come to yourself is only one of 32 the possible meanings of the Greek word), they would—unlike Judas—survive the ordeal.

The last section of Jesus' speech bears more closely still on what was 25–37 about to happen. All the gospels record that when Jesus was arrested in Gethsemane at least one of those who were with him was carrying a sword and attempted to use it (John's gospel actually gives the name of the slave who was wounded). This appeared to be incompatible with the instructions which Jesus had previously given to his followers (10.3–4), quite apart from being contrary to the spirit of Jesus' teaching, and from carrying with it the danger of trouble with the Roman authorities. Luke explains the circumstance by recording a saying of Jesus which seemed (if it was really spoken on this particular occasion) to authorize exceptional preparations. 'We have 38 two swords here'—certainly not enough for serious resistance, but enough (as perhaps Luke was the first to notice) to give fulfilment to an important 37 prophecy. One of the first clues which the early church found to the meaning of Jesus' person and work (a clue which may indeed have been given by Jesus himself) was the "suffering servant" of Isaiah 53. But one verse of that prophecy ran, "He was counted among the outlaws" (53.12). How could this be true of Jesus? In what sense could his disciples be regarded as "outside the law" or "transgressors of the law" (both nuances are present in the word translated **outlaws**)? A possible answer lay in the firm tradition that one of them had used a sword in Jesus' defence. From the strict Jewish point of view simply carrying a sword on the Sabbath (and so, *a fortiori*, on a festival such as the Passover) was probably forbidden, and from the Roman point of view its use in resisting arrest would have incurred severe penalties. If two of Jesus' disciples had swords on that particular night, this would have been **enough** to make the prophecy, "**he was counted among the outlaws**", seem to have come true.

39 **Then he went out and made his way as usual to the Mount of Olives.** Luke has a version of the following scene which is rather different from that of Matthew and Mark. The main elements are the same—the words of Jesus'

40 prayer, the disciples falling asleep, and the warning about '**the hour of testing**'. But all this is told more briefly, as if it were already well known to Luke's readers. Luke does not mention Gethsemane by name; he simply calls it **the place**, and suggests (rather to our surprise, since Matthew and Mark give the impression of a unique occasion) that Jesus made a habit of going

39 there (**as usual**)—which perhaps explains how Judas was able to find him. Further, the sequence of events in Mark's version is drastically shortened; only a summary of Jesus' hours of prayer is given, and much less is said about the disciples—indeed their falling asleep is made to seem less culpable: Luke

45 suggests they could not stay awake because they were **worn out by grief**.
But in return, Luke offers a description of Jesus at prayer which is quite

41 unparalleled. To pray, Jesus **knelt down**, an unusual attitude (Jews usually stood to pray, sometimes prostrated themselves, only occasionally knelt). He

43 received a vision of an **angel from heaven bringing him strength**: angels appear often enough in Luke's narrative, but nowhere in a rôle quite like this. Evidently the struggle was exceptionally severe (Luke probably thought of it as a struggle between Jesus and the devil rather than as a psychological struggle within Jesus himself), and despite the angel's help,

44 Jesus underwent **anguish of spirit**. The Greek word so translated is *agōnia*, from which our word "agony" is derived. It means, not so much an acute conflict of emotions, as an intense anxiety about what is going to happen. Jesus, we must suppose, was in suspense whether Satan would after all prevail, and Luke, by using the violent metaphor of "bloody sweat", [a] leaves his readers in no doubt of the reality of Jesus' agitation.

47 **While he was still speaking.** Once again, the main points of Mark's narrative are here, but are much more briefly told; on the other hand, Luke

48 adds one or two new details. The kiss, for Matthew and Mark, was simply

[a] Like clots of blood falling to the ground is a bizarre image (sweat can hardly be compared to bits of *congealed* blood) and, though accurate, is probably an over-pedantic translation. Luke doubtless meant "drops" of blood. The metaphor occurs in Greek literature from the time of Homer.

the signal pre-arranged between Judas and the armed band; here it is the
cue for outraged comment by Jesus. The momentary resistance of his 49
followers is placed, perhaps more logically, before the arrest of Jesus instead
of after it, and is followed by a miracle of healing (which only Luke mentions,
perhaps to indicate that Jesus did not intend his instructions about carrying 36
swords to have such bitter consequences). The flight of the disciples is not
mentioned (Luke seems to be avoiding anything which would discredit
them); on the other hand, point is given to Jesus' reply to his captors by
bringing on to the scene people of some responsibility—not just servants
and police, but some of the **chief priests** and **elders** themselves (represent- 52
ing the Sanhedrin), and **officers of the temple police** who were responsible
for public order in the temple area, and would have been the men to take
action had Jesus' conduct been in any way irresponsible when, **day after** 53
day, he was in the temple. 'But this is your moment—the hour when
darkness reigns'. It was no good arguing. It was not just that Jesus and his
followers were utterly outnumbered; behind the crowd of armed men were
supernatural forces of evil which were to be allowed a temporary victory.
Satan (euphemistically called **darkness**) had already claimed Judas (22.3),
though he was to be denied the other disciples (22.32); he still had more to
gain before the end.

They brought him to the High Priest's house. Luke arranges the 54
next events somewhat differently from Mark and Matthew. If we had only
his account we should not suspect that there were any legal proceedings
during the night. Jesus seems to have been brought to Caiaphas' house
simply for safe detention until the morning session, and this period of
waiting provided a natural context for the stories of Peter's denial and the
mocking of Jesus. **They lit a fire in the middle of the courtyard** for 55
warmth and light. Peter, sitting in the group gathered round it, was three
times identified. Jesus, meanwhile, was presumably held by the guards
somewhere in the courtyard where he could turn and look at Peter—which, 62
in Luke, is the climax of the episode, [a] and we are left to imagine Peter's
feelings. The mockery and insults heaped on Jesus are described as the
guards' way of passing the time—not, as in Mark and Matthew, as a deliberate test of Jesus' Messiahship.

At this point Luke's account is quite different from Mark's and is, in many
ways, more plausible. **When day broke.** The session of the Sanhedrin (of 66

[a] Most manuscripts add, after verse 61, "He went outside and wept bitterly". These
words are exactly as in Matthew's account, though different from Mark. If Luke wrote
them here, it would seem to follow that he was making use, not only of a source of his own
and of Mark, but also of Matthew. But on other grounds it is not very likely that he knew
Matthew's gospel, at least in its finished Greek form; and it is perhaps easier to assume, as
the NEB translators do, that the words crept into most manuscripts of Luke through
assimilation with Matthew.

which the elders of the nation, chief priests, and doctors of the law together made up the membership) is described as taking place, not at night, but at the more normal time of early morning—official business, even at Rome, and still more in the east, was done between dawn and midday—and for all Luke says may have been held, not in the High Priest's house, but in the usual assembly chamber of the Council. No witnesses were called, no evidence presented. The object of the session seems to have been simply to establish from Jesus' own lips whether he admitted to being the Messiah 70 and therefore (in that sense at least) the Son of God. Jesus' reply was 67 guarded, but for good reason. 'If I tell you . . . you will not believe me; and if I ask questions, you will not answer'. Jesus could not admit to being the Messiah without qualification; to give a truthful answer, he would need opportunity to explain and define, and this was being denied him. However, the judges took this reserve as tantamount to a confession.

As soon as the council was satisfied that Jesus admitted to being (at least in 23. 1 some sense) the Messiah, they brought him before Pilate: Jesus was a threat to public order, and it was the governor's responsibility to deal with him. In this, they were acting as proper citizens of a country governed by Rome. A Roman official did not normally institute proceedings against criminals and troublemakers, but received charges brought by a third party against them. Having heard the charges and questioned the witnesses and the accused, it was for him to decide upon the legal nature of the alleged offence, and to pronounce the verdict and the sentence. Luke gives fuller details than the other gospels do of the charges that the Jewish authorities brought against Jesus. These charges appear as deliberate but entirely credible misrepresentations of events which are actually recorded in the gospel. Pilate seized upon Jesus' admission that he was the Messiah, which 2 implied, in some sense at least, the claim to be a king. If Jesus seriously claimed to be "king", then there might well be grounds for a charge of sedition against Rome. So Pilate questioned Jesus on this point. But he evidently did not regard Jesus' reply as sufficiently incriminating to proceed with the matter.

Jesus' accusers then slightly changed their tactics, and picked up in more 5 detail one of their earlier charges. 'His teaching is causing disaffection among the people all through Judaea. It started from Galilee and has spread as far as this city'. Galilee was in the jurisdiction of the tetrarch Herod Antipas, and Pilate immediately remitted the prisoner to him (an episode which Luke alone records). It is unlikely that Pilate was obliged to do this merely because Jesus' country of origin lay outside his own jurisdiction: the misconduct of which Jesus was accused had come to a head in Jerusalem, and he had a perfect right to deal with it himself. On the other hand, the accusers of Jesus were now alleging charges which arose out of events in Galilee and which Pilate had no means of verifying, and he could well have felt that this part of the case would be much better heard by the local ruler, who happened to be available in Jerusalem at that time. In addition, the remission of Jesus to Herod was perhaps intended as a courtesy. Luke says that it was anyhow received as such, and healed the strained relations between the two men. We have no other evidence that there had been **a standing feud between them**; but it is not improbable that the 12 Roman administrator had frequent causes of difference with the part-Jewish ruler in the adjoining territory. Herod Antipas apparently had some influence with the Emperor at Rome—it was not for nothing that he had named his capital Tiberias, after the reigning Emperor. Pilate's gesture towards his influential neighbour is perfectly understandable.

We know from Josephus where Herod would have been: not in the great palace built by his father, for this was now the Roman governor's *praetorium*, but in the older palace built by the Hasmoneans, close to the walls of the temple area. **When Herod saw Jesus he was greatly pleased.** Hints of 8 Herod's interest in Jesus were given earlier in the gospel (9.9; 13.31); but the hearing does not seem to have advanced matters, and it ended once again in a scene of mockery. Presumably the question of kingship was still the main charge against Jesus. Herod obviously regarded it as preposterous, and **sent** 11 **him back to Pilate dressed in a glorious robe.**

Pilate now called together the chief priests, councillors, and people. 13 Neither Pilate nor Herod having found Jesus guilty **on a charge of sub-** 14 **version,** Pilate now publicly delivered his considered decision. He would let Jesus off with a warning, probably accompanied by a light **flogging** (which 16 was usual enough in such cases (Acts 22.25), though here the Greek word is a general one and could mean a "warning" alone). But at this point the crowd intervened to upset the normal course of justice. Mark and Matthew provide the explanation (which has found its way into many ancient manuscripts of Luke, but is probably not part of the original text) that it was customary for Pilate to release a prisoner at the festival—which also explains incidentally what the crowd was doing there: they had come to claim their prisoner. Luke merely represents the crowd as demanding that if any prisoner were to be released it should be, not Jesus, but a certain Barabbas, who, because of his connection with **a rising** against the Romans, was perhaps understandably 19 the more popular of the two. Not merely this, but they clamoured for Jesus' crucifixion, even though neither the Jewish authorities, nor Herod, nor Pilate, had **found him guilty of any capital offence.** The result of their 22 clamour, in Luke's account, was a total miscarriage of justice. **Their shouts** 24 **prevailed and Pilate decided that they should have their way.** There was no pretence at a fair trial or a regular verdict: it was the rule of the mob, connived at by the Roman governor. Luke, by this means, reaches the same conclusion as Matthew and Mark: it was the Jews who were guilty of Jesus' death, even though the punishment—crucifixion—was one that could only have been inflicted by the Roman authorities. But his presentation, if it exculpates Pilate from direct responsibility for Jesus' death, leaves him with a strange reputation for the administration of justice in his province, and also has the implication that it was not just the Jewish leaders, but the people of Jerusalem as a whole, who secured Jesus' condemnation.

26 By a very slight change, Luke has made the episode of **Simon from Cyrene** carry a load of symbolic meaning. Simon does not just "carry Jesus' cross" as in Matthew and Mark; he walks **behind Jesus carrying it,** and so becomes the first to fulfil the condition of discipleship, 'he must take up his cross, and come with me' (9.23).

27 **Great numbers of people followed.** Luke's interest, throughout the gospel, in the **people** as a whole, and particularly in the group of women who followed Jesus, was perhaps his reason for mentioning this; and it
28 gave him a cue for recording a further saying of Jesus. '**Daughters of Jerusalem**'. The tone is prophetic, both in its language and in its intention. The women were weeping, ostensibly for Jesus. But the real meaning of their tears (this is how the Old Testament prophets worked, giving the true interpretation of signs that were misread by their contemporaries) was that they presaged the fate of Jerusalem. Jesus had already prophesied about the future: 'Alas for women who are with child in those days, or have children at the breast' (21.23). Here the same thing is expressed in different words, and an oracle from Hosea is added, which showed that the impending catastrophe must not be regarded as a transient disaster, but as the decisive judgement
30 of God. Rather than face that, people would '**start saying to the mountains, "Fall on us", and to the hills, "Cover us"**' (Hosea 10.8). Jesus
31 ends his speech with a proverb. '**If these things are done when the wood is green, what will happen when it is dry?**' To give the proverb its most immediate application (though we cannot be sure that this is what Jesus intended): if this sort of thing can happen even to a harmless preacher, what may not happen when there are real revolutionaries at work? This prophecy, at least, was gruesomely fulfilled during the Jewish rebellion against the Romans, A.D. 66–70.

34 '**Father, forgive them; they do not know what they are doing.**' Luke is the only evangelist to record this saying.[a] In its setting, the prayer appears to be for the executioners who were acting under Roman orders: they knew nothing of the issues involved, and they must not be held to bear the blame for the crucifixion any more than Pilate himself. But Luke doubtless saw more in the saying than this. The unconditional and radical character of God's forgiveness is often stressed in his gospel; and in Acts he makes it clear that this pardon was available even for the Jews, who through ignorance

[a] And not all manuscripts of his gospel contain it (see NEB footnote) so that we cannot be sure that it is authentic.

and failure to understand (Acts 13.26) had crucified their own Messiah (Acts 2.36–8). Even they had the excuse that "they did not know what they were doing". Even they could be forgiven.

In his gospel Luke often abbreviates an episode we know from Mark and Matthew, and then adds a new element of his own. So here: the mockery is told more economically, but a new light is thrown on it by the reactions of the two criminals. To one criminal, as to all the mockers, Jesus was a false 39 pretender: his impending death proved the absurdity of his claims. But the other criminal accepted that Jesus would, nevertheless, "come to his throne" 42 —that is, that there was some sense in which the title over Jesus' head would be shown to be true. This could doubtless only happen in that hoped-for age when the Messiah would inaugurate the glorious kingdom of his elect people. The criminal begged that, through Jesus' "remembrance" of him, he too would have a place in that kingdom. "He got more than he asked for" is an old comment on this passage. Whatever theoretical picture the Jews officially held of the after-life (involving first a period of waiting, then the moment of general resurrection, judgement, and apportioning of reward), there was another far simpler way of talking about life after death which perhaps the majority of people in Palestine tended to adopt and which Jesus himself felt able to make use of (for instance, in the parable of the rich man and Lazarus): immediately after death, the individual expected to be judged by God and awarded his appropriate punishment or reward. It is this more popular way of seeing the matter that seems to be reflected in Jesus' reply to the criminal, 'Today you shall be with me in Paradise.' As in all languages and 43 cultures, there were many names for the reward of the just (as for the condemnation of the wicked). **Paradise** was originally the sumptuous garden of a Persian monarch. When the Jews used the word, they probably thought of the Garden of Eden. Jesus' promise to the criminal was in language he could easily understand: God would grant him the reward of the just. His faith that Jesus was after all a "king" made him the first to inherit the glorious destiny of all who acknowledged Jesus as their Lord.

The sun's light failed. This was Luke's explanation of the darkness. If 45 he meant that there was an eclipse (which is the usual meaning of the Greek word he uses), [a] his explanation was physically impossible: there can be no eclipse of the sun at full moon (the Passover was always at full moon), and in any case an eclipse lasts only a few minutes. But Luke certainly regarded the darkness as a miracle, and these objections will hardly have occurred to him; one way or another, he was convinced that **the sun's light failed.** Mark and Matthew both report that Jesus died with a cry, Luke alone informs us what it was: a verse from a psalm, 'Father, into thy hands I commit my 46 spirit' (Psalm 31.6). Perhaps someone heard it, perhaps it was an early Christian intuition that Jesus had made his own this serene Old Testament

[a] It is so translated in the First Edition of NEB.

prayer (drawn from another of the "righteous sufferer" psalms) and prefaced it with his characteristic address to God, 'Father'. The last word rests (as

47 in Mark and Matthew) with **the centurion**. What impressed him was evidently Jesus' bearing on the cross (and not the supernatural portents which accompanied his death, as in Matthew's version). But his exclamation is given in a form which would perhaps have come more naturally to such a man than the theologically pregnant confession ('Son of God') attributed to him by Mark and Matthew. **'Beyond all doubt'**, he said, **'this man was innocent.'** [a]

At this the mood of the onlookers seems to change from mockery to

48 sympathy or remorse. With the rather stylized literary expression, **beating their breasts**, the crowd is described as already perhaps regretting its part in the crucifixion of Jesus and preparing for the repentance which (as Luke will soon describe in his second volume) will be induced in many of them by the preaching of the apostles.

49 **Jesus' friends, and the women who had accompanied him from Galilee,** showed their loyalty by remaining near by until the end. And Joseph of Arimathaea, out of sympathy with Jesus' cause, obtained from Pilate the body for burial. Luke tells this episode in his own way. In Mark, Joseph's motive seems to be one of ordinary Jewish piety: no dead body must be left exposed after nightfall. In Matthew, Joseph is a secret disciple, and acts out of loyalty to the master. But in Luke, Joseph takes his place among the other

51 pious Jews (men who **looked forward to the kingdom of God**) on the fringe of the gospel story who, without being disciples, were **good** and **upright** (like Zechariah and Elizabeth, 1.6, and Simeon, 2.25); and his goodness and uprightness were shown precisely in that he dissociated himself from the action of the Council, and wished to make some kind of amends—in other words, Luke characteristically offers a moral explanation for Joseph's action which, in its main details, he records exactly as it stands in Mark.

54 **It was Friday, and the Sabbath was about to begin.** This is a very precise note of time: [b] the Sabbath began at sunset on what non-Jews would naturally call "Friday evening". Luke is carefully building up his effect: the women evidently meant to return, and we are told exactly how they spent

24.1 the intervening time, and why they came back only **on the Sunday morning** —if they had come earlier they would have broken the Sabbath command-

[a] Literally, "just" or "righteous". But the point of the sentence was not to pass a relative moral judgement on Jesus, but to show which side the centurion had taken: guilty or innocent, blasphemer or man of God, false or true. The translation "innocent" catches this well enough.

[b] The Greek word means, not "about to begin", but "dawning", and is an odd way of saying that the Sabbath *evening* was beginning. But the translation given, which assumes that the word could be used very loosely, seems the only way to make sense of Luke's sentence. There is some evidence that contemporary Jewish writers used a similar idiom, which may have been translated literally into Greek at an early stage of the gospel tradition.

ment. In what follows, the details (including the improbable one that they
still thought of anointing Jesus' body with **spices**) are as in Mark, but the
emphasis is slightly shifted. The main fact in the story is still that the tomb
was empty; but this only put the women **utterly at a loss.** The important 4
element is now the declaration of the angels (two angels have taken the place
of one in Mark, but the effect is the same: the essential thing is the angelic
vision, not the number of angelic beings). No more than an echo remains of
the puzzling promise that Jesus will meet his disciples in Galilee (Mark 16.7;
Matthew 28.7). Galilee is only mentioned as the place where Jesus uttered a
prophecy of his resurrection. And the resurrection was now proved to have
taken place, not so much by the empty tomb, as by the realization that the
prophecy had been fulfilled. It was this realization which the women hastened
to tell the apostles. Luke does not name them until this point. His list agrees
with that of Mark and Matthew, except that Joanna (see above on 8.2) takes
the place of Salome. Like both Mark and Matthew, he has his own explanation of why their experience did not pass straight into the proclamation of
the first Christians: they were not believed.

That same day. This story occurs only in Luke; indeed, all the gospels, 13
after having run closely together in their accounts of the trial and execution,
diverge markedly when they come to the circumstances of the resurrection,
and it is impossible to fit their accounts together into a single coherent scheme.
The reason for this may well be that the conviction that Jesus had "risen
from the dead" was not reached at the same time and in the same way by all
the disciples, and many different stories about these critical days must have
been current (we know in any case from 1 Corinthians 15.5–7 that there were
more appearances of the risen Christ than are recorded in the gospels). Each
evangelist will have chosen to narrate the particular experiences which seemed
to bring out most clearly the meaning of this almost unimaginable event—
something **too good to be true,** as the NEB expresses it with perhaps 41
unnecessary banality—and we can expect to find a vein of deliberate teaching
in each of the episodes. Luke's story, even though the mysterious stranger
and his mysterious disappearance give it at first a slightly fairy-tale atmosphere, is nevertheless precise in its details. The name of the village is given,
and its distance from Jerusalem; and though there are certain difficulties
in identifying it, there is every reason to believe that it existed. [a] One of the 18

[a] The present village of *Amwas* stands on the site of the important Roman town of
Nicopolis, some eighteen miles north-west of Jerusalem. In the third century this town was
firmly believed to be the Emmaus of the gospel, and there are the remains of a large
Byzantine basilica there. But the distance does not agree with Luke's figure of "60 stades"
(**seven miles**). Consequently the Crusaders built a church exactly 60 stades along the same
road, and thereby started a second tradition. A third possibility is a village which was
called *Koloniyeh* after the Romans had planted a "colony" there, but which in Jesus' time
was certainly called Emmaus. This lies on the Jaffa road, some four miles north-west of
Jerusalem. If this is the true site, the discrepancy of Luke's **seven miles** is not serious.

two disciples is also named: Cleopas (short for Cleopatros, a not uncommon name: he may have been the Clopas who was the husband of a certain Mary, John 19.25). Presumably his home was at Emmaus; and the disciples' offer of hospitality to the stranger rings true for the east: by early afternoon the main part of the day is thought to be over. The stranger made the proper show of reluctance—**he made as if to continue his journey**—but no one liked to be still on the road too late in the day (for darkness falls very rapidly in Palestine), and he soon gave in and stayed for a meal. At his sudden departure the disciples could still have had an hour or two's daylight in which to walk back rapidly to Jerusalem.

The significance of the story is concentrated in two points. First, Jesus
27 **explained to them the passages which referred to himself in every part of the scriptures.** The various beliefs which Jesus' contemporaries held about the coming Messiah were all based on passages of Scripture which could be interpreted as prophetic references to him. But the picture which was usually obtained from these sources was of a glorious and powerful figure who would immediately inaugurate a new age. In the course of his teaching, Jesus had frequently tried to modify this picture by replacing the central figure with another, the Son of Man, and by insisting on the suffering which must precede glorification, both for himself and for those who followed him. Nevertheless, he had not succeeded in preparing his disciples for the apparent catastrophe of the crucifixion, which they found quite impossible to reconcile with any of their existing ideas of what a Messiah should be. Nevertheless, after the resurrection, they came to see that Jesus' humiliation and death did in fact "fulfil" Scripture as much as his glorification; or (to put it the other way round) that the many passages in the Old Testament about a Righteous Sufferer pointed to the same person as those which were more usually quoted in support of the expectation of a divinely sent Deliverer. Thus Christianity very soon gave to its adherents a distinctive approach to the Old Testament quite different from that current among the Jews; and Jesus is here shown to have given his authority to this method of interpretation.
31 The other point of significance is the moment at which **their eyes were**
30 **opened, and they recognized him.** Jesus **took bread . . . said the blessing . . . broke the bread**—the precise actions of his solemn last supper three days previously. That last supper was continued by Christians whenever they met together for the Eucharist. It was their experience that when they did this the Lord was there. The meal was the right and inevitable moment for the two strangely blinded disciples to recognize the risen Christ.
34 They returned to Jerusalem and found that meanwhile Jesus had **appeared to Simon**—that is, to Simon Peter: this is confirmed by Paul (1 Corinthians 15.4) though it is not narrated in any of the gospels. Jesus' next appearance
37 is also clearly recorded for a purpose. **They thought they were seeing a**

ghost; and the emphasis on their being able to touch Jesus, and on his human appetite, was meant to show them that this was not a ghost-story. But not only them: doubtless there were still many people when this gospel was written who thought they could explain away the resurrection (and so discredit Christianity) by suggesting that the disciples had only seen a ghost. The evidence of Jesus' tangibility continued to be important long after the first Easter day.

Then he opened their minds to understand the scriptures. Jesus' 45 magisterial lesson in the right understanding of the Old Testament is repeated—but with an important addition: all this was **to be proclaimed** 47 **to all nations.** How this came to be fulfilled is the subject of Luke's next volume, Acts of the Apostles, and there is no real break in the story. Nevertheless, the narrative up to this point has been a "gospel", like the other gospels, and needs to end, as they do, with Jesus' last appearance on earth. So a brief summary is given of the events which fill the first chapters of Acts, [a] and the gospel ends, as it began, in the temple at Jerusalem. But this is not really the end. The disciples only **begin from Jerusalem.** Luke has 48 still to tell the story of how Christianity reached Rome.

[a] Some manuscripts make this summary correspond more closely to the account of the Ascension in Acts 1. See the footnote in NEB.

THE GOSPEL ACCORDING TO JOHN

The coming of Christ

The purpose of the Gospel according to John is declared, not at the beginning, but at the end: 'in order that you may hold the faith that Jesus is Christ, the Son of God' (20.31).

To anyone (other than a Christian) who understood what was meant by the term "Christ" (Messiah, Anointed One), it would have come as a surprise that a book should have to be written for this purpose. "Christ", by definition, was a figure of power and glory. When he came, it would be impossible not to be aware of the fact. His destiny was to restore a kingdom of unprecedented splendour and justice to God's elect people among the Jews. Once his reign had begun, it would hardly be necessary to write a book to prove that he had come.

Nevertheless, Christians were not deterred from calling Jesus "Christ", even though the fact that the Christ had come was not recognized by the majority of the human race, not even by the Jews, who for centuries had been praying for his coming. This technical term of Jewish religion seemed the natural way to describe one who had actually been among them on earth, who was now at God's right hand in heaven, and who was the source of new life for his followers. They were able to find Old Testament texts which not only prophesied his glory but also implied a destiny of suffering and rejection; and the more they reflected on the life and teaching of Jesus, the better they began to understand the mysterious necessity that 'the Christ was bound to suffer' (Luke 24.26) and that his reign was to be, at least for the present, unrecognized by all but a few.

However, they soon came to realize that Jesus was more than this. He had power, not only over the hearts of men, but over the elemental and demonic forces of the universe; he gave meaning, not only to human life, but to the whole created order; he belonged, not only to time, but to eternity. But if so, then the problem of his rejection became more acute than ever. If Jesus belonged to the very structure of the world, why did the world not accept him? How could one possibly explain the bitter reality of the crucifixion?

John's gospel is an attempt to tackle the wider implications of this problem. The technical terms of Jewish religious expectation which are found in the other gospels—Christ, Son of God, Son of Man—were no longer adequate to describe the depth and universality of the Christian's understanding of Jesus. Accordingly, John uses a new vocabulary. Jesus is light, and life, and truth: words which belong more to religious poetry than to the prosaic language of doctrine, and which set Jesus in a much larger frame than could be provided by the traditional categories of the Jewish religion. These words need no explanation, though they take on new depths of meaning as they are put to work in the course of the gospel.

The distinctive character of John's gospel is apparent in the way it begins. The other gospels, confining themselves to a more modest programme, and mainly concerned to show that Jesus was—in some sense—the Christ of Jewish expectation, were each content to describe some of the circumstances in which this Christ made his appearance among men. But John, having so greatly enlarged the scale on which he proposed to tackle his subject, could not regard the story as beginning only with the birth or the first public appearance of Jesus. He needed some way of describing Jesus which would show him to have been an integral element in the created universe from the beginning. For this purpose he chose another suggestive term which featured in the vocabulary of both religion and philosophy: the Word.

No single English word conveys the associations which the word *logos* would have had for an educated Greek. It meant far more than a mere unit of spoken language: it included any articulate thought, any logical and meaningful utterance; it was that which gave order and shape to the process of thinking—proportion in mathematics, rational intelligibility in the study of the natural world, an ordered account of human affairs. It was almost equivalent to "rationality". As such, it was a convenient tool for philosophy: the Stoics, indeed, used the word *logos* for the immanent rational principle of the whole universe, the single divine system which (according to their philosophy) underlay the multiplicity of the visible world; and doubtless their use of the word had already begun to influence the everyday speech of many Greek-speaking people who had never troubled to explore the theoretical implications of Stoicism.

To a Greek-speaking Jew, the word had a still wider range of meanings. In the Bible, God's "word" was not only the means by which (as it might be through a prophet) God communicated with men and brought them into obedience to his Law; it was also the expression of his relationship with the whole created universe: God said . . . and there was, God spoke . . . and it was done. "My word . . . shall not return to me fruitless without accomplishing my purpose" (Isaiah 55.11). God's word was an expression of his creative power.

A term which embraced so many ideas could be put to many uses. For Philo of Alexandria, whose life was devoted to the task of expressing the essence of the Jewish religion in terms borrowed from contemporary philosophy, the *logos* became a philosophical entity in its own right, and seemed to offer the key to understanding the relationship between the transcendent God of the Bible and the world that is known to the human senses. But there is no reason to think that John was addressing his gospel to readers who were accustomed to any particular or technical use of the word *logos*: they spoke Greek, and therefore shared the usual Greek understanding of it as a word with a wide range of meanings to do with the rational use of the intellect; but they were also familiar with Jewish traditions, and knew something of the power and vigour associated in the Old Testament with the Word of God. They were therefore prepared for this *logos* of John to mean a great deal more than can be expressed in English by "word"; and it was for John to show, by some specimen phrases, in exactly what sense he wished to apply it to Jesus Christ. The first eighteen verses of his gospel may be regarded as a kind of poem in which successive stanzas seek to draw out the implications of this single word, *logos.*[a]

1. 1 **When all things began.** In the Greek, the first two words of the gospel are the same as the first two words of the Old Testament; and there can be little doubt that this echo is intentional. The first image brought to mind is the creation. But whereas, in Genesis, the sentence continues with a state-ment about the first thing that happened—God made the heavens and the earth—here it goes on quite differently: **the Word already was.** It is as if something is being said, not about creation itself, but about the conditions under which creation was brought about. This was in fact an old line of thought: surely God was not to be imagined as personally supervising every detail of the universe that was being brought into being? The omniscient intelligence which could be seen to underlie all created things, and which indeed rendered them intelligible to man's own power of reasoning—this intelligence was surely not identical with God himself (as some philosophers would have said, who denied the existence of any God beyond that which is revealed in the rational system of the universe)? An answer to these questions had been already supplied in some of the later writings of the Old Testament: God was assisted at the creation by the figure of Wisdom.

"The Lord created me when he began his work . . .
When he marked the foundations of the earth
    then I was beside him like a master-workman."
(Proverbs 8.22–31)[b]

[a] These verses are poetical in the further sense that they are more evocative than precise; hence many of them can be translated in more than one way, as can be seen from the number of alternatives offered in the NEB footnotes. Moreover the sequence of thought seems less than perfectly logical; and it is possible (as some have supposed) that the writer did not in fact compose the poem himself but found it already in existence and, in adapting it to his purpose, made changes and additions which interrupted its continuity and disturbed its logic. On the other hand, it is not to be expected of poetry—and certainly not of poetry inspired by the Old Testament—that it should say things in perfectly logical order, any more than that each of the concepts it uses should be capable of exact definition.

[b] This translation follows, not the Hebrew text, but the Septuagint Greek version. It was this version that John's readers were familiar with; and it contains certain small changes in the sense which make it seem to bear more directly on the part played by Wisdom at the creation.

"With thee is wisdom who knows thy works
and was present when thou didst make the world."

(Wisdom 9.9)

No Jew would ever have been tempted to think of this "wisdom" as a separate deity, usurping the honour of the one true God. On the contrary, wisdom provided a way of speaking of God with greater respect, avoiding the somewhat crude and anthropomorphic idea of God actually at work on the details of his creation, and yet conceding that, in the last analysis, wisdom was nothing other than God, though it was God conceived under the particular aspect of the physical and moral laws of the universe. Nevertheless, it was the way of religious poetry to allow this figure of wisdom to take on almost a life of its own. Wisdom was "beside" God (Proverbs 8.30), it "went forth to make its dwelling among the children of men, and found no dwelling" (Enoch 42.2—an apocryphal Jewish scripture compiled during the second and first centuries B.C.). John clearly stands in this tradition when, in his opening verses, he says similar things about the Word. Only, by using that term (instead of "Wisdom") he brings this old image of Jewish religious poetry within reach of a more philosophical reader. The Jesus who can be described in such terms is not a figment of the Hebrew imagination, but has to do with those essential and rational principles of the universe that must have existed from the beginning: **no single thing was created without** 3 **him.**

By a progression which is again more poetical than logical, two further ideas are associated with the Word: life, and light. Both of these are 4 developed as the gospel proceeds; but the second serves to lead into the next great theme of the prologue. **The light shines on in the dark**: the concept 5 of light presupposes its opposite; light would not be recognized as light if there were no darkness with which to compare it. A scientist would doubtless express the matter differently; but a poet speaks naturally of a light that shines **in the dark**, and goes on from there to imagine a kind of contest between the light on the one hand and the darkness on the other, the darkness surrounding the light and trying to quench it. This image is the first hint of the mystery with which the gospel is concerned: the rejection of Christ by mankind. Christ is the Word, an agent of creation, a principle of the universe. As such he is eternal, he can never be **mastered** or "quenched",[a] as a light can; but, just as light presupposes darkness, so the Word presupposes a world which does not understand and acknowledge. It need be no more paradoxical

[a] **The darkness has never mastered it** is a brilliant rendering, suggested also by R. A. Knox in his own translation (1945), of an ambiguous Greek expression. The words can mean either, "the darkness has never quenched it" (NEB, First Edition), or "the darkness has never understood it", an interpretation which became popular in the Middle Ages, and has found its way into many English versions. Linguistically, the first of these meanings is more probable; but John may well have intended a *double entendre*. In 12.35 the same word is translated 'overtake'.

to say that the divine Word was not received than that a light is surrounded by darkness.

But this admission raises a new question. If it was of the nature of this Word that, although integral to the created order, it could yet be ignored and rejected by men, what assurance was there that it would ever be recognized and acclaimed at all? The answer was that there must be "witnesses" to it, men and women whose lives, by being dedicated to the Word and entirely determined by it, would be powerful arguments for its existence and power. Here was a way to understand that strange figure who always stood on the
6 first page of the Christian story. **There appeared a man named John**— the sentence is suddenly in the style of the Old Testament, and we are reminded at once of the other gospels, where it is as a man in the tradition of the Old Testament prophets—an ascetic preacher of the desert, with something of Elijah about him—that John the Baptist makes his appearance. He fulfils prophecies, he revives the long-silent gift of prophetic speech, he foretells his greater successor and places him in the flaming scenery of the Last Judgement—in short, a figure only comprehensible in a culture shaped by the Bible and conditioned by urgent expectation of a new world-order that is about to come. The writer of this gospel suggests a different and less esoteric
7 rôle for him: **he came as a witness to testify to the light.**
9 **The real light which enlightens every man was even then coming into the world.** A strictly chronological scheme would yield a different order: Jesus' birth would come before John the Baptist's preaching. But this is poetry, not history: John's sequence of ideas reflects, not the passage of time, but a movement of thought, a movement from the metaphysical implications of the Word which was present with God 'when all things began', to that moment in time when there was on earth a person—Jesus— whose appearance challenged mankind to accept the Word. The description of that unearthly presence on earth is the climax of the prologue; but lest it should be supposed that the splendour of that moment commanded the assent of all who saw it, John first reminds his readers of the point already made: there was darkness around the light, the Word was inevitably not
10 received, it needed witnesses to commend it. **The world, though it owed its being to him, did not recognize him.** That was true of the world in general; but certain people did recognize him, and these—that is, Christians,
12 **those who have yielded him their allegiance**—experienced a relationship with God which could be described as that of **the children of God** (for a new appreciation of the personal fatherhood of God was one of the distinctive marks of early Christianity).
14 **So the Word became flesh.** John makes no attempt to soften the harshness of this terrific proposition. The man Jesus was now at the right hand of God: that was an easy way of putting it, given the limitations of such naïvely pictorial language (it was the way most early Christians did put it). But this

"Christ" was also—had always been—part of the structure of the universe, something that is essential to understanding the created order; and all this was somehow concentrated in one individual who fully shared the human condition. John had no alternative but to bring into one sentence words which would normally seem to belong to totally different worlds of discourse: **the Word became flesh.**

He came to dwell among us. The man Jesus was also the Word. An easier way to conceive of this double aspect of Jesus' person is that adopted by most New Testament writers: the two aspects are assigned to two different periods of time. After (and perhaps also before) his life on earth, Jesus was a figure of glory, seated at the right hand of God, superior to all heavenly and earthly powers. But when he was literally 'among us', he was simply man— a unique and exceptional man, no doubt, but so far as his humanity went indistinguishable from other men. By contrast, John makes no such clear distinction between Jesus in heaven and Jesus on earth. Throughout his gospel he invests Jesus with something of the divinity and the glory which belongs to the Word, even though this Word became absolutely flesh, even though Jesus was absolutely human; and so here, his brief description of the manner in which Jesus was **among us** contains more than a hint of a presence that was all the time something more than merely human, merely 'flesh'. **He came to dwell.** The translation is as correct as any English rendering can be; but the Greek word has far more overtones than its English equivalent. Originally it meant "dwell in a tent": it was in a "tent" that God had dwelt when he first accompanied his people in their travels across the desert. Moreover, the same Greek word was reminiscent of a Hebrew expression for the glory of God "dwelling" on earth. **He came to dwell among us** is therefore a phrase which, with its Old Testament associations, already suggests a more than human side to the period of Christ's humanity. The following words—**glory, grace, truth**—are equally charged with meaning by their use in the Old Testament, where they belong to the vocabulary of God's care for his people; yet almost all these words are ones which will take on new meaning as the gospel unfolds. For the present, they serve as a summary of what it could be said that **we saw**—that is, not the subjective impressions of one man or of a group of people, but the essential double aspect of Jesus' life on earth to which witness was borne by the whole community of those who had actually acknowledged him, whether after seeing him themselves, or after hearing the testimony of others.

Here is John's testimony to him. The synoptic gospels present a 15 simpler view of John the Baptist's work: John prophesied that a greater than himself would come, and a greater did come. But in this gospel John is not so much a prophet as a witness: he was the first to recognize and give testimony that a greater *had* come. Jesus' appearance was such as, in a sense, to put one off the scent. It was John who was drawing the crowds; Jesus only came **after** (perhaps as a disciple, perhaps simply later in time). On the face of it, it was John who marked the arrival of something new. But his real importance was in the testimony he gave that, despite appearances, Jesus was of superior **rank**, of another order altogether: '**before I was born, he already was**'.

17 **The Law was given through Moses.** This was one of the basic premises of Jewish religion. From this flowed the tremendous benefits and privileges which the Jewish people believed they had received from God: the Law was the expression and guarantee of the 'grace and truth' with which God had consistently treated his people. John boldly corrects this ancient belief: **grace and truth came through Jesus Christ.** But of course it was not just a matter of Jesus having replaced Moses as the bearer of the same benefits as before. The 'grace' received through Jesus Christ was greater than anything received through the Law of Moses: it was **grace upon grace**.

18 **No one has ever seen God.** Pagan religions might speak lightly of gods appearing to men; but the seriousness with which the Jews took the idea of God forbade any such fantasy. God was far too terrible to be 'seen' by men; at most they might expect to have to face him at the moment of Judgement. Therefore the Jesus whom men had "seen", despite all the near-divine titles given to him, was not in every sense identical with God. [a] He revealed God only to the extent that men could bear it. John uses what in Greek was almost a technical term for the inspired activity of one who imparted truths about God: **he has made him known.** Men did not literally "see" God in Jesus: this would have been inconceivable. Through Jesus, they came to "know" God.

19 **This is the testimony which John gave.** Jesus' work and message burst upon the Jews of Palestine as something entirely new and original; but it was immediately preceded by a movement which was itself quite out of the ordinary, that of John the Baptist. The gospels differ among themselves in the picture they give of him, and drop occasional hints that there was a good deal more to him than they have chosen to record; and the contemporary historian Josephus also sketches a portrait of him which is recognizably of the same person, and yet is seen from a quite different point of view. The main question to which Christian writers had to address themselves was this: the movement of John and the movement of Jesus was each in its own way unique; yet the one came immediately before the other, and there were

[a] As can be seen from the footnote in NEB, the evidence of the manuscripts is divided on this point. Since the exact relationship of Christ to God was one of the most burning questions which agitated the church in the early centuries, it is perhaps not surprising that a verse which had such bearing on it as this one should have been quoted in different versions by theologians of different persuasions. The version given in the text is that which seems to give the best sense. But the much more difficult reading, which calls Jesus "himself God", is offered by our earliest papyrus manuscripts, and must therefore have been current within a century of the writing of the gospel.

clear points of contact between them, so much so that it was impossible to tell the story of Jesus without first referring to the story of John. What then was the relationship between the two? Out of what was clearly a mass of tradition about John, the writers of the other gospels selected three points in particular which seemed to point towards an answer. First, John fulfilled an Old Testament oracle about **a voice crying aloud in the wilderness** 23 (Isaiah 40.3) which clearly cast him in the rôle of a person preparing for an event of universal importance; secondly, he was the precursor of someone infinitely greater than himself—he had used words like those of the humblest of servants about his master, '**I am not good enough to unfasten his** 27 **shoes**'; and thirdly (the most obvious point of contact) he had baptized Jesus.

John's gospel, where it uses the same material, uses it in a quite different way. The quotation from Isaiah, the sayings about the superiority of the Baptist's successor, and the description of **the Spirit coming down from** 32 **heaven like a dove** (one of the phenomena accompanying the baptism of Jesus, according to the other gospels) are all phrased, not as news, but as reminiscences. They describe, not what John did, but what he said. They are his **testimony**. Accordingly, no interest is shown in what was, after all, his main activity—baptizing. This (as we know both from Josephus and from the other gospels) was a ritual of great significance: it was 'for the forgiveness of sins' (Mark 1.4). But for this writer it had only one meaning: it was the prototype—the first inkling, as it were—of that infinitely more profound experience offered by Jesus to his followers, baptism **in Holy Spirit**. In itself, it was unimportant: this writer does not even mention that John baptized Jesus. For him, the whole importance of John lay, not in his being a "baptist", but in his being the first "witness" to Jesus Christ.

This is subtly emphasized at the beginning. John, while working at a place *a* called **Bethany beyond Jordan,** was confronted by **the Jews of** 28, 19 **Jerusalem**—that is to say, by that element in the total Jewish population which was to show itself consistently opposed to Jesus: the men of influence in Jerusalem. Here, they are represented first by some of those concerned with the administration and worship of the temple (**priests and Levites**), and subsequently by more learned men whose interests extended particularly to the interpretation of the Law—**some Pharisees**. His reply to them is 24 introduced by a curious phrase: **He confessed without reserve and** 20

[a] The site of this **Bethany** had been forgotten even by the time Origen looked for it early in the third century A.D., and there was a tendency to insert into the manuscripts the name *Bethabara*, the site of which could still be identified. But a possible derivation for the name Bethany is *bet aniyyah*, House of the Boat—a very plausible name for a small place on the bank of the river which subsequently disappeared. At any rate, an early tradition fixed the place of John's baptism on the east bank of the Jordan, near the ford closest to Jericho, just below the small mountain which was believed to be the place where Elijah ascended into heaven—for John had much about him which seemed deliberately to recall the figure of Elijah, even though he is here said to have denied that he was Elijah.

avowed. In the Greek, as in the English, this sentence appears cumbrous and over-emphatic. But the emphasis of the words is surely deliberate: John's "testimony" to Jesus demanded, in the first place, that he should make it absolutely clear that his own rôle, though unique and significant, did not detract in any way from the weight of the titles which would soon be suggested for Jesus. (On Jesus' reaction to a similar question, and on the titles themselves, see above on Mark 8.28.)

26 However, John's "testimony" does not consist only of statements familiar from the other gospels. '**Among you, though you do not know him, stands the one who is to come after me**'. This is something new. One of the many current beliefs about the coming Messiah was that he already existed, and might even be already on earth, but that he was to remain "unknown" until the day when he would be revealed. This idea was rich in

11 possibilities for explaining the paradox that Jesus, 'the Word', **entered his own realm, and his own would not receive him.** Jesus conformed to the traditional type of a hidden Messiah; it was only the way in which he was revealed which was totally different from what his contemporaries expected.

31, 33 He was hidden, at first, even from his first witness: John says twice over, '**I did not know him**'. There is evidence in the other gospels that John continued for some time to be in doubt about him. But here, he has now seen

34 enough to give his precious evidence: '**I have borne witness. This is God's Chosen One**'. [a]

29 '**There is the Lamb of God**'. This too is something quite new; but it is hard to know how to interpret it. By the time the gospel was written, the phrase had a rich store of meanings: the death of Jesus, occurring as it did in the course of the Passover festival, could be described as the sacrifice of a Passover lamb (1 Corinthians 5.7); and his glorious ascension into heaven as Messiah is represented in the Revelation as the exaltation of a slaughtered Lamb in heaven. If John the Baptist used this phrase about Jesus, he can hardly have foreseen all this, and the only clue to his meaning is in the sequel, '**it is he who takes away the sin of the world**'. There was nothing in the Jewish sacrificial system about a "lamb" which could have such atoning power; but the words, **takes away the sin of the world,** are reminiscent of just one passage in the Old Testament, which describes a Servant of God who was "led like a sheep to the slaughter", and who "bore the sin of many" (Isaiah 53.7,12). It is even possible that the original Aramaic word used by John the Baptist was one which meant both "lamb" and "servant"; if so, John may have been the first to recognize in Jesus the mysterious Servant prophesied in Isaiah 53. However that may be, this is

[a] Another Old Testament title, probably derived, like "Beloved" in Mark 1.11 and Matthew 3.17, from Isaiah 42.1: "... my chosen in whom I delight; I have bestowed my spirit upon him". Here, as in Mark and Matthew, the reading of some manuscripts gives the much less technical and allusive title, "Son of God".

only the first of a series of related images in this gospel: here Jesus is the lamb, later he is the door of the sheepfold, and finally he is the shepherd himself.

After John the Baptist, the gathering of disciples—an episode which necessarily stands near the beginning in all the gospels. John again has a particular interest in it—not so much in the fact that certain disciples decided to follow Jesus, or in the reasons why they did so, but because they too could be called as early "witnesses" to the true nature of Jesus. The first two, for instance, called him 'Rabbi' (which means a teacher), and 38 their question 'where are you staying?' showed what they meant by it: a man of fixed abode, who gathered a group of pupils—a kind of "school" —around him. True, Jesus certainly deserved the title Rabbi, and much of his work consisted of teaching; and the prosaic question about his lodging received a prosaic answer. But his pupils were soon to find that he was a great deal more besides. Indeed, one of these two, Andrew, immediately went on to give a more significant testimony: 'We have found the Messiah' 41 (John characteristically both offers the original Hebrew word and explains that its Greek equivalent is 'Christ'). This led to the adherence of Simon Peter. In the other gospels, the call of these two men takes place beside the Sea of Galilee. Here the setting is quite different; but John's account includes one of the most certain facts in the New Testament: that Jesus gave Simon the name Cephas, of which the Greek equivalent is Peter, the Rock.   42

Philip appears in the lists of the Twelve given in the other gospels. His 43 testimony is much the same as Andrew's: 'we have met the man spoken 45 of by Moses in the Law, and by the prophets'—the person, that is to say, to whom so many passages of the Old Testament were believed to point forward, the Messiah, the Christ. It was not in itself implausible that this Messiah should turn out to be identical with a particular man Jesus, of known family (Joseph) and home (Nazareth): many believed that the Messiah would first appear *incognito*. But what the next disciple, Nathanael, found hard to accept was that the incognito should be so complete. Nazareth was a small, remote place, without even a mention in the Old Testament to give a clue to its future distinction. 'Can anything good come from 46 Nazareth?' Nevertheless, his initial doubt soon yielded to recognition, and he gave the most important testimony so far: 'You are the Son of God; 49 you are king of Israel'. Like the titles already given, these will be shown to be true (in a sense) as the gospel proceeds.

Nathanael is not in any surviving list of the Twelve, and in fact it is not 45 said here that he became a disciple. He is brought in, again, entirely because of the value of his testimony. But there was reason to place him as the last and most decisive witness in the series. Jesus said, 'Here is an Israelite 47 worthy of the name; there is nothing false in him'. He was, in short, the exact opposite of Jesus' Jewish opponents in Jerusalem: he was a true

Israelite, one whose Jewish nationality and upbringing were to yield their proper fruit in making him a man who recognized and acclaimed Jesus for what he was. But how did Jesus know this about him? Was it a guess? Or had he a true gift of prophecy? This time it was Jesus' turn to be a witness. If you wished to give evidence about a scene you had witnessed, you could be asked about the exact place and time. The question might take the form (as in Daniel and Susanna 51–8), "What kind of tree did it happen under?" Jesus passed the test; he then went on to cap the series of testimonies with 51 a startling statement of his own: '**You shall see heaven wide open, and God's angels ascending and descending upon the Son of Man.**'

Here again, the synoptic gospels preserve elements out of which this saying could have been constructed. At Jesus' baptism, the heavens were 'torn open' (Mark 1.10); immediately after, in the temptation story, 'angels waited on him' (Mark 1.13); and there are a number of places where Jesus appears to refer to himself in this same oblique way as **the Son of Man**. But even if these elements were the original material out of which this saying in John's gospel was composed, the result suggests a quite different picture. "Jacob dreamt that he saw a ladder, which rested on the ground with its top reaching to heaven, and angels of God were going up and down upon it" (Genesis 28.12). Grammatically, the last word in the Hebrew could equally well mean "upon him", that is, on Jacob; and in due course Jewish scholars came to be attracted by the possibility. Jacob, after all, was Israel, and the Israel on earth had surely some kind of spiritual counterpart in heaven; might it not be that the verse in Genesis was intended to illustrate the relationship of the earthly and the heavenly Israel? We do not know how much of this kind of speculation was going on in John's day, but it is tempting to see a similar train of thought here: when Nathanael saw Jesus it was as if the true Israelite saw the true Israel in heaven, and his true counterpart on earth. At any rate, the allusion to the Jacob story is unmistakable, and the picture is one which emphasizes what (at least for John) was an essential feature of the mythological title, Son of Man: it meant a figure whose destiny was to be played out both on earth and in heaven.

Christ the giver of life

2. 1 **On the third day there was a wedding.** We can fill in a few of the details. The wedding took place in a small town, Cana, which was about nine miles north-east of Nazareth. [a] It was the home-town of Nathanael (21.2) and a

[a] The modern *Khirbet Kana*, now a mound of ruins. Another possible site is *Kefar Kenna*, rather closer to Nazareth on the road to Tiberias. Here, two churches have been built to commemorate the miracle; but the tradition that this was Cana-in-Galilee seems not to be older than the Middle Ages.

place, according to this gospel, visited more than once by Jesus. Certainly, his family was well known there, for the mother of Jesus was present at the festivities, helping with the domestic arrangements (for only men were invited to the actual meal). **Jesus and his disciples were guests also:** 2 whether he was invited because of a family connection, or out of a new respect for him as a teacher, it would have been normal and courteous to include in the invitation those who had begun to form a regular group of disciples around him. Five have been mentioned: there may already have been more. They will have gone, not merely to receive hospitality, but to assist the bridegroom in the formalities and the entertainment which were a necessary part of the wedding and which usually went on for several days.

On the face of it, the story describes how Jesus spared his host a serious social embarrassment. It is possible that Jesus had been partly responsible for the crisis (hence his mother's unexpected approach to him to tell him of the alarm felt in the domestic quarters). He had arrived with a large party, but without bringing the kind of contribution expected of such guests—food and wine. If so, his deed may have been originally understood as a miraculous resourcefulness in the face of an obligation which his chosen way of life made it impossible for him to meet out of his own resources (the story of the tribute-money found in a fish's mouth—Matthew 17.24–7—is on the same lines). In any case, he acted with great discretion. The other guests were spared the shock of knowing anything about it, and even **the steward of** 8 **the feast** (who was probably a kind of head waiter or master of ceremonies) was not in the secret.

Reduced to these simple terms, the story yields no very obvious moral: like many of the stories which must have circulated about Jesus, it could only qualify to stand in a gospel if it could be shown to contain some deeper meaning. John describes it as one of **the signs by which Jesus revealed** 11 **his glory**, and characteristically places a load of significance upon some of the most banal details. In the brief dialogue, for instance, between Jesus and his mother the sentence, **'Your concern, mother, is not mine'**, can bear 4 more than one meaning. The tone is a little formal (**'mother'** translates the Greek word meaning "woman", and would have been the correct form of address on such an occasion) and the idiom is the same as that used by the demons to Jesus in Mark 1.24 and 5.7 ('what do you want with me?'). At its simplest level, it need be no more than an expression of surprise and slight annoyance that his mother should have come in to interrupt his attention to the festivities. But (as the NEB rendering suggests) a further meaning is possible: "you are worried about the supply of wine, but my concern is with more important things". Again, the **six stone water-jars** were nothing out 6 of the ordinary, and their impressive size simply underlines the miraculous abundance created by Jesus; but when John adds the detail that they were **of the kind used for Jewish rites of purification**, we can be sure that we

are intended to draw a moral: the ritual observances of the Jews had given
10 place to the spiritual sacraments of the Christians. Finally, the comment of
the steward, which rounds off the episode, sounds like a trite piece of con-
vivial small talk; but for Christian readers it bears more than a hint of those
sayings of Jesus in which the old wine of the Jewish religion is shown to be
infinitely inferior to the new wine of the gospel.

12 **After this he went down to Capernaum.** John gives a quite different
picture of Jesus' movements from that in the other gospels. There, Jesus
makes Capernaum his base for much of his work in Galilee; here, Jesus
makes Cana (if anywhere) his base, and only makes one brief visit to Capernaum. Again, in the other gospels Jesus (after his baptism) makes only one
pilgrimage to Jerusalem, the pilgrimage which ends in his death; all the
Jerusalem episodes are therefore concentrated in the last few days of Jesus'
life. But in John's gospel Jesus makes several journeys to Jerusalem (a fairly
frequent pilgrimage for the great festivals was customary for such a person),
and his drastic action with regard to the temple is accordingly placed near
the beginning of the gospel instead of towards the end. If we wish to know
in what order things actually happened, we have to make our choice between
the two versions, and allow for the fact that one or the other (or both) may
have been deliberately rearranged in order to bring out better the significance
of each period of Jesus' life.

15 **Jesus made a whip of cords.** This is one of the small details by which
John succeeds in conveying a slightly different and more agitated picture
than the other gospels. Jesus' action was not just a prophetic gesture: he
effectively drove the animals out of the precincts with his whip, causing
chaos among the money-changers, and finally ordering out the **dealers in
pigeons** with their caged birds. What was his reason for this action? In the
other gospels, the question is a complicated one (see above on Mark 11.15–
16 19); here, there is a simpler answer. **'You must not turn my Father's
house into a market'.** This is a fairly plain allusion to the last words of
Zechariah (14.21), "There shall no longer be a trader in the house of the
Lord of hosts on that day": Jesus was deliberately fulfilling this oracle, and
his deed proclaimed the imminence of that "day of the Lord" which the
prophet had foretold. For the disciples, on the other hand, the episode came
17 to have another meaning. **'Zeal for thy house will destroy me'** is a
quotation from Psalm 69.9—and the subject of that psalm is one of the
nameless righteous sufferers of the Old Testament: even the devotion and
piety of the man towards the temple had been held against him. These **words
of Scripture** seemed to fit Jesus perfectly.

18 **The Jews challenged Jesus.** As in the other gospels, the action inevitably
provoked a controversy. The reply of Jesus is a saying that is reported by the
New Testament writers in different forms and contexts. Speaking sacri-

legious words against the temple could have been a serious offence, possibly even punishable by death; and a charge of this kind was evidently brought against Jesus at his trial. It caused the evangelists some embarrassment: could Jesus really have threatened to destroy the temple? Various solutions are suggested in the gospel accounts (see above on Mark 14.58). Here, the saying (as John reports it) is not so much an attack on the temple, as a claim that, if it were destroyed, Jesus could rebuild it in three days. With characteristic irony, John makes the Jews take this quite literally: the temple had been begun by Herod the Great in 20–19 B.C., and was not in fact finished until A.D. 63, though the main work may have been completed after **forty-six** 20 **years**—by, say, A.D. 27, which is about the time this conversation could have taken place. It is pedantic to ask whether John knew that work was still in progress a generation later: the point is simply to contrast the immense labours of the builders with Jesus' grandiose claim to accomplish something comparable in three days. The claim was absurd—taken literally; but that its literal meaning was absurd or sacrilegious was (according to John) quite beside the point. **The temple he was speaking of was his body**—a hidden 21 meaning which could only be grasped in the light of the resurrection and of the many scriptures which were thereby fulfilled.

Many gave their allegiance to him. The response to Jesus' 'signs' was 23 positive. How could it be said, therefore, that 'his own would not receive him' (1.11)? The full answer lay in the sequel; but in the meantime a sufficient reason could be found in the attitude of Jesus himself: he **would** 24 **not trust himself to them. He knew men so well.**

There was one of the Pharisees named Nicodemus. He was evidently 3. 1 more sympathetic to Jesus than most of the influential people in Jerusalem: he recognized Jesus as a **teacher** (like himself) and acknowledged that the 2 **signs** he performed indicated that he had a divine mission on the level at least of one of the great figures of the Old Testament. Nevertheless, though a **famous teacher of Israel**, this Pharisee could not advance to any real 11 understanding of Jesus. He was a case in point of a man who was ready to "give his allegiance" to Jesus, but to whom, because of the limitations of his understanding, Jesus could not 'trust himself'.

So far as the narrative goes, this Nicodemus has a humble function. He simply provides the questions and comments that are needed to draw out a discourse from Jesus, and his contribution is of a kind that occurs again and again in this gospel: by understanding a saying of Jesus in its most literal and banal sense ('**how is it possible…for a man to be born when he is** 4 **old?**') he gives the dramatic cue for a more subtle explanation from Jesus. Indeed, the whole episode is characteristic of the way in which the writer of this gospel presents the teaching of Jesus, a way which is quite different from that of the other gospels. In them, Jesus' teaching takes the form of brief and memorable sentences, usually evoked by some question or incident, sometimes running over into a parable or illustration, but never offering a systematic development of a particular line of thought. Even where we find substantial paragraphs entirely devoted to teaching (as in the Sermon on the Mount, or in the discourse on the future), they turn out to consist of collections of sayings, many of which were remembered separately and were only later brought together into a composite discourse. But in this gospel the style of teaching is quite different. Starting from a particular episode, or question, or comment, Jesus develops his thought on a given subject, and ranges over a wide field of ideas. Sometimes his words are reminiscent of sayings recorded elsewhere; but more often they are expressed in the more sophisticated and philosophical idiom which is characteristic of this gospel. Theoretically, it is possible that Jesus actually spoke like this, and that we have here an authentic style of teaching which is unaccountably missing from the other gospels. But this is hardly the most likely explanation. The sayings in the other gospels are pungent, poetic and easily memorable: many of them are in exactly the form to be expected of teaching given in a Semitic language, and there is no difficulty in imagining how they could have been preserved in people's memory until they came to be written down. The discourses in John, on the other hand, are literary and artificial. They are cast in the form of dialogues or monologues such as are familiar from some of the philosophical literature of the time; they are carefully composed around a group of concepts which occur again and again, with different variations, as the gospel proceeds; and they seem to presuppose a writer meditating in his study rather than a teacher responding spontaneously to the questions of his hearers. In other words, Jesus did not deliver the discourses that are attributed to him in this gospel. But nor (in all probability) did he deliver the "Sermon on the Mount" in the form in which Matthew has recorded it. The gospels present us with different attempts to gather the teaching of Jesus into a form which would bring out its meaning and meet the needs of subsequent generations of Christians. The author of this gospel has done this in a more systematic way than the others. If, in the process, he has recast it in a somewhat different idiom, it is still possible that he has come at least as near as any other New Testament writer to its essential meaning.

3   'Unless a man has been born over again he cannot see the kingdom of God'. This saying, introduced by the solemn and distinctive formula which so often goes with a pronouncement of Jesus in this gospel ('In truth, in very truth I tell you') is the substance of the discourse; the rest, in a sense, is commentary. The idea that, by committing himself to a new religion or philosophy, a man might be "reborn", was not unheard of in antiquity. But what precisely did this mean in Christian terms? In the subsequent experience of Christians, the obvious moment when this "rebirth" took

place was at baptism (in Titus 3.5 baptism is actually called "rebirth"). The elements of Christian baptism were the **water** which symbolized the washing 5 away of sin, and a new **spirit** which was received; of these, it was the spirit which (to this writer at least) gave meaning to the notion of rebirth. It has already been said in the prologue (1.13) that those who accept Jesus as Christ are born, not 'by fleshly desire', but 'of God himself'. Here the same point is made by means of the psychology of flesh and spirit (see also Romans 8.5–8). "Flesh" is the whole of the human person as it were in its crude state, untouched by God: physical birth in itself can bring forth nothing more. "Spirit" is that aspect of the personality which is capable of responding to God, and which is brought to life when the Spirit of God touches it. The argument is an example of the old philosophical principle that "like begets like". If Christian baptism was "in spirit", it evidently caused a rebirth in the spirit of a man: '**it is spirit that gives birth to spirit**'. Jesus may 6 originally have meant something much less technical; but John, in his commentary, makes sense of the saying about being **born over again** in terms of Christian baptism.

John's gospel contains only one explicit parable (10.1–6); but there are occasionally other illustrations which, like the parables in the other gospels, invite the reader to do some thinking for himself. '**The wind blows where** 8 **it wills**' is one of these. The point of comparison seems to be the freedom and unpredictability of the wind: in the same way, Christian "rebirth" is not tied to physical laws and long processes like physical birth, but is sudden and unpredictable. Indeed you can take the comparison as far as you like; it happens that in Greek, as in Hebrew, the same word is used for both wind and spirit.

However, there is still more to be said about the concept of being "born again". In Greek the words have a double meaning: "**born over again**" or "**born from above**". This second meaning suggests a whole new line of thought. Baptism is something which happens **on earth**: the spirit is received 12 as an enrichment of the possibilities of human life; it does not follow that it reveals to the Christian the **things of heaven**. But if rebirth is also "from above", then it must also introduce him to the divine world above. The clue to this aspect of it is in Christ himself. Rebirth is faith in Christ; and Christ is a figure who belongs to both worlds. The title which most clearly brings this out is **Son of Man**. It has already occurred once (1.51) with precisely 13 this significance of uniting the two worlds. And here are two more Son of Man sayings which make the same point. This figure is one who is not only a special and perhaps representative Man on earth, he also has a place on the right hand of God in heaven. The conception of such a Son of Man belongs to both worlds; and if Jesus was in fact (as he appears to have claimed in a number of sayings) the eventual embodiment of this Son of Man conception, then he was the unique link between the two worlds. '**No one ever went** up into heaven except the one who came down from heaven, the Son of Man.' And how was the believer helped by this? Many of the Son of Man sayings in the other gospels seemed anything but illuminating. The Son of Man was to suffer and to die: how then could he help the believer to draw near to heaven, and give him a rebirth "from above"? John's version of

14 these sayings (for that is what verse 14 appears to be) is that the **Son of Man must be lifted up**. This had all kinds of possible meanings—lifted up on the cross, lifted up to heaven—which could be said to have been fulfilled in what happened to Jesus. But for the present, we are left to grapple with a single image from the Old Testament. To end an attack of fiery serpents on the people of Israel in the wilderness,

> "the Lord told Moses to make a serpent of bronze and erect it as a standard, so that anyone who had been bitten could look at it and recover. So Moses made a bronze serpent and erected it as a standard, so that when a snake had bitten a man, he could look at the bronze serpent and recover."
>
> (Numbers 21.8–9)

This serpent, according to later tradition, was "raised on high" by Moses; it was a "token of deliverance" for the people (Wisdom 16.6). The parallel is subtle but illuminating: by "looking at" and believing in Jesus in the various ways in which he was "lifted up", the Christian may find deliver-

15 ance, **possess eternal life**, and so be brought by the Son of Man into heaven.

16 'God loved the world so much'. Is Jesus still speaking? The original text, having no inverted commas, leaves the question open, and modern translators have to make a choice. Perhaps in fact it makes little difference. The whole discourse is a commentary on some basic affirmations of Jesus, and is the work of the writer. His task is to show what Jesus meant, not to provide a transcript of his actual words, and it does not much matter how much of the commentary is actually placed in Jesus' mouth. The object of these final paragraphs, in any case, is to get rid of a misconception. Mention of the Son of Man suggests judgement; for, in the classic Old Testament passage about him—Daniel 7—it is at God's final judgement that he makes his triumphant appearance. But if now this Son of Man has already appeared

13 and gone **up into heaven**, does this mean that it is too late for any more rebirth, are men already lined up for judgement, is their fate already sealed? The answer lies in a radical reformulation of traditional beliefs about God's judgement. The old conception was of a moment at the end of time when all men, the living and the dead, would be summoned to appear before the divine tribunal. To some extent that picture may still be valid; but now, much of what was traditionally thought of as belonging to the ultimate

19 future must be realized as taking place in the present. **Here lies the test**— here and now. Judgement has indeed begun, but it consists in the challenge

now presented to mankind by Jesus: men are judged when they declare for
or against the light. Rebirth, involving salvation, is still an option for all.
Thus it can be said, '**It was not to judge the world that God sent** 17
his Son into the world, but that through him the world might be
saved.'

Jesus . . . baptized. John too was baptizing. This gospel records a period 22–3
when both men were apparently doing identical work simultaneously. Such
a period is not mentioned in the other gospels; indeed it seems to be implied
that Jesus did not begin his public activity until after John had been imprisoned (Mark 1.14). John's gospel explicitly contradicts this: **This was** 24
before John's imprisonment. There was an initial period when both John
and Jesus were "baptists".

Nevertheless, the activity of the two men was quite distinct. First with
regard to geography: **John . . . was baptizing at Aenon, near to Salim.** 23
We cannot locate this precisely. Aenon is probably simply a form of an Aramaic word meaning "springs", and in later centuries travellers were
doubtful just where Salim was. But all traditions point to the northern end
of that part of the Jordan valley which runs from the Sea of Galilee to the
Dead Sea. If this is correct, it is certainly true that **water was plentiful in**

that region; and there is the further point that it lay in the territory of one of the cities of the Decapolis, Scythopolis (Bethshan). There would still have been a substantial Jewish population there, but politically it was outside the jurisdiction either of Herod Antipas or of the Roman governor of Judaea.

22 Meanwhile, Jesus was baptizing in **Judaea**—that is to say, probably lower down the Jordan valley. The two baptizers were some way apart, in different political territories.

Secondly, the two men, even if they were both baptists, were not strictly comparable. This has already been shown by John's 'testimony' (1.26–30), and the reader is given a further reminder of that testimony here, along with

29 a brief parable to illustrate how the two men stood in relation to each other (as the bridegroom's friend to the bridegroom on the wedding day). The

25 conversation arose out of **a dispute with Jews** [a] **about purification.** This is something we hear nothing about elsewhere; there was clearly a great deal more to be known about John the Baptist than the gospels tell us, and this may be a genuine fragment of history. Possibly this gospel recorded it because of the word "purification": John's baptism remained on the level of outward observance and ritual purification, but Jesus, who had turned water intended for Jewish purification into wine, had a baptism which far transcended such things. Furthermore, John the Baptist's followers were evidently looking askance at the success of Jesus. Whatever John himself may have said, a certain sense of competition may have persisted between the two groups, and if this was still alive at the time this gospel was written, it could explain the particular emphasis with which, on several occasions, John the Baptist is made to disclaim any rivalry with Jesus.

Finally the difference is brought out in the terms already explored in the previous discourse. Once again, there is no indication in the original text whether verses 31–6 are intended to be read as a speech of John the Baptist or as a comment of the writer. This time the NEB chooses the second alternative. But again, it makes little difference. Coming from above—

36 witness—Spirit—judgement (here, for once in this gospel, called **wrath**) are concepts which have already been put to use. Here they stand in a new combination, and serve to summarize the stage reached so far in defining the status and authority of Jesus.

In John's gospel, the opposition to Jesus always comes from "the Jews", that is, people of influence in Jerusalem, represented sometimes by the priests

4. 1 or High Priests, sometimes (as here) by the **Pharisees.** Exactly what had

[a] There is a well-attested manuscript reading at this point (not recorded in NEB) which appears to mean "with a Jew". This is hard to make sense of; and it is possible that John originally wrote "with Jesus", and that this was accidentally copied as "with a Jew" and then changed to **with Jews** in order to yield better sense.

aroused them on this occasion is a little obscure. It has just been said (3.26) that Jesus was baptizing, and crowds were flocking to him; but now a correction is made: **in fact, it was only the disciples who were baptizing and** 2 **not Jesus himself.** This certainly matches better with the other gospels, where it is taken for granted that Jesus was not a "baptist". But in this gospel Jesus certainly had a "baptist" period, whether or not he did the actual baptizing himself (the correction, in fact, is impossible to reconcile with John's narrative, and may have been added by a later editor to remove the apparent discrepancy with the other gospels). In the face of some sort of threat from the Pharisees, he brought this period to an end, and moved to Galilee, where he was to make use of a different kind of water-symbolism.

He had to pass through Samaria. In practical terms, this was not 4 absolutely necessary: it was possible to travel from the lower Jordan to Galilee without climbing into the Samaritan hill-country. But it was common for Jewish travellers (despite the hostility of the Samaritans) to take the higher road through the mountains of Samaria: walking there was very much easier than in the stifling climate of the Jordan valley. Jesus' route was therefore perfectly normal. Moreover, there are several examples in Luke of Jesus' attitude towards the feud between Jews and Samaritans; in part, this episode in John's gospel clearly has the same intention.

Near the place where the road which Jesus would have taken from the Jordan valley joins the mountain road from Jerusalem there is a deep well. Recent archaeological evidence has shown that it was in continuous use from 1000 B.C. until A.D. 500. There is no other well in the area, and there can be no doubt that it was here that Jesus stopped on his journey. Later in the 12 conversation it is explained why it was called "Jacob's well": it was '**Jacob our ancestor, who gave us the well, and drank from it himself, he and his sons, and his cattle too**'. This too fits the spot. Nearby was the ancient city of Shechem, which had particular associations with Jacob (Genesis 33.18–20, Joshua 24.32), and the burial place of Joseph, Jacob's son, is still venerated a few hundred yards away. Even if the neighbouring towns all had springs of their own (as they have today), a watering place outside would have been important for herds of cattle, and would have been kept in constant use. The tradition that this was "Jacob's well" does not rest on any text in the Old Testament but was doubtless already a very old one in the time of Jesus. It was beyond doubt the same "Jacob's well" which is still shown to visitors today.

The nearby city of Sichem (Shechem) had been in ruins ever since its destruction in war more than a century before. Nevertheless, there were certainly towns and villages in the area. We cannot identify the one men-
5 tioned here, **a Samaritan town called Sychar**, though it is quite likely that its name has survived in the modern village of *Askar*, less than a mile away.

Why should a Samaritan woman have walked out from Sychar (where
7 there was probably a spring) **to draw water** at this well? It is possible that its water was thought to be especially pure or even medicinal (this was certainly the case as recently as the nineteenth century), given the great depth and antiquity of the well; but John gives no hint of anything of the kind. However, from this point on the story fits perfectly into its setting. Jesus was in Samaria—that is to say, a country of people who, though closely related to the Jews, had their own customs and religion, and who were liable to be unfriendly to Jewish visitors. The distrust was mutual, and a generation later it found expression in a Jewish decree that all Samaritan women must be regarded by strict Jews as ritually unclean. "Unclean" persons automatically made all their household vessels "unclean". It followed that Jews who wished to remain ritually clean could not eat or drink from the household
9 vessels of a Samaritan woman: in John's words, **Jews and Samaritans, it should be noted, do not use vessels in common**. This was true by the time the gospel was written. That it was true in the time of Jesus is questionable; but the anachronism (if it is one) is not serious. Relations were certainly strained between the two races, even if the decree about Samaritan women was not yet in force.

There was therefore some justification for the disciples' astonishment when they found Jesus **talking with a woman**. There was no Jewish 27 convention forbidding a man to converse with a female stranger. On the other hand, there was a fairly strong prejudice against the idea of a learned teacher spending any time giving instruction to women; and the fact that the woman was a Samaritan must have made the scene which greeted them seem even odder.

However, the story is not told for this reason, but for the sake of the conversations which took place. First, the simple request by Jesus for a drink leads into some teaching about '**living water**'. This expression, in 10 the Greek, can also mean fresh or running water, so that the woman's mis-understanding of Jesus' meaning—though it is an example of John's most characteristic device for keeping this kind of conversation going—is not wholly implausible. Her mind remains on the level of wells and buckets; Jesus is speaking (in words which Jewish writers sometimes liked to use when describing the Law of Moses) of '**an inner spring always welling** 14 **up for eternal life**'.

Then the conversation makes a fresh start. Telepathic knowledge (as we should call it) marked a man as a prophet. If a prophet, then perhaps the Messiah himself—an inference which the Samaritans may have been par-ticularly ready to draw, since they accepted only the first five books of the Old Testament, and the only reference there to any Coming One was to a "prophet like Moses" (Deuteronomy 18.18). The reaction of the woman was thus typically Samaritan (though many Jews might have had the same question): '**Could this be the Messiah?**' 29

But again, some deeper teaching is worked into the conversation. Just as, for the Jews, one of the tasks of the Messiah would be to restore the purity and splendour of the temple worship at Jerusalem, so, according to Samaritan belief, the Messiah would re-consecrate the Samaritan sanctuary which now lay in ruins on Mount Gerizim. This, in fact, was the point of the deepest cleavage between Jews and Samaritans. For the Jews, the place where God "made his name to dwell" (as the Book of Deuteronomy puts it) was un-questionably Jerusalem; for the Samaritans, it was Gerizim, one of the three great mountains of the country, to which the Samaritan woman could have pointed with a wave of the hand when she referred to '**this mountain**' (she 20 and Jesus were actually at the foot of it). Jesus' attitude to this dispute was frankly Jewish: the Samaritans' eccentric cult was due to an ignorant inter-pretation of Scripture. '**You Samaritans worship without knowing what** 22 **you worship, while we worship what we know**'. However exclusive the Jewish religion seemed for the moment, there could be no question that it provided the only possible basis for a universal religion. '**It is from the Jews that salvation comes**'. For many Jews, Jerusalem itself was doubtless mainly a symbol: it was not the actual city with its temple which was important, but the deeper realities it stood for. Nevertheless, they felt the need for some focus for their worship. Their conception of God was transcendent, yet it was still localized. **Worship** meant turning in the direction of Jerusalem, orientating oneself towards that place on earth which God had made 24 particularly his own. To this, Jesus now opposed the conception of **worship in spirit and in truth**. The terms have a rich load of philosophical and religious meaning. There was a sense, for instance, in which any Stoic might have agreed that **God is spirit** (it was a possible way of defining God's substance). In the Old Testament, on the other hand, the words would have meant that there is a spirit which is God's Spirit, and that God therefore has that freedom and spontaneity which goes with wind or spirit. Here, these terms serve to hint at the possibilities of a worship which is totally detached from the limitations of any particular place.

33 '**Can someone have brought him food?**' This time it is the disciples who keep the conversation going by their prosaic understanding of Jesus' 32 words, '**I have food to eat of which you know nothing**'. But then a few verses follow which read more like a recollection of some isolated sayings of Jesus (in the manner of the other gospels) than like the kind of continuous 35 discourse into which this writer usually casts his material. '**Do you not say, "Four months more and then comes harvest"?**' This sounds like a proverb (especially in the Greek, which scans like a line of verse): in Palestine the interval between sowing and harvest was regularly about four months. '**But look, I tell you**'. Jesus is evidently not just commenting on the actual season of the year: the **harvest** stands for something else. In the other gospels, as in the Bible as a whole, it is a constant symbol of the Last Judgement. The same meaning fits here. Men have seldom expected the Last Judgement to come inconveniently soon: when you sow your corn, harvest seems a long time ahead; when you look at your moral record, the reckoning seldom seems imminent. But Jesus, in his own person, brought judgement into the present. He put an end to the comfortable sense of delay which belonged to the old way of looking at things. At the same time he brought the joy of a future heavenly reward within the grasp of human life. This, at least, seems to be the drift of his words. But we have little to go by, and we 37 are still more at a loss when it comes to the other proverb, "**One sows, and another reaps**". This was usually said from the point of view of the sower: it was the expression of a gloomy recognition of the inherent injustice of life. But here it is said from the point of view of the reaper, and has a cheerful note. It is possible to think of circumstances in the history of the church to which the saying might have applied by the time the gospel was written. The first "toiling" for the gospel in Samaria, for instance, was done by a group of "Hellenists" (Acts 8.4–13); when the Jerusalem leaders arrived, they simply 38 came in '**for the harvest of their toil**'. But if Jesus used the proverb, he must have meant something different. '**I sent you to reap**'. That his followers

were to have a part in the "reaping" that was the prelude to the judgement of the world, was something which Jesus certainly hinted at (Matthew
9.37). But who were the mysterious **others** who would have already done the
hard work? The Samaritan religious leaders who had prepared their people
so well for the coming of a great "prophet"? A group of Samaritans who
came to believe in Jesus as a result of this very visit? We cannot tell.

The Samaritan woman had believed in Jesus because of his apparently
psychic powers (**'He told me everything I ever did'**). He was a prophet, 39
and therefore he might well be the awaited Messiah. But after Jesus had
stayed with the Samaritans for two days, **many more became believers** 41
because of what they heard from his own lips. A feat of telepathy was
only the prelude to much more serious pronouncements; and the idea that
Jesus might be the Messiah gave place to the realization that he was a
more universal figure than their religion allowed for: '**the Saviour of the** 43
world'.

A prophet is without honour in his own country. This saying is recorded 44
in all the gospels, but here it has a completely new context. Jesus' "own
country", in the most literal sense, was Nazareth, a village in Galilee; and
the other three gospels record, as an apt setting for the saying (which was
probably in fact already a proverb), an occasion when honour was withheld
from Jesus in his home town (Matthew 13.57; Mark 6.4; Luke 4.24). But
the literal meaning was not the only possible one, nor even the most plausible
one. John took the phrase **his own country** in a much deeper sense: Jesus
was sent to the Jewish people, the centre of whose religion and national life
was Jerusalem. But "the Jews" (as John usually calls Jesus' influential
opponents at Jerusalem, by contrast with the ordinary Jewish inhabitants of
Palestine) consistently "dishonoured" him—this was the true application
of the proverb. Jesus' **own country** was the place where, above all, he
should have been accepted—Jerusalem. In due course, Jesus would deliberately face this hostility; but for the present he returned to the more welcoming **Galileans.** 45

An officer from Capernaum, whose son (or servant) was dangerously ill,
is the subject of an episode recorded by Matthew (8.5–13) and Luke (7.1–10).
These two accounts each tell the story in a somewhat different way, but both
include a dialogue between Jesus and the officer which stresses the officer's
exceptional faith; and there is the further point (especially in Luke) that the
officer was a Gentile who showed very marked deference to Jesus. In John,
the story is again different. The **officer** was not necessarily a soldier at all; he 46
was simply **in the royal service,** that is to say, probably an official in the
household of Herod Antipas, and therefore just as likely to have been a Jew.
Moreover, Jesus' rejoinder to him was reminiscent of the rebuke which Jesus
gave to Jewish people in general in Matthew 12.38–9, 'It is a wicked, godless

generation that asks for a sign'; despite which, the boy's father continued to plead with him. Thus the interest arising from Jesus' first confrontation with a Gentile, and the whole dialogue that turns on a comparison between the authority of a soldier and that of Jesus, is absent from John's version. On the
50 other hand, the emphasis is once again on faith. **The man believed what Jesus said,** and this initial act of faith turned into a whole-hearted acceptance of the gospel: in a phrase curiously reminiscent of the later history of
53 the church as it is recorded in Acts, **he and all his household became believers.**

5. 1 **Later on Jesus went up to Jerusalem for one of the Jewish festivals.** In this gospel, unlike the others, Jesus makes frequent visits to Jerusalem as a pilgrim: the festivals offered the most natural reason for a Galilean
2 teacher to "go up". **Now at the Sheep-Pool in Jerusalem there is a place with five colonnades.** Archaeology has shown John's information to be correct. Architecturally, five colonnades is a puzzling number; but Cyril, a fourth-century bishop of Jerusalem, provides the solution: "four ran round the sides, but the fifth, where the crowd of sick lay, ran across the centre". We are therefore to imagine a pool enclosed by a colonnade on each of the four sides, the pool being in fact a double pool, divided by a fifth colonnade running down the middle. An arrangement of this kind has been excavated in the north-east corner of Jerusalem. No colonnades have been found, though there may well have been some in the time of Jesus; but water can still be seen in the two largest pools. It may be only an accident that there is still a sheep market in the vicinity; but there is little reason to doubt John's statement that this pool was in some way associated with sheep and was called **Bethesda.**[a]

7 One more piece of information is given by implication. **'I have no one to put me in the pool when the water is disturbed'.** Evidently the pool was thought to have miraculous power, and this was connected with a mysterious "disturbance" of the water. This could have been the result of a peculiarity of the spring which fed the pools (at least one intermittent spring, which produced a kind of siphon-action when it failed, has been known to exist in Jerusalem); and an occasional unexplained eddy in the pool would have been enough to account for the legend which drew a crowd of sick people to it.[b]

[a] The NEB does not record that the manuscripts offer more than one version of these names. In particular, one very slight variant gives the meaning, "At the Sheep Gate in Jerusalem there is a pool with five colonnades", which fits the archaeological evidence more neatly. Bethesda also appears in some manuscripts as Bethzatha or Bethsaida; but Bethesda (meaning "House of Mercy") is probably correct.

[b] Most of this is made explicit in the additional sentences given in the NEB footnote. But these sentences, which occur only in some manuscripts, look like an intelligent inference from John's text, and not a piece of independent tradition.

Jesus' cure of the cripple is told, not just as a spectacular miracle, but as a meaningful encounter between healer and healed. It begins with a searching question—'**Do you want to recover?**', after which, despite his relatively 6 trivial answer, the man is cured. Subsequently, Jesus adds, '**leave your** 14 **sinful ways, or you may suffer something worse.**' The other gospels see most of Jesus' cures as exorcisms: when the demon had been driven out of a man, there was always a danger of a worse one coming in, and Jesus was remembered to have made a vivid comment on precisely this danger (Matthew 12.43–5; Luke 11.24–6). Here, it is as if the same idea is translated into terms of a more sophisticated view of disease, though still with the presupposition (which lay deep in Hebrew culture and is sometimes reflected in sayings of Jesus) that disease is the result of sin.

But the story gains its dramatic point from the circumstance that **that day** 10 **was a Sabbath.** The easiest offence to establish was that of the cripple himself: it was forbidden to carry any burden on the Sabbath, and so **the Jews** (who stand again, evidently, for the authorities) were justified in saying, '**You are not allowed to carry your bed**', even though the bed in 9 question may have been no more than a stretcher. However, the cripple disclaimed responsibility, and passed the blame on to Jesus. In fact, far more than a case of "carrying" was involved: the healing itself was the real cause of offence. This is exactly the situation so often described in the other gospels: **it was works of this kind done on the Sabbath that stirred** 16 **the Jews to persecute Jesus.**

It was certainly arguable that to heal was a form of "work", and therefore prohibited on the Sabbath. Jesus was impatient of this attitude. Sometimes (according to the other gospels) he simply poured contempt on it in the name of sheer humanity, sometimes he found in Scripture a precedent for his exceptional authority to waive the Sabbath regulations. His defence here was both more subtle and more far-reaching. '**My Father has never yet** 17 **ceased his work, and I am working too**'. There was certainly debate in Jesus' time on the implications of Genesis 2.2–3: "On the sixth day God completed all the work he had been doing, and on the seventh day he ceased from all his work. God blessed the seventh day and made it holy . . ." This, it was supposed, was the origin of the Sabbath. But could it be the case that God, who is now enjoying his own "Sabbath", does no "work" of any kind? Surely God is still active; how then does he avoid breaking his own Sabbath regulations? Different answers were suggested to this question; but it was generally admitted that there must be some sense in which God is still "working", and that the Sabbath prohibition of work therefore does not apply to God in the same sense that it applies to men. Jesus seems to have been alluding to this debate when he said, '**My Father has never yet ceased his work**'; but when he went on, '**and I am working too**', he clearly implied that the special exemption from the Sabbath rest which

applied to God applied equally to himself. His opponents were quick to see
18 that thereby **he claimed equality with God.**

This was a serious matter, more serious even than breaking Sabbath
regulations. The God of the Old Testament was unique and absolute. For
any man to compare himself with God was blasphemous: even to claim an
attribute like "goodness", which properly belonged only to God, was to
show irreverence (Mark 10.18). It was true that the Jews claimed a special
relationship with God: in a certain sense, they were his "children", he was
their "father". But this did not affect the immense distance which necessarily separated any individual from God. The claim Jesus had just made,
and the form in which he had expressed it (**calling God his own Father**,
as if he had a special and intimate relationship with him), went far beyond
anything a Jew would normally dare to utter. It sounded like a direct assault
on the basic monotheism of their faith. Did Jesus claim to be some sort of
second "god"? The question could have been a burning one for John's
readers as much as for Jesus' original hearers. Jesus' reply was a preliminary
answer to it.

19 '**The Son can do nothing by himself**'. In this and the following verse,
it would be perfectly correct (so far as the Greek goes) to write Father and
Son without capital letters. When this is done, the saying reads almost like
one of Jesus' parables in the other gospels: the picture is of a boy appren-
ticed to his father and learning his trade entirely under his father's super-
vision. But it would be clear, even without the capital letters, that in fact
Jesus was applying the parable to himself: just as a boy-apprentice learns
all his skill and derives all his knowledge from his craftsman-father, so Jesus,
far from claiming "equality" with God, was completely dependent on his
heavenly Father. But that is only one side of the parable's meaning. The
other side is more startling. If Jesus was God's apprentice-son, then Jesus'
work was God's work. This would be innocuous enough if it were meant in
the general sense that all men are doing "God's work" (though some more
than others, and Jesus to an exceptional degree). But the application Jesus
made of it was to a "work" that would normally be thought to be the
21 prerogative of God alone. '**As the Father raises the dead and gives them
life, so the Son gives life to men**'. God (it had always been believed) was
the supreme judge of mankind; but even this had now been learnt and
22 carried on from him by the apprentice: **God has given full jurisdiction
to the Son**. Jesus pretended to no "equality" with God, he was no "second
god" himself; yet in virtue of all that he had learnt from God and which he
23 did with God's authority, '**all should pay the same honour to the Son
as to the Father**'.

Raising the dead and giving them life, judging—these terms belonged to
the standard Jewish picture of the destiny which awaits every man after
death: at a given moment, God will "raise" all who have died, so that they

may stand before him for judgement; the righteous he will reward with an everlasting life of felicity, the unrighteous he will consign to an appropriate punishment. To put it in its simplest terms, 'those who have done right will rise to life; those who have done wrong will rise to hear their doom'. Jesus nowhere explicitly rejects this traditional picture; but in what has just been said he claims to occupy a significant place in it. It appears that he is to take over from God the actual administration of the final judgement: he is to have full jurisdiction. What is the importance of this? Is it simply a redistribution of rôles in that mythological drama which is the way men tend to imagine the judgement of God? Does it mean that in any picture of the last things the traditional representation of the divine Judge at the centre must now be replaced by the figure of Jesus? Doubtless, yes—so long as the old picture is kept at all. But in this gospel Jesus' words, though still using the old language, suggest a different picture altogether.

The furthest possible extremes of human experience are represented by the two words, life and death. If one wants to describe two kinds of living as totally different from each other, one can draw a metaphor from the same antithesis. The old, poor kind of life one can call "death", the new and splendid dimension one can call "life", "real life", or better still, borrowing a term from the traditional picture of the life of the blest after death, "eternal life". In doing this, one is not necessarily denying that the old picture of a final judgement after death is in some sense valid; but one is deliberately using the old imagery to describe the intensity of a new way of life which is now attainable in the present.

This is what John is doing here. His interpretation of Jesus' parable about father and son begins with a preliminary definition of what this new kind of living consists of: 'anyone who gives heed to what I say and puts his trust in him who sent me has hold of eternal life, and does not come up for judgement, but has already passed from death to life'. The old imagery is pressed into service to show how radically different this new kind of life is from the old. The traditional concepts are not necessarily cancelled (the restatement of them in verses 28–9 is completely ambiguous: it could be an endorsement of them or a total reinterpretation of them). But now, the "judgement" which matters consists in the way a man reacts to Jesus, eternal life is what is experienced as a result of reacting warmly. This is all new; and yet it is an expression of the unchanging justice of the judgement of God: 'I judge as I am bidden, and my sentence is just, because my aim is not my own will, but the will of him who sent me'.

Reacting warmly to Jesus, however, meant believing him to be what he claimed to be; and it was legitimate to ask (as one would ask in a court of law) what the evidence was for such tremendous claims. In this sense, however compelling some people might find Jesus' own sayings, what he said himself could not count as evidence: to be believed, he must have independent

witnesses. From this strictly legal point of view, it was correct for him to
31 say, 'If I testify on my own behalf, that testimony does not hold
good'. Now in fact two particular kinds of testimony to Jesus have already
been mentioned, that of John the Baptist, and that of the scriptures. But
both these were cogent only for those already disposed to believe. Most
35 people saw significance in John the Baptist's movement only for a time:
they failed to see its lasting significance as a testimony to Jesus. And as for
39 the scriptures, the duty of studying them diligently was recognized by
every Jew who took his religion seriously, and no one doubted that this was
the surest way of securing the prospect of eternal life after death; but the
40 Jews still missed the true meaning of those scriptures (that 'their testimony
points to me'), and so failed to come to him who could offer them 'that
life' here and now. For anyone who was beginning to believe in Jesus, both
these kinds of testimony were exceedingly important. About that of John,
34 for instance, Jesus could say, 'I remind you of it for your own salvation'.
But, for those who remained unconvinced, Jesus' ultimate appeal was to a
36 testimony higher than John's, a testimony more explicit than that of the
scriptures—the testimony of God himself, not in the form of a crude and
dazzling appearance of the divine (for the Jews quite rightly thought of
37 God as far too transcendent a figure for anyone to have heard his voice or
36 seen his form), but expressed in the works of Jesus, which testified to the
true nature of him who performed them. It is of these "works" and of the
testimony they gave to Jesus that John's gospel is principally a record.
41 'I do not look to men for honour'. There was of course something else
which might have caused people to believe in Jesus. There is normally no
difficulty in believing that a certain man is, say, a king: the fact becomes
evident from the honour which people pay to him, and from the prestige
which he acquires in the performance of his exalted office. The same kind
of "honour" could conceivably have been concentrated in the person of
Jesus, and so have convinced people of who he was. But "honour" of this
44 kind is a purely human category, something which men receive from one
another. It could be of no value in attesting Jesus' relationship with God.
41 'I do not look to men for honour'. On the other hand, there was a kind of
44 honour which he did possess, 'the honour that comes from him who
alone is God'. Here there is a word-play which can hardly be reproduced
in English. When the Hebrew Bible was translated into Greek, the Septuagint translators used the word *doxa*, "honour", to translate the Hebrew
expression which in English we usually call "the glory of God". This was
an extension of language: it was as if God could be said to have an "honour"
which (unlike honour in the ordinary sense) is given to him by no one else,
but belongs to him by right, and is an expression of his transcendence and
power, his "glory". Jesus' argument (at least as reported in Greek by John)
makes deliberate play with this double meaning of the word *doxa*. No human

"honour" would add any weight to Jesus' claims; but if people only had an eye for the kind of *doxa* which is the glory of God, they would realize that this was something which did attach to Jesus and showed him to have been accredited by his Father. 43

'Do not imagine that I shall be your accuser'. If everything depends 45 on how a man reacts to Jesus, then it could be expected (given the traditional picture of the Last Judgement, when each man's words and deeds will be held against him) that Jesus himself would be the "accuser", saying to God (in effect), This man did not accept me. But this would be to suggest that Jesus introduced a new criterion of judgement—no longer right or wrong, good or evil, but for or against Jesus. In fact, the criterion is the same as it always was. Rightly understood, the whole of Scripture points to the same criterion. 'Your accuser is Moses'.

Some time later. A miracle performed by Jesus, in which a great crowd 6. 1 was fed from a small number of loaves and fishes, is told twice over by Mark and Matthew, and once each by Luke and John. In all these accounts, the main elements of the story are the same: the two episodes that are reported in Mark and Matthew differ only in relatively unimportant details, and Luke appears to follow Mark's first account. The version in John, like that of the second miracle in Mark and Matthew, places the episode on **the farther shore of the Sea of Galilee (or Tiberias),** [a] but in other respects it comes closer to the first (Mark 6.33–44). A single well-remembered episode evidently forms the basis of these various accounts (even if Jesus, as Mark and Matthew record, actually repeated the miracle on a second occasion). But John characteristically tells the story in his own way, and, by a slight shift of emphasis, makes it yield a new meaning.

According to all the other accounts of this miracle, the crowd was hungry, the hour was late, the place deserted. A compassionate concern for the pilgrims' needs was the spring of Jesus' action. But John says nothing of this. Instead, he simply records that **it was near the time of Passover, the** 4 **great Jewish festival.** Our attention is drawn, not to the urgent need for food, [b] but to the imminence of the one symbolic meal of the Jewish year. The food Jesus was about to provide must not be understood, any more than the Passover lamb, merely as a means of satisfying hunger.

When everyone had had enough. Five thousand men had been satisfied 12

[a] Tiberias is on the west shore of the lake. It was built by Herod Antipas for his capital city, and its name was intended as a compliment to the reigning Emperor, Tiberius. To Gentiles, it would have been natural to call the lake by the same name. But the Jews, who disliked the new pagan city, preferred to call it either by its biblical name, the Lake of Gennesaret (Luke 5.1), or else (as usually in the gospels) the Sea of Galilee.
[b] Most of Galilee, in the time of Jesus, seems to have been about as densely populated and cultivated as modern rural Surrey. Even on the mountains one could never have been far from towns. In this respect, John's account is perhaps more plausible than the others.

with five barley loaves and two small fishes: this was surely a sufficiently sensational fact to make the narrator pause a moment. But John allows it 13 only a passing reference, and hurries on to another point: they **filled twelve baskets with the pieces left uneaten of the five barley loaves.** Why was this so important? On the face of it, it was the feeding that mattered, not what was left over. Admittedly, the detail is mentioned in the other gospels, and it may have seemed to the writer to be almost a necessary part of any story of this kind. A miracle performed by Elisha, for instance, included the same point (and also has other features in common with this one):

"A man came from Baal-shalisha, bringing to the man of God some of the new season's bread, twenty barley loaves ... Elisha said, 'Give this to the people to eat.' But his disciple protested, 'I cannot set this before a hundred men.' Still he repeated, 'Give it to the people to eat; for this is the word of the Lord: "They will eat and leave over"'. So he set it before them, and they ate and left some over, as the Lord had said." (2 Kings 4.42–4)

And there is also something similar in the story of Ruth: "Boaz passed her some roasted grain. She ate all she wanted and still had some left over" (Ruth 2.14). Moreover, when Jesus (according to the other gospels) later alluded to this miracle, he referred deliberately to this point of bread having been left over: 'When I broke the five loaves among five thousand, how many basketfuls of scraps did you pick up?' (Mark 8.19). Gathering up scraps of bread after a meal was certainly an ingrained habit. Bread was eaten with everything. It was the only implement for eating, and was used for wiping the fingers. To leave substantial pieces lying about was dirty, wasteful and irreverent. But on this occasion there was far more to it than that. It is important to visualize the quantities involved. A modern baker's loaf may feed several people; but the loaves of Jesus' time were the small, round, flat ones still used by Semitic peoples. Three of them were needed to give a man a meal (Luke 11.5). Twenty of them, in the Elisha story, seemed absurdly little to set before a hundred men. Any basket would hold at least 13 a dozen such loaves, if not many more. On this occasion, they **filled twelve baskets with the pieces left uneaten of the five barley loaves.** In other words, even after the meal, they were left with many times more than they started with. We can now see why this detail is the real climax of the story. How much bread the men needed to eat could not be calculated. Perhaps (a cynic might have said) they were not very hungry. But this did not matter. The real evidence for the miracle lay in those twelve baskets full of scraps. 14 This was the **sign** that **the people saw.** Moreover, it gave John the cue 27 for adding some teaching of Jesus about **food that lasts, the food of eternal life.** Like the 'water' which is 'an inner spring always welling up for eternal life' (4.14), the bread which Jesus gives is always there, even after it has fed multitudes.

The word went round, 'Surely this must be the prophet that was to 14 come into the world'. The Jewish religion encouraged people to pin their hopes on a figure "who was to come", even though it allowed a wide variety of opinions on what kind of figure this would be. Speculation ranged from a purely human warrior-king to an almost transcendental being who would usher in a new age. One text which was often quoted in this connection was that in which Moses foretold that God would "raise up a prophet from among you like myself" (Deuteronomy 18.15). Moses had miraculously fed the people with manna, and here was Jesus doing much the same thing. It was not difficult for the crowd to guess that Jesus 'must be the prophet', and the subsequent dialogue shows that this was the way their minds were working. But this kind of religious excitement could easily spill over into something more practical and dangerous. There were several "prophets" in this period who promised to show an authoritative "sign" and then to lead the Jewish people against their Roman conquerors. It needed no more than what Jesus had just done for the crowd to come and seize him to proclaim 15 him king.

Jesus . . . withdrew. In Matthew and Luke, the possibility of an earthly kingship was one of the "tests" to which Jesus was exposed by the devil. In all the gospels, the point was important when it came to Jesus' trial; and there were many earlier occasions on which his words and actions had political implications. This is the only place in any of the gospels where the possibility of a political movement starting outside Jerusalem is explicitly referred to; but it would have been natural for the evangelists to play down this motif, and John may well preserve something here which the others have passed over. In any case, the danger (as Jesus saw it to be) provides a convincing motive for Jesus separating himself from his followers and for his disciples taking to their boat—an episode which also comes in this place 16-21 in Mark (6.45–52) and Matthew (14.22–32).

'It is I; do not be afraid'. All the accounts of this episode contain these 21 words; but the story itself is told by John in a rather different way. Matthew and Mark leave the reader in no doubt that Jesus miraculously walked across the water. In John, the details are not so clear: Jesus could have been in shallow water near the edge of the lake. But (as the sequel shows) the writer certainly believed he was describing a supernatural event. Next morning 22 the crowd tried to work out what had happened to Jesus, and found his disappearance inexplicable. [a] When they finally tracked him down in Capernaum, this was the first thing they wanted to ask him. 'Rabbi', they said, 26 'when did you come here?'

It looked, then, as if the crowd's motives in following Jesus were pure curiosity and a desire for more free bread. Jesus ignored the first and poured

[a] Verses 22–4 are somewhat obscure in the original; but the essential point seems to be that there was originally only one boat, and Jesus was known not to have embarked in it.

scorn on the second. The miracle of the loaves was not intended just to satisfy their hunger. It was a "sign" of something more important—something the crowd had failed to grasp. To turn the discussion in the right
27 direction, Jesus used a form of words they could easily understand. '**You must work, not for this perishable food, but for the food that lasts, the food of eternal life**'.

This was the familiar choice offered by religious teachers: either "perishable food"—that is, the material rewards of a wholly this-worldly life—or the kind of god-fearing and obedient living which would secure a favourable judgement on the Last Day and the reward of **eternal life**. Jesus' next words seemed at first sight to fit into the same picture: '**This food the Son of Man will give you**'. The Son of Man (in Daniel 7 and also probably in popular belief) was a figure associated with the Last Judgement. So, missing the real point of Jesus' saying (which only becomes clear later in the chapter), [a] they asked him the usual question about the way of life which would secure their acquittal on the day of Judgement and entitle them to receive
28 food from the Son of Man. '**Then what must we do**', they asked him, '**if we are to work as God would have us work?**'

This was a stock question. In the other gospels it is put to Jesus in the form, 'What must I do to inherit eternal life?' (Mark 10.17); and Jesus' answer is, 'Follow me'. Here, his answer is similar, though "following" has
29 given place to "believing": '**believe in the one whom God has sent**'.

But how were they to believe? Jesus must do something, give some sign, to show who he was. Of course (John would have us understand) this is exactly what Jesus had been doing; but the "signs" Jesus gave were too subtle, and demanded too much readiness of acceptance, to be generally understood. The crowd was thinking of something more obvious, such as
31 Moses providing the people with manna (Exodus 16; the quotation, "**He gave them bread from heaven to eat**", does not occur in the Old Testament in precisely this form: it is a recollection of such passages as Psalm 78.24, Nehemiah 9.15). If Jesus were similarly to arrange a miraculous supply of bread, they would believe in him. Perhaps; but that was not Jesus' way. Believing in Jesus did not depend on happening to have witnessed a miracle. 'His own would not receive him' (1.11) expressed a greater mystery than
44 this. Ultimately, believing was something given by God. '**No man can come to me unless he is drawn by the Father who sent me**'. This

[a] '**He it is upon whom God the Father has set the seal of his authority**' is a sentence open to many interpretations. The crowd would presumably have understood it as a piece of normal Son of Man doctrine: God had in some sense marked out and chosen the figure who would ultimately be revealed as Son of Man. The metaphor of a "seal" could have been one way of saying this (though it could also perhaps have suggested another popular doctrine about the Son of Man, that he was "hidden"—shut away and kept secure under a seal—until the day when he was to be revealed). But later Christian readers would certainly have understood it quite differently. God "set his seal" on Jesus at any of those moments in his life—perhaps particularly his baptism—which marked him out as someone unique.

sounds like the harshest determinism. But consider how God does in fact "draw" men: through the revelation of himself in the Bible. Jesus was witnessed to by Scripture; it was open to anyone to be "drawn". In this sense, those who came to Jesus were those who read Scripture aright— 'who . . . listened to the Father'—and who could be described in the 45 words of a prophecy of Isaiah (54.13), **"And they shall all be taught by God."**

'**The truth is, not that Moses gave you the bread from heaven, but** 32 **that my Father gives you the real bread from heaven**'. The manna was supernatural bread, certainly, but it did no more than satisfy physical hunger. Even if Jesus were to provide bread on that supernatural scale (instead of just once in the mountains beyond the lake), nothing would be achieved of real significance. What Moses had done in the wilderness was at most a shadow of what Jesus now proposed to do. He was offering, not the satisfaction of physical hunger, but **real bread**, real sustenance. '**Whoever** 35 **comes to me shall never be hungry**'. Jesus' claim was that in his own person he represented the spiritual values, the authentic experience, the true goal of existence, which until then had been envisaged only as a gift which God would give to the righteous after death. The old language of the after-life was doubtless still valid: '**I will raise him up on the last day**' 40 was a perfectly conventional promise that, at the Last Judgement, Jesus would secure for his followers a favourable verdict and a share in the promised blessings. But by now the reader of this gospel has learnt that after-life language is also a way of talking about a new kind of life in the present. '**Eternal life**' was attainable here and now, given a certain relationship with Jesus.

At this the Jews began to murmur disapprovingly. Such a claim, 41 from any man who seemed in so many respects like other men, provoked incredulity and censure. '**Surely this is Jesus son of Joseph; we know** 42 **his father and mother.**' [a] Jesus recognized this obstacle to belief, and accepted the consequence that only some would be led to believe. Undeterred, he went on to give a further turn to the idea of 'real bread' which this time led **to a fierce dispute among the Jews** and caused many even of his 52 disciples to withdraw from him. '**The bread which I will give is my own** 51 **flesh**'.

This is the climax of the chapter, the point towards which the discussion has been leading from the beginning. The Christians for whom this gospel was written were already accustomed to holding a solemn supper at which the bread and wine were affirmed to be the body and blood of Christ; and

[a] Did John know (as Matthew and Luke did) that Jesus had no human father, but was conceived 'by the Holy Spirit' (Matthew 1.18)? It is hard to be sure. The most one can say is that Jesus' miraculous birth is fully compatible with John's understanding of his nature. The present passage, in any case, hardly bears upon the question; the Jews merely echo the usual opinion at the time. Jesus was 'the son, as people thought, of Joseph' (Luke 3.23).

they knew that the institution of this new and distinctive act of worship went back to some explicit teaching of Jesus himself. They will have been prepared by a number of hints earlier on in the chapter to expect such teaching here

11, 23 (**Jesus took the loaves, gave thanks, and distributed, and the bread over which the Lord gave thanks,**[a] are phrases which are characteristic of the New Testament accounts of the Lord's Supper); and they will have

51 found what they were expecting in the words, 'The bread which I will give is my own flesh; I give it for the life of the world'. These words are strikingly similar to those used by Jesus in the other gospels' accounts of the last supper, celebrated by Jesus with his disciples on the night before the crucifixion. Here, however different the setting, the substance of the teaching is the same. Indeed, it seems likely that John chose this point in his gospel to

50 gather together all Jesus' teaching on '**the bread that comes down from heaven**', the bread which is Jesus' own body and which gives eternal life. In the context of his narrative, this teaching had the effect of still further shocking those who heard it into belief or disbelief. But for his readers, the whole chapter took on its full meaning only when read in the light of their own experience of the eucharist.

59 **This was spoken in synagogue when Jesus was teaching in Capernaum.** Considering the dramatic series of episodes which led up to the discourse, it seems both unnecessary and inappropriate to suggest that by the end it had become an ordinary synagogue sermon. But perhaps a new point is being made. This, in John's gospel, is Jesus' last public appearance in Galilee; and, just as in the other gospels it was **in synagogue** that the decisive confrontations between Jesus and the religious leaders in Galilee took place, so here it is fitting that Galilee's final judgement on Jesus' words and works should have been passed at the local centre of religious worship and religious education: the synagogue at Capernaum.

62 '**Does this shock you?**' Taken at all literally, Jesus' words about himself as "bread" to be eaten were of course shocking. Jews, in any case, had a horror of consuming the blood of any slaughtered animal. Therefore Jesus'

53 statement, '**Unless you eat the flesh of the Son of Man and drink his blood you can have no life in you**' seemed an almost deliberate affront to their sensibilities, however figurative the language was supposed to be. Jesus does little to soften the shock; but he adds a brief pointer to the way in

62 which his words should be interpreted. '**What if you see the Son of Man ascending to the place where he was before?**' It is not as an ordinary man that Jesus can give his flesh to eat, but as Son of Man, that is, as a person who belongs both to heaven and earth. There have been hints of this

[a] This second hint may be due, not to John himself, but to a later copyist anxious to make the symbolism more explicit. If so, this would explain why some manuscripts omit the phrase. See the footnote in NEB.

earlier. The bread—or Jesus himself[a]—'comes down from heaven'. He 33
belongs (and is soon to ascend) to the realm above, which is the realm of
spirit. 'The spirit alone gives life; the flesh is of no avail'. To think only 63
of the flesh of the human Jesus is to fail to see the meaning of the "bread".
The Jesus who feeds others is a person who belongs to heaven, and whose
real nature is therefore spirit. Unless one believed this, one could make
nothing of Jesus' teaching.

Nevertheless, the shock remained, and many found it too much for them.
The rejection of Jesus is necessarily a theme of all the gospels, though they
treat it in different ways. Usually there is a clear distinction between the
crowds on the one hand and the disciples on the other. Here, the dividing
line runs right down the group of disciples themselves: the Twelve were
only the remnant of a larger number who had once followed Jesus (there may
be a hint of this in Luke 22.28). It was only from that time on that there 66
was a sharply defined group of twelve disciples corresponding to the Twelve
of the other gospels.

So Jesus asked the Twelve, 'Do you also want to leave me?' In 67
Mark 8.27–33 (and in the corresponding passages of Matthew and Luke)
there is an important scene in which Peter recognizes Jesus' true nature, and
in which Jesus then predicts what is to befall him in Jerusalem. This brief
dialogue in John contains the same elements. Peter calls Jesus, not 'the
Messiah' (as in Mark), but the Holy One of God. Doubtless it came to 69
much the same thing: it was the title given to Jesus by a demon in Mark 1.24,
and the demons knew who Jesus really was. In any case, it was a decisive
confession of faith. It marked out those who were Jesus' "followers" (not
of their own merit, but by Jesus' call)—except, of course, that even in that
small group there was one who would betray him. 71

The great controversy

The new heading marks a new stage in the narrative. It was said at the outset
that Christ 'entered his own realm, and his own would not receive him' (1.11).
What has just been described is the refusal of some to believe, and the
defection of others who had begun to believe. But in the story of Jesus, the
failure of his own to receive him was to take a much more drastic form than
this. It was not merely that they refused to believe in him. In the end they
actually put him to death. That they did so was admittedly the result of a
combination of circumstances: Jesus' execution followed a formal trial and
was ordered, not by 'his own' (the Jews) but by the Roman governor. But
this terrible dénouement was not a sudden reversal of fortune. The intention

[a] Verse 33 is perhaps deliberately ambiguous. See the footnote in NEB.

was there from the moment Jesus arrived in Jerusalem: the arrest, trial and crucifixion were simply the historical form taken by the principle that 'his own would not receive him'. Much of *The great controversy* which follows turns on points that have been made earlier; but there is now a more

7. 1 threatening factor. **The Jews were looking for a chance to kill him.**

Why did they not immediately succeed? On a practical level, it might be said that the appearance of the Son of God was too complicated a phenomenon for that. People who saw and heard Jesus were both attracted and

32 scandalized by him; even the **temple police,** sent by the authorities to

46 arrest him, found it impossible to carry out their orders—'**No man',** they answered, '**ever spoke as this man speaks**'. These alternating reactions of exasperation and respect provide the dramatic framework of the controversy. But meanwhile there was another reason for Jesus' repeated escapes from his enemies, a reason of a different kind. Jesus' death, and the glorification which was to go with it, was something determined in advance by God. When the time came, it would take place inexorably; but for the

30 present, **his appointed hour had not yet come.**

There was also another side to this alternation of admiration and enmity.

10 It was as if Jesus was not fully showing his hand: he was present, **not**

5 **publicly, but almost in secret.** To his brothers, who **had no faith in him,** and therefore represented the attitude of those who did not understand the nature of Jesus' person and work, it seemed obvious that one must either be resigned to the obscurity of a provincial existence in Galilee, or else

4 "show oneself to the world" in Jerusalem: '**Surely no one can hope to be in the public eye if he works in seclusion**'. But again, the presence of Jesus in the world, the coming of the Word 'into his own realm', was too complex a phenomenon to be expressed in such simple terms. A certain secrecy (as is particularly evident in Mark's gospel) was a necessary condition attached to the appearance of the Messiah. Those who recognized him did so because they discerned who he really was, not because his real nature was so apparent that it could not be denied. To evoke true faith, Jesus necessarily showed the world a face that was challenging and ambiguous. *The great controversy* provoked by his appearance in Jerusalem consists of a series of brief dialogues which lay bare different aspects of this essential ambiguity. The curiously non-committal way in which Jesus makes his pilgrimage to Jerusalem sets the tone for the conversations which follow.

2 **The Jewish Feast of Tabernacles** was the greatest of the year—and this may be a sufficient reason for John mentioning it: Jesus went up to Jerusalem on that occasion in the year when the largest number of Jews regularly made their pilgrimage. It was an autumn festival, to mark the safe gathering in of crops and fruit. It involved the setting up of token "tabernacles", or huts made of branches (the origin of which is uncertain), and there were processions with greenery and fruit; the services and festivities in the temple lasted

for a week. It is true that certain subsidiary rites, such as the ceremonial pouring of water over the altar, or the lighting of candles in the court outside the temple, would have provided cues for sayings of Jesus about 'living 38 water' and 'the light of the world'. But in John's narrative these allusions 8. 12 to little-known ceremonies, if they were intentional, would have been very recondite, particularly since nothing is said of the "tabernacles" themselves, which were the best-known feature of the festival. For the most part, the festival seems merely to provide the occasion for Jesus' sudden appearance in Jerusalem.

Jesus **began to teach.** This immediately raised the question of his authority 7. 14 to do so. 'How is it', they said, 'that this untrained man has such 15 learning?' All authority to teach normally came to the pupil from his master; but Jesus had been to no professional school to study the interpretation of Scripture. So far as anyone knew, he was **untrained.** So where did he get his authority? Jesus' answer was that his authority lay in no exterior qualification, but in the teaching itself. Anyone who sincerely had **the will** 17 **to do the will of God** as it was revealed in the Law of Moses would find that Jesus' teaching enabled him to understand how to do so. The teaching authenticated itself: instead of giving **honour** to Jesus, it gave "glory" to 18 God (there is the same play on the meanings of a single Greek word as in 5.41–4 above).

'Did not Moses give you the Law? Yet you all break it.' The 19 majority of the Jews did not aspire to observe every detail of the Law of Moses; but the Pharisees, despising this lack of seriousness, set themselves a very rigorous discipline by which they believed they could avoid even an inadvertent transgression. Yet even they were not always successful: the apostle Paul was a Pharisee who ultimately confessed himself defeated by the complexity of the demands which he believed the Law laid upon him. There may have been those standing by who would have personally denied Jesus' charge that they broke the Law; but they would have been ready to admit that the majority of Jews did so in one way or another. Why, in that case, single out Jesus and try to kill him for one transgression?

But of course Jesus' transgression was a serious one: 'Once only have I 21 done work on the Sabbath', but breaking the Sabbath was an offence against a basic principle of the Jewish religion, and it has already been said (5.16) that it was Jesus' deliberate healing on a Sabbath which aroused powerful opposition. The gospels all contain instances of such Sabbath **work** by Jesus, and record various lines which he adopted to justify his actions. Here is yet another (of a kind which some Jewish scholars of the time actually used themselves). Some commandments (such as that to circumcise a baby on the eighth day) inevitably conflict occasionally with resting on the Sabbath, but must still be carried out. If circumcision, affecting only one

member of the body, is permissible on the Sabbath, how much more an act
23 giving health 'to the whole of a man's body'?

27   'When the Messiah appears no one is to know where he comes
from'. Popular belief, picturing the coming Messiah, tended to wrap him
in mystery: he would be a person of unknown origin, appearing from some
secret recess of the world at the time appointed for him to perform his great
work. On the face of it, the known facts of Jesus' home and origin did not
fit the conventional picture. Jesus' reply is characteristic of this gospel.
Knowing the village "where Jesus came from" was irrelevant: what mattered was whether (in a much more fundamental sense) he "came from"
God. This was harder to tell. Some judged the claim to be blasphemous,
31 others reflected on the 'signs' he had done. Once again, there were conflicting reactions to him.

After the event, we can see that this "having come" from God implied
also that Jesus would soon "go to" God. But at the time Jesus' sayings
33 about going could well have seemed enigmatic, and have led to speculation
35 that Jesus proposed to leave Palestine (in which, of course, there was an
element of prophetic truth: by the time the gospel was written, it could be
said that a great part of the ultimate purpose of Jesus' work had been to
'teach the Greeks'.)

38 'If anyone is thirsty let him come to me; whoever believes in me, let
him drink'. By itself, this belongs naturally to a whole series of sayings in
this gospel in which Jesus likens himself to real food and real drink; but
here, it gains added point from the context in which it is given. John tells
37 us that it was delivered on the last and greatest day of the festival. The
festival lasted eight days in all, and it is the way of such religious functions
to be best attended at the end; this fact alone would be sufficient to give
particular emphasis and solemnity to Jesus' pronouncement. (Exactly what
stage had been reached in the ceremonies, and whether it was a day when the
ritual of fetching and pouring out water was performed, are questions which
John's sketchy indications do not allow us to answer; but his first readers
can hardly have been much better informed than we are, and it is not likely
that John intended them to be picturing any particular ceremonies when they
read Jesus' words.) But his words also had strong Old Testament overtones. [a]
It was prophesied in Zechariah 14.8 that "in that day" (that is, at the beginning of a new age) "living water shall issue from Jerusalem"—a prophecy
greatly elaborated by Ezekiel (47.1–12), who shared the same vision of the
arid hills and valleys of Judaea being watered by a miraculously abundant
spring flowing out of the temple itself (a vivid symbol of the place of Jeru-

[a] The punctuation of the saying is uncertain, and it is possible that the quotation from
Scripture is actually part of it, instead of being a comment on it (see the footnote in NEB).
But this yields a meaning which seems to fit less naturally into the sequence of Jesus'
teaching.

salem in the religious life of the world). Moreover, when Moses struck a rock at Horeb, water came out for the thirsty people to drink (Exodus 17.6). There is no phrase in Scripture exactly corresponding to the quotation, '**Streams of living water shall flow out from within him**'; it was 38 probably a composite text, the result of scholars having constantly seen the possibilities of combining the story of the desert Rock with the prophecy of an abundance of water in the temple.

These Old Testament overtones raised questions. Admittedly Christians held the real clue to the interpretation of the saying: water, in Jesus' teaching, was a symbol for **the Spirit,** a gift which they received in abundance 39 when the church came into existence after the resurrection of Jesus. But Jesus' hearers did not have this clue. Thinking more literally of water (and not of that which the water symbolized) they reflected that it was Moses who found the miraculous supply of water in the desert (and that **the expected** 40 **prophet,** like Moses, would doubtless do something similar), and that it was **the Messiah** who would initiate the new age when water would flow from the temple in Jerusalem. '**If anyone is thirsty let him come to me**'—did 38 this mean that Jesus was the Messiah? There seemed to be the fatal objection that Jesus had '**come from Galilee**', whereas the Messiah, being a succes- 41 sor to David, was expected to come '**from David's village of Bethlehem**'. 42 John's readers doubtless knew the answer to this: Jesus was in fact born in Bethlehem. But Jesus' hearers could not be expected to know this: for them, Jesus both was and was not like the Messiah. This is the theme of the whole scene: the challenge and ambiguity of the person of Jesus. This time, it **caused a split among the people.** The Pharisees, however, were quite 43 clear in their own mind: his Galilean origin was fatal to Jesus' claims. No passage of Scripture could be quoted to show that any important figure or prophet would come from there. It made not the slightest difference what ordinary people thought. The Pharisees firmly believed that it was only the members of their own fellowships who made a serious attempt to observe the Law, and many of them regarded their less disciplined fellow-Jews as undoubtedly beyond salvation. '**As for this rabble, which cares nothing** 49 **for the Law, a curse is on them**', was typical Pharisees' language.

(In most older translations of the New Testament, *An incident in the temple* 7. 53–**8.** 11 follows here, but is almost certainly out of place. See below, p. 395.)

'**I am the light of the world**'. After water, light. Jesus' great affirmations **8.** 12 about himself use one great poetical concept after another. "Light" and "life" were two of the evocative words used in the prologue: they are about to be explored in the following chapters. Here they simply serve as an example of the kind of thing Jesus was saying about himself. He was making great claims, and the objection of his enemies at this stage was not so much

to the language he was using about himself as to the fact that he was making
13 such claims at all. 'You are witness in your own cause; your testimony
is not valid'.

When a person made some claim, he normally had to support it with
independent evidence. Jesus' enemies were saying, in effect, that to make the
kind of claims he was making, Jesus ought to produce some independent
evidence. But it could happen that under exceptional circumstances no such
evidence was available: suppose, for example, a man's title deeds to a particular property had been lost, and there was no other evidence of his ownership; in that case a judge or arbitrator would have no choice but to decide
whether or not to accept the man's "witness in his own cause". This was
Jesus' defence. His claim to recognition rested ultimately upon his origin
and his destiny. But the previous dialogue had proved that only Jesus knew
14 what these were. 'I know where I come from, and where I am going.
You do not know'. His case rested on facts to which only he had access.
He was in the exceptional position of a claimant whose testimony about
himself was the only evidence available. Therefore his testimony was
valid.

15   'You judge by worldly standards.' One reason why at this point the
argument becomes hard for us to follow is that we are accustomed to make
a sharp distinction between judging and giving evidence. To us, judges are
utterly distinct from witnesses; their task is to determine impartially whether
the evidence offered by the witnesses is true. But in a Jewish court, if the
witnesses were persons generally accepted as reliable, if they could not be
shown to have lied, and if their testimony agreed, there was no more to be
said: judgement followed automatically. Indeed, since the penalty for
criminal offences was prescribed by the Law, there was no need even for a
judge to pronounce the sentence; the witnesses were entitled to see that it
was carried out themselves. Thus, "judging" might often include framing
an accusation, testifying as a witness, and carrying out the sentence. The
Jews were concerned to "judge" Jesus on his claim to be the light of the
world. Jesus had shown that only he had access to the kind of evidence
which would support such a claim. The Jews had mistaken the nature of the
case when they demanded independent evidence; they were judging by
worldly standards. But suppose now the tables were turned. The Jews had
failed to accept Jesus' claims. He could now "judge" them for their dis-
16 belief. True, that was not his purpose. I pass judgement on no man. But
suppose he did (if I do judge): he accepted, as they did, the basic proposition
of the Jewish law of evidence (Deuteronomy 19.15) that "a charge must be
established on the evidence of two or three witnesses". It followed from this
17 that the testimony of two witnesses is valid. If Jesus were bringing a
charge against the Jews, his own evidence would count: he would be one
witness (not quite "in his own cause", as the NEB puts it, for it was now

the Jews who were on trial for refusing to accept Jesus' claims). Where was the other? 'My other witness is the Father who sent me'. Taken literally, 18 this would not count—and the Jews, by their question, 'Where is your 19 father?' showed that they did take it literally. One's own relative could not normally be produced as an independent witness. But Jesus' real Father was God; and to call God as a witness was equivalent to swearing an oath that one's statement was true. Jesus' other witness was such that his words had 18 the force of a solemn oath. This put Jesus' opponents in a difficult position. It was as sinful to disbelieve a statement made on oath as it was to make a statement on oath that was not true. It was only because they did not recognize that Jesus' Father was God that the Jews were indifferent to the consequences of refusing to believe Jesus' testimony.

'Where I am going you cannot come'. When Jesus said this earlier 21 (7.34), his opponents could do no better than imagine that he meant he was leaving Palestine. This time their suggestion was less improbable: 'Perhaps 22 he will kill himself'—though this was still a total misunderstanding of Jesus' meaning. Jesus' origin and destiny belonged to a different order of things. A fairly obvious way of putting it was in terms of the world above 23 as opposed to this world below. Admittedly this was not quite the language the Jews were used to: if asked to think of a world more real than this one, they conceived it as something in the future, the "age to come", as opposed to "the present age". Again and again, Jesus used this traditional language of future expectation to describe a present experience: what they believed would come to pass one day was already a reality, even if as yet they had no experience of it. There existed, not just an age to come, but a world above. With their present attitude, the Jews could have no part in that world; they remained in this world below, the world where death still has its old power, and where there is no escape from sin.

They asked him, 'Who are you?'. A true answer to this question could 25 only have been in terms of the world above of which they had no know- 23 ledge. It was therefore impossible for Jesus to give them any answer they could understand which would not have been misleading. They did not even grasp what he meant when he talked about himself having been "sent". All he could do was to offer them an apparently enigmatic phrase, 'I am what 28 I am'. On the level of grammar this was almost meaningless. But there is a grammar of religion as well as of ordinary speech. In that grammar, the Jews were accustomed to use the future tense. Reality, for them, was something which would come one day: God would act, there would be a Person among them bringing about a new age. But Jesus' grammar was all in the present. 'I am what I am', whatever else it might mean, at least showed that Jesus was not merely a hint of what was to be, but was a reality already present. Of course, Jesus' words could have meant more than this. If you knew "what he was", you could fill in the meaning from what you knew. But ultimately,

Jesus was of God, and God is essentially indefinable. It is probably no accident that the phrase seems to echo the mysterious words spoken by God to Moses, "I AM; that is who I am" (Exodus 3.14—compare Isaiah 43.10, "... know that I am HE"). All this would be easier to grasp (again, for those who could grasp it at all) when the destiny of the Son of Man was fully

28 played out: the "lifting up" of that figure (on the cross, up to heaven) would make a bridge between the two worlds such that it would at last be possible to see how Jesus belonged to both.

31 **Turning to the Jews who had believed in him.** Jesus' words and actions had been evoking varied reactions: while there was strong opposition, nevertheless some were tempted to accept the claims he was making for himself. Suppose, now, that some Jews came to "believe in him". What difference was this going to make to them? In what sense could their ancestral religion be said to be so inadequate and incomplete that it left room for the radical new factor introduced by Jesus? Was not their Jewish inheritance of more ultimate importance than any new teaching that could be added by Jesus? This question, we know, was to be raised in a sharp form by Jewish groups within the early church—Paul's letter to the Galatians is concerned with little else. It may well have occurred to some of Jesus' original followers; but John can hardly have written this paragraph without being aware how relevant it was to the church of his own day.

33 The argument turned on Abraham. 'We are Abraham's descendants' was the basic premise of the case for the religious superiority of the Jew. Abraham had been a man of exceptional faith, piety and merit. In reward for these qualities, God had made great promises to him about his descendants; on the strength of these promises, the Jews believed that, whatever might be the destiny of the rest of mankind, they themselves could look forward to a privileged place in that new order which God ultimately intended for the universe. It was true, of course, that Jewish thinkers also saw that this could not be entirely automatic: personal integrity and righteousness must always be some kind of precondition for inheriting God's salvation. Nevertheless, it was a very deeply rooted presupposition that, in the last analysis, the fact of being a Jew was the most important factor of all in the judgement which God would pass on human beings. Again and again in the New Testament we meet the same exclusive claim to special consideration: 'We are Abraham's descendants'. However hard political circumstances might have borne on the Jewish nation (and the occupation of Palestine by the Romans seemed to some of them like virtual slavery), their sense of superiority to all other nations remained: even the Romans showed them exceptional consideration in allowing them to continue the practice of their own religion. In everything that mattered, they felt justified in saying, 'We have never been in slavery to any man'.

To non-Jewish thinkers, this would have sounded like nonsense. It is righteousness, self-understanding, self-control, not belonging to a particular race, which give men confidence and peace of mind. 'The truth will set 32 you free' . . . 'everyone who commits sin is a slave'—such phrases were 34 often on the lips of Greek philosophers. It is perhaps a little difficult to imagine Jesus using such philosophical language himself (though it would probably have come quite naturally to John). But in essence his protest against the traditional Jewish attitude was the same as that of any thinker who took the facts of human sinfulness seriously. Indeed, it was a protest that was written into the Old Testament itself and had recently found a powerful spokesman in the person of John the Baptist.

The point would apply in the first instance to Jewish Christians: their new faith, however much it owed to their old, was concerned with the realities of an individual's relationship with God, and no appeal to the privileged history of a particular race was relevant to the one really important question of a man's own attitude to Christ. But the same point could also be turned against Jews who were opposed to Christianity—and Jesus seems to continue with his enemies in mind rather than his friends. 'Abraham is our father.' 39 This, to the Jews, was a statement of fact. It was their guarantee of special rights and privileges. But there were other senses, apart from the purely physical one, in which one could call a great figure of the past one's father. [a] In particular, one could mean by it that one modelled one's conduct on his. The Jews' present conduct was sufficient to show that they could not be Abraham's children in this deeper, more ethical sense. They were bent on killing Jesus. 'That is not how Abraham acted.' 40

The Jews were ready to accept this more significant sense of "father". Indeed, this was part of what they meant when they said, 'God is our 41 father'. They professed to take all instruction on how to live their lives from God alone. Whether this claim was justified depended of course on how one conceived of God. If the Jews had had a true understanding of the nature of God (through their understanding of the Law of Moses), it might have been arguable that their lives were indeed modelled on his will, and that they were therefore justified in calling God their "father". But Jesus claimed to have "come from God", to have been "sent by God". This gave him a unique position from which to pass judgement on Jewish pretensions. Their failure to understand his language showed that they had no true understanding of 43 God. They did not know what they were modelling their lives on. Therefore they could not be 'God's children'. 47

'You are doing your own father's work . . . your father is the devil'. 41, 44 What in fact were the Jews modelling their conduct on? They were seeking to kill an innocent man; and they were refusing to listen to a truth which nevertheless they could not refute. This suggested a "father" from mythology. The devil had been 'a murderer from the beginning'—he had 44

[a] This is Paul's argument in Galatians 3.

been the cause of the death of Adam; and one of his most important rôles, especially in the period immediately preceding the Last Judgement, was to be that of misleading men whose faith was weak, and, by deceiving them, of bringing them into condemnation: he was 'a liar and the father of lies'. An apt "father" for the Jews who opposed Jesus! And in so far as the devil was not merely a figure of mythology but an active and objective force in the world, here was perhaps a partial explanation of the Jews' attitude to Jesus: it was the work of the devil.

48   'A Samaritan'—this was a studied insult: the Jews not merely disowned Jesus from membership of their race, they identified him with their bitterest enemies. 'Possessed'—this time something more than an insult: it was a sinister explanation of Jesus' words and deeds (Mark 3.22). Jesus of course denied the charge; but (here as in the other gospels), by denying that he was 'possessed', he did not thereby take personal credit for what he said and did. By so acting and speaking, he acted for God, he was "honouring his Father"; their reaction to him affected, not Jesus himself, but the judgement God would pass on them. The other gospels go so far as to call this blasphemous reaction an unforgivable sin. Here the same reality of judgement is expressed

51   the other way round, in its positive form: 'if anyone obeys my teaching he shall never know what it is to die'.

"Death" and "life" in Jesus' vocabulary had a special meaning. Missing

53   this, the Jews asked the obvious question. 'Are you greater than our father Abraham, who is dead? . . . What do you claim to be?' This had, in effect, been the question all along. So far, Jesus' answers had been tantalizing and ambivalent; he was now about to make a claim that was absolutely decisive. But before doing so, he made an important reservation. Any answer he could give to the Jews' question would inevitably draw attention to himself, whereas his whole purpose was to draw men, not to himself, but to his Father (there is the same word-play on "honour" and "glory" as before). Whatever answer he gave must be understood as a statement, not about himself, but about God, or at most about himself in relation to God. The Jews' real error was not that they did not recognize Jesus for what he was, but that they did not "know God". And so Jesus made his reply in terms of that same Abraham whom the Jews believed to be the key to the history of

56   God's relationship with men. 'Your father Abraham was overjoyed to see my day'. There was a tradition among Jewish scholars (for which there is evidence not long after the date of the writing of this gospel) that Abraham was given a vision of things to come. Whether or not Jesus was referring to this, his meaning is clear: Abraham may have been the key figure in the Jewish national mythology, but that was not to say that he was the last word in God's dealings with men. The form in which Jesus expressed this, if taken literally, suggested that Jesus must have been alive in Abraham's time, many centuries ago. This, as usual, was how the Jews took it: how could a

man, who had not yet even become **old** himself,[a] reach back across the 57
centuries? Understood in this way, the proposition was absurd. But at the
hands of the writer of this gospel, whose first sentence proclaimed that
'when all things began, the Word already was', it was meaningful and true.
'Before Abraham was born, I am'. The statement at last brought Jesus 58
into the open: the speaker could belong to no human category. But to the
Jews it seemed axiomatic that only God could make such a statement, and
it followed that Jesus must be blaspheming. Death by stoning, even if dis-
allowed by the Romans, would have been the proper Jewish punishment.
Once again his life was threatened; once again he avoided the threat, though
this time John does not even offer an explanation. Mysteriously, **Jesus was** 59
not to be seen.

Jesus saw a man blind from his birth. Then as now, the spectacle of 9. 1
human suffering posed an acute religious question: how could a good and
just God allow such things? The usual answer given by Jewish thinkers was
that suffering and misfortune must be regarded as punishments for sin; and
if, as in the present case, it appeared that the individual concerned could
hardly have brought it upon himself, then there was still the possibility that
it was the parents who had sinned and that the son or daughter was bearing
the consequences. This somewhat naïve way of looking at suffering needed
considerable refinement if it was to account satisfactorily for all the facts, and
it was by no means held uncritically by everyone. Nevertheless, the natural
Jewish reaction to a case of illness or personal calamity was that the individual
concerned, or possibly his parents, must have committed some sin. The
disciples' question takes this for granted.

In the other gospels, Jesus seems occasionally to work from the same
presupposition. But here he explicitly rejects it. **'He was born blind so that** 3
God's power might be displayed in curing him.' This was certainly a
sufficient explanation in this particular case, and in any other case (such as
that of Lazarus later on, 11.15) when Jesus was there himself to turn tragedy
into joy. But was it relevant to the innumerable other sufferers who could
have no hope of a personal cure by Jesus? The unexpected "we" of verse
4—**'we must carry on the work of him who sent me'**—is perhaps a hint 4
deliberately given by the writer that Jesus' saying applied to more than his
own miracles of healing: it was addressed to "us", that is, the Christian
church which found itself able to exercise something of Jesus' power over
suffering and thereby (whether actual physical healing was involved or not)
to find a meaning in suffering as one of the circumstances under which God
makes himself known to men. At any rate, this healing was "God's work";

[a] The phrase, '**not yet fifty years old**' was understood by many early Christian writers
to mean that Jesus was between forty and fifty. But this contradicts Luke's clear statement
(3.23) that Jesus was about thirty years old, and in any case does not follow from John's
words.

that is to say, it was of a different order from the "work" to which the Jewish Sabbath rules applied (for this, here as in chapter 5, was to be the main cause of Jewish opposition); it could go on being done continuously until that period of **night** when it would seem that the opposition of men had finally

5 extinguished the **light** of Jesus. Meanwhile, Jesus was still '**the light of the world**', of which the curing of a blind man was an apt illustration.

6 **He spat on the ground and made a paste with the spittle.** Outwardly, the procedure was old-fashioned magic. Such treatment would normally be followed by a careful washing or anointing. In Jerusalem there was only

7 one place where fresh spring water could be had, at **Siloam,** the outlet of the only spring which the city possessed. The spring still exists: it runs through the long underground tunnel originally made for it by King Hezekiah, and emerges at the lowest point of the old city, at the south-east corner of the city walls. In this area there has always been a pool (though its exact position has changed over the centuries). Here the blind man went to wash the paste from his eyes. It was the obvious place to do so; but it also had a name which (whatever it really meant) sounded like the Hebrew word for 'sent'. The symbolism was obvious: the blind man was cured, not by any magical properties of the water, but by Jesus, the man "sent" from God.

14 **It was a Sabbath day when Jesus made the paste.** This, as with the cure of the cripple in chapter 5, was the immediate cause of the controversy. But this time Jesus was absent, and the scene is played out between the man who

13 had been cured and the Jews (mainly represented by **the Pharisees,** who were in fact the authors of much of the detail of the Sabbath regulations). As a result the episode moves more rapidly, and gives the narrator scope for working in some lively repartee on both sides. One detail, perhaps, betrays

22 his hand: it is true that in the time of Jesus individuals were **banned from the synagogue** for specified periods as a punishment for certain offences; but it is unlikely that this rule could have been applied to people who merely held a certain opinion, such as acknowledging **Jesus as Messiah.** It was only at the end of the century that the Jewish leaders revised their rules in such a way as deliberately to exclude Christians, and it looks as if John is here reading back this recent development into the time of Jesus. In other respects his narrative is entirely lifelike.

The point at issue was quite simple. A man born blind had been given his

17 sight. In the popular view this showed that Jesus was, at the very least, 'a prophet'. There must have been a special reason why God had answered

31 Jesus' prayer: '**It is common knowledge that God does not listen to sinners; he listens to anyone who is devout and obeys his will.**' To ordinary people it was obvious where Jesus "came from"—from God; and there is a hint here that some of the Pharisees were prepared to take the

16 same view. But other Pharisees saw it differently. '**How could such signs**

come from a sinful man?' was not an entirely convincing argument. There were magicians and exorcists about who certainly achieved remarkable feats, but who were very far from being sinless. Moreover, by their own principles, Jesus had been shown to be "sinful": '**This fellow is no man of God; he does not keep the Sabbath**'. No one who deliberately set aside such an important commandment could possibly be **devout**, let alone 17 **a prophet.** These uncertainties made it impossible for some of the Pharisees 31 to join in the popular acclamation of Jesus. Their best course seemed to be to try to cast doubt on what had actually happened. When this failed, they simply resorted to abuse. '**Who are you to give us lessons**', they re- 34 **torted, 'born and bred in sin as you are?**' This, again, was the authentic Pharisaic tone of voice towards the undisciplined multitude of their fellow-Jews in general, sharpened in this particular case by the fact that they, unlike Jesus, took it for granted that a man born blind must have been '**born and bred in sin**'.

The man's own acceptance of Jesus was as definite as the Jews' rejection—and this is the moral of the whole episode. The person of Jesus brought into the world of the present that divine judgement which men usually conceived of as lying in the remote future. The blind man recovering his sight was symbolic: those who before had no pretensions that they could "see" came to believe in Jesus; those who relied on their "sight" were shown to be "blind". Jesus' final rejoinder to the Pharisees is full of irony. '**If you were** 41 **blind . . . you would not be guilty**'. This was the exact reversal of their presupposition that a man, because he was blind, was bound to be guilty. The only form of guilt that mattered now was that of those who could not "see" who Jesus was.

A parable that Jesus told them. In the other gospels, parables are one of 10. 6 the most distinctive elements in the teaching of Jesus. Of these, some are complete stories, some are simply pointed descriptions of familiar scenes. In this gospel, Jesus' teaching is more discursive, and makes comparatively little use of parables; when it does (and this passage is the only one where an illustration is explicitly called a parable), they belong to the second kind, that is to say, they are brief and memorable descriptions of something already familiar to the hearer, but with an emphasis on certain details which suggests a particular application. So here: the "parable" consists of a straightforward description of Palestinian shepherding. In the evening (or before a storm, or at any other time when protection is necessary) the shepherd may bring the entire flock into the walled courtyard of a house (the translation **sheep-** 1 **fold,** suggesting fences or hurdles, is misleading). The street door of this courtyard is kept by a door-keeper, who keeps the door closed against marauders, but opens it to the shepherd when he comes next morning to lead the sheep out to pasture. European shepherds drive their sheep from behind; but in the east the shepherd usually walks ahead of his flock: he has special calls which his own sheep know and respond to; indeed he knows his flock so well that he has a name for each sheep, just as an English farmer has a name for each of his cows. The flock is exposed to many dangers: on the mountains, there may be wild animals who will attack it; even inside the courtyard, a robber may climb in during the night and open the door from inside. The robber will not be able to lead away the entire flock, for the sheep will not follow him and will scatter as soon as he lets them out; but in fact

10 he comes only **to steal, to kill, to destroy.** If he can get the meat and the wool of a few, he will have done a good night's work.

The image of a shepherd at the head of his flock occurs again and again in ancient literature. It was an obvious one for the ruler of a people or the general of an army. It occurs constantly in the Old Testament: the leaders of the Jewish people were its "shepherds", and in Ezekiel 34 (a chapter which has many points in common with this parable) those shepherds are subjected to fierce criticism on the grounds of their selfishness and rapacity, and threatened with being replaced by a new shepherd (David, or a descendant of David) who would make the flock into a single one, obedient to its Lord (who is God). Had Jesus' parable been purely in this tradition, it would have contained a thinly veiled attack on the present "shepherds" of Israel, and would doubtless have been easily understood by his hearers. The reason

6 why, on this occasion, **they did not understand what he meant by it,** was perhaps because it did not exploit the obvious theme of good and bad shepherds, but concentrated on certain small details, accurately observed from real life, which in fact distinguished the real shepherd from a thief: his free access to the courtyard, and his familiarity with the sheep. These details are never mentioned when the shepherd-image is used in the Old Testament; and Jesus' hearers did not immediately grasp what he meant.

The parable is given an interpretation which makes it bear directly upon the person of Jesus. First (somewhat unexpectedly) one small detail is taken

7 from the parable as a clue to Jesus' nature: '**I am the door**'—a pictorial symbol of the truth he is to make explicit later, 'No one comes to the Father except by me' (14.6), and also a very definite claim that he possesses an authority of a different order altogether from all previous teachers. But there

11 is a far more important point of comparison than this: '**I am the good shepherd**'. This goes beyond anything in the parable. There, two points have been mentioned which serve to distinguish the shepherd from a thief or impostor: his right of free access to the sheepfold, and the fact that the

14 sheep have got used to him. Jesus refers to one of these again—'**I know my own sheep and my sheep know me**'—but the thing which fundamentally distinguishes **the good shepherd** from all others is something that has not been mentioned in the parable and possibly would not have occurred to his

11 hearers: he '**lays down his life for the sheep**'. Such heroic conduct in a

sheep-owner faced with the prospect of losing his flock to a wolf was conceivable; applied to the "shepherds" of nations or armies, it was something which might on occasion be called for, say in time of war. But in what sense could it be said of a religious leader-shepherd that it belonged to his rôle deliberately, of his own free will, to lay down his life? Christians, after the 18 event, could understand this; they could understand also how Jesus' death had been of service, not just to those within the Jewish fold, but to the 16 Gentiles outside. But Jesus' hearers were as bewildered by the idea as by his other references to "going away". These words once again caused 19 a split among the Jews. Until the story was finished and all the clues fell into place, Jesus' words and deeds continued to display a tantalizing ambiguity.

The festival of the Dedication. Festivals, rather than seasons, offered to 22 a Jewish writer the most natural way of marking the time of year. Like Luke, who dates important events in the history of the early church by reference to the Jewish religious calendar (see also Acts 2.1), John separates the various episodes of Jesus' life by connecting each with a certain festival. Chapter 6 was dated by Passover to the spring, chapter 7 by Tabernacles to the autumn; and now it is Dedication, a winter festival instituted by Judas Maccabaeus in 164 B.C. to mark the re-dedication of the temple after its profanation by Antiochus Epiphanes. In this eight-day festival there were lights, processions, singing; but John clearly mentions it, not because of anything distinctive about the celebrations, but because it gives the episode an approximate date (we should say, "some time in December"). It was in any case a likely time for Jesus and many other visitors to be in Jerusalem.

It was winter. To a European, this suggests the cold months of December, January and February. But in Palestine, as indeed in most Mediterranean countries, there were only two seasons, that of hot, dry, settled weather (roughly from May to September) and that of periodic rainfall (October to April). In Jerusalem, wintry weather—whether it be snow and frost, wind and rain, hail and thunder—can occur at almost any time during the second of these seasons, between long periods of fine days and warm sun. In this sense, "winter" is half the year. No one would think of dating anything by it. John's words probably mean that it was rough weather; and the other details he gives would then fall into place. **Solomon's Portico** (see 23 also Acts 3.11) offered protection from rain and wind; but it also gave proceedings a more formal character than the open spaces of the **temple precincts.** Such porticos were regularly used for teaching and disputations in any city where there were philosophers or religious teachers. But they were also used as courts of law; and what follows is no longer a mere controversy, but is in all but name a trial. **The Jews gathered round** 24 him—in the Greek, the expression is distinctly aggressive, evoking the picture of an army encircling a besieged city, or of a court like the Sanhedrin seated in a semicircle around the accused; and the dialogue follows the same pattern (and indeed uses many of the same words) as that which, in Luke's gospel (22.67–71), takes place at the formal hearing of Jesus' case before a Jewish court: Jesus is directly challenged to say whether he is the Messiah, refuses to give an explicit reply on the grounds of his judges' unbelief, but then makes a claim (in Luke, to be at the right hand of God, in John to be

30 "one with the Father") which makes him appear guilty of blasphemy and liable to the death penalty. All this, in the other gospels, takes place in the course of a formal trial, and leads directly to Jesus' crucifixion. John places it here, and has no record of a formal trial later (its place is taken by a kind of private interrogation by the High Priest). That is to say, John uses this occasion instead of the later one to lay bare the issue between Jesus and the Jewish authorities. Once again, Jesus' immediate execution is averted only by the strange elusiveness which he has displayed throughout *The great*

39 *controversy*: **he escaped from their clutches.**

The scene, nevertheless, is worked carefully into the pattern of the whole section. The parable of the shepherd is developed a little further; and the

25 discussion of Jesus' **'credentials'** is brought to a conclusion. Jesus had made various claims for himself; but the testimony of his words, even though there was a sense in which it was legally valid (8.14), had not been accepted. However, there was still another kind of evidence to be considered. '**My deeds done in my Father's name are my credentials**'. These were done

32 according to his Father's will and in his **Father's power.** Their purpose is

38 now finally defined: '**that you may recognize and know that the Father is in me, and I in the Father**'. John's readers were by now prepared for this kind of language, which belonged to a wider religious culture than that of the Jews: Jesus' relationship with God could not be described only in terms of the Jewish concepts of Messiah or Son of God. Indeed, Jewish thinking tended to draw a sharp line between language appropriate to men and language appropriate to God. Jesus' description of himself seemed to them

33 to be overstepping that line: '**You, a mere man, claim to be a god.**' To

34 this, Jesus replied, in effect, that they had drawn their line too sharply. Consider these verses of Psalm 82:

> "God takes his stand in the court of heaven
> To deliver judgement on the gods themselves . . .
> I said: you are gods,
> And all of you sons of the Most High.
> Yet you shall die like mortals . . ."

The psalm was originally written against a background of a lingering belief in heathen gods alongside the one true God of Israel. Later interpreters, anxious to banish the idea that any such "gods" could exist, suggested that the beings meant were angels, demonic powers, or even men. We do not know what Jesus' hearers thought the psalm meant; but whatever view they took, they would have been bound to concede Jesus' point that it showed that the word "god" could be used of someone who is less than God. If so, then it was not so easy to draw the line between language that was and was not blasphemous. Jesus could truthfully say, '**I am God's son**'. Even if his adversaries did not admit that it was true, they still could not prove that it was blasphemous. 36

Victory over death

Jesus withdrew again across the Jordan. For a moment before the final conflict in Jerusalem, the contact with John the Baptist's work is renewed, and a last tribute is paid to John's "witness" to Jesus, which alone caused many **to believe in him** there. The interlude also prepares for the next scene; for the drama of Lazarus' death depends on Jesus being **across the Jordan**, a long day's journey from the scene of events. 40 42 40

There was a man named Lazarus who had fallen ill. The characters in this scene are first carefully identified—and we receive an unexpected reminder that the readers of this gospel were assumed to be already so familiar with the events of Jesus' life that John could point forward to an episode he had not yet recorded (12.1–8) in order to identify Mary. [a] The family were friends of Jesus, and it was to be expected that he would use his undoubted power to cure one of them of an illness. This, in fact, is what everyone—the two sisters and their friends—assumed would happen; and they were naturally dejected (verses 21, 32), if not cynical (verse 37), when it failed to happen. What no one dared to hope was that anything could be done once Lazarus had died. Raising the dead, though not unheard of, was a rare and exceptional miracle, and Jesus was not assumed to have the power to perform it. Jesus, however, saw Lazarus' illness as an occasion for doing precisely this. '**It has come for the glory of God, to bring glory to the Son of God.**' This was to be the climax of his works of power, and a visible demonstration of the seriousness of his teaching about life and death. Two comparable miracles are related in the other gospels (Mark 5.21–43; Luke 7.11–17); but this is by far the most spectacular, and is the only one which teaches such a clear lesson of Jesus' *Victory over death*. 11. 1 2 4

'**This illness will not end in death**'. By the time the reader has reached the end of the story, he will have grasped the meaning of this reaction of Jesus. But it was naturally taken by Jesus' disciples to mean that there was 4

[a] Two sisters named Mary and Martha had their home in "a village" in Luke 10.38–9. We cannot be certain that they are the same; though the reference below (12.2) to Martha "serving" makes it likely that they were.

nothing further to worry about in Lazarus' illness, and they were therefore

7 surprised when, two days later, Jesus suggested returning to Judaea, and exposing himself to the danger he had just left behind. Jesus answered them,

9 first, with a parable. 'Anyone can walk in day-time without stumbling' —it was a vivid way of saying that even near Jerusalem he would be safe for the time being: his "hour", his "night", had not yet come (but the tell-tale phrase, the light of this world, shows that the parable, by the time this gospel was written, had come to mean more than this: the Christian, walking in the light of Christ, is safe from stumbling). Secondly, Jesus had a positive

11 reason for going back, which he gradually unfolded to his disciples. 'Lazarus has fallen asleep'. In Greek, as in English, this was ambiguous. The

4 disciples remembered that Jesus had said, 'This illness will not end in death', and seized eagerly on what was apparently hopeful news (known apparently by intuition to Jesus): falling into a calm sleep was a sign that a

14 fever was passing. Then Jesus spoke out plainly: 'Lazarus is dead'. Before, the journey seemed pointless because Jesus had said that Lazarus would not die. Now it seemed pointless because he was already dead. Nothing but certain death awaited Jesus in Jerusalem. One at least of the disciples

16 made up his mind what was expected of them. 'Let us also go, that we may die with him.'

We can reconstruct what had happened. Lazarus had died soon after the sisters sent their message to Jesus. As was usual, he was buried the same

38 day. The tomb was a cave, with a stone placed against it. There are thousands of such tombs in Palestine: they consist of a rock chamber, with small horizontal niches or tunnels hewn out of the sides. The corpse was wrapped in linen and laid on one of these rock shelves. The tomb was then sealed by a large flat stone placed over the entrance to the cave. The mourning continued for some days. It was a highly esteemed act of charity to visit and console the bereaved. Mary and Martha were naturally surrounded by

17 their friends from the city. Moreover, Jesus found that Lazarus had already been four days in the tomb. There is probably a touch of folklore in this. For three days, it was believed, the soul continued to haunt the body, and a return to life might still seem just conceivable. After that, decomposition began and death was irrevocable. We are told twice over that Jesus did not arrive until the fourth day. What he was about to do exceeded the bounds even of imagined possibility.

In the main the episode is left to speak for itself. But it contains a charac-

23 teristic piece of dialogue. Jesus said, 'Your brother will rise again'. This sounded like ordinary spiritual comfort: most people believed in a

24 resurrection on the last day, and it could be consoling to know that one's dear ones would be there. But of course, this was not what Jesus meant. Lazarus was to rise again now; and this would demonstrate in visible form

that the categories of life-after-death were being brought by Jesus into the present. The quality of living offered by Jesus was such that even physical death could not impair it. Martha could hardly yet grasp all this; but she did get so far as to make a correct confession of who Jesus was. Her confession was a limited one: Messiah was no more than a Jewish title. But at least she knew that the arrival of this Messiah **who was to come into the** **world** must be the signal for something radically new in the experience of mankind.

Towards the end, Jesus showed signs of strong emotion, sighing and weeping. It is possible that he was simply entering into the general grief: this, at any rate, is what the Jews thought—'**How dearly he must have** **loved him!**' But we must beware of assuming that they were right. It is a recurring feature of the style of this gospel that the bystanders are made to misinterpret the words and actions of Jesus. Moreover, it is clear from the very beginning of the narrative that Jesus, far from being disconcerted by Lazarus' death, welcomed it as an opportunity to show forth the glory of God. It would have been surprising (though perhaps only human) if, when it came to the point, he felt it to be a calamity to be wept over. Finally, the Greek word translated **sighed heavily** or **sighed deeply** is one which usually expresses anger or indignation rather than grief—in Mark 14.5 it is translated 'turned upon her with fury'; in Mark 1.43 it expresses a 'stern warning'. In all the gospels Jesus has moments of anger, and his anger is usually provoked by the inhumanity and hypocrisy of people and institutions. The same may well be the case here. All these Jewish people, who professed a belief in the resurrection of the dead, were weeping their eyes out as if the death of their friend Lazarus was something tragic and final. This exhibition of superstitious weakness moved Jesus to tears of indignation (mistaken as sympathy by the Jews). He was to show them how foolish their weeping had been.

Now many . . . But some . . . Even this most sensational of all Jesus' actions did not convince everyone who saw it. Many **put their faith in him**; but the continued hostility of others resulted in a meeting of the Council— the only such meeting recorded in this gospel.

It is possible to question John's account of this scene on points of historical detail. If the meeting was a formal session of the Sanhedrin, and not just a hurried conference of influential people (John's words would fit either interpretation), **the Pharisees** as such would have had no official right to convene it; and John's language about Caiaphas being **High Priest that year** makes one wonder whether he knew that he was in fact High Priest continuously from A.D. 18 to 36. On the other hand, in general the episode is entirely convincing. All the gospels agree that the arrest and execution of Jesus was the result of plotting by the Jewish authorities; and one of the most plausible motives for their action was fear of what the consequences might be if someone who called himself the Messiah were allowed to gather 48 a considerable following. 'The Romans will come and sweep away our temple and our nation'. This had happened by the time the gospel was written: it could well have happened earlier if a serious insurrectionary movement had got under way under the leadership of a man such as they took Jesus to be.

On the face of it, Caiaphas' advice was sound political sense: the judicial murder of one scapegoat was a small price to pay for avoiding serious trouble. But what might have been merely the practical wisdom of a political leader 51 was seen by John as an instance of inspired **prophesying** such as might be expected from a High Priest. Jesus did indeed **die for the nation**, not to save it from Roman oppression, but to make possible a new kind of life. And John adds that there were to benefit from this many who did not belong to "that nation", but would be brought by Christ into a new community of the 52 **children of God.**

In any case, Jesus once more retired from the neighbourhood of Jeru-54 salem. The other gospels do not mention this withdrawal, and **a town called Ephraim** occurs nowhere else in the New Testament. It is probably to be identified with a place some $12\frac{1}{2}$ miles north-east of Jerusalem, on the edge of the arid range of mountains that fall down to the Jordan valley.

55 **The Jewish Passover was now at hand.** In this gospel, all Jesus' visits to Jerusalem have been associated with a festival. His last, which ends in his death, is placed by all the gospels at the time of the Passover. John opens his narrative with the first influx of visitors: those who, either by living abroad or for some other reason, had made themselves ritually "unclean" and had to be in Jerusalem for seven days in order to complete the rites of purification which would enable them to approach the temple on the day of the festival (see also Acts 21.26). This was a day or two before the main crowd of pilgrims would arrive. It was the moment for the authorities to make their plans, and for the beginning of popular speculation about Jesus' intentions.

12. 2 **A supper was given in his honour.** A somewhat similar episode is recorded in all the gospels. In Luke (7.36–50) it has nothing to do with Jesus' approaching death; the woman who anoints Jesus' feet, after washing them and wiping them with her hair, is a stranger who intends simply to express her gratitude and love. In Mark on the other hand (14.3–9)—who is followed on most points by Matthew (26.6–13)—the woman's action is presented as a kind of rehearsal for the anointing which should have been administered to the body of Jesus before his burial: as such, it was a notable "act of kindness", and therefore far more meritorious than an ordinary contribution to the needs of

the poor. Most of these elements are present here, but in a slightly different arrangement. First, the characters are all identified. The scene is once again Bethany, and of the three people already known to us there each is given a part: **Lazarus sat among the guests**, Martha was behind the scenes 2 serving (characteristically, if she was the same Martha as appears in Luke 10.40), Mary came into the room to perform her extravagant act of devotion to Jesus. The shocked reaction which this caused is ascribed to Judas Iscariot, and gives John an opportunity to fill in a trait of Judas' character in advance of the betrayal itself: he used **to pilfer the money put into the** 6 **common purse, which was in his charge.** This precision about the people involved goes with a vivid telling of the story (**the house was filled with the** 3 **fragrance** is a touch not found in any of the other accounts). But John has not made it clear how he understood the story. If he had wished to emphasize Mary's humble service to Jesus, he would surely have mentioned what was in fact the main point of a similar service performed by Jesus later—the washing of the guest's feet. Indeed, had he done so, it would have made his description much clearer. In Luke, the woman washes Jesus' feet with her tears, dries them with her hair, and then anoints them with ointment. John also says that Mary **wiped them with her hair**—but apparently after putting on the ointment! John may in fact mean that (as in Luke) she washed them first, and then dried them before anointing them; but if so, his description is so condensed that he certainly cannot have intended to put any stress on the actual washing. Nor does he make anything of the contrast between giving money to the poor and performing exceptional acts of kindness (which seems to be the main point of the scene in Mark); and as for the point about anticipating Jesus' burial, it is expressed so obscurely that it is impossible to be sure what he thought it meant. [a] We are left with the impression that on this occasion John was content to set down the story for its own sake, without attempting to give it a fully consistent interpretation.

The next day. Jerusalem had now begun to fill up with the great body of 12 pilgrims, who were moved to give Jesus a royal acclamation. The **palm** 13 **branches** were appropriate for greeting a king; the chanting of a psalm, '**Hosanna! Blessings on him who comes in the name of the Lord!**' (Psalm 118.25-6), though it was primarily a song for a religious festival, was apt enough with the addition of the words, '**God bless the king of Israel!**' On a previous occasion, when there had been an attempt to make Jesus king (6.15), Jesus had hastily withdrawn from the scene. Here, his response was similar to that which he was to make when Pilate questioned him on the

[a] 'Let her keep it until the day when she prepares for my burial' would make sense as an answer to Judas if Mary had not in fact already used it to anoint Jesus; and even so, we should have to reckon with the fact that, at Jesus' burial, it was not Mary's pound of ointment, but Nicodemus' hundred pounds, that were used (19.39).

14 matter: he accepted the title, but in a special sense. **Jesus found a donkey and mounted it.** A warrior king would have chosen a horse; Jesus' action
15 was that of a man of peace. When Zechariah had prophesied (9.9), '**See, your king is coming, mounted on an ass's colt**', it was obvious that the prophet envisaged no ordinary king, but a figure who combined authority with a singular humility—in short, a universal peacemaker, a divinely appointed Messiah. Jesus allowed himself to be acclaimed king only on such terms as these.

The accounts of this episode in the other gospels contain much the same elements, but they leave tantalizing questions unanswered. What did the crowds recognize in Jesus which made them follow the disciples' lead and give him a triumphal entry? And why did the demonstration peter out as suddenly as it had begun? John's version makes it all sound more rational. The crowds acclaimed Jesus because of the sensational raising of Lazarus which they had seen or heard about; and far from petering out, the demonstration went on for as long as was to be expected; for some time it could be
19 said, '**All the world has gone after him!**' This popular emotion was of course transient and superficial: the crowd would follow Jesus only so long as the impression of Lazarus' resurrection was fresh in their minds. Nevertheless, the episode had a deeper significance: in a certain sense, Jesus was truly a king, although even the disciples (who in the other accounts play a larger part in the scene, and might have been expected to grasp its real
16 meaning) **did not understand this.** In this gospel, Jesus' triumphant entry into Jerusalem was one more of those moments when his presence was half-accepted, half-rejected, his true nature at best half-understood.

A festival at Jerusalem not only drew a great crowd of Jewish pilgrims: people of other nationalities, whether they were full proselytes or merely sympathetic to the Jewish religion, also made the journey to visit the holy city. It
20 was convenient to call such people **Greeks**, though they might come from almost anywhere in the eastern part of the Roman empire. Their common language would be Greek; and the main thing that was meant by the word was that they were not Jews by birth. Some of them expressed a desire to see Jesus—which sounds a simple enough request; but the fact that it elicited from Jesus a series of exceedingly solemn sayings shows that we must
19 be prepared to look for a deeper significance in it. The Jews had said, '**Why, all the world has gone after him**', meaning simply that Jesus had attracted a crowd. But, taken literally, their words suggested something more sensational. Jesus was attracting, not only his fellow-Jews, but **the world,** that is, strangers and foreigners, people who had no allegiance to the Jewish religion. An example is immediately given in the Greeks who approached Philip. But every reader of the gospel knew that the real fulfilment of these words was the existence of the Christian church, which had by now far out-

grown its Jewish origins and was mainly composed of people who were, not Jews, but "Greeks".

The process by which this was to happen had already begun. 'The hour 23 has come for the Son of Man to be glorified.' In straight Jewish terms, this would probably have meant that the person whose destiny it was finally to unite the two worlds of earth and heaven was now to be endued with supernatural splendour and lead his people to heaven. But John has been working out a different meaning for these terms. The "glorifying" of the Son of Man consisted in his being "lifted up" on the cross, it was the other side of what appeared to be a dark destiny of condemnation and death. The reader is helped to understand this first by a brief parable. 'A grain of 24 wheat remains a solitary grain unless it falls into the ground'. The parable of a single seed growing into a great fruitful plant occurs in the other gospels (see especially Mark 4.26–32) as an illustration of spectacular growth from tiny beginnings. But now a new idea is added: 'if it dies, it bears a rich harvest.' The idea that a seed (and indeed nature itself) dies in the dead season of winter and comes to life again in the spring underlies a great deal of religious symbolism (it occurs again in 1 Corinthians 15.36–8). The seed, when it falls into the ground, enters the yearly cycle of death and rebirth. In this sense, it dies; and by this small elaboration, the parable of a rich harvest from a tiny grain is made to turn on that death—the death of Jesus which is also his glorification—which must precede the prodigious growth which is to follow. But this death involves others, it conditions the way in which men must seek to serve and follow Jesus. In a sequence of ideas and sayings very similar to those in Mark 8.34–8, the implications for Jesus' followers are spelled out.

'Now my soul is in turmoil'. All the gospels record a moment before 27 *The final conflict* when Jesus seems suddenly to have had a moment of irresolution. Here the setting is different from that in the other gospels, but it is clear that the experience being described is the same. We must beware of psychologizing. Jesus' words are not chosen because these alone exactly describe his emotions, but because (being an allusion to Psalm 42) they evoke a classical expression of the agony of one whose faith in God is stretched to breaking-point. Both here and on the cross, Jesus uses the traditional language of Hebrew spirituality to show that he, like countless just men before him, is in a position where circumstances make it hard to continue to believe in God. The admission is unexpected: apart from this one moment, Jesus moves with a serene sense of purpose. It is also short-lived. In the other gospels, the prayer for deliverance gives place to acceptance: 'not what I will, but what thou wilt' (Mark 14.36). Here, the same is said in the distinctive idiom of John's gospel. Until now, the glory attending the person of Jesus (which is God's glory) has been ambiguous and incomplete: it will be fully realized only in Jesus' death and resurrection. So Jesus' acceptance

27 of his destiny takes the form, 'Father, glorify thy name'. And the supernatural answer to this prayer (corresponding perhaps to the 'angel from heaven bringing him strength' in Luke's account of Gethsemane, 22.43) is in effect that the glory already attendant upon Jesus is now to be consummated by that supreme act of glorification by which the Son of Man will be 32 **lifted up,** on the cross, to heaven.

Jesus, after his brief moment of hesitation, firmly accepted this uniquely demanding mode of glorification. But for men there was still the great difficulty of seeing the glory in the humiliation, of accepting that Jesus' death was an expression of God's glory on earth. Jesus' teaching had been preparing 30 them for this; now a voice from heaven declared it was so. '**This voice spoke for your sake, not mine**'. Even this, of course, was ambiguous. Most people **said it was thunder.** The events leading up to the crucifixion itself 31 were to be the decisive challenge to declare for or against Jesus: '**Now is the hour of judgement for this world**'. Many would doubtless declare against; but this would not rob the crucifixion of its power. It was a firm Christian belief—supported by a number of Jesus' sayings—that the devil himself ('**the Prince of this world**') was vanquished by the crucifixion (compare Hebrews 2.14); and it was the crucifixion which finally broke through the exclusiveness of the Jewish religion and enabled Jesus to "draw all men to himself".

32 '**Lifted up**'. The expression seems to have been deliberately ambiguous —indeed the macabre pun was apparently quite well known (it is exploited for instance, in Genesis 40.12–19). Its most natural meaning was "exalted"; but it could also mean "lifted up (on the cross) for execution". John puts 33 his readers wise to this second meaning—**This he said to indicate the kind of death he was to die**—and then tells us that this was in fact the meaning which Jesus' listeners seized on, and found inconsistent with their 34 conception of a glorious Deliverer. '**Our Law teaches us that the Messiah continues for ever**'. There were varying interpretations of those passages in the Law which pointed foward to a Messiah; but most interpreters agreed that he must be an eternal figure. Call him what they would—Messiah in their own terminology, or Son of Man (apparently) in that of Jesus—the splendid figure they expected was surely not to be **lifted up**—to die! This of course was the question posed by the gospel right from the beginning: how could the Word be rejected, how could the Son of God be crucified? Jesus, in his last response to this question, simply recalled answers he had given before. Light presupposes darkness, day presupposes night. Rejection by men belongs to the conditions under which the Word can dwell on earth. 36 The essential thing is to make the right response: '**Trust to the light, so that you may become men of light.**'

37 Nevertheless, these people had actually seen **the many signs which Jesus had performed in their presence.** They, of all people, ought surely to

have been prepared to believe. Yet it was the Jews of Jerusalem who were responsible for Jesus being condemned to death, and at the time this gospel was written it was still the Jewish nation which was the most unwilling to accept the Christian gospel. This was the extreme case of the paradox stated at the beginning, 'He entered his own realm, and his own would not receive him' (1.11). Concluding this part of his narrative, John offers two more explanations, the first theoretical, the second practical. The theoretical explanation was the one which was seized on most eagerly by Christians right from the beginning, and may indeed go back to Jesus himself: **the** 38 **prophet Isaiah's utterance had to be fulfilled.** Scripture, rightly interpreted, foretold the rejection of Christ. Isaiah 53, with its description of a suffering servant who nevertheless bore the sins of many, was one of the passages most frequently invoked (it opens, '**Lord, who has believed what we reported . . .**'). Another was Isaiah 6.9, '**He has blinded their eyes . . .**', 40 which in all the gospels (though in a slightly different way in each) is used to explain the failure of Israel to accept and understand Jesus (see above on Mark 4.11–12). However mysterious the fact of this rejection, and however brutal and fatalistic this explanation might sound, it remained true that these things were predicted in Scripture, and must therefore be the will of God.

The second explanation was quite practical. There was a powerful incentive not to acknowledge Jesus: **fear of being banned from the synagogue.** 42 In this form, the threat was probably more of a reality at the time the gospel was written than in the time of Jesus (see above on 9.22). But the general point was valid at any time and could be neatly expressed in a pun that has already been exploited earlier (see above on 5.41–4). One word meant both human "honour" and divine "glory". Men are men, and it was only to be expected they would prefer the former sense of the word: **they valued their** 43 **reputation with men rather than the honour which comes from God.**

So Jesus cried aloud—but there is no audience, no occasion (Jesus, so 44 far as we have been told, is still in **hiding**). What we have here is a final 36 comment on the argument as it has been unfolding throughout these chapters. This argument has necessarily thrust Jesus into the centre of the picture. It is the Jesus who did these deeds and spoke these words about whom men must make up their minds. It is for Jesus or against Jesus that they must decide. But now comes the corrective. '**When a man believes** 44 **in me, he believes in him who sent me rather than in me**' . . . '**There** 48 **is a judge for the man who rejects me**'. The words and ideas have all occurred earlier; but here the emphasis is all on one point: Jesus is no independent divinity, no isolated challenge. Declaring for or against Jesus is nothing more nor less than declaring for or against God.

Farewell discourses

'He entered his own realm, and his own would not receive him' (1.11). The first part of the gospel has been wrestling with this paradox. It has illustrated the ambiguity necessarily involved in the appearance of the Son of God on earth, and the diversity of response which he elicited. It has described the words and actions by which Jesus sought to confront men and women with the challenge of his presence, and it has recorded the strength of the opposition which he aroused. There were certainly many who 'believed in him'; but so far the main emphasis has been on those who rejected him and who were soon to bring him to his death.

Yet the story of Jesus was not only a story of rejection. When this gospel was written, the Christian church had already taken firm root in many parts of the world; and this church traced its origin to those who in Jesus' lifetime had given their undivided allegiance to him. By some, Jesus was accepted. And to them, Jesus gave a great deal in return. As was said in the prologue, 'To all who did receive him . . . he gave the right to become children of God' (1.12). The first Christians possessed in common, not only their faith that Jesus was the Christ, but a conviction of his continuing presence among them, and a relationship with him and with each other which was strong and new. It is to this aspect of Jesus' work that the writer now turns.

The other gospels all contain sections of teaching given privately by Jesus to his disciples, but this teaching is usually spread over the whole course of Jesus' activity. Only in Matthew is there a serious attempt to gather it together into substantial discourses; and even there the discourses occur at intervals throughout the gospel. In John all this teaching comes together at the end, and fills several pages. In part it makes use of ideas already introduced in earlier chapters; but in part it works out a new set of concepts, in particular the 'love' which is to bind Jesus' followers together and the effects of Jesus' "going to his Father" upon the nature of his continuing presence with them on earth.

In form, these chapters are unlike what has gone before: no longer a series of dramatic episodes followed by dialogue, but a long speech of Jesus interrupted only by occasional questions from the disciples. It is of course entirely probable that Jesus devoted much of the last night of his life on earth to talking with his disciples. At the same time, when John came to write this part of his gospel, he was doubtless influenced by the historian's convention of writing up a long parting speech purporting to have been made by the hero shortly before his death. An appropriate occasion for such a speech was a final meal shared with friends. John's is not the only gospel to make use of this convention: in Luke's gospel, Jesus' last supper is also made the occasion for a parting speech to the disciples. But in John, the opportunity to gather together Jesus' private teaching at this point is exploited much more systematically, and that moment in Jesus' life which in Mark and Matthew is described simply as a solemn meal and is made to carry only a few important sayings of Jesus, becomes here an occasion for a series of what may appropriately be called *Farewell discourses*.

In the other gospels this meal is stated to have been a Passover supper, celebrated by Jesus with his disciples according to Jewish custom; in the course of it, Jesus spoke certain words over the bread and the wine which gave the meal an altogether new significance and made it the origin and prototype of the Christian eucharist. John says nothing of all this (though he has made clear allusions to the eucharist in chapter 6); indeed the chronology he follows for the last days of Jesus' life makes it impossible for this supper to have been a regular celebration of the Passover: as he says himself, it was before the Passover. From the historical point of view this creates 13. 1 difficulties. The meal he describes was no ordinary meal. It was a sufficiently formal occasion for the guests to be reclining on couches around the table; 23 and it was held, not in the afternoon (the usual time for the main meal of the day), but at night. These details would fit a dinner party or a solemn festivity 30 such as a wedding. They would also fit a Passover supper, which is in fact the only kind of occasion which we should expect Jesus and his disciples to have marked with such careful formality. But by John's reckoning, Passover night, when a meal of this character would be enjoyed by all the Jews in Jerusalem, was the following night. It is not easy to imagine Jesus deliberately holding his own celebration of the festival one day earlier than everyone else. However, behind this historical difficulty lies a real difference of approach between John's gospel and the other gospels. All the gospels agree that the crucifixion happened at Passover time: they differ over the exact significance and timing of this connection. According to Mark (apparently followed by Matthew and Luke), Jesus was crucified on the day following Passover night, and the effect of this coincidence was to give Jesus' last meal with his disciples the character of a Passover supper. In John, on the other hand, the Passover came twenty-four hours later, so that Jesus' death was simultaneous with the slaughter of the lambs on the afternoon before the Passover supper. This made it possible to understand Jesus' death as that of a Passover victim; but it necessarily removed any specifically Passover associations from Jesus' own last supper.

Nevertheless, the meal had its own drama. Part of this drama was caused (as in the other gospels) by the presence of Judas Iscariot who was about to betray his master—a betrayal which was made still more horrifying by the fact that the betrayer had just shared this meal with Jesus and so was to betray, not just a friend, but the table-fellowship which such a meal was held to establish between friends. "He who eats bread with me has turned 18 against me" (Psalm 41.9) was one of the classic Old Testament formula-

tions of such a betrayal. Jesus was well aware of what was to happen (another
21 sign that he was no ordinary person) and was moved by it to **deep agitation
of spirit.** He then identified the traitor. In all the gospels the question why
Judas did what he did (which we would tend to explore in psychological
2 terms) is answered quite simply: **the devil had already put it into the
mind of Judas.** But John is careful not to give the impression that the devil
held the initiative: it was only after Jesus had deliberately singled out Judas
27 for his sinister role that **Satan entered him**; then, with Jesus' connivance,
Judas slipped away to perform his deed without arousing the other disciples'
suspicions. John allows us to visualize the scene: Jesus lay on his left side
with his head towards the table, and his right arm free to help himself to
food. The disciple on his right was in the same position; his head would have
23 been at about the level of Jesus' chest (which is what the Greek of **reclining
close beside Jesus** actually implies), and he would have been in a better
position than anyone to whisper to Jesus. Jesus' gesture to Judas was entirely
natural. Bread was the main implement used at table: one dipped it like a
spoon into the common dish, and it was polite to do so for a guest. It could
well have escaped the notice of all present except **the disciple he loved** (the
first appearance of this cryptic phrase—see below on 21.24); but it was a
poignant signal for the traitor to begin his work.

But the main element of drama is provided by an action of Jesus which is
recorded only in this gospel (though it may be alluded to in Luke 22.27).
4 Jesus **rose from table, laid aside his garments, and taking a towel,
tied it round him.** This was the uniform of the slave whose special task it
was to carry out the hospitable act of washing the guests' feet before supper.
The act itself was one which a Jew felt to be very much beneath his dignity;
indeed, a Jewish slave was usually spared the task if a gentile slave was
available; otherwise it was performed by a woman (as in Luke 7.38; 1 Tim-
othy 5.10). The shock and surprise caused by Jesus' action was voiced by
6 Peter: 'You, Lord, washing my feet?' But, as so often in this gospel, this
naïve reaction was merely the cue for Jesus to continue the conversation on
a deeper level.

On this occasion, the deeper meaning is no more than hinted at, and it is
not easy to be sure how these hints should be interpreted. The first hint is
7 one which occurs elsewhere in these discourses: '**You do not understand
now what I am doing, but one day you will**'. One of the themes of these
chapters is the connection between the short period of Jesus' activity on
earth and the subsequent life of the church. '**One day**' meant after the resurrection, the time when Jesus' presence would be known mainly through the
Spirit. Now in this gospel a constant symbol of the Spirit is water; and it is
at once obvious that Jesus' act of washing his disciples' feet is intended to
symbolize their possession of the Spirit after his resurrection. But we can
probably go further: the rite by which Christians received the Spirit was

baptism; and all the things which Jesus said about his action of washing his disciples' feet could also in fact be said about the symbolic washing of baptism. It was baptism which marked the moment when a believer found himself in fellowship with Jesus. Baptism was effective once and for all 8 (the convert needed no further washing). And baptism, since it procured 10 forgiveness of sins, made any other purification ceremony (such as the Jews believed in) entirely unnecessary: after baptism, the Christian was altogether clean. All this teaching about the future rite of Christian baptism was elicited by Peter's unperceptive reactions to Jesus' wish to wash his feet. Indeed it could even perhaps be said (in case anyone wondered whether the disciples themselves had ever been baptized) that this *was* their baptism.

Nevertheless, if the deeper meaning of Jesus' action was to symbolize Christian baptism, it also had a more direct message: 'I have set you an 15 example: you are to do as I have done for you.' If Jesus' mastership and lordship could be expressed by such a startling reversal of the usual conventions, the relationship of Christians to each other must be expected to follow a similarly radical pattern. This, in short, is the first example of Jesus' love for his own. So far, his disciples have been there merely to listen and to question and to make their own decision in the face of the challenge of his work and teaching. But now we are taken far below this surface impression and shown something of the strength of that solidarity which binds Jesus to his followers. When Jesus washes his disciples' feet, we have the first and most striking illustration of a theme which runs right through these discourses: now he was to show the full extent of his love. 1

The scene also provides a new application for a proverb-like saying which elsewhere (both in John 15.20 and Matthew 10.24) is intended to show that a disciple cannot expect to receive less persecution than his master: 'A 16 servant is not greater than his master.' Here, it is clearly meant to silence any protest that washing a fellow-Christian's feet is beneath one's dignity. The addition, 'nor a messenger than the one who sent him' makes the same point, but leads on to a further illustration of the relationship between Jesus and his disciples. It was an old principle that a messenger is equivalent in dignity to him who sent him: to maltreat an ambassador is to dishonour a foreign power, to welcome him is to welcome him whom he represents. Here (as in Matthew 10.40) the analogy is applied to the followers of Jesus who (as will soon be shown) are "sent" by Jesus, just as Jesus was "sent" by his Father.

'Now the Son of Man is glorified'. For some time the reader has been 31 prepared for a fulfilment of this saying in a more subtle sense than was suggested by the conventional picture of an individual who, after a period of obscurity, was to be manifest to all, clothed in the visible glory of God. The moment of Jesus' final rejection and deepest humiliation was to be the moment when in fact this "glorification" would take place, since the crucifixion itself, followed immediately by the resurrection and by the emergence of a church endued with the Spirit, was that which would enable all men to come to God through him. Once again, there is an important proviso: this "glory" attaching to the Son of Man was not intended for his own glorification in competition with God. It must always be remembered that 'in him God is glorified'.

34   'Where I am going you cannot come.' To Jesus' adversaries this had been a riddle they were unable to answer (7.33–6). They were unable to understand the sense in which Jesus belonged to another world. But even for his disciples the saying caused difficulties. It was natural for them to think that Jesus' progress towards glorification was one on which they would be privileged to accompany him. A period of separation from him, even if temporary, was hard to understand. A full explanation was about to be given;

37 but another false answer had to be disposed of first. Peter said, 'Lord . . . I will lay down my life for you.' Hints have already been given that Jesus' departure would involve him in "laying down his life" for others. Why should not his disciples do the same? The short answer to this was that they simply were not capable of it. Peter was in fact to deny Jesus (all the gospels record this prediction, though in somewhat different contexts). No, they would have to be separated from Jesus. The followers would be left without their master. What would hold them together then, and how would their

34 allegiance be known? The answer lay in a 'new commandment' (new, at least, in the narrative of this gospel, and new in the radical interpretation Jesus was to put upon it): 'love one another'.

14. 1   'Set your troubled hearts at rest. Trust in God always'. This is the traditional language of faith: it is the spirituality of many of the psalms in the Old Testament. But Jesus goes on, 'trust also in me'. Jesus himself is a decisive new factor in a man's faith in God. He affects even one's belief in

2 life after death. 'There are many dwelling-places in my Father's house'—this much was agreed by most people: the usual picture of the after-life was of a number of different "places" to which people would be allotted depending on the virtues or vices they had shown during their life on earth. But faith in Christ introduced a new element into this picture. The "place" of Christians would be such that after death they would certainly be with Christ. As Paul expressed it, 'the Lord himself will descend from heaven; first the Christian dead will rise, then we who are alive shall join them, caught up in clouds to meet the Lord in the air. Thus we shall always be with the Lord' (1 Thessalonians 4.16–17). The formulation in John is

3 more abstract, but expresses the same truth: 'I shall come again and receive you to myself, so that where I am you may be also'. What then must a Christian do to be sure of coming to that "place"? What was his "way" to get there? One of the disciples, Thomas, is made to ask this

question in a crudely literal form, as if a knowledge of the geography of heaven were necessary in order to be sure of finding oneself in the right part of it. Jesus characteristically seizes on this to give a new twist to the metaphor: 'I am the way'. Solidarity with Jesus here and now is the guarantee 6 of being with him hereafter.

'Lord, show us the Father and we ask no more.' The request was 8 natural: instead of constantly straining to glimpse and understand how God was brought near to them by Jesus, the disciples yearned for a direct vision of the Father. But the request only showed how little they had grasped of what Jesus was. In him, they had seen and known as much of God as man is capable of knowing in this world. Jesus' words and deeds constituted the 10, 11 final evidence on which a man must base his faith in God. This was to be true, not only during Jesus' visible presence on earth, but in the subsequent life of the church. The authority of Jesus' words and deeds was due to his closeness to his Father: 'it is the Father who dwells in me doing his own 10 work'. But Christians, through their faith in Christ, would be equally close. Through prayer, they could do things at least as great as Jesus had done, which would have the same effect of bringing men to God, 'so that the 13 Father may be glorified in the Son'.

'Your Advocate'. When (according to the traditional picture) men came 16 before the judgement seat of God, they would find themselves facing formidable charges. Sins which they had forgotten would be brought against them; and the devil would be there, seeking to make them appear in the worst possible light. But there would be certain things on the other side. Good deeds they had committed might speak in their favour, and outweigh all contrary evidence. To borrow a technical term from Jewish legal procedure: they would find that they had a *paraclete*, an advocate (the original word *paraklētos* was Greek, but it had been taken over into Jesus' own language, Aramaic, in the form *paraclete*). In a Jewish court, a plaintiff or a defendant was entitled to enlist the help, not only of witnesses to the facts, but of a person of high standing who might give him personal support before the judge and, by his intervention, make the case appear in a more favourable light. This was not "advocacy" in the western, professional sense: the paraclete influenced the judge's decision, not by his knowledge of the law (for this was the judge's business) but by the weight of his personal authority as a man enjoying the esteem of society. Nevertheless, the nearest word in English is probably "advocate", so long as this is understood in a nonprofessional sense.

In Jewish writing, the most common metaphorical use of the term *paraclete* was in the context of God's final judgement upon men. The Jews believed that when they came before God they would find they had an Advocate in such things as their own good deeds and the merits of their ancestors. But in John, language that was conventionally used of the Last

Judgement is frequently applied to the present; and it is clear that in this passage Christians are promised an Advocate, not only when they come before God after death, but from the very moment that Jesus has left them. Given that John (alone of the New Testament writers) is using this title for the Holy Spirit, it is not too difficult to see why. Christians had been promised that, when they found themselves on trial for their faith, the Spirit would prompt them with the right words for their defence (Mark 13.11): in this sense, the Spirit was already their **Advocate**. Moreover, John is about to make Jesus depict the present confrontation between Christianity and the world as a trial, in the course of which the Spirit plays its part as the Christians' **Advocate**. But neither of these explanations fully accounts for all the things said of the **Advocate** here—that it will be **the Spirit of Truth,**
26 **that it dwells with you, that it will teach you everything, and will call to mind all that I have told you.** It is just possible that John saw a further possibility in the metaphor of a *paraclete*. A man of standing who took up a friend's cause before a judge and obtained favourable terms for him would then find himself in the position of reporting back to his friend and having to persuade him to accept the judgement of the court. He would be in the position of a go-between, interpreting the law, as propounded by authoritative judges, to the individual whose interests were affected. In this rôle, he perhaps furnished to John (or to whatever Christian had previously used this title for the Holy Spirit) an illustration of that continuing relationship between Christ and his followers which is one of the principal themes of
15 these *Farewell discourses*. **'If you love me you will obey my commands'.** This had been the principle of Jesus' relationship with his disciples from the beginning. His **'commands'** were simply the will of the Father; like an "advocate", he had been commending these commands to them all the
16 time he was with them. When he left them, there would be **'another to be**
26 **your Advocate'** [a] to continue the same work: he would **teach you everything.** In this sense (though only in this rather technical sense) it is possible to understand a different translation of the word *paraklētos* which was adopted by Greek commentators some centuries after John's time and which found its way into most older English versions: "Comforter". The Advocate "comforts" the individual by explaining and so far as possible lightening the judicial "commands" by which the individual is bound. In some such way as this, the lives of Christians would continue to be quite different even after Jesus' departure. Here was one way of realizing the fulfilment of Jesus'
18 promise, **'I will not leave you bereft; I am coming back to you.'**
22 **Judas asked him.** Throughout this chapter, the discourse is kept going by questions from different disciples in turn. A Judas, other than Iscariot, is

[a] The Greek means literally "another advocate". There was a sense in which Jesus himself had been, and continued to be, the Christians' "advocate", and the word is actually used of him in 1 John 2.1.

known only from the list in Luke (6.16). 'Lord, what can have happened, that you mean to disclose yourself to us alone and not to the world?' This was indeed the greatest reversal of their presuppositions which the disciples had to face. They could perhaps understand how it was that the person of Jesus, during his time on earth, presented a humble appearance and provoked indifference or rejection instead of eliciting universal homage. But this period, Jesus had said again and again, was merely a prelude to his "glorification". Their whole notion of a Messiah was of a figure who would finally dispel the doubts and ambiguities of religious faith and present all men with a decisive manifestation of the power of God and the vindication of the righteous. But Jesus' words seemed to suggest a further period—even after his glorification—when things would not be so plain, and when faith still would not have given place to sight. And indeed, after the resurrection, the church found itself with the task of explaining why, since Christ was now glorified and God's kingdom was a reality, the world seemed to be going on exactly as before, and the glory of God was still perceptible only to those who believed. The answer was that God was now present in a new and unique way in the church. The old concept of a glorious Messiah-king, establishing the rule of God by force, had to give place to that of a new relationship between God and man: 'then my Father will love him, and we will 23 come to him and make our dwelling with him'.

'Peace is my parting gift to you'. Semitic peoples (and not only they) 27 have always "given peace" to one another at greeting or parting. Jesus' parting from his disciples was not to be an ordinary human one, since he would soon be present with them again. This peace, too, was more than a mere word. The disciples would have real peace, 'peace, such as the world cannot give'.

'Up, let us go forward!' Almost exactly the same words occur in Mark 31 and Matthew just before the arrival of the party sent to arrest Jesus in the garden of Gethsemane. Taken in the same sense here, they suggest that Jesus has done with talking and now resolves to go to meet his fate. This is in fact what happens—but only three chapters later. It is tempting to think that something may have gone wrong with John's text, and that these words appear in the wrong place. [a] Nevertheless, this apparent anomaly is not un-characteristic of John. In the first place, it is in his manner to add a passage amplifying what Jesus has just said, even though the scene itself has come to an end (compare the concluding paragraph of chapter 3). In the second place, the literal meaning of Jesus' words is often no more than a decoy: the real meaning lies below the surface. Here perhaps a further explanation is being given for the course of Jesus' passion. It was not that the devil was in command, but that Jesus had to show his obedience. He would do so in

[a] It is possible to understand the whole sentence in more than one way: see the footnote in NEB. But this does not greatly affect the question.

action a little later: meanwhile, on the spiritual level, his words show that he was prepared for whatever might come.

15. 1 'I am the real vine'. Vines grow slowly. In a vineyard in Palestine it was three years before any grapes could be gathered from new plants. They needed constant training and pruning. And any damage done to them could destroy in an hour the patient labour of years. Tending vines (the occupation of countless Palestinian farmers) naturally suggested itself as an illustration of the care with which God tended his people (Jeremiah 2.21; Isaiah 5), and the sudden destruction of a vine was a poignant image for national calamities (Psalm 80.8–16; Ezekiel 19.10–14). It was characteristic of Jesus to use such a familiar example in his own teaching. The other gospels preserve a parable about a vineyard (Mark 12.1–9); but it is only here that anything is made of the actual technique of vine-growing.

The solidarity of Jesus with his disciples (which is the main theme of these chapters) could be expressed as that of the stem with the vine-branches. But everyone knew that there was more to it than just letting the vine grow. Not all the branches would survive: there must be constant tending and pruning. The metaphor was easy to apply. A ruthless politician, for example, could be said to do some "pruning" in the state. So, among Jesus' disciples, God (who is **the gardener**) would do some rigorous selection and training.

But "pruning" really involved two processes: breaking unwanted shoots off the branches, and tending the shoots which remained. This made it possible to use the metaphor in two ways. Some disciples would forfeit their solidarity with Jesus and be pruned off altogether. This would amount to total rejection, for which the reward was loss of all possibility of new life:

6 'The withered branches are heaped together, thrown on the fire, and burnt'—a sentence which has more than an echo of the traditional language used of the Last Judgement (and John again and again shows that he understands this Last Judgement as a thing of the present: it is what a man brings upon himself by his attitude to Jesus). Those disciples, on the other hand, who maintained their solidarity with Jesus still needed that further tending which is here called "cleaning" or "cleansing". Precisely what this means is obscured by the fact that the discourse is on two levels. In its context it is addressed to the disciples, who in some sense (though in what sense is not

3 quite clear, either here or in the previous reference, 13.10) had 'already been cleansed'. But on another level it is addressed to the subsequent church, whose members would certainly need "cleansing", both when they entered it (by baptism) and doubtless thereafter (in a more metaphorical sense). The essential thing, in any case, was the solidarity; and the essence of this solidarity was love and obedience. Given this, Christians would be so much at one with Christ and God that prayer would be answered and the

remaining term of the vine-image would be fulfilled: they would **bear** 8 **fruit.**

The inspiration for such love could only be the example of Christ himself. 'Love one another, as I have loved you'. And this in turn was inspired 12 by God: 'As the Father has loved me, so I have loved you'. What such 9 love involved has been illustrated already by the washing of the disciples' feet: it is about to be seen to its full extent in Jesus' own death. '**There is no** 13 **greater love than this, that a man should lay down his life for his friends.**' As a general proposition, most people might have agreed with this. But friendship was usually defined in terms of mutual advantage. In what sense could it be said that Jesus had **friends**? The answer could lie only in a new definition of friendship. Jesus had no common interest with his disciples, he did not stand to gain anything by their friendship. He was their master, and it would have been natural to think of them as his pupils or his servants. But now he called them his friends, for no other reason than that he had chosen them to be his friends, and had loved them to 'the full extent of his love' (13.1). Love, friendship—these words took on a new meaning in the light of Jesus' relationship with his disciples. All this was implied in Jesus' reiterated commandment: 'love one another'. 17

"**A servant is not greater than his master.**" In 13.16 this saying was 20 put to a new use. Here, it is given the meaning it has in the other gospels: persecution will come as much to the one as to the other. But persecution was never regarded in the early church as an avoidable evil, something which might just blow over. Many Christians saw it in terms which they had inherited from the Jewish way of looking at world history: it was a part of that necessary intensification of evil which would be the prelude to the Last Judgement. But there was also another way of looking at it. Just as the world, far from spontaneously acknowledging Jesus, treated him with such indifference or animosity that it could be said to have actually **hated** him, so it 24 would hate his followers. The manner of his continuing presence among them would provoke exactly the same hostile reaction as he had provoked during his time on earth. '**If I had not come and spoken to them . . . If I** 22, 24 **had not worked among them**'. Jesus' words and works were the ultimate criterion: to reject them was to be **guilty of sin.** In view of what was soon to happen, "hatred" of Jesus and the Father was not too strong a word for their attitude; it was also a word used in a psalm which was found again and again to have been fulfilled in the events of Jesus' life and death: "**They** 25 **hated me without reason**" (Psalm 69.4). Yet not everyone hated: some believed. How did they come to believe? In Jesus' lifetime, they had been persuaded by the **witness** of John the Baptist, and (in a certain sense) by the 26 witness of Jesus himself. Such witness would still be available when men were challenged to believe by the disciples. It would be one of the functions of the Spirit (which has already been described as the **Advocate** in 14.16) to

bear witness and to lend weight to the Christians' cause; and the disciples themselves would be powerful witnesses, having been eyewitnesses of
27 Jesus' acts from the first.

The other gospels record detailed prophecies by Jesus of the persecutions and tribulations which would be suffered by the church. John gives only
16. 2 two: 'They will ban you from the synagogue'—a stiffening of the Jewish attitude towards Christians which we know to have taken place within a few decades of Jesus' resurrection; and, 'anyone who kills you will suppose that he is performing a religious duty'—again, the Jews did believe that in certain circumstances it was a religious duty to punish blasphemy with death, and in due course they certainly came to regard Christians as blasphemers. These were the dangers which lay before any Jews who became Christians. We can glimpse (in the very narrow range of these prophecies compared with those in the other gospels) the specific readership for which John's gospel was written: Greek-speaking Christians of Jewish origin, exposed to hostile pressure from the Jewish communities in the cities where they lived. The persecution they would be exposed to, like other kinds of persecution which would fall upon other parts of the church, was all part of a picture which had been carefully painted by Jesus. To know this was to
1 be guarded against the breakdown of one's faith.
6 'You are plunged into grief because of what I have told you'. On the human level, the prospect of Jesus' departure from the disciples on the eve of this period of troubles was daunting. But in the future, what the followers of Jesus would need most was the conviction that, through all their vicissitudes, they were in the right and had the truth on their side. Persecution is intolerable if you are not sure of that for which you are being persecuted. This would never happen to Christians because of the reality of their experience of the Spirit among them. This Spirit, in these discourses,
7 is called the Advocate; and the scene of its action is again imagined as a law-court. Each encounter between the world and the church is like that of two opposing parties before a judge. The world sets out to show (i) that the Christians have sinned (done wrong) in adopting their new faith (which, from the Jewish point of view, involved the blasphemy of using divine titles of Jesus); (ii) that they cannot be in the right after pinning their faith to one who ended his life on the cross; and (iii) that Jesus' death itself, secured according to the principles of the Jewish faith, was a clear instance of the proper course of divine justice. The appearance of the Advocate on the Christians'
9 side completely turns the tables on the accusers. (i) 'He will convict them of wrong', in that, by being clearly on the side of the Christians in all they do, he will show that their faith has been vindicated, and that it is their enemies'
10 refusal to believe which is wrong; (ii) 'He will convince them that right is on my side', since he will strengthen and validate the Christians' faith that Jesus, by his resurrection and glorification, has been shown to be in the

right despite the cross; and (iii) 'he will convince them of divine judge- 11
ment' by showing that what they took to be the condemnation of Jesus was
in reality the condemnation of the devil, the Prince of this world. All
this fits easily enough into the conventional picture of the Last Judgement.
When all the world comes before God to be judged, Christians will certainly
have an Advocate who will give decisive evidence in their favour. But this
Advocate (in John's presentation of Jesus' teaching) is none other than the
Holy Spirit who is present even now in the church. As so often in this gospel,
'now is the hour of judgement for this world' (12.31). The Advocate at the
Last Judgement, and the Spirit which is on the Christians' side today, are
one and the same.

'There is still much that I could say to you'. All the gospels report 12
that Jesus gave his disciples some teaching about the conditions under
which they would find themselves exercising their discipleship (conditions,
it is explained in John, which were only the logical sequel of those under
which Jesus himself made his appearance among men). In Matthew, Mark
and Luke, these conditions are interpreted in terms of traditional Jewish
expectation: their meaning was to be found in the fact that they formed a
part of that great drama of inevitable sufferings which would be the prelude
and earnest of the imminent end of the world. Given this traditional picture,
it was not difficult to fill in the details of the kind of tribulations which the
righteous were to endure. In John, this traditional view of the future is
taken less for granted, and it is suggested that Jesus, instead of giving his
disciples the conventional blueprint, as it were, of what was in store for
them, forbore to overwhelm them with predictions of their sufferings ('the
burden would be too great for you now'), but promised instead that
they would receive enlightenment when the time came from the Spirit of 13
truth. 'He will make known to you the things that are coming'. One
of the ways in which the church actually experienced the Holy Spirit was as
a spirit of prophecy, speaking through individual Christians and predicting
events that were about to happen. But we need not suppose that it is only
this literal kind of prophecy which is meant here. The essential thing for
Christians was to know, not exactly what was about to happen, but the
meaning of what was actually happening (which was in fact the main
function of Old Testament prophecy). Jesus gave a certain amount of teaching on the subject. But the Spirit was to bring the same prophetic understanding of events into every situation that would be encountered by the
church.

In all this, the phenomenon to be described was the continuing experience
of the church that, after Jesus' death, they were nevertheless not bereft. For
this purpose, it was necessary to use three apparently personal and distinct
terms: Father, Son, and Spirit (or Advocate). This might seem a dangerous
way of talking, as if there were more than one separate deity involved. Did

Christianity, after all, ask for a belief in many gods? Did it ask Jews to abandon their fundamental doctrine of the one true God? The answer to these
fears was to be found in the intimate relationship between the three; and a
13-15 few words are added here to show how tightly the circle is drawn which
includes Father, Son and Spirit.

16 'A little while'. Any reader of the gospel who knew what was about to
happen could see one obvious meaning of this pregnant little phrase. In "a
little while" Jesus would be arrested, tried and executed; and "a little
while" after that he would rise from the dead. We read in the other gospels
that Jesus predicted his death and his resurrection on the third day (see
above on Mark 9.9), and that his predictions were simply not understood by
18 the disciples. On the face of it, this is exactly the situation here. 'What
is this "little while" that he speaks of? We do not know what he
means'.

But this "little while" was also a standard phrase in the vocabulary of any
Jewish teacher who professed to have an insight into the future. If you
believed (as most Jews did, and as Christians certainly did to an intense
degree) that world history was tending towards a climax, and that God was
about to act, then at any moment when faith in this cosmic dénouement
seemed to be slackening, you would recall your hearers or your readers to a
proper pitch of expectation by reminding them that all this must surely come
to pass "in a little while". The phrase is in the Hebrew prophets, it is in the
Christian book called the Revelation (6.11). Jesus, in this part of his discourse, had been saying something about what the future had in store for his
followers. This "little while" was just what might have been expected: a
cryptic reference to the period before the End, when history would at last
be hastening towards its consummation. Teaching of this kind about the
pattern of the future necessarily sounded cryptic to outsiders. But the intimate followers of such a teacher would expect to be let into the secret
meaning. They would hardly remain content to say, 'We do not know what
he means'.

Nor is this the only hint that the paragraph is cast in the mould of traditional esoteric teaching about the imminent crisis of history. It was commonly
accepted (at least within certain circles of Jewish teachers) that the period
before the end would be one of intensified violence and tribulation: the joys
of the age to come would be heralded by unprecedented sufferings. To describe this period, one of the metaphors which suggested itself was that of a
woman giving birth to her first child: the suffering would be such as she had
never suffered before, but it would be short-lived, and the memory of it
would be swallowed up in the joy which followed it. The metaphor had been
worked out already in Isaiah 26.16–18, a passage which has many echoes
in this chapter of John; and in the time of Jesus (or at least very soon after)

the 'birth-pangs of the new age' (Mark 13.8) was almost a technical expression for the last period of world history. When, therefore, Jesus, in the context of his teaching about the future, elaborated the metaphor of 'a woman in labour', and then described a state of affairs in which his disciples would be so close to God that their prayers would be certain of an answer (one of the standard blessings in the age to come), there can be little doubt where these 'figures of speech' came from. Jesus, here as in the other gospels, was making use of the traditional repertory of those who claimed to have insight into the coming last days of the world and the new age which was to follow them.

But in John's gospel, when Jesus uses language of this kind, it tends to bear a radically original meaning. What his contemporaries described as belonging to a world of the future, Jesus showed to be realities belonging to a kind of life which men may experience here and now. The whole of this section plays upon new meanings of the old language: both the "little while" of apparent dereliction, and the joy of communion, are simultaneous experiences in the life of the Christian. This actualization of traditional hopes becomes explicit towards the end of the section. According to the traditional scheme, one of the conditions of living in the time before the end was having to be content with partial vision, partial understanding. The signs of the times were puzzling and ambiguous, one got no nearer the truth than figures of speech. But when the end came the veil would be lifted, the obscurities would be removed. As Paul puts it, 'Now we see only puzzling reflections in a mirror, but then we shall see face to face' (1 Corinthians 13.12). Figures of speech would give place to plain words, the truth would be known, no longer through anxious questioning and dimly understood answer, but by direct communication. Jesus had already talked many times about "going to the Father", but had never been understood, even by his own followers. Now, suddenly, they grasped what he meant, and the truth seemed to burst in upon them. It was as if the perfection of knowledge and clarity of vision which they believed they would have only in heaven was available to them here and now. 'Why, this is plain speaking; this is no figure of speech.' Here was an earnest of what Jesus had promised: an experience hitherto conceived as only possible in an imagined future was already breaking into the present.

Jesus answered, 'Do you now believe?' In the Bible, this period of "trouble" for the righteous was an element common to all inspired prophecies about the future. Nothing Jesus had said must be interpreted as if his followers would be spared this trouble. He was still exhorting them to bear it. But traditionally, every exhortation to bear trouble steadfastly was based on the promise of ultimate victory: in "a little while", those who now were oppressed and persecuted would conquer. The new factor in Jesus' exhortation was that he did not have to leave his followers with a mere promise. The

victory had already been won. That which made the trouble worth bearing
33 was already possessed. 'The victory is mine; I have conquered the
world.'

17. 1 **After these words Jesus looked up to heaven.** It is easy enough to imagine
Jesus concluding this long discourse to his disciples with an act of prayer.
Equally, it is easy to imagine that when John came to arrange and reformulate
the teaching of Jesus he should have thought it appropriate to round it off
with a prayer. In fact, however, this final address of Jesus to his heavenly
Father includes rather more than we normally look for in a "prayer". It
expresses, certainly, the perfect resolution of Jesus to undergo his destiny—
a resolution which had seemed to falter for a moment on a previous occasion
(12.27); and it contains a number of petitions for the welfare of his followers
15 (including what appears to be an allusion to the Lord's Prayer: '**keep them
from the evil one**'). But it also consists (particularly in its opening phrases)
of a solemn summary of what has been said earlier about the nature of Jesus
19 and the faith of his disciples; and with the words, '**I now consecrate
myself**', it marks the actual moment when Jesus might be said to have
committed himself irrevocably to his act of sacrifice '**for their sake**'. All
this is not quite "prayer" in the sense the word bears today. On the other
hand, it falls well within the function which a prayer was deemed to have in
antiquity, that is, not only supplicating and praising God, but defining carefully those beliefs about God and man which justify us in attempting to
pray at all.
1   '**Glorify thy Son**'. That Jesus' "glorification" was to take place on the
cross is a paradox which has already been hinted at more than once. But here
2 it is related to an image more characteristic of the other gospels: '**For thou
hast made him sovereign over all mankind**'. Jesus was the Son of
Man; and it was prophesied of this Son of Man that he would be installed at
the right hand of God, and that all mankind would be made subject to him.
Eternal life, which elsewhere in this gospel is usually defined in terms of
believing in Jesus Christ, is here described as a matter of "knowing" God
and Christ. To put these ideas together: the Christian is one who "knows"
that the humble Son of Man who was crucified is now sovereign, that the
crucifixion was in reality Jesus' glorification, that to recognize Jesus' glory
is to see God's glory and to enter upon that new quality of living which can
4 be called eternal life. Jesus' **work** on earth has had the purpose of making all
this credible. But it is something which has always been true. This glory of
Jesus, which Christians come to understand through his life and death, has
5 in fact existed (as the very first words of the gospel proclaim) since **before
the world began.**
    The main part of the prayer is for the disciples. They have just reached a
8 decisive point in their apprenticeship: '**they have had faith to believe**

374

that thou didst send me'. They are now to continue in the world in something of the same conditions under which Jesus himself taught and lived, that is, with the same sense of belonging to two worlds, of being **strangers in** 16 **the world**. The inherent ambiguity of this relationship with the world sets the tone for the prayer which Jesus now makes for them.

He prays first for their safety. This is not just a matter of physical security: the stakes are higher than that. They must be protected, not so much from the danger of suffering and death, as from the danger of being forced by these things to renounce their faith and forfeit their new life. '**Protect by** 11 **the power of thy name those whom thou hast given me**'. God's name was an expression used in the Old Testament to describe the fact that God was believed to be present to a particular degree in a particular place: God made his **name** dwell in the temple of Jerusalem. Jesus' presence among his disciples was equivalent to this "power of the name", this presence of God on earth; and Jesus prays that the disciples may continue to have this power[a] to protect them from disaster. If it were objected that Jesus' presence did not in fact protect Judas from his fate, the answer was that Judas was a special case; he was **the man who must be lost**, a traditional phrase for 12 one who, in the current mythology about the future, would appear as a kind of personification of wickedness (2 Thessalonians 2.3); and his special rôle had been amply foretold by **Scripture** (13.18).

Secondly, Jesus prays that **they may be one**. For Christianity, as for any 22 religious movement, unity among its adherents was of course essential for its survival (and indeed, by the time John wrote, the church had been exposed to serious threats to its unity). Jesus' prayer doubtless embraces this functional unity; but it also envisages something more fundamental. The intense solidarity between Jesus and his disciples has already been expounded. Here it is developed still further: '**as thou, Father, art in me, and I in thee, so** 21 **also may they be in us**'. The implication of this relationship between men and God is a new unity among men themselves; and this is to be embodied, not only in the original disciples, but in subsequent generations of Christians. 20 (Jesus may or may not have foreseen such a long history for his followers; but John already knew at least several generations of them.)

Thirdly, Jesus prays that they may be **consecrated by the truth**. The 19 metaphor belongs to temples and sanctuaries. A priest consecrates himself by separating himself from the ordinary concerns and squalor of the world, in order to make himself a fit person to draw near to the presence of God in ritual and service. The metaphor can of course be refined and spiritualized: consecrating oneself need mean no more than simply committing oneself wholeheartedly to a particular task or form of service. But there is always in

[a] However, the "name" does not necessarily imply power. It might also mean simply the common name shared by all who have a common loyalty. Hence the alternative translation offered in the NEB footnote.

it a hint of separation: consecration implies freeing oneself from certain things in order to be fully available for something else. In this sense, it was an appropriate word for the disciples who, for the sake of Christ, had become 14 **strangers in the world.** But again, their solidarity with Christ implied that they would share something of his consecration, a consecration which amounted to utter self-sacrifice.

The whole of the discourse has been exploring the manner in which Jesus would continue to be present with his disciples after the crucifixion and resurrection. Something of heaven, he has been saying, would attend their life on earth. But one could put it the other way round. It was not only that life in this world would be transformed by influences from another world: human beings, while still in this world, could have an experience of heaven. This was the climax of the possibilities of Christian discipleship, and the 24 final subject of Jesus' great prayer for his followers: '**I desire that these men . . . may be with me where I am, so that they may look upon my glory**'.

The final conflict

This is the heading given by the translators to the last section of all four gospels; and indeed at this point the gospel according to John, which up to now has followed a strikingly different pattern from the others, suddenly begins to run closely parallel to them. The differences no longer lie in the grand design, but in the details.

18. 1 **After these words, Jesus went out with his disciples, and crossed the Kedron ravine.** The name occurs nowhere else in the New Testament; but we know exactly what it stands for: it is the deep river-bed (or *wady*) which separates the hill on which Jerusalem was built from the range of higher hills to the east which includes the Mount of Olives. John tells us, therefore, which side of the city Jesus came out of, and when he goes on to say that **there was a garden there,** it is obvious that he means the place which appears in the other gospels as Gethsemane, on the slopes of the 2 Mount of Olives. The detail (also hinted at in Luke 22.39) that Jesus **had often met there with his disciples** casts Judas in a clear rôle: he was able to pass on information to Jesus' enemies on which they could act. But this, according to John, was the full extent of his treachery. His traitor's kiss is not mentioned: there was no need to identify Jesus, for Jesus immediately identified himself, causing some consternation to his captors. Whether or not they originally intended to arrest Jesus' followers as well (a possibility John leaves open), Jesus insisted that they should let them go, and in so doing gave, as it were, a literal demonstration of the truth of a promise he had made earlier in general terms (6.39), '**I have not lost one of those**

whom thou gavest me'. There is no question in this account of the disciples running away.

Jesus' captors are described as a **detachment of soldiers, and police** 3 **provided by the chief priests and the Pharisees.** In the other gospels it is clear that they were sent by the Sanhedrin. John's description is less precise. The chief priests *ex officio*, and the Pharisaic party in fact, each formed an influential section of the Sanhedrin, and John doubtless meant the **police** to be understood as coming from that authority. But what about the **detachment of soldiers?** In the Greek, this is the correct term for a Roman cohort, and means a force of several hundred men. Apart from the fact that such a large detachment seems quite inappropriate, it is a surprise to find Roman soldiers involved at this stage. John may have known, independently of the other gospels, that Roman soldiers were in fact present, or he may perhaps have wished to tell the story of Jesus' arrest, trial and execution in such a way as would seem to implicate the Roman administration right from the start. Alternatively, just as in Mark 6.21 the senior officers in Herod's private army could be called 'commanders' (which, in Greek, was the correct title for a tribune in the Roman army), so John may have been using military language rather loosely, and have meant, both by this phrase and by **the** 12 **troops with their commander** in verse 12, nothing more than a mixed force of Jewish armed men. At any rate, the brief scuffle took place just the same. John gives the names of both the disciple and the slave, and in Jesus' rebuke—'**This is the cup the Father has given me**'—makes a suggestive 11 allusion to the scene of Jesus at prayer in the garden (Mark 14.36), which he may have known about even though he has omitted it from his own narrative.

They took him first to Annas. This is a significant departure from the 13 account in the other gospels. Matthew and Mark report that Jesus was immediately brought before a meeting specially convened during the night; Luke describes Jesus being held prisoner in Caiaphas' house until dawn. John introduces a new element altogether with the mention of Annas. Annas had been deposed from the office of High Priest, which he had held for ten years, in A.D. 15, but he remained a person of influence, for apart from his son-in-law Caiaphas, who was high priest from A.D. 18 to 36, five of his sons also held the office, and it is not in itself unlikely that he was behind Jesus' arrest and was given an opportunity to conduct the first examination. John, however, combines this new piece of tradition with one that he shares with all the other gospels: the story of Peter's denial. Here too he has a fresh piece of information to give. Peter's presence in the courtyard was made possible by **a disciple who was acquainted with the High Priest.** We are not told who 15 this was; and the fact that Jesus' following included people with connections of this kind is new to us. It does not look, therefore, as if John was simply rewriting the story from a version like that in Mark. He seems to have had an independent source of information which allowed him to identify some of the characters in the scene.

19 **The High Priest questioned Jesus about his disciples and about what he taught.** This suggests, not formal legal proceedings, but an informal interrogation. To the High Priest's questions, Jesus replied (as in the other gospels he replied to his captors in the garden) that after all his public

20 teaching **in synagogue and in the temple** such a procedure was pointless. John gives no further details; he is hastening on to a new issue altogether, that between Jesus and the Roman governor. He pauses only to finish off the story of Peter, and to give his own very mild and attenuated version (which hinges on Exodus 22.28 "You shall not revile God, nor curse a ruler of your people") of the insults suffered by Jesus at the hands of the Jewish authorities. Here it is no more than a single blow struck by an officer; and

23 Jesus replies by insisting upon the conditions of a fair trial: '**If I spoke amiss, state it in evidence**'.

24 **So Annas sent him bound to Caiaphas the High Priest.** John has

13 already said that Caiaphas, Annas' son-in-law, was **the High Priest for that year.** This is correct, in so far as Caiaphas was certainly High Priest at the time, but misleading in that it suggests that the office was held for one year only—Caiaphas held it for 18 years. Possibly John was confused by the fact that a number of high priests did in fact hold office for not more than a year in the first half of the century. A further complication is that Annas, though no longer in office as High Priest, was still a member of the class of "High Priests", and therefore a person of great influence. John is therefore

15 correct, though a little confusing, in referring to him too as **the High Priest.**

28 **From Caiaphas Jesus was led into the Governor's headquarters.** All the other gospels give some account of a session of a Jewish court, presided over by Caiaphas the High Priest; during this session, Jesus made a statement which the court judged to be blasphemous and punishable by death. Whether or not such a session actually took place, John makes no mention of it here. He has already recorded (10.22–39) an occasion when Jesus was heard committing blasphemy (as they thought) by the Jewish authorities. Even if John knew that a similar scene took place in the presence of Caiaphas, he had no need to delay his readers by repeating the details here. It was clearly the trial before the Roman authorities to which he wished to give the greatest emphasis in this chapter; and his account of it is a great deal fuller than that of the other gospels.

The trial scene itself is also conceived somewhat differently. Instead of hearing the case of accusers and accused together, Pilate has Jesus held prisoner inside his headquarters, but interviews the Jews outside, so that the prosecution and the defence are heard in different places, and Pilate, as judge, moves in and out from one to the other. John provides a reason for this: the Jews themselves stayed outside the headquarters to avoid 28 defilement, so that they could eat the Passover meal. From an antiquarian point of view, this was probably (though not certainly) correct: the Jews who celebrated the Passover at Jerusalem, and in particular the priests who had ceremonial duties to attend to during the afternoon, were obliged to make themselves ritually "clean" beforehand; and the houses of Gentiles were regarded as places of possible ritual contamination (there was the danger, for instance, that there might be a grave underneath, which would make a Jew ritually "unclean" for a week). To this extent, the reason John gives for their remaining outside is plausible, though a little recondite. A more obvious reason would have been that it was customary for a Roman magistrate to set up his tribunal in a public place, and not inside his house, and what really needed explaining was, not that the Jews remained outside, but that Jesus was brought inside. However, the significance of the statement (certainly for us, and probably also for John) is that it clearly dates the Passover festival to the evening following the crucifixion, [a] whereas the other gospels equally clearly place it on the evening before. The day of the week is the same in all accounts: Jesus was crucified on a Friday. But according to the first three gospels, Friday that year fell on 15th Nisan, the day after the celebration of the Passover meal, and Jesus' last supper was in fact a Passover celebration. According to John, on the other hand, the feast fell a day later that year, and Jesus hung on the cross while the lambs for the feast were being sacrificed at the temple. Both cannot be right, and a choice has to be made between them. But each, in its different way, exploits the fact that it was the season of Passover, in order to set the last events of Jesus' life against the background of a Jewish religious festival.

It was the duty of the Roman governor to hear charges laid against his subjects, to check their accuracy, and to decide on the action to be taken under Roman law. Pilate's first question to the Jews was the normal opening of this procedure: 'What charge do you bring against this man?' But 29 their answer was curiously evasive. 'If he were not a criminal', they 30 replied, 'we should not have brought him before you.' It is not clear how John means us to understand this; but the fact that they did not immediately bring forward a charge apparently made Pilate assume that the matter was a technical one of Jewish law which the Jews were not disposed to explain to him and on which, in any case, he could not be expected to give a ruling (this, at any rate, was the reaction of the Roman governor of Corinth on a similar occasion, Acts 18.14–15). But the Jews replied to this that, even if it was a technical matter of their own law, it was a capital case, and they

[a] If the translation given in the footnote were correct, this inconsistency would disappear, since the "Passover season" lasted for a week. But it is very doubtful whether the Greek words can bear this meaning.

31 had no competence to carry out the death penalty. 'We are not allowed to put any man to death.'

This statement provides, almost casually, the answer to the main problem posed by the gospel accounts of Jesus' trial and death. Jesus was crucified, a form of execution carried out only by the Romans; but the blame for his condemnation is placed by all the evangelists, not on the Romans, but on the Jews. How were these two facts to be reconciled? The solution offered is that it was indeed the Jews who found Jesus guilty of blasphemy; but that they prevailed upon the Roman authorities, in the person of Pilate, to carry out the execution. And the clue to this surprising procedure is provided by a chance remark made in John's narrative (and nowhere else in any of the gospels) that, at this time, the Jews themselves did not have the power to carry out the death penalty. That this was true is at least probable: we have no decisive evidence, but it is consistent with what we know of the Roman administration of the provinces of the empire. But it has to be admitted that this is the one single reference in the New Testament to a fact which is of critical importance to understanding the trial and execution of Jesus. John underlines the significance of the fact in his own way. That Jesus was

32 crucified was not merely the result of historical circumstances: it was the only form of execution which would have been consistent with what Jesus himself had said about the symbolism of his death (12.32). If the Jews had executed him, they would have done it by stoning, and this could never have been described as a "lifting up". To those mysterious obstacles which prevented the Jews from summarily doing away with Jesus earlier (see above, p. 336) is now added a purely technical one: they were not allowed to by the Roman regulations.

We must assume that more passed in the conversation between Pilate and the Jews than is actually recorded here, for when Pilate went inside to examine

33 the defendant he put to him a specific charge ('Are you the king of the Jews?') and admitted that the charge was one put forward by the Jews. In the accounts in the other gospels, Jesus' reply to the charge, though he never altogether denied it, was always marked by a certain reserve. Here the same reserve is expanded into a definition of the exact sense in which Jesus claimed to be a king. This convinced Pilate that, if Jesus' kingship operated only with

38 abstractions such as truth, no action need be taken. He consequently returned outside to inform the Jews of his decision. He also entertained the hope that he could at the same time exploit the situation by making his release of Jesus satisfy the Jews' customary demand for the release of one prisoner at Passover. But in this he was disappointed. Instead of being able to get away with releasing the harmless Jesus, he was forced to release one who was a bandit, that is, perhaps a member of one of the armed resistance groups which constantly harried the Roman occupying forces: Barabbas.

19. 1   Pilate now took Jesus and had him flogged. Events were still taking a

normal course according to Roman justice. The flogging was the Roman equivalent to "letting him off with a warning"; and the soldiers' mockery, and the public exhibition which followed, may have been a legitimate extension of it. But from this point the proceedings became more political than judicial. By Roman law Pilate had found Jesus innocent—indeed that no case had been made out against him at all. But by Jewish law (the chief priests maintained) Jesus had been proved to have committed blasphemy ('**he** 7 **has claimed to be Son of God**') for which the penalty was death; and Pilate was now being subjected to pressure to carry out the sentence of a Jewish court which that court was not competent to carry out itself. At first Pilate was merely impatient. '**Take him and crucify him yourselves**,' he said sarcastically, knowing that they had no power even to stone him, let alone to use the Roman method of crucifixion. But then the strength of the Jewish agitation seems to have unnerved him; he became **more afraid than** 8 **ever,** and went inside for a further interview with Jesus, doubtless hoping to discover at least some reason why the Jews were so anxious to see the death sentence carried out. His question, '**Where have you come from?**' cer- 9 tainly sounded like the opening of a general interrogation. **But Jesus gave him no answer.** This motif of Jesus' silence appears in all the gospel accounts. Here it is made the cue for a brief dialogue about authority, and a further indication of where the main responsibility lay for Jesus' condemnation.

In Pilate's final interview with the Jewish leaders, the issue once again entered a new phase. Having failed to get their way so far, the Jews brought forward something of a threat: '**If you let this man go, you are no friend** 12 **to Caesar**'. "Friend of Caesar"—*amicus Caesaris*—this is what, under the empire, every Roman official aspired to be: to have the Emperor's ear, to be known for one's loyalty. A few years later Pilate was deposed from office at the instigation of one who was more of a "friend of Caesar" than he. At any time, the possibility of reports reaching home that he was allowing disloyalty to Caesar among his subjects in Judaea would have alarmed him. Finally, therefore, he determined to put the matter to the test: if the crowd showed that they were prepared to acknowledge Jesus as king, clearly the man was dangerous after all, and action must be taken. For the first time he brought the prisoner outside his headquarters to confront his accusers. The scene is carefully and solemnly set. The Roman governor normally set up his **tribunal** for the purpose of giving judgement *a* in a public place outside his 13 residence. John knows the name of the place. Greek-speaking people called it '**The Pavement**': streets and squares paved with smooth and massive

[a] The phrase, "took his seat on the tribunal", certainly suggests that Pilate is about to give judgement. But in fact he has given judgement already, and what follows is hardly judicial. Another possible translation of the Greek is, "he set Jesus on the tribunal". If this were correct, it would add point and drama to the scene: Pilate would be deliberately challenging the Jews to show their allegiance to a usurper of his own authority.

stone blocks were characteristic of Herodian Jerusalem, and it would not be surprising if there were a particularly fine one outside the Governor's residence (which was formerly Herod the Great's palace). [a] **In the language of the Jews it was called 'Gabbatha'**, which probably represents a Hebrew or Aramaic word meaning "a high place": and again, in a city built on steep hills, this would be an obvious name for any public square in the higher parts

14 of Jerusalem. John also appears to know the exact time: **It was the eve of Passover,** [b] **about noon.** This conflicts with the other gospels, where Jesus is crucified in the morning. John may have had other information; on the other hand, if he knew that on the eve of Passover the sacrificial lambs were slaughtered at the temple in the early afternoon, and if he wished to make Jesus' death carry some of the symbolic meaning of these sacrifices, he may have deliberately pictured Jesus' final condemnation as taking place at the last moment when work was permissible on the eve of Passover: **about noon.**

15 **Pilate said to the Jews, 'Here is your king.'** This was a direct challenge to the Jews. But the Jews replied with a vigorous protestation of their loyalty to Caesar, and demanded Jesus' execution. The demand may have been unjust, but it could be taken as an expression of allegiance to the power of Rome; and Pilate yielded to it.

To this extent John's narrative permits us to make a possible reconstruction of the original events. At the same time, it is clear that here, as throughout his gospel, John is doing a great deal more than merely recording events as they happened. Like the authors of the other gospels, he has certain points that he wishes to make. Jesus was put to death by the Romans, allegedly as a claimant to the treasonable title, "King of the Jews": this was the basic fact known to anyone who had heard anything about Jesus at all. But two obvious inferences from this fact needed to be corrected. First, the execution was not

12 the Romans' fault; on the contrary, **Pilate tried hard to release him.** It was the Jews, not the Romans, who were mainly responsible. Secondly, Jesus was not a traitor to Rome: his "kingship" was not political, and therefore his followers need not be regarded as disloyal citizens by the Roman authorities (a point of importance by the time John's gospel was written). It

[a] An impressive area of such paving has been found on the site of one of Herod the Great's buildings in Jerusalem, the fortress-palace called Antonia which lay next to and dominated the temple area. It is tempting to believe that this was the site of Jesus' trial; but unfortunately this identification is not certain. It is in many ways more likely that Pilate had his headquarters (*praetorium*) in the main palace of Herod the Great that was situated in the highest part of the city (and which it has not yet been possible to excavate), than in the Antonia; and in any case the archaeological evidence suggests that the paving at the Antonia dates from the time of Hadrian, a century after the trial of Jesus.

[b] The alternative rendering given in the footnote would eliminate the second of the two statements in John's gospel which show that this author believed the crucifixion to have taken place before, not after, the Jewish Passover (the other is 18.28), and would make it possible to reconcile his chronology with that of the other gospels. But it is very doubtful whether the Greek words could bear the sense proposed.

was true of the trial of Jesus—as it was true of the ensuing trials of Christians in Roman courts—that it was not the Roman administration which was ultimately to blame: '**the deeper guilt lies with the man who handed** 11 **me over to you**'. [a] But John's account of the trial, though it is in many ways so similar to that in the other gospels, is at the same time characteristic of him. For he uses it, as he uses many episodes, to explain to the reader the significance of some of the concepts used by Jesus. In particular (since it was known that Jesus was crucified as "king of the Jews") there is a conversation between Jesus and Pilate which, whatever may have passed between them (which John could hardly have had any means of knowing), fills a gap in this gospel's presentation of the person of Jesus by explaining what Jesus meant by the title. '**My task is to bear witness to the truth**.' 18. 37

Carrying his own cross. John appears not to know of the tradition (vouched 19. 17 for by the man's own sons in Mark's account) that a certain Simon of Cyrene was forced to carry the cross for Jesus. It may be, in any case, that Jesus did in fact carry the beam of his own cross at least some of the way, until he had to be relieved of it through exhaustion. John may have known of Jesus' saying that stands in Luke 14.27 in the form, 'No one who does not carry his cross . . . can be a disciple of mine'; if so, he may have deliberately concentrated on the early stages of the procession, during which Jesus was as it were setting an example to his future disciples.

Not far from the city. This detail, given only by John, is exactly what 20 we should expect: the Romans crucified insurrectionists to set a public example, and though custom forbade them to do this in the most public place of all (inside the city), they normally chose a place not far outside, where the victims would be seen by a large number of people. John also gives very plausible details about **the inscription** (which he calls by the technical Latin name, *titulus*). Hebrew can mean (as often in the New Testament) the language actually spoken by the inhabitants of Palestine; **Latin** was the native language of the Roman administrators; **Greek** was the common language in fact used for official purposes throughout the eastern part of the empire. Thus publicly displayed, the charge against Jesus could well have seemed to the chief priests a deliberate insult to their nation.

'**They shared my garments among them, and cast lots for my** 24 **clothing**'. This quotation (Psalm 22.18) occurs in all the gospel accounts, and indeed the psalm, with its classic description of the predicament of a righteous sufferer, evidently offered a convenient and traditional framework in which to set the remembered details of the crucifixion of Jesus. But John seems to have worked out the exact way in which this **text of Scripture**

[a] In its context this saying is ambiguous: it could mean Judas or Caiaphas. But the vagueness may be deliberate. It would have made it easier for Christians to quote the saying when they found themselves on trial before the Roman authorities.

came true. Even though, in Hebrew poetry, the two halves of a line are often intended to balance each other, and to yield, not two statements, but two ways of making the same statement, nevertheless John takes the whole line quite literally, and appears to ask himself how, if the four soldiers **shared** Jesus' garments by dividing them among themselves, they could also find

23 anything to **cast lots** about. He found the answer in Jesus' **tunic**, which might well have been the one really valuable object among the spoils to which the soldiers were entitled: the tunic (*chitōn*) was the long shirt (usually with short sleeves) which was worn under a cloak. Obviously it would have been silly to "share" this by tearing it up (even if it were not **in one piece throughout**, as John painstakingly assures us it was); therefore they "tossed for it", and thus fulfilled the prophecy to the letter.

25 **That is what the soldiers did.** With considerable artistry John builds up a surrounding frame of onlookers before coming to the centre of the picture, Jesus himself. All the gospels refer to the women who were present at the crucifixion, although they differ in the details: only John reports that they were actually **near the cross**, and that Jesus' mother was among them. We do not know who **her sister** was—the Greek, like the English, is ambiguous, and so far as grammar goes she could be the same person as **Mary wife of Clopas**: but it is perhaps not very likely that two sisters would both have been called Mary. Otherwise, the only woman of the group who can be certainly identified is **Mary of Magdala**, who is known from Luke 8.2. In any case their presence enables John to record a further saying of

26 Jesus, '**Mother, there is your son**'. This is evidently more than a last-minute concern for the welfare of a bereaved mother. If it had been merely

27 this, it would have been sufficient to say to the disciple, '**There is your mother**'; there would have been no need for Jesus to address his mother as well. In any case, the form of address is strange and solemn. Literally, the Greek gives "woman", for which **mother** is only a rough equivalent: the word was not rude (as "woman" would be in English), but it was formal (in a way that "mother" is not). Jesus addressed his mother in the same way at Cana (2.4 above), and on that occasion too his utterance had a solemn and formal ring. Clearly there is a hidden meaning, and subsequent Christian meditation has found the germ of many doctrines about the church, about womanhood, and about Mary herself in this single sentence. One point at least seems fairly certain. The **disciple whom he loved** (whoever he was) stands on this occasion for more than one individual: he represents the whole company of followers of Christ; and the saying falls into line with those great affirmations of Paul that Christians are Christ's "brothers", and share his sonship.

28, 29 '**I thirst**'. All the gospels mention that Jesus was offered **sour wine**, and a verse from Psalm 69 (which was one of the classic descriptions of a righteous sufferer) must have helped to determine the words in which the incident was recorded: "for my thirst they gave me vinegar for drink" (Ps. 69.21). John, too, may well have had this text in mind when he added, **in fulfilment of Scripture.** But he also refashioned the incident in his own way. It would be a little strange if Jesus were really yielding to acute thirst at this point. It would be his only expression of physical suffering in any of the gospel accounts, and it would be surprising if John had chosen to record something so trivial at this critical moment. More probably, Jesus' "thirst" was (characteristically in this gospel) metaphorical: it was an intense longing for God. The word was misunderstood, and taken literally by the soldiers [a]— this again was a favourite device of the writer when he wished to draw attention to the deeper meaning of a saying of Jesus. Its true meaning is given in another psalm (63.1):

> "O God, thou art my God, I seek thee,
> my soul thirsts for thee."

This psalm begins, in Hebrew, *elohim eli*. Mark and Matthew both record that Jesus cried *eli* from the cross, and that this was misunderstood as 'Elijah' by the bystanders. John may have assumed that the cry was a prayer of Jesus based on this psalm and that the misunderstanding consisted in his "thirst" being taken literally.

That Jesus' life and work was a perfect unity, a work to be finished and a destiny to be accomplished, is one of the themes of John's gospel (4.34; 5.36; 17.4). Aptly, John records, as his final cry, '**It is accomplished!**' 30

Because it was the eve of Passover. [b] It was laid down in Deuteronomy 31 that a criminal executed by "hanging on a tree" must be buried before nightfall. Moreover, the day on which Jesus was crucified was a Friday: the Sabbath began at dusk, and was a day that must not be profaned by dead bodies in public places—especially (as John adds, perhaps unnecessarily) since **that Sabbath was a day of great solemnity,** being the first day of the 31 festival. The request of the Jews was therefore reasonable. The "defilement of the land" (Deuteronomy 21.23) which would have ensued otherwise would have been a serious matter for the consciences of strict Jews who had come to Jerusalem to keep the festival. Execution by crucifixion was a slow death—sometimes it could take up to thirty-six hours. Breaking the legs of the victims was a recognized way of hastening death. But Jesus was **already** 33

[a] A javelin is the translation of the Greek word *hyssos*. The manuscripts all give *hyssōpos*, "marjoram", which makes little sense. It was conjectured in the sixteenth century that John must originally have written *hyssos*, and that an easy slip of an early copyist produced the reading of all our existing manuscripts—except one of the thirteenth century which, perhaps by accident, supports the conjectural reading, "javelin".

[b] The translation, "eve of Passover", is a correct inference rather than an exact rendering. The Greek word means simply "Friday"; but it is true that, at least by John's reckoning, the Passover was about to begin at nightfall, and so, in that sense, this Friday was the "eve" of Passover. The alternative translation given in the footnote is a further attempt to harmonize John's dating with that of the other gospels. See above on 18.28 and 19.14.

dead, so they did not break his legs. Why did John mention this? We know that many Jews at this time were beginning to have scruples about deliberately breaking a man's bones (for example, by stoning): might it not affect the victim's chances of bodily resurrection at the last day? Possibly John shared this concern, and thought it necessary to show that Jesus was not

36 affected; or possibly he was impressed by the text, 'No bone of his shall be broken'. It is not quite certain what text he was referring to. Exodus 12.46 reads (of the lamb eaten at Passover), "You shall not break a bone of it". If John intended his readers to have in mind the fact that Jesus was crucified at the same time as the lambs were being slaughtered in the temple, then this might have been meant as a further detail in the symbolism of Jesus' death. Alternatively, the allusion is to Psalm 34.20, which describes how the Lord protects the righteous: "He keeps all his bones; not one of them is broken".

Instead of having his legs broken, Jesus was stabbed in the side with a

34 lance. There was a flow of blood and water. This is said to be physiologically possible—a white fluid could have been released by the wound. But John, who lays great stress on the reliability of his report, obviously saw more in it than a mere physical phenomenon. Blood and water were both highly significant symbols; at the very least, they suggested the two sacraments of eucharist and baptism. In addition, the whole incident fulfilled

37 another prophecy (quoted also in Revelation 1.7), 'They shall look on him whom they pierced'. This is certainly a quotation of Zechariah 12.10—and the last chapter of Zechariah provided a number of prophecies which seemed to have been fulfilled in the passion of Jesus.

38 After that, Pilate was approached by Joseph of Arimathaea. Different suggestions are made by the evangelists about the motives of this Joseph. In Mark and Luke, he is a pious and influential Jew, anxious to avoid the ritual defilement which would ensue if a dead body were left exposed overnight, or else moved to make some amends for the injustice of the Sanhedrin's action. John comes closer to Matthew's explanation: Joseph was a secret disciple and was joined by another person of influence, Nicodemus (3.1), who was doubtless also obliged to keep his discipleship secret. They evidently intended to bury Jesus with the full honours that were customary among the

42 Jews. They were pressed for time: it was the eve of the Jewish Sabbath, and once the sun had set their activity would no longer be permissible. They therefore made use of a new tomb that happened to be near at hand in a garden. [a] But they did not (as in the other gospels) neglect to anoint the corpse. On the contrary, they brought with them a prodigious quantity of

39 spices for the purpose (more than half a hundredweight). Such things

[a] The traditional site of the Holy Sepulchre is about twenty yards from the rock of Calvary, and since the area was certainly not built over in the time of Christ, a part of it could well have been under cultivation.

were precious, and were normally packed in small jars with long narrow necks, so that they could be used sparingly; and since it was usual to anoint a corpse with olive oil, one would have expected them simply to mix a little of the perfume with it. John perhaps means to emphasize that the two distinguished Jewish disciples gave Jesus a burial worthy of the 'King of the Jews'.

Early on the Sunday morning. Ultimately, the faith of the first Christians **20.** 1 that Jesus had risen from the dead rested on the conviction that they, or at least certain witnesses whom they had reason to trust, had seen him with their own eyes. But all the gospels tell of a sensational event which preceded any appearance of Jesus: the discovery that the tomb was empty. Exactly how this discovery was made, and why it was not immediately seized upon by the disciples as convincing proof of the resurrection, are questions which receive a different answer in each gospel. Clearly there was some uncertainty in the writers' minds about the importance of the discovery, in view of the fact that it was so soon followed by an encounter with the risen Jesus himself. This gospel, however, seems to present a more considered account. John takes for granted many of the details recorded in the other gospels: his readers are evidently expected to know, without having been told, that Jesus' tomb had been sealed with a massive stone, and they are given no explanation how Mary, having left the tomb in verse 2, is back again weeping there in verse 11. In other words, John is evidently working with a narrative similar to the others; but not only does he offer certain details which are different and add whole episodes which are new to us: he arranges the material in such a way that it shows a clear progression from simple consternation to assured belief.

This is at its clearest in the first paragraph. The first reaction to the discovery that the tomb had not remained as it was left on the Friday was that of Mary of Magdala (in John she is alone, in the other gospels there is a group of women). She drew the obvious conclusion: **'They have taken the** 2 **Lord out of his tomb',** she cried, **'and we do not know where they have laid him'** (the other women of the other gospel accounts seem to have left their mark in the word we). The second reaction was that of a disciple, and was much more perceptive. Here there is an elaborate distribution of rôles between Simon Peter and **the other disciple, the one whom** 1 **Jesus loved.** From a formal point of view, Peter seems to be given precedence (he was, after all, and was intended to be, the chief of the apostles). But in reality the decisive reaction belonged to the other disciple. He, like Peter, noticed both the linen wrappings (19.40) and the **napkin** (such as 6 was wrapped round the head of Lazarus 11.44) still lying in the tomb. It was inconceivable that anyone stealing the corpse should have first unwrapped it and left the wrappings in a neat pile. Something of a different order altogether must have happened. There were of course prophecies in the scriptures about a "rising from the dead", but **until then** these had been but 9

387

dimly understood. The disciple now grasped the significance of this puzzling
8 discovery: **he saw and believed.**

This is the only occasion in the New Testament on which it is said that
someone believed as a result of the empty tomb. In principle, all the apostles
came to believe because they saw the risen Jesus. But subsequent generations
of Christians were required to believe on the basis of something far less
sensational; their faith was, so to speak, at second-hand. It was for such
Christians that this gospel was written; and John shows how much he had
29 them in mind when he records Jesus saying, '**Happy are they who never
saw me and yet have found faith**'. This disciple had not yet seen the
risen Christ; he had not received that decisive experience which was to give
the other disciples their faith in the resurrection. He had merely noticed a
strange fact about the wrappings in the tomb. But this was enough for him:
8 **he saw and believed.** We do not know who this disciple was. He appears,
again in close company with Peter, both in chapter 13 and in chapter 21.
Whether or not he stands for the author of the gospel (see below), he was
certainly a person whom the first readers of the gospel knew and whose
memory (if he was dead) they revered. His was a powerful example to appeal
to; and he, despite such slender and puzzling evidence, had come to that
faith in the resurrection which was to be the cardinal belief of the whole
church.

However, events moved quickly. According to Matthew and Luke, the
discovery of the empty tomb was followed almost at once by supernatural
appearances, first to the women, then to the disciples. John faithfully follows
the same pattern. Mary of Magdala continues to take the place of the whole
group of women, and her vision of angels corresponds to the scene in the
other gospels. But this vision leaves her still assuming that there must be
some natural explanation of the body's disappearance, so much so that, when
Jesus himself appears to her, she immediately (since she does not recognize
him) puts the same explanation to the stranger, and asks for his help.

16 **Jesus said, 'Mary!'** That simply addressing her by name was enough to
open her eyes is a piece of vivid and convincing reporting. The scene is told
with a rare simplicity and economy of words. It is of course possible that
John meant his readers to have in mind some words that Jesus had spoken
earlier: 'he calls his own sheep by name' (10.3). At any rate, there is some
17 serious teaching in the rest of the dialogue. '**Do not cling to me, for I
have not yet ascended to the Father.**' In Matthew, the women who first
saw the risen Jesus 'clasped his feet, falling prostrate before him' (28.9).
This (John may have felt) was to attach the wrong significance to these
appearances of Jesus. They were intended to convince, not to excite homage.
The reader must not be given the impression that the women, or in this case
Mary, or indeed any disciple, had been given a chance to know and worship
the risen Christ in a way more direct, more personal, more privileged than

was given to any subsequent Christian. The Christ whom Christians worshipped was the Christ who had **ascended to the Father.** If this were imagined in spatial terms, it could be said that Mary saw him, so to speak, on his way to heaven. But the truth behind this naïve form of expression was that Mary's experience, though at that particular place and time it was decisive in convincing her and others of the fact of Jesus' resurrection, was in no way more direct or more privileged than all Christians have when they worship their ascended Lord. [a]

'But go to my brothers'. That Jesus' followers are his **brothers** is implied by a saying recorded in the other gospels (Mark 3.35) and is a presupposition of much of his teaching in Matthew's gospel—indeed, in Matthew the risen Jesus actually says to the women who have seen him 'Go and take word to my brothers' (28.10). In this gospel the idea is a new one (though it is perfectly consistent with the teaching so far about Christians being children of God, and friends of Jesus); but even if John was faithfully reproducing some tradition that the risen Jesus had used this very word, he did not miss the opportunity to draw the consequence: God was '**my Father and your Father, my God and your God'.** For all the majesty implied in Jesus' ascension, his followers remained in close solidarity with him. In their relationship with God, they were privileged to be his equals.

Mary of Magdala went to the disciples with her news. Each of the other gospels suggests an answer to the question why this news had no immediate effect on the disciples (see above on Mark 16.8). John ignores the question. It is as if he is simply following the traditional pattern of Jesus' appearances: first he was seen by some women (or Mary of Magdala), then by the disciples all together. He makes little attempt to link these appearances together in a single coherent narrative. The appearance of Jesus to his disciples **late that** Sunday **evening** takes place exactly as if it were the very first of its kind. This, in any case, was doubtless the appearance which was remembered as the most important and authoritative of all. Paul mentions an appearance 'to the Twelve' (1 Corinthians 15.5); and Luke also gives an account of it (24.36–43) which is in many respects similar to this one. John's version has details which are characteristic of this gospel. '**Peace be with you'** is doubtless intended (as in 14.27) to be understood as more than a formal greeting; and '**As the Father sent me, so I send you'** belongs to the pattern of Jesus' teaching as it is often presented in the *Farewell discourses*. But the scene as a whole falls into place alongside passages in the

[a] It is impossible to be sure of the exact sense of Jesus' words in the Greek (see the footnote in NEB), and their interpretation must remain uncertain. It is possible that John chose the word "touch" (as it is rendered in the footnote) in order to make a deliberate reference to the eucharist: Christians "touch" the Lord in the bread they share (compare 1 John 1.1), and this is the authentic way of experiencing him. Jesus forbade Mary to "touch" him in a literal sense, pending the time when all Christians would be able to "touch" him in the eucharist.

other gospels. Just as in Luke there is much emphasis on the fact that the risen Jesus was no mere ghost, so here the apparition, though he enters
19, 20 through **locked doors,** shows the disciples **his hands and his side.** Again, the ending of the scene represents a formal commission given by Jesus to his
22 disciples. **Then he breathed on them, saying, 'Receive the Holy Spirit!'** It was the distinctive experience of the earliest Christians that, as soon as the church began its existence, it possessed the gift of the Holy Spirit. This spirit was understood in different ways, and had a variety of manifestations. Moreover, there was evidently some doubt about the exact occasion on which it could be said that this new factor had entered the lives of men and women. But all agreed that the Holy Spirit was a reality in the church, and had been so ever since the church began to exist. To describe how in fact it had been given necessarily involved using highly metaphorical language. In Acts 2, Luke narrates a particularly sensational phenomenon which he saw as the definitive irruption of this new power into human lives. Here, John uses a metaphor straight from the Old Testament. "The Lord God formed a man from the dust of the ground and breathed into his nostrils the breath of life" (Genesis 2.7; compare Ezekiel 37.7–14). "Breath", in Hebrew, is the same word as "spirit": the giving of the Spirit by Jesus lent itself easily to being described in the same terms as the original giving of the breath of life by God.

23 **'If you forgive any man's sins, they stand forgiven'.** It is clear (and not at all surprising) that Jesus was remembered to have given to his disciples—and thereby, it has usually been understood, to their successors—a definite authority over the lives of their fellow-Christians. In Matthew (16.19 and 18.18) this is expressed in terms of "forbidding" and "allowing"— apparently an idiom of Jesus' own language, and one that could have been understood in certain rather technical senses. Here, the saying has the same form, but concerns the disciples' power to pronounce the forgiveness of sins. It is likely that it was in this way that Greek-speaking Christians understood the original saying: in the life of the church, it was necessary sometimes to decide whether the conduct of a member made it necessary to exclude him. Authority to do this was found in a saying of Jesus; and John, although he does not elsewhere show interest in the concept of the forgiving of an individual's sins, nevertheless records that Jesus gave this authority to the disciples.

There are traces elsewhere in the gospels that not all the disciples were immediately convinced of the resurrection. In Matthew, there is the laconic statement that 'some were doubtful' (28.17). John, alone of the gospel
24 writers, gives a concrete instance. **Thomas, that is 'the Twin',** has already been named twice in the course of the gospel (11.16; 14.5); here he is an example of one who refuses to believe without incontrovertible and tangible evidence. When it comes to the point, Jesus' appearance elicits from him

what is probably intended to be the most significant confession of faith that has been made by anyone in the gospel: 'My Lord and my God'. Earlier 28 in the narrative this might have been misunderstood: Lord and God were titles which, in the Old Testament, belonged to God alone, and to address Jesus so might have seemed like calling him another "god". But by now the reader knows more of the relationship between Jesus and his Father. Jesus had even said, 'Anyone who has seen me has seen the Father' (14.9). Thomas, like the whole church after him, acknowledged Jesus as Lord; but he now understood also that his Lord was (in one sense at least) God. Nevertheless, in this story, Thomas is no more than a foil to the true picture of the Christian believer. To convince Thomas, Jesus had to make, so to speak, a special appearance. But John was writing for Christians who had come to their faith without demanding an impossible confirmation of it. Fittingly, Jesus' last words are addressed to them: 'Happy are they who 29 never saw me and yet have found faith.'

There were indeed many other signs . . . which are not recorded in 30 this book. The writer now addresses his readers directly. The signs, in this gospel, are mostly what we should now call miracles; and from a comparison with the other gospels it is quite clear that John has recorded only a small selection of those that were ascribed to Jesus. The same indeed is true of Mark's gospel (1.34); and it is also true that Mark tended, like John, to narrate only those miracles which had a bearing upon faith. John now makes this explicit: Those here written have been recorded in order that you 31 may hold the faith that Jesus is the Christ, the Son of God. From our point of view, the phrase is disappointingly ambiguous.[a] It does not make it clear whether John was writing a missionary book for unbelievers or a treatise for people who were already Christians (an answer to this question can only be given on the basis of the work as a whole). Nevertheless, it effectively sums up the grand purpose for which the gospel was written. The purpose, indeed, was the same as that for which any gospel was bound to be written. Any gospel was, almost by definition, 'of Jesus Christ the Son of God' (Mark 1.1), and it can hardly have had any other purpose than to awaken or to strengthen faith in those who heard it or read it. John's gospel is only different from the others in the way in which he approaches his task. As a summary of the writer's aims, the sentence could stand appropriately at the end of any of the gospels. Only the word life is distinctive: almost from the beginning, this has been John's most characteristic and emphatic way of describing the benefits and possibilities which are now open to mankind as a result of the story he has been telling.

Normally, it was only by way of a preface or an epilogue that a writer addressed his readers about his own book. The last verse of chapter 20 is a typical way

[a] It also appears in more than one form in the manuscripts. See the footnote in NEB.

of ending a book; and it is astonishing to find that in fact another chapter follows. This alone would be sufficient to make one suspect that chapter 21 was added after the main work was finished. But there are other oddities. The scene is set by the Sea of Tiberias. Nothing has prepared us for this. The disciples were last heard of in Jerusalem. Yet we read that Simon Peter said, 'I am going out fishing', as if he was living the normal life of a fisherman in Galilee. Apart from a kind of editorial comment—**this makes the third time that Jesus appeared to his disciples after his resurrection from the dead**—there is nothing to suggest that the episode belongs to the sequence of events that has just been related. If it is an afterthought by the author of the whole work, one would have expected him at least to have worked it in more neatly. The style is very similar (though there are a few points of detail where one would have expected the writer of the rest of the gospel to express himself differently), and many of the idioms and ideas are found elsewhere in the gospel. But the awkwardness of the join is such that, even though all the manuscripts run straight on from chapter 20 to chapter 21, it seems almost impossible to resist the apparent implication of 21.24 that someone else has had a hand in writing the end of the gospel.

The episode is made up of a number of different elements. The main plot, so to speak, is the story of a group of Galilean fishermen who, after a night's unsuccessful fishing, are told by Jesus to try once more; they then make an astonishingly large catch. A story of this kind is also told by Luke (5.1–11), who places it near the beginning of Jesus' activity, and uses it to explain how Jesus attracted his first disciples. Here it has a more unearthly quality, for it is placed after the resurrection, and Jesus' sudden appearance is as inexplicable as the catch of fish. It is still a wonder story; but its real significance is in the by-plots. The first of these is a delicate balancing of priorities between Peter and **the disciple whom Jesus loved**, very much as in the discovery of the empty tomb (20.1–9): Peter took action, but it was the other disciple who first recognized (and believed) that the figure on the shore was Jesus. The second by-plot (which is rather loosely integrated into the main plot, since there is no obvious reason why Jesus should have asked for the disciples' catch of fish, when he already had other fish laid on the fire) is a meal shared by the risen Jesus with his disciples. This, again, has a parallel in Luke (24.30, 36–43), and is described in a way which might well be intended to make the reader think of the eucharist, for the eucharist, the original meal in which Jesus **took the bread, and gave it to them,** was celebrated again and again in the church in the conviction that the risen Lord was present. Besides all this, there is a rich load of symbolism. We are told that the net **was full of big fish, a hundred and fifty-three of them.** The writer hardly intends us to think that someone present counted and remembered the exact number: to give an idea of the size of the catch, a round number would have been at least as impressive. In a culture where the symbolism of numbers meant far more than it does now, it would have been even more obvious that this number had a secret meaning. It happens that the sum of the numbers $1 + 2 + 3 + \ldots$ up to 17 is 153; $17 = 10 + 7$, and ten and seven were each numbers signifying a perfect whole. By such reasoning, 153 could have been understood to stand as a symbol for the whole of something (the whole of mankind, or the whole of the church). Alternatively, the explanation may be that some naturalists (again perhaps influenced by the arithmetical properties of the number rather than by actual observation) allowed for exactly 153 different species of fish—in which case the number would again be a symbol of totality. Whether either of these explanations is correct we shall never know; but we can be fairly sure that the writer intended something of the kind. And when he goes on to tell us another quite unimportant detail —the net was not torn—we can hardly be wrong in seeing here another symbolical statement. Again, we cannot be sure what is meant; but if the fish in the net represented the totality of peoples who would be brought into the church then the fact that the net was not torn would stand for the unity of the church: for all the great number and diversity of its members, there was no division, no schism. All this may seem rather recondite. But it was Jesus himself who started the metaphor: 'I will make you fishers of men' (Mark 1.17). The rest is only elaboration of this basic idea.

Jesus said to Simon Peter. Sayings of Jesus which seemed to assign a special place to Peter among the apostles are recorded in Matthew (16.18) and Luke (22.31–2). At the same time, all the gospels faithfully record Peter's threefold disowning of Jesus during the trial. Here Peter's threefold profession of love [a] for Jesus may be intended to balance his threefold denial; and certainly Jesus' final command to him, '**Follow me**', seems to refer back to 13.36, where Jesus said, 'You cannot follow me now, but one day you will'. But the actual form of the commission to Peter is new: '**Feed my sheep**'. Up to now, Jesus has been the only shepherd. In the period of the church, the shepherding is to be continued by a disciple.   *15* *19* *17*

'**And further**'. What follows has a proverbial ring. To walk any distance, a man must hitch up his long clothes by making a fold over his belt, and then fasten his belt tighter. A young man is perfectly independent; but an old man is dependent on others, he can only **stretch out** his **arms** for other people to arrange his clothes for him and lead him where they will. Taken by itself, this reads like a pessimistic aphorism, of the kind that is so brilliantly elaborated at the end of Ecclesiastes (12.1–8). What was the application of it for Peter? The writer tells us: **He said this to indicate the manner of death by which Peter was to glorify God**—in other words, Peter   *18* *19*

[a] Two different Greek words are used in this brief dialogue. One of them (*agapō*) is the one characteristically used in the Gospel and Letters of John for the "love" of Christ and of Christians; the other (*philō*) is the commonest Greek word for human affection in general. This alternation may be just a question of style. But in case a distinction is intended, the footnotes in NEB offer a translation which preserves it.

was to find himself as helpless as an old man in the face of those who would put him to death as a martyr for his faith. This comment was clearly written after the event, and is one of our first pieces of evidence that Peter was in fact martyred (probably in Rome, soon after the middle of the first century A.D.). Tertullian, writing a century or so later, knew (or assumed) that Peter had been crucified (and Origen, later still, says that he was crucified, at his own request, head downwards), and saw a prophetic significance in the words
18 **stretch out your arms** and **bind you fast**. But this interpretation involves a certain forcing of the Greek words. "Another will do up your belt" is a more accurate translation than **a stranger will bind you fast**. Taken as it stands, the prophecy seems to mean only that Peter would not die a natural death.

On two occasions already in these last chapters, there has been a careful
20 balancing of honours between Peter and **the disciple whom Jesus loved**. If Jesus had made a prophecy about Peter's death (and at the time of writing the death of a Christian martyr was much honoured: it was the most esteemed
19 way of all **to glorify God**), had he not also said something to the other
22 disciple? He had: '**If it should be my will that he wait until I come, what is it to you?**' On the face of it, this was less mysterious. For many
23 years after the resurrection, it was believed by the church (here called **the brotherhood**, a word more familiar in Acts than in this gospel), that, though some Christians might die, the majority, or at least a certain number, would "wait until the Lord's coming". This disciple, it seemed, was intended to be one of these. But the "coming" of Jesus did not take place in this way—indeed it has been one of the themes of this gospel that such naïve language about the future was in reality only a way of speaking about a new dimension of the present. The disciple died. And it became necessary to draw attention to the oracular ambiguity of what Jesus had said. Correcting this misunderstanding was doubtless one of the objects for which this chapter was added to the
25 completed gospel. The writer then provided a new ending, which is little more than a rhetorical flourish such as many ancient writers used, and answers somewhat colourlessly to the real ending of the gospel in 20.30–1. The proper conclusion of this chapter is in the previous verse. Peter may
24 have glorified God by his death; but this disciple gave **testimony** of another kind: **it is this same disciple who attests what has here been written. It is in fact he who wrote it.** We hear the voice now, no longer of an author, but of the community which used and treasured this book. They believed, rightly or wrongly, that they had the clue to the mysterious phrase, 'the disciple whom Jesus loved'. It was the author himself. This meant, moreover, that this chapter at least, if not the whole book, had been written by an eye-witness. In an account of Jesus' life and teaching where so much was said to depend on "witness", **testimony**, here was the ultimate ground for confidence. The author had been there himself. **We know that his testimony is true.**

An incident in the temple

This passage did not form part of the original gospel according to John. In its traditional place (7.53–8.11) it clearly disturbs the sequence of John's narrative; and in any case most of the early manuscripts omit it altogether, and some manuscripts have it in a different place. In style, it is more like a passage from one of the other gospels (especially Luke, to which one group of manuscripts actually ascribes it). What appears to have happened is that an isolated story about Jesus was somehow preserved without having been incorporated into any gospel until it was ultimately slipped in at some point where it did not seem inappropriate.

A great many stories about Jesus circulated in the first few centuries of the Christian era, but were never incorporated in the New Testament, and are preserved in what are called the Apocryphal gospels. Almost all of these can be recognized as being of considerably later date than the New Testament. By contrast, this one falls well into place beside all that we know of Jesus from the New Testament gospels, and seems (so far as we can tell) to reflect the conditions of Jesus' own time. Even if it is impossible to find a place for it in any of the four gospels, there is no reason to doubt that it preserves an authentic memory of an episode in the life of Jesus.

It is necessary to fill in the background of the incident. The immediate result of a woman committing adultery would have been that her husband would be entitled to divorce her without any financial loss, and that the woman would bear the disgrace of the act among her own family. Where there was doubt about whether adultery had been committed, further evidence might be collected, or the woman might be subjected to a primitive kind of ritual test (Numbers 5). But in this case we are told that the woman was **caught in the very act of adultery**, so that there was presumably no **8.4** doubt about the facts, and the divorce would have followed almost automatically. And there, normally, the affair would have ended. Adultery and divorce in most societies are subjects of civil litigation, and carry no graver consequences; and although laxity in sexual matters was very strongly disapproved of in Jewish society, there was seldom any punishment beyond a certain degree of social disgrace. Nevertheless, in the Law of Moses a more serious view was taken. Adultery was conceived of as something which was both against the will of God and a source of harm to the community as a whole. Consequently the Law (which was still the law by which the Jewish people lived) laid down nothing less than the death penalty (Deuteronomy 22.22). It is unlikely that in more recent times this law was often invoked: adultery, after all, is hard to prove conclusively, and most courts are loth to impose the death penalty unless they have to. On the other hand, there were certainly sections of Jewish opinion which zealously tried to bring the society in which

they lived into full conformity with the Law of Moses, and to eradicate
3 conduct which was inconsistent with its demands. Among **the doctors of the law and the Pharisees** who make their appearance in this story, there
4 may well have been some who felt that this case of an adulteress **caught in the very act** offered an opportunity for applying the law in all its rigour.

The situation was complicated by the fact that, under the Roman administration, the Jewish authorities had apparently lost the power to impose the death penalty (John 18.31). Those wishing to see the law enforced in its full severity therefore could not hope to get what they wanted through a public trial. Their only course was to constitute themselves as a court and, after making sure that their action was strictly legal according to the Law of Moses, to see justice done themselves. As for the sentence, the relevant passage of Deuteronomy did not prescribe exactly how this was to be carried out; but death by stoning was one of the standard punishments mentioned in the Law, and it is fairly certain that this was the accepted penalty for adultery in the time of Jesus (though it was later changed to the somewhat more humane one of strangling). It was therefore a fair summary of the
5 situation to say that '**in the Law Moses has laid down that such women are to be stoned**'.

In this particular case, zeal for the full application of the Law was doubtless combined with a desire to compromise Jesus. It was courteous and reasonable to invite someone who had made a name for himself in expounding the Law to give his judgement in such a matter; but against the background of a growing conspiracy against Jesus, the case seemed to offer a handle to his enemies. If Jesus recommended the Mosaic Law to be enforced, he could be accused to the Roman authorities of interfering in their administration of the province. If he did not, he would be showing that he did not take the Law seriously, and therefore had no right to expound it. In some such way as this,
6 the narrator may be right in saying, **They put the question as a test, hoping to frame a charge against him.**

Jesus bent down and wrote with his finger on the ground. It is possible that he wrote some Hebrew characters, say the first few words of a text from the Law which bore on the case at issue; the advantage of doing this would have been that it is sometimes possible to read Hebrew words with more than one pronunciation, and so to give them more than one meaning: writing the words, instead of speaking them, would have been a way of pointing out a number of possible meanings in a clause of the Law. Alternatively, Jesus was just thinking—his writing on the ground may simply be a vivid touch by which the narrator tells his readers that, on this occasion, Jesus gave no snap answer.

And no wonder. Not only his own position, but the woman's life, was at stake. When it did come, his answer did not for a moment take lightly the binding force of the law about adultery; but by invoking another basic principle of the Law, it at once cast the whole matter in a different light. To convict on a capital charge, the evidence of at least two witnesses was necessary. To a certain extent their evidence could be checked by examination in court. But in a Jewish court, what carried weight most was the known character and probity of the witnesses. The judges required, not so much independent proof of their story, as reason to believe that the witnesses were trustworthy. If the court was convinced of this, no more questions need be asked: sentence was given and the witnesses had the right and the duty to throw the first stones (Deuteronomy 17.7). In view of this heavy responsibility of the witnesses, there was a large number of conditions they had to fulfil before their word could be accepted. If their probity was questioned, they had to show that they had not been implicated in any way with the crime they had witnessed nor with any other unlawful proceeding. The penalties for giving and accepting evidence when all these conditions were not fulfilled were heavy: both witnesses and judges would be implicated in the grave sin of bearing false witness. Jesus was in effect challenging those who in this case had claimed to have been witnesses of the **very act** of adultery. It was all very well to insist on a literal application of the Law of Moses in the interests of a high standard of morality. But had these zealous reformers considered that they must also observe an equally high standard of probity as witnesses and judges? **'That one of you who is faultless** 7 **shall throw the first stone.'**

Jesus had extricated himself and saved the woman. Under these circumstances, no one had dared pronounce the death sentence, no witness had dared insist on exercising the witnesses' right to cast the first stone. In the absence of the witnesses, Jesus, even if he had wanted to, was in no position to do so himself. **'Do not sin again'.** From a judge, this would have been a significant warning: on a subsequent occasion, the woman would have been that much more obviously guilty. But Jesus was now alone with her. His words were not the decision of a court, but expressed what he really felt. The letter of the Law of Moses was not to be enforced. There would be no punishment. But this made no difference to the seriousness of the woman's offence. **'Do not sin again'.**

INDEX

INDEX